Constructing European Intellectual Property

EUROPEAN INTELLECTUAL PROPERTY INSTITUTES NETWORK SERIES

Series editors: Manuel Desantes, *University of Alicante, Spain,* Josef Drexl, *Max Planck Institute for Intellectual Property and Competition Law, Munich, Germany,* Christophe Geiger, *CEIPI, University of Strasbourg, France,* Anselm Kamperman Sanders, *IPKM, Maastricht University, the Netherlands* and Guido Westkamp, *Queen Mary, University of London, UK*

This innovative book series features the results of high-quality legal and interdisciplinary research undertaken in the area of intellectual property law from international, European, national and comparative perspectives, carried out under the auspices of the European Intellectual Property Institutes Network (EIPIN). The series provides a platform for dissemination of thinking at the forefront of the discourse on complex matters of intellectual property law, and aims to develop a sound analytical and factual basis for balanced and well-informed policy making in Europe and beyond. It is edited by five prominent scholars representing some of Europe's leading programs of intellectual property research and education composing the EIPIN: Manuel Desantes from the Magister Lvcentinvs at the University of Alicante; Josef Drexl from the Munich Intellectual Property Law Center (MIPLC); Christophe Geiger from the Centre for International Intellectual Property Studies (CEIPI) of the University of Strasbourg; Anselm Kamperman Sanders from the Intellectual Property Law and Knowledge Management (IPKM) at Maastricht University; and Guido Westkamp from the Queen Mary Intellectual Property Research Institute (QMIPRI) at Queen Mary, University of London.

Constructing European Intellectual Property

Achievements and New Perspectives

Edited by

Christophe Geiger

Associate Professor, Director General and Director of the Research Department of the Centre for International Intellectual Property Studies (CEIPI), University of Strasbourg, France

EUROPEAN INTELLECTUAL PROPERTY INSTITUTES NETWORK SERIES

Edward Elgar
Cheltenham, UK • Northampton, MA, USA

Published by
Edward Elgar Publishing Limited
The Lypiatts
15 Lansdown Road
Cheltenham
Glos GL50 2JA
UK

Edward Elgar Publishing, Inc.
William Pratt House
9 Dewey Court
Northampton
Massachusetts 01060
USA

A catalogue record for this book
is available from the British Library

Library of Congress Control Number: 2012938074

This book is available electronically in the ElgarOnline.com Law Subject Collection,
E-ISBN 978 1 78100 164 6

FSC
www.fsc.org
MIX
Paper from
responsible sources
FSC® C018575

ISBN 978 1 78100 163 9

Typeset by Cambrian Typesetters, Camberley, Surrey
Printed and bound by MPG Books Group, UK

Contents

PART II DEVELOPING THE EUROPEAN IP SYSTEM

Section 3 Trademarks and Geographical Indications at EU Level

Section 4 Patents and Plant Variety Protection

Section 5 Copyright Protection in the EU

Section 6 Databases, Design Protection, Unfair Competition and/or New IP Rights in the EU

Contributors

Christian Archambeau, Vice-President of the Office for Harmonization in the Internal Market (Trade Marks and Designs), Alicante, Spain

Estelle Derclaye, Dr., Professor of Intellectual Property Law, University of Nottingham, School of Law, UK

Roberto D'Erme, Research Assistant, Centre for International Intellectual Property Studies (CEIPI), University of Strasbourg, France

Thomas Dreier, Prof. Dr. iur., M.C.J. (New York University); Professor of Intellectual Property Law; Director of the Institute for Information and Economic Law, Karlsruhe Institute of Technology (KIT); and Honorary Professor at the University of Freiburg, Germany

Séverine Dusollier, Prof., Professor at the University of Namur, Belgium; Director of the Research Center in Information, Law and Society (CRIDS)

Gail Elizabeth Evans, BA (Hons), Dip.Ed, LLB, SJD, Reader in International Trade and Intellectual Property Law, Centre for Commercial Law Studies, Queen Mary, University of London, UK

Christophe Geiger, Associate Professor, Director General and Director of the Research Department of the Centre for International Intellectual Property Studies (CEIPI), University of Strasbourg, France; Affiliated Senior Researcher, Max Planck Institute for Intellectual Property and Competition Law, Munich, Germany

Jonathan Griffiths, Senior Lecturer, School of Law, Queen Mary, University of London, UK

Henning Grosse Ruse-Khan, Dr., Senior Research Fellow, Max Planck Institute for Intellectual Property and Competition Law, Munich, Germany; Associate Fellow, Centre for International Sustainable Development Law, Montreal, Canada

Christian Heinze, Dr. jur., LL.M., Max Planck Institute for Comparative and International Private Law, Hamburg, Germany

P. Bernt Hugenholtz, Professor of Intellectual Property Law, University of Amsterdam, and Director, Institute for Information Law (IViR), the Netherlands

Thomas Jaeger, Senior Research Fellow, Max Planck Institute for Intellectual Property and Competition Law, Munich, Germany

Anselm Kamperman Sanders, Professor of Intellectual Property Law at

Maastricht University Faculty of Law, the Netherlands; Director Institute for Globalisation and International Regulation (IGIR); Director Advanced Masters Intellectual Property Law and Knowledge Management (LLM/MSc); Academic Director IEEM Intellectual Property Law School, IEEM Macao SAR, China; Professeur Invité à l'Université de Liège, Belgium; Adjunct Professor at Jinan University Law School, Guangzhou, China

Jan Krauss, Dipl.-Biol. Dr., Part-Time Lecturer, University of Washington School of Law, Seattle, USA; Patentanwalt, European Patent and Trademark Attorney, Boehmert & Boehmert, Munich, Germany

Annette Kur, Prof. Dr. jur., Max Planck Institute for Intellectual Property and Competition Law, Munich, Germany

Raimund Lutz, Vice-President, European Patent Office, Munich, Germany

Rita Matulionyte, Senior Research Fellow, Institute for Legal Informatics, Leibniz University Hannover, Germany

Luke McDonagh, Dr., LSE Fellow, Department of Law, London School of Economics and Political Science (LSE), UK

Axel Metzger, Professor of Civil Law and Intellectual Property, Institute for Legal Informatics, Leibniz University Hannover, Germany

Tuomas Mylly, LL.D., LL.M. Eur., Professor of European Law, Faculty of Law, University of Turku, Finland

Jacques Raynard, Agrégé des Facultés de Droit, Professor at the University of Montpellier I and at the Centre for International Intellectual Property Studies (CEIPI), University of Strasbourg, France; Director of the Centre for Corporate Law, Montpellier, France

Marco Ricolfi, Prof., Faculty of Law, University of Turin, Italy

Jens Schovsbo, Prof., Dr. jur., PhD, Centre for Information and Innovation Law, University of Copenhagen, Denmark

Vincenzo Scordamaglia, Hon. Director General of the Council of the European Union

Martin Senftleben, Ph.D., Professor of Intellectual Property, VU University Amsterdam; Senior Consultant, Bird & Bird, The Hague, the Netherlands

Xavier Seuba, Ph.D., Senior Associate Researcher, Centre for International Intellectual Property Studies (CEIPI), University of Strasbourg, France

Uma Suthersanen, Prof. Dr., Professor in International Intellectual Property Law, Centre for Commercial Law Studies, Queen Mary, University of London, UK

Toshiko Takenaka, Ph.D., Professor of Law, Director of Center for Advanced Study and Research on Intellectual Property (CASRIP), University of Washington School of Law, Seattle, USA

Geertrui Van Overwalle, Prof. Dr., Centre for Intellectual Property Rights (CIR), University of Leuven, Belgium; Tilburg Institute for Law, Technology and Society (TILT), Tilburg University, the Netherlands

Michel Vivant, Professor at Sciences Po Law School (Paris) and at the Centre for International Intellectual Property Studies (CEIPI), University of Strasbourg, France; Doctor honoris causa University of Heidelberg, Germany

Abbreviations

ACTA	Anti-Counterfeiting Trade Agreement
Am.U.Int'l L.Rev	*American University International Law Review*
BCLR	Butterworths Constitutional Law Reports
CDPA 1988	Copyright, Designs and Patents Act 1988
CDR	Community Design Regulation
CEIPI	Centre for International Intellectual Property Studies
Chicago-Kent L. Rev.	*Chicago-Kent Law Review*
Cir.	US Circuit Court of Appeals
CJEU	Court of Justice of the European Union
CLJ	*Cambridge Law Journal*
CMLR	Common Market Law Reports
Columbia L. Rev.	*Columbia Law Review*
COM	European Commission
CP	Community Patent
CPVO	Community Plant Variety Office
CTM	Community Trade Mark
CTMR	Community Trade Mark Regulation
EC	European Community
ECDR	European Copyright and Design Reports
ECHR	European Convention on Human Rights
ECJ	European Court of Justice
ECR	European Court Reports
ECT	Treaty establishing the European Community
EHRR	European Human Rights Reports
EIPIN	European Intellectual Property Institutes Network
EIPR	*European Intellectual Property Review*
EJHG	*European Journal of Human Genetics*
EPC	European Patent Convention (Munich Convention)
EPN	European Patent Network
EPO	European Patent Office
ETMR	European Trade Mark Reports
EU	European Union

EWCA Civ	Civil Division of England and Wales Court of Appeal
EWHC	England and Wales High Court
F.	Federal Reporter (US)
F. Supp.	Federal Supplement (US)
Fed. Cir.	US Court of Appeals for the Federal Circuit
GATT	General Agreement on Tariffs and Trade
GI	geographical indication
GRUR	*Gewerblicher Rechtsschutz und Urheberrecht*
Harv. Int'l L.J.	*Harvard International Law Journal*
ICTSD	International Centre for Trade and Sustainable Development
IIC	*International Review of Intellectual Property and Competition Law*
IMPACT	International Medical Products Anti-Counterfeiting Taskforce
IP	intellectual property
IPR	intellectual property rights
IPQ	*Intellectual Property Quarterly*
JBL	*Journal of Business Law*
J. Cop. Soc.	*Journal of the Copyright Society of the USA*
JIPITEC	*Journal of Intellectual Property, Information Technology and E-Commerce Law*
JIPLP	*Journal of Intellectual Property Law and Practice*
L. Ed.	Lawyer's Edition
MPI	Max Planck Institute for Intellectual Property and Competition Law
OECD	Organisation for Economic Co-operation and Development
OHIM	Office for Harmonization in the Internal Market (Trade Marks and Designs)
OJ	Official Journal (EC, EU)
PCT	Patent Cooperation Treaty
PDO	protected designation of origin
PGI	protected geographical indication
QMJIP	*Queen Mary Journal of Intellectual Property*
S. Ct.	Supreme Court Reporter (US)
SDNY	US District Court for the Southern District of New York
SMU Law Review	*Southern Methodist University Law Review*
STOA	Science and Technology Options Assessment

TEU	Consolidated version of the Treaty on the European Union
TFEU	Consolidated version of the Treaty on the Functioning of the European Union
TGI	Paris Tribunal de grande instance de Paris
TMD	Trade Mark Directive
TRIPS	Agreement Agreement on Trade-Related Aspects of International Property Rights
TSG	Traditional Specialities Guaranteed
UNCTAD	United Nations Conference on Trade and Development
UNTS	United Nations Treaty Series
US	United States
U.S.	United States Reports
USC	United States Code
USPQ	*United States Patent Quarterly*
USPTO	United States Patent and Trademark Office
WCT	WIPO Copyright Treaty
WIPO	World Intellectual Property Organization
WL	Westlaw
WTO	World Trade Organization

Introduction to the series

EUROPEAN INTELLECTUAL PROPERTY INSTITUTES NETWORK (EIPIN): OUR COMMON HISTORY

1. Once consolidated, projects recreate their lives. Dreams and legends mix with reality to define their own existence. This is the case of EIPIN. In 1994 while walking up and down the beach of San Juan, Alicante, Professor Dieter Stauder, at that time Director of the international section of the CEIPI (University of Strasbourg) shared his vision of 'bringing our students together' with Manuel Desantes, Professor at the University of Alicante. This vision was to become a shared obsession.

2. The idea, simply stated, was that there will be no truly unified Europe unless people from different cultures know one another, understand one another and work with one another. Consequently, it was imperative for intellectual property institutions to create a network offering students the possibility to do precisely that – to meet, to understand and to work together. They posited that common enrichment would radiate from these 'physical contacts', and correctly so, as EIPIN collaboration has been enhancing the academic experience of countless students and professors for more than a decade.

3. It took almost six years, however, to realise this vision for the first time. Years during which the relations between the four founding institutions gradually moved from competitive to cooperative. Years in which bilateral contacts and visits among the partners multiplied. Years in which the partners grew to know each other. Years in which the concept was fine-tuned. Years during which the partners all realised that EIPIN could be a win-win for all if the EIPIN dream could be kept alive.

4. And, thankfully, it was!

5. From 11 to 13 May 2000, almost one hundred students and professors, representing four European intellectual property institutions – Centre d'Etudes Internationales de la Propriété Intellectuelle (CEIPI,

Strasbourg, France); Eidgenössische Technische Hochschule (ETH, Zurich, Switzerland); Queen Mary Intellectual Property Research Institute (University of London, UK); and Magister Lvcentinvs (University of Alicante, Spain) – met together on the Campus of the University of Alicante for the I EIPIN Congress (1999-2000). The press published that:

> The University of Alicante held the I Inter European Conference of Postgraduate Programs on Intellectual Property, the aim of which was to create the basis for strengthening the co-operation between the European academic programs specialized in this matter. For three days, students, professors and renowned specialists from the OHIM discussed the Community Trademark.

Needless to say, when we recall this first EIPIN Congress what first comes to mind is great fun, many nice surprises, – we can do it!!! – three completely sleepless days and the firm resolve to repeat the experience the following year.

6. And repeat it we did! In January 2001 the II EIPIN Congress took place at the University of Alicante, and for the first time we staged a mock trial with teams comprised of students belonging to the different EIPIN Partners and participation of specialized judges.

7. The III EIPIN Congress (2001–2002) was organized by the Queen Mary Intellectual Property Research Institute in the historic Cumberland Lodge, Windsor, and took place in April 2002.

8. CEIPI assumed the lead of the IV EIPIN Congress (2002–2003) and for the first time EIPIN travelled to Strasbourg in April 2003. This was a milestone event as it signified both the further consolidation of the EIPIN network and continued development of the EIPIN Congress methodology. It was at the IV EIPIN Congress that the students were first organized into international teams (advised by Ph.D. students of the participating institutions) and required to meticulously prepare for the Congress. The teams were given a variety of assignments such as delivering presentations, participating in mock court competitions, and writing reports on the topics addressed at the Congress. The students' preparation prior to the Congress was done mainly by means of a 'virtual classroom' website on which the works-in-progress were posted. This methodological innovation has stood the test of time and continues to provide a successful structure for our common endeavor.

9. The V EIPIN Congress (2003–2004) also brought further innovation and change. For the first time, the Congress was divided into several conferences hosted by the respective EIPIN partner institutes. Each institute hosted a meeting: ETH in Zurich, 4–6 December 2003 (Patent Litigation); Second, Magister Lvcentinvs in Alicante, 5–7 February 2004 (Design and Trademark Litigation); Third, CEIPI in Strasbourg, 1–3 April 2004 (Technology Transfer); finally, Queen Mary in London, 6–8 May 2004 (Patenting and the Life Sciences).

10. The academic year 2004–2005 was particularly important for the history of the network. First of all, the Munich Intellectual Property Law Center (MIPLC) became a member of EIPIN. MIPLC sent students to the meetings which took place in Zurich, 2–4 December 2004 (Patent litigation), in Alicante, 17–19 February 2005 (Trademark and Design Litigation), and in London, 29 April–1 May 2005 (Technology Transfer). Second, ETH hosted the I EIPIN Doctoral Meeting in Zurich, 28–29 September 2005. Since then, every year around twenty Ph.D. candidates whose research focuses on IP matters come together to meet colleagues, to learn from the experience of the commentators, – all of them Ph.D. – to exchange their ideas and viewpoints, and, above all, to share research methodologies, rationales for structuring the written presentation of the Thesis in a given way, and experiences on how to properly identify a suitable topic for research purposes.

11. The VII EIPIN Congress (2005–2006) was comprised of three conferences which were organized under the common theme of 'IP in the Digital Age' (Zurich/Gerzensee, 2–4 December 2005, IP in the Digital Age; London, 17–19 February 2006, The Legal Response to New information Flows; and, for the first time, Munich, 28–30 April 2006, IP Aspects of Digital Technology). This year, ETH hosted the II EIPIN Doctoral meeting in Zurich, 31 March–1 April 2006. It was also in this year that Queen Mary offered the organization of a new remarkable event, the I EIPIN Job Fair, which took place in London, 13 May 2006. The EIPIN Job Fair was designed to facilitate the meeting between EIPIN students and potential future employers, both private enterprises and public institutions.

12. Three EIPIN meetings, devoted to the same overall theme were organized in the academic year 2006–2007 (VIII EIPIN Congress). The first one, in Munich, 1–3 December 2006 (Information Flows, Software Protection and Standardization); the second, in Zurich/Gerzensee, 16–18 February 2007 (New Business Models: DRM's Collective

Societies and Open Source); and the third, in Alicante, 4–6 May 2007 (Domain Names, Trademarks and Licensing). The III EIPIN Doctoral Meeting took place in Zurich on 13–14 April 2007, and the II EIPIN Job Fair was again organized in London on 12 May 2007 with the participation of Novartis, Bovard, Jones Day, Wuesthoff, Covington & Burling and Procter & Gamble.

13. It is also worth mentioning that a regional conference on IP Education and Networking was co-organised by the EC-ASEAN Intellectual Property Rights Co-operation Programme (ECAPII) and the ASEAN Universities Network (AUN) on 28–30 May 2007 in Bangkok, Thailand, with the co-operation of the Chulalongkorn University. Over 50 academics from AUN member universities and EIPIN representatives combined their efforts to identify needs on IP education in the ASEAN region, and to customize national IP curricula and to further develop the ECAP II Regional Handbook on IP teaching prepared under the cooperation framework of EIPIN and AUN.

14. The IX EIPIN Congress (2007–2008) was divided into five events. Three EIPIN student meetings, which addressed the topic of IP enforcement: Zurich/Gerzensee, 30 November–2 December 2007 (Enforcement Framework and Civil Enforcement); Strasbourg, 14–16 March 2008 (Enforcing Industrial Property in Europe); and London, 18–20 April 2008: (Criminal Enforcement)). The IV EIPIN Doctoral Meeting was hosted, once again, by ETH in Zurich, 23–25 May 2008. The III EIPIN Job Fair, which took place in Munich under the auspices of the MIPLC on 10 May 2008.

15. During the academic year 2008–2009 the number of EIPIN meetings was limited to two, as experience had shown that the organization of three big events during the same year was a disproportionate effort. This X EIPIN Congress was again devoted to issues of IP enforcement and was organized by ETH (Zurich/Gerzensee, 23–25 January 2009: Enforcement Framework and Civil Enforcement) and CEIPI (Strasbourg, 27 February–1 March 2009: Criminal Enforcement of Intellectual Property). MIPLC organized the IV EIPIN Job Fair.

16. The organization of the XI EIPIN Congress (2009–2010) was led by QMIPRI (London, 26–28 February 2010: Intellectual Property, Privacy and Publicity) and by MIPLC (Munich, 9–11 April 2010: Intellectual Property and Unfair Competition). The V EIPIN Doctoral Meeting took place in London on 26 February 2010.

17. Sadly, this was the last year for the participation of our colleagues from ETH, as the Program so successfully run in Zurich came to a close this year. Needless to say, we are all deeply indebted to the outstanding commitment of both professors and students from the Eidgenössische Technische Hochschule, and most particularly to EIPIN co-founder, Professor Gerard Hertig.

18. The XII EIPIN Congress (2010–2011) also consisted of two conferences. The first one was organized by CEIPI and took place at the premises of the European Parliament in Strasbourg on 24–25 February under the title 'Constructing European Intellectual Property: Achievements and New Perspectives'. The second conference was held in Alicante, 8–10 April 2011. In Alicante, the students and professors presented and debated on the subject of 'New Trends in Intellectual Property Protection'. Part of the meeting was generously hosted by the Office for Harmonization of the Internal Market (OHIM). The VI EIPIN Doctoral Meeting also took place in Alicante on 7 April 2011.

19. The academic contributions of the conference which took place in Strasbourg will be the basis for the first volume of the 'European Intellectual Property Institutes Network (EIPIN) Series', a new publication series which provides a platform for dissemination of results of the forefront thinking on matters related to intellectual property law discussed during the EIPIN Congresses and which will come to life during the year 2012.

20. Finally, the XIII EIPIN Congress rounds the 2011–2012 academic year around the topic 'Imitation as Innovation'. The first session took place in Munich in the premises of the European Patent Office on 3–5 February 2012 with MIPLC also hosting the VII EIPIN Doctoral Meeting on 2 February 2012. The second session brought all the participating institutions to London from 20 to 22 April, where the network was enlarged by its fifth member, the Intellectual Property Law and Knowledge Management (IPKM) at Maastricht University (Netherlands).

21. The next XIV EIPIN Congress of the academic year 2012–2013 will be hosted by the IPKM, in Maastricht, and the CEIPI, in Strasbourg.

22. EIPIN is a very healthy institution which has shown during last thirteen years how powerful networking between postgraduate students and between doctorates coming from different institutions and cultures can

be. More than six hundreds 'eipiners' testify year after year that having had the opportunity to participate in an EIPIN Congress or an EIPIN Doctoral Meeting was one of the most outstanding landmarks of their professional and academic training and brought them a new perspective of international relations. Above all, bringing people together is a must and largely justifies the efforts of so many scholars from so many places of Europe. Long live EIPIN!!!

From Alicante, London, Maastricht, Munich and Strasbourg, 22nd April 2012.
The EIPIN series editors

Introduction

Christophe Geiger

Europe today stands at a crossroads. In fact, the European model based on a high level of social protection and a welfare state is currently under pressure. Shaken by the economic crisis and already seriously in debt, the European states, devoid of natural resources, have no option for recovery other than by making full use of their trumps. In order to do this, they can, in particular, rely on the existence of relatively high-performing educational systems that allow the emergence of new ideas, sources of economic development. With labour being considerably cheaper elsewhere, the Old World is faced with a relatively simple equation: 'innovate or disappear', and has thus no choice but to rely on its brain power. High hopes are undeniably being placed on what economists call the 'knowledge economy',[1] and the European Council in Lisbon already made this one of its priorities at the turn of the century in the year 2000. More than ten years later, recent strategic documents from the European Union have emphasized the extreme importance of sectors based on intangibles and new technologies for the development of the European economy.[2] However, the objectives set today go considerably further than strictly economic preoccupations. In fact, a recent

---

1 *See* e.g. D. Foray (2004), *The Economics of Knowledge*, Cambridge: MIT Press; OECD, 'Innovation in the Knowledge Economy, Implications for Education and Learning' (Paris, OECD Publishing, Centre for Educational Research and Innovation, 2004).

2 *See* the 'Europe 2020' strategy (COM (2010) 2020) and the Digital Agenda for Europe (COM (2010) 245). This view is shared at a more global level by the OECD and WIPO. In a recent report examining the major trends of knowledge and innovation within the global economy, the OECD in effect emphasized that the role of innovation will be essential 'in lifting economies out of the downturn and finding new and sustainable sources of growth and competitiveness' (OECD Science, Technology and Industry Scoreboard 2011, 'Innovation and Growth in Knowledge Economies', Paris, OECD, 2011, Summary). According to a recent study done by the WIPO, intellectual property rights have thus become a central element for the strategies adopted by innovative firms worldwide as the knowledge markets based on intellectual property rights continue to grow. As a result, policies in the field of intellectual property have become the very first priority in innovation-related policies (WIPO, 'World Intellectual Property Report 2011 – The Changing Face of Innovation', WIPO Economics & Statistics Series, Geneva, November 2011).

Commission document entitled 'A single market in intellectual property rights' dated 24 May 2011 emphasizes that,

> innovation not only helps the European economy to flourish. It is indispensable to address the challenges that humankind is facing in the 21st century: ensuring food security, containing climate change, dealing with demographic change and improving citizen's health. It also has an essential role to play in the quality of daily life by fostering cultural diversity.[3]

And the document concludes that it is the system of intellectual property rights that will have to bear the main responsibility for achieving all these objectives!

Intellectual property law, or more generally the law on intangibles, will therefore inevitably play an essential role in the future, since it will have the delicate function of giving a framework to a rapidly expanding array of activities, regarded by decision makers as being the main factor for development and the guarantee for the survival of the competitiveness of the European economy.[4] However, the topic is complex. In fact, intellectual property has become a sensitive subject. Astonishingly, the more intellectual property rights have become the centre of economic activity, the more their legitimacy has been contested within public opinion and in various circles. Amongst economists in particular, certain voices have been raised against a development of the law that tends towards 'over-protection' and the consequences of which on the economy and the collective well-being have in part been insufficiently evaluated.

The task for lawmakers is thus crucial but likewise difficult. Of course, the European legislator is not starting from scratch. Legislative activity in the field of intellectual property has been significant, given the number of directives and regulations that have been adopted over the last 20 years. Intellectual property has thus been the subject of considerable sectorial regulatory initiatives at European Union level. Despite this, however, the construction of a coherent European intellectual property law is still to be undertaken. The task is important. Of course, certain areas of intellectual property have benefitted

---

[3] *See* the Communication from the Commission to the European Parliament, the Council, the European Economic and Social Committee and the Committee of the Regions, 'A single market for intellectual property rights: Boosting creativity and innovation to provide economic growth, high quality jobs and first-class products and services in Europe', Brussels, 24 May 2011, (COM (2011) 287 final, p. 3).

[4] *Ibid.* p. 3: 'A modern, integrated European IP regime will make a major contribution to growth, sustainable job creation and to the competitiveness of our economy [...], objectives which are essential to sustain the EU's recovery from the economic and financial crisis. It will enable the development of sectors such as commerce and digital industries which offer the greatest potential for future growth.'

from more attention than others: some fields have been considerably harmonized, others – much less; some areas benefit from unitary rights while others do not (or, at least, not yet). Certain initiatives have likewise been subject to serious blockages during the legislative process and have not reached their conclusion. However, the establishment of a truly European intellectual property model, a balanced model that could ensure growth while at the same time being supported by public opinion, still requires considerable reflection. This is the aim of this volume, the result of a conference organized at the European Parliament in Strasbourg on 24 and 25 February 2011 within the framework of the EIPIN network (European Intellectual Property Institutes Network). This volume reflects the structure of the conference, namely the first part containing an evaluation of the European intellectual property law system ('Assessing the European Intellectual Property System') and the second part analysing the prospects for the development of this system ('Developing the European Intellectual Property System'). While the majority of the oral contributions have led to a chapter in this book, not everything that was said on the occasion of the conference was laid down in written form. This is particularly the case of the very stimulating discussions held on the occasion of the final round table closing the conference, which were moderated with great talent by Professor Manuel Desantes of the University of Alicante, during which speakers, in particular the representatives of the principal European institutions and intellectual property organizations, replied very freely and without stonewalling to questions prepared in advance by the conference participants. Moreover, certain other chapters have been added in order to complete the discussion. This is for instance the case for the chapter by Xavier Seuba on the European Union's free trade agreements and the rules on enforcement of intellectual property rights, which has been specially written for this volume, or the joint article on the Impact of the Anti-Counterfeiting Trade Agreement on the Legal Framework for IP Enforcement in the European Union. The final result, it is hoped, might serve as an inspiration in putting forward useful ideas for the elaboration of a genuine European intellectual property law.

Anyhow, there is still much work to do. The definition of a European identity will require the continuation of the development of common visions, in the field of intellectual property as well as in other fields. As rightly emphasized by the Romanian political scientist, Cristian Pârvulescu, 'Europe is neither a geographical area nor a market, it is a state of mind based on values.'[5] It is surely this state of mind that gave rise to the creation of the EIPIN network in 1999, and which still inspires it today. There is no doubt that its future work

[5] C. Pârvulescu, interview published in Libération, Monday 30 June 2008, p. 19.

will continue to contribute to the progress of the European spirit in the field of IP. At this point, it is appropriate to express our warmest thanks to the directors and members of the European Intellectual Property Institutes Network (currently made up of the Queen Mary Intellectual Property Research Institute (QMIPRI) at Queen Mary, University of London; the Magister Lycentinvs at the University of Alicante; the Intellectual Property Law and Knowledge Management (IPKM) at Maastricht University; the Centre for International Intellectual Property Studies (CEIPI) of the University of Strasbourg; and the Munich Intellectual Property Law Center (MIPLC)), in particular Professors Guido Westkamp, Josef Drexl, Manuel Desantes, Anselm Kamperman Sanders, Aurelio López-Tarruella, Dieter Stauder and Yves Reboul, as well as Dr Nari Lee and Seth Ericson of the MIPLC for chairing some of the panels, and of course to all the students from the four academic institutions who participated at the conference and whose enthusiasm contributed to its success. Enormous thanks are also due to Mrs Catherine Trautmann, Member of the European Parliament and a confirmed European, for having agreed to be the patron of the conference and for having delivered an inspiring closing speech. We are extremely grateful to her for this important support.

However, this work could not have been possible without the meaty contributions of the speakers at the conference who have been so kind as to submit a written version of their contributions in the form of chapters, and the decisive assistance provided by Roberto D'Erme and Oleksandr Bulayenko, research assistants and doctoral students at the CEIPI. Mr D'Erme was particularly involved in the organization of the conference and participated very actively in its preparation, while Mr Bulayenko carried out impressive work during the editing phase, thus permitting the results of the conference to be accessible in the form of this volume. Our warmest thanks are addressed to all of them.

PART I

Assessing the European intellectual property system

Section 1

IP and European Construction

1. The construction of intellectual property in the European Union: searching for coherence

Christophe Geiger

There is no doubt anymore: European Union law has become the main source of influence on the national laws of the Member States. Today, the European Union constitutes a model of regional legal integration. It has been attributed broad powers by the Member States for the purpose of achieving their common objectives[1] and has set up numerous institutions to implement them.[2] Initially hesitant, the European Union has gradually become interested in intellectual property ('IP') and adopted a variety of legislative acts, which were subsequently supplemented by numerous decisions of the Court of Justice of the European Union (the 'CJEU'). This contributed to the elaboration of a new legal framework in this field, so that it is today possible to speak of a veritable 'European intellectual property law'.[3] However, this construction has not been systematic but has arisen more or less without organization, often following the agenda of the various institutions. Moreover, as a sign (indeed even proof?) of this lack of unity, there are still very few works that present European intellectual property law in an organized manner.[4] Is such a task impossible given the lack of coherence in European legislative provisions? This is the question that we shall attempt to answer in the following. It is today

1 See Article 1 of the Treaty on the European Union (hereinafter the 'TEU') as well as of the Treaty on the Functioning of the European Union (hereinafter the 'TFEU'): *OJ* 30 March 2010, 2010/C 83/01.

2 Article 13 TEU.

3 This study does not concern the Europe of the Munich Convention dated 5 October 1973 (the 'EPC'), which resulted from an international agreement, but rather the European Union.

4 Mention should be made, however, of the work edited by G. Tritton (2008), *Intellectual Property in Europe*, 3rd ed., London: Sweet & Maxwell, which was the first to attempt this difficult task. See also B. Harris (2005), *Intellectual Property law in the European Union*, New York: W.S. Hein & Co, and more recently C. Seville (2010), *EU Intellectual Property Law and Policy*, Cheltenham, UK and Northampton, MA: Edward Elgar; T. Cook (2010), *EU Intellectual Property Law*, Oxford: OUP.

essential to ask whether the construction is coherent, since this will permit an assessment of the legislation and thus allow us to identify the direction for the future development of intellectual property within the European Union.

There are four possible stages of a reply to the question about coherence of the construction of European law in the field of intellectual property. First of all, we must recall that the activity of the European legislature has been made difficult in the absence of explicit powers of the Union in this field (1). Then, we will see that for a certain number of reasons, the numerous advances in the legislation were not always well thought out (2). Subsequently, we will examine the prospects that have opened up, following the entry into effect of the Treaty of Lisbon, for the development of a coherent law at Union level (3). Finally, in the form of a conclusion, we shall briefly study what work still needs to be done in the field of European intellectual property law (4).

1. A DIFFICULT STARTING POINT: THE ABSENCE OF EXPLICIT COMPETENCE OF THE EU IN THE FIELD OF INTELLECTUAL PROPERTY

First of all, it is appropriate to remember that the EU institutional framework did certainly not facilitate the emergence of coherence in the development of a European intellectual property law. As we know, the European Union has one jurisdiction *ratione materiae*: its intervention must be based on a provision of the Treaty that authorizes it to act.[5] However, at the beginning, there was no provision in the Treaty of Rome that explicitly granted competences to the European Community in the field of intellectual property. The founding treaties are silent on the question, and the Treaty establishing the European Community (the 'ECT') even seemed to be hostile to the intervention of the Community legislature; Article 295 ECT,[6] for instance, stated that the 'Treaty shall in no way prejudice the rules in Member States governing the system of property ownership'. Consequently, a European framework in the field of intellectual property could only be constructed on a fragmented legal basis, i.e., general provisions; such fragmentation would obviously have an important influence on the coherence of the construction. For purposes of simplification, we will only address here two provisions (even though there are obviously others[7]): former Articles 95 and 308 of the ECT. First, the former

---

[5] Article 5(1) and 5(2) TEU.

[6] Now Article 345 TFEU.

[7] A certain number of more specific legal bases have occasionally been used as the main legal basis or as a supplement to the general legal basis. Mention could be

Article 95,[8] which permits the Union to act in order to approximate legislations with the object of the 'establishment and functioning of the internal market', served as the legal basis for the majority of the directives in the field of intellectual property. In this context, it should be recalled that the procedure of joint decision-making with the European Parliament was only introduced with the Treaty of Maastricht in 1992, i.e. until that date the European Parliament lacked this power, which did not remain without consequences for the legitimacy of the regulations.[9] Second, there is the general clause of the former Article 308 of the ECT,[10] which allows the European Union to take measures when it is required to act in order to achieve one of its objectives, but where no explicit power has been granted. We have seen that this was the case for intellectual property. This provision was thus the only option when it was decided to set up Community IP rights.[11] Accordingly, it was on this legal basis that the rules concerning the Community trademark,[12] Community plant variety protection[13] or the Community designs[14] were adopted. However, the recourse to this general clause has one disadvantage: the procedure is cumbersome since it needs the unanimity of the votes in the Council. It is for this reason that, with politically very sensitive issues such as the European Union

---

made of the former Article 37 ECT (now Article 43 TFEU) on the Common Agricultural Policy which was used as the main legal basis in the field of geographical indications and appellations of origin, or the Articles of the Treaty concerning the free movement of services (former Articles 47(2) and 55 ECT) that served as supplementary legal basis in the field of approximation of copyright and neighbouring rights.

[8] Now Article 114 TEU.

[9] To which we shall return below, 2.

[10] Now Article 352 TFEU.

[11] Except for the provisions concerning geographical indications and appellations of origin, which were adopted on the basis of the former Article 37 ECT concerning the Common Agricultural Policy (Council Regulation (EEC) No. 2081/92 of 14 July 1992, on the protection of geographical indications and appellations of origin for agricultural products and foodstuff (*OJ* 24 July 1992, L 208), replaced by Council Regulation (EC) No. 510/2006 of 20 March 2006 on the protection of geographical indications and appellations of origin for agricultural products and foodstuff (*OJ* 31 March 2006, L 93); see also, in this field, Council Regulation (EC) No. 479/2008 of 29 April 2008 on the common organisation of the market in wine: *OJ* 6 June 2008, L 148). Council Regulation (EEC) No. 1768/92 of 18 June 1992 concerning the creation of a supplementary protection certificate for medicinal products (*OJ* 2 July 1992, L 182) was adopted on the legal basis of Article 100A of the Treaty of Rome (former Article 95 ECT).

[12] Council Regulation (EC) No. 40/94 dated 20 December 1993 on the Community Trademark: *OJ* 14 January 1994, L 11.

[13] Council Regulation (EC) No. 2100/94 dated 27 July 1994 on Community plant variety rights: *OJ* 1 September 1994, L 227.

[14] Council Regulation (EC) No. 6/2002 dated 12 December 2001 on Community designs: *OJ* 5 January 2002, L 3.

patent, it is very difficult to bring the procedure to a conclusion, with the result that such a right has still not been adopted.

2. A PROGRESSIVE CONSTRUCTION, OFTEN AMBITIOUS BUT NOT ALWAYS COHERENT AND WELL THOUGHT OUT IN ADVANCE

This difficult starting point did not prevent significant action on the part of the European legislature on the basis of the above-mentioned provisions, leading to the gradual construction of its own EU system in the field of intellectual property. The action was often ambitious. The result is that today we have Union rights that tend to function well[15] and, in various fields, an approximation of legislation that renders trade easier and contributes to the creation of a true European identity in the field of intellectual property. Having said that, the construction of European IP law was not always coherent or well thought out. One of the reasons has already been mentioned: it is probably due to the absence of the Union's explicit competences, which meant that it was always necessary to act 'in the light of the functioning of the internal market', i.e. to approach the subject entirely from the economic point of view. However, we know that intellectual property can also have huge cultural, social, environmental and even philosophical implications.[16] To name but two examples, copyright covers access to culture and information,[17] while patents on living organisms involve important ethical questions.[18] Gradually, this 'societal'

---

15 Of course, in addition to the Union rights, there is also the European patent conferred in accordance with the Munich Convention, which is an international agreement.

16 On the 'social function' of intellectual property rights, see C. Geiger (2006), '"Constitutionalizing" Intellectual Property Law? The Influence of Fundamental Rights on Intellectual Property in Europe', *IIC*, 375; C. Geiger (2010), 'La fonction sociale des droits de propriété intellectuelle', *Recueil Dalloz* (D.), 510.

17 As an example, see C. Geiger (2004), *Droit d'auteur et droit du public à l'information, approche de droit comparé*, Paris: Litec; C. Geiger (2007), 'Author's Right, Copyright and the Public's Right to Information: A Complex Relationship', in F. Macmillan (ed.), *New Directions in Copyright Law*, Vol. 5, 24, Cheltenham, UK and Northampton, MA: Edward Elgar Publishing.

18 As an example, see J. Koopman (2008), 'Human Rights Implications of Patenting Biotechnological Knowledge', in P. Torremans (ed.), *Intellectual Property and Human Rights*, Austin, Boston, Chicago, New York, Netherlands: Kluwer Law International, 53; F. Franconi (ed.) (2007), *Biotechnologies and International Human Rights*, Oxford: Hart Publishing; G. Van Overwalle (2010), 'Human Rights' Limitations in Patent Law' and D. Matthews (2010), 'Intellectual Property Rights, Human Rights and the Right to Health', in W. Grosheide (ed.), *Intellectual Property*

dimension entered the discussions more and more frequently, and the European Parliament would give voice to the latter. A study conducted by the Centre for International Intellectual Property Studies (CEIPI) showed that the Parliament, over the course of the years, developed a position of its own in the field of intellectual property.[19] By allowing debate to take place on a certain number of controversial subjects, the European Parliament has not been reluctant to take up courageous positions and to intervene in a reasoned manner in the adoption of an appropriate legal framework for intellectual property rights at EU level. This led to important corrections to certain of the proposed texts (such as was the case for the Directive concerning the legal protection of biotechnological inventions[20]) and also to large-scale rejections, when the texts failed to obtain support and were not sufficiently 'prepared' in advance (as was the case for the proposed Directive on the patentability of inventions implemented by computer, rejected by the European Parliament by a majority of 95%).[21]

This new role of the European Parliament is very important since it means that discussion can take place on subjects that are closer to the heart of public opinion. This, ultimately, can only increase the legitimacy of the activities of the Union legislature in this field. An example is the resolution[22] adopted by the European Parliament by a wide majority demanding full information from the European Commission on the progress of the negotiations concerning the proposed Anti-Counterfeiting Trade Agreement (ACTA).[23] As we know, the

---

Rights and Human Rights: A Paradox, Cheltenham, UK and Northampton, MA: Edward Elgar, 236 and 118.

19 See C. Geiger and E. Py, La législation communautaire en matière de propriété intellectuelle et le rôle du European Parliament, Study for the European Parliament, Strasbourg, May 2009, available at the CEIPI website (www.ceipi.edu). This study was published in French and English in a revised version entitled 'Droit de propriété intellectuelle de l'Union européenne', in: Etat des lieux et perspectives dans le domaine des questions juridiques et du droit parlementaire, European Parliament, Brussels, 27 May 2009, JURI_4_1.

20 Directive 98/44/EC of the European Parliament and Council dated 6 July 1998 on the legal protection of biotechnological inventions: *OJ* 30 July 1998, L 213/13. This Directive followed the rejection by the European Parliament on 1 March 1995 of a first draft Directive dated 21 October 1988, COM(1988) 0496.

21 Proposal for a Directive of the European Parliament and of the Council on the patentability of computer-implemented inventions dated 20 February 2002, COM(2002) 92 final, rejected by the European Parliament on 6 July 2005 after numerous modifications of the text. See on the issue R.M. Hilty and C. Geiger (2005), 'Patenting Software? A Judicial and Socio-Economic Analysis', *IIC*, 615.

22 See the resolution of the European Parliament dated 10 March 2010 on the transparency and state of progress of the ACTA (Anti-Counterfeiting Trade Agreement) negotiations P7_TA-PROV(2010)0058.

23 On this agreement see C. Geiger (2012), 'Weakening Multilateralism in

secret negotiations on this agreement, conducted for three years outside any official multilateral body between the Commission and ten other countries, gave rise to considerable concern within public opinion,[24] thus emphasizing the feeling of exclusion sometimes felt with respect to regulations in the field of intellectual property rights at EU level. In compliance with this resolution, the Commission made a version of the proposed agreement public on 21 April 2010;[25] following the last cycle of negotiations in Tokyo, it published a consolidated version on 2 October 2010,[26] and then a final version on 3 December 2010 following the legal verification meeting held in Sydney.[27] On 24 November 2010 the European Parliament adopted a resolution in favour of the October version of the project, which it considers to be fully compatible with the 'acquis communautaire'.[28] This was surprising, especially in light of

---

Intellectual Property Lawmaking: A European Perspective on ACTA', W.I.P.O.J., **3**(2), 166, enhanced version of a Study made on the request of the Committee on International Trade (INTA), Directorate-General for External Policies of the European Parliament, 'The Anti-Counterfeiting Trade Agreement (ACTA): A Comprehensive Assessment from a European Perspective', March 2012. A. Metzger (2010), 'A Primer on ACTA, What Europeans Should Fear about the Anti-Counterfeiting Trade Agreement', *Journal of Intellectual Property, Information Technology and Ecommerce Law (JIPITEC)*, 109; P. Arhel (2011), 'L'accord commercial anticontrefaçon: version finale', *Propr. industr.* March, 13; M. Stieper (2011), 'Das Anti-Counterfeiting Trade Agreement (ACTA)', *GRUR Int.*, 124; P. Yu (2011), 'Six Secret (and Now Open) Fears of ACTA', *SMU Law Review*, **64** (3), 975; K. Weatherall (2011), 'Politics, Compromise, Text and the Failures of the Anti-Counterfeiting Trade Agreement', *Sidney Law Review*, **33**, 229, and by the same author: (2011) 'ACTA as a New Kind of International IP Law Making', *Am.U.Int'l L.Rev.*, **26** (3), 839; J.-C. Galloux, *RTDcom*. January/March 2011, 81.

24 See the critical comments by C.R. McManis (2009), 'The Proposed Anti-Counterfeiting Trade Agreement (ACTA): Two Tales of a Treaty', *Houston Law Review*, **46** (4), 1235.

25 ACTA, consolidated text prepared for public release, April 2010, available at: http://trade.ec.europa.eu/doclib/docs/2010/april/tradoc_146029.pdf (last accessed 19 July 2012).

26 Anti-Counterfeiting Trade Agreement, Consolidated text, Reflects changes made during September 2010 Tokyo Round, Informal Predecisional/Deliberative Draft 2 October 2010.

27 The definitive text is available at the website of the Trade DG of the European Commission, which negotiated the Agreement, http://trade.ec.europa.eu/doclib/docs/2010/december/tradoc_147079.pdf (last accessed 19 July 2012). This Agreement was signed on 1 October 2011 in Tokyo by the representatives of eight of the negotiating parties (Australia, Canada, Japan, Republic of Korea, Morocco, New Zealand, Singapore and the United States) and on 26 January 2012 by the European Union and 22 of its Member States (Austria, Belgium, Bulgaria, Czech Republic, Denmark, Finland, France, Greece, Hungary, Ireland, Italy, Latvia, Lithuania, Luxemburg, Malta, Poland, Portugal, Romania, Slovenia, Spain, Sweden and the United Kingdom).

28 Resolution of the European Parliament dated 24 November 2010 on the Anti-Counterfeiting Trade Agreement (ACTA), P7_TA-PROV (2010)0432.

the fact that numerous provisions clearly go beyond the current EU legal framework. The most flagrant example is that the agreement includes an important section on criminal enforcement, while the European Union does not at present have any approximated legislation in this field.[29] This led a group of European academics to draft an Opinion aimed at drawing the attention of the Union institutions, and of the European Parliament in particular, to the differences between the ACTA and European and international intellectual property law, and to the modifications to European law that the ratification of this agreement would involve.[30] After months of intense debates in its various Committees,[31] the European Parliament finally rejected ACTA on 4 July 2012 with an overwhelming majority.[32] Coherence can therefore also be achieved through transparency.

---

[29] This also raises the question of the competence of the Union, since traditionally criminal law has been left to the Member States. Article 83(2) TFEU only provides for the possibility of adopting, by means of a directive, 'minimum rules concerning the definition of criminal offences and penalties' when 'the harmonisation of the legislative provisions proves to be *indispensible* to ensuring the effective implementation of Union policy' (emphasis added). The 'indispensible' nature of criminal penalties for all the offences envisaged would have to be proven in the light of the fact that there is already a harmonized element for civil penalties, which might be considered sufficient and better suited in many cases. See on these questions, A. Ramalho (2011), 'The European Union and ACTA – Or Making Omelettes without Eggs (Again)', *IIC*, 97. A different solution would amount to using an international approach to circumvent the Union's (limited) competences. Moreover, in its Opinion No. 1/94, the Court of Justice stated that the power to ratify TRIPS was divided, i.e., the agreement required ratification by the Union and the Member States (Opinion of the Court of 15 November 1994 on the Competence of the Community to conclude international agreements concerning services and the protection of intellectual property – Article 228(6) of the EC Treaty, *European Court reports* 1994 Page I-05267, paras 59–60).

[30] See the 'Opinion of European Academics on Anti-Counterfeiting Trade Agreement', 2011 *JIPITEC* **2**.

[31] Because of the vague and uncertain nature of some provisions of the Agreement, the European Parliament rapporteur on ACTA, David Martin, recommended that the 'European Parliament declines to give consent to ACTA' (Draft Recommendation on the draft Council decision on the conclusion of the Anti-Counterfeiting Trade Agreement, 12 April 2012 (2011/0167(NLE)), PR\898850EN.doc). Following the recommendation, the International Trade Committee, the Committee responsible for ACTA, voted on 21 June 2012 'to decline to consent to conclusion of the agreement' (Recommendation on the draft Council decision on the conclusion of the Anti-Counterfeiting Trade Agreement, 22 June 2012 (12195/2011 – C7-0027/2012 – 2011/0167(NLE)).

[32] European Parliament legislative resolution of 4 July 2012 on the draft Council decision on the conclusion of the Anti-Counterfeiting Trade Agreement between the European Union and its Member States, Australia, Canada, Japan, the Republic of Korea, the United Mexican States, the Kingdom of Morocco, New Zealand, the

The second element of the Community construction might paradoxically be related to the excessive activism of the European Commission, which has in the past sometimes been accused of giving way too easily to the pressures of the lobby and of being too willing to adopt legislation at the request of sectorial interests. To put it simply, priority is said to have been given to quantity over quality, without checking (specifically by means of serious economic studies) the usefulness of the legislative activity. Mention might be made here of, for example, legal protection of databases, where a very complicated legal instrument has been set up that according to the Commission's own admission has probably not had the expected success.[33] Another example is copyright, where rapid action was taken in order to protect exclusive rights and technical protection measures, without taking sufficient account of exceptions and limitations to those rights, which however play an essential role in the dissemination of works within society.[34] A recent example is the Directive extending the term of neighbouring rights from 50 to 70 years,[35] which was based on no independent economic study and has been massively rejected by the majority of European academics.[36]

Republic of Singapore, the Swiss Confederation and the United States of America (12195/2011 – C7-0027/2012 – 2011/0167(NLE)), P7_TA-PROV(2012)0287).

[33] See the evaluation of Directive 96/9/EC on the legal protection of databases published by the European Commission on 12 December 2005. On this text, see A. Kur, R.M. Hilty, C. Geiger and M. Leistner (2006), 'First Evaluation of Directive 96/9/EC on the Legal Protection of Databases – Comment by the Max Planck Institute for Intellectual Property, Competition and Tax Law, Munich', *IIC*, 551.

[34] Directive 2001/29/EC of the European Parliament and of the Council dated 22 May 2001 on the harmonisation of certain aspects of copyright and neighbouring rights in the information society: *OJ* 22 June 2001, L 167/10. This text has been the subject of a number of critical comments, see for example C. Geiger, 'The Future of Copyright in Europe: Striking a Fair Balance between Protection and Access to Information', Report for the Committee on Culture, Science and Education – Parliamentary Assembly, Council of Europe, Strasbourg, October 2009, available at: www.ceipi.edu. Published in a revised version in: (2010), *IPQ*, 1.

[35] Directive 2011/77/EU of the European Parliament and of the Council of 27 September 2011 amending Directive 2006/116/EC on the term of protection of copyright and certain related rights, *OJ* L 265, 11 October 2011, pp. 1–5 (for a comment see V.-L. Benabou (2011), *Propr. intell.*, **41**, 411). The Directive was adopted by the Council of the European Union on 12 September 2011 (press release 303, 13972/11). The Commission's proposal was for a term of 95 years (Proposal for a directive of 16 July 2008 amending Directive 2006/116/EC of the European Parliament and Council on the terms of protection of copyright and certain related rights, COM(2008) 464 final), which was reduced to 70 years thanks to the intervention of the European Parliament (legislative resolution of the European Parliament of 23 April 2009 on the proposed directive of the European Parliament and Council amending Directive 2006/116/EC of the European Parliament and Council on the terms of protection of copyright and certain related rights, P6_TA (2009)0282).

[36] See for example the joint position adopted by a certain number of European

A third vector of incoherence paradoxically derives from the CJEU's creative interpretation of the acquis communautaire in the field of intellectual property. Through the mechanism of preliminary rulings at the request of national judges in the Union, the Court of Justice has been able to interpret certain key concepts of European IP law; it could thus exercise considerable power in the direction of approximation,[37] since the national courts are subsequently bound by these interpretations. The problem is that the interpretations proposed by the judges are not always clear. Moreover, the decisions are sometimes contradictory, making it even more difficult to understand EU law. However, it must be conceded that this judicial activity also has its advantages; it pushes the dynamics of harmonization, the CJEU being able to succeed in areas where the Union's legislature has failed. In effect, in certain cases, one can see that gradually certain coherence is emerging as the decisions are being rendered. To take one example, the criteria for an abuse of a dominant position as applied to intellectual property law were refined between the *Magill* decision in 1995[38] and the *Microsoft* decision in 2007.[39] Thus, it is to be hoped that future decisions will further perfect the developed criteria.[40] One way of improving the quality of the decisions might result in the future from a greater dialogue between European judges and academics, enabling the former to

---

academics: (2008), 'Creativity stifled? A Joint Academic Statement on the Proposed Copyright Term Extension for Sound Recordings', *EIPR*, 341; C. Geiger, J. Passa and M. Vivant (2009), 'La proposition de directive sur l'extension de la durée de certains droits voisins: une remise en cause injustifiée du domaine public', *Propr. intell.*, **31**, 146; C. Geiger (2009), 'The Extension of the Term of Copyright and Certain Neighbouring Rights – A Never Ending Story?', *IIC*, 78.

[37] See on this issue in the field of copyright, L. Bently, 'Harmonization by Stealth: The Role of the ECJ', Paper presented at the conference 'Ten Years after the EU Directive on Copyright in the Information Society: Looking Back and Looking Forward', European Parliament, Brussels, 13 January 2012; A. Metzger (2012), 'Der Einfluss des EuGH auf die gegenwärtige Entwicklung des Urheberrechts', *GRUR*, 118.

[38] Joined cases C-241/91 P and C-242/91 P, *Radio Telefis Eireann (RTE) and Independent Television Publications Ltd (ITP) v Commission of the European Communities*. Judgment of the Court of 6 April 1995, ECR 1995 Page I-00743.

[39] Case T-201/04, *Microsoft Corp. v Commission of the European Communities*, Judgment of the Court of First Instance (Grand Chamber) of 17 September 2007, ECR 2007 Page II-03601.

[40] The conditions under which the refusal of a licence constitutes an abuse of a dominant position within the meaning of the EU Treaty have been specified since the *Magill* ruling, specifically in *IMS Health* (Court of Justice, 29 April 2004, Case No. C-418/01, ECR. I, p. 5039) and in the *Microsoft* decision of the General Court, even if there remain some uncertainties regarding the exact scope of the criteria. On these cases and more generally on the interface of intellectual property and competition law in the EU, see G. Ghidini (2010), *Innovation, Competition and Consumer Welfare in Intellectual Property Law*, Cheltenham, UK and Northampton, MA: Edward Elgar, 218 *et seq*.

benefit from the expertise of the latter when drafting their decisions. In this way, the judicial power could become an important vector for improved coherence of Union law in the field of intellectual property.

3. THE NEW PERSPECTIVES CREATED BY THE TREATY OF LISBON

The third stage in the construction of Community legislation is probably forthcoming, since the entry into effect of the Treaty of Lisbon on 1 December 2009 opened up new perspectives.[41] In fact, the Treaty of Lisbon set up a specific legal basis for the creation of European property rights. According to Article 118, the legislature, acting in accordance with the ordinary legislative procedure, can provide for uniform protection of intellectual property rights throughout the Union. This provision finally gives legitimacy to the efforts of the European Union; however, it might be regretted that the provision does not go all the way, since according to Paragraph 2 of Article 118, the question of the language arrangements for these rights continues to be subject to the rule of unanimity. This is obviously important for the implementation of a European Union patent, since, as we know, it is precisely the sensitive question of languages that in the past proved to be an obstacle to the adoption of a Regulation on this issue. Having said this, the Article may give a new impetus to the elaboration of an effective legislative framework. One might even dream of the implementation of a unitary copyright of the European Union, which would constitute the logical conclusion of the integration process.[42] On

---

[41] Treaty of Lisbon amending the Treaty on European Union and the Treaty establishing the European Community, signed at Lisbon, 13 December 2007: *OJ* 17 December 2007, 2007/C 306/01. The Max Planck Institute for Intellectual Property and Competition Law has launched a project aimed at studying the multiple potential consequences of the Treaty on intellectual property in Europe. For a first overview, see T. Jaeger, K.-D. Beiter, O. Fischer, A. Früh, R. Kordic and M. Postl (2009), 'Lessons from Lisbon', *The European Legal Forum*, 90. On this question, see also Scordamaglia (2010), 'Les dispositions relatives à la propriété intellectuelle dans le Traité de Lisbonne', *Propr. industr.*, March, focus 28; C. Geiger (2010), 'Intellectual "Property" after the Treaty of Lisbon, Towards a Different Approach in the New European Legal Order?', *EIPR*, 255.

[42] Numerous authors have spoken out in favour of creating a unified EU copyright law, see for example R.M. Hilty (2004), 'Copyright in the Internal Market. Harmonisation vs. Community Copyright Law', *IIC*, 760; C. Geiger (2009), 'Drafting the Appropriate and Balanced Scope of Copyright Protection in the European Union – What Language can Contribute to the Debate', in Y. Gendreau and A. Drassinower (eds), *Language and Copyright/Langues et droit d'auteur*, Québec and Brussels: Carswell and Bruylant, 93; F. Gotzen (2007), 'Copyright in Europe: *quo vadis*? Some

this subject, a proposed European Copyright Code drawn up by a group of university academics (the 'Wittem Group') was recently published and could serve as inspiration.[43] Implementation of a unitary copyright law appeared utopian only a short while ago but is now generating considerable interest, and the European Commission has recently even referred to this hypothesis as a conceivable option.[44]

Another change introduced by the Treaty of Lisbon is the linking of the Charter of Fundamental Rights of the European Union (the 'Charter') to primary law. This is of considerable importance, since one of the Articles of the Charter lays down that 'intellectual property is protected' (Article 17, para. 2). Intellectual property is thus consecrated at the very top of the pyramid of European Union norms,[45] a powerful symbol and a clear sign of the legitimacy of the Union in dealing with this subject. Nevertheless, intellectual property exists alongside other fundamental rights with which it will have to be

---

Conclusions after the Implementation of the Information Society Harmonisation Directive', *RIDA*, **211**, 2; P.B. Hugenholtz (2009), 'Copyright without Frontiers: the Problem of Territoriality in European Copyright Law', in E. Derclaye (ed.), *Research Handbook on the Future of EU Copyright*, Cheltenham, UK and Northampton, MA: Edward Elgar, 26: 'The potential advantages of a Community copyright are undeniable. A Community Copyright Regulation (or "European Copyright Law") would immediately establish a truly unified legal framework'; T. Cook and E. Derclaye (2011), 'A EU Copyright Code: What and How, if Ever?', *IPQ*, 259.

43 The 'European Copyright Code', released on 26 April 2010, available at: www.copyrightcode.eu. Version published in *EIPR* 2011, p. 76. For a comment see J.C. Ginsburg (2011), 'European Copyright Code – Back to First Principles (with some Additional Detail)', Columbia Public Law Research Paper, No. 11-261; E. Rosati (2010), 'The Wittem Group and the European Copyright Code', *JIPLP*, 862; R. Kuhlen (2011), 'Richtungsweisend oder eine nur begrenzt wahrgenommene Chance? Der Copyright-Code des Wittem-Projekts', *JIPITEC*, 18; L. Belder, L.E. Dijkman and A.E.M. Mombers (2011), 'The Age of Copyright: Wittem's Copyright Reform Proposal Compared to Samuelson's Preliminary Thoughts', *QMJIP*, **1** (3), 200; C. Castets-Renard (2012), 'La réforme du droit d'auteur en Europe: vers un code européen?', *Recueil Dalloz*, **15**, 955.

44 See Communication from the Commission to the European Parliament, the Council, the European Economic and Social Committee and the Committee of the Regions, 'On a Single Market for Intellectual Property Rights – Boosting creativity and innovation to provide economic growth, high quality jobs and first class products and services in Europe', Brussels, 24 May 2011, COM(2011) 287 final, p. 14, and the Green Paper on the online distribution of audiovisual works in the European Union: opportunities and challenges towards a single digital market (Brussels, 13 July 2011, COM(2011) 427, p. 14), which states that 'an optional unitary copyright could be envisaged' which 'could be made available on a voluntary basis and coexist alongside the national rights'.

45 The European Charter of Fundamental Rights of the European Union, which until now has not had any binding force, acquires 'the same legal value as the Treaties' and thus is integrated into European Union primary law (Article 6(1) TEU).

balanced, as well as other founding principles of the common market such as free competition and the free circulation of goods. This implementation of what has sometimes been called a 'European economic constitution'[46] might permit the development of a balanced approach in the field of intellectual property, since the top of the EU legal system will be composed of a mixture of utilitarian (economic approach in terms of the market, originating from competition law) and ethical (approach in terms of fundamental rights) sources.[47]

4. AS A CONCLUSION: WHAT WILL BE THE FUTURE FIELDS OF ACTION TO BUILD A TRUE EUROPEAN INTELLECTUAL PROPERTY LAW?

In conclusion, we can state that there are already significant legal provisions for intellectual property within the European Union; it seems, however, necessary to work towards ensuring the coherence of said provisions so that they can constitute both an effective framework for the knowledge economy and a regulation that can inspire popular support amongst the people of Europe. The Treaty of Lisbon has created the tools for working towards this objective, but there remains much to be done.[48]

Amongst these future actions, we have already mentioned the implementation of a European Union patent, which will have to be accompanied by the

---

[46] T. Mylly (2009), *Intellectual Property and European Economic Constitutional Law*, Vaajakoski: Gummerus Kirjapaino Oy, 232: 'The European economic constitution can be seen as an open constitution accommodating different competing values between free competition and economic and social cohesion'. This idea had already been used before the adoption of the Treaty of Lisbon, see in particular J. Baquero Cruz (2002), *Between Competition and Free Movement. The Economic Constitutional Law of the European Community*, Oxford: Hart Publishing.

[47] Mylly, *ibid*, 33. According to this author, following the entry into effect of the Treaty of Lisbon, economic considerations based on an analysis of the market drawn from competition law are corrected by ethical and democratic considerations drawn from the fundamental rights, and *vice versa*, thus reconciling the idealist and the utilitarian approaches in the field of intellectual property.

[48] As a sign of a strong political will to make progress in this field, the European Commission also adopted a 'global strategy in the field of intellectual property rights' on 24 May 2011, the aim of which is to re-adjust the applicable European legal framework (see Commission press release, IP/11/630 and *supra* note 44), in particular to adapt it to technological development and the increasing importance of online activities. In this document, the Commission thus proposes a series of major short and long term measures in numerous fields of intellectual property.

establishment of an advanced judicial system to guarantee its effectiveness, and hence its attractiveness.[49] The question of the creation of a separate jurisdiction at Union level is very complex, and the works are currently under way.[50] Recently, at the European Council meeting of 28-29 June 2012, participating Member States at least reached an agreement on the location of such a specialized court. The seat of the Central Division of the Court of First Instance of the Unified Patent Court and of the President of the Court of First Instance will be located in Paris. It was also decided to create specialized

---

[49] See also the independent report 'Digital Opportunity, A Review of Intellectual Property and Growth' presented to the British Prime Minister by Prof. Ian Hargreaves in May 2011, p. 3, identifying the creation of the European Union patent and a unitary judicial system as being the main priorities. On this question, see A. Poore (2011), 'The European Union Patent System: Off Course or On the Rocks?', *EIPR*, 409 and the proceedings of the CEIPI Conference on the topic: 'What Patent Law for the European Union?', organized at the European Parliament, Strasbourg, on 26 and 27 April 2012 (forthcoming).

[50] On the question, see the presentations made at the CEIPI conference entitled 'Towards a European Patent Court' organized at the European Parliament on 16 and 17 April 2010 (available at: www.ceipi.edu), and J.-C. Galloux and B. Warusfel (2009), 'Aspects juridictionnels et procéduraux des brevets européens et communautaires', *Propr. intell.*, **30**, 9; B. Warusfel (2010), 'La juridictionnalisation du droit européen de la propriété industrielle', in *Droits de propriété intellectuelle, Liber amicorum Georges Bonet,* Paris: Litec, 533. On 23 March 2009, the European Council published a proposed international agreement aimed at creating a jurisdiction with competence for disputes concerning the European patent and the future Community patent (Draft Agreement on the European and Community Patents Court and Draft Statute – Revised Presidency text, Doc. No. 7928/09 PI 23 COUR 29; for a comment, see V. Scordamaglia (2009), *Propr. industr.* May, Study No. 9, 11). The Court of Justice of the European Union, requested to assess the compatibility of the project with Union law, however, issued a negative comment (ECR, Notice 1/09 of 8 March 2011). For a comment, see J.-C. Galloux (2011), *Propr. intell.*, No. 39, 233), emphasizing the problems of competences and of the reconciliation of the rules concerning the operation of this international jurisdiction with the Union's institutional rules. The project will probably have to be amended in order for it to fit better into the institutional framework of the EU treaties. The Commission also announced that it intends to pursue these works as far as concerns the proposals aimed at creating a unitary and specialized jurisdiction for the classical European patent and the future European patent with unitary effect (press release, 24 May 2011, *supra* note 48, p. 2). The Presidency of the Council of the European Union has since published, on 14 June 2011, a new proposal for an agreement aimed at taking account of the remarks made by the Court (Note of the General Secretariat, Council of the European Union, Draft agreement on a Unified Patent Court and draft Statute, 11533/11, PI 68, COUR 32), followed by a revised version of the project on 2 September 2011 (Revised Presidency text, 13751/11 PI 108 COUR 48). For a comment, see T. Jaeger (2012), 'All Back to Square One? - An Assessment of the Latest Proposals for a Patent and Court for the Internal Market and Possible Alternatives', *IIC*, 286.

thematic clusters in two sections of the Central Division, one in London and the other in Munich.[51]

The adoption of an EU patent right is also difficult and is the subject matter of a blockade within the Council on the question of translations (it should be recalled that any language arrangements need unanimous agreement). For this reason the Commission has now turned towards a system of 'enhanced co-operation' between a majority of Member States with the aim of creating a unitary patent within the Union with a language arrangement based on that of the European Patent Office (EPO), thus permitting the grant of a unitary patent valid in all the countries participating (currently all Member States except Italy and Spain).[52] On 14 December 2010, the Commission proposed, having recourse to the procedure of 'Enhanced cooperation' as provided for in Article 20 of the EU Treaty,[53] a procedure to which the European Parliament gave its consent on 15 February 2011.[54] The Competitiveness Council had, in turn, authorized this approach in a decision dated 10 March 2011.[55] The Commission presented two legislative proposals on 13 April 2011 concerning

---

[51] Conclusions of the European Council (28/29 June 2012), EUCO 76/12, available at: http://www.consilium.europa.eu/uedocs/cms_data/docs/pressdata/en/ec/131388.pdf (last accessed 23 July 2012). Important to note that the conclusions of the European Council on the outstanding and final issue of the so-called 'patent package' were supposed to be followed by a vote of the European Parliament at its recent plenary session of 2-5 July 2012. However, Parliament's scrutiny of the EU draft patent legislation was postponed due to the suggestion of the Council to delete the three key Articles, 6, 7 and 8, of the Regulation implementing enhanced cooperation in the area of the creation of unitary patent protection to be adopted by the Council and the European Parliament. Press Release, European Parliament, EU unitary patent: Council move would infringe EU law, says EP rapporteur, REF.: 20120709IPR48484, available at: http://www.europarl.europa.eu/news/en/pressroom/content/20120709IPR48484/html/EU-unitary-patent-Council-move-would-infringe-EU-law-says-EP-rapporteur (last accessed 23 July 2012).

[52] On this question, see N. Binctin (2011), 'Le projet de brevet européen à effet unitaire: en attendant un brevet de l'Union?', *Propr. intell.*, **40**, 270; M. Lamping (2011), 'Enhanced Cooperation – A Proper Approach to Market Integration in the Field of Unitary Patent Protection?', *IIC*, 879; H. Ullrich, 'Harmonizing Patent Law: The Untamable Union Patent', *Max Planck Institute for Intellectual Property & Competition Law Research Paper* No. 12-03.

[53] Proposal for a Council Decision authorising enhanced cooperation in the area of the creation of unitary patent protection, COM(2010) 790 final Brussels, 14 December 2010. See on the issue F. Sieber (2011), 'How does "Enhanced Cooperation" work?', *epi Information*, **3**, 103.

[54] European Parliament legislative resolution of 15 February 2011 on the draft Council decision authorising enhanced cooperation in the area of the creation of unitary patent protection (P7_TA-PROV(2011)0054).

[55] Council Decision of 10 March 2011 authorising enhanced cooperation in the area of the creation of unitary patent protection (2011/167/EU).

the system of enhanced co-operation, which were submitted to the Council and Parliament for examination.[56] On 27 June 2011, the Council of the European Union reached an agreement on the general lines of the proposals.[57] This development certainly constitutes a significant step forward towards a unitary right, and hence progress towards the development of a unified intellectual property law within Europe. However, it has alas not yet led to the creation of a true EU right,[58] which will mean delicate references to national law in the event of conflict.[59] In addition, in the long term it will not be possible to avoid the question about the sense of having three different patent systems coexisting in Europe: the national patent, the European patent and, tomorrow, the European Union patent system. Certain economists, in any event, have pointed out the risks of inefficiency of such structure.[60]

The question of the approximation of the criminal penalties for counterfeiting, revived by the proposed ACTA agreement that was already referred to, will probably also arise soon. It might be recalled that a proposed directive on the topic was recently the subject of impassioned discussions and ultimately failed to be adopted.[61] It will then be the moment to carefully draw up a text

---

56 Proposal for a Regulation of the European Parliament and of the Council implementing enhanced cooperation in the area of the creation of unitary patent protection, COM(2011) 215 final Brussels, 13 April 2011; and Proposal for a Council Regulation implementing enhanced cooperation in the area of the creation of unitary patent protection with regard to the applicable translation arrangements, COM(2011) 216 final Brussels, 13 April 2011. For a comment *see* E. Treppoz (2011), 'Le brevet unitaire est-il enfin pour demain?', *RTDeur*, 864; J. Pagenberg (2012), 'Die EU-Patentrechtsreform – Zurück auf Los?', *GRUR*, 582.

57 Press release by the Council of the European Union, Luxembourg, 27 June 2011, 11831/11, Press 184.

58 The right will be the result of a regional international agreement, the Munich Convention, and will be issued by the European Patent Office.

59 See Binctin, *supra* note 52, 275.

60 B. Van Pottelsbergue de la Potterie (2010), 'Patent fixes for Europe', *Nature* 23 September, **467**, 395.

61 Amended proposal for a Directive of the European Parliament and of the Council on criminal measures aimed at ensuring the enforcement of intellectual property rights dated 26 April 2006, COM(2006) 168 final. For a review of this text see R.M. Hilty, A. Kur and A. Peukert (2006), 'Statement of the Max Planck Institute for Intellectual Property, Competition and Tax Law on the Proposal for a Directive of the European Parliament and the Council on Criminal Measures Aimed at Ensuring the Enforcement of Intellectual Property Rights', *IIC*, 970. The Commission finally withdrew its proposal on 18 September 2010 (*OJ* 18 September 2010, 2010/C 252/9). On the changes to EU law on criminal enforcement that would result from ACTA, see C. Geiger (2012), 'The Anti-Counterfeiting Trade Agreement and Criminal Enforcement of Intellectual Property: What Consequences for the European Union?', in J. Rosen (ed.), *IP Rights at the Crossroads of Trade*, Cheltenham, UK and Northampton, MA: Edward Elgar, 167.

on the topic and to propose a fully transparent and differentiated approach; such approach might inspire support and enable the effective combat of counterfeiting when it involves dangerous consequences in terms of innovation and, above all, risks to consumers (specifically in the field of pharmaceutical products).[62] It is moreover possible that the ACTA treaty, if adopted, would have required a modification of the European legal provisions on civil enforcement.[63] More generally, the question of the opportunity of an amendment of the Directive of 29 April 2004 on the enforcement of intellectual property rights[64] was recently raised by the European Commission in an evaluation report of 22 December 2010 on the application of this text by the Member States.[65] It is obvious that the issue of enforcement remains essential, since the attractiveness of these rights risks being considerably limited in the future if their enforcement proves to be impossible or involve serious difficulties. However, precipitate action should be avoided.[66] Implementation of the Directive in national law only ended in 2009, the Commission itself admitting that 'experience in applying the Directive is limited and only few court cases have been reported'.[67] Before proposing a complete redrafting of the European

---

62 See C. Geiger (ed.) (2012), *Criminal Enforcement of Intellectual Property: A Handbook of Contemporary Research*, Cheltenham, UK and Northampton, MA: Edward Elgar.

63 See the Opinion of European Academics on Anti-Counterfeiting Trade Agreement, *supra* note 30.

64 Directive 2004/48/EC of 29 April 2004 on the enforcement of intellectual property rights: *OJ* L 157 of 30 April 2004, corrected in *OJ* L 195 of 2 June 2004, 16.

65 Report by the Commission to the European Parliament, the Council, the European Economic and Social Committee and the Committee of the Regions, on the application of Directive 2004/48/CE of the European Parliament and Council of 29 April 2004 on the enforcement of intellectual property rights, Brussels, 22 December 2012, COM(2010) 779 final.

66 See C. Geiger, J. Raynard and C. Rodà (2011), 'What Developments for the European Framework on Enforcement of Intellectual Property Rights? A Comment on the Evaluation Report of the European Commission dated 22 December 2010', *EIPR*, **33**(9),543.

67 Report, *supra* note 65, p. 4. In the analytical document on the application of the 2004 Directive that accompanies the report, the Commission also clearly admits that the information available is limited and hence that a complete evaluation of the text was not possible at that time:

> Due to the late transposition of the Directive in many Member States and the fact that some Member States did not provide the application report provided for in the Directive or provided only some information of a very general nature, *the information available on the impact of the directive is too limited to allow a full assessment of its effectiveness at this stage*' (emphasis added).

Commission Staff Working Document, Analysis of the application of Directive

legal framework concerning enforcement, it would be more useful to first carry out a critical economic analysis of the effect of the Directive on innovation and development of the information society,[68] an analysis that, moreover, is recommended by Article 18 of the said Directive. As we have already emphasized, actions of the European legislature will increase in efficiency and legitimacy if its initiatives are founded on a solid basis.

At EU level, the field of copyright is probably currently the one that leaves the most questions unanswered in terms of approximation of laws. Yet, the possibility of the creation of a European copyright code was explicitly expressed by the Commission in a recent document of 13 July 2011.[69] A large number of texts will probably be needed to perfect the current legal framework,[70] which is judged as unsatisfactory by many authors.[71] However, *better* legislation sometimes means *less* legislation, and should specifically imply a refusal to legislate under pressure. Hence, future initiatives by the European legislature will have to be based more frequently on serious (and above all independent) economic data and on impact studies that will make it possible to measure the probable consequences of the legislative activity.[72] The legislature

2004/48/EC of the European Parliament and the Council of 29 April 2004 on the enforcement of intellectual property rights in the Member States, 22 December 2010, SEC(2010) 1589 final.

68 According to the Commission's admission, such an analysis has not yet been carried out (report, *supra* note 65, p. 4). Accordingly, it is surprising that the Commission has announced, although the results of the evaluation are not yet known, a proposed amendment of the Directive on the enforcement of intellectual property rights (see the Communication of 24 May 2011, *supra* note 44, p. 3).

69 Green Paper on the online distribution of audiovisual works in the European Union, *supra* note 44, p. 14. According to the Commission, 'such a unitary European Copyright Code could be based on a codification of the existing EU copyright directives' and that 'the need to go beyond the current harmonisation will be examined.'

70 Listing the work still to be done, see C. Geiger, M. Bouyssi-Ruch and R.M. Hilty (eds) (2007), *Perspectives d'harmonisation du droit d'auteur en Europe*, Paris: Litec.

71 See on this question M. van Eechoud, P.B. Hugenholtz, S. van Gompel, L. Guibault and N. Helberger (2009), *Harmonizing European Copyright Law, The Challenge of Better Lawmaking*, Alphen aan den Rijn, the Netherlands: Kluwer Law International, a consolidated version of two studies carried out by the Institute for Information Law (IViR), University of Amsterdam, for the European Commission and containing interesting proposals for improving the legal framework of copyright in the European Union.

72 See also the report 'Digital Opportunity, A Review of Intellectual Property and Growth' *supra* note 49, p. 1, inviting the legislature 'to ensure that in the future, policy on Intellectual Property issues is constructed on the basis of evidence, rather than weight of lobbying'. For a comment of this report, see J. Smith and R. Montagnon (2011), 'The Hargreaves Review – A Digital Opportunity', *EIPR*, 596; Members of Hogarth Chambers (2011), 'The Hargreaves Review – Another Mixed Bag', *EIPR*,

will likewise have to request the advice of independent experts in advance and during the process of the adoption of the legislation.[73] This would lead to a greater coherence of the legislative structure and above all improve the wording of the texts. In effect, one of the principal characteristics of European Union intellectual property law is its complexity and, consequently, its opaqueness, which does not facilitate its acceptance. A future simplification, possibly even codification,[74] might have a beneficial effect. This would require a more fundamental identification of the common principles of intellectual property law within the countries of the European Union,[75] accompanied by a veritable review of the correspondences and differences in the approaches. Comparative law studies could then serve as the basis for informed activity on the part of the Commission, which would permit the adoption of the solutions that have proven to work best within the different Member States. It must not be forgotten that the content of the Europe of intellectual property, as of many other domains in Europe in general, is still to be defined, at least in part. If it is to be accepted, it cannot be imposed from above but must result from a synthesis of the different traditions of the Member States in order to be able to 'capture' what might constitute a European identity. This will probably require actors in the future that are able to understand how to 'think through' the differences and similarities in order to be able to give sense and content to the construction.

In order to do this, one of the principal means will certainly be education and research. From this perspective, it will in the future be important to include a larger number of courses on European intellectual property law in the current IP education programs, while at the same time continuing to make considerable efforts towards improving and creating a common basis by means of research. This certainly implies the teaching of existing rules (the number of courses at university level dealing with this is still insufficient) and a greater sensitization of students to European aspects of the subject, but also a certain anticipation by means of the creation of specific training courses that would give life to this 'European intellectual property law'. It is important to

599; G. Roberts (2011), 'The Hargreaves Review reviewed: a missed opportunity to help the dragons in their den?', *QMJIP*, **1**(3), 280.

[73] Academics could play a major role here. On this subject, see D. Visser, *The Role of Legal Academia in the Process of IP Harmonization in Europe* (forthcoming).

[74] See the interesting reflections of N. Binctin (2010), 'Pour un Code communautaire de la propriété intellectuelle', in *Droits de propriété intellectuelle, Liber amicorum Georges Bonet*, Paris: Litec, 51.

[75] On this question see A. Ohly (ed.) (2012), *Common Principles of European Intellectual Property Law*, Mohr Siebeck: Tübingen, proceedings of a very interesting conference organized on the topic at the University of Bayreuth on 20 and 21 November 2009.

ensure that students and professionals from various countries come together in joint training courses and to encourage exchanges and partnerships between the various national education systems. This will also help the creation of a network that might one day give rise to a feeling of true membership of a European legal system.[76] This would obviously need a greater cultural and linguistic effort from all sides. However, this effort is essential and it seems to us that this is the price to be paid to build a true Europe for intellectual property. Let us not forget, to paraphrase Democritus, that it is often the struggle between opposites that creates the most beautiful harmony.

---

76 The 'European Intellectual Property Institutes Network' (EIPIN), the current members of which are the Queen Mary Intellectual Property Research Institute (QMIPRI) at Queen Mary, University of London, Magister Lvcentinvs at the University of Alicante, the Intellectual Property Law and Knowledge Management (IPKM) at Maastricht University, the Centre for International Intellectual Property Studies (CEIPI) at the University of Strasbourg and the Munich Intellectual Property Law Center (MIPLC), has been a pioneer in this regard and could serve as a basis for implementing a broader network.

2. Pruning the European intellectual property tree: in search of common principles and roots

Séverine Dusollier

A few years ago, William Cornish wondered whether intellectual property had not become 'omnipresent, distracting, irrelevant'.[1] Many others now doubt the coherence of the intellectual property regime and denounce its excessive development. Taking stock of these sound and always well-reasoned critiques, the conference organized in Strasbourg in the frame of the EIPIN assumed the uneasy task of reconstructing European intellectual property.

This reform of the IP regime ought necessarily to begin with an assessment of the existing rules and their relevance. As the European Union knows a multiplicity of IP rights, from classical ones (copyright, patent, trademark or design) to more marginal ones, in terms of the economic sectors concerned (rights in databases, in plant varieties, in semiconductors, in geographical indications), the quest for consistency could integrate a reflection on the common core embedded in that diversity. Is there (and should there be) common ground and uniform principles across all intellectual property rights? And to what extent should diversity and specificity of intellectual property rights give way to a common approach?

This paper aims at identifying and assessing the existing similarities or common principles in intellectual property rights in the European Union. Despite their apparent diverging functions, subject-matter and scope of protection, copyright, trademark, patent and the other intellectual property rights share at least the fact that they belong to a set of rules granting some exclusive rights in intangible assets, whether creation or signs. Their inclusion under the same label 'Intellectual Property' should at least count for something and induce some joint ends and means.

I strongly believe that belonging to a broader field of intellectual property matters. It obliges us to form unified perspectives, questions and answers as to

[1] W. Cornish (2004), *Intellectual Property – Omnipresent, Distracting, Irrelevant?*, Oxford: Oxford University Press.

how immaterial resources deserve protection and how limits to that protection should be more central than in tangible property. This common approach is probably vanishing in the legislative work of the European Union that tends to deal separately with each IP right on an ad hoc basis, with no permeability with other rights. This is regrettable, for the way Europe conceives its intellectual property regime as a whole will ultimately shape its innovation, economic development and knowledge wealth. This paper is a very modest attempt to seek overall rules in intellectual property, or at least a more systematized ordering of the many protections, to serve as a first skeleton for a reform of intellectual property.

In 2008, in a conference organized by the University of Helsinki, Andrew Christie sketched a vision of a unified system for intellectual property, where all rights would merge into a single one, protecting diverse subject-matter.[2] To that end, he borrowed the metaphor of a tree from an intervention made the day before by Annette Kur[3]: intellectual property could be portrayed as a tree whose many branches represent all the protections granted by literary and artistic property or industrial property. I will take over this image. Intellectual property is a tree, an old one, a big one, a very luxuriant tree, one that seems to have grown a bit too much, without control and in an anarchic manner. It has many branches, some of them threatening to break under their own weight. The tree looks pretty and rich, but it also seems to suffer from suffocation, from lack of space. Tree specialists all agree that it is time to prune the tree, in order to make it breathe and blossom again. It will probably require some difficult cuts and the removal of some lively branches, but it is to make it develop better in the end.

To start the actual work, a preliminary step would be to agree on the common design its many branches should take. It requires the identification within the diverse regimes of intellectual property of the common features upon which further convergence could be built. The actual pruning will be however left to others.

The regimes surveyed by this paper will primarily be copyright, trademark, patent and design rights, which can be considered as the sequoias of the IP jungle. The other varieties, i.e. related rights, the *sui generis* right in databases, the geographical indications or appellations of origin, plant variety rights or

---

2 A. Christie (2008), 'A Possible Vision of a One Right System for IP', *One Right System for IP – Vision Impossible?*, IPR University Center International Conference, Helsinki, 3 October.

3 A. Kur (2008), 'Differentiated Protection Based on Unitary Ground – A Feasible Approach?', *One Right System for IP – Vision Impossible?*, IPR University Center International Conference, Helsinki, 3 October.

even the protection of semiconductors (that is a plant that not so many people can claim to have actually seen), will be addressed only incidentally or for comparison purposes.

Questions that will be successively addressed are the following: the justification of the granted protection (the *why* of the protection) (2), the subject-matter (the *what*?), requirements for protection (the *how*?), as well as the exclusions from protection (the *what not*?) (3), the scope of protection (the *what for*?) (4), the limitations and exceptions to such protection (the *not for what*?) (5), the duration (the *when*?) (6).

Contractual protection, rules of ownership, management of the rights will be left out, as the analysis is already broad enough. The enforcement or remedies conferred to all intellectual property rights will not be touched upon as they have been largely harmonized by Directive 2004/48 on enforcement.[4]

Unfair competition law will not be addressed either, even though it forms a relevant protection of creation, signs or other intangible items.[5] Nevertheless, the choice to omit it is justified by its less structured protection regime (in terms of rights conferred, limitations, conditions) and by its lack of exclusive and exploitable rights, replaced by a rule of liability to be enforced *ex post*. That does not diminish the evidence that unfair competition, as well as competition law, plays a role in the intellectual property landscape, that I will not have time to develop.

Before addressing the many elements of the protection, a first step will be to underline the variable intensity put by the European lawmaker into each IP right, which influences the level of harmonization and configuration of the EU intellectual property regime (1).

1. LEVEL OF EUROPEAN INTERVENTION

Diversity in IP rights can be partially explained by the many levels of European lawmaking. Not all rights have been tackled by EU lawmaking with the same intensity, and the European gardener has not treated all branches of the IP tree alike.

---

4 Directive 2004/48/EC of the European Parliament and of the Council of 29 April 2004 in the enforcement of intellectual property rights, hereafter 'the enforcement directive'.

5 See Directive 2005/29/EC of the European Parliament and of the Council of 11 May 2005 concerning unfair business-to-consumer commercial practices in the internal market.

The more thorough intervention is the creation of an EU-wide right, as has occurred in trademark,[6] design right[7] and plant variety right.[8] Geographical indications and appellations of origin can also be granted at the EU level,[9] which generates a title superseding the national protection. Such community rights have the desirable effect of granting a title of protection valid on the whole internal market. Provided for by Regulations, they can be said to genuinely construct a European intellectual property regime.

Less integrative are harmonization efforts that tend to provide common principles to national intellectual property protection, without encroaching upon the national sovereignty and territoriality of the protection. The most successful and comprehensive harmonization endeavour has arguably occurred in trademark,[10] where only one directive has managed to bring together the laws of Member States on many aspects.[11] The same process of coupling a harmonization directive with a community right regulation along the same rules has occurred for design.[12] Harmonization can also be called a success for the protection of unoriginal databases by the *sui generis* right[13] and of semiconductors,[14] as two brand new rights have been created on similar principles (even though the latter has not been applied much by courts).

Copyright, despite no fewer than eight directives, remains a largely national matter.[15] Harmonization has occurred on specific points. Technical subject-

---

[6] Council Regulation (EC) No. 207/2009 of 26 February 2009 on the Community trademark (codified version), hereafter 'the Community trademark regulation'.

[7] Council Regulation (EC) No. 6/2002 of 12 December 2001 on Community designs, hereafter 'the Community design regulation'.

[8] Council Regulation (EC) No. 2100/94 of 27 July 1994 on Community plant variety rights, hereafter 'the Community plant variety rights regulation'.

[9] Council Regulation (EC) No. 510/2006 of 20 March 2006 on the protection of geographical indications and designations of origin for agricultural products and foodstuffs, hereafter 'the Community geographical indications regulation'.

[10] Directive 2008/95/EC of the European Parliament and of the Council of 22 October 2008 to approximate the laws of the Member States relating to trademarks (codified version), hereafter 'the trademark directive'.

[11] See the Max Planck Institute for Intellectual Property and Competition Law (2011), *Study on the Overall Functioning of the European Trade Mark System*, February.

[12] Directive 98/71/EC of the European Parliament and of the Council of 13 October 1998 on the legal protection of designs hereafter 'the design directive'.

[13] Directive 96/9/EC of the European Parliament and of the Council of 11 March 1996 on the legal protection of databases, hereafter 'the database directive'.

[14] Council Directive 87/54/EEC of 16 December 1986 on the legal protection of topographies of semiconductor products.

[15] B. Hugenholtz (2009), 'Copyright Without Frontiers: the Problem of Territoriality in European Copyright Law', in E. Derclaye (ed.), *Research Handbook on the Future of EU Copyright*, Cheltenham, UK and Northampton, MA: Edward Elgar Publishing, pp. 12–26.

matter such as computer software or databases have received a harmonized protection within copyright, in terms of definition, criteria of protection, ownership, exclusive rights, exceptions.[16] But questions of interpretation challenging the actual level of harmonization have been recently brought to the attention of the Court of Justice of the European Union, as in the *Football Dataco* case for copyright in databases,[17] the *Softwarova* case[18] or the *SAS Institute* one[19] for copyright in software. Those references to the Court indicate that harmonization still leaves many questions open.

Other fields for harmonization in copyright have been related rights,[20] the determination of some exclusive economic rights, e.g., cable and satellite rights,[21] the *droit de suite,*[22] lending and rental rights,[23] reproduction, distribution, communication and the making available rights, redefined to fit the digital age,[24] the duration of copyright and related rights,[25] the protection of digital management of rights.[26] The infosoc directive also had the ambition of

---

16 See for databases, the database directive, and for computer programs, Directive 2009/24/EC of the European parliament and of the Council of 23 April 2009 on the legal protection of computer programs (codified version), hereafter the 'software directive'.

17 CJEU, 1 March 2012, *Football Dataco Limited v Yahoo UK Limited*, C-604/10. The question here was precisely the extent of harmonization brought by the directive and the freedom that is left to Member States to keep their own national interpretations and rules, in parallel to that of the directive.

18 CJEU, 22 December 2010, *Bezpečnostní softwarová asociace*, C-393/09.

19 CJEU, 2 May 2012, *SAS Institute Inc. v World Programming Ltd*, C-406/10.

20 Directive 2006/115/EC of the European Parliament and of the Council of 12 December 2006 on rental right and lending right and on certain rights related to copyright in the field of intellectual property (codified version), hereafter 'the rental and lending directive'.

21 Council Directive 93/83/EEC of 27 September 1993 on the coordination of certain rules concerning copyright and rights related to copyright applicable to satellite broadcasting and cable retransmission, hereafter 'the satellite and cable directive'.

22 Directive 2001/84/EC of the European Parliament and of the Council of 27 September 2001 on the resale right for the benefit of the author of an original work of art.

23 See the rental and lending directive.

24 Directive 2001/29/EC of the European Parliament and of the Council of 22 May 2001 on the harmonisation of certain aspects of copyright and related rights in the information society, hereafter 'the infosoc directive'.

25 Directive 2006/116/EC of the European Parliament and of the Council of 12 December 2006 on the term of protection of copyright and certain related rights (codified version), hereafter 'term directive', amended by the Directive 2011/77/EU of the European Parliament and of the Council of 27 September 2011 amending Directive 2006/116/EC on the term of protection of copyright and certain related rights.

26 Provided for the software directive for technical protection of the computer programs and by the infosoc directive for the rest of copyright, related rights and *sui generis* rights.

harmonizing copyright exceptions, but everybody would agree that this attempt has failed[27] as the directive only provides for an exhaustive list of 23 exceptions from which the Member States are free to choose both to adopt the exception and to decide upon its conditions of application. It results in the impossibility of knowing for sure that an exploitation of a work (for example the use of works in online teaching) across European borders will benefit from exceptions in the whole territory of the internal market.

Still in copyright, a draft directive on collective management has been announced, which makes the EU lawmaker step into a new territory, formerly reserved to Member States, and a directive on orphan works has just been released.[28] For the latter, it is difficult to talk about real harmonization as the directive only provides a mutual recognition of the status of an orphan work granted in one Member State and recommends some guidelines to carry out the diligent search of the rights owners that is required as a preliminary step to acknowledge a work as orphan.

Patent has been the *parent pauvre* of the EU legislative efforts. There is no need to recall the unhappy saga of the community patent, still wishful thinking after more than 30 years of discussion. Besides, no directive has been adopted to harmonize the general rules of patent in the Member States. The only achieved intervention of the European Union in the patent arena has been to sustain the patentability of biotechnological inventions,[29] hereby enhancing a thriving new industry in Europe. As a result, patent laws remain largely fragmented in the Member States, even though the rules of the EPO patent might have influenced national laws, all Member States being part of the Munich Convention.[30]

Last but not least, the European Union has tried to better secure the enforcement of its intellectual property by enacting a horizontal directive dealing with enforcement and remedies in all intellectual property rights.[31]

---

[27] Amongst many others, L. Guibault, G. Westkamp, T. Rieber-Mohn, P.B. Hugenholtz, et al. (2007), *Study on the Implementation and Effect in Member States' Laws of Directive 2001/29/EC on the Harmonisation of Certain Aspects of Copyright and Related Rights in the Information Society*, report to the European Commission, DG Internal Market, February; M.-C. Janssens, 'The Issue of Exceptions: Reshaping the Keys to the Gates in the Territory of Literary, Musical and Artistic Creation', in *Research Handbook on the Future of EU Copyright, supra* note 15, p. 332.

[28] Directive 2012/28/EU of the European Parliament and of the Council on certain permitted uses of orphan works, 25 October 2012.

[29] Directive 98/44/EC of the European Parliament and of the Council of 6 July 1998 on the legal protection of biotechnological inventions, hereafter 'the biotechnology directive'.

[30] The TRIPS Agreement and the Paris Convention on Industrial Property also ensure that key rules in patent are similar in all European Member States.

[31] Directive 2004/48/EC of the European Parliament and of the Council of 29 April 2004 on the enforcement of intellectual property rights.

2. THE JUSTIFICATION AND OBJECTIVES OF INTELLECTUAL PROPERTY

The quest for a common ground for IP rights proves to be hazardous. The European legal texts applicable in intellectual property refer to diverse grounds for legislation. A common justification could well be found in article 17 of the EU Charter of Fundamental Rights that solemnly declares that 'Intellectual property shall be protected'.[32] But can it be inferred from that rather blunt formulation that the protection of intellectual property is an end in itself, hence not needing any further justification? Despite the apparent strength and self-confidence of this declaration, many scholars agree that it should not be construed as providing a free rein to IP protection.[33] The Charter only follows previous qualification of the right to property, as it includes intellectual property, as a fundamental right,[34] without settling the ultimate justification of this protection.

Beyond this overall affirmation, a common rationale for intellectual property protection, whatever its type, is still lacking in the *acquis communautaire* and in legislative debates. Each directive or regulation tends to offer a series of objectives and foundations to the protection it provides. Justifications that are usually proffered can be categorized in different types.

A classical economy-based rationale is the role of exclusive rights *to provide a necessary incentive to creation or innovation*. This appears in the enforcement directive that states in its first recital that 'the protection of intellectual property is important [...] for promoting innovation and creativity'. The same recital links the achievement of the internal market to the need to create 'an environment conducive to innovation and investment', which can find satisfaction in IP protection. Similar objectives are mentioned in the infosoc directive ('to foster substantial investment in creativity and innovation [...] and lead in turn to growth and increased competitiveness of European industry'[35]), in the community design regulation ('enhanced protection for industrial design [...] encourages innovation and development of new prod-

[32] Article 17(2), European Charter of Fundamental Rights, OJ, 18 December 2000, C 364/01.

[33] See notably J. Griffiths and L. McDonagh, 'Fundamental Rights and European IP Law – the Case of Art 17(2) of the EU Charter', in this volume; C. Geiger (2008), 'Intérêt général, droit d'accès à l'information et droit de propriété : la propriété intellectuelle analysée à la lumière des droits fondamentaux', in S. Dusollier and M. Buydens, *L'intérêt general et l'accès à l'information en propriété intellectuelle*, Bruxelles: Bruylant, p. 249.

[34] See the Opinion of the Advocate General, 14 April 2011, *Scarlet Extended SA v Sabam*, C-70/10, §90.

[35] Infosoc directive, recital 4.

ucts and investment in their production'[36]), in the database directive,[37] as well as in the community plant varieties rights regulation ('to stimulate the breeding and development of new varieties'[38]).

Closely related to the incentive reasoning, intellectual property rights are also considered as a desirable *protection of investment*, hereby offering some return on production costs and remunerating the actors involved. This appears in copyright, patent or design protection and is often coupled with innovation-based motives.

For instance, in copyright, the infosoc directive explains that:

> if authors or performers are to continue their creative and artistic work, they have to receive an appropriate reward for the use of their work, as must producers in order to be able to finance this work. The investment required to produce products such as phonograms, films or multimedia products, and services such as 'on-demand' services, is considerable. Adequate legal protection of intellectual property rights is necessary in order to guarantee the availability of such a reward and provide the opportunity for satisfactory returns on this investment.[39]

This rationale is explicit in the protection of subject-matter for related rights that merely consists in economic contribution to creation, such as the rights in phonograms, first fixation of films or broadcasts. 'The possibility of securing [the income of performers] and recouping [the investment required for the production of phonograms and films]'[40] justifies the legal protection conferred to the rightholders concerned by the directive on rental and lending rights that harmonized the protection of related rights in the European Union. Similar justifications are found in the software directive,[41] the biotechnology directive,[42] the database directive[43] and in the resale right directive that insists on the adequate remuneration of artists.[44]

---

[36] Community design regulation, recital 7.

[37] See recitals 9–12 of the database directive.

[38] Community plant variety rights regulation, recital 5.

[39] Infosoc directive, recital 10. The next recital even mentions 'safeguarding the independence and dignity of artistic creators and performers'.

[40] Rental and lending directive, recital 5.

[41] See the software directive, recital 2.

[42] See the biotechnology directive, recitals 2 and 3 ('maintain and encourage investment in the field of biotechnology').

[43] See the database directive, recital 12 ('Whereas such an investment in modern information storage and processing systems will not take place within the Community unless a stable and uniform legal protection regime is introduced for the protection of the rights of the makers of databases').

[44] See recital 3 of Directive 2001/84/EC of the European Parliament and of the Council of 27 September 2001 on the resale right for the benefit of the author of a original work of art ('The resale right is intended to ensure that authors of graphic and plastic works of art share in the economic success of their original works of art').

Return on investment is also proffered as a ground for protection of trademarks, as the ECJ has recently admitted the need to protect other functions of trademark, in particular 'those of communication, investment or advertising'.[45] The protection of investment in a brand as a publicity signal is now recognized as an objective of trademark, whether famous or not.[46]

The diversification of agriculture and its positive effects on the incomes of farmers equally appears in the objectives of the protection of geographical indications.[47] Likewise, protection of investment often results in the protection of a specific economic sector, agriculture for geographical indications, the information market for the *sui generis* right,[48] the nascent biotechnology industry for the biotechnology directive.[49]

A last type of justification, still rooted in economic considerations, is *to prevent free riding* and ensure that *competition is not distorted*, even though that last motive aligns itself on the very objective of harmonization directives to achieve an internal market by removing the differences of protection amongst the Member States. Trademark protection clearly comes within that scope,[50] but traces of that rationale can be tracked in the protection of databases and software when copies are said to be possible at a fraction of the cost needed for their development.[51]

Each intellectual property right also has ancillary and specific objectives linked to its own subject-matter. Protection of geographical indications and appellations of origin purports to ensure some product quality,[52] an objective that has been gradually acknowledged also in trademark. The Court of Justice has indeed recently insisted on the protection of the function of guaranteeing the quality of the goods or services,[53] beyond the protection of the function of origin and has applied this function even to trademark with no reputation. Here

---

45 ECJ, 18 June 2009, *L'Oreal v Bellure*, C-487/07, §58 *in fine*.

46 CJEU, 22 September 2011, *Interflora*, C-323/09, §40

47 See recital 2 of the geographical indication regulation.

48 See recital 7 of the database directive.

49 See recital 1 of the biotechnology directive ('Whereas biotechnology and genetic engineering are playing an increasingly important role in a broad range of industries and the protection of biotechnological inventions will certainly be of fundamental importance for the Community's industrial development').

50 See recital 2 of the community trademark regulation and the recital 2 of the trademark directive.

51 See the identical formulation in recital 2 of the software directive and recital 7 of the database directive.

52 See recital 3 of the geographical indication regulation ('a constantly increasing number of consumers attach greater importance on the quality of foodstuffs in their diet rather that to quantity. This quest for specific products generates a demand for agricultural products or foodstuffs with an identifiable geographical origin').

53 ECJ, 18 June 2009 *L'Oreal v Bellure*, C-487/07.

also, it is not certain that the Court wished to limit this function to trademarks with a reputation.[54]

Literary and artistic creation brings with it some cultural aspects. The cultural importance of copyright protection is underlined in many directives, without playing a central role. For instance, the infosoc directive reminds us of the 'great importance from a cultural standpoint' of copyright and related rights,[55] referring immediately to the former article 151 of the treaty mandating the cultural competence of the Community.[56]

All those justifications might look a bit messy and inconsistent. Surprisingly, EU legislative texts do not mention much the balance that is generally said to be embedded in intellectual property protection. The directive on enforcement of 2004 is remarkable in that regard as it clearly affirms that:

> the protection of intellectual property should allow the inventor or creator to derive a legitimate profit from his/her invention or creation. It should also allow the widest possible dissemination of works, ideas and know-how. At the same time, it should not hamper freedom of expression, the free movement of information, or the protection of personal data, including on the Internet.

This statement is echoed in the infosoc directive that opposes freedom of expression and the public interest to the fundamental protection of intellectual property. However in many copyright legal texts, it is said that any harmonization of copyright must take as a basis *a high level* of protection,[57] which inclines to tilt the balance in favour of one side of the scale only.

The reluctance of the European lawmaker to specifically address the overall objective of intellectual property, beyond classical incentives-based arguments, is puzzling. Recitals about the effect of a high protection on the European competitiveness sound like a well-learnt script. Reforming the intellectual property system and trying to make it more comprehensive and convergent would at least require providing the same roots for all protection of intellectual property under an overall objective of enhancement of creation, innovation and competition.

---

54 CJEU, 22 September 2011, *Interflora*, C-323/09.

55 Infosoc directive, recital 12.

56 See also recital 3 of the rental and lending directive insisting on the cultural development of the Community.

57 See recital 9 of the infosoc directive, and particularly recital 11 of the term directive ('The level of protection of copyright and related rights should be high, since those rights are fundamental to intellectual creation. Their protection ensures the maintenance and development of creativity in the interest of authors, cultural industries, consumers and society as a whole').

3. OBJECT OF PROTECTION

Addressing the object of intellectual property requires analysing first the type of immaterial content that is liable for protection, i.e. the subject-matter (3.1), then the fundamental exclusion of ideas from intellectual property (3.2), the requirements for protection (3.3) and finally, the cases of exclusions and their motives (3.4).

3.1 Subject-matter of Intellectual Property

Each intellectual property right protects a differently defined subject-matter: literary and artistic work for copyright, invention for patent right, sign for trademark, the appearance of a product for design right, a database for the *sui generis* right, the creation of a plant variety for plant variety right, or names of regions or specific places for geographical indications and designations of origin.

The divergence of subject-matter seemingly displays the heterogeneous nature of intellectual property and jeopardizes any project trying to put some order in the different branches thereof. Some would say that it is impossible to conceive similar principles and rules to protect so dissimilar objects of protection.

Actually, one can distinguish three categories of subject-matter. The first one encompasses all types of 'creation', whether a work in copyright, an invention in patent, the appearance of a product in design or a plant variety in the plant variety right. All those rights protect some activity of innovation or creation, but separate them from each other depending on the field or means of creation. Copyright protects artistic and literary creation, not limited to the arts, but rather conveying expression in a visual, sound or language medium. The related rights of performers are enjoyed in performances, which are another form of creation. Patent protects creation in the technical field expressed in technical means. The plant variety right vests upon botanical variations of plants. As to industrial designs, they are hybrids between artistic and technical creations. Both the directive and the regulation define the 'design' as 'the appearance of the whole or a part of a product resulting from the features of, in particular, the lines, contours, colours, shape, texture and/or materials of the product itself and/or its ornamentation'. Design cannot be exclusively technical as the right does not subsist in features of appearance of a product, which are solely dictated by their technical function (see *infra*). With that limit in mind, a vast range of designs can be protected, from mere artistic shapes with no specific function to appearances of technical components of a product.

A second category includes 'signs or denominations', either protected by trademark or by the right in geographical indications. The notion of 'sign' is very broad, for it gathers all forms of expressions conveying some meaning, from words, numbers, sentences, to images, shapes, sounds or colours. A sign is to be set apart from the notion of creation. Trademark does not need the sign to be created specifically to distinguish a product or service in order to enter into function. Existing words, images, colours or sounds can perfectly apply for trademark protection. Instead of a creation, the very focus of the protection in trademark, and incidentally in the protection of geographical indications, is the use of a sign, existing or not, in relation to products or services.

Aside from those two categories of subject-matter eligible for IP protection, some productions are protected as mere 'investments'. This is the case of non-original databases when protected by the *sui generis* right or of related rights protecting first fixations of films or phonograms and broadcasts.

Classifying the subject-matter of intellectual property in these three key categories (creation – sign – investment) could form three main branches with rules adapted to the type of object to be protected, whether a creation, a sign or an investment. Reasonably, the objectives of regulating creations, whatever their field, would obey similar considerations and differ from those governing signs or investments. For instance, the economic reasoning about incentives only play a role for creation, and partially for investments, but not for signs whose use does not need to be incentivized. Investments might not even need to be incentivized but need a protection against free-riding. Balancing protection with public interest would also be differently shaped as the effect of protecting a creation or a sign is necessarily different. Another key difference between creation and sign is that the first one should be protected against copying by an absolute protection whereas for signs, it is their use in relationship with products or services that matters, which only leads to a relative protection.

The three big branches of the tree might then be separated again to set up different principles of protection depending, for instance, on the artistic or technical nature of the creation.

3.2 The Exclusion of Ideas

Whatever the subject-matter of protection, an underlying principle is shared by all intellectual property rights: ideas should remain free. As a rule, no intellectual property applies to abstract ideas or principles, but it appears more clearly in some rights than in others.

It is a key and explicit rule in copyright that is strongly affirmed in many legal texts under the idea/expression dichotomy. It is surprising that almost no community legislative act – but the software copyright directive[58] – expressly

[58] Article 1(2) of the software directive: 'Ideas and principles which underlie any element of a computer program, including those which underlie its interfaces, are not protected by copyright under this directive'.

repeats that foundational principle. Arguably that can be explained by the fact that no directive addresses the subject-matter of copyright in a comprehensive way. On the other hand, the idea/expression dichotomy is more visible in international texts, such as the WIPO Copyright Treaty, in its article 2, or the TRIPS Agreement, in its article 9(2).

This paradigmatic criteria for copyright protection is however unsteady in the *acquis communautaire*. Despite the upfront affirmation in the software directive that ideas and functional elements are not protected, the protection of computer programs hides very badly the difficulty of keeping ideas free from the effect of copyright protection in the expression of the program, as demonstrated by the intricate provision of decompilation, required to uncover mere ideas behind the protection of unavailable source code. The Court of Justice of the European Union has recently answered questions referred by a UK judge about the infringing nature of the replication of functional aspects of the program that did not require any copying of its source code.[59] This gave the opportunity to the court to insist on the key principle that ideas are not protected by copyright, which it justified by the encouragement of 'technological progress and industrial development'.[60]

The exclusion of ideas is a well-known mantra in copyright but it is also valid in other intellectual property rights, yet more implicitly. Patent, for instance does not protect abstraction, but only technical features, as implied by the list of exclusions of article 52(2) of the European Patent Convention, most of which are explained by their abstract dimension (e.g. discoveries, scientific theories and mathematical methods, schemes, rules and methods for performing mental acts, or presentations of information). An idea, understood as any abstract concept with no concrete application or materialization in a technical solution or process, is not eligible for patentability.

By its very nature and definition, a design has a material character, concretized by the lines, shapes, texture or materials of a product that form the very object of the protection. The exclusion of an idea or abstract feature is here self-evident.

Even in trademark protection, an abstraction or concept is not liable for protection, as was clearly reminded by the European Court of Justice in the *Dyson* case,[61] which is rarely presented under that aspect. In that decision, the judges have excluded the protection of a transparent bin forming part of the external surface of a vacuum cleaner. The Court held that a trademark constituted by all the conceivable shapes of a product, in a general and abstract

59 CJEU, 2 May 2012, *SAS Institute Inc. v World Programming Ltd*, C-406/10.
60 *Ibidem*, §40.
61 ECJ, 25 January 2007, *Dyson v OHIM*, C-321/03.

manner, is not a sign in the meaning of trademark law.[62] Without clearly considering that such subject-matter would actually be an idea or a concept by nature excluded from IP protection, this decision can be construed as admitting the protection of trademark only for specific and determined signs and not for abstract matter.

Pruning the IP tree shall require strong affirmation of the principle of exclusion of ideas in all fields of intellectual property and its inscription in the *acquis communautaire*. Instead of leaving more or less implicit traces of this fundamental paradigm, a clear statement should ascertain the necessary freedom of using ideas, principles or methods. That would provide some solidity to resist attempts of commodification over those building blocks of innovation, creation and industrial or commercial development, as it was witnessed in the computer program area.

3.3 Requirements for Protection

Requirements for protection logically depend on the type of intellectual property right concerned: originality for copyright, a set of three conditions for patent (novelty, inventiveness and industrial application), mainly distinctiveness for trademarks, novelty and individual character for design.

One can however find some common features in those apparently diverging conditions. Indeed, they can be arranged in a continuum comprising four levels: creation – novelty – adequacy – investment. *Creation* includes all conditions that require, in one way or another, some level of intellectual intervention, beyond mere financial or technical contribution. Conversely, *novelty* is strictly objective and means that something that did not exist before has now been produced. What I refer to by *adequacy*, for want of a better term, is the capability to satisfy the objectives of the intellectual property protection, in other words, the fact that the subject-matter requesting protection is fit for its purpose. As we will see, trademark, and to some extent, patent law, impose conditions for protection related to the very objective of the right granted. *Investment* is the lower requirement as it only implies a financial contribution in producing the intellectual object.

Copyright is clearly related to the creation criteria. A work has to be original to be eligible for protection. The requirement of originality is only partially harmonized by EU law, for software, photographs and databases, are defined as 'the author's own intellectual creation'. This Community definition of originality has been extended by the European Court to all copyrighted works.[63]

62 *Ibid*, §35.

63 ECJ, 16 July 2009, *Infopaq v DDF*, C-5/08, §37. It has been upheld in CJEU, 22 December 2010, *Bezpečnostní softwarová asociace*, C-393/09, §46.

Considering originality as a Community notion that needs to receive a uniform interpretation will force the choice of which conception of originality will prevail amongst the many comprehensions of that notion in the Member States. One often opposes the subjective approach of the civil law countries, focusing more on the imprint of the creator to the objective approach of the UK and Ireland that rather insist on skill and labour.[64] The EU decision in the *Football Dataco* case might be construed as rejection of the 'skill and labour' test,[65] even though it remains controversial. Whatever the conception, originality belongs to the 'creation' requirement in the sense that copyright protection is triggered when there is an intellectual creation emanating from the author, which the European court has defined as the possibility, for the author, to express his creative abilities in the production of the work by making free and creative choices.[66]

Design lies between creation-based and novelty-based systems. A first condition is that the design must be new, which is satisfied if no identical design has been made available to the public before the registration. A second condition is that the design must have an individual character, defined as the fact that the overall impression the design produces on the informed user differs from the impression produced by the existing designs. It departs from novelty as the test is not purely objective but integrates some creative involvement of the designer, perceptible by the user, thereby entering into the realm of creation-based requirements.

Plant varieties have to be distinct, uniform, stable and new, which puts them in the category of novelty, the other conditions not revealing any test of creation.

Trademarks do not have to show creation or novelty to be protected. The key requirement of distinctiveness more particularly refers to the fact that signs should be able to perform their function of origin of the product or service. In Community law, the distinctiveness of a trademark has been defined as 'the greater or lesser capacity of the mark to identify the goods or services for which it has been registered as coming from a particular undertaking, and thus to distinguish those goods or services from those of other undertakings'.[67] In other words, trademark must be fit for the purpose of distinguishing goods or services: a sign that would be perceived by the consumers as referential or descriptive qualities of the product or as mere

---

64 A. Strowel (1993), *Droit d'auteur et Copyright – Divergences et convergences*, Bruxelles: Bruylant; R. Casas Valles, 'The Requirement of Originality', in *Research Handbook on the Future of EU Copyright*, *supra* note 15, p.102.

65 CJEU, 1st March 2012, *Football Dataco*, C-604/10.

66 CJEU, 1st December 2011, *Painer*, C-145/10.

67 ECJ, 22 June 1999, *Lloyd v Loint's*, C-342/97, §22.

ornamentation of the product or of its packaging is not apt to serve as a trademark.

The requirement of distinctiveness can thus be qualified as a test of adequacy: only signs that can accomplish the very function of the trademark, i.e. distinguishing products or services, are eligible to the protection. Trademark law excludes descriptive, generic or customary signs, which by themselves are inappropriate to operate as trademarks, as the public will not perceive them as indications of origin of the product or service.

There is however a small touch of novelty in trademark conditions for protection in the fact that the sign should not be already registered in an identical or similar form for identical or similar products or services.[68] This intervention of novelty is rather limited as it is not absolute but relative in two respects. Firstly, only the owner of a former trademark or other protected sign is entitled to complain about the registration of a sign similar to his own. Second, the protection of a sign being limited to similar products or services, by the speciality principle, the trademark does not have to be absolutely new, as in patent law, but should only not have been registered already in the same field of commercial production.

Patent is a very peculiar case, as inventions have to comply with requirements that mix creation, novelty and adequacy. The key criterion is certainly novelty: the invention should be new and not exist already. But there is also some creative aspect in the condition of inventive step: the invention should not be obvious to a person skilled in the art, having regard to the state of the art. It should not be an obvious step in technical progress, thereby requiring some innovation from the inventor.

And finally, the condition of industrial application relates to the usefulness of the invention, its capacity to serve industry, and can be attached to the notion of adequacy, mentioned above.[69] Only inventions that can serve to 'something' and lead to production of goods or services are fit for protection.

A final type of requirement in intellectual property is investment. It applies to databases that can pretend to the protection of the *sui generis* right if they have necessitated a substantive investment. No creation, novelty of adequacy here, but merely some degree of financial contribution.

Surprisingly, related rights do not obey to any requirements for protection. The rights of performers are granted as soon as there is a performance that has some artistic dimension. Arguably, the condition of performance is not even a test for protection but its very subject-matter. Deciding that the artistic performance is a condition might to some extent include the right of performers in

---

68 Even for different products in the case of protection of famous trademarks.

69 The condition of industrial application also reflects the technical feature of an invention, thereby excluding abstract matter.

the 'creation' category, as something has to be created by the performer. It is more disturbing that producers of phonograms or films do not have to demonstrate a significant level of investment to enjoy related rights. This is one of the only cases where an intellectual property right is granted with no formalities or specific conditions to fulfil. This explains that their specific rights cannot rejoice the *sui generis* right on databases in the investment category of conditions for protection.

This lack of any qualitative or quantitative threshold, compared to the many requirements applicable to the other forms of intellectual property, raises a legitimate concern of overprotection. There is no reasonable ground explaining this lack of any condition for protection, except maybe the presumption that any phonogram or film production requires a high amount of investment. At least some level of investment could be required.

Despite the relative differences in the conditions for protection, all intellectual property rights recognize a twofold principle of non-discrimination. On one hand, there is no minimal threshold of protection in many IP rights; on the other hand, the protection is applied independently of the type of creation or sign.

On the first element, intellectual property rights generally grant protection to eligible subject-matter, even though the satisfaction of the conditions to be met is minimal. For instance, trademark can have a weak distinctive character (but it will have consequences on the degree of their protection to some extent). The originality required for copyright protection does not function quantitatively or qualitatively, and the author's own intellectual creation has been construed very broadly by the European Court in the *Painer* case,[70] following national case law that generally applies a low threshold. Likewise, the test of non-obviousness in patent seems easily passed, even for mundane inventions.

A second factor of non-discrimination lies in the generosity of intellectual property rights that welcome all types of creations or signs. Copyright is not limited to works in the artistic field, but protects, as required by the Berne Convention for that matter, scientific, informational, functional creations. Article 27 of the TRIPS Agreement imposes the patentability of 'all fields of technology', an expression that has been used in article 52(1) of the EPC, in its revised version of 29 November 2000. As to trademark, all imaginable signs have knocked on the door of registration and have been broadly welcomed in to the extent of the satisfaction of the requirement of graphical representation.[71]

70 CJEU, 1 December 2011, *Painer*, C-145/10.

71 See for colours (admitted), ECJ, 6 May 2003, *Libertel Croep BV v Benelux-*

Taken together, both refusals to discriminate on subject-matter in intellectual property result in a very broad protection in the key fields of intellectual property. Copyright, trademark, design and patent rights have gained a catch-all character, which raises concerns of overprotection and, in practice, enables overlapping rights in a same subject-matter.[72] Categories of IP subject-matter might appear as being properly delineated and separated (artistic creations for copyright, technical ones for patent, signs for trademark, appearance of a product for design). Yet the actual munificence of intellectual property tends to multiply the situations where several rights apply to the same object, even though they might protect different aspects thereof. The shape of technical components might be protected by national copyright or design, as the artistic purpose of the creation is not required and the level of originality is very low. Software is now protected by copyright and by patent, despite the formal exclusion contained in article 52(2)(c) of the EPC.[73] This is probably one of the densest parts of the IP tree that can give an impression of an anarchic and overgrown foliage.

3.4 Exclusions from Protection

Exclusions from protection are largely linked to each intellectual property with no overall approach. Two major causes for exclusion can however be systematized.

The first one is justified by *public order* or *ethics considerations* and can be found in almost all intellectual property rights. Contradiction with public policy excludes signs from trademark protection. Article 3(1)(f) of the trademark directive and article 7(1)(f) of the community trademark regulation reject the registration of trademarks which are contrary to public policy or accepted principles of morality. Two other absolute grounds for refusal or invalidity are related to public policy, i.e. the exclusion of deceptive signs and of trademarks concerned with article 6*ter* of the Paris Convention (official signs, flags, State emblems, of countries or international intergovernmental organizations).

Contradiction of public policy or morality provides a similar ground for exclusion in design right, also under the harmonizing directive and the regulation creating a community protection.

Merkenbureau, C-104/01; for sounds (admitted in principle but with a subsisting difficulty of graphical representation), ECJ, 27 November 2003, *Shield Mark BV v Joost Kist*, C-283/01; for smells (rejected so far), ECJ, 12 December 2002, *Ralf Sieckmann*, C-273/00.

72 S. Dusollier and A. Cruquenaire (eds) (2009), *Le cumul des droits intellectuels*, Bruxelles: Larcier; E. Derclaye, and M. Leistner (2011), *Intellectual Property Overlaps: A European Perspective*, Oxford: Hart Publishing.

73 EPO Enlarged Board of Appeal, 19 February 2010, G-2/08.

Public order is more articulated in patent protection. The European Patent Convention provides that inventions the commercial exploitation of which would be contrary to 'ordre public' or morality will not be patented. The EPO case law has built some interpretation of this notion by specifying that the bar to patentability grounded in public order mainly depends on a careful weighing up of the negative effects of the invention and of its beneficial outcome for humankind.[74] More recently, both the EPO Enlarged Board of Appeals and the European Court of Justice, in cases of a patent involving embryonic human stem cells, have pointed out that:

> it is not the fact of the patenting itself that is considered to be against *ordre public* or morality, but it is the performing of the invention, which includes a step (the use involving its destruction of a human embryo) that has to be considered to contravene those concepts.[75]

Grounds for excluding inventions from patent protection based on public order or ethics have also materialized in a list of unpatentable inventions in the directive on biotechnological inventions,[76] encompassing processes for cloning human beings, processes for modifying the genetic identity of human beings, the use of human embryos for industrial or commercial purposes and the modification of the genetic identity of animals without any substantial medical benefit. Equally related to ethical debates about life patenting, the biotechnology directive excludes the patenting of the human body and the simple discovery of one of its elements, plant and animal varieties, and essentially biological processes for the production of plants or animals. But those exclusions can equally be justified by the lack of a technical invention in such subject-matter, which could be described as mere discoveries, and the exclusion for plants does not prevent the grant of a plant variety right. More generally, the exclusion of therapeutic methods can be explained by a strong public policy motive.

Only copyright avoids exclusion based on public policy. Having said that, most Member States exclude official documents from protection, which can also be explained by public policy and the objective to keep legal norms available to citizens. But this exclusion is not included in the *acquis communautaire*.

---

[74] EPO Board of Appeal, 3 October 1990, T-19/90 (Oncomouse), OJ EPO, 1990/476, Reason 5.

[75] EPO Enlarged Board of Appeal, 25 November 2008, G-2/06, §29; CJEU, 18 October 2011, *Brüstle*, C-34/10, §52.

[76] Article 6(1) of the biotechnology directive. See also, for the European patent, the similar list in Rule 28 of the Implementing Regulations to the Convention on the Grant of European Patents.

A second ground for exclusions is the need *to keep some resources available for competitors*. This explains many exclusions from trademark protection, such as descriptive signs (trademarks which consist exclusively of signs or indications which may serve, in trade, to designate the kind, quality, quantity, intended purpose, value, geographical origin, or the time of production of the goods or of rendering of the service, or other characteristics of the goods or services), usual signs (signs or indications which have become customary in the current language or in the bona fide and established practices of the trade), and for three-dimensional signs, the exclusion of the shape of which results from the nature of the goods themselves and the shape of goods which is necessary to obtain a technical result. A similar competitive consideration lies in the exclusion from protection by design rights of designs dictated by their technical function and of designs of interconnections.

This is an essential ground for exclusion that responds to the competition dimension of intellectual property, sometimes evoked in the rationale or context of the legislative action of the European Union.

Excluding some subject-matter is an important policy option, useful to organize competition or to choose not to protect some matter, for ethical, public order or economic reasons. Paradoxically, the determination of excluded subject-matter mainly appears as being bound to each IP right with no real overall perspective. This separated approach is understandable, as exclusions should also be devised according to the specific subject-matter of each protection. However, it has some side effects, as the categories of subject-matter for each intellectual property right are not perfectly closed or coherent, and some creations or signs are increasingly protected by overlapping rights. As a consequence, excluded matter can enjoy protection by other types of right than the one that excludes it. It is not always problematic, since the ground for exclusion might be the need to properly delineate each intellectual property field, as is the case with aesthetical presentations, excluded from patent protection, but protected under copyright. Another example is the exclusion by trademark law of shapes that give a substantial value to the product, which can be partially explained by the more adequate protection of such shapes by design right.

The two grounds for exclusion that we have underlined are particularly relevant. They could be better systematized and cross, when necessary, all IP rights, while taking the particularity of each right and its subject-matter into account.

3.5 Formal Requirements

With the noteworthy exception of literary and artistic property, intellectual property rights are subject to formality requirements. Patent, trademark, design right (even though a reduced protection exists for unregistered design), plant variety right, geographical indication and appellation of origin are all governed by a rule of registration-based acquisition of right and transfer.

Formalities, it is well known, are prohibited by the Berne Convention as a precondition to the existence and exercise of copyright. The advent of the digital environment, that abounds with creations difficult to retrace to their copyright owners, has revitalized that question.[77] Formal requirements in copyright are not a taboo anymore and parallels are drawn with trademark and patent law registration systems. If one could liberate copyright from the restraining anchor of the Berne Convention in one way or another, a common ground could well be found across the different intellectual property rights to align the regimes of formalities, while preserving particular interests of copyright, such as the moral right. At least nothing prevents, under current international copyright law, formalities from being imposed to make transfer of rights valid against third parties.[78] That would be a first step in the direction of a more efficient and easier identification of copyright owners.

More surprising is the absence of any formalities to enjoy and exercise related rights, the *sui generis* right in databases or the protection of technological measures and rights management information against circumvention and removal, despite some proposals to that effect.[79] The case of the performer set aside, nothing explains that formalities cannot be required from the industrial and economic entrepreneurs who are the producers of phonograms and films, the broadcasters, the producers of databases or the providers of works in a DRM-protected format. Registration of their production or of the application of the technology they deploy in their business models would in our view be necessary and justified.[80]

4. SCOPE OF PROTECTION/RIGHTS CONFERRED

At first blush, the rights conferred by each intellectual property right appear to be rather different. In copyright, moral rights set aside, rights to control *repro-*

---

77 S. Van Gompel (2011), *Formalities in Copyright Law – An Analysis of Their History, Rationales and Possible Future*, Kluwer Law International, pp. 2–8.

78 S. Dusollier (2011), '(Re)introducing Formalities in Copyright as a Strategy for the Public Domain', in L. Guibault and C. Angelopoulos (eds), *Open Content Licences from Theory to Practice*, Amsterdam University Press, p. 75.

79 Ibid, pp. 92–94.

80 Registration of DRM could also provide some solution to users wishing to benefit from exceptions, to help the interoperability and to resist the obsolescence of the lock-ups affixed to digital content.

duction, *public communication* and *distribution* are granted to the right owner.[81]

Patent rights protect against any *making* and any *use* of the invention, but for private purpose. Whereas trademark defines its scope of protection as the *use* of the protected sign in the course of trade, which includes, but not exhaustively,[82] affixing the sign to the goods or to the packaging thereof; offering the goods, putting them on the market or stocking them for these purposes under that sign, offering supplying services thereunder; importing or exporting the goods under that sign; or using the sign on business papers and in advertising.[83]

The design regulations also refer to a protection against unauthorized *use* of the design, which is further defined as 'the making, offering, putting on the market, importing, exporting or using of a product in which the design is incorporated or to which it is applied, or stocking such a product for those purposes'.[84]

The realm of the rights conferred on each type of IP rights appears rather specific, both in technical and legal terms. Indeed, what could be similar between a copy of a work, the use of an invention itself and the use of a trademark in relation to a product? Actually, those notions are not so distinct as they seem to be. They all fit under a broader notion of *exploitation*: whatever the type of intellectual property, the exclusive rights delineate the power of the owner to take an effective benefit of her property. The scope of her rights covers uses of the protected subject-matter that presumably tend to achieve the purpose of its protection. This explains why, technically speaking, definitions of the rights slightly differ and take form according to the type of subject-matter.

Exploiting a literary or artistic work means to achieve its circulation in the public, which can be done directly and with no mediation (hypotheses covered by the communication right) or indirectly through a copy (hypotheses of the reproduction right, but also of the distribution, lending and rental rights).

A patent entitles its owner to control any making or use of the invention, beyond the private use, which is equivalent to say that the invention is exploited, for the technical solution is put into operation in such use or making. The patent holder's interest is to capture the benefits of her invention when it is applied in a product, technology or process.

---

81 Other exclusive rights in copyright are the rights to control rental, lending, resale for artistic works, and adaptation.

82 CJEU, 23 March 2010, *Google*, C-236/08, C-237/08, C-238/08.

83 See article 9(2) of the Community trademark regulation and the article 5(3) of the trademark directive.

84 Article 9(1) of the Community design directive, as well as article 12 of the design directive.

As to trademark, its function and benefit are to serve to distinguish products or services of one undertaking from another. Exploiting a trademark hence covers any use of the mark to designate a product or service, whether in direct relation to a product or service, or in marketing or publicity.

Insisting on this common feature of all intellectual property rights would reinforce the consistency of the intellectual property framework. One could go as far as acknowledging that one single right, called the *right of exploitation*, could be adopted to encompass all the rights granted to IP owners, whatever subject-matter is concerned.[85] The unique umbrella of the right of exploitation would not only be a matter of systematization and convergence but it would also, and perhaps more fundamentally, serve as a useful concept to refocus all technical or incidental acts of use that have gradually entered into the scope of the rights, thanks to this unlimited list of rights contained in each intellectual property regime. Let me give two examples.

The copyright case law of the last two years shows some uncertainty, perhaps even a disorienting confusion, when dealing with new technological developments that challenge technically-defined exclusive rights. It has happened with the communication to the public and the reproduction right. As to the communication to the public, the European Court had put forward a sound criterion in the *SGAE* case: the new public,[86] and has gradually developed it in any case related to the communication to the public[87] There is an act of communication to the public if the work is communicated to a public different from the public at which the original act of communication of the work is directed.

Aligning the scope of the communication right with the transmission to a new public arguably follows the notion of exploitation, as works are exploited when they are reaching different publics, who can hence enjoy, view or listen to the content so received. It can also serve to determine, amongst many technical acts that contribute to the transmission of a work to its final public, which ones should be covered by the exclusive right.[88] Yet, a recent decision has shown confusion by adding a supplementary element to the communication right, that of the possible access by the public to the essential element of the work.[89] Facts of the case related to the television broadcasting of the graphic

85 Christie, *supra* note 2.

86 ECJ, 7 December 2006, *SGAE v Rafael Hoteles*, C-306/05, § 40.

87 See CJEU, 4 October 2011, *Football Association Premiere League*, C-429/08; CJEU, 13 October 2011, *Airfield,* C-431/09 & C-432/09; CJEU, 15 March 2012, *Phonographic Performance*, C-162/10; CJEU, 15 March 2012, *SCF*, C-135/10.

88 See an application to technical acts required by broadcasting, the Opinion of the Advocate General, 17 March 2011, *Airfield*, C431/09 and C-432/09.

89 CJEU, 22 December 2010, *Bezpečnostní softwarová asociace*, C-393/09, §57.

user interface of a computer program, which the Court did not consider as an act of communication covered by copyright as the interaction with the user, deemed to be an essential element of such interface, was impossible. Beyond the puzzled reaction that many scholars had when discovering this unexpected condition for the communication right and its blatant contradiction with the refusal of the Court to qualify the user interface as a computer program (which conversely could have explained the requirement of an interaction), the only way to understand and accept this element might be to attach the ruling to the notion of exploitation. Should not the communication to the public be restricted to cases where the work is indeed achieving its purpose of being transmitted to the public, and effectively received by the public? The difficulty comes from the fact that the graphic user interface should indeed ensure some interactivity with the user to be properly received, but that the European judges could not consider it as a software. As a consequence, the decision seems to imply that the requirement of interaction applies to all works protected by copyright, whereas what is at stake is rather the communication of the essential elements of the work, in other words that the work is really exploited when communicated, meaning that it is capable of reaching its new public.

I doubt however that this was the implicit intention of the European Court, since, in other decisions dealing with reproduction right, and more particularly the temporary right of reproduction, its approach was rather attached to technical definitions of the act, than on a purpose-bound notion of exploitation. Indeed, in the *Infopaq* case, the European judges did not enter into a discussion of the ultimate purpose of the copies that occurred, but only touched upon their genuine transient nature, by requiring that 'the process must be automated so that it deletes that act automatically, without human intervention, once its function of enabling the completion of such a process has come to an end'.[90]

As a reminder, the infosoc directive includes in principle temporary copying within the scope of the reproduction right but exempts acts that are only transient or incidental, are an integral and essential part of the technological process of a network transmission or of a lawful use and have no independent economic significance.[91] Many have denounced the lack of clarity of that demarcation line between unauthorized and authorized copying.[92] It would be

90 ECJ, 16 July 2009, *Infopaq v DDF*, C-5/08, §64.

91 *Ibid.*

92 For instance A. and H.-J. Lucas (2006), *Traité de la propriété littéraire et artistique*, Lexis-Nexis, 3ème éd., p. 205, n°245; S. Dusollier (2005), 'Technology as an Imperative for Regulating Copyright: From the Public Exploitation to the Private Use of the Work', *EIPR*, 201–4.

clearer to embrace acts of transitory copying only when they can be qualified as exploitation of the work, meaning that a further circulation of the work can occur from the temporary copy itself. This would rejoice the purpose of the reproduction right that is to grant a control over the public circulation of the work, not over its mere use. The copy should not in itself enter into the realm of the exclusive rights, but only when it is the means of a further exploitation of the work. Transposed to the temporary copy, the fact that they are technically copies (which is the view of the infosoc directive) does not suffice to make them relevant for copyright: it is also necessary that they can trigger a new act of communication. The Advocate General Kokott, in her opinion on the *Football Premier League* case, seems to follow that reasoning when she considers that the exemption of temporary copying allowed in article 5(1) of the infosoc directive is precisely 'to permit acts of reproduction which are the condition for actual exploitation'.[93] But her conclusion, according to which a temporary reproduction on the television screen is not exempted under article 5(1) of the infosoc directive, ruins that hope. Her mistake is to consider that 'however, the economic significance of a broadcast is, as a rule, based on its reception'. Reception of a work as a principle eludes the realm of copyright, but providing the possibility for the public to receive and get access to a work does not, as it is the key matter for exploitation. The Court of Justice has rightfully corrected the opinion of its Advocate general on that point.[94] In our view, the notion of 'independent economic significance' that has appeared in the *acquis communautaire* to separate controlled temporary copies from exempted ones, can only be understood as 'being able to trigger a new exploitation'.

This single notion of exploitation could further simplify the definition of exclusive rights in copyright by not artificially separating the many technical acts of reproduction or communication that follow one another in one exploitation, and require all, under the current state of copyright, a distinct authorization, and generally an additional remuneration.

A second example of a possible reorientation of intellectual property around the notion of exploitation is the recent evolution of the European case law in trademark that attaches the counterfeiting of the trademark to the verification that the use of the protected sign has infringed one of the functions of the trademark.[95] By establishing a link between the scope of protection and the

---

93 Opinion of the Advocate General, 3 February 2011, *Football Association Premier League Ltd and Others v QC Leisure and Others*, C-403/08 and C-429/08, §92.

94 CJEU, 4 October 2011, *Football Association Premier League*, C-403/08 and C-429/08, § 171.

95 See, in chronological order, ECJ, 12 November 2002, *Arsenal v Reed*, C-206/01; ECJ, 25 January 2007, *Adam Opel*, C-48/05; ECJ, 18 June 2009, *L'Oréal*

very objective of the trademark grant, it indirectly installs the notion of exploitation on the throne of the protection. Indeed, the control of the trademark owner will only be limited to cases where her trademark has been exploited without any authorization, and not merely used. The difference between exploitation and use in trademark would be that for a trademark to be exploited, the capacity of the trademark to accomplish one of its functions in the use made by a third party would be affected. As in copyright, the notion of exploitation would adapt to the intellectual property right in question and would follow the function of the circulation of the protected subject-matter that the intellectual property protection aims to control. It would be circulation to the public for copyright, and public use of the sign to distinguish products or services for trademark.

True, the evolution of the European Court of Justice around the requirement of some harm to one of the functions of the trademark is somewhat bothering, particularly in double identity cases of infringements (i.e. use of a sign similar to the registered trademark for similar products) where no likelihood of confusion is required.[96] Other puzzling consequences of such case law are the extension of the protection of the image of a brand beyond the trademark with a reputation and the difficulty to allow for referential exceptions when some infringement to the functions of a trademark has been proven.[97] However, imposing a single right of exploitation in trademark would not give an autonomous role of the functions of the trademark, and certainly not to the vague functions of investment or publicity. On the contrary it could help draw a clear line between prohibited use of a protected trademark and referential use that should still be allowed for they are not acts of exploitation of the sign.

The same argument is equally valid for patent: the scope thereof should be limited to acts of use and making that correspond to a notion of exploitation tailored to technical inventions. Their purpose being the application of technical solutions and process, any use that puts the protected invention into operation is an act of exploitation of the patent that should be exclusively reserved to its owner. One could find traces of this exploitation-based reasoning in one

Bellure, C-487/07; CJEU, 23 March 2010, *Google*, C-236/08, C-237/08, C-238/08; CJEU, 8 July 2010, *Portakabin*, C-558/08; and the comment of this evolution in M. Senftleben, 'Adapting EU Trademark Law to New Technologies – Back to Basics?', in this volume.

96 For a critique of the CJEU recent case law in that regard, see *Max Planck Study*, *supra* note 11, pp. 103 *et seq.*

97 A circular reasoning then applies: there is an infringement if the indication of origin is troubled or the image of the brand is prejudiced, and a limitation is only valid if the use was fairly made, which is almost impossible to admit if some prejudice to the trademark has already been proven. See the *Portakabin* case, *supra* note 87, for a fine example of the dead-end situation when limitations of trademark are invoked.

of the rare CJEU decisions in patent law. In the *Monsanto* case, the CJEU has refused the protection of the patent to 'a patented DNA sequence which is not able to perform its function'.[98] Even though the question referred to the Court dealt with the object of the protection, not its scope or the rights conferred to the patented invention, both are interrelated. One way to interpret this decision is to consider that the patent protection cannot cover inventions when they are not operating as technical mechanisms. In the case of the soy flour fabricated from patented soy, the import thereof was only related to a dead matter, an invention incapable at the moment of the import, to exert its technical function. It follows that the patent owner being only entitled to stop uses of the invention in operation, her control amounts to the exploitation of the invention. The notion of use and making in patent law should be understood in that sense.

I have deliberately left aside the issue of moral right. Specific to copyright protection and performers rights,[99] such a right adds a subjective touch to protection of economic exploitation and cannot be reduced to the notion of exploitation I have just defined.

5. LIMITATIONS AND EXCEPTIONS

5.1 Exceptions to the Exclusive Rights

Limitations and exceptions to the protection are amongst the thickest and most entangled branches of the IP tree. It is even difficult to sketch a common picture here.

Copyright recognizes a long list of exceptions ranging from private copy, exceptions for education and libraries, for disabled people, for social institutions, to news reporting, quotation, parody, use during religious or official celebrations, for the purpose of advertising an exhibition, and so on. Copyright in software and databases have their own list of exceptions, tailored to the technical subject-matter at stake.

Patent is generally limited by private use and use for research, as well as by compulsory licensing that could be granted to manufacturers of the invention in the case of dependent inventions, unexploited inventions, or to cater to the needs of countries with public health problems in the case of pharmaceutical

98 CJEU, 6 July 2010, *Monsanto*, C-428/08, §49.

99 It also appears in patent law where the paternity of the inventor is guaranteed by the mention of his/her name in the application.

products. The only community legislation in patent, the biotechnology directive, applies the first case of compulsory licensing, by authorizing a breeder that cannot exploit a plant variety right without infringing a prior patent, or reciprocally the holder of a patent who cannot exploit a biotechnological invention without infringing a prior plant variety right, to apply for a compulsory licence.[100] It also introduces a specific exception that replicates the well-known farmers' privilege in the plant variety rights legislation, allowing the farmers to use the patented seeds, their harvest or breeding stock for their own farm.[101]

Actually, it is too hasty to say that the biotechnology directive is the sole EU intervention in patent. The European Parliament and Council have enacted in 2006 a Regulation organizing a system of compulsory licensing of patents permitting the manufacture of pharmaceutical products for export to countries suffering with public health issues,[102] which is a rare case of an EU piece of legislation that only deals with a limitation to intellectual property.

Limitations to trademark protection are mainly referential uses (including the use by a third party of his own name and address, of indications about characteristics of the product or service or to indicate the intended purpose of a product or service).[103]

Design exceptions borrow from copyright and patent and include private use, experimental use, citations or illustrations for teaching, as well as a right of prior use.[104]

Stand-alone justification can equally explain some limitations such as health consideration in patent or necessary use in copyright (namely justifying the temporary copy, back up copy, ephemeral recordings by broadcasting organizations, incidental inclusion of a work or the normal use in software and database protections and many others), whereas the rationale of the exception might be even more difficult to assess (think only of the use of works during celebrations!).

The overall impression of the exceptions twigs of the intellectual property tree is disorder. Diverse limitations appear to be justified when exclusive rights and subject-matter are diverse, but once again, when intellectual property admits many situations of overlapping rights in the same object, a better

---

100 See article 12 of the biotechnology directive.

101 See article 11 of the biotechnology directive.

102 Regulation (EC) No. 816/2006 of the European Parliament and of the Council of 17 May 2006 on compulsory licensing of patents relating to the manufacture of pharmaceutical products for export to countries with public health problems.

103 See article 7 of the trademark directive and article 12 of the Community trademark regulation.

104 See articles 20 and 22 of the Community design regulation, as well as the more limited exception allowed by article 13 of the design directive.

harmonization of exceptions across the different rights, might be needed. Efforts to systematize those diverse limitations could draw upon different grounds for allowing exceptions and be organized around key boxes where existing exceptions could be arranged. They would create a sort of Charter of User's Rights,[105] benefiting users, independently of the type of intellectual property right.

Private use could be a first category of limitation, as it is generally acknowledged as a natural boundary of the exclusivity in copyright, patent, trademark and design laws. Maybe it should not even be considered as an exception but as the logical reverse of the notion of exploitation delimitating the rights conferred.

Close to private use, a second category of exceptions would encompass all *necessary or incidental uses*. It would absorb the normal use of software and databases, the temporary reproduction in copyright (that could also disappear thanks to a reorientation of the rights around the notion of exploitation), the incidental use in copyright, the use during repair, and maybe referential uses in trademark.

Then, exceptions pursuing an objective of *competition or promoting innovation* could form a third block that would already include many existing exceptions (such as the decompilation of software, the compulsory licences for dependent inventions or unexploited ones, the farmers' privileges, the rights of prior use in design and patent laws). The referential uses of protection trademark could also belong here, as they are justified under the free movement of goods or freedom of services.

This category could be expanded to introduce new or redefined exceptions in some intellectual property regimes. A good example is the exception pertaining to research that exists in many intellectual property rights but not to the same extent. Design law admits the acts done for experimental purposes, copyright mentions an exception for illustrations of research (aligning blindly this motive with the illustration for teaching, without a more tailored application), and authorizes the reproduction of software when conducted to study the program. But a harmonized research exception is still lacking in European patent law, apart from the possibility to get access to deposited biological samples for experimental purposes as laid down by the biotechnology directive.[106]

Transformative uses could enter into intellectual property in a more direct way by taking over exceptions based on the right to express oneself or freedom of the press. It would encompass the quotation, parody and news report-

105 This expression is taken from Kur, *supra* note 3.

106 Article 13(3) of the biotechnology directive.

ing exceptions in copyright but is oddly absent in the other IP rights. This absence can be easily explained in patent where exploitation does not touch upon the expressiveness of an invention (and it is difficult to imagine cases where it would). Conversely, an exception for parody in trademark has recently invited itself in court cases, by reason of the increasingly cultural and semantic value of brands. Indeed, trademarks are used to convey meaning in our liberal economies, and constitute signs with an expressive force, that can be used to criticize for political or artistic motives. Rather than relying to the freedom of expression itself, which implies striking a fair balance between the IP rights and the restriction it imposes on the fundamental rights, with uncertain outcome, an overall exception for free speech could be introduced in all IP rights, including trademark. For that matter, such an introduction in trademark has been advocated in the recent study of the Max Planck Institute on the Community Trademark, under a broader exception of 'honest referential use'.[107] An exception for free speech would also prove useful in design law to avoid unnecessary litigation such as the case brought by Louis Vuitton against a Dutch artist who had reproduced one of its design-protected bags in a painting denouncing the lack of attention to the Darfur situation (in contrast with excessive attention to show-business stars).[108] The freedom of speech of the artist has prevailed in the Netherlands but not in France where she was enjoined to stop selling T-shirts reproducing the art work, which illustrates the uncertain result of applying freedom of speech directly against intellectual property.

Access to knowledge or essential resources would be another important category of limitations. It already pertains to the copyright exceptions enjoyed in teaching, by libraries or persons suffering from a disability. In parallel to knowledge, access to other resources might be essential and justify a limitation to intellectual property, as the access to medicines and its correlative compulsory licensing in patent. Farmers' privileges in plant variety rights or biotechnological patent follow a similar rationale, as the access of farmers to seeds of their harvest can be considered as essential to ensure their subsistence. Food security or biodiversity could in the near future give good reason for other cases of compulsory licensing in patent or plant variety rights.

Finally, *de minimis* exceptions could be admitted, but rather than relying on a closed list of all imaginable cases where countries have exerted enough

---

[107] Max Planck Institute for Intellectual Property and Competition Law, *Study on the Overall Functioning of the European Trade Mark System*, February 2011.

[108] See the decision refusing the design right infringement on free speech grounds, Rechtbank's-Gravenhage, 4 Mai 2011, n°389526/ KG ZA 11-294, available (in Dutch), at http://www.mediareport.nl/wp-content/uploads/2011/05/kvdl-727526-v1-vonnis_d_ d__4_mei_2011.pdf

influence, as in article 5 of the infosoc directive, it might be useful to introduce in all intellectual property rights a *fair use* clause, provided that the use does not conflict with normal exploitation of the subject-matter concerned.

One finds here one key element of the three-step test that now applies to all exceptions of copyright according to article 5(5) of the directive of 2001. Exceptions are only permitted in certain special cases, which do not conflict with a normal exploitation of the work and do not unreasonably prejudice the legitimate interests of the rightholders. A similar test exists in patent law in the TRIPS Agreement that admits limitations in the absence of an unreasonable conflict with the normal exploitation of the invention and with the legitimate interests of the patent owner, as well as in trademarks. Also for trademarks, the case law has construed the obligation to comply with honest practices in industrial or commercial matters when using the protected sign for referential purpose or comparative advertisement, by aligning it with the absence of any likelihood of confusion.[109] If the notion of exploitation in trademark amounts to the capacity to control the use of the sign to distinguish products or services, likelihood of confusion harms the normal exploitation.

Some coherence could be gained in using a two-step test or three-step test, including the respect of the normal exploitation of the protected subject-matter and the legitimate interests of the intellectual property owner, not as a limiting device to existing exceptions, but as a further breathing space to assess fair use of the creation or sign.[110] It would be then a reverse three-step test, allowing some fair use beyond what is explicitly authorized by the law.

5.2 The Rule of Exhaustion

The principle of exhaustion is a common limitation to trademark, copyright, patent and design. It prevents the enforcement of an intellectual property right

---

[109] ECJ, 11 September 2007, *Céline SAR v Céline SA*, C-17/06, §34:

> The issue of whether that condition has been satisfied must be assessed by, inter alia, taking account of the extent to which the use by the third party is understood by the relevant public, or at least by a significant section of that public, as establishing a link between the third party's goods and those of the trade mark proprietor or a person authorised to use the trade mark, and of the extent to which the third party ought to have been aware of that.

See also CJEU, 8 July 2010, *Portakabin*, C-558/08, §67; concerning comparative advertising see ECJ, 12 June 2008, *O2 Holdings*, C-533/06.

[110] This proposal has been made by some scholars for copyright, see C. Geiger (2007), 'The Role of the Three-Step Test in the Adaptation of Copyright Law to the Information Society', *e-Copyright Bulletin*, January-March, and the Wittem Code, article 5.5.

against further commercialization of goods that have been put on the European market with the consent of the intellectual property owner. Details of the application of exhaustion might slightly differ from one right to another. But the principle is shared by all rights in intellectual property, as well as its rationale rooted in the principle of the free movement of goods within the internal market. What is also common is the geographical scope of the exhaustion that has been determined by the ECJ as covering the European Union territory.[111]

6. DURATION

IP students generally learn that intellectual property is by nature limited in time, and that inherent quality is what makes it differ from tangible property that is inherently perpetual.

Copyright lasts for 70 years after the death of the author(s); patents are valid for a maximum of 20 years; community design for a maximum of five successive terms of five years; related rights for 50 years and the *sui generis* right applies to databases for 15 years.

This last duration can be extended for a renewed term each time a substantial investment is made to the database. This possibility to renew protection upon each substantial change, begs the question of the target of this lengthened duration: would it only vest in the contents resulting from the new investment or in the database as a whole?[112] Opting for the second interpretation would offer a protection potentially unlimited in time to databases.

Trademarks enjoy a specific situation as the protection lasts as long as the sign is genuinely used as a trademark and remains distinctive. However the effect of this limitless duration is relative as the protection only pertains to determined products and services and the protection, in opposition to other intellectual property rights, does not vest in a creation whose access by the public after some time would be essential.

The principle of a limited duration has been implicitly reasserted by the General Court of the European Union in the *Astra Zeneca* case. On the basis of competition law, the Court has found an abuse of dominant position in the false information given by a pharmaceutical firm to the patent office in order

---

[111] In copyright the community exhaustion, rather than an international one, has been confirmed in ECJ, 2 September 2006, *Laserdisken*, C-479/04; in trademark, see ECJ, 16 July 1998, *Silhouette*, C-355/96.

[112] On that question, see E. Derclaye (2008), *The Legal Protection of Databases – A Comparative Analysis*, Cheltenham, UK and Northampton, MA: Edward Elgar, pp. 139–40.

to get a longer period of supplementary protection certificate.[113] This decision tends at least to safeguard the rule of a limited duration strictly determined by the law, and dares to have recourse to the arm of competition law to enforce it.

However, this decision appears to run against the current, conveyed by the tendency to prolong whenever possible the duration of protection. A notable example is the directive lengthening the duration of performers' and producers' right in music,[114] which does not give sufficient account to the principle of a limited duration.

Beyond this principle, what is at stake is the immutability of the public domain. Rarely mentioned in intellectual property legislation, the public domain is mainly conceived as the repository of works or inventions whose term of protection has lapsed.[115] The European Union has not developed a strong position on the public domain, for all efforts focus on development of intellectual property. Consequently, the public domain is what is left after the intellectual property has taken its toll, and extending duration of a right is only analysed through the lens of economic development, not through the impoverishment of the public domain. Such a biased approach underlines cases where restoration of rights is admitted on purely technical application of legal provisions, without any consideration of the effect of such renewal of rights on the public domain where such creations stood. The ECJ has namely restored related rights in a phonogram, for a country where this phonogram was never protected by virtue of article 10(2) of the term directive.[116]

Pruning the intellectual property tree would require leaving breathing space for the leaves to fully blossom. Public domain, comprising unprotected resources (such as ideas or abstract matter) but also resources whose term of protection has ended, gives to subsequent creation the raw material to build upon. The total absence of public domain as a common principle of European intellectual property is unfortunate. It is time for the public domain to justify some legislative attention in itself and be addressed for what it is, and not only as an unintended counterpart of intellectual property.[117]

---

113 Gen. Court, 1 July 2010, *AstraZeneca v Commission*, T-32/05.

114 Directive 2011/77/EUof the European Parliament and of the Council of 27 September 2011.

115 For a broader conception of the public domain, see S. Dusollier, *Scoping Study on Copyright and Related Rights and the Public Domain*, WIPO, 2010.

116 ECJ, 20 January 2009, *Sony v Falcon*, C-240/07.

117 On the issue of the public domain in intellectual property, see S. Dusollier & V.L. Benabou (2007), 'Draw me a public domain', in P. Torremans (ed.), *Copyright Law: A Handbook of Contemporary Research*, Edgar Elgar, pp. 161–184 ; S. Dusollier (2009), 'The Public Domain in Intellectual Property: Beyond the Metaphor of a

7. CONCLUSION

At the end of this botanical journey, the realities and principles common to all intellectual property rights are rather scarce. There is the overarching principle, laid down in the EU Charter of Fundamental Rights, that intellectual property should be protected. The fact that ideas should remain free is another important motto in European intellectual property. The principle of exhaustion applies across all exclusive rights, and enforcement and remedies are almost similar whatever the right infringed.

Beyond these common lines, traces of similarities can perhaps be detected in formalities (save for copyright and related rights), in exclusive rights conferred, or in the rule of a limited duration. However, justifications, subject-matter, rights and exceptions largely remain fragmented and leave ample manoeuvre for uncontrolled extension of intellectual property and overlapping of rights.

What tree would we like in intellectual property? Should we focus on a unitary system, valid for all subject-matters? Or should we admit a hybrid mix of commonalities and diversity? My choice would be to have at least common roots in the form of an overall foundation sustaining intellectual property and based on innovation and promotion of knowledge, including a necessary balance, and a solid trunk based on some overarching principles. Those principles should be a proper limitation of subject-matter,[118] a registration-based grant of protection, a unitary right of exploitation for all intellectual property rights, though adjustable to the subject-matter concerned, a common catalogue of exceptions and limitations, as well as an effective public domain.

The branches of intellectual property could develop under their own rules and specificity to cater to the needs and mechanics of the diverse subject-matter concerned.

It is time to start pruning the tree. Gardeners know quite well that the very objective of pruning, however radical and destructive it might seem, is to get a blossoming tree that, after its forced reduction for some time, will grow bigger and in a more harmonious fashion. Who would refuse such a special treatment to intellectual property?

Domain', in P.L. Jayanthi Reddy (ed.), *Intellectual Property and Public Domain*, Hyderabad: Icfai University Press, pp. 31–69.

118 The objective would be to see what deserves exclusive protection and what, on the contrary, could develop under the normal conditions of the market with no protection, but that of unfair competition.

Section 2

The European Legal Framework

3. The legal framework of the legislative activity concerning intellectual property rights at European regional level

Vincenzo Scordamaglia

In this chapter I shall try to present the legal framework in which most of the legislative activity concerning IP rights takes place at European regional level. This legal framework is the result of a development characterized in a first phase by a traditional intergovernmental approach, followed from 1980 onwards by a growing European Communities (EC), later on European Union (EU), legislative approach. The most important part of this activity has been and is being carried out today in the framework of the EC, now EU. The intergovernmental approach, which was at the origin of one of the most successful achievements, the creation of the European Patent Organisation, continues to play some role also today. The two approaches have strongly influenced each other and continue to do so at present, as witnessed by the current initiative to create an international Patent Court to decide actions concerning European Patents and EU patents.

It goes without saying that this regional activity must be assessed in connection with the international activity at worldwide level, mainly in the framework of the World Intellectual Property Organization (WIPO), the UN Agency specializing in IP rights, but lately also of the World Trade Organization (WTO), particularly since the 'Trade Related Aspects of IP rights' have become part of its objects of activity. The peculiar nature of the IP rights, the principle of territoriality that characterizes them, has made this specific sector of law a favourite object of international cooperation. The Paris Convention for the Protection of Industrial Property of 1883, the Bern Convention for the Protection of Literary and Artistic Works of 1886 and the number of special agreements which have since been concluded under these two Conventions witness to the level of international cooperation that States have established. The drafting of national laws, a matter of exclusive sovereignty of each State, has been strongly influenced by the various international instruments of which the States were becoming parties. This explains the homogenous character of most of these legislations, with differences persisting mainly due to specific national interests or to differing legal traditions.

After the Second World War the cooperation in IP matters at European level followed quite naturally the traditional pattern of multilateral intergovernmental negotiations. Early outstanding results of this cooperation are:

- the Convention of 6 June 1947 setting up the 'Institut International des Brevets' at the Hague, concluded between France and Benelux and successively extended to several other European countries and eventually absorbed in the European Patent Organisation in 1976,
- the Convention of 27 November 1963 on the Unification of Certain Points of Substantive Law on Patents for Invention concluded in the framework of the Council of Europe.[1]

In 1958 the six original EEC Member States adopted the view that there was no Community competence to deal with IP rights under the new EEC Treaty. This resulted explicitly from Art. 295 EEC[2] and from Art. 36 EEC,[3] according to which the protection of IP rights justified a derogation from the fundamental rule on the free circulation of goods. According to this view IP rights remained entirely a subject of national sovereignty. To avoid the risk that the functioning of the 'Common Market' be hampered by these national territorially limited rights the six Member States envisaged the conclusion of conventions unifying the law of patents, trademarks and design.

The six EEC Member States set up in 1958 three Intergovernmental Working Parties. Each Working Party was composed of national experts and appointed its own President. The European Commission took part in the work. The Working Parties reported in 1962 to the Governments, but their reports have been considered by the Ministers and the Commission meeting within the EEC Council. The ambiguity of this activity, institutionally separated but functionally linked to the Community, has been present from the entry into force of the EEC.

---

1 The text of the Convention can be found at http://conventions.coe.int/Treaty/en/Treaties/Html/047.htm.

2 Now Art. 345 TFEU: 'The Treaties shall in no way prejudice the rules in Member States governing the system of property ownership.'

3 Now Art. 36 TFUE:

> The provisions of Articles 34 and 35 shall not preclude prohibitions or restrictions on imports, exports or goods in transit justified on grounds of [...] the protection of industrial and commercial property. Such prohibitions or restrictions shall not, however, constitute a means of arbitrary discrimination or a disguised restriction on trade between Member States.

Two of these Working Parties, on Patents and Trademarks,[4] produced preliminary Draft Conventions aiming at the creation of a unitary 'Community IP right', granted and managed by a 'Community Office'. The Draft Convention on Patents was received with high interest at the political level of the Ministers, but in 1964 failed to be adopted for political reasons (the wish that the UK should accede to the Convention clashed with the French veto putting an end to the first negotiations for accession of the UK to the European Communities).

From 1964 to 1968 no IP rights negotiations took place at European regional level. The interest was concentrated on the worldwide WIPO initiative on Patents which was going to lead in 1970 to the Patent Cooperation Treaty (PCT).[5]

In 1968 the positive conclusion of the future PCT was clearly in view and, at Community level, the accession of the UK to the European Communities appeared close at hand. There was a need for a patent initiative at broader European level, more far reaching than the PCT. This need found expression in a French initiative presented in the EEC Council. The French initiative was based on the well-known dichotomy between European and Community Patents, both to be realized by internationally negotiated conventions. The initiative has been approved by the six Member States and the Commission.

The preparation of the European Patent Convention (EPC) was entrusted to a European Conference to which 21 European States had been invited. It operated in Luxembourg from 1968 to 1972. The Commission took full part and the EEC Council and EFTA put at disposal their secretariats. These negotiations had therefore again a functional but no institutional link with the EEC.

The working method was strictly intergovernmental. The President and Vice-Presidents of the Conference had been appointed by the Conference which had its own rules of procedure. Each delegation contributed with proposals. The results of the deliberations of the Conference were translated into draft provisions of the future Convention by a permanent Drafting Committee and submitted to the Conference. The progress was ensured by the personal involvement of the heads of the main national patent offices, who contributed the best practices of their offices. The interested circles were regularly invited to the meetings, following the practice of WIPO negotiations. The

---

4 The Working Party on Design was unable to reach any common view and it is only almost 40 years later that a unitary solution could be found in the framework of the EU (European Parliament and Council Directive of 13 October 1998 on the legal protection of Design and Council Regulation of 12 December 2001 n. 6/2002 on the Community Design).

5 The full text of the PCT can be found at http://www.wipo.int/pct/en/texts/articles/atoc.htm.

result was a Draft Convention which became the basic document for the Diplomatic Conference held in Munich in 1973, where the EPC was concluded and opened to signature.[6]

The EPC sets up a new international organization, the European Patent Organisation, of which the European Patent Office (EPO) is an organ. This organization had no institutional link with the Community, nor did the situation change when the EU succeeded the EC. The Commission has always had so far a status of observer in the meetings of the Administrative Council.

The EPC entered into force in 1976. The EPO started its successful operation in 1977. At present 38 European States, including the 27 EU Member States, are parties to it.

There have been clear advantages in the intergovernmental form of negotiations at the origin of the EPC, in the technocratic composition of the Administrative Council and in the institutional independence of the EPO from the EU.

The EPC is a wonderful fruit of technocratic cooperation. The EPO has made of Munich one of the world capitals for patents. It employs 7000 highly specialized officials from 38 European countries. It has made of the European Patent the most important tool for protection of any new development of technology in Europe.

Patent law is only occasionally a hot topic for politics. The negotiations of the EPC and, later on, the patent activity of the EPO have been largely preserved from the political troubles of the Community life. This has been confirmed by the way the EPO has absorbed the EC results on the issue of biotechnology or the lack of results on the issue of patentability of software.

The low political profile has facilitated accession to the EPC of non-EU countries, those whose accession to the EU is still under consideration (Croatia, Iceland, Turkey, FYROM) and those which do not wish or cannot yet file a request for accession to the EU (Switzerland, Lichtenstein, Norway, Principality of Monaco, San Marino, Albania, Serbia).

The intergovernmental procedure followed to conclude the EPC continues to characterize more recent international instruments connected with this Convention, where the functional support is now ensured by the EPO. This procedure was used for the two revision conferences of the EPC held in 1991 and 2000 in application of Art. 142 EPC. The same procedure was followed for the 2000 London Agreement on the application of Article 65 EPC[7] on the issue of translations and had been envisaged for the negotiation, now aban-

---

[6] The complete and updated text of the EPC can be found at http://www.epo.org/law-practice/legal-texts/html/epc/2010/e/index.html.

[7] The text can be found at http://www.epo.org/law-practice/legal-texts/london-agreement.html.

doned in this form, of the European Patent Litigation Agreement (EPLA),[8] with the aim of instituting an international Court for litigation concerning European Patents. It is worth noting that the political difficulties now prevailing over the technocratic approach have compelled the negotiators to give these last instruments an optional character, thus instituting a kind of 'enhanced cooperation', or a 'two speed Europe' among the parties to the EPC.

The second element of the 1968 French initiative was the creation of a Community Patent (CP), a unitary European Patent designating all the EEC Member States, granted and managed by the EPO. The instrument instituting this Patent should have been a Convention restricted to the EEC Member States. The preparation was entrusted to a Working Party operating within the framework of the EEC Council, but making use of negotiating methods similar to those used by the Conference for the European Patent. The functional link with the EEC was much stronger, but from an institutional point of view the work had a very different nature from that of other Working Parties preparing Community secondary legislation. The Commission had full right of participation, but no monopoly of initiative. In fact its contribution was mainly concerned with the codification in the Convention of the principle of Community exhaustion of IP rights which was being developed by the Court of Justice around that period. For other aspects the technocratic approach of the experts in the delegations prevailed. The only problem having a real political dimension was the linguistic regime of the CP, which was to represent a kind of permanent curse hanging over the whole history of this project. A draft Convention was prepared by the Working Party according to a procedure very similar to the one used for the preparation of the EPC. The Drafting Committee had an important role.

A Conference of the nine Member States[9] took place at Luxembourg in December 1975 and as a result the 1975 Community Patent Convention (CPC)[10] was signed. A clever compromise was found to the problem of the linguistic regime (the number of languages involved was six). The entry into force of the CPC, expected more or less at the same time as the EPC, was delayed by constitutional difficulties in Denmark and Ireland, linked with the ambiguous nature of this instrument. For the CPC was an international Convention, but also an instrument aiming at a better functioning of the common market and giving new competences to some EEC institutions, particularly the Court of Justice, without any reference to a legal basis in a provision of the EEC Treaty.

---

8 The text of the latest draft can be found at http://www.epo.org/law-practice/legislative-initiatives/epla.html.

9 The UK, Ireland and Denmark had joined the EEC.

10 Convention for the European patent for the common market (Community Patent Convention) OJ L 17 of 26 January 1976.

The work continued in the same form during the 1980s to take account of the accession of Greece, Spain and Portugal and to improve the text of the CPC, particularly concerning the litigation regime. Two further Conferences were held in Luxembourg in 1985 and 1989. The 1989 Conference adopted the Agreement relating to Community Patents, containing a revised version of the 1975 CPC and a Protocol of litigation.[11]

The entry into force of the 1989 Agreement was dependent upon the ratification by all the 12 signatory Member States. This condition was never fulfilled, partly because of the excessively costly solution found for the linguistic regime (nine languages were now involved), partly because of the persistent ambiguous nature of the instrument with respect to Community law.

The Community Patent story does not end here, but it continues in the framework of the different model, the Community model, which takes over from the 1980s onward.

The European cooperation in IP matters was based on the conclusion of conventions following the traditional procedure under public international law as a consequence of the firm belief that IP rights were national matters, entirely outside the scope of the Community competence.

This conviction, which was maintained by some Member States until 1995, when the Court of Justice swept it away definitely,[12] started however to lose its absolute character very soon, in the late 1960s–early 1970s. The Court clarified in a number of decisions that some EEC Treaty rules had a direct impact on the national IP rights.

- The Community rules on competition[13] also found application to the behaviour of undertakings based on the use of IP rights.
- The doctrine of Community exhaustion of these rights, directly enshrined in the text of the EEC Treaty[14] required an appropriate amendment of the national rules defining the rights attached to any IP right.

During the 1970s the European Commission became aware that the absolute denial to the Community of any competence to adopt secondary legislation in IP matters was simply wrong and that there was space for Community legislative initiatives. It was obviously correct that the Community did not possess any exclusive internal competence in this field, but IP rights had a strong impact on the functioning of the common (later internal) market. This market

11 OJ L 401 of 30 December 1989.
12 See Decision of 13 July 1995 on the case C-350/92 *Spain v Council*.
13 Arts 85–86 EEC Treaty, later Arts 81–82 EC Treaty, now Arts 101–102 TFEU.
14 Arts 30 and 36 EEC Treaty, later Arts 28 and 30 EC Treaty, now Arts 34 and 36 TFEU.

is one of the shared competences of the EU (Art. 4 TFEU). The EEC was entitled, under Art. 100 EEC Treaty, to 'issue directives for the approximation of such laws, regulations or administrative provisions of the Member States as directly affect the establishment or functioning of the common market'. National IP legislation undoubtedly falls under this definition. It was therefore possible, by making use of Art. 100 EEC Treaty as a legal basis, to adopt Directives approximating the IP legislations of the Member States when the differences were sufficiently important to represent an obstacle for the smooth functioning of the internal market.

Art. 100 EEC Treaty[15] required unanimity in Council; the European Parliament was only consulted and the only accepted measure was the Directive. In 1986 the Single European Act introduced an Art. 100A EEC Treaty,[16] which recognized the Community competence under basically the same conditions as Art. 100 EEC Treaty, but the measure only required a qualified majority in Council, was subject to the cooperation procedure with the European Parliament and could differ from a Directive. The Maastricht Treaty, signed in 1992, further amended the procedure under Art. 100A EC Treaty by making the adoption of the measure subject to the co-decision procedure with the European Parliament.

Since the Maastricht Treaty this legal basis is generally accepted and regularly used. Only the numbering of the article has been changed: Art. 95 EC Treaty after the Amsterdam Treaty, Art. 114 TFEU after the Lisbon Treaty. It has given rise to a corpus of measures, mainly Directives, which have strongly influenced all aspects of the national IP legislations and conditioned their evolution. The principle of national territoriality of IP rights is preserved but the autonomy of the national legislator in establishing the applicable rules is now seriously limited.

The need to avoid that the functioning of the internal market be hampered and to establish fair conditions for competition between undertakings has been a sufficiently convincing argument to justify a complete and systematic approximation, at substantive level, of the national rules governing trademarks[17] and design[18] and, at procedural level, of the national rules concerning

---

15 Later Art. 94 EC Treaty, now Art. 115 TFEU.

16 Later Art. 95 EC Treaty, now Art. 114 TFEU.

17 Council Directive 89/104/EEC of 21 December 1988 to approximate the laws of the Member States relating to trade marks. A codified version of this Directive is to be found in Directive 2008/95/EC of the European Parliament and of the Council of 22 October 2008 to approximate the laws of the Member States relating to trade marks, OJ L 299 of 8 November 2008.

18 Directive 98/71/EC of the European Parliament and of the Council of 13 October 1998 on the legal protection of designs, OJ L 289 of 28 October 1998.

measures, procedures and remedies ensuring the enforcement of IP rights.[19] The same argument has justified measures approximating on specific points the rules governing copyright, with as the main example the term of duration of copyright.[20]

But this legal basis did in particular allow, every time the technological or cultural development required new IP instruments or adaptation of the existing instruments, the realization of this progress in a uniform manner, by introducing on specific issues unified rules in the national legislations, thus avoiding the risk of divergent developments. The Directive on topographies of semiconductor products[21] was not only a typical example of this type of measure, but also the first Directive on IP rights in absolute to be adopted by Council in 1986. Many other Directives of this type followed, most of them adapting the instrument of copyright to its new technological functions. Let's just mention the Directives on software,[22] on databases,[23] on satellite broadcasting and cable retransmission[24] and on the information society.[25] In the field of patents the Directive on biotechnology[26] also belongs to this category of measures.

Art. 100A EEC Treaty had opened to the Community a large perspective for legislative action, but the very nature of the measures adopted, applicable to national IP rights, could not affect the territorial limitation of each right to the

---

[19] Directive 2004/48/EC of the European Parliament and of the Council of 29 April 2004 on the enforcement of intellectual property rights, OJ L 204 of 4 August 2007.

[20] Council Directive 93/98/EEC of 29 October 1993 harmonizing the term of protection of copyright and certain related rights. A codified version of this Directive is to be found in Directive 2006/116/EC of the European Parliament and of the Council of 12 December 2006 on the term of protection of copyright and certain related rights, OJ L 372 of 27 December 2006.

[21] Council Directive 87/54/EEC of 16 December 1986 on the legal protection of topographies of semiconductor products, OJ L 24 of 27 January 1987.

[22] Council Directive 91/250/EEC of 14 May 1991on the legal protection of computer programs. A codified version of this Directive is to be found in Directive 2009/24/EC of the European Parliament and of the Council of 23 April 2009 on the legal protection of computer programs OJ L 111 of 5 May 2009.

[23] Directive 96/9/EC of the European Parliament and the Council of 11 March 1996 on the legal protection of databases, OJ L 77 of 27 March 1996.

[24] Council Directive 93/83/EEC of 27 September 1993 on the coordination of certain rules concerning copyright and rights related to copyright applicable to satellite broadcasting and cable retransmission, OJ L 248 of 6 October 1993.

[25] Directive 2001/29/EC of the European Parliament and of the Council of 22 May 2001 on the harmonization of certain aspects of copyright and related rights in the information society, OJ L 167 of 22 June 2001.

[26] European Parliament and Council Directive 98/44/EC of 6 July 1998 on the legal protection of biotechnological inventions, OJ L 213 of 30 July 1998.

Member State having granted it. The negotiations on the Community Patent had made the Commission aware how important it was for large companies, but also for active medium and small companies, to dispose of unitary IP rights covering the whole territory of the Community.

Alas, even perusing attentively the Treaty, no provision could be found giving explicitly a competence to institute such unitary rights. A provision was however found which could be interpreted as giving implicitly such a competence, Art. 235 EEC Treaty, later Art. 308 EC Treaty:

> If action by the Community should prove necessary to attain, in the course of the operation of the common market, one of the objectives of the Community, and this Treaty has not provided the necessary powers, the Council shall, acting unanimously on a proposal from the Commission and after consulting the European Parliament, take the appropriate measures.

In 1973 the Commission started preparation of two instruments: a Directive approximating the substantial rules of the legislation governing national trademarks and a Regulation instituting a Community Trademark, in order to test the two legal bases identified above, Arts. 100 and 235 EEC Treaty. The two proposals were presented as a whole. The basic consideration was that national trademarks would continue to play an important role even in an integrated market, but a unitary right covering the whole of the Community could usefully supplement such national rights. This unitary right, the Community Trademark, would coexist with the national trademarks and be created in the Community legal order, whose existence as an independent order separate from the national orders, but also from the international legal order, had been recognized by the Court of Justice. It would be registered and managed by a Community agency to be created under the same legal basis.

The two proposals were the object of thorough preparation by the Commission. Most of the techniques of the intergovernmental patent negotiations had been taken over: close cooperation with the best national experts, consultation of the interested circles, discussion of successive versions of the draft proposals during public hearings. Eventually the two proposals were submitted officially to Council in 1980. The proposals were initially received with mistrust concerning the legal basis by the Working Party in Council, but progressively, during the 1980s, the validity of the Commission's approach was recognized. Any doubt concerning the admissibility of this legal basis has been dispelled by the Court of Justice in its Opinion 1/94.[27]

---

27 S. paras 55–71 of the Opinion 1/94 of 15 November 1994.

It took 13 years for the Council to adopt, in 1993, the Regulation instituting the Community Trademark.[28] The negotiations concerning the substantive aspects of trademark law were completed in 1988 when the Directive approximating the national legislations on trademarks was adopted, because of the fundamental unity of the system governing national and Community rights. Five years were needed to find solutions to political issues like the seat of the Office for Harmonisation in the Internal Market (Trademarks and Designs) (OHIM) and its linguistic and financial regime. Only the intervention of the European Council in October 1993 allowed an agreement to be reached.

As soon as the road toward the creation of unitary rights was opened two new initiatives were successfully launched by the Commission: the unitary rights on plant varieties and on designs. The EU right on plant varieties was adopted in 1994[29] and is granted and managed by the Community Plant Variety Office (CPVO) based in Angers (France), the EU design was adopted in 2001[30] and is registered and managed by the OHIM based in Alicante (Spain).

An initiative was undertaken in 2000 by the Commission to institute an EU unitary patent using the same legal basis, Art. 308 EC Treaty. The proposal took over the unsuccessful results of the two 1975 and 1989 Conventions on the Community Patent, but it adapted them to the clear institutional framework created by choosing the instrument of an EU Regulation. The proposal was inspired by the precedent of the Trademark Regulation, but it contained at least two interesting features which constituted innovative elements from an institutional point of view. First of all the EU did not aim at setting up a new Patent Office operating as an EU agency, as it did with the OHIM. In the case of patents it was reasonable, not to say inescapable, to make use of the existing structure of the EPO. The EU patent has therefore been conceived as a European Patent designating the EU, granted by the EPO under the EPC procedure. To obtain this result the EU would have acceded to the EPC of its own right, next to its Member States, following a revision of that Convention which is currently open to accession only for States. The second element differentiating this proposal from the trademark solution concerned the litigation regime. The litigation concerning EU trademarks was reserved to the

[28] Council Regulation (EC) No 40/94 of 20 December 1993 on the Community trade mark. A codified version of this Regulation is to be found in Council Regulation (EC) No 207/2009 of 26 February 2009 on the Community trade mark, OJ L 78 of 24 March 2009.

[29] Council Regulation (EC) No 2100/94 of 27 July 1994 on Community plant variety rights, OJ L 227 of 1 September 1994.

[30] Council Regulation (EC) No 6/2002 of 12 December 2001 on Community designs, OJ L 3 of 5 January 2002.

national courts both for infringement actions and invalidity counterclaims, only the direct actions on invalidity being brought directly before the OHIM first and the EU General Court and Court of Justice for judicial control. The proposal for an EU patent, making use of Arts. 225A and 229A EC Treaty, two new provisions introduced by the Nice Treaty, suggested concentrating the whole of the litigation concerning the EU patent, infringement and invalidity actions, before a special court to be instituted in the framework of the EU Court of Justice.

Intense negotiations went on concerning this proposal before Council from 2000 until the end of 2009. Several times the proposal came for consideration before the Council at ministerial level, but every time the unanimity required by Art. 308 EC could not be reached on the issue of the linguistic regime of the EU patent (the EU official languages have now reached, since the last accessions to the EU, the number of 23).

An entirely new development in terms of legal basis resulted from the entry into force of the Lisbon Treaty on 1 December 2009. A new Treaty provision, Art. 118 TFEU, explicitly recognizes an EU competence to institute unitary IP rights '*in the context of the establishment and functioning of the internal market*'. The procedure no longer requires unanimity in Council, but only the qualified majority, and the European Parliament is now fully involved under the '*ordinary legislative procedure*', the new terminology for '*co-decision*'. There is however a limitation: the language arrangements for the EU unitary rights continue to be established by the Council alone, acting unanimously on a proposal by the Commission and after consulting the European Parliament.

In July 2010 the Commission transformed its original proposal on the linguistic regime of the EU patent into a new proposal based on this new provision. The discussion was pursued on this basis in Council during the last semester, but the extensive efforts of the Belgian Presidency did not succeed. The Council reached the conclusion in December 2010 that 'it was impossible to reach on this issue a decision requiring unanimity at present and in the foreseeable future'. Under these circumstances several delegations requested the Commission to take the initiative in order to create a unitary patent protection in the framework of a procedure of 'enhanced cooperation', as foreseen by the Lisbon Treaty. The Commission has positively reacted to this request and a proposal for a Council decision authorizing enhanced cooperation in the area of the creation of a unitary patent protection was submitted in December 2010. According to recent information 25 Member States wish to participate in this enhanced cooperation, only Italy and Spain maintaining an objection to this procedure. The European Parliament has approved this proposal and the Council should adopt in March 2011 the decision authorizing the enhanced cooperation.

The negotiations on the EU patent entailed another consequence. The Council reached in December 2008 a political agreement on a document called 'Enhanced Patent System in Europe'. One of the elements of this system should be 'the setting up of an integrated specialised and unified jurisdiction for patent related disputes thus improving the enforcement of patents and enhancing legal certainty'. This should be realized by a Convention to be negotiated by the EU, its Member States and the other States parties to the EPC. An international court should be created having exclusive competence for actions concerning validity and infringement of European Patents and EU Patents. A preliminary project of this Convention has been prepared and it has been submitted to the Court of Justice by the Council, to ascertain its compatibility with Community law. The opinion of the Court is shortly expected and it will no doubt point to several aspects where changes or improvements are required. The main problem will however be how this construction, originally conceived for the EU Patent, can now be adapted to a situation where the unitary title of protection within the EU will be created in the framework of a procedure of enhanced cooperation.

The development of the EU legislative activity on IP rights also had an impact on the status and activity of the EU in the international WIPO and WTO frameworks. In the 1970s and 80s, before the EU Member States recognized the internal EU competence, a practice had been progressively developed to present coordinated positions in the WIPO meetings. These were prepared in coordination meetings with the participation of the Commission, but in the absence of any voting rule they were useful only to the extent that the Commission and the delegation holding the Presidency in Council succeeded in obtaining a consensus on some compromise. This practice had however the advantage that the third countries were getting used to the idea that they should expect the group of EU countries to operate as a unit.

The development of the EU internal competence entailed the recognition of the existence of a double external competence:

- an exclusive competence for the trade related aspects of IP rights, contained in the EU exclusive competence for the common commercial policy;
- an implicit external competence based on the doctrine of 'implied powers', resulting from the internal EU legislation.

The fight against the international commerce of counterfeit and pirated goods had led the Community in the 1980s to adopt unilateral internal measures authorizing the custom authorities to take measures under a suspensive procedure for goods imported within the EU suspected of infringing IP rights. These measures were compatible with the obligations under the General Agreement on Tariffs and Trade (GATT) and belonged to the field of common commercial policy. This action has been developed in the following years and it covers today, under Council Regulation (EC) No 1383/2003 of 22 July 2003,[31] the whole spectrum of IP rights, including patents.

The negotiations concerning the TRIPs Agreement[32] led to the full recognition of the external competence of the EU in this field. The accent put on the trade related aspects of IP rights gave the EU the right to be recognized as a future party to this Treaty and to sign it. During the ratification procedure the question arose of the extent of this competence. The Commission traditionally maintained the argument that any negotiations with third countries concerning IP rights belonged to the common commercial policy and therefore the EU had an exclusive competence. This argument had never been accepted by the Council. The ratification procedure of the Treaty instituting WTO gave the Commission the opportunity of testing its argument: the Commission took the view that the TRIPs should be ratified exclusively by the EU and not by its Member States. The Council asked the opinion of the Court of Justice on this issue by making use of Art. 300(6) EC Treaty. The Court took a clear position in its Opinion 1/94: the EU competence is limited to matters concerning the fight against international counterfeit and pirated goods, but does not extend to provisions of substantive or procedural law concerning IP rights. Here the external competence is in principle reserved to the Member States, except when the EU has adopted internally common rules and the exercise of the competence by the Member States would be likely to affect them or to alter their scope.[33]

Now Art. 207 TFEU concerning the common commercial policy expressly mentions the commercial aspects of intellectual property as object of this policy.

The current international negotiations concerning the Anti-counterfeiting Trade Agreement (ACTA) the final draft of which was released on 15 November 2010, have seen the full participation of the EU acting by virtue of this aspect of its exclusive external competence.

The implicit external competence of the Community to conclude agreements with third countries or international organizations even when this was not expressly foreseen by the Treaty has been recognized by the Court of Justice

---

[31] Council Regulation (EC) No 1383/2003 of 22 July 2003 concerning customs action against goods suspected of infringing certain intellectual property rights and the measures to be taken against goods found to have infringed such rights, OJ L 196 of 2 August 2003.

[32] The text of the TRIPs Agreement is to be found at http://www.wto.org/english/docs_e/legal_e/27-trips_01_e.htm.

[33] S. Art. 216(1) TFEU.

since 1971 in the famous decision AETR.[34] The doctrine of 'implied powers' represents a cornerstone of the system of external competences of the EU.

This doctrine has naturally found application to the area of intellectual property. To the extent that approximation Directives had been adopted, Member States are no longer allowed, either individually or collectively, to negotiate agreements with third countries which could affect the obligations resulting from those Directives. This was particularly the case with the negotiations of the WIPO Copyright Treaty[35] and of the WIPO Performances and Phonograms Treaty,[36] both of 1996, of which the EU has become a member in 2010, next to its Member States.

The unitary EU rights instituted by Regulation were also quickly affected by negotiations with third countries. In this case the EU external competence was exclusive, but subject to an important restraint: as the Regulations adopted internally were based on Art. 308 EC Treaty, requiring unanimity, the same voting rule was required for the various stages of the negotiations procedure affecting these rights. This has not prevented the successful conclusion of two international instruments, the 1989 Protocol Relating to the Madrid Agreement on trademarks[37] and the 1999 Geneva Act of the Hague Agreement on Industrial Design[38] to both of which the EU has become a party. The rule of unanimity has changed since the entry into force of the Lisbon Treaty. Art. 118 TFEU provides as a basic voting rule the qualified majority, with the consequence that the procedure for negotiations affecting EU unitary rights will be based on the same voting rule. An exception remains with regard to negotiations affecting the linguistic regime of such IP rights that are still to be decided by unanimity.

---

34 Case 22/70 '*AETR*' (Commission/Council) Decision of 31 March 1971:

> In particular, each time the Community, with a view to implementing a common policy envisaged by the Treaty, adopts provisions laying down common rules, whatever form they may take, the Member States no longer have the right, acting individually or even collectively, to undertake obligations with third countries which affect those rules or alter their scope.

35 The text can be found at http://www.wipo.int/treaties/en/ip/wct/trtdocs_wo033.html.

36 The text can be found at http://www.wipo.int/treaties/en/ip/wppt/trtdocs_wo034.html.

37 Protocol Relating to the Madrid Agreement Concerning the International Registration of Marks, adopted at Madrid on 27 June 1989. The text can be found at http://www.wipo.int/madrid/en/legal_texts/trtdocs_wo016.html.

38 Geneva Act of the Hague Agreement on Industrial Design Concerning the International Registration of Industrial Designs Adopted by the Diplomatic Conference on 2 July 1999. The text can be found at http://www.wipo.int/hague/en/legal_texts/wo_haa_t.htm.

4. Fundamental rights and European IP law: the case of Art 17(2) of the EU Charter

Jonathan Griffiths and Luke McDonagh

1. INTRODUCTION

There is a large and ever-growing literature on the relationship between fundamental rights and intellectual property law.[1] Particular attention has been devoted to a number of specific issues. These include the impact of the rights to health, medicine and life on patent law,[2] the potential conflict between freedom of expression and the laws of copyright and trade marks[3] and the privacy

[1] See for example, C. Geiger [2006], '"Constitutionalising" Intellectual Property Law? The Influence of Fundamental Rights on Intellectual Property in the European Union', *International Review of Intellectual Property and Competition Law* 371; T. Mylly (2009), *Intellectual Property and European Economic Constitutional Law*, Vaajakoski: Gummerus Kirjapaino Oy; J. Cornides [2004], 'Human Rights and Intellectual Property, Conflict or Convergence?', *Journal of World Intellectual Property*, 1423; P. Torremans (ed.) (2008), *Intellectual Property & Human Rights*, Alphen aan den Rijn, the Netherlands: Kluwer; L. Helfer and G. Austin (2011), *Human Rights and Intellectual Property: Mapping the Global Interface*, Cambridge: Cambridge University Press; D. Matthews (2011), *Intellectual Property, Human Rights and Development, The Role of NGOs and Social Movements*, Cheltenham, UK and Northampton, MA: Edward Elgar; W. Grosheide (ed.) (2009), *Intellectual Property Rights and Human Rights: A Paradox*, Cheltenham, UK and Northampton, MA: Edward Elgar.

[2] See D. Matthews (2009), 'Intellectual Property Rights, Human Rights and the Right to Health', in W. Grosheide (ed.), *Intellectual Property Rights and Human Rights: A Paradox*, Cheltenham, UK and Northampton, MA: Edward Elgar; H. Hestermeyer (2007), *Human Rights and the WTO: The Case of Patents and Access to Medicines*, Oxford: Oxford University Press; Matthews, *supra* note 1.

[3] N.W. Netanel (2008), *Copyright's Paradox*, Oxford: Oxford University Press; J. Griffiths and U. Suthersanen (2005), *Copyright & Free Speech*, Oxford: Oxford University Press; C. Geiger [2007], 'Trade Marks & Freedom of Expression – the Proportionality of Criticism' *IIC*, 317; J. Griffiths (2008), 'Is there a Right to an Immoral Trade Mark?' in P. Torremans (ed.), *supra* note 1, p. 309; *Laugh it Off Promotions CC v South African Breweries International (Finance) BV* [2005] ZACC

implications of intellectual property remedies and sanctions.[4] These issues, amongst others, have been explored in a range of national and international legal contexts. However, the role of fundamental rights within European Union (EU) intellectual property law has not yet been fully explored.[5] It is, nevertheless, likely to become a subject of increasing significance. Following the coming into force of the Lisbon Treaty, EU bodies have clear obligations to take fundamental rights into consideration in all their activities.[6] Under Art 6(1) of the Treaty of European Union (TEU), rights granted under the Charter of Fundamental Rights of the EU ('the EU Charter')[7] have the same legal value as those established under the foundational treaties. Furthermore, under Art 6(3) TEU:

> Fundamental rights, as guaranteed by the European Convention for the Protection of Human Rights and Fundamental Freedoms and as they result from the constitutional traditions common to the Member States, shall constitute general principles of the union's law.[8]

7, [2005] BCLR 743 (Constitutional Court, South Africa); *Alles Wird Teurer* [1999] ETMR 49 (KG Berlin Court of Appeal); *Sté Gervais Danone v Société Le Riseau Voltaire, Société Gandhi, Valentin Lacambre* [2003] ETMR 321; *Association Greenpeace France v SA Société Esso* [2003] ETMR 867 (Cour d'appel de Paris); *SA Société des Participations du CEA v Greenpeace France et al* [2003] ETMR 870 (Cour d'appel de Paris).

4 See, for example, S. Catal (2004), 'Privacy v Piracy', *Yale Journal of Law and Technology* 7, 222; J. Griffiths (2011), 'Criminal Liability for Intellectual Property Infringement in Europe – the Role of Fundamental Rights', in C. Geiger (ed.), *Criminal Enforcement of Intellectual Property: A Blessing or a Curse?*, Cheltenham, UK and Northampton, MA: Edward Elgar.

5 Although, see C. Geiger (2009), 'Copyright's Fundamental Rights Dimension at EU level', in E. Derclaye (ed.), *Research Handbook on the Future of EU Copyright*, Cheltenham, UK and Northampton, MA: Edward Elgar, 27; Mylly, *supra* note 1.

6 For a thorough assessment of the application of the EU Charter post-Lisbon, see P. Craig (2010), *The Lisbon Treaty: Law Politics, and Treaty Reform*, Oxford: Oxford University Press. See also S. Peers (2011), *EU Justice and Home Affairs Law*, 3rd ed., Oxford: Oxford University Press. For a general assessment of fundamental rights in an EU context see P. Craig and G. De Burca (2007), *EU Law: Text, Cases and Materials*, 4th ed., Oxford: Oxford University Press, pp. 379–427. See also D. Ehlers (ed.) (2007), *European Fundamental Rights and Freedoms*, Berlin: De Gruyter Recht and T. Ahmed and I. de Jesús Butler [2006], 'The European Union and Human Rights: An International Law Perspective', *European Journal of International Law*, 771.

7 EU Charter of Fundamental Rights, as signed and proclaimed by the Presidents of the European Parliament, the Council and the Commission at the European Council meeting in Nice on 7 December 2000.

8 The EU is itself under an obligation to accede to the European Convention on Human Rights (ECHR) as a result of Article 6(2) Treaty on European Union ('TEU'), original treaty signed at Maastricht, 7 February 1992, and amended by the Treaty of Lisbon amending the Treaty on European Union and the Treaty establishing the

In such circumstances, a fundamental rights dimension applies to all areas of law within the EU's competence, which clearly includes most areas of intellectual property law. The obligation to comply with fundamental norms applies not only to the EU legislature, the Court of Justice of the European Union and other EU bodies, but also to national institutions when acting within the sphere of EU competence.

The enhanced status of the rules and jurisprudence of fundamental rights law under the Lisbon arrangements is likely to have an impact in a number of different areas of intellectual property law. However, in this chapter, we intend to focus on only one particularly interesting aspect of the relationship between these two bodies of law. Art 17(2) of the EU Charter grants intellectual property itself a fundamental status, providing that: 'Intellectual property shall be protected.'

The intention and effect of this provision have been controversial[9] Nevertheless, it has already been referred to on a number of occasions within the EU's intellectual property system. In this chapter, we seek to address some of the uncertainty concerning the aim and scope of Art 17(2) by exploring the interpretation of its historical antecedents. In so doing, we hope to dispel a number of misconceptions concerning its supposed effects.

2. FUNDAMENTAL RIGHTS IN EU INTELLECTUAL PROPERTY LAW

Even prior to the coming into force of the Lisbon Treaty, the relevance of fundamental rights to intellectual property law had been acknowledged by the institutions of the EU. Fundamental rights have, for example, been advanced as a justification for legislative activity on a number of occasions. In the Information Society Directive, it was claimed that:[10]

> The proposed harmonisation will help to implement the four freedoms of the internal market and relates to compliance with the fundamental principles of law and especially of property, including intellectual property, and freedom of expression and the public interest.[11]

European Community, signed at Lisbon, 13 December 2007, entered into force on 1 December 2009. The Council of Europe introduced Protocol No. 14 ECHR (entered into force 1 June 2010) in order to allow the EU to become a party to the ECHR.

[9] See C. Geiger [2009], 'Intellectual Property Shall be Protected!? – Article 17(2) of the Charter of Fundamental Rights of the European Union: a Mysterious Provision with an Unclear Scope' [2009] *EIPR*, 115.

[10] Directive 2001/29/EC of the European Parliament and of the Council of 22 May 2001 on the harmonisation of certain aspects of copyright and related rights in the information society (OJ L 167, 22.06.2001).

[11] Ibid, recital 3.

In patent law, the recitals to the Directive on the legal protection of biotechnological inventions make a similar claim:

> Whereas pursuant to…the Treaty on European Union, the Union is to respect fundamental rights, as guaranteed by the European Convention for the Protection of Human Rights and Fundamental Freedoms signed in Rome on 4 November 1950 and as they result from the constitutional traditions common to the Member States, as general principles of Community law.[12]

The Enforcement Directive is also presented as serving goals grounded in respect for fundamental rights:

> This Directive respects the fundamental rights and observes the principles recognised in particular by the Charter of Fundamental Rights of the European Union. In particular, this Directive seeks to ensure full respect for intellectual property, in accordance with Article 17(2) of that Charter.[13]

On occasion, such assertions of compatibility with fundamental rights norms have also been tested before the EU courts in the context of intellectual property law. Notably, for example, it was argued in *The Netherlands v European Parliament and EU Council*[14] that the fundamental right to human dignity was infringed by the Directive on biotechnological inventions. The Netherlands, supported by Norway and Italy, argued that the patenting of any invention derived from human DNA constituted an affront to the fundamental right to human dignity and integrity because it envisaged using the human body as a 'means to an end'. The ECJ rejected this assessment, noting that Art 5(1) of the Directive clearly states that the human body cannot constitute a patentable invention during its various stages of formation and development. Furthermore, no element of the human body is patentable of itself; inventions are only patentable when they combine a natural element with a technical process with the purpose of undertaking an industrial application.

The Court of Justice has also heard challenges to the compatibility of EU legislation with fundamental norms in the area of copyright law. In *Laserdisken*,[15] the validity of Art 4(2) of the Information Society Directive

---

12 Directive 98/44/EC of the European Parliament and of the Council of 6 July 1998 on the legal protection of biotechnological inventions, (OJ L 213, 30.7.1998), recital 43. See also recital 16.

13 Directive 2004/48/EC of the European Parliament and of the Council of 29 April 2004 on the enforcement of intellectual property rights (OJ L 157, 30.4.2004), recital 32.

14 C-377/98 [2001] 3 CMLR 49. Most recently, see (C-34/10) *Brüstle v Greenpeace*, 18th October 2011 (Court of Justice, Grand Chamber).

15 C-479/04 [2007] 1 CMLR 6.

was questioned by the proprietor of a business selling copies of cinematographic works, who argued that it violated the right to freedom of expression protected under Art 10 of the ECHR.[16] In particular, it was claimed that the public's right of access to information, a right falling within the ambit of Art 10, was breached by Art 4(2)'s prohibition of national rules providing for 'international exhaustion of rights' in the case of copyright and related rights. In rejecting the challenge, the ECJ held that, even if Art 4(2) were to be regarded as an interference with the right established under Art 10(1) ECHR, its effects were justified by the need to protect intellectual property.

As demonstrated by these two cases, frontal challenges to the compatibility of intellectual property legislation with the norms of fundamental rights law have not been successful in the Court of Justice.[17] Nevertheless, the Court has confirmed that EU legislation must be interpreted in a manner that secures effective protection for fundamental rights. This was made clear in the judgment in *Promusicae*,[18] which concerned a national application for an order requiring an ISP to disclose the identity of clients engaged in unlawful file-sharing. The Court held that, in the absence of specific EU rules, national courts or other relevant authorities are obliged to arrive at a 'fair balance' between the rights to privacy of the ISP's customers on the one hand and the right-holders' rights to property and to an effective remedy on the other. Similar fundamental rights constraints have also been noted in relation to copyright exceptions in *Stichting de Thuiskopie v Opus Supplies Deutschland GmbH*[19] and, in trade mark law, in proceedings concerning the attempted registration of 'immoral' marks at OHIM.[20]

---

16 Directive 2001/29/EC of the European Parliament and of the Council of 22 May 2001 on the harmonisation of certain aspects of copyright and related rights in the information society.

17 However, in two recent instances, the Court of Justice has held that *national* measures in the area of intellectual property law violated the requirements of the EU Charter. See (C-70/10) *Scarlet Extended SA v SABAM* [2012] ECDR 4 (Court of Justice); (C-277/10) *Luksan v van der Let*, 9th February 2012 (Court of Justice).

18 *Productores de Musica de Espana (Promusicae) v Telefonica de Espana SAU* (C-275/06) [2008] ECR I-271. See now also *Scarlet Extended SA v Société Belge des auteurs, compositeurs et éditeurs (SABAM)* (C-70/10) (AG Cruz Villalón), Opinion of 14 April 2011.

19 *Stichting de Thuiskopie v Opus Supplies Deutschland GmbH* (C-462/09), Opinion, 10 March 2011(AG Jääskinen) and Judgment of the Court, 16 June 2011, [2011] ECDR 18. In particular, the judgment notes that: 'A "fair balance" must be maintained between the rights and interests of the authors, who are to receive the fair compensation, on one hand, and those of the users of protected works, on the other' [25].

20 See, for example, *Application of Kenneth (trading as Screw You)* [2007] ETMR 7 (OHIM, Grand Board).

3. EXAMINING ART 17(2)

As noted above, the meaning of Art 17(2)'s short instruction that 'intellectual property shall be protected' is controversial. Commentators have noted that the phrasing of the English version of the provision differs subtly from that in other languages.[21] For example, in French, Art 17(2) states that '*La propriété intellectuelle est protégée*' and the German version declares that '*Geistiges Eigentum wird geschützt*'. These could be translated as 'intellectual property *is* protected', rather than as 'intellectual property *shall be* protected'. Such ambiguities of translation serve only to heighten the mystery surrounding the provision. How then are we to understand its intended effect? One possible interpretation which seems to accord closely with the French and German versions, would be that Art 17(2) simply declares, as a matter of fact, that intellectual property is protected within the EU and, perhaps, that such protection serves to promote the fundamental norms embodied in the Charter. However, such a purely descriptive reading seems unlikely. Art 17(2), after all, is to be found in the Charter of Fundamental Rights of the EU, a constitutional document of declaratory and aspirational significance. Such a factual and descriptive interpretation would surely be out of place in that context. At the opposite end of the spectrum of potential meanings, Art 17(2) may be argued to be the constitutional expression of a maximalist approach to intellectual property. As such, could it perhaps be intended to require EU bodies, and national authorities acting within the scope of EU law, to accord intellectual property the highest possible degree of protection at all times? Some right-holder organizations would undoubtedly find such an interpretation appealing. However, in reality, it is just as implausible as the purely descriptive reading canvassed above. EU intellectual property law is a complex body of rules under which the interests of right-holders give way to public and third party interests in a variety of ways. Against such a background, the enigmatic formula of Art 17(2) surely cannot have been intended to form the basis for a radical disruption of this settled balance or for a system under which the policy options available to EU law-makers are radically curtailed.

A more plausible interpretation has been advanced by Geiger, who suggests that Art 17(2) should be read as confirmation that intellectual property is a form of property covered by Art 17(1)'s general property guarantee.[22] There are a number of reasons for believing this interpretation to be correct. First, it

[21] See C Geiger [2009], 'Intellectual Property Shall be Protected!? – Article 17(2) of the Charter of Fundamental Rights of the European Union: a Mysterious Provision with an Unclear Scope', *EIPR*, 115; A. Peukert [2011], 'Intellectual Property as an End in Itself?', *EIPR*, 67, 68–70.

[22] See Geiger, *supra* note 20.

makes sense of the overall structure of Art 17, under which Art 17(2) is subservient to the more generally worded Art 17(1). Secondly, there are suggestions to this effect in the explanatory memoranda to the Charter.[23] Thirdly, it has recently been confirmed by the Court of Justice that Art 17(2) does not offer absolute protection[24] and fourthly, as is the case with other provisions in the Charter, such an interpretation would give explicit recognition to the interpretation of the equivalent Article in the Charter's predecessor, the ECHR, by the European Court of Human Rights. As discussed further below, that Court has, on a number of occasions, confirmed that intellectual property is a form of property that is covered by the right to peaceful enjoyment of possessions. [25]

If this interpretation is correct, the text of Art 17(1) is clearly crucial to the determination of the meaning and scope of Art 17(2). Art 17(1) provides that:

> Everyone has the right to own, use, dispose of and bequeath his or her lawfully acquired possessions. No one may be deprived of his or her possessions, except in the public interest and in the cases and under the conditions provided for by law, subject to fair compensation being paid in good time for their loss. The use of property may be regulated by law in so far as is necessary for the general interest.

This right establishes a number of related guarantees (including, for example, guarantees against deprivation and use) and sets out the conditions under which interferences with lawfully acquired possessions are permissible. Cases involving *deprivation* of possessions are only permitted where, inter alia, compensation is paid. However, simple control of the *use* of possessions may be 'regulated by law in so far as is necessary for the general interest'.

Art 17(1) has its historical origin in Art 1, Protocol 1 of the ECHR and in the jurisprudence of the European Court of Human Rights on that provision.[26] Art 1, Protocol 1 provides that:

> Every natural or legal person is entitled to the peaceful enjoyment of his possessions. No one shall be deprived of his possession except in the public interest and subject to the conditions provided for by law and by the general principles of international law.

---

[23] See Explanations Relating to the Charter of Fundamental Rights (2007/C 303/02)

[24] See (C-70/10) *Scarlet Extended SA v SABAM* [2012] ECDR 4, [43].

[25] See cases discussed below. See also *Smith Kline and French Laboratories Ltd v the Netherlands* (1990) 66 DR 70, 79 (European Commission of HR); *Melnychuk v Ukraine* (2006) 42 EHRR 42.

[26] Note, for example the explicit reference to the general requirement to pay compensation in the case of deprivation of possessions. See *Lithgow v United Kingdom* (1986) 8 EHRR 324.

> The preceding provisions shall not, however, in any way impair the right of a state to enforce such laws as it deems necessary to control the use of property in accordance with the general interest or to secure the payment of taxes or other contribution or penalties.

There are differences between the two provisions. Art 17(1) offers a more general, idealized form of protection and omits some of the specific detail to be found in Art 1, Protocol 1.[27] Nevertheless, there are close similarities in overall structure. Both Articles apply to 'possessions' and permit interferences with the enjoyment of those possessions in 'the general interest'. Similarly, both provisions have a sliding scale of impact – with right-holders appearing to be protected more strongly against *deprivation* of possessions than simple *use* of possessions.

Given this historical relationship and these similarities of structure, it can be assumed that the extensive jurisprudence of the European Court of Human Rights on the application of Art 1, Protocol 1 will be relevant to the interpretation of Art 17(1) of the Charter and, in so far as the Charter's property guarantee applies to intellectual property, to the interpretation of Art 17(2). The Charter and the ECHR have different functions. As applied to EU institutions, the Charter is a constitutional document and has the potential to have direct impact in proceedings between private parties. The ECHR, by contrast, is an international treaty and only directly binds state parties. Nevertheless, this structural distinction ought not to affect the interpretation of core concepts shared by both property guarantees, including 'possessions', 'the general interest', 'deprivation' and 'use'. The concept of the 'margin of appreciation', which has played a significant role in the Strasbourg jurisprudence on Art 1, Protocol 1, will undoubtedly have diminished relevance within the EU legal system. Nevertheless, the European Court of Human Rights' reasons for according a broad zone of discretion to law-makers in implementing this right will apply equally under EU law. Legislatures and executive bodies will generally be in a better position than courts to identify the appropriate balance between private property rights and other complex social interests in particular cases. It can therefore reasonably be supposed that an understanding of the European Court of Human Rights' jurisprudence on Art 1, Protocol 1 will continue to provide valuable help in resolving some of the current uncertainty concerning the meaning and scope of Art 17(2). Accordingly, it is to this jurisprudence that we now turn.

---

[27] See, for example, the specific references to international law and to the payment of taxes in Art 1, Protocol 1, ECHR.

4. EXAMINING THE MEANING OF ART 1, PROTOCOL 1 OF THE EUROPEAN CONVENTION ON HUMAN RIGHTS

The European Court of Human Rights has settled the limits of the right to peaceful enjoyment of property in a number of important respects. [28] Art 1, Protocol 1 states that:

> Every natural or legal person is entitled to the peaceful enjoyment of his possessions. No one shall be deprived of his possessions except in the public interest and subject to the conditions provided for by law and by the general principles of international law.
>
> The preceding provisions shall not, however, in any way impair the right of a state to enforce such laws as it deems necessary to control the use of property in accordance with the general interest or to secure the payment of taxes or other contributions or penalties.

The Strasbourg Court has confirmed that this Article establishes three related rights – the general right to the peaceful enjoyment of property and the specific rights against deprivation of property and against the regulation of the use of property. [29] The first element, the right to the peaceful enjoyment of possessions, is of a general nature and may come into play in cases in which there is no deprivation or control of the use of property, but where there has nonetheless been an interference with the enjoyment of the right to property.[30] For instance, in the case of *Sporrong and Lönnroth v Sweden*, expropriation permits were issued by the state in relation to a number of privately owned properties in central Stockholm in expectation of urban development. The existence of the expropriation permits meant that the properties were much less attractive for buyers than they would have otherwise been. The Court found that, as the owners remained free to sell or dispose of the property, there had been no deprivation of property in accordance with the second element. However, the right to peaceful enjoyment of property under the first sentence of the first paragraph was relevant because the owners' peaceful enjoyment of the property had been disrupted.

---

[28] For an examination of the case law on this right, see A. van Rijn (2006), 'Right to the Peaceful Enjoyment of One's Possessions', in P van Dijk, F. Van Hoof, A. Van Rijn and L. Zwaak (eds), *Theory and Practice of the European Convention on Human Rights*, 4th ed, Intersentia Publishers, p. 863; D.J. Harris et al, *Harris, O'Boyle & Warbrick: Law of the European Convention on Human Rights*, 2nd ed., Oxford: Oxford University Press, 2009, p. 655.

[29] The three categories were first identified by the European Court of Human Rights in *Sporrong and Lönnroth v Sweden* (1982) 5 EHRR 85. For discussion of the Article's structure, see Harris et al, *supra* note 25, pp. 666–72.

The right not to be deprived of property under the second sentence of the first paragraph of the Article will be applicable where there has been a formal transfer of ownership[31] or where de facto expropriation has taken place.[32] Typical examples of the regulation of a property's use under the second paragraph of the Article are provided by the exercise of planning restrictions,[33] rent control powers[34] or powers of taxation.[35]

The concept of 'possessions' under Art 1, Protocol 1 has also been interpreted by the Court, which has confirmed that the protected rights apply only to 'existing possessions'. These include rights arising by virtue of legitimate expectations (such as the legitimate expectation that proper administrative procedures will be followed).[36] An example of a case in which legitimate expectations were protected is provided by *Pressos Compania Naviera SA v Belgium*. Following a number of shipping accidents involving the alleged negligence of state employees, the Belgian state enacted specific legislation to prevent tort claims from being brought in relation to losses incurred by private individuals. The Court held that the failure to fulfil the prior existing legitimate expectation that a claim in tort would be possible constituted an interference with the applicant's rights under Art 1, Protocol 1.[37] *Pine Valley Developments Ltd v Ireland*[38] concerned an applicant who had purchased a plot of land for which planning permission for industrial development had been granted. However, subsequent to the purchase of the land, the Irish Supreme Court upheld a decision that the grant of planning permission had

---

30 *Sporrong and Lönnroth v Sweden* (1982) 5 EHRR 85. See also *Stran Greek Refineries and Stratis Andreadis v Greece* (1994) 19 EHRR 293.

31 See, for example, *The Former King of Greece and Others v Greece* (2001) 33 EHRR 21, in which a formal transfer of property from a natural person to the state was held to breach Art 1, Protocol 1.

32 *Sporrong and Lönnroth v Sweden* [1982] 5 EHRR 85. In this case, the Court found that, because the owners were nonetheless free to sell or dispose of the property, there had been no formal or de facto expropriation of property. On the other hand, in *Papamichalopoulos v Greece* (1993) 16 EHRR 440, the Court found that there was a de facto expropriation of property amounting to deprivation under Art 1, Protocol 1. In *Papamichalopoulos*, the property in question comprised of a piece of land formally owned by the applicants but upon which the Greek navy had constructed a naval base. The title in the property remained with the applicants but due to the actions of the state it was held that the applicants' rights under the second aspect of Art 1, Protocol 1 had been breached. See also *Brumarescu v Romania* (2001) 33 EHRR 36.

33 *Pine Valley Developments Ltd v Ireland* (1991) 14 EHRR 319.

34 *Mellacher v Austria* (1989) 12 EHRR 391.

35 *Gasus Dosier- und Fordertechnik v the Netherlands* (1995) 20 EHRR 403.

36 *Marckx v Belgium* (1979) 2 EHRR 330. See also *Anheuser-Busch Inc v Portugal* (2007) 45 EHRR 36.

37 *Pressos Compania Naviera SA v Belgium* (1997) 21 EHRR 301.

38 *Pine Valley Developments Ltd v Ireland* (1991) 14 EHRR 319.

been illegal and as a result had been void *ab initio*. The Strasbourg Court held that because the applicant was entitled to rely on the legitimate expectation that planning permission had been granted, there had been an interference with the applicant's rights under Art 1, Protocol 1.

Art 1, Protocol 1 does not, however, cover claims to be entitled to property in future. As Harris et al have explained: 'The Convention protects an applicant's existing possessions and assets against interference. It is not a right to be put into the possession of things one does not already have, however strong the individual's interest in this happening may be.'[39] Thus, for example, in *Marckx v Belgium*,[40] the applicant claimed that a national law restricting the inheritance rights of children born to unmarried parents breached Art 1, Protocol 1. The Court disagreed, holding that the property guarantee under the ECHR does not guarantee the right to acquire possessions in future, whether through intestacy or via voluntary disposition.[41]

Whichever of three rights established under this Article is at issue, the Court will apply a 'fair balance' test in deciding whether an interference with the right can be justified. The application of this test requires the public interest and the affected fundamental rights to be balanced in proportionate manner.[42] In investigating this issue, the Court has accorded states a considerably wider margin of appreciation than has been permitted in the case of interferences with other qualified rights protected under the ECHR. Particular flexibility has been shown where the interference at issue can be defined as 'use' rather than as total deprivation of property. However, even in the case of

---

39 Harris et al, *supra* note 25, p. 660.

40 *Marckx v Belgium* (1979) 2 EHRR 330.

41 See also *Inze v Austria* (1987) 10 EHRR 394, where an illegitimate child who had already inherited part of an estate was able to make arguments based on Art 1, Protocol 1 in relation to other aspects of the inheritance because his interest in the estate constituted an 'existing possession'. See, however, the case of *X v the Federal Republic of Germany* (1979) 18 DR 170, where the facts concerned a change to the law which reduced the amount chargeable as a notary fee. A notary argued that this affected his ability to earn future revenue. The Court rejected the argument that he had a 'possession' for the purpose of Art 1, Protocol 1. The Court stated that the mere expectation that the state legal regulations on notary fees would not be reduced could not be considered a property right. In *Müller v Austria* (1975) 3 DR 25 the Court held that a person could claim his or her own pension contributions as a 'possession' under Art 1, Protocol 1. Furthermore, the Court acknowledged that the right may be affected by the way the pension fund is distributed. Nonetheless, the Court held that there was no right to claim that any particular amount of final pension payment was guaranteed by Art 1, Protocol 1.

42 *Sporrong and Lönnroth v Sweden* (1982) 5 EHRR 85. In this case it was found that there had been no fair balance and therefore that the interference with the right under Art 1, Protocol 1 could not be justified.

deprivation, the Court has accepted that private property interests may legitimately be regulated in the 'general interest'.[43] An example of this deference is provided by *James v United Kingdom*,[44] which concerned the transfer of privately-owned properties to longstanding tenants at less than market value. The United Kingdom argued that this transfer was in accordance with national legislation and was in the 'public interest' as an attempt to combat social injustice. The Court found that the aim of the legislation was reasonable and the means of achieving it were not disproportionate. The Court went on to say that it would not intervene, so long as a national authority's assessment of the public interest was not manifestly without reasonable foundation. It also noted that, even in the case of a deprivation of property, it would not always be necessary for full compensation to be paid. As long as compensation is proportionate, the terms of Art 1, Protocol 1 will be satisfied. States are also granted a wide margin of appreciation in assessing proportionality.[45] The Court's willingness to allow extensive leeway to states under Art 1, Protocol 1 means that this provision has served predominantly as a guarantee of legality and fair procedure, rather than as a strongly entrenched bulwark for private property.[46]

5. INTELLECTUAL PROPERTY UNDER ART 1, PROTOCOL 1

The relatively loose standard of review described above has also been apparent in the few cases in which the Court has given direct consideration to the application of Art 1, Protocol 1 to intellectual property.[47] The case of

---

[43] For discussion of the 'margin of appreciation' under the ECHR see *Handyside v United Kingdom* (1976) 1 EHRR 737; Harris et al, *supra* note 25, pp. 11–14.

[44] *James v United Kingdom* (1986) 8 EHRR 123. See also *Scollo v Italy* [1995] 22 EHRR 514

[45] See also *AGOSI v United Kingdom* (1986) 9 EHRR 1. A further example of a justifiable interference is provided by *Tre Traktörer Aktiebolag v Sweden* (1989) 13 EHRR 309, where a licence to serve alcohol at a restaurant was withdrawn by the state due following a dispute over taxation issues. The Court decided that while a restaurant's licence to serve alcohol could constitute a possession, there was no interference with the right under Art 1, Protocol 1 because the withdrawal of licence was lawful, proportionate and in the general interest.

[46] *Hentrich v France* (1994) 18 EHRR 440.

[47] See cases discussed below. See also *Smith Kline and French Laboratories Ltd v the Netherlands* (1990) 66 DR 70, 79 (European Commission of HR); *Melnychuk v Ukraine* (2005) 42 EHRR 42. For discussion, see L. Helfer (2008), 'The New Innovation Frontier? Intellectual Property and the European Court of Human Rights', in P Torremans (ed.), *Intellectual Property & Human Rights*, Leiden: Kluwer, p. 25; J. Weiss [2011] 'Commercializing Human Rights: Trademarks in Europe After

Anheuser-Busch Inc v Portugal[48] is the most famous of these. The proceedings in that case arose from the long-running dispute between the American company, Anheuser-Busch Inc, and the Czech brewer, Budějovický Budvar. Anheuser-Busch claimed that the Portuguese Court had violated Art 1, Protocol 1 in upholding the national authority's refusal to register its application for registration of the trade mark, 'Budweiser'. The decision to refuse the application had been based on the fact that Budějovický? Budvar owned a registered 'protected geographical indication' for 'Budweiser Bier', a registration which the national decision-maker held to take precedence over Anheuser-Busch's trade mark application by virtue of the complex effect of an international treaty on domestic law. The Court held that the mere application for trade mark registration could qualify as a 'possession' for the purposes of Art 1, Protocol 1 and, therefore, that Anheuser-Busch's claim fell within the scope of the protected right. The application constituted a possession because an applicant had a legitimate expectation that it would be handled fairly by national authorities and because there was evidence that such applications were, as a matter of fact, tradeable. However, having held that the application was *covered* by the property guarantee, the Court noted that the national court had simply interpreted an uncertain aspect in national intellectual property law and it was not the Court's role to review such a determination of the competing claims to entitlement to a mark, stating that:

> ...[T]he Court reiterates that its jurisdiction to verify that domestic law has been correctly interpreted and applied is limited and that it is not its function to take the place of the national courts, its role being rather to ensure that the decisions of those courts are not flawed by arbitrariness or otherwise manifestly unreasonable.[49]

A similar conclusion was reached in *Dima v Romania*,[50] which concerned a design submitted to a government-sponsored competition and which was ultimately chosen as an official state emblem. The dispute in the national courts centred on the question of who ought to be recognized as the 'author' of the emblem – Dima, the original creator, or the Romanian Parliament, which had commissioned the design. Dima claimed that the use of his creation without payment breached his rights under national copyright law. The Romanian Supreme Court decided that the Parliament was to be deemed the 'author' of the design in such circumstances and therefore that no fee was payable. Dima

Anheuser-Busch v Portugal', *Journal of World Intellectual Property,* 176 and B. Goebel (2005), 'Geographical Indications and Trademarks in Europe', *Trademark Reporter*, 95, 1165.

48 *Anheuser-Busch Inc v Portugal* (2007) 45 EHRR 36.

49 *Ibid*, [83].

50 *Dima v Romania* (58472/00), admissibility decision of 26 May 2005.

brought a complaint under the ECHR, claiming that this decision violated his rights under Art 1, Protocol 1. However, his claim was held to be inadmissible.[51] The national court had simply resolved a dispute about the interpretation of the scope of a property right in national law in a manner that was not arbitrary and, therefore, it was inappropriate for the Strasbourg Court to intervene.[52]

By contrast, the case of *Balan v Moldova*[53] demonstrates that there are limits to this deference in cases in which a state effectively expropriates an intellectual property right. *Balan* concerned a photographer's work, which had been used by the state without payment in the production of national identity cards. The photographer had succeeded in a legal action against the state in March 1999 and had been awarded an amount of compensation regarding use of the photograph up to that date. However, the state continued to use the applicant's photograph on identity cards until May 2000. The applicant received no further compensation for this period of use and the applicant brought proceedings before the national court, seeking compensation for the use of his creation by the state on identity cards between March 1999 and May 2000. The Moldovan Supreme Court refused this claim, holding that the applicant was not entitled to compensation for the use of the photograph because he had already received compensation resulting from the earlier successful legal action and had not requested a prohibition on future use during the earlier action. Balan applied to the European Court of Human Rights, claiming that his rights under Art 1, Protocol 1 had been violated. In this instance, by contrast with *Anheuser-Busch* and *Dima*, the Court found that the photographer's rights had been breached. The national court's assessment that the applicant had tacitly accepted the state's use of his photograph was untenable. In fact, its application of national law appeared not even to have been compatible with the Convention's conception of 'lawfulness'. In any event, whether the national court had acted lawfully or not, it had interfered with a copyright interest protected under national law disproportionately and without justification. Accordingly, it had failed to strike a 'fair balance' between the interests of the parties to the national proceedings.

---

51 A separate procedural complaint under Art 6(1), ECHR was subsequently upheld, see *Dima v Romania* (58472), Judgment of 16 November 2006.

52 Although, see now (C-277/10) *Luksan v van der Let*, 9 February 2012, which suggests strongly that the Court of Justice would come to a different conclusion on such facts.

53 *Balan v Moldova* (19247/03), Judgment of 29 January 2008.

6. THE TRUE SCOPE OF ART 17(2)

Having investigated the case-law on Art 1, Protocol, 1 and having seen that this jurisprudence must guide the meaning and scope of Art 17(2) of the Charter, it is now possible to investigate the likely impact of Art 17(2) upon EU intellectual property law in greater detail. As an initial step, it may be helpful to identify certain situations in which it will *not* apply. There are certain claims to which it will have no relevance at all. As we have seen, Art 17(2) regulates interferences with *existing* possessions only and cannot, therefore, form the basis of a claim to property that has no current legally-recognized form. Art 17(2) will not, therefore support a claim to be entitled to intellectual property protection where none is currently enjoyed. Thus, for example, proponents of a right to control the second-hand trade in legitimately distributed reproductions of copyright works would not be able to argue in favour of the introduction of such a right on the basis of Art 17(2).

A second important limitation on the application of Art 17(2) is provided by the fact that , even where an interference with an existing possession is established, extensive leeway is permitted for the regulation of property in the general interest will also limit the impact of this provision in intellectual property law.

Despite these limitations, it is nevertheless possible to identify situations in which Art 17(2) may have an impact in European intellectual property law. One such situation is exemplified by the *Balan* judgment described above. The fundamental guarantee of the peaceful enjoyment of intellectual property rights will prohibit any arbitrary, or manifestly disproportionate, refusal to register a claim to an intellectual property right or to uphold a clearly valid claim.[54] This effect of the fundamental right to intellectual property falls very close to the core of protection offered by the European property guarantee.[55] Such violations of the basic principles of legality may, at first sight, seem unlikely to occur very often. However, it is important to bear in mind that the concept of 'legality' has been interpreted broadly by the Strasbourg Court. Legal regulation must be both reasonably ascertainable and reasonably predictable if it is to be entitled to be described as 'law' for the purpose of the

---

[54] The recent Judgment of the Court in (C-277/10) *Luksan v van der Let*, 9 February 2012, suggests that Art 17 will also apply where a national law fails to implement the relevant European Union rules on the ownership of intellectual property rights.

[55] This will be the case even when that guarantee is interpreted in its narrowest form (a form described by Helfer as the 'rule of law' paradigm). See Helfer, *supra* note 44, pp. 25, 51.

ECHR.[56] Accordingly, in the case of an unforeseeably unfavourable interpretation of the scope of an intellectual property right, or of an exception to that right, a right-holder may be entitled to rely upon Art 17(2) in objecting to that interpretation.

A further potential situation in which Art 17(2) may have an impact arises as a result of the European Court of Human Rights' recognition that Art 1, Protocol 1 will, to some extent, require the establishment of enforcement mechanisms that allow property right-holders to seek redress for interferences with their property rights. This will be the case, even where the interference in question has been committed by a third party.[57] Art 17(2) may also have relevance where an EU or national authority abolishes, or curtails the scope of, existing intellectual property rights. In such a case, there would be a clear interference with an existing possession which would only be permissible if justifiable under the Charter. Consider, for example, a decision taken by an EU or national authority to reduce the term of protection of an intellectual property right[58] or to introduce a new limitation upon an existing intellectual property right. Such decisions would undoubtedly fall within the scope of Art 17(2), although they would be likely to be considered as 'uses' rather than

---

[56] Article 7 ECHR states that:

> '(1) No one shall be held guilty of any criminal offence on account of any act or omission which did not constitute a criminal offence under national or international law at the time when it was committed. Nor shall a heavier penalty be imposed than the one that was applicable at the time the criminal offence was committed.
> (2) This Article shall not prejudice the trial and punishment of any person for any act or omission which, at the time it was committed, was criminal according to the general law recognised by civilised nations'.

The principle of legality requires that laws be sufficiently clearly formulated to be reasonably predictable in their operation, so that it is possible for individuals to regulate their conduct in line with the 'law'. For application of the principle, see *Kafkaris v Cyprus* (2009) 49 EHRR 35; *SW & CR v UK* (1996) 21 EHRR 363. In the intellectual property context, see *Scarlet Extended SA v Société Belge des auteurs, compositeurs et éditeurs (SABAM)* (C-70/10) (AG Cruz Villalón); Opinion of 14 April 2011.

[57] See *Sovtransavto Holding v Ukraine* (2004) 38 EHRR 44; *Broniowski v. Poland* (2004) EHRR 1, 56 (Grand Chamber); *Iatridis v Greece* (2000) 30 EHRR 97; *Immobiliare Saffi v Italy* (1999) EHRR 73, 90–92 (Grand Chamber). Helfer has described this broader understanding of the impact of the property guarantee as the 'enforcement paradigm' for human rights intervention in intellectual property law. See Helfer *supra* note 44, pp. 25, 51, noting that the maintenance of effective enforcement mechanisms is also a requirement of TRIPS.

[58] The provision of transitional protection for existing right-holders may, of course, remove any issue relating to the property guarantee.

'deprivations'.[59] This potential impact of Art 17(2) may, at first sight, appear to place a significant obstacle in the path of balanced policy-making. However, it is important to bear in mind that decision-makers are granted a very wide margin of appreciation in determining the necessity of interfering with the enjoyment of possessions in the general interest under Art 1, Protocol 1. It can be suggested that this deferential approach ought to continue to apply under Art 17(2).[60]

7. CONCLUSION

The admission of intellectual property to the category of EU fundamental rights is clearly related to broader trends towards 'propertization' in intellectual property law. Peukert has noted that descriptions of intellectual property as a fundamental right underpin a 'self-sufficient property logic' that has developed in intellectual property law.[61] He suggests that recent ECJ jurisprudence in this area has aligned itself with this 'property logic', through acceptance of the notion that maintaining the highest possible level of intellectual property protection is always desirable.[62] In such a climate, it is not surprising that advocates of stronger intellectual property rights have already sought to rely upon the fundamental rights status of intellectual property rights. In this concluding section, we briefly consider a number of such claims.

An example of such an argument can be seen in the submission of the Motion Picture Association (MPA) to a recent United Kingdom consultation exercise on a proposal to expand the scope of certain copyright exceptions and

---

59 The case law from the European Court of Human Rights is useful in the context. As noted in *Lithgow v United Kingdom* (1986) 8 EHRR 324, 'deprivation' will only occur where all rights in the property are extinguished. Furthermore, as noted in *Sporrong and Lönnroth v Sweden* (1982) 5 EHRR 85 and *Baner v Sweden* (1989) 60 DR 125, *de facto* deprivation will only occur where an interference with the rights of the property owner are so extensive as effectively to deprive the owner of the property, even where he, she or it retains the formal title.

60 Helfer, *supra* note 44, pp. 25, 51–2. Helfer has stated that an expansive view of the role of the ECHR, under which the European Court of Human Rights would have broader powers to rule on cases involving 'balancing' IP protection with other rights such as freedom of expression and privacy, would not be in line with the spirit of Art 1 Protocol 1, or with current ECHR jurisprudence

61 Peurket, *supra* note 20, 69–70.

62 Nonetheless, there are also some recent cases in which the ECJ has not necessarily taken a 'maximalist' approach to IP protection. See, for example, (C-49-09P) *Lego Juris v OHIM* [2010] ECR 0000 [43]–[48]; (C-236/08 to C-238/08) *Google/Louis Vuitton* [2010] ECR 0000 [75]-[98]; (C-428/08) *Monsanto/Cefetra* [2010] ECR 0000, [43]–[50].

limitations.[63] The MPA's submission begins by reminding national authorities that: '[I]n weighing the various proposals, it should be borne in mind that copyright is a fundamental right...'[64]

On the face of it, this statement is accurate. Copyright undoubtedly falls within the ambit of Art 17(2).[65] However, in the context of the consultation, the statement appears to be intended to dissuade the United Kingdom authorities from expanding the scope of the statutory copyright exceptions. It implies that copyright's status as a fundamental right militates against the liberalization of the existing regime of exceptions. This, as we have learned from a closer analysis of the jurisprudence on Art 1, Protocol 1, is not really accurate. The case-law indicates that, as long as a legislator acts legally (in the Strasbourg sense), does nothing that is manifestly disproportionate and applies a procedure that is fair, it will have a high degree of discretion in framing laws 'in the general interest', even where such laws interfere with the enjoyment of private 'possessions'. It is important that law-makers understand the true scope of Art 17(2) and are not deterred from serving the general interest through misplaced fear of committing a violation of fundamental rights.

Rhetorical references to intellectual property's status as a fundamental right are not only to be found in submissions by lobbyists.In an earlier section of this chapter we quoted the recital to the Enforcement Directive (IPRED), which claims Art 17(2) as a justification for legislative intervention. The form of words employed in that recital was subsequently repeated verbatim in the preamble to the ill-fated draft Directive on criminal enforcement of intellectual property rights (IPRED 2):

> This Directive respects fundamental rights and observes the principles recognised by the Charter of Fundamental Rights of the European Union. In particular, this Directive seeks to ensure full respect for intellectual property, in accordance with Article 17(2) of the Charter. [66]

These words suggest that IPRED2's harmonization and expansion of criminal sanctions in the field of intellectual property law is motivated by a requirement

---

[63] UK-IPO, *Taking Forward the Gowers Review of Intellectual Property – Second Stage Consultation on Copyright* (2009).

[64] At the time of writing, the submissions have not been published by the UK-IPO. The submission of the MPA is on file with the authors. The submission goes on to acknowledge the competing rights of users of copyright works.

[65] See also Art 27, Universal Declaration of Human Rights, adopted and proclaimed a the General Assembly of the United Nations on 10 December 1948.

[66] Amended Proposal for a Directive of the European Parliament and of the Convention on criminal measures aimed at ensuring the enforcement of intellectual property rights COM (2006) 168 final, 26 April 2006, recital 12.

to act 'in accordance with' Art 17(2). We have noted above that Art 1, Protocol 1 requires parties to the ECHR to implement systems permitting the enforcement of property rights and it has been suggested that this principle will extend to intellectual property rights under Art 17(2). Nevertheless, it cannot reasonably be suggested that Art 17(2) requires the introduction of any *specific* form of enforcement mechanism. While criminal sanctions may be the only permissible response to certain violations of fundamental rights,[67] there is nothing to suggest that such sanctions are mandatory in the case of intellectual property infringements. In this instance, it is difficult to escape the conclusion that the recital's reference to fundamental rights is little more than an attempt to bolster the draft legislation's claim to legitimacy through reference to fundamental norms. The increasing prevalence of such ill-founded rhetoric is disturbing. It is not only misleading, but may eventually lead to scepticism of all claims based on fundamental rights in the sphere of intellectual property law. The more things that are claimed as being 'fundamental' or 'human' rights, the greater the risk that rights language will become less persuasive. It is accordingly important that claims concerning the scope and effect of Art 17(2) are advanced, and scrutinized, carefully.

---

[67] See, for example, *X & Y v The Netherlands* (1986) 8 EHRR 235; *MC v Bulgaria* (2005) 40 EHRR 459; *A v UK* (1999) 27 EHRR 611; *Opuz v Turkey* (2010) 50 EHRR 28; *Siliadin v France* [2006] EHRR 16.

5. Intellectual property and competition law in the information society

Tuomas Mylly

1. INTRODUCTION

The European Commission keeps on insisting in its intellectual property strategies that 'rigorous application of competition rules' could counterbalance its intellectual property policy based on strong protection and enforcement of intellectual property rights.[1] The statement presumes that competition is needed in addition to strong exclusive rights, that strong intellectual property laws enable and facilitate market power they are ill equipped to handle with, and that existing competition law could fulfil that function adequately. What kind of values competition law *could* bring in to intellectual property contexts depends on our construction of competition law and its basic societal functions and objectives. What it *should* bring in also depends on what in our view is lacking in intellectual property law. The present chapter argues that the reference to competition law as a counterweight to strong intellectual property rights functions as a mere legitimation for the Commission's proprietarian-minded intellectual property strategy. However, this chapter also elaborates whether EU competition law could be re-imagined to integrate freedom of expression-related values in contexts involving intellectual property rights.

Such re-imagining of EU competition law is inevitably utopian, as the Chicago School has marginalized non-efficiency-related objectives in antitrust on both sides of the Atlantic. In the USA, the Supreme Court has cleaned antitrust case law from 'populist sentiments' reflecting democratic concerns.[2] Arguments related to democratic values have to be smuggled in to the antitrust

---

1 Communication from the Commission: A Single Market for Intellectual Property Rights. Boosting creativity and innovation to provide economic growth, high quality jobs and first class products and services in Europe, Brussels, COM(2011) 287 final, p. 6. See also the previous Communication from the Commission: An Industrial Property Rights Strategy for Europe, Brussels, COM(2008) 465/3, pp. 2 and 9.

2 See in particular *Verizon Communications Inc v Law Offices of Curtis V. Trinko, LLP*, 540 U.S. 407 (2004) and *Pacific Bell Telephone Co. v linkLine Communications, Inc.*, 129 S. Ct. 1109 (2009), decided 25 February 2009.

discourse by using the language of microeconomics, like in the infrastructure theory developed by Frischmann and others.[3] EU competition law seems to follow a somewhat similar trajectory. Intended to produce convergence with US law, it is now referred to as antitrust. Calls for renewing EU competition norms are automatically based on microeconomic models. Economic analysis – or at least declarations of the proposed outcomes representing 'sound economics'[4] or a 'more economic approach'[5] – is becoming the norm also for intellectual property–competition law scholarship in Europe. The change of paradigm from form-based ordoliberal competition law to effects-based microeconomic antitrust thus seems inevitable for many, including the Commission.[6]

From this perspective, it appears unlikely that competition law could be developed to counterbalance the proprietarian trend of intellectual property law or to tame societally harmful informational power enabled and facilitated by intellectual property rights. At most, it could strengthen microeconomic efficiency argumentation also in the application of intellectual property law. This could lead to seeing excesses of intellectual property-enabled power as economic waste or 'deadweight loss', but not as something requiring control for the sake of the informational power and constitutional values involved. Moreover, the norms and persistent doctrines of intellectual property and competition law inhibit competition law from assuming functions related to constitutional values. They may constrain legislative choices and judicial activism threatening proprietarian interests. For example, the competition norms of TRIPS could constrain the application of competition

---

[3] B. M. Frischmann (2005), 'An Economic Theory of Infrastructure and Commons Management', *Minnesota Law Review*, 917 and B. M. Frischmann and S. Weber Waller (2008), 'Revitalizing Essential Facilities', *Antitrust Law Journal,* 1. See more closely the subsequent discussion of this theory.

[4] See for example J. Kallaugher and B. Sher (2004), 'Rebates Revisited: Anti-competitive Effects and Exclusionary Abuse under Article 82', *European Competition Law Review*, 263 and J. Drexl (2004), 'Intellectual Property and Antitrust Law – IMS Health and Trinko – Antitrust Placebo for Consumers Instead of Sound Economics in Refusal-to-Deal Cases', *International Review of Intellectual Property and Competition Law,* 788.

[5] See J. Drexl (2008), 'Is There a "More Economic Approach" to Intellectual Property and Competition Law?', in J. Drexl (ed.), *Research Handbook on Intellectual Property and Competition Law,* Cheltenham, UK and Northampton, MA: Edward Elgar, p. 27.

[6] See the document published in 2009 by the Commission 'Guidance on the Commission's enforcement priorities in applying Article 82 of the EC Treaty to abusive exclusionary conduct by dominant undertakings', as well as the preceding 'Discussion Paper on the Application of the Prohibition on the Abuses of a Dominant Position to Exclusionary Abuses', OJ 24.2.2009 C 45/7.

law to intellectual property. Such 'new constitutionalist' measures place limits on national and European legislators and courts alike.[7]

Yet at the same time competition law cases against Microsoft and Google,[8] among others, indicate that the application of competition law may increasingly involve concerns related to informational power and freedom of expression, in particular. In information society, economic power based on intellectual property has often social and political dimensions: the technological architectures of communication based on the Internet are simultaneously structures of competition. This development is likely to deepen in the on-going transition to a networked information society. Competition law should be prepared for such transformations. Otherwise it risks losing its societal legitimacy.

The chapter proceeds as follows. The next sub-section will discuss the reasons why competition law in the information society should sometimes consider questions resonating on the level of constitutionalism. After that, the chapter discusses some of the constraints for such a change. The final substantive sub-section will discuss the ways competition law could be modified to integrate freedom of expression values.

2. INFORMATION SOCIETY AND THE NEED TO RENEW COMPETITION LAW THINKING

In the Google case referred to above the Commission investigates whether Google Inc. has abused a dominant position in online search by lowering the ranking of unpaid search results of competing services specialized in providing users with specific online content, such as price comparisons (so-called vertical search services), and by giving preferential placement to the results of its own vertical search services in order to exclude competing services. The Commission also investigates other potential manipulations of search results, exclusivity obligations placed on advertising partners preventing them from placing certain types of competing advertisement on their websites, as well as similar obligations placed on computer and software vendors, with the aim of excluding competing search tools. Furthermore, the Commission investigates

7 See more closely T. Mylly (2013), *Intellectual Property and New Constitutionalism*, Cheltenham, UK and Northampton, MA: Edward Elgar, forthcoming.

8 See T-201/04, *Microsoft Corp. v Commission*, [2007] ECR II-3601, Commission's Decision Case COMP/C-3/37, 792 *Microsoft* and about the allegations of competition law violations by Google Inc., the Commission's Press Release IP/10/1624, Brussels, 30 November 2010.

suspected restrictions on the portability of online advertising campaign data to competing online advertising platforms. National competition authorities in France, Italy and the US have also investigated Google's measures.[9] There have also been allegations that Google codes YouTube videos discriminatorily, thereby harming its competitors' search engines, such as Microsoft's Bing.

Such alleged practices would affect not only economic efficiency, but also freedom of expression, communicative diversity and thus ultimately the freedom and autonomy of individuals using the Internet. If consumers lack a meaningful alternative, search engine bias could jeopardize online information credibility and accessibility. A super-dominant search engine like Google could distort online reality and our access to information and services to favour its own and its customers' information. Yet it should be recognized that every search engine design choice unavoidably reflects some normative values. The recently introduced term "search neutrality" could thus be seen as misleading, as it implies the existence of neutral search engines.[10] Moreover, designing effective but proportionate remedies for search engine bias could prove difficult. This is likely why the Google case in the EU seems to be leading to a commitment decision.[11]

Similar considerations may be connected to the Microsoft case, also referred to above. Microsoft's attempt to leverage the near monopoly position of Windows operating system to other markets at least equally important for global Internet-based communications appears as a threat not only to economic efficiency, but above all to democratic values and fundamental right-related collective goods like communicative diversity. Although the relevance of intellectual property rights for the alleged abuses of Google Inc. remains to be seen, in Microsoft intellectual property became decisive for the way the Commission and the General Court had to argue the case. The mere potential existence of intellectual property rights raised the threshold required for finding an abuse of a dominant position.

The cases demonstrate that the effects of competition law application cannot be restricted to the economy. Its application or non-application may increasingly affect the information and communication structures relevant for the civil society. Communicative interaction is culturally, symbolically and

---

9 See S. van Loon (2012), 'The Power of Google: First Mover Advantage or Abuse of a Dominant Position? ', in A. Lopez-Tarruella (ed.), *Google and the Law: Empirical Approaches to Legal Aspects of Knowledge-Economy Business Models*, the Hague, the Netherlands, Springer, 10-35.

10 E. Goldman (2011), Revisiting Search Engine Bias, *William Mitchell Law Review*, 107.

11 See Statement of VP Almunia on the Google antitrust investigation, 21/05/2012, SPEECH/12/372.

technologically mediated, implying the centrality of indirect social relationships in the discursive practices of the civil society.[12] This trend finds its apex in the networked information society, where the lived experiences and the cultural life of individuals and communities increasingly become mediated by the digital networks and commodified forms of communication. The structure of our information environment is constitutive of our autonomy, not only functionally significant to it. As Benkler argues:

> All of the components of decision making prior to action, and those actions that are themselves communicative moves or require communication as a precondition to efficacy, are constituted by the information and communications environment we, as agents, occupy. Conditions that cause failures at any of these junctures, which place bottlenecks, failures of communication, or provide opportunities for manipulation by a gatekeeper in the information environment, create threats to the autonomy of individuals in that environment. The shape of the information environment, and the distribution of power within it to control information flows to and from individuals, are, as we have seen, the contingent product of a combination of technology, economic behavior, social patterns, and institutional structure or law.[13]

An essential condition of self-direction is hence the capability to perceive the state of the world, to conceive available options for action, to connect actions to consequences, to evaluate alternative outcomes, and to decide upon and pursue an action accordingly. Online service providers, search engines and makers of software used to access the information structures may select, pre-structure and filter content. The existence of alternatives and diversified competition on the provision of access to the structures of information thus facilitates individual autonomy and communicative diversity.[14] A variety of technologies and business or net-cultures enabled by interoperability between technologies generates possibilities of autonomy.[15]

---

12 C. Calhoun (1992), 'The Infrastructure of Modernity. Indirect Social Relationships, Information Technology, and Social Integration', in H. Haferkamp and N.J. Smelser (eds), *Social Change and Modernity,* University of California Press, p. 205. The networked information society has expanded the technological mediation of lifeworld interaction, leading to *sociodigitization*, the rendering in a digital form not only of information and artifacts, but the logics of social organization, interaction and space. See about sociodigitization R. Latham and S. Sassen (2005), 'Digital Formations: Constructing an Object of Study', in R. Latham and S. Sassen (eds), *Digital Formations. IT and New Architectures in the Global Realm,* Princeton University Press, p. 89.

13 Y. Benkler (2006), *The Wealth of Networks. How Social Production Transforms Markets and Freedom,* Yale University Press, p. 146–7.

14 T. Vesting (2004), 'The Autonomy of Law and the Formation of Network Standards', *German Law Journal,* 639, 666–7 and Benkler, *supra* note 13, pp. 147–9.

15 See also Vesting, *supra* note 14, 667 (in the context of network standards).

Although technological design has assumed an unprecedented role as a regulator of behaviour in the networked information society,[16] intellectual property and competition laws do not lose their relevance. Quite the opposite. Intellectual property restricts patterns of human actions and thus individual freedom. It enables and modifies informational and technological power positions in complex processes involving the evolution of markets and technologies. Competition laws could be used, among others, to control abuses of such positions. Intellectual property and competition laws thus play a major immediate role in the public regulation of technological environments and informational power. They participate in establishing the 'rules of the game', the forms of power, selectivity and exclusion inherent in communication. The existence and scope of patent rights underlying technologies, freedom of others to experiment with them, the transparency and openness of technological design, access and use rights, the binding or non-binding nature of contractual clauses limiting these, and the positive and negative obligations placed on dominant technology owners are neither inherent features of technological design nor merely dependent on the deployment of the technologies in society, but something essentially constituted by legal rules.

European intellectual property developments underline the need to integrate balancing elements in the application of competition law. The Commission's expressed policy based on strong intellectual property rights reflects a *structural proprietarian bias*.[17] Outside trademark and design law, European intellectual property measures do not typically integrate compulsory exceptions based on economic or public policy concerns. Quite the contrary, for example the permitted exceptions and limitations to copyright have been exhaustively enumerated in the Information Society Copyright Directive.[18] Yet the exclusive rights are typically defined broadly on the European level. According to Article 2 of the Information Society Copyright Directive, the reproduction right is the exclusive right 'to authorise or prohibit direct or indirect, temporary or permanent reproduction by any means and in any form, in whole or in part'.[19] In Infopaq the European Union Court of Justice (EUC)

---

16 This is already becoming a cliché in some academic circles, not least because of Lawrence Lessig's bestsellers. See for example L. Lessig (1999), *Code and Other Laws of Cyberspace,* New York: Basic Books.

17 See more closely T. Mylly, *supra* note 7.

18 Directive 2001/29/EC on the harmonisation of certain aspects of copyright and related rights in the information society, Article 5.

19 The wording of the Article is reminiscent of the famous *Dassonville* formula in the area of free movement of goods which the EUC had to limit in the *Cassis de Dijon* and *Keck* case law. See more closely about this case law for example P. Craig and G. de Búrca (2008), *EU Law. Text, Cases and Materials*, 4th ed., Oxford: Oxford University Press, pp. 668–720.

concluded that the already broad language of Article 2 'must be given a broad interpretation'. Moreover, as the only compulsory exception in the Directive derogates from a general principle established by the Directive, it must be interpreted strictly. The EUC construed the general principle underlying the Directive to be 'the requirement of authorisation from the rightholder for any reproduction of a protected work'. It also invoked the notion of legal certainty, but not as a general concept guiding interpretation. Instead, 'legal certainty for authors with regard to the protection of their works' was the kind of legal certainty desired. Finally, the 'three-step test' of the TRIPS Agreement and the Information Society Directive supported a narrow interpretation of exceptions and limitations to copyright.

The example reflects a more generic structural problem of European intellectual property protection outside trademark and design law, namely very broadly defined exclusive rights and the relative absence of compulsory, harmonized exceptions and limitations on the European level. This causes an imbalance on the European level of protection: the values and interests behind exceptions and limitations become considered only negatively when testing whether they fall within the categories of exhaustively enumerated exceptions in the European legislative measures or whether they satisfy the criteria imposed by the three-step test as interpreted in European law. Moreover, if the EU courts follow the interpretations of the WTO panels in applying the three-step test, there would be no substantive evaluation of the public policy reasons behind the exception or limitation even at this stage, but rather formal application of each prong of the test. In any case, the outcome of this evaluation would not likely be that the national exception or limitation is inadequate with respect to the values and interests it is intended to protect.[20] The role of the EU level is thus typically to establish a strong or high level of protection throughout the Union and to censor the existence and application of exceptions and limitations. Such regulation of intellectual property protection on the European level is deformed. The informational and market power produced with European intellectual property rights is consensually left for the EU competition law and the application of the nationally determined exceptions. The European-level exclusive rights hence produce economic and informational power they are unable and unwilling to handle.

---

[20] In principle, the Member States must fulfil the European Union standard of fundamental rights protection when implementing EU directives. See for example case 5/88, *Wachauf v Germany* [1989] ECR 2609, at paragraph 22. However, considering the fundamental right-based judicial review of European Union intellectual property measures by the EUC (see the subsequent discussion), it appears very unlikely that this standard would not be fulfilled by a domestic measure implementing an EU intellectual property directive.

The Member States' existing record of taking full benefit of exceptions and limitations is not necessarily very promising. For example, the granting of compulsory patent licences for any permitted purposes seems to be very rare in most EU Member States.[21] There has been only one case in Finland before courts dealing with compulsory licensing of patents.[22] In Germany, since 1950 no compulsory licences have been granted by final judgment. This international trend has led some commentators to argue that the institution of compulsory licences has in industrialized countries lost its practical significance.[23]

Nevertheless, as both national and European-level case law indicates, competition law may create an obligation to license intellectual property.[24] This proposes a functional hierarchy of values, in which the preservation of competition ranks higher than the traditional compulsory licensing bases under patent laws. In the absence of compulsory licensing taking place under patent law in the industrialized countries, the values underlying the traditional bases may become relevant in the application of competition law, where *de facto* compulsory licensing is still possible. Article 31(k) of the TRIPS Agreement, which treats compulsory licensing based on competition grounds more leniently than other causes, strengthens this conclusion. It is thus feasible that for example non-working or dependency patent situations could become constructed as instances of competition law application, provided it is possible under competition law doctrine.[25] Likewise, for example many of the historical public interest grounds mentioned in the German *Interferon-gamma*

---

[21] See for example K.J. Koelman (2006), 'An Exceptio Standardis: Do We Need an IP Exemption for Standards?', *International Review of Intellectual Property and Competition Law*, 823, 835; W. Cornish and D. Llewelyn (2007), *Intellectual Property: Patents, Copyright, Trade Marks and Allied Rights*, 6th ed., London: Sweet & Maxwell, p. 301; R.M. Hilty and C. Geiger (2005), 'Patenting Software? A Judicial and Socio-Economic Analysis', *International Review of Intellectual Property and Competition Law*, 615, 641 (Germany and France).

[22] See N. Bruun (2001), *Intellectual Property Law in Finland,* The Hague: Kluwer Law International, p. 87.

[23] F.-K. Beier (1999), 'Exclusive Rights, Statutory Licenses and Compulsory Licenses in Patent and Utility Model Law', *International Review of Intellectual Property and Competition Law*, 251, 259–60.

[24] See for example *Standard-Spundfass*, Decision of 13 July 2004, KZR 40/02 (*Bundesgerichtshof*), translated into English in *International Review of Intellectual Property and Competition Law*, (2005) **36**(6), 741–54 and case T-201/04, *Microsoft Corp. v Commission*, [2007] ECR II-3601, Commission's Decision COMP/C-3/37.792 and the pre-existing case law referred to in them.

[25] For non-working and technology suppression as instances of US antitrust law application, see K.M. Saunders (2002), 'Patent Nonuse and the Role of Public Interest as a Deterrent to Technology Suppression', *Harvard Journal of Law and Technology*, 389, 434.

decision,[26] like danger to entire sectors of industry, prevention of the closure of businesses or large-scale redundancies or guaranteeing the uninterrupted supply of electrical energy, could well be connected to the current or historical functions and objectives of EU competition law.

Even if the European intellectual property legislation is deformed and structurally biased, could not the fundamental rights of the EU function as a counterweight to proprietarian interests? Before year 2011 the EUC was likely to reject most challenges of EU intellectual property legislation even when the balance of fundamental rights in the legislative measure in question was distorted. For example, in *Laserdisken* the mere notion of intellectual *property* insulated the choices made by the Union legislator from any constitutional review and arguments based on freedom of expression.[27] The EUC has also taken the overprotective trend as reflected in the TRIPS Agreement as a factor further shielding intellectual property from fundamental rights-based judicial review.[28] The *Promusicae* case anticipated the change of course in the EUC. The Court emphasized that when the Member States transpose copyright directives, they must take care to rely on an interpretation that allows a fair balance to be struck between the various fundamental rights protected by the Union legal order. This obligation also extends to the authorities and courts when interpreting the national rules deriving from the directives.[29] However, for example the *Infopaq* case referred to above shows that even the EUC does not necessarily follow these interpretative guidelines.

Recent case law indicates that the EUC may actually strike down norms of EU secondary law as contrary to fundamental rights.[30] This stronger emphasis on fundamental rights protection continued in intellectual property cases from years 2011 and 2012: *Scarlet Extended, Netlog* and *Bonnier Audio*.[31] In these cases the EUC placed limits on the possibility to impose filtering, monitoring

---

[26] *Interferon-gamma*, Decision of 5 December 1995, X ZR 26/92 (*Bundesgerichtshof*), translated into English in *International Review of Intellectual Property and Competition Law*, (1997) **28**(2), 242–50.

[27] Case C-479/04, *Laserdisken ApS v Kulturministeriet* [2006] ECR I-8089.

[28] Case C-200/96, *Metronome Music v Music Point Hokamp* [1998] ECR I-1953.

[29] Case C-275/06, *Productores de Música de España (Promusicae) v Telefónica de España SAU* [2008] ECR I-271.

[30] Joined cases C-92/09 and C-93/09, *Volker and Schecke*, judgment of 9 November 2010, nyr. Case C?236/09, *Association belge des Consommateurs Test-Achats ASBL and Others v Conseil des ministres*, judgment of 1 March 2011, nyr.

[31] Case C-70/10, *Scarlet Extended SA v SABAM*, judgment of 24 November 2011, nyr., case C-360/10, *SABAM v. Netlog NV*, judgment of 16 February 2012, nyr. and case C-461/10, *Bonnier Audio AB and others v. Perfect Communication Sweden AB*, judgment of 19 April 2012, nyr.

and user-identification obligations on Internet access and platform providers for the protection of copyright. Filtering and monitoring obligations could risk freedom to conduct a business, as well as the customers' data protection and their freedom to receive or impart information. It is still uncertain whether the trend emphasizing the need to balance fundamental rights continues in cases where the Union's secondary IP norms are challenged.

However, these cases also reflect the fact that the interference of intellectual property norms with rights is now regularly explained as a conflict of property ownership with other rights. This metamorphosis of intellectual property from a policy, to be checked under fundamental rights limitations test, into a fundamental right in itself, to be balanced on an equal footing with other rights, is strengthened by Article 17(2) of the European Charter of Fundamental Rights (European Charter). It declares, 'Intellectual property shall be protected'. It is located under right to property and could be interpreted rationally as being declaratory only, subject to the limitations of the preceding paragraph and case law of the European Court of Human Rights interpreting protection of property ownership under the European Convention of Human Rights.[32] Nevertheless, by mentioning intellectual property out of all possible categories of law-created rights and by using strict and unconditional language, the European Charter enables the invocation of the said norm in lobbying, legislative discourse and judicial proceedings in favour of strong exclusive rights. It in practice shifts the burden of argumentative proof to the one defending the right of legislators to enact and courts to expand exceptions and limitations to exclusive rights. It makes steps backwards in protection less feasible. Yet effective fundamental rights review would be particularly significant in the area of intellectual property, as the EU measures now typically reflect proprietarian bias and pre-empt the comparable national competence to legislate. This results in persistent but single-sided intellectual property legislation throughout the Union.

Taken as a whole, the relevant fundamental rights case law of the EUC has still had the function of legitimating a strong form of intellectual property ownership and the intellectual property institution in general. The recent positive developments in the EUC's fundamental rights case law hardly overturn the fact that even if fundamental rights would be extended to the private sphere more extensively than currently, no direct conclusions could be made of the increased role of fundamental rights law in controlling private informational power or putting significant limits to the single-sided proprietarian bias prevalent in intellectual property legislation during the recent years.

---

[32] See Griffiths and McDonagh, in this volume.

However, the existing record of EU courts does not frustrate the potential of fundamental rights discourse to improve interpretations of intellectual property and competition law alike, in individual instances or on a more lasting basis by affecting the doctrines and systematizations of the relevant laws. What the discussion of the problems inherent to existing fundamental rights case law serves is to avoid naïve expectations of any such increased interaction.

The structural problems and proprietarian biases of European intellectual property law and similar problems in the operation of Union-level fundamental rights suggest that the problems related to informational power, communicative diversity and freedom of expression are to a significant extent left for the application of competition law. As argued above, the networked information society increasingly produces instances in which economic power is also informational power. As informational power is a co-product of intellectual property law and market processes, competition law as *ex post* regulation could in theory well assume the function of controlling such power. However, in addition to the Chicago School neoliberalism affecting the current competition policy of the Commission, there are additional constraints on making European competition law concerned with informational power.

3. CONSTRAINTS ON THE CONSTITUTIONALIZATION OF COMPETITION LAW

The doctrines developed by the EU Courts for analysing the refusal to license intellectual property rights under Article 102 TFEU are in many respects problematic. They could constrain the development of competition law in the direction suggested in this chapter. The General Court's *Microsoft* judgment will be treated as an example. On one hand, it liberated the notion of exceptional circumstances required for a refusal to license to constitute an abuse from some of the formalism of the pre-existing case law, but on the other hand also created new ones. Although the core of Microsoft's power was the strategic control over technological trajectories and activities of others based on the Windows-platform, the General Court used traditional methods for the finding of a dominant position. Competition law doctrine is underdeveloped in recognizing that informational power contributes to dominance in network environments, as argued in more detail subsequently. Also the analysis of abuse was defective.

When applying the additional *criterion of a new product* required for competition law-based obligation to license intellectual property, the General Court concentrated on the incentives of competitors to develop products distinguished from those of the dominant intellectual property owner under the notion of a limitation of technical development to the prejudice of consumers. It thus shifted the focus from the individual applicant to the potential of the platform to generate value more generally. This broadens the utility of the new product-criterion, which has otherwise been subjected to criticism.[33] However, the analysis of abuse may be criticized for being too innovation-centric at the expense of possibilities to comprehensively evaluate the effects caused by Microsoft's measures. The General Court did not discuss the particular significance of the markets affected by Microsoft's actions. The leveraging of market power to work group server operating systems and streaming media players with further effects on several markets and new leverages affected the gravity of the competition law infringement and thus the amount of the fines imposed, but did not constitute an integral part of the analysis of abuse. The Court did not evaluate the scope and especially the quality of downstream activities prevented by the refusal. These had to do with communicative diversity in the Internet environment.

Moreover, the General Court's interpretation of the objective justification based on innovation incentives was problematic. In the General Court's interpretation, the objective justification does not enable weighing of the respective effects on innovation, but on the other hand may function as an absolute justification for a *prima facie* abuse, irrespective of its effects. This interpretation could insulate any restriction of competition from the application of Article 102 TFEU provided the threshold of *a significant negative impact* on the dominant firm's incentives to innovate becomes fulfilled. Such a formalistic standard would in fact establish a hierarchy of values, whereby the protection of the innovation incentives of the dominant enterprise would be on the top, capable of pardoning any conduct excluding competitors, leveraging the dominant position to other markets. If generalized, such objective justification related to innovation incentives could lead to a more generic insulation of some property rights from the reach of competition law, provided they are the result of sufficient investments. The test manages to be simultaneously too limited and too far reaching with regard to intellectual property protection. Its basic presumption is that intellectual property rights do not incentivize their owners, as the intellectual property owner must invoke this justification and demonstrate that the duty to license would have a significant negative impact on its incentives to innovate. On the other hand, provided the threshold set by the General Court becomes fulfilled, the *prima facie* abuse is justified – in conformity with the logic of objective justification and as explicitly confirmed

---

33 For example, Drexl 2008, *supra* note 5, p. 37, states that '*the new-product rule is not consistent with any economic rationale*'.

by the General Court – irrespective of the market power present and anticompetitive effects caused.

In addition to the competition law doctrine as developed by EU courts, the competition norms of TRIPS (Articles 8, 31(k) and 40) could also restrict competition law evaluation of refusals to license intellectual property. They could be seen as an attempt to constitutionalize the intellectual property standards defined in the same agreement from the obvious external threat competition laws pose to them.[34] Perhaps the original idea of these competition norms was to relax some concerns of the developing countries by securing them the right to apply and develop their competition rules with regard to abuses of intellectual property law.[35] Yet, as adopted the norms contain *limits* on the application of domestic competition laws. They require *consistency* of the domestic competition law measures with the other provisions of TRIPS. The strictest interpretation of this requirement allows no competition law-based derogation from the substantive TRIPS standards even on the level of individual cases.[36] This would effectively immunize substantive intellectual property standards required by TRIPS from the application of competition laws.

The Agreement could thus enable application of competition law to the extent it does not interfere with the substantive TRIPS standards, *also provided* that the practices under scrutiny constitute an abuse of intellectual property rights *and* have an adverse effect on competition. The requirements of abusive behaviour and adverse effect on competition could *strengthen* factual intellectual property protection under TRIPS by sheltering licensing practices from competition law also when the interference would *not* frustrate the substantive TRIPS standards. In any case the competition norms of TRIPS may have the likely function of directing the basic orientation of competition law authorities and courts: international law norms 'with teeth' somehow seem to limit the application of competition law to intellectual property rights. Even if – or rather because – the demands of these norms are vague, it is always safer to refrain from the application of competition law to intellectual property, or limit its application to the extent possible. In particular, integrating freedom of expression considerations may appear particularly suspicious from the perspective of these norms.

---

34 See more closely Mylly, *supra* note 7.

35 H. Ullrich (2005), 'Expansionist Intellectual Property Protection and Reductionist Competition Rules: A TRIPS Perspective', in K.E. Maskus and J.H. Reichman (eds), *International Public Goods and Transfer of Technology Under a Globalized Intellectual Property Regime,* Cambridge: Cambridge University Press, pp. 726, 752 and 755.

36 See D. Gervais (1998), *The TRIPS Agreement. Drafting History and Analysis,* London: Sweet & Maxwell, 68–9.

4. INTEGRATING FREEDOM OF EXPRESSION VALUES IN COMPETITION LAW APPLICATION

Despite the current ideological and legal constraints to integrate freedom of expression considerations in the application of competition law, the possibilities for doing so should nevertheless be considered. The EUC's recent fundamental rights cases discussed above demonstrate that the Court now takes fundamental rights more seriously than before. This approach could in theory be extended to competition law.

By its very nature, competition law involves delicate balancing between private and governmental power and between private and government-imposed restrictions on the freedom of the markets and market participants.[37] Irrespective of one's wishes, it determines in an important way the kind of competition a society is willing to pursue: the diversity of market actors, the fairness of transactions, the prospects of small and medium-sized enterprises and the degree of economic power tolerated are constituents of an economic culture greatly affected by the competition law institution. Workable markets characterized by a diversity of types of actors may be seen to represent the collective good aspect of many economic rights among the objectives of competition law. Such collective goods need constitutional protection against abuses of power in order to enable the exercise of fundamental rights in the economic sphere.

Similar considerations apply to freedom of expression and its meaning for an open society. In the current communicative environment the guarantee of pure formal liberty to speak relies largely on a technological and regulatory infrastructure. Power over distribution channels and technologies may confer power over content reaching their users. When the user has no choice of distribution channels and technologies, she is at the mercy of the owner of the distribution channel or technology in question. As Balkin argues, we should shift our focus from free speech rights narrowly construed to free speech values.[38]

The free press clauses and other provisions guaranteeing media freedom should be interpreted broadly to cover all communications media – not only the established press and broadcasting media.[39] In the information era, media

---

[37] See generally G. Amato (1999), *Antitrust and the Bounds of Power. The Dilemma of Liberal Democracy in the History of the Market*, Oxford: Hart Publishing, for an argumentation in this direction.

[38] J.M. Balkin (2004), 'Digital Speech and Democratic Culture: A Theory of Freedom of Expression for the Information Society', *New York University Law Review*, 1, 51–2.

[39] Similarly E. Barendt (2005), *Freedom of Speech*, 2nd ed., Oxford: Oxford University Press , p. 424.

should not be equated with traditional media companies, which act as intermediaries filtering and selecting content for particular media outlets and distribution channels.[40] Communicative diversity, more broadly conceived, should be facilitated as one collective good aspect of the protection of freedom of expression. This notion is not restricted to the diversity of goods and services available on the markets, which is the consumer aspect of the diversified possibilities for innovation and economic action. Rather, it refers to users of communication networks and information resources as active participants of the emerging digital culture and hence also to the variety in types of actors and types of goods and services offered. As the core information processing platforms now constitute of computer programs characterized by the presence of strong network effects, there are particular reasons for a positive obligation on governments to promote communicative diversity in this environment. There is no less reason to worry about excessive dependency of media companies and users on a dominant software platform than there is to worry about dependency on a single content provider. Despite the EU's dismal record of protecting media plurality or communicative diversity through concrete actions, the capacity to protect these interests in Europe lies predominantly on the Union legislature, administration and judicature. In addition to the Member States, the Union organs thus also have an obligation to actively protect media pluralism and communicative diversity in Europe. This obligation could also be pursued in the interpretations of intellectual property and competition laws, when the context of application so requires.

Certainly competition law is not a perfect, and alone a sufficient, instrument to secure communicative diversity. Typically complex concerns related to cultural and symbolic power may escape its traditional methodologies and standard orientation. With regard to merger control, in particular, concentrations reducing pluralism may not always be regarded as impeding competition. Specialized regulation for the communications, media and broadcasting sectors is also required for the protection of communicative diversity. However, the ideal of communicative diversity may be seen to overlap with the more traditional competition law objective related to market pluralism, diversity of economic actors and avoidance of excessive market power. Price competition and economic efficiency should be complemented with other possible objectives of competition law overlapping with communicative diversity when the sector of application is about information and discourse. In such instances, interpretive flexibility in market definition and other competition law analysis should be utilized to favour an outcome being consistent with

---

40 See also B. Rotenberg (2004), 'The European Regulation of Communications Software: Building a "Plattform" for Freely Interoperable Digital Expression?', *International Journal of Communications Law and Policy*,1, 36.

communicative diversity. This is so especially when specialized communication, media and broadcasting laws do not apply to the situation at hand or do not sufficiently secure communicative diversity. In any event, such laws do not apply generally, thus precluding a consistent policy. Moreover, specialized communication regulation on EU level has increased rather than decreased the role of competition law in controlling market power in the communications sector. Communicative diversity could thus increasingly become something to be considered in the application of competition law.

Integrating such considerations in the application of competition law is not necessarily unheard of, as the example of merger control and individual cases from other areas of competition law demonstrate. In its *Associated Press* decision the US Supreme Court stated the following:[41]

> The First Amendment, far from providing an argument against application of the Sherman Act, here provides powerful reasons to the contrary. That Amendment rests on the assumption that the widest possible dissemination of information from diverse and antagonistic sources is essential to the welfare of the public, that a free press is a condition of a free society.

Economic welfare could thus in some instances be complemented with considerations related to societal welfare. The openness of the core communication networks, information platforms, as well as the freedom of information in general constitute pre-requisites related to workable competition and freedom of market values in the information and network-based economy. Protecting such values is thus in line with the traditional interest of competition law to secure workable and diversified competition also in the longer-term perspective.

With regard to the Internet, the paradigmatic core of the competitive process functions within the central communicative structures of the civil society and affects them directly. The techno-economic structures of communication are simultaneously structures of competition, which the firms may affect directly by various techniques of private regulation. Exclusion of distribution channels, information sources or alternative access points to communication affect not only economic competition, but diminish individual and collective autonomy. As these central communicative structures also enable new forms of cross-border political action bypassing central authority,[42] the firms' regulation of these structures also affects the forms and feasibility of such political processes. It may also affect open source development by excluding some

---

41 *Associated Press et al. v United States*, 326 U.S. 1 (1945), at paragraph 20.

42 See S. Sassen (2006), *Territory, Authority, Rights: from Medieaval to Global Assemblages,* Princeton University Press, pp. 366 and 374.

technological trajectories through patenting or by lessening the viability of open source products through reductions of interoperability. Although the actions of firms are not usually based on political motivation but on commercial interests, they have the capacity to affect the public sphere and the collective goods related to social subsystems at least partially outside the economy. While aiming to affect various economic parameters of the Internet environment, firms cannot avoid the political function of these actions, as they have direct repercussions in lifeworld and politics without any further mediation of politics.

The role of competition law in controlling both economic and political power is thus not being lost, as sometimes argued,[43] but transformed. Besides the indirect political power of firms to affect legislation, the ability of enterprises to regulate the communication infrastructures through code has emerged as now perhaps a more important aspect of their politically significant market power, having direct repercussions for democratic culture, individual autonomy and also the legitimacy of law.[44]

It is necessary to concretize the foregoing with examples of how competition law could be developed to integrate freedom of expression-related values. These include competition law's position with regard to the end-to-end principle of the Internet, the meaning of informational power on dominance and finally the possibilities to develop the analysis of abuse with the infrastructure theory mentioned above.

Competition law should be concerned with facilitating the end-to-end principle of the Internet, as innovation competition on the Internet has been dependent on its open nature and absence of central authority determining which activities are permissible and which are not. As Lemley and Lessig have noted, the end-to-end principle:

> expands the competitive horizon by enabling a wider variety of applications to connect to and use the network. It maximizes the number of entities that can compete for the use and applications of the network. As there is no single strategic

---

43 Cf. Amato, *supra* note 37, pp. 104–5, arguing that competition law has lost the potential to control the effects of market power in political process, as the markets have globalized and the control of market power existing nationally is being gradually lost.

44 Republican and deliberative democratic theories concentrate on the qualities of public discourse preceding the legislative process as well as the legislative process itself. According to Habermas legitimate law is rooted in the lifeworld through the democratic procedure of legislation, based on the transformation of communicative power through law into administrative power See J. Habermas (1996), 'Three Normative Models of Democracy', in Benhabid, Seyla (ed.), *Democracy and Difference. Contesting the Boundaries of the Political,* Princeton University Press, p. 21.

> actor who can tilt the competitive environment (the network) in favour of itself, or no hierarchical entity that can favor some applications over others, an e2e [end-to-end] network creates a maximally competitive environment for innovation.[45]

The principle relaxes the fear of strategic capture of both innovation competition and individual freedom in the Internet environment. Hence, with regard to the end-to-end principle communicative diversity and an ideal of dynamic competition overlap to a great extent. Facilitating the end-to-end principle in the application of competition law would thus also be in conformity with the objectives of competition law.

Informational power could also be considered in the analysis of dominance. For example, Microsoft's market power emanated not only from its long-lasting very high (above 90%) market share or from high entry barriers. Its power to affect the technological trajectories and economic activities of others stemmed from the central importance of personal computer operating systems in the technological paradigm of communication and economic action based on computers and the Internet. The competitive threats on Microsoft's dominance emerged partially – and typically in information society contexts – from outside its own markets and thus from products not in direct competition with Windows operating system. Microsoft's proprietary platform and conduct also affected non-commercial activities. Its market power comprised significant political and social dimensions capable of being internalized in the analysis of its market power and dominant position. Such effects could be used to strengthen the *prima facie* finding of dominance, to implicate super-dominance implying more rigorous treatment, or to speak in favour of active *ex officio* investigations and measures on the part of competition law authorities. In addition to catching the most relevant aspects from market power in the networked information society, such discrimination between different relevant markets would imply active and rigorous application of competition law in markets central for communication and communicative diversity.

Thus, rather than seeing a particular proprietary platform and the enterprises active in the related fields in isolation, the platform in question should be seen in the context of the broader communicative ecosystem and the networks of related and dependent technologies. In the *Microsoft* decision such analysis can be found in the analysis of abuse, but not in the preceding analysis of dominance, as already the traditional methodology indicated super-dominance based on the near monopoly position on the operating system markets for personal computers.[46] Neither the Commission nor the General

[45] See M.A. Lemley and L. Lessig (2001), 'The End of End-to-End: Preserving the Architechture of the Internet in the Broadband Era', *UCLA Law Review* 925, 930–1.

[46] See about the concequences of super dominance case C-333/94 P, *Tetra Pak International SA v Commission*, [1996] ECR I-5951.

Court had to devise any new, contestable theories regarding dominance. Yet, the core features of Microsoft's market power, and the multiple potential and actual effects of its actions and inactions, become intelligible only after an analysis of the communicative and informational structures as well as the networks of related technologies whereby the operating system and other technologies involved are embedded. Microsoft's market power is centrally technology-enabled power to structure communication and information flows and exclude competition far beyond the primary markets of the operating systems for personal computers. Its control over the dominant operating system for personal computers had been, and could in the future increasingly be, used to structure the communicative environment built around the Internet.

The traditional methodology is not sufficient, as it does not distinguish between cases where the market position enables power over price only from cases where it also enables power over technological trajectories and activities of others. A firm may have market power conceived of as pricing freedom, but may lack power to affect technological trajectories or economic activities of others. This distinction becomes of central importance when the case involves intellectual property rights. This is so because the function of most intellectual property rights is to enable, through the manipulation of property rights and the incentives of firms, some power over price. The traditional methodology for establishing dominance, designed to discover power over price, is thus problematic as the only or principal criterion for establishing a dominant position based on intellectual property.

Due to digitization and convergence of technologies and information resources around the Internet, the whole communicative system increasingly has the characteristics of a highly complex system good consisting of several subsystems. Both the openness of the subsystems, as well as competition within them, varies to a considerable extent. Some of the technological standards may be interchangeable; some may be fixed relatively permanently. In either case, they may be secret and proprietary or freely accessible and usable to all. The system good-nature of the current communicative system built around the Internet connotes that market power can no more be evaluated atomistically, as the various subsystems are connected through protocols, interoperability and on-going multi-level convergence: the measures within one subsystem may reach multiple other subsystems. In industrial society contexts the traditional measurement of market power based on market share and additional factors was justified, as the effects of products and technologies on other products and technologies were rather incidental, and as the market position of an enterprise was not determined as a function of its product's or technology's strategic place in a system, but rather individually as a function of the enterprise's products' or technologies' position among other similar, substitutable products or technologies.

To comprehend the market power of a given enterprise with a given technology in communicative contexts thus requires systemic evaluation capable of positioning the technology or information resource in question on the broader communicative system. Such analysis should *complement* the more traditional market power analysis. This would connote not the demise, but the return of structural competition analysis in a modified form: whoever controls the flows and structures of communication holds both strategically and socially the most important form of power, as power over the communicative structures of the civil society and market power largely overlap. The system good-nature of the current communication paradigm connotes that there are several points of partial control, none of them complete, but many of them having the capacity to affect the lifeworld interaction and economic action based on the communicative structures pervasively.

The most relevant market power in the information society is exclusionary market power, which should be evaluated from the perspective of anticompetitive effects and impact on the markets. Dominance and abuse thus should not be analysed separately. Dominance should not constitute the first filter definable in isolation from the impact of the abusive measure on the markets. Infrastructure theory as first formulated by Frischmann and others will be briefly discussed in the following as a direction for the Community Courts to develop the decision-making doctrines concerning abuse.[47] As already mentioned, the theory is based on microeconomic vocabulary. This improves its possibilities of penetrating the relevant competition law discourses now increasingly reflecting microeconomic theory.

The key element addressed in infrastructure theory is how and to what extent infrastructure resources generate value for society. The focus is thus on the demand-side, outputs capable of being produced, instead of supply-side, the indispensability of the input needed. From this perspective, distinctions could and should be made among resources or inputs that are in themselves indispensable in the sense that there are no existing or potential substitutes for them. In other words, the mere indispensability of a resource does not have to lead to the need to open the resource for use by others with competition law or other regulation. What becomes decisive is the *non-rivalrous nature* of the resource, its *capacity to function as an input in the production of a wide variety of outputs* as well as the *particular context and the mix of outputs* it generates. Frischmann identifies three qualities of infrastructure: 1) the resource may be consumed non-rivalrously; 2) social demand for the resource is driven primarily by downstream productive activity that requires the resource as an

47 Frischmann, *supra* note 3. Frischmann and Waller have applied infrastructure theory to the essential facilities doctrine. See Frischmann and Weber Waller, *supra* note 3.

input; and 3) the resource may be used as an input into a wide range of goods and services, including private goods, public goods, and non-market goods.[48]

The more clearly a given resource satisfies the above criteria, the stronger the case for managing it in an openly accessible manner, without discrimination on the basis of the identity of the end-user or the end-use. In contradistinction to products consumed directly by end-users, intermediate goods or inputs capable of being used non-rivalrously in multiple downstream activities present a stronger case for open access. Infrastructure resources are thus essentially 'enabling platforms' upon which others may build.[49] They facilitate downstream competition, inventive activities and experimentation with new uses, typically resulting in positive externalities and large social gains.[50] There are specific reasons for an open access regime for inputs enabling the production of public and non-market goods, in particular.[51] In such instances the social value generated by permitting additional users to utilize the resource may be substantial, but very difficult or even impossible to quantify. The infrastructure owners (typically) cannot 'internalize the complementary externalities', when these are public or non-market goods. Such outputs may be produced without the motivation or ability to appropriate the value created, still generating considerable value for the society as a whole. Also members of the society who do not directly use the infrastructure in question may benefit from the outputs produced, thus making the internalization of all benefits very unlikely. Such 'external effects' or spillovers, when pervasive, should become an integral part of the welfare analysis. This is the core insight of infrastructure theory, also worth elaborating in European competition law doctrine in its relationship to intellectual property rights.

The basic implication of the infrastructure theory is simple, intuitive and often emphasized in democratic theory: price signals and market forces alone do not guide the commercially motivated owners and developers of techno-

---

48 Frischmann, *supra* note 3. Public and non-market goods differ from each other through the way they create value for society. The value of public goods is realized upon consumption, whereas non-market goods modify the societal conditions and social interdependencies so as to increase social welfare. These can relate to facilitating an open public sphere, education or freedom to experiment with new ideas and solutions, thus also benefiting non-participants in these processes. See *ibid.*, 964–7.

49 Frischmann, *supra* note 3, 949–51 and 957 and also *passim*.

50 Frischmann, *supra* note 3 and Frischmann and Weber Waller, *supra* note 3, 12.

51 Frischmann divides infrastructures into commercial, public and social infrastructure, depending on the downstream activities produced. Commercial infrastructure enables the production of commercial goods, public infrastructure the production of public goods and social infrastructure the production of non-market goods. However, *many important infrastructures (like the Internet) are mixed in the sense that they enable the production of all these goods.* See Frischmann, *supra* note 3, 959–69.

logical resources towards democratic design maximizing public and non-market values, but to design maximizing private commercial benefit and hence private goods.[52] As an economic theory, infrastructure theory provides a terminology familiar for competition law experts for discussing the effects of competition law application on issues like communication, democratic participation and self-expression. As such, it could enable critique and re-interpretation of some of competition law's central concepts and currently underlying presumptions on competition law's own territory and within its specialized discourse. Yet, although it manages to demonstrate the value of open access from the perspective of consumer welfare, it could not answer – practically or theoretically – where to draw the line between incentivizing the creation of infrastructures and enabling the production of public and non-market goods based on their use. Moreover, as an application of economic theory it merely presents one alternative economic perspective among others which the competition law courts, authorities and scholars could embrace. Hence, its recommendations obviously could not penetrate the doctrine by design. Finally, it is also a bit sad if courts and competition law authorities and scholars cannot discuss the implications of competition law for societal objectives, collective goods and democratic ends without resorting to terminology borrowed from microeconomics. The present chapter would thus recommend the courts and scholars to address the democratic issues underlying competition law also more directly. Like merger control in the media sector and individual competition law decisions like *Associated Press* demonstrate, constitutional concerns have not been wholly beyond competition law even in the absence of a coherent competition law theory accommodating such interests. Should this prove impossible in the current ideological stage of European antitrust, building on the insights of infrastructure theory in European competition law scholarship remains the second best alternative.

5. CONCLUSIONS

This chapter has argued that the developments related to networked information society imply major challenges for competition law. They should lead to re-evaluating not only some of its individual doctrines, but more critically its

52 From the perspective of democratic theory see for example J. Habermas (2001), 'The Postnational Constellation and the Future of Democracy', in M. Pensky (ed. transl.), *The Postnational Constellation. Political Essays*, Cambridge: Polity Press, p. 95 and E. Iversen, T. Vedel and R. Werle (2004), 'Standardization and the Democratic Design of Information and Communication Technology', *Knowledge, Technology & Policy*, 104–26, 109.

relationship to constitutional values, as in the information society competitive processes are increasingly embedded in the communicative structures built around the Internet. The proposals made do not mean that wealth maximization or other mainstream objectives of competition law should be rejected. Rather, in appropriate cases considerations related to them should be complemented with questions resonating on the level of constitutional values and freedom of expression, in particular.

In the current communicative environment the guarantee of pure formal liberty to speak relies largely on a technological and regulatory infrastructure. The power over distribution channels and technologies may confer power over content reaching the users over the channels and technologies. The structures of competition increasingly overlap with the structures of communication. Privately imposed restrictions of competition often directly translate into restrictions of communication or communicative diversity. The ideal of communicative diversity overlaps with the competition law objective related to market pluralism, diversity of economic actors and avoidance of excessive market power. Even though competition law has its own limitations, it may in some contexts be the best available instrument for controlling excessive, intellectual property-enabled informational power generated through market developments like network effects or standardization. This is well demonstrated by the Microsoft and Google cases. Effects related to communicative structures and informational power should increasingly be considered under competition law. This is necessary if competition law seeks to maintain its societal legitimacy by controlling competitively and societally the most harmful forms of market power.

For example, in the conditions of the *Microsoft* case, the attempt to leverage the near monopoly position of Microsoft on the markets for operating systems for personal computers to other markets equally central for the global Internet-based communications appears as a threat to democratic and constitutional values. Asking whether the market power and abusive practices extending it to new markets could pose a threat to such values and interests is relevant as a potential challenge for the straightforward application of the mainstream doctrines and propositions emanating from the microeconomic-oriented competition law discourses. Could competition law be seen from this perspective to have the function of also complementing intellectual property law in the sense that it enables the control of informational power exercised as techno-economic action, which is enabled or facilitated by the intellectual property institution? Could competition law be seen to foster the plurality and diversity of actors and types of actors the intellectual property institution and economic phenomena like globalization of production, network effects and standardization are likely to produce?

Even if competition law developed in the direction proposed in this chapter, most of the problems generated with strong intellectual property protection remain outside its potential scope of application. It cannot remedy the general expansion of intellectual property protection. Market power or dominance as such, facilitated by strong intellectual property protection, is not within the reach of competition law. The possibilities of competition law are thus limited. The application of competition law also entails inherent risks related to excessive imposition of either economic or bureaucratic rationality on social spheres and markets. Building too heavily on competition law to fix intellectual property law might also reduce the pressure to seek more rational solutions within intellectual property law.

Taking into account the apparent inherent limitations of competition law in controlling the societal problems and informational power caused by strong rights, the relaxation of European competition law, as well as the new constitutionalist measures seeking to immunize intellectual property from the application of competition law, the notion of 'rigorous application competition rules' seems to function as a mere legitimation for a scheme based on strong intellectual property rights. However, recognizing this should not prevent us from seeking to develop competition law so that it could better consider concerns related to informational power of the information age.

PART II

Developing the European IP system

Section 3

Trademarks and Geographical Indications at EU Level

6. Evaluation of the functioning of the EU trademark system: the Trademark Study

Annette Kur

1. INTRODUCTION

The EU trademark system in its current form came into existence in the mid-nineties of the last century. As is well-known, it consists of two tiers: the national trademark systems which were harmonized by the Trademark Directive (TMD) and the overarching regime established by the Community Trademark Regulation (CTMR). The Community Trademark (CTM) is a unitary right extending over the entire Community, while the national rights remain confined to their respective territories. Both regimes – the CTM system and national rights – coexist with each other. Due to the exclusive character of rights existing at the national or Community level, the systems are interdependent in the sense that all prior national marks (and other signs used in the course of trade) form obstacles for protection of subsequent CTMs, and all prior CTMs form obstacles to subsequent national marks.

From the very beginning, the CTM system has been a tremendous success. Already in the first year, the number of applications surpassed by far any previous expectation. While this is a source of pride for those who established the system, it also meant that the revenues from application fees received by the Office for Harmonization in the Internal Market (OHIM), which had been entrusted with the administration of the system, were much higher than had been estimated. As it had been envisaged, and was set out in the text of the CTMR, that the OHIM should be self-supporting, no legal basis existed for dealing with the surplus, for instance by feeding it into the general EU budget, or by disposing of it in any other manner. As the income proved to be relatively stable over the following years, the accumulation of surplus continued, finally reaching a critical point.

One obvious solution, also preferred by OHIM itself, would have been to lower the fees to a level where surplus would no longer be generated. However, such plans did not meet with approval by EU Member States. From their perspective – though to a varying degree – their own trademark systems were already in jeopardy because of the strong pulling effect exerted by the CTM system. To an increasing extent, companies doing business in the EU tend to revert to OHIM instead of the national offices in order to secure their trademark rights, causing most national offices to lose a (more or less) substantial part of their business. As any lowering of fees would likely create an additional incentive to substitute national applications with those of CTMs, no support from their side for any such plans could be mustered. However, as the need to dispose of the surplus became increasingly pressing, a political compromise was found which attempts to encompass the interests of all sides involved. First, the fees taken out by OHIM where lowered moderately, in two subsequent steps. Second, it was agreed among the Commission and the representatives of Member States that an amount equivalent to 50 per cent of the revenue from renewal fees should be distributed to the national offices, under the condition that the money was spent not on general budgetary issues, but on purposes connected to CTMs, or at least to trademark protection in general. Finally, it was decided that before the actual implementation of the compromise, which requires an amendment of the CTMR, an overall evaluation of the actual functioning of the EU trademark system should be carried out, so as to identify potential problems and lacunae which could be tackled in the same legislative context. As an element of that evaluation, the Max Planck Institute for Intellectual Property and Competition Law (MPI) was awarded the task to investigate aspects and areas of trademark law which could be of relevance for the purpose, so as to provide a basis for the EU Commission to elaborate their own proposals.

After concluding the contract with the Commission, the MPI study team[1] embarked on a fact-finding mission consisting of the following elements: consultations with organizations of stakeholders, interviews – in personal talks or in written form – were conducted with national trademark offices, and, as the most extensive part of the fact-finding efforts, a survey was carried out by a market survey company with ample experience in the field. Parallel to that, the statistical data available from OHIM as well as from certain national offices were evaluated from an economic perspective by an institute (INNO-tec) based at the Ludwig-Maximilians-University in Munich. The insights gathered from the fact-finding were then employed as basis for the legal analysis forming the main part of the Trademark Study ('Study').

1 Apart from the author herself, the team consisted of Dr. Roland Knaak (MPI) and Dr. Alexander v. Mühlendahl (attorney at law, former vice president of OHIM). The team was supported by a number of MPI scholarship holders as well as by Prof. Dr. Ansgar Ohly (University of Bayreuth).

The final text of the Study[2] comprises an account of general principles of EU trademark law, a discussion of legal issues which are common for the TMD and the CTMR, issues concerning the functioning of the CTM system, the task and mandate of OHIM, and considerations regarding further harmonization of trademark law in the EU. In the following text, only a few of those topics will be addressed, namely the principle of coexistence and its (perceived) imbalance, and, as matter of specific interest in an academic setting, the issue of rights conferred and their limitations.

2. COEXISTENCE ('SYSTEM COMPETITION')

2.1 The Issues

As set out above, most EU Member States in recent times have experienced a certain decline in the numbers of applications they receive, both from national and also from foreign enterprises. The size of the downturn varies: while some national offices fear that their very existence as an independent agency may be at stake if the current tendencies continue, others only had to suffer very small losses, or none at all. On the other hand, even those offices that did relatively well statistically do not get close to the increase in applications which OHIM as well as national offices in non-EU countries such as Switzerland and Norway could record during the same period. Thus, it is claimed by certain Member States, supported by part of the stakeholder organizations, that the system of coexistence has become imbalanced, and that measures should be taken to assure its integrity in the future. The following topics are debated in that context:

- *Fees*: As said above, it is a widespread feeling in (most) Member States that registration of a CTM is 'too cheap' as compared to national registrations. Whereas CTMs do come with a price – the basic fee for application and registration of a mark, covering three classes of the Nice classification system, is currently 1050 EUR, or 900 EUR if filed electronically – it becomes financially superior to national filings if the proprietor intends to claim protection in more than three Member States (depending on the national fees, which also vary among countries). Also, after the link has

[2] http://www.ip.mpg.de/shared/data/pdf/mpi_final_report.pdf (last accessed 20 July 2012). For reasons of convenience and easiness of reference, it had been planned by the MPI to publish the Trademarks Study as a book; however, this was prohibited, under the threat of legal prosecution by the Commission.

been established between the CTM system and international registration based on the Madrid protocol, filing for the entire Community instead of selected individual countries has become very simple, and has also led to fee reduction.

- *Use requirement*: While CTMs, just as national trademarks in the EU, do not have to be used at the time of registration, they become unenforceable and are subject to revocation if they are not put to genuine use in the Community upon the lapse of a five-year grace period. Regarding the interpretation of that requirement, it is regular practice at OHIM to assume that use made in one Member State is sufficient to maintain the right in the CTM for the entire Community. In recent times, the validity of that principle has been challenged by national offices, claiming that as a result, CTMs of which only minimal use has been made entail a disproportional blocking effect.
- *Cluttering* It is argued that the high and steadily increasing number of CTM registrations leads to substantial impediments for newcomers in search of available trademarks. Relatively low fees and generous assessment of what constitutes genuine use are considered as factors contributing to the phenomenon; in addition, it is claimed that other features of the CTM system, such as the basic fee covering three classes instead of only one, and also the practice established by OHIM that all goods and services in a Nice class are assumed to be covered by the respective class heading, are exacerbating the problems perceived.

In the following, these issues are addressed in turn.

2.2 Level and Distribution of Fees

Fees are certainly a core aspect in the architecture of the EU trademark system, though it is rather of a political than of a legal nature. Nevertheless, the issue also involves certain legal questions, in particular whether it forms part of established principles of EU law that an authority can only take fees that are measured according to the actual workload involved in the activities. This would be crucial not only for the level of the basic fee – which is arguably more than enough to cover the pertinent activities by OHIM – but even more so regarding the fee for renewal, which is much higher than what is actually needed for administration of the relevant task. On the contrary, the fee required for filing an opposition is significantly lower than the actual costs it entails for the Office. Therefore, the fee structure at OHIM would have to be completely rearranged if a principle requiring full proportionality of fees to the tasks performed were to be respected. Without being able itself to investigate the issue, the study team, upon advice by the Commission, proceeded from the assumption that no such principle existed, and that a certain discretion of the competent bodies exists as to the level and structure of fees claimed. On that basis, no changes were suggested with regard to the current fee system. In particular the position was endorsed that renewal fees should remain relatively high, so as to provide a certain counterweight to the risk that trademarks are maintained for more than the regular registration period which are not used at all, or which should rather be protected on the national level only. Furthermore, it was also considered as well-founded to keep opposition procedures relatively cheap, in order to ensure that proprietors of earlier rights are able to prevent the registration of conflicting CTMs, irrespective of their own size and financial means.

Regarding the distribution of fees, it was found that the envisaged flow of revenue from OHIM to the national offices is justified because and in as far as it serves to ensure that the principle of coexistence is maintained and supported. In essence, this means that the income should be used to help national offices shape up their performance, and thus preserve or re-gain their competitiveness. As a crucial element of their performance, the national offices should engage in a stronger cooperation among each other and with OHIM, to the benefit of the users of the system, for instance by providing common information or – in the longer run – registration platforms, and/or by establishing common databases containing decisions and guidelines of mutual interest, etc. As to the key governing the distribution of fees, it is recommended that, in addition to a gross sum to be distributed equally among the Member States, the shares attributed to the national systems should preferably reflect as closely as possible the actual proportion of costs generated for the respective system by the influx of the CTM system. Such costs are primarily generated by the fact that conflicts between CTMs and national trademarks are solved either in (not cost-efficient) opposition proceedings or within the national court system. As the probability of such conflicts rises with the number of national trademarks, the Study suggests that the most adequate distribution key is found in the number of trademark applications received by the national offices.

2.3 Genuine Use

When the CTM was passed in December 1993, the Council and the Commission released a Joint Statement holding that: 'The Council and the Commission consider that use which is genuine within the meaning of Article 15 in one country constitutes genuine use in the Community' (Joint Statement of 20 December 1993). That statement has formed the basis for the practice of OHIM in the relevant aspect. The reason is that the term 'in the Community', in light of the concept on which the CTM is founded (unitary right; 'single market' theory), cannot be understood as requiring use in more than one country, or any other qualification referring to national boundaries. On the other hand, it has been remarked that by applying too lenient standards for the assessment of genuine use, the balance between the systems would be seriously distorted. Much attention was raised in this context by the decision of the Benelux Trademark office of 15 January 2010 (ONEL/OMEL):[3] Pointing out that the Joint Statement stems from a time when the European Community was much smaller in terms of geographical coverage and membership, it was held that use in one Member State should not 'by definition' constitute use in the Community. A similar view was also endorsed by the Hungarian trademark office.[4]

Whereas the attitudes endorsed on this issue seem to be highly controversial, the large majority of opinions, including those reflected in the decisions by the Hungarian and Benelux offices, do not diverge on the essential point, namely that the sufficient scale of genuine use cannot be determined on the basis of a quantitative approach linked to national borders. The more challenging question rather concerns the aspect of substantiality of the use made. In that regard, it must be noted that the Joint Statement can be read in two different ways: it may mean that any use which is sufficient to maintain a national trademark is automatically also sufficient for a CTM. On the other hand, the Statement may also simply mean that if the use as such is genuine in the meaning of Article 15 CTMR, that result is not countered by the fact that it was made in one country only. The latter understanding appears to be correct; it means that the scope, volume and extent of use which must be made of a CTM are not the same as for national marks. Whether the necessary threshold is met must be assessed on the basis of a case-by-case analysis, guided by the principle of proportionality, which takes into account all circumstances, such as in particular the nature of the goods and services, as well as the size and type of business activities of the proprietor.

Whereas it should be possible in most cases to arrive at a satisfactory solution on the basis of that formula, it is assumed that in exceptional cases, the current scheme – even when interpreted in the manner suggested above – could lead to inadequate results. For instance, if a CTM was used, over a long period of time, in only a small part of the European Union, without any indication that the use might be extended to other parts as well, it appears disproportionate to accept that the mark nevertheless has a blocking effect vis-à-vis subsequent national marks for which protection is sought in a Member State

3 *Leno Merken/Hagelkruis Beheer B.V.* (ONEL/OMEL), now pending before the ECJ as Case C-149/11.

4 Decision of 11 February 2010, Case No. M0900377 – *C City Hotel.*

which is remote, in geographical and/or economic terms, from the part of the European Union where the CTM is actually used. The Study proposes therefore that in such a situation (after more than 15 years from registration), the CTM cannot be enforced against registration and use of the younger sign, provided that the latter was applied for in good faith. As a result, both marks will have to coexist with each other. In its structure and consequences, the proposed rule is similar to that of acquiescence, according to which a trademark can no longer be enforced vis-à-vis a younger sign if the proprietor was aware of the younger sign for more than five years, unless the person adopting the younger sign has acted in bad faith.

It must be emphasized in that context that while enforceability of the CTM is blocked in these cases, this does not mean that the proprietor of the CTM is prohibited from entering the territory where the younger right exists. The CTM remains a unitary right, i.e. it is valid and can be used without restriction throughout the European Union. It is true that this would lead to a situation where two basically conflicting marks exist in the same territory, thereby arguably giving rise to a likelihood of confusion. However, that situation is by no means unique – it also arises in consequence of acquiescence, or in other constellations when the enforceability of trademarks is excluded vis-à-vis younger marks. In all those cases, it needs to be assessed how serious the risk for confusion actually is. If such risks are pertinent, measures must be taken to avoid consumers being deceived about the identity of goods and services. In that regard, the Study suggests that the burden of taking such measures should be on the proprietor of the younger sign.

2.4 Cluttering

Wide diversity of opinion exists in Europe as to whether the registers at OHIM (and also in the Member States) are actually 'cluttered' in the sense that accessibility of new trademarks is substantially impeded. The issue can be divided into two separate elements, one concerning the absolute size of a register – whether it contains 'too many' marks – and the other relating to the question whether the register is cluttered by too much 'deadwood', i.e. marks which are either not used at all, or are only used for a part of the goods and services covered by the registration. Regarding the first element, the answer can hardly be other than negative. In terms of absolute numbers, the OHIM register is still much smaller than that in the United States, or China, or even some of the bigger European Member States. Also, it appears hardly possible to establish a bright line indicating the 'maximum size' of registers, beyond which they would be regarded as cluttered. On the other hand, it cannot be denied that the difficulties for newcomers to find a sign which is not blocked by a prior mark – and which can easily be pronounced and remembered, and gives rise to positive associations without being descriptive – are bound to increase in proportion with the size of registers.

Regarding the second element, there is no doubt in principle that trademark systems such as the European one attract a certain number of 'void' registrations. CTMs as well as national marks can be registered without actual use, and if not challenged after five years of non-use, they will remain in the register for the full registration period, and eventually even beyond – they can be renewed without difficulty.[5] The system therefore inevitably involves a certain amount of cluttering in the sense that unused trademarks are found in the registers and will show up in searches, even when they cannot be validly enforced. Further features arguably contributing to the accumulation of 'deadwood' at OHIM (and at national offices following the same model) concern the basic fee covering three classes, which may invite overbroad registrations, or the use of class headings as designations covering all goods or services under that heading.

Whereas those issues may give rise to concern, it should not be ignored that they are expressions of a general policy choice on which European trademark law is built: unlike, for instance, its American counterpart, the European system is geared towards fast and cost-efficient procedures, which implies that private actors must be alert and defend their interests in a pro-active manner instead of relying on the 'watchdog-function' of the register. Thus, if a person finds that his way into the trademark register is blocked by an earlier mark, it is up to him to find out about the state of use of that mark, and to challenge its validity or the scope of protection claimed, if doubts exist in that regard. If the system were changed, this would necessarily result in longer and more costly procedures.

Respecting those basic choices, the question whether and which measures should be taken to address the cluttering issue becomes first and foremost a matter of cost-benefit analysis. As a basis for that exercise, it would be useful to know whether the impediments resulting from unused or unnecessary registrations are substantial in their dimensions, and whether possible countermeasures would give rise to disproportional costs. As it turned out, it is all but easy to arrive at a clear picture regarding those aspects. It is plausible that if a cluttering problem exists, it would primarily affect CTM applications, which are liable to opposition not only from prior CTMs, but also from an aggregated number of national registered marks and other signs used in the course of trade. However, as is emphasized by OHIM, statistical data do not support such assumptions: the opposition rate has remained stable throughout the

[5] Whether such marks are actually renewed depends primarily on the willingness of the proprietor to pay the relatively high renewal fee; see above.

years or is even slightly declining, showing that the growing number of trademarks has not led to a rising portion of conflicts. Interestingly, statistics also show that very crowded classes[6] attract a relatively low opposition rate (between 14 and 15 percent). On the other hand, those figures are not entirely conclusive. Apart from the absence of conflicts, an explanation for the low opposition rate could lie in the fact that more efforts are undertaken in those classes to clear the rights before filing an application, thus adding to the pre-filing costs incurred by the companies. Concrete data are not available on that point, and inquiries among companies and agents equally lead to inconclusive results: in the user survey conducted in the framework of the Study, it was found that a relatively high percentage of agents, but only a – not quite insubstantial – number of proprietors was of the opinion that the number and breadth of trademark registrations at OHIM posed a problem. Differing views were also proffered by stakeholder organizations.

All in all, it must be concluded that the evidence gathered in the course of the Study did not allow drawing definite conclusions. There is no sustainable documentation showing that access to trademarks is substantially impaired by congestion of registers; on the other hand, it appears equally unwise to contend that the features of the present system that tend to invite a certain amount of cluttering do not give rise to any problems at all, and will not do so in the future. Some amendments in that regard were therefore proposed in the Study; for instance, it is suggested that in the future, only one Nice class should be covered by the initial fee (which would then have to be lowered accordingly). Furthermore, it is proposed that 'overbroad' and imprecise class headings should be reconsidered and re-formulated, in cooperation with the national offices, so as to allow for a more accurate representation of the goods and services covered thereby, and furthermore, it should be clarified that only those goods or services can actually be considered as being covered, which, according to a normal understanding of the class heading used, are considered to fall into that class.[7] The Study also considered more 'radical' measures such as imposing on trademark proprietors an obligation to file, five years following registration, a statement with OHIM indicating that, and for which goods or services, the mark was actually put in use. However, as hard and fast evidence is lacking as to serious problems resulting from unused marks, no such proposals were included in the final text.

6 Such as 9, 35, 42 and 41.

7 In the meantime, a very similar position was endorsed by the ECJ in the Case C-307/10 – *CIPA/Registrar of Trade Marks* ('IP TRANSLATOR').

3. RIGHTS CONFERRED AND LIMITATIONS

3.1 Rights Conferred

3.1.1 'Use as a mark' and trademark functions

The provisions defining the scope of trademark protection in an infringement situation, Articles 5 TMD and 9 CTMR, require a sign to be used 'in relation to goods and services' in order to find for infringement. In an early decision dealing with use of the trademark 'BMW' by a person offering used BMW cars and offering repair services (case C-63/97 – *BMW/Deenik*), the ECJ interpreted the latter criterion as meaning that the trademark must be used 'as a mark', i.e. so as to 'identify and distinguish' goods or services from those of different commercial origin. In the case at hand, use as a mark was found to exist, as 'BMW' had been used by the alleged infringer so as to identify the object of his services and to distinguish it from other car brands. While it was suggested by that ruling that use of trademark for the purpose of referring to the proprietor's products was sufficient to constitute use as a mark, the ECJ later on insisted that the case had been an exception, and that in principle, the use made must relate to the alleged infringer's own goods or services case (case C-48/05 – *Opel/Autec*). However, the restriction seemingly intended thereby was rendered practically meaningless, when the ECJ held in another decision that a competitor using another person's trademark in comparative advertising uses that mark in relation to his own, i.e. the competitor's, goods or services (case C-533/06 – *O2/Hutchison*).

Throughout its meandering course, the ECJ constantly claimed that its decisions were based on an analysis of the trademark functions which are addressed in recital 10 of the preamble to the TMD. In the beginning, the Court in that context regularly emphasized the importance of the origin function of the mark, and denied (though not in a consequent manner) the applicability of the provision granting absolute protection in case of identical marks being used for identical products (Article 5(1)(a) TMD) in situations when the origin function was not (likely to be) jeopardized. However, in its more recent jurisprudence, the ECJ went further by pointing out that protection under Article 5(1)(a) TMD is also granted if other trademark functions, namely the quality, advertising, communication and investment functions are affected.[8] While that seemed to indicate an extension of trademark protection, such expectations were dampened by subsequent case law, which applied a rather strict interpretation of the question whether those additional functions are actually affected.[9]

---

8 Case C-487/07 – *L'Oréal/Bellure*.
9 Joined Cases C-236-238/08 – *Google/Vuitton*.

All of this has caused much confusion about the actual state of European trademark law, in particular regarding the ambit of the 'double identity clause' in Articles 5(1)(a) TMD and 9(1)(a) CTMR. The principal cause for the problems appears to lie in the fact that the ECJ has not found a clear and consistent way to integrate cases of 'referential use' – i.e. use made in order to refer to goods or services as those of the proprietor – into the current structure of Articles 5 TMD and 9 CTMR. One way to overcome the difficulties would have been to change that structure, and promulgate two different provisions, one addressing use of a mark to indicate the commercial origin of products not originating from the proprietor, and another one relating to referential use. However, in order to confine changes of the current text to a minimum, the Study only proposes to clarify in the preamble of the TMD and CTMR that Article 5(1)(a) and 9(1)(a) CTMR apply to both situations alike. In the same context, it should also be stated that only in the first type of cases, protection is 'absolute' in the sense that it regularly results in infringement, whereas use made of a mark for identifying the goods or services as those of the proprietor will only be found infringing if it does not comply with honest commercial practices, as specified in the limitations. No further functional analysis is needed to motivate that result.

3.1.2 Likelihood of confusion and extended protection

Concerning likelihood of confusion, the Study also proposes certain clarifications to be set out in the preamble. In particular, the principle that the scope of a mark is measured according to the 'strength' of the mark – whether inherent or acquired – should be emphasized as a fundamental guideline informing the practice of courts and authorities.

Clarifications and smaller amendments are also called for with regard to protection of trademarks having a reputation against unfair advantage being taken of, or detriment being inflicted on, the distinctive character of reputation of the mark. The respective provision in the TMD, Article 5(2), is only optional, meaning that Member States are not obliged to implement it in their national laws. However, with very few exceptions, all Member States currently provide for such extended protection. It must also be considered in the context that an international obligation exists under Article 16(3) TRIPS to grant at least a certain degree of protection against use of a mark for dissimilar goods. The Study therefore concludes that Article 5(2) should become a mandatory part of the TMD. Furthermore, the wording of Article 5(2) currently only refers to use made for *dissimilar* goods or services. As the ECJ has clarified, it would be mistaken to infer from that wording that no extended protection is available against use for identical or similar goods.[10] In order to

---

[10] Case C-292/00 – *Davidoff/Gofkid* (*Davidoff/Durffee*).

prevent any misunderstanding about that point, the formulation of Article 5(2) should be amended accordingly.

3.1.3 Marks having a reputation and well-known marks under Article 6bis Paris Convention

Another, more substantial point addressed by the Study, in connection with extended protection for trademarks having a reputation, concerns the relationship between that concept and the notion of well-known marks under the Paris Convention and TRIPS, which has remained unclear so far. On the basis of ECJ jurisprudence elaborated on the concept of reputation[11] and its comparison with the WIPO Recommendations on the protection of well-known marks,[12] it is concluded that the two actually coincide. (Unregistered) trademarks are therefore entitled to claim protection under Article 6bis Paris Convention if they live up to the threshold required for marks having a reputation, meaning that they must be known to a substantial part of the relevant public in a substantial part of the respective territory, weighted in connection with other factors such as duration and intensity of use, marketing efforts, etc. It is submitted that the proposal is uncontroversial so far. However, two thornier issues remain: first, whether unregistered marks are well-known should also be entitled to claim extended protection under Article 5(2) TMD, and second, whether protection for unregistered well-known marks should also form part of the infringement provisions of the CTMR.

Regarding extended protection of unregistered marks, it must be noted first that such protection is not mandatory under Article 16(3) TRIPS, which only refers to registered marks. However, the WIPO Recommendations stipulate that registration should not be a requirement for protection beyond likelihood of confusion.[13] Although the Recommendations are not binding, they have considerable political weight, and should therefore not be disregarded without substantial reason. As such reasons, according to the Study, do not exist, it is proposed that unregistered marks should actually be considered as eligible for extended protection under EU law, if the necessary requirements are met.

Regarding protection of unregistered well-known marks on the Community level, current legislation only lists such marks as prior national rights in the catalogue of mandatory relative grounds for refusal set out in Article 8(1), (2) CTMR. In contrast to that, no protection is granted under the

---

[11] Cases C-375/97 – *General Motors/Yplon S.A.* (Chevy) and C-328/06 – *Nieto Nuño/Franquet*.

[12] WIPO Joint Recommendation Concerning Provisions on the Protection of Well-Known Marks (JR 1999), available at http://www.wipo.int/about-ip/en/development_iplaw/pub833.htm (last accessed 20 July 2012).

[13] Article 2(3) in connection with Article 4 JR 1999.

CTMR against infringing use of marks that are well-known in the Community; instead, such marks must seek protection on the national level. It is debatable whether the EU thereby violates its obligations under the TRIPS Agreement and, by inclusion, of the Paris Convention,[14] or whether it is sufficient that the protection required is granted by the Member States. In order to avoid any such debates, the Study recommends that protection against infringing use of unregistered well-known marks should likewise be anchored in the CTMR. However, as this is ultimately a political question, no explicit proposals are formulated in that regard.

3.2 Limitations and Exceptions

Even if a conflict is found to exist, the trademark proprietor cannot enforce the right if the use is found to be admissible under the provision allowing for use that is fair for reasons set out in Article 6 TMD/12 CTMR, or if it concerns the commercialization of products that were released on the market in the Community by the proprietor or with his consent (exhaustion; Article 7 TMD/13 CTMR). At present, the catalogue of limitations in Article 6 TMD/12 CTMR refers to use of a mark as a name or address, use for descriptive purposes, and use to indicate purpose, in particular of spare parts or accessories. The Study proposes changes with regard to the use of names, and it also proposes to enlarge the current list of acceptable uses with a view to honest referential use.

Regarding use of a name which is privileged under Article 6(1)(a) TMD/12(1)(a) CTMR, it was documented in a Joint Statement by the Commission and the Council at the time of enactment of the TMD that it was intended only to cover use of personal names. However, the ECJ declared that the Joint Statement was not binding for its interpretation of the clause, and judged instead that the privilege should extend to all kinds of names, including trade names, whether or not they contain the personal name of the owner.[15] The Study concludes that there is no clear justification for such a wide interpretation, and proposes to change the wording so as to make clear that only personal names are covered by the provision.

Apart from that, an extension of the current catalogue of limitations was found necessary as a corollary to the proposal made in the Study that referential use of trademarks should be encompassed by Article 5(1)(a) TMD/9(1)(a)

---

[14] In that respect, it might be argued that by restricting protection to the national level, unregistered marks which are well-known in the EU are disadvantaged vis-à-vis CTMs insofar as they do not have access to the jurisdiction system established under the CTMR, and thus have to be enforced in a fragmented manner.

[15] Case C-245/02 – *Anheuser Busch/Budějovický Budvar*.

CTMR. Otherwise, the enlargement of the ambit of trademark law might lead to imbalanced results that run counter to important principles such as freedom of speech and free competition. It should therefore be clarified that use of a mark is admissible if it serves purposes of critique and comment, including parodies.[16] The same must apply, quite obviously, to the use of marks in comparative advertisement, under the conditions set out in the relevant Directive (2006/114/EC). A clause to that effect is proposed to be included Articles 5 TMD and 9 CTMR.

4. CONCLUDING REMARKS

The topics addressed in this brief chapter as well as the many other suggestions made in the Study have been submitted to the EU Commission for consideration. It is important to note in this context that they represent only one – albeit important – element in the overall evaluation undertaken by the Commission, and that our findings will by no means prejudice the final result, or the legislative proposals to be made for the reform of EU trademark law.

Also for the MPI, delivering the final version of the Study to the Commission does not mark the end of work focused on the future of EU trademark law. In the course of a larger academic project, if possible with the assistance of colleagues from other academic disciplines such as economics, it is intended to elaborate on a variation of 'scenarios for the future', trying to anticipate future trends of development in order to discuss issues connected therewith and devise possible strategies for their solution.

16 For a recent example (concerning, however, Community Design protection), see Rechtbank s'Gravenhage, 21 May 2011, *Nadia Plesner/Louis Vuitton Malletier*.

7. Adapting EU trademark law to new technologies: back to basics?

Martin Senftleben

INTRODUCTION

In recent years, the Court of Justice of the European Union (CJEU) has continuously expanded the scope and reach of trademark protection in the EU. With the challenges arising in the digital environment, however, this expansionist approach becomes more and more questionable. The current problems arising from keyword advertising shed light on areas of overbroad, excessive trademark protection created by the Court. Moreover, inconsistencies in the Court's system of infringement criteria clearly come to the fore. Against this background, the present analysis explores ways out of the dilemma.

After a short introduction to basic notions of EU trademark law (section 1), the problematic expansion of trademark protection in recent years (sections 2 and 3), and current problems arising in the digital environment (section 4), will be analysed in more detail. Addressing potential solutions, it will be argued that in spite of current difficulties, it would be naive to assume that the Court is prepared to restrict the scope of EU trademark law to traditional protection against confusion with only minor extensions concerning dilution (section 5). Instead, the need for an appropriate, more flexible limitation infrastructure will be emphasized (section 6 and concluding section 7).

1. BASICS

According to traditional trademark theory, trademarks primarily serve the purpose of indicating the commercial origin of goods and services offered in the marketplace.[1] The CJEU refers to

[1] For an overview of trademark functions, pointing out this traditional focus on identification and distinction functions and potential extensions with regard to communication, investment and advertising functions, see R. Keim (2009), *Der markenrechtliche Tatbestand der Verwechslungsgefahr*, Baden-Baden: Nomos, pp. 37–61.

> the essential function of the trade mark, which is to guarantee the identity of the origin of the trade-marked product to the consumer or final user by enabling him to distinguish without any possibility of confusion between that product and products which have another origin.[2]

To enable trademarks to fulfil the essential origin function, trademark law offers enterprises the opportunity to establish an exclusive link with a distinctive sign. As a result, the protected sign is rendered capable of functioning as a source identifier in trade. In this way, trademark law guarantees market transparency. It ensures fair competition, protects consumers against confusion and contributes to the proper functioning of market economies by allowing consumers to clearly express their preference for a particular product or service. From an economic perspective, it can be added that the clear indication of the commercial origin of goods and services reduces consumers' search costs.[3]

To enable trademarks to fulfil this essential origin function, defensive[4] protection is sufficient. As long as the trademark owner is capable of preventing other traders from using identical or similar signs for identical or similar goods or services, the clear identification of the commercial source of goods and services can be guaranteed. As highlighted by the CJEU, the protection of trademarks as identifiers of commercial source aims at the exclusion of 'any possibility of confusion.'[5] Accordingly, this protection is to be granted only if use of a conflicting sign is likely to cause confusion.[6] In cases of double iden-

---

2 For an early use of this formula, see CJEU, 3 December 1981, case C-1/81, *Pfizer v Eurim-Pharm*, para. 8. As to the reappearance of the same formula in later judgments, see particularly CJEU, 12 November 2002, case C-206/01, *Arsenal/Reed*, para. 48. Cf. I. S. Fhima (2005), 'How Does "Essential Function" Doctrine Drive European Trade Mark Law?', *IIC*, **36**, 401.

3 With regard to the search costs argument, see J. Griffiths (2008), 'A Law-and-Economic Perspective on Trade Marks', in L. Bently, J. Davis and J.C. Ginsburg (eds), *Trade Marks and Brands – An Interdisciplinary Critique*, Cambridge: Cambridge University Press, p. 241; M. Strasser (2000), 'The Rational Basis of Trademark Protection Revisited: Putting the Dilution Doctrine into Context', *Fordham Intellectual Property, Media & Entertainment Law Journal,* **10**, 375, 379–82. With regard to questions arising in the digital environment, see S.L. Dogan and M.A. Lemley (2004), 'Trademarks and Consumer Search Costs on the Internet', *Houston Law Review*, **41**, 777.

4 This protection is defensive in the sense that it aims at the prevention of confusing use and is not concerned primarily with the exploitation of brand value as an enterprise's intellectual property asset. Cf. M.R.F. Senftleben (2009), 'The Trademark Tower of Babel – Dilution Concepts in International, US and EC Law', *IIC*, **40**, 45, 47, online available at http://ssrn.com/abstract=1723903.

5 See the references provided *supra*, note 2.

6 Apart from the introduction of 'absolute protection' in cases of sign and prod-

tity (an identical sign used for an identical product), this risk of confusion may be deemed so obvious that it can be presumed.[7] However, this presumption must not be misunderstood as a departure from the general requirement to show that confusion is likely to arise from the use at issue.

Given these clear conceptual contours of traditional trademark protection against confusion, it is not surprising that agreement on this limited scope of protection was reached in the European Union. By virtue of Art. 5(1) of the Trademark Directive (TMD),[8] the grant of this basic protection is mandatory in all EU Member States. It gives trademark owners limited control over communication concerning their marks – control that only covers the identification and distinction of the goods or services they offer in the marketplace. According to the CJEU, the condition of a likelihood of confusion may be satisfied where the public confuses the sign and the mark in question (direct confusion), or where the public makes a connection between the proprietors of the sign and those of the mark and confuses them (indirect confusion).[9]

---

uct identity (which will be dealt with below), this basic requirement is clearly reflected in Recital 11 of the EU Trademark Directive:

> The likelihood of confusion, the appreciation of which depends on numerous elements and, in particular, on the recognition of the trade mark on the market, the association which can be made with the used or registered sign, the degree of similarity between the trade mark and the sign and between the goods or services identified, should constitute the specific condition for such protection.

[7] At the international level, this concept of presuming a likelihood of confusion in cases of double identity is clearly reflected in Art. 16(1) TRIPS:

> The owner of a registered trademark shall have the exclusive right to prevent all third parties not having the owner's consent from using in the course of trade identical or similar signs for goods or services which are identical or similar to those in respect of which the trademark is registered where such use would result in a likelihood of confusion. In case of the use of an identical sign for identical goods or services, a likelihood of confusion shall be presumed.

[8] Directive 2008/95/EC of the European Parliament and of the Council of 22 October 2008, to approximate the laws of the Member States relating to trade marks (codified version) (OJ 2008 L 299, 25), which entered into force on 28 November 2008, and repealed the earlier Directive 89/104/EEC of the Council of 21 December 1988.

[9] See CJEU, 11 November 1997, case C-251/95, *Puma/Sabel*, paras 16–26. For an overview of the EU approach to anti-confusion protection, see G. Würtenberger (2002), 'Risk of Confusion and Criteria to Determine the Same in European Community Trade Mark Law', *EIPR* 20. For critical comments on the need for additional anti-dilution protection, see J.T. McCarthy (2004), 'Dilution of a Trademark: European and United States Law Compared', *The Trademark Reporter,* 94, 1163, 1170–2, online available at http://ssrn.com/abstract=1350045.

Moreover, trademarks with a particularly distinctive character may give rise to a greater likelihood of confusion.[10] The EU concept also covers post sale confusion that might arise after the place of purchase with a clear notice concerning the commercial origin of goods has been left.[11]

2. EXTENSIONS

In all these cases, EU protection against confusion can be understood to serve the rather defensive purpose of preventing competitors from use that would interfere with the basic communication of information about the commercial origin of goods and services offered by the trademark owner. It is this prevention of confusing use that constitutes the core rationale of protection.[12] Nonetheless, the exclusive rights necessary for ensuring protection against confusion can be used strategically by the trademark owner to realize additional benefits. To allow trademarks to convey reliable information on the commercial origin of goods or services, it is indispensable to reserve use of the trademark exclusively for the trademark owner in all market segments where use of identical or similar signs could lead to confusion.[13] As a result, the

---

10 CJEU, 11 November 1997, case C-251/95, *Puma/Sabel* , para. 24. The degree of distinctiveness is one of the factors to be considered in the framework of the infringement analysis. See CJEU, 29 September 1998, case C-39/97, *Canon/Cannon*; CJEU, 22 June 1999, case C-342/97, *Lloyd/Loint's*.

11 See CJEU, 12 November 2002, case C-206/01, *Arsenal/Reed*, para. 57, with regard to cases of double identity.

12 For an alternative view, emphasizing the attention devoted to the trademark owner's interest in exploiting brand value in the context of protection against confusion, see T. Cohen Jehoram and H. Van Helden (2011), 'Bekend, bekender, bekendst: Goodwill-bescherming van merken', in Benelux Office for Intellectual Property (ed.), *In Varietate Concordia? National and European Trademarks Living Apart Together*, The Hague: Benelux Office for Intellectual Property, 111; M. Buydens, 'Pouvoir distinctif de la marquee et risque de confusion: larvatus prodeo?', in Benelux Office for Intellectual Property, *ibid*, p. 33; A.A. Quaedvlieg (2007), 'Verwaterd of verward, een kwestie van bekendheid?', in D.J.G. Visser and D.W.F. Verkade (eds.), *Een eigen, oorspronkelijk karakter – Opstellen aangeboden aan prof. mr. Jaap H. Spoor*, Amsterdam: DeLex, p. 275.

13 In the case of collective trademarks, this exclusive reservation of a sign concerns an association of enterprises who use the trademark in trade. The basic mechanism, however, remains unchanged. The information conveyed via the trademark, by contrast, will focus on certain product characteristics rather than one particular commercial origin. Cf. A. Peukert (2011), 'Individual, Multiple and Collective Ownership of Intellectual Property Rights – Which Impact on Exclusivity?', in A. Kur and V. Mizaras (eds), *The Structure of Intellectual Property Law: Can One Size Fit All?*, Cheltenham UK and Northampton, MA: Edward Elgar Publishing, online available at http://ssrn.com/abstract=1563990.

trademark owner obtains an exclusive channel of communication in several areas of the market. In principle, only the enterprise holding trademark rights is entitled to convey information to consumers via the trademark in this protected area.[14]

Through investment in advertising, the trademark owner can easily use this exclusive communication channel to add messages that are unrelated to the underlying objective of ensuring accurate information about the commercial source of goods or services. In particular, an enterprise can start advertising campaigns to teach consumers to associate a certain attitude or lifestyle with the trademark.[15] The moment a trademark 'speaks' to consumers about a particular image that can be associated with the trademarked product, consumers no longer simply buy products from a particular source. They also buy the respective 'trademark experience' and 'brand image.'[16]

Inevitably, the exclusive rights necessary to ensure protection against confusion, therefore, also protect the investment made in the creation of a favourable trademark image. Basic protection against confusion safeguards the exclusive link between an enterprise and its trademark. In this way, it also offers legal security for substantial investment in the evocation of brand-related associations in the minds of consumers. The WTO Panel dealing with EC protection for trademarks and geographical indications for agricultural products and foodstuffs described this protection reflex as follows:

> The function of trademarks can be understood by reference to Article 15.1 [TRIPS] as distinguishing goods and services of undertakings in the course of trade. Every trademark owner has a legitimate interest in preserving the distinctiveness, or capacity to distinguish, of its trademark so that it can perform that function. This

---

14 As in other fields of intellectual property protection, it is indispensable to set certain limits to the exclusive rights of trademark owners. The principle of an exclusive communication channel, therefore, is limited in several respects. See the general limitations set forth in Art. 6 TMD. With regard to comparative advertising, see CJEU, 12 June 2008, case C-533/06, *O2/Hutchison*, para. 45; CJEU, 18 June 2009, case C-487/07, *L'Oréal/Bellure*, para. 54.

15 Cf. R.S. Brown (1999), 'Advertising and the Public Interest: Legal Protection of Trade Symbols', *Yale Law Journal*, **108**, 1619, 1619–20; K.H. Fezer (2003), 'Entwicklungslinien und Prinzipien des Markenrechts in Europa – Auf dem Weg zur Marke als einem immaterialgüterrechtlichen Kommunikationszeichen', *Gewerblicher Rechtsschutz und Urheberrecht*, 457, 461–2; S. Casparie-Kerdel (2001), 'Dilution Disguised: Has the Concept of Trade Mark Dilution Made its Way into the Laws of Europe?', *EIPR*, , 185, 185–6; M. Lehmann (1986), 'Die wettbewerbswidrige Ausnutzung und Beeinträchtigung des guten Rufs bekannter Marken, Namen und Herkunftsangaben – Die Rechtslage in der Bundesrepublik Deutschland', *Gewerblicher Rechtsschutz und Urheberrecht International*, 6, 14–17.

16 See J.E. Schroeder (2008), 'Brand Culture: Trade Marks, Marketing and Consumption', in Bently, Davis and Ginsburg, *supra* note 3, p. 161.

> includes its interest in using its own trademark in connection with the relevant goods and services of its own and authorized undertakings. Taking account of that legitimate interest will also take account of the trademark owner's interest in the economic value of its mark arising from the reputation that it enjoys and the quality that it denotes.[17]

The WTO Panel was not called upon to discuss the protection of trademark reputation and brand image in more detail. It could content itself with the indication of a connection between the protection of trademark distinctiveness and trademark repute. The delicate question to be answered in advanced trademark protection systems, such as the EU system, however, is whether – in addition to the described protection reflex inherent in basic protection against confusion – the creation of a brand image should additionally be rewarded with enhanced protection covering cases of dilution.[18] In other words: does the marketing effort made by the trademark owner justify an additional layer of protection against dilution besides the basic protection against confusion?

The problem with this additional layer of protection is that the creation of a brand image is a selfish endeavour. When a trademark triggers a whole bundle of lifestyle messages and positive associations, the trademark experience itself becomes an independent product for which consumers are willing to pay. Realizing the economic potential of the trademark, the brand owner will seek protection for the brand image as such.[19] Once sufficient protection is acquired, the marketing and commercialization of the brand can easily be extended to additional products. The owner of a prestigious clothing brand, for

---

[17] See WTO Panel, 15 March 2005, WTO Document WT/DS174/R, para. 7.664, based on a complaint by the US. A second and almost identical report, WTO Document WT/DS290/R, deals with a parallel complaint by Australia. The reports are online available at www.wto.org. For a discussion of the reports, see M.R.F. Senftleben (2006), 'Towards a Horizontal Standard for Limiting Intellectual Property Rights? – WTO Panel Reports Shed Light on the Three-Step Test in Copyright Law and Related Tests in Patent and Trademark Law', IIC, **37**, 407, online available at http://ssrn.com/abstract=1723871.

[18] With regard to the basis of this discussion in trademark law, see F.I. Schechter (1927), 'The Rational Basis of Trademark Protection', *Harvard Law Review*, **40**, 813. With regard to current problems, see Casparie-Kerdel, *supra* note 15; McCarthy, *supra* note 9; Senftleben, *supra* note 4; G. Bonet (2010), 'La protection de l'image de la marquee dans la jurisprudence de la Cour de Justice', in C. Geiger and J. Schmidt-Szalewski (eds), *Les défis du droit des marques au XXIe siècle*, Strasbourg: Litec, p. 105; G.B. Dinwoodie, M.D. Janis (2006), 'Dilution's (Still) Uncertain Future', *Michigan Law Review First Impressions*, **105**, 98.

[19] See the position taken by the US Supreme Court, *Moseley v V Secret Catalogue ('Victoria's Secret')*, 537 U.S. 418 (2003): '[u]nlike traditional infringement law, the prohibitions against trademark dilution are not the product of common-law development, and are not motivated by an interest in protecting consumers.'

instance, may consider also selling jewellery and perfume under the trademark or decide to grant licences for this purpose. Through product diversification of this type, the revenue accruing from the creation of a powerful brand can be maximized.[20]

As a result of these marketing strategies, trademark rights lose their defensive nature. Seeking enhanced protection against dilution, the brand owner asks for control over the use of the trademark across all markets and regardless of whether there is a likelihood of confusion. This brings anti-dilution rights close to exploitation rights. However, unlike other intellectual property owners enjoying exploitation rights, such as inventors and authors, the brand owner cannot validly claim to have created intellectual property that furthers science or art. The trademark does not even fall into the public domain after a limited period of time. By contrast, brand protection is protection of investments that are made to improve an enterprise's market position. It is not evident that this selfish investment decision also furthers the overall welfare of society.

Against this background, it is unclear why trademark law should offer brand exploitation rights.[21] Typical rationales underlying the grant of exploitation rights in intellectual property law, such as the incentive rationale and the reward rationale, are inapplicable in this context. It is not obvious that the extra incentive of brand exploitation rights is needed to spur investment in brand creation. In fact, there is little evidence of any need for brand image creation in society that would justify the invocation of this rationale and an extra incentive for brand image creators.[22] By contrast, it may be argued that

---

20 The result of these marketing efforts, however, is 'self-dilution'. As the trademark owner herself engages in the establishment of links with additional products, she could hardly care less about the immediate association of the mark with a specific product in the minds of consumers. Cf. S. Stadler Nelson (2003), 'The Wages of Ubiquity in Trademark Law', *Iowa Law Review,* **88**, 731.

21 For a detailed analysis of potential justifications, see W. Sakulin (2010), *Trademark Protection and Freedom of Expression – An Inquiry into the Conflict between Trademark Rights and Freedom of Expression under European Law*, The Hague, London and New York: Kluwer Law International, pp. 35–67, who also casts doubt upon the justificatory basis of protection against dilution. Proponents of brand image protection in the framework of trademark law particularly point to the effort and financial expenses made by the brand owner. For instance, see A. Breitschaft (2009), 'Intel, Adidas & Co – Is the Jurisprudence of the European Court of Justice on Dilution Law in Compliance with the Underlying Rationales and Fit for the Future?', *EIPR*, 497, 499. Considering the costs for society involved in the grant of brand image protection – in particular restrictions of freedom of expression and freedom of competition – this fact alone, however, can hardly be deemed sufficient for the grant of broad exclusive rights.

22 See D. Scott, A. Oliver and M. Ley-Pineda, 'Trade Marks as Property: a

seductive lifestyle messages conveyed by a trademark distract from a product's genuine qualities, thereby rendering consumers' buying decisions less objective and depriving the trader with the objectively best offer of corresponding market success.[23] Potential economic arguments, such as the facilitation of competition in mature markets and the enhancement of product popularity, are outweighed by social and cultural concerns about the privatization of words and phrases.[24]

The reward argument hardly offers stronger support.[25] Admittedly, it is the trademark owner who spent time and money on the creation of a particular brand image. Feelings of rightness and justice, therefore, suggest that the result of these efforts be due to her. Comparing brand image with other intellectual creations, however, it becomes doubtful whether the trademark owner deserves this reward. Whereas works and inventions contribute to mankind's treasury of cultural expression and technical knowledge once they fall into the public domain, a trademark carrying a particular brand image can be monopolized *ad infinitum* by the trademark owner by constantly renewing registration. As emphasized above, the investment in the creation of a brand image remains an individual, selfish marketing decision for which the trademark owner cannot necessarily expect a reward from society as a whole.[26]

Philosophical Perspective', in Bently, Davis and Ginsburg, *supra* note 3, pp. 285, 296–7, who consider product differentiation, facilitation of consumer choice and incentives to purchasing and, nevertheless, reject utilitarian arguments. Cf. M.A. Lemley (1999), 'The Modern Lanham Act and the Death of Common Sense', *Yale Law Journal* **108**, 1687, 1694–6); R.S. Brown (1999), 'Advertising and the Public Interest: Legal Protection of Trade Symbols', *Yale Law Journal,* **108**, 1619, 1622–34.

[23] See Brown, *ibid*, 1635–7, who points out that '[t]he classical economists who enthroned the consumer never dreamed that he would make his decisions under a bombardment of stupefying symbols.' However, see also the economic analysis conducted by R. van den Bergh and M. Lehmann (1992), 'Informationsökonomie und Verbraucherschutz im Wettbewerbs- und Warenzeichenrecht', *Gewerblicher Rechtsschutz und Urheberrecht International*, 588, 589–93).

[24] See Strasser, *supra* note 3, 389–90 and 412–14, on the one hand, and Lemley, *supra* note 22, 1694–8; R. Cooper Dreyfuss (1996), 'We Are Symbols and Inhabit Symbols, so should we be Paying Rent? Deconstructing the Lanham Act and Rights of Publicity', *Columbia-VLA Journal of Law & Arts,* **20**, 123, 128, on the other hand.

[25] For an analysis of Lockean justification models, see Scott, Oliver and Ley-Pineda, *supra* note 22, pp. 297–305; Sakulin, *supra* note 21, pp. 63–6.

[26] Cf. B. Beebe (2006), 'A Defense of the New Federal Trademark Antidilution Law', *Fordham Intellectual Property, Media & Entertainment Law Journal,* **16**, 1143, 1159, stating that a court 'should not grant antidilution protection to reward – i.e., to promote – spending on advertising, just as it should not grant such protection in recognition of something like the plaintiff's good faith in trying as hard as it can to make its mark famous.'

With classical rationales being unavailable in the case of brand exploitation rights, law and policy makers in the field of trademark law should be cautious with regard to the extension of trademark protection beyond the traditional field of protection against confusion. Not surprisingly, the legal framework set forth in the EU Trademark Directive includes several safeguards against inappropriately broad protection in this area. For EU Member States, the grant of enhanced protection against dilution is optional under Art. 5(2) TMD. If the provision is implemented into national law,[27] the brand owner still has to surmount several hurdles to obtain protection. Besides the obligation to satisfy the general protection requirements of use in the course of trade and use in relation to goods or services, the brand owner must show that her trademark has a reputation, and that a conflicting sign is used in a way that takes unfair advantage of, or is detrimental to, the distinctive character or the repute of the trademark. Moreover, Art. 5(2) TMD provides for a flexible defence of 'due cause' to counterbalance the grant of anti-dilution protection.

With these safeguards, the EU trademark system seems unlikely to succumb to the temptation of granting unjustified brand exploitation rights. The phalanx of infringement criteria clearly indicates that the mere use of a sign similar to a mark with a reputation is not intended to give rise to an infringement action based on dilution. Anti-dilution protection should not readily be awarded whenever a sign calling to mind a mark with a reputation is used in some area of the market. Otherwise, the brand owner would obtain an exclusive right that, *de facto*, can be equated with exploitation rights conferred in copyright and patent law. Instead, the conditions laid down in Art. 5(2) TMD call upon courts in the EU to embark on a careful case-by-case analysis to ascertain whether the individual circumstances of the case brought before them justify anti-dilution protection.[28]

3. EXCESSES

The CJEU, however, is reluctant to follow this cautious approach. Instead of seeking to give individual meaning to the various protection requirements, the Court seems determined to systematically lower the threshold for anti-dilution protection and cut up the safety net of infringement criteria that was tied to prevent overbroad brand image protection. Step by step, the Court has relaxed

---

[27] In fact, all EU Member States implemented Art. 5(2) TMD in their national trademark laws. On the basis of this provision, anti-dilution protection is thus available throughout the European Union.

[28] For a more detailed discussion of an approach avoiding an unjustified protection automatism in EU trademark law, see Senftleben, *supra* note 4, 59–64.

the applicable protection requirements in recent years.[29] As a result, anti-dilution rights in the EU come closer and closer to unjustified brand exploitation rights. Brand owners may soon be able to invoke anti-dilution protection to control any use of signs similar to a mark with a reputation in trade.

Under the aegis of the CJEU, the general protection requirements of use in the course of trade[30] and use in relation to goods or services do not constitute substantial hurdles for trademark owners seeking protection. In particular, the requirement of use in relation to goods or services is applied flexibly by the CJEU.[31] In principle, this general prerequisite for protection could be understood to require 'use as a trademark'. It may be applied to confine the scope of trademark rights to instances where another's trademark is employed as an identifier of commercial source with regard to one's own goods or services.[32] Following this approach, access to trademark protection could be contained from the outset.[33] The entrance requirement of trademark use would already serve as a filter to exclude claims that are unrelated to the identification and distinction of goods and services. Nonetheless, this notion of trademark use

---

29 In particular, see CJEU, 14 September 1999, case C-375/97, *General Motors v Yplon ('Chevy')*; 23 October 2003, case C-408/01, *Adidas/Fitnessworld*; 18 June 2009, case C-487/07, *L'Oréal/Bellure*.

30 Use of a trademark constitutes use in the course of trade in the EU where it occurs 'in the context of commercial activity with a view to economic advantage and not as a private matter.' See CJEU, 23 March 2010, cases C-236/08-238/08, *Google/Louis Vuitton et al.*, para. 50; CJEU, 12 November 2002, case C-206/01, *Arsenal/Reed*, para. 40.

31 For an overview of developments in this area, see A. Kur (2008), 'Confusion Over Use? Die Benutzung "als Marke" im Lichte der EuGH-Rechtsprechung', *Gewerblicher Rechtsschutz und Urheberrecht International,* 1, 11.

32 CJEU, 25 January 2007, case C-48/05, *Opel/Autec*, para. 24, pointed in this direction. The course adopted in this judgment, however, was not followed in further decisions. Cf. P.J. Yap (2009), 'Essential Function of a Trade Mark: From BMW to O2', *EIPR*, 81, 86–7.

33 With regard to similar proposals in the US, see S.L. Dogan and M.A. Lemley (2008), 'The Trademark Use Requirement in Dilution Cases', *Santa Clara Computer & High Technology Law Journal,* **24**, 541, 542: 'By maintaining the law's focus on misleading branding, the trademark use doctrine keeps trademark law true to its ultimate goal of promoting competitive markets.' However, see also G.B. Dinwoodie and M.D. Janis (2007), 'Confusion Over Use: Contextualism in Trademark Law', *Iowa Law Review,* **92**, 1597, 1657–8, doubting that problems arising in the current 'expansionist climate' could be solved by recalibrating the notion of trademark use: 'Trademark use is simply too blunt a concept, no matter how defined, to capture the full range of values at play in these debates.' For a summary of the debate, see M. Davison and F. Di Giantomasso (2009), 'Use as a Trade Mark: Avoiding Confusion When Considering Dilution', *EIPR*, 443. With regard to the EU, see Kur, *supra* note 31, who warns of limiting trademark protection from the outset on the basis of a restrictive notion of trademark use, in particular with regard to Community trademarks.

would cover instances of dilution where harm to a mark with a reputation flows from a conflicting sign used by a third party as a source identifier. In the 1975 landmark *Claeryn/Klarein* decision of the Benelux Court of Justice – an important source for the later harmonized EU anti-dilution regime – use of the sign KLAREIN as a source identifier for a cleaning detergent gave rise to an infringement action based on dilution because it was similar to the well-known gin trademark CLAERYN and encroached upon that trademark's 'potential for raising a desire to buy'.[34]

Instead of sharpening the conceptual contours of trademark use in this way, the CJEU has constantly weakened this general protection requirement. The Court found use for the purpose of informing the public about repair and maintenance services offered with regard to trademarked products to constitute relevant trademark use.[35] The CJEU also qualified use in comparative advertising as trademark use on the grounds that the advertiser made use of a competitor's trademark to distinguish her own products from those of the competitor.[36] Summarizing the notion of trademark use, the Court held that for satisfying the requirement of trademark use, it was sufficient that a link was established with the trademark.[37] As a result, the basic requirement of trademark use does not prevent trademark owners from asserting their rights against references to the trademark even though the public does not perceive these references as an indication of commercial source. By contrast, referential use is brought within the reach of the exclusive rights of trademark owners.

---

[34] See Benelux Court of Justice, 1 March 1975, case A74/1, *Claeryn/Klarein*, published in Nederlandse Jurisprudentie 1975, 472; Ars Aequi 1977, 664; Bijblad bij de Industriële Eigendom 1975, 183. Cf. Casparie-Kerdel, *supra* note 15, 189–90. See also Opinion of Advocate General Jacobs, 10 July 2003, concerning CJEU, case C-408/01, *Adidas/Fitnessworld*, para. 38, stating that 'the concept of detriment to the repute of a trade mark [...] describes the situation where – as it was put in the well-known Claeryn/Klarein decision of the Benelux Court of Justice – the goods for which the infringing sign is used appeal to the public's senses in such a way that the trade mark's power of attraction is affected.'

[35] See CJEU, 23 February 1999, case C-63/97, *BMW/Deenik*, para. 42. For an overview of the development of the trademark use requirement in CJEU jurisprudence, see Kur, *supra* note 31.

[36] See CJEU, 12 June 2008, case C-533/06, *O2/Hutchison*, paras 35–6. As to keyword advertising on the basis of services offered by a search engine, use of a competitor's trademark as a keyword for a sponsored link with one's own advertising has been found to constitute trademark use on similar grounds. See CJEU, 23 March 2010, cases C-236/08-238/08, *Google/Louis Vuitton et al.*, para. 71.

[37] See CJEU, 19 February 2009, case C-62/08, *UDV/Brandtraders*, para. 47. The emphasis on the criterion of a mere link with the goods or services offered under a conflicting sign was particularly confirmed in cases dealing with keyword advertising. See CJEU, 23 March 2010, cases C-236/08-238/08, *Google/Louis Vuitton et al.*, para. 72; 12 July 2011, case C-324/09, *L'Oréal/eBay*, para. 92.

In the case of marks with a reputation, even decorative use that merely calls to mind the protected trademark may be held to constitute relevant trademark use on the basis of CJEU jurisprudence. The case 'Lila Postkarte' of the German Federal Court of Justice, for instance, concerned the marketing of postcards that alluded ironically to trademarks and advertising campaigns of the chocolate producer Milka. On purple background corresponding to Milka's abstract colour mark, the postcard sought to ridicule the nature idyll with cows and mountains that is evoked in Milka advertising. It showed the following poem attributed to 'Rainer Maria Milka':

> Über allen Wipfeln ist Ruh,
> irgendwo blökt eine Kuh.
> Muh![38]

Assessing this ironic play with Milka insignia, the German Federal Court of Justice confirmed the broad notion of trademark use following from the jurisprudence of the CJEU.[39] It held that for the use of Milka trademarks to constitute trademark use in the sense of Art. 5(2) TMD, it was sufficient that the postcard called to mind the well-known Milka signs.[40] In spite of being decorative, the use in question therefore gave rise to the question of trademark infringement. Accordingly, the German Federal Court of Justice embarked on a scrutiny of the trademark parody in the light of the infringement criteria of detriment to distinctive character or repute, and the taking of unfair advantage. Weighing Milka's concerns about a disparagement of the trademarks against the fundamental guarantee of the freedom of art, the Court finally concluded that the freedom of art had to prevail in light of the ironic statement made with the postcard.[41] The use of Milka trademarks was found to have taken place with 'due cause' in the sense of Art. 5(2) TMD.[42]

---

[38] 'It is calm above the tree tops, somewhere a cow is bellowing. Moo!' The attribution to 'Rainer Maria Milka' is an allusion to the famous German writer Rainer Maria Rilke. See German Federal Court of Justice, 3 February 2005, case I ZR 159/02, *Gewerblicher Rechtsschutz und Urheberrecht* 2005, 583, *Lila Postkarte*, online available at www.bundesgerichtshof.de. Cf. C. Born (2006), 'Zur Zulässigkeit einer humorvollen Markenparodie – Anmerkungen zum Urteil des BGH "Lila Postkarte"', *Gewerblicher Rechtsschutz und Urheberrecht*, 192.

[39] See the reference to CJEU, 23 October 2003, case C-408/01, *Adidas/Fitnessworld*, para. 39, in the decision *Lila Postkarte* of the German Federal Court of Justice, *supra* note 38, 584. With regard to the qualification of decorative use as relevant trademark use, see also Kur, *supra* note 31, 5–6.

[40] See German Federal Court of Justice, *supra* note 38, 584.

[41] See German Federal Court of Justice, *supra* note 38, 584–5. For a further case in which freedom of speech prevailed over trademark protection, see German Federal Court of Justice, 11 March 2008, case VI ZR 7/07, *Neue Juristische Wochenschrift* 2008, 2110, *Gen-Milch*, online available at www.bundesgerichtshof.de.

[42] German Federal Court of Justice, *supra* note 38, 585.

Examples of this kind show that, with jurisprudence encouraging the inclusion of referential and decorative use in an elastic concept of trademark use, the CJEU has opened the doors wide to trademark protection.[43] Trademark rights become generally available when a protected sign is used in the context of presenting or discussing goods or services. This general control over communication involving a trademark paves the way for the extension of trademark rights to exploitation rights comparable to those conferred in copyright and patent law. The mere use of a trademark in some relation to goods or services is sufficient to lodge an infringement claim.[44] In the Milka case, for instance, the infringement action could not be stopped at an early stage by holding that the use did not constitute actionable trademark use. Instead, the parodist had to invoke the defence of due cause and argue the case in several instances until the German Federal Court of Justice took a final decision.

Admittedly, the CJEU need not necessarily employ the basic requirement of use in relation to goods or services as a means to draw clear boundary lines of trademark protection in the EU. The general requirement of trademark use is followed by several more specific conditions. As indicated above, a brand owner seeking protection under Art. 5(2) TMD must also show that her trademark has a reputation. This further protection requirement only applies in the specific context of anti-dilution protection. Therefore, it could be embraced by the CJEU as a tool to regulate access to this problematic enhanced layer of protection. With a nuanced concept of reputation, the Court could ensure that anti-dilution protection is awarded only if a trademark has a brand image that is likely to be harmed or unfairly exploited because of its particular value and attractiveness. The requirement of 'having a reputation' could become an important eligibility criterion in the case of brand owners seeking protection against dilution.

---

43 The requirement of trademark use is even less relevant in EU Member States that, in line with Art. 5(5) TMD extend trademark protection to forms of use 'other than for the purposes of distinguishing goods or services'. In these Member States, not only the requirement of 'use in the course of trade' but also the requirement of 'use in relation to goods or services' does not apply in this area of extended protection. See Art. 2.20(1)(d) of the Benelux Treaty Concerning Intellectual Property. Cf. T. Cohen Jehoram, C.J.J.C. van Nispen and J.L.R.A. Huydecoper (2008), *Industriële eigendom – Deel 2: Merkenrecht*, Deventer: Kluwer, 366–7; C. Gielen (2007), 'Merkenrecht', in C. Gielen (ed.), *Kort begrip van het intellectuele eigendomsrecht*, Deventer: Kluwer, pp. 256 and 286–7.

44 This risk of creating an automatism of property claims ('Eigentumslogik') is also pointed out by proponents of an elastic notion of trademark use. See Kur, *supra* note 31, 12. For similar concerns expressed against the background of developments in the US, see S.L. Dogan and M.A. Lemley (2008), 'Grounding Trademark Law Through Trademark Use', *Trademark Reporter*, **98**, 1345.

Instead of establishing an appropriate test that regulates eligibility for anti-dilution protection, the threshold for assuming that a trademark has the necessary reputation is remarkably low in the EU. In *Chevy*, the Court explained that 'the market share held by the trade mark' and 'the size of the investment made by the undertaking in promoting it' had to be taken into account in this context.[45] However, the Court also explained that:

> [t]he public amongst which the earlier trade mark must have acquired a reputation is that concerned by that trade mark, that is to say, depending on the product or service marketed, either the public at large or a more specialized public, for example traders in a specific sector.[46]

Moreover, the Court clarified that:

> [t]he degree of knowledge required must be considered to be reached when the earlier mark is known by a significant part of the public concerned by the products or services covered by that trade mark.[47]

This clarification shows that the Court considers knowledge among the individual target group of the product concerned sufficient, even though this target group may be a specialized public in the case of specific products or services. The Court favours a niche reputation approach. Further findings in *Chevy* confirm this conclusion. In respect of the necessary territorial expansion of the mark's reputation, the Court held the view that:

> [i]n the absence of any definition [in Art. 5(2) TMD] in this respect, a trade mark cannot be required to have a reputation 'throughout' the territory of the Member State. It is sufficient for it to exist in a substantial part of it.[48]

Hence, the CJEU follows a niche reputation approach focusing on knowledge among a significant part of a potentially specialized public in a substantial part of an EU Member State. Introducing this low standard, the Court is far from exerting efficient access control on the basis of the reputation requirement. Instead of actively regulating access to enhanced protection against dilution, the door to anti-dilution rights is kept wide open.[49] Not only the general

---

[45] See CJEU, 14 September 1999, case C-375/97, *General Motors v Yplon ('Chevy')*, para. 27.

[46] CJEU, *ibid*, para. 24.

[47] CJEU, *ibid*, para. 26.

[48] CJEU, *ibid*, para. 28. In respect of the territorial expansion required in the case of Community trademarks, see CJEU, 6 October 2009, case C-301/07, *Pago/Tirolmilch*, paras 29–30.

[49] Cf. the critique by F. Pollaud-Dulian (2001), 'Marques de renommée: Histoire de la dénaturation d'un concept', *Propriétés intellectuelles*, 43.

requirement of trademark use but also the specific eligibility criterion of 'having a reputation' is virtually eroded instead of being employed to keep trademark protection within reasonable limits.

The erosion of a further prerequisite for protection seems inevitable in the context of anti-dilution protection. As pointed out above, traditional protection against confusion requires some likelihood of confusion. Protection against dilution, however, is not primarily concerned with the prevention of confusing use. It aims at preserving the particular distinctive character and the repute of marks with a reputation. A trademark's particular distinctive character or repute, however, may be harmed or unfairly exploited without causing a risk of confusion. The mere allusion to the mark with a reputation can be sufficient. Accordingly, the CJEU adopted an elastic association test in *Adidas/ Fitnessworld*. In line with this ruling, enhanced protection against dilution becomes available when a competing sign calls to mind a mark with a reputation.[50]

After this erosion of safeguards against overbroad brand image protection, the seemingly robust edifice of EU infringement criteria is about to crumble. To obtain protection against dilution, however, the brand owner still must provide evidence that the conflicting use takes unfair advantage of, or is detrimental to, the distinctive character or the repute of the mark with a reputation. This remaining condition constitutes the last bastion against overbroad brand image exploitation rights. Against this background, the decision *Intel/CPM* gave hope that the CJEU would defend at least this remaining barrier. With regard to proof of detriment to the distinctive character of a mark with a reputation, the Court required:

> evidence of a change in the economic behaviour of the average consumer of the goods or services for which the earlier mark was registered consequent on the use of the later mark, or a serious likelihood that such a change will occur in the future.[51]

From a practical perspective, one may wonder how the required 'evidence of a change in the economic behaviour of the average consumer' can ever be produced.[52] Considering the need to balance protection, however, it is consistent

50 See CJEU, 23 October, 2003, case C-408/01, *Adidas/Fitnessworld*, para. 29.

51 See CJEU, 27 November 2008, case C-252/07, *Intel/CPM*, para. 77.

52 Cf. A. Bouvel, 'Marques et renommée: À propos de l'arrêt "Intel" rendu par la Cour de justice des communautés européennes le 27 novembre 2008 (aff. C-252/07)', in Geiger and Schmidt-Szalewski, *supra* note 18, p. 123; A.A. Quaedvlieg (2009), 'INTEL en verwatering: Economisch gedrag en juridisch bewijs', *Bijblad bij de industriële eigendom.*, 253; A.A. Quaedvlieg (2009), 'Herkomst- en goodwill-inbreuk in het merkenrecht na INTEL en l'Oréal', *Ars Aequi*, 799; S. Middlemiss and S. Warner (2009), 'The Protection of Marks with a Reputation: Intel v CPM', *EIPR*, 326, 331–2.

to pose a difficult hurdle. With the general requirement of trademark use and the specific eligibility criterion of having a reputation being rendered meaningless, it is justified to set a high threshold when it comes to the final question of taking unfair advantage or causing detriment.

The *Intel/CPM* decision, however, was followed by the *L'Oréal/Bellure* judgment in which the CJEU lowered this final threshold substantially. Dealing with comparison lists concerning cheap imitations of well-known L'Oréal perfumes, the Court stated that a mere attempt to ride on the coat-tails of a mark with a reputation could be sufficient to assume that unfair advantage had been taken. It explained that

> where a third party attempts, through the use of a sign similar to a mark with a reputation, to ride on the coat-tails of that mark in order to benefit from its power of attraction, its reputation and its prestige, and to exploit, without paying any financial compensation and without being required to make efforts of his own in that regard, the marketing effort expended by the proprietor of that mark in order to create and maintain the image of that mark, the advantage resulting from such use must be considered to be an advantage that has been unfairly taken of the distinctive character or the repute of that mark.[53]

The fundamental change with regard to the availability of anti-dilution protection becomes apparent the moment the relationship between the different final infringement criteria is considered. The three modes of infringement – detriment to distinctive character (blurring), detriment to repute (tarnishment), unfair advantage from distinctive character or repute (free-riding) – constitute alternative conditions in accordance with Art. 5(2) TMD. By setting a low standard for the taking of unfair advantage, the Court thus creates a loophole that can be used when a showing of detriment is impossible. The brand owner who does not succeed in providing 'evidence of a change in the economic behaviour of the average consumer' can insist on the taking of unfair advantage instead. For this alternative basis of her claim, she merely has to argue that the defendant attempts (!) to ride on the coat-tails of the mark with a reputation.

With the creation of the coat-tail formula in *L'Oréal/Bellure*, the CJEU, therefore, abandoned the remaining bastion of final infringement criteria. Under Art. 5(2) TMD, brand owners seeking anti-dilution protection can benefit from an elastic entrance requirement of trademark use, encompassing referential and decorative use, a remarkably low eligibility criterion of having a reputation, an elastic association test of calling to mind the mark with a reputation and, finally, a flexible unfair advantage criterion that is already fulfilled

---

[53] See CJEU, 18 June 2009, case C-487/07, *L'Oréal/Bellure*, para. 49.

the moment a third party attempts to ride on the coat-tails of the mark with a reputation. Surveying these broad, elastic, and flexible conditions for protection against dilution, one can hardly deny that anti-dilution protection under Art. 5(2) TMD requires little more than showing that a conflicting sign in some area of the market triggers an association with a mark with a reputation.[54] The CJEU, therefore, has brought anti-dilution rights very close to the exploitation rights offered in copyright and patent law.

In *L'Oréal/Bellure*, however, the Court did not content itself with this remarkable step in respect of Art. 5(2) TMD. It also transformed Art. 5(1)(a) TMD into a powerful instrument for brand image protection. The provision regulates protection in cases of double identity – a sign identical to the protected trademark used for identical goods or services. In this regard, the CJEU held that, besides the essential origin function, a trademark's quality, communication, investment, and advertising functions enjoy *absolute* protection under Art. 5(1)(a) TMD.[55] These functions, however, are typically fulfilled by marks with a reputation. As elaborated above, a strong brand is capable of conveying lifestyle messages that are the result of substantial investment in advertising. Protection of a trademark's communication, investment, and advertising functions is thus protection of the investment in the creation of a favourable brand image and the brand communication based on this image.

In line with Recital 11 of the EU Trademark Directive, the CJEU assumes that the protection of these additional trademark functions under Art. 5(1)(a) TMD must be absolute. Indeed, the Recital stipulates that:

> [t]he protection afforded by the registered trade mark, the function of which is in particular to guarantee the trade mark as an indication of origin, should be absolute in the case of identity between the mark and the sign and the goods or services.

---

54 However, see also the practical considerations by C. Morcom (2009), 'L'Oréal v Bellure – Who Has Won?', *EIPR*, 627, 634–5: 'The law reports include many cases which demonstrate that whatever the ECJ may rule, it may be dangerous to assume that a mark is so well-known that little evidence is needed in claims invoking art. 5(2) of the Trade Marks Directive and corresponding provisions elsewhere. Perhaps Intel provides an example.' Nonetheless, the crucial point here is that the CJEU lowered the conditions for a showing of infringement under Art. 5(2) TMD substantially by providing the coat-tail formula as a vehicle to bypass the higher infringement standard developed in *Intel*. The practical difficulties with regard to sufficient evidence, therefore, have been reduced significantly.

55 CJEU, *supra* note 53, para. 58. Cf. F. Hacker (2009), 'Funktionenlehre und Benutzungsbegriff nach 'L'Oréal', *Markenrecht*, 333.

However, this Recital must be seen in the context of the Directive's particular structure. The drafters intended protection against confusion under Art. 5(1) TMD to be mandatory, whereas protection against dilution under Art. 5(2) TMD remained optional. The statement about absolute protection in double identity cases falling under Art. 5(1)(a) TMD, therefore, only concerns mandatory protection against confusion. Including typical functions of marks with a reputation in this system of absolute protection, the Court crossed this boundary line drawn in the Directive. As protection of marks with a reputation is optional under Art. 5(2) TMD, the protection of specific functions of these trademarks also remains optional. The protection of the specific functions of marks with a reputation under the mandatory Art. 5(1)(a) TMD encroaches upon the freedom left to EU Member States.

The *contra legem* inclusion of communication, investment, and advertising functions in Art. 5(1)(a) TMD is a further step in the transformation of trademark rights into brand exploitation instruments. According to the Court, absolute protection under Art. 5(1)(a) TMD merely requires that one of the protected functions of a trademark is 'adversely' affected by the use of an identical sign for identical goods or services.[56] It remains to be seen how the Court further develops this criterion of adverse effect.[57] Considering the continuous relaxation of infringement criteria in the field of Art. 5(2) TMD, it cannot be excluded that the threshold for a showing of adverse effect is fairly low.[58]

---

56 With regard to the requirement of adverse effect, see the explications given in CJEU, 23 March 2010, cases C-236/08-238/08, *Google France and Google/Louis Vuitton et al.*, paras. 75–9.

57 It is doubtful whether the breathing space created in this way is sufficient to satisfy freedom of speech concerns. See A. Ohly (2009), 'Keyword-Advertising auf dem Weg von Karlsruhe nach Luxemburg', *Gewerblicher Rechtsschutz und Urheberrecht*, 709, 711–12; A. Kur, L. Bently and A. Ohly, 'Sweet Smells and a Sour Taste – the ECJ's L'Oréal Decision', Max Planck Institute for Intellectual Property and Competition Law Research Paper Series No. 09-12, online available at http://ssrn.com/abstract=1492032.

58 However, in CJEU, 22 September 2011, case C-323/09, *Interflora/Marks & Spencer*, the Court pointed out that the advertising function would not be adversely affected simply because the trademark owner, as a result of keyword advertising, would have to intensify its own advertising to maintain or enhance its profile with consumers (para. 57). Similarly, the Court held that the investment function would not be adversely affected by keyword advertising simply because the trademark owner was obliged to adapt its efforts to acquire or preserve a reputation capable of attracting consumers and retaining their loyalty (para. 64). These statements may be seen as an indication that the Court, in any case, is prepared to preserve some freedom of competition in the area of advertising.

An elastic test of adverse effect, however, would be even more problematic than a low threshold for anti-dilution protection under Art. 5(2) TMD. As indicated above, a flexible defence of 'due cause' is available under Art. 5(2) TMD to safeguard comparative advertising and parody. A similar balancing tool is sought in vain in Art. 5(1)(a) TMD.[59] Comparative advertising and parody almost inevitably interfere with brand communication, investment, and advertising. A biting parody impacts deeply on the way in which consumers perceive the target trademark. It is likely to have a corrosive effect on a favourable trademark image that is the result of substantial investment in advertising and product control.[60] Harm to the investment and advertising function of a trademark can also flow from comparative advertising that sheds new light on a trademark by informing consumers about better offers in the marketplace. As the product comparison interferes with the trademark communication initiated by the owner, affects prior investment in a favourable trademark image, and reduces the trademark's advertising power, it is difficult to see how advertisers could escape a finding of adverse effect under Art. 5(1)(a) TMD. The verdict of infringement seems unavoidable.[61]

---

59 See the critique by A. Ohly (2010), 'Keyword Advertising auf dem Weg zurück von Luxemburg nach Paris, Wien, Karlsruhe und Den Haag', *Gewerblicher Rechtsschutz und Urheberrecht*, 776, 780 and 782; Hacker, *supra* note 55, 337. Cf. also Max Planck Institute for Intellectual Property and Competition Law (2011), *Study on the Overall Functioning of the European Trade Mark System*, Munich: Max Planck Institute, online available at http://ec.europa.eu/internal_market/indprop/tm/index_en.htm, para. 2.260, stating that the present state of law is unsatisfactory because of absolute protection 'in the sense that it does not depend on any balancing of interests, apart from a functional analysis.'

60 T-shirts or cartoons parodying the trademarked Mickey Mouse drawing can serve as an example of a parody falling under Art. 5(1)(a) TMD. See the international Madrid registration no. 296478 of Mickey Mouse relating, among various other products, to printed matter (class 16) and clothing (class 25). The particulars of the registration can be consulted online at <http://www.wipo.int/ipdl/en/madrid/search-struct.jsp>. In the copyright fair use case *Campbell v Acuff Rose*, the US Supreme Court solved the problem by stating that 'when a lethal parody, like a scathing theater review, kills demand for the original, it does not produce a harm cognizable under the Copyright Act.' See *Campbell v Acuff-Rose*, 510 U.S. 569 (1994), II D. A similar denial of 'adverse effect' by the CJEU would be necessary to safeguard parody under Art. 5(1)(a) TMD.

61 However, the indications given by the Court in *Interflora/Marks & Spencer*, as explained *supra* note 58, must be considered in this context. Nonetheless, the mere presumption of confusion in double identity cases would offer more flexibility. In cases of comparative advertising meeting the requirements stated in the EC Comparative Advertisement Directive, it could be concluded that the presumption has been rebutted.

In *L'Oréal/Bellure*, the CJEU solved this dilemma by invoking the rules of the EC Comparative Advertisement Directive.[62] Using the criteria for permissible comparative advertising as an external balancing tool, the Court arrived at the conclusion that a case of infringement would only arise where a trademark was used for the purpose of comparative advertising without all the requirements stated in the Comparative Advertisement Directive being satisfied.[63] To add flexibility to its overbroad system of trademark function protection under Art. 5(1)(a) TMD, the Court thus had to resort to the rules on comparative advertising outside the Trademark Directive. Whether the Court will make similar efforts for parodists remains to be seen. In any case, the developments in the area of Art. 5(1)(a) TMD confirm the Court's intention to give brand owners rather general control over any communication involving their marks with a reputation. Besides flexible anti-dilution protection under Art. 5(2) TMD, they can rely on protection under Art. 5(1)(a) TMD that only requires a showing of adverse effect on brand communication, investment, and advertising.

4. NEW TECHNOLOGIES

After this excessive broadening of brand protection, it is an open question how the CJEU will adapt trademark law to new technologies. The Internet, bringing along the challenge of keyword advertising, may have a mitigating effect on the further development of trademark protection in the EU. In particular, it allows the CJEU to reconsider the balance between trademark protection and fundamental freedoms, such as freedom of expression and freedom of competition.[64] It is obvious that the extension of trademark rights in recent years

---

[62] The Court dealt with the Misleading Advertisement Directive 84/450 of 10 September 1984, as amended by the Comparative Advertisement Directive 97/55 of 6 October 1997. These two Directives are now consolidated in the Misleading and Comparative Advertisement Directive 2006/114/EC of 12 December 2006.

[63] See CJEU, 18 June 2009, case C-487/07, *L'Oréal/Bellure*, paras 54 and 65.

[64] With regard to the mitigating effect of fundamental rights on intellectual property protection regimes, see C. Geiger (2008), 'The Constitutional Dimension of Intellectual Property', in L.C. Torremans (ed.), *Intellectual Property and Human Rights*, The Hague, London and New York: Kluwer Law International, p. 101; L.R. Helfer (2007), 'Toward a Human Rights Framework for Intellectual Property', *University of California, Davis Law Review*, **40**, 971, online available at http://ssrn.com/abstract=891303; T. Mylly (2005), 'Intellectual Property and Fundamental Rights: Do They Interoperate?', in N. Bruun (ed.), *Intellectual Property Beyond Rights*, Helsinki: WSOY, p. 185; C. Geiger (2004), 'Fundamental Rights, a Safeguard for the Coherence of Intellectual Property?', *IIC*, **35**, 268.

endangers artistic and commercial freedom of expression and information.[65] As explained above, the Court included referential and decorative trademark use in its flexible concept of trademark use. As a result, trademark rights can be asserted against mere references to a protected sign even though these references are not perceived as an indication of commercial origin by the public. With this approach, references to trademarks in comparative advertising and parody have become actionable under EU trademark law. Given the elastic infringement tests applied by the Court in the context of Art. 5(2) and 5(1)(a) TMD, they may easily amount to infringement. Under these circumstances, sufficient breathing space for freedom of speech and freedom of competition depends on appropriate defences that are scarce at least in the case of Art. 5(1)(a) TMD.

The Advocates General (AG) in keyword advertising cases openly address this dilemma in opinions concerning trademark use in the digital environment. The need to strike a proper balance between trademark protection and freedom of expression and competition has become a recurring theme. In his opinion in *Google France*, AG Poiares Maduro underlined the importance of appropriate counterbalances in the light of broad brand protection:

> Nevertheless, whatever the protection afforded to innovation and investment, it is never absolute. It must always be balanced against other interests, in the same way as trade mark protection itself is balanced against them. I believe that the present cases call for such a balance as regards freedom of expression and freedom of commerce.[66]

Similarly, AG Jääskinen urged the Court in his opinion in *L'Oréal/eBay* not to forget:

> that the listings uploaded by users to eBay's marketplace are communications protected by the fundamental rights of freedom of expression and information provided by Article 11 of [the] Charter of Fundamental Rights of the EU and Article 10 of the European Convention on Human Rights.[67]

---

65 With regard to the digital environment, cf. Dogan and Lemley, *supra* note 40, 1372–3. See also R. Tushnet (2008), 'Gone in Sixty Milliseconds: Trademark Law and Cognitive Science', *Texas Law Review*, **86**, 507, pointing out that even a minimalist anti-dilution statute is likely to impact deeply on freedom of speech.

66 See AG Poiares Maduro, opinion of 22 September 2009, cases C-236/08-238/08, *Google France and Google/Louis Vuitton et al.*, para. 102.

67 See AG N. Jääskinen, opinion of 9 December 2010, case C-324/09, *L'Oréal/eBay*, para. 49. For an overview of decisions concerning keyword advertising by online auction providers, see A.S.Y. Cheung and K.K.H. Pun (2009), 'Comparative Study on the Liability for Trade Mark Infringement of Online Auction Providers', *EIPR*, 559.

In his further opinion in *Interflora/Marks & Spencer*, Jääskinen again invited the Court to recalibrate the EU brand protection system in light of the need to reconcile trademark protection with competing fundamental rights. The case concerned an infringement action brought by Interflora on the grounds that Marks & Spencer bought the well-known Interflora trademark and several variants thereof as keywords for the advertising of its competing flower delivery service via the Google AdWords system. Addressing the coat-tail formula developed in *L'Oréal/Bellure* with regard to Art. 5(2) TMD, Jääskinen wondered why the Court did not make the existence of unfair advantage dependent on the conflicting use being detrimental to the trademark proprietor. In *L'Oréal/Bellure*, the CJEU had awarded protection against the taking of unfair advantage even though the trademark owner had failed to demonstrate the existence of any harm, such as an impairment of sales or a loss of reward for the promotion and maintenance of the trademark.[68] With regard to freedom of competition, Jääskinen warns against this background of:

> a move away from a Pareto optimal situation. The situation of the trade mark proprietor would not improve as he by definition would not suffer any detriment because of the use, but the competitor's situation would worsen because he would lose a part of his business. Also the situation of the consumers who had not been misled by the ad but consciously preferred to buy the competitor's products would be impaired.[69]

Seeking to safeguard Marks & Spencer's endeavours to present a commercial alternative to Interflora flower delivery services, Jääskinen proposes not to condemn the advertising simply because Marks & Spencer is taking advantage of the repute of Interflora's trademark, but to focus on the fairness of that use instead. In Jääskinen's view, the purpose of presenting a commercial alternative to the goods or services protected by a mark with a reputation should count as due cause in the context of modern marketing relying on keyword advertising on the Internet. Otherwise, keyword advertising using a third party's mark with a reputation would readily amount to prohibited free-riding. Such a conclusion, however, could not be justified in view of the need to promote undistorted competition and the possibilities of consumers seeking information about goods and services.[70]

Although Marks & Spencer neither compares its goods and services with those of Interflora, nor presents its goods as imitations or copies, or even

---

68 See CJEU, 18 June 2009, case C-487/07, *L'Oréal/Bellure*, paras 30 and 43.

69 See AG N. Jääskinen, opinion of 24 March 2011, case C-323/09, *Interflora/Marks & Spencer*, para. 94.

70 See Jääskinen, *ibid*, para. 99. The need to further develop the condition of unfairness under Art. 5(2) TMD has also been pointed out by Kur, *supra* note 31, 6 and 10.

expressly presents them as alternatives, the importance attached to freedom of competition and freedom of information prompts Jääskinen to conclude that the mere choice of Interflora keywords in search engine advertising implies a marketing message that Marks & Spencer offer an alternative service. Given this implied message, the keyword advertising, according to Jääskinen, does not constitute free-riding in the sense of the coat-tail formula developed by the Court in *L'Oréal/Bellure*.[71] Virtually, the Advocate General, therefore, calls upon the Court to drop the infringement automatism created in *L'Oréal/Bellure* and apply a strict test of unfairness instead. This proposal could pave the way for a more balanced approach to Art. 5(2) TMD after the continuous relaxation of infringement requirements in recent years.

In its judgment in *Interflora/Marks & Spencer*, the CJEU did not follow this proposal to reconsider the elastic test of unfairness. Instead, the Court confirmed the broad coat-tail formula developed in *L'Oréal/Bellure*. In the view of the Court, an advertiser deriving benefits from a trademark with a reputation by selecting that trademark as a keyword for its own advertising, in principle, takes unfair advantage of the trademark with a reputation.[72] The Court added, however, that:

> where the advertisement displayed on the internet on the basis of a keyword corresponding to a trade mark with a reputation puts forward – without offering a mere imitation of the goods or services of the proprietor of that trade mark, without causing dilution or tarnishment and without, moreover, adversely affecting the functions of the trade mark concerned – an alternative to the goods or services of the proprietor of the trade mark with a reputation, it must be concluded that such use falls, as a rule, within the ambit of fair competition in the sector for the goods or services concerned and is thus not without 'due cause' for the purposes of Article 5(2).[73]

Instead of relaxing infringement criteria, the Court thus introduces a 'due cause' defence covering the use of trademarks for the purpose of informing Internet users of alternatives in the marketplace. In previous decisions, the Court has already shown its willingness to offer breathing space for keyword advertising services.[74] In *Google France and Google*, the CJEU held that the

---

71 See Jääskinen, *supra* note 70, paras 104–5.

72 See CJEU, 22 September 2011, case C-323/09, *Interflora/Marks & Spencer*, paras 86–9.

73 CJEU, *ibid*, para. 91.

74 With regard to the development of jurisprudence concerning keyword advertising in the EU, cf. Ohly, *supra* note 59; M.R.F. Senftleben (2010), 'Keyword advertising – Geldend Europees recht en daaruit volgende systematiek', *Bulletin industriële eigendom*, 346; J. Cornthwaite (2009), 'AdWords or Bad Words? A UK Perspective on Keywords and Trade Mark Infringement', *EIPR*, 347; R. Knaak (2009), 'Keyword Advertising – Das aktuelle Key-Thema des Europäischen Markenrechts',

search engine offering a keyword advertising service – in this case Google with its AdWords service – did not use affected trademarks in the sense of trademark law. It could not be inferred from the fact of creating the technical conditions necessary for the use of a trademark as a keyword, and receiving a payment for that keyword advertising service, that the search engine itself used the sign.[75] The Court confirmed this approach in *L'Oréal/eBay* by stating that the use of trademarks in offers for sale on the eBay platform did not amount to use of those trademarks by eBay itself. Instead, the use was made by eBay's customers placing the respective offers on the website.[76] Given the flexible approach to trademark use in recent years, these rulings come as a welcome surprise.[77] They place keyword advertising services offered by search engines beyond the direct control of trademark owners. Search engines may be held liable, however, for infringing advertising made by the users of the service, if they do not meet the requirements of the exemption for hosting in Art. 14 of the EU E-Commerce Directive.[78]

Gewerblicher Rechtsschutz und Urheberrecht International, 551; C. Well-Szönyi (2009), 'Adwords: Die Kontroverse um die Zulässigkeit der Verwendung fremder Marken als Schlüsselwort in der französischen Rechtsprechung', *Gewerblicher Rechtsschutz und Urheberrecht International*, 557; G. Engels (2009), 'Keyword Advertising – Zwischen beschreibender, unsichtbarer und missbräuchlicher Verwendung', *Markenrecht*, 289; M. Schubert and S. Ott (2009), 'AdWords – Schutz für die Werbefunktion einer Marke?', *Markenrecht*, 338; O. Sosnitza (2009), 'Adwords = Metatags? Zur marken- und wettbewerbsrechtlichen Zulässigkeit des Keyword Advertising über Suchmaschinen', *Markenrecht*, 35; Ch. Gielen (2008), 'Van adwords en metatags', in N.A.N.M. van Eijk et al. (eds.), *Dommering-bundel*, Amsterdam: Cramwinckel, p. 101; O. van Daalen and A. Groen (2006), 'Beïnvloeding van zoekresultaten en gesponsorde koppelingen. De juridische kwalificatie van onzichtbaar merkgebruik', *BMM Bulletin*, 106.

75 See CJEU, 23 March 2010, cases C-236/08-238/08, *Google France and Google/Louis Vuitton et al.*, para. 57.

76 See CJEU, 12 July 2011, case C-324/09, *L'Oréal/eBay*, paras 101–5.

77 With regard to opposite developments in the US and a critique of these developments, see S.L. Dogan (2010), 'Beyond Trademark Use', *Journal on Telecommunication and High Technology Law,* **8**, 135. However, see also Dinwoodie and Janis, *supra* note 33, 1629–32, warning of an information overload that may result from widespread and unregulated sale of trademark-generated sponsored links.

78 CJEU, 23 March 2010, cases C-236/08-238/08, *Google France and Google/Louis Vuitton et al.*, para. 114. A more detailed discussion of the safe harbour for hosting can be found in CJEU, 12 July 2011, case C-324/09, *L'Oréal/eBay*, paras 112–24, where the Court establishes the standard of a 'diligent economic operator' (para. 120) to be met by online intermediaries. As to the regulation of hosting service outside trademark law, see also the fundamental critique expressed by G.B. Dinwoodie and M.D. Janis (2007), 'Lessons From the Trademark Use Debate', *Iowa Law Review,* **92**, 1703, 1717, who point out in the light of developments in the US that 'the sale of keyword-triggered advertising and the manner of presentation of search results potentially create independent trademark-related harm, thus making it an appropriate subject of direct liability.'

The *Google France* decision is also important with regard to the broad function theory governing Art. 5(1)(a) TMD after *L'Oréal/Bellure*. Discussing the liability of the advertiser using keyword advertising services, the Court held that using another's trademark as a keyword for one's own advertising did not encroach upon the advertising function of the affected trademark.[79] The CJEU comes to this conclusion by assuming that the website of the trademark owner would feature prominently among the natural search results, and that this prominent position would be sufficient to safeguard the advertising function.[80] This doubtful assumption[81] appears as a strategic argument to bypass the new function theory altogether – at least with regard to the functions of communication, investment, and advertising that are typically fulfilled by marks with a reputation.[82] The fact that the Court does not even address the communication and investment function in *Google France* confirms this impression. In the later *L'Oréal/eBay* decision, the Court also avoids a discussion of the communication, investment and advertising functions in the context of Art. 5(1)(a) TMD.[83] In *Interflora/Marks & Spencer*, however, the function theory features prominently again. The Court confirms the recognition of additional trademark functions under Art. 5(1)(a) TMD and devotes particular attention to potential encroachments upon the advertising and investment function.[84]

5. BACK TO BASICS?

In an ideal world, the steps taken by the CJEU in keyword advertising cases would herald a fundamental change in the Court's attitude towards brand image protection. They would indicate that the Court is determined to bring trademark protection back into shape after the excesses of recent years. With a further sharpening of the conceptual contours of the notion of trademark

---

79 CJEU, *supra* note 78, para. 98.

80 CJEU, *ibid*, para. 97.

81 See Ohly, *supra* note 59, 782, who rightly points out that the assumption becomes questionable in the case of 'normal' trademarks not having a particular reputation. Webpages concerning these marks need not necessarily feature prominently among the natural search results. The argument even becomes invalid if the trademark owner does not have webpages.

82 With regard to the essential origin function that is traditionally protected under Art. 5(1)(a) TMD, the Court did not hesitate to hold keyword advertising liable of having an adverse effect. See CJEU, *supra* note 78, para. 90.

83 See CJEU, 12 July 2011, case C-324/09, *L'Oréal/eBay*, paras 94–7.

84 CJEU, 22 September 2011, case C-323/09, *Interflora/Marks & Spencer*, paras 37–40 and 56–64.

use,[85] a high threshold for assuming an adverse effect on newly protected trademark functions under Art. 5(1)(a) TMD, and a strict test of unfairness under Art. 5(2) TMD in line with the *Interflora* opinion of AG Jääskinen, the questionable protection of brand value would become subject to a careful case-by-case analysis again. A protection automatism that brings trademark rights close to exploitation rights could be avoided. Traditional protection against confusion could be brought into focus again. The risk of encroachments upon freedom of expression and freedom of competition could be reduced.

For several reasons, however, this return to trademark protection of less extravagant proportions is not very likely. First of all, it must not be overlooked that the *Google France* decision need not be interpreted as a radical departure from the expansionist course adopted by the Court in recent years. Besides the outlined cautious approach to the notion of trademark use and the protection of new trademark functions under Art. 5(1)(a) TMD, the decision also contains elements that point towards a further strengthening of protection. In particular, the CJEU imposed new obligations on advertisers with regard to the prevention of consumer confusion. As to the essential origin function traditionally protected under Art. 5(1)(a) TMD, the Court stated:

> In the case where the ad, while not suggesting the existence of an economic link, is vague to such an extent on the origin of the goods or services at issue that normally informed and reasonably attentive internet users are unable to determine, on the basis of the advertising link and the commercial message attached thereto, whether the advertiser is a third party vis-à-vis the proprietor of the trade mark or, on the contrary, economically linked to that proprietor, the conclusion must also be that there is an adverse effect on that function of the trade mark.[86]

In the almost simultaneous *BergSpechte* decision, the Court extended this specific standard to Art. 5(1)(b) TMD.[87] Both the origin function analysis under Art. 5(1)(a) TMD and the likelihood of confusion test under Art. 5(1)(b) TMD, therefore, now include the test whether the advertising is too vague to exclude a potential risk of consumer confusion. This recalibration of protection against confusion is nothing less than a shift from proof of likely confusion by the trademark owner to an obligation on all third parties to secure

---

85 For an alternative concept focusing on contextual factors rather than the 'wonder drug' of trademark use as a limiting theory, see Dinwoodie and Janis, *supra* note 33, 1657–61.

86 See CJEU, 23 March 2010, cases C-236/08-238/08, *Google France and Google/Louis Vuitton et al.*, para. 90.

87 See CJEU, 25 March 2010, case C-278/08, *BergSpechte/Trekking.at*, paras 36 and 38–40.

market transparency when using keyword advertising services.[88] This change seems to corroborate the Court's efforts to overcome the rather defensive nature of traditional trademark rights. Instead of conceiving of trademark rights as instruments that shield trademarks from confusing use by third parties at the initiative of the trademark owner, the Court redefines protection against confusion as a positive obligation of third parties to keep a sufficient distance from the origin information conveyed via the trademark. *Google France*, therefore, does not necessarily put an end to the continuous broadening of trademark rights in recent years.

Moreover, it must not be overlooked that there are strong structural incentives for the Court to apply at least the eligibility criteria laxly. In Art. 5 TMD, for instance, a boundary line is drawn between use qualifying as trademark use in the sense of EU trademark law and falling under the harmonized rules set forth in Art. 5(1) to (4) TMD, and protection against use of a sign 'other than for the purposes of distinguishing goods or services' that, in accordance with Art. 5(5) TMD, remains unaffected by the Directive. The regulation of 'other use' of this latter nature, therefore, is left to the discretion of EU Member States. Apart from the Benelux countries that implemented Art. 5(5) TMD in regional trademark legislation,[89] this means that 'other use' is governed by the various protection mechanisms against unfair competition in EU Member States.[90] Whenever the CJEU finds a particular form of trademark use not to

---

88 Cf. Ohly, *supra* note 59, 780; N. van de Laan (2010), 'Die markenrechtliche Lage des Keyword Advertising', in J. Taeger (ed.), *Digitale Evolution – Herausforderungen für das Informations- und Medienrecht*, Oldenburg: Oldenburger Verlag für Wirtschaft, Informatik und Recht, p. 597 at p. 605), who refer to active information obligations in unfair competition law. The practical consequences of this shift must be clarified in further case law. From the perspective of the trademark owner, the new formula may also be understood differently in the sense indicated in Max Planck Institute, *supra* note 59, para. 2.171, that 'the origin function would be adversely affected (only) in the case where a third party's ad suggests that there is an economic link between that third party and the proprietor of the trade mark.' For an overview of recent national case law, see N. van der Laan, 'The Use of Trade Marks in Keyword Advertising: If Not Confusing, Yet Unfair?', in N. Lee, G. Westkamp, A. Kur and A. Ohly (eds), *Property and Conduct: Convergences and Developments in Intellectual Property, Unfair Competition and Publicity*, Cheltenham, UK and Northampton, MA: Edward Elgar, forthcoming, chapter 11, section 5.

89 See Art. 2.20(1)(d) of the Benelux Treaty Concerning Intellectual Property. Cf. Cohen Jehoram, van Nispen and Huydecoper, *supra* note 43, pp. 366–7; Gielen, *supra* note 43, pp. 256 and 286–7.

90 With regard to the state of law against unfair competition in the EU and the interplay between harmonized EU law and national regimes, see F. Henning-Bodewig (2010), 'Die Bekämpfung unlauteren Wettbewerbs in den EU-Mitgliedstaaten: eine Bestandsaufnahme', *Gewerblicher Rechtsschutz und Urheberrecht International*, 273; F. Henning-Bodewig (2010), 'Nationale Eigenständigkeit und europäische Vorgaben

constitute relevant trademark use, the Court thus foregoes the opportunity of bringing that form of use under the umbrella of harmonized EU trademark law.

The exclusion of referential use from the notion of trademark use would prevent the Court, for instance, from setting an EU-wide standard for the way in which the public may be informed about repair and maintenance services offered with regard to trademarked products.[91] A less flexible concept of trademark use, therefore, would reduce the level of harmonization which the Court can attain on the basis of the Trademark Directive.[92] Against this background, the Court is unlikely to abandon the elastic interpretation of the notion of trademark use developed in past cases.[93] In *Google France* and *L'Oréal/eBay*, the Court may have felt that, nonetheless, it was unnecessary to qualify keyword advertising services provided by search engines or offers for sale displayed by online marketplaces as relevant trademark use. At least formally, the resulting harmonization vacuum could be filled by invoking the hosting rules laid down in the E-Commerce Directive instead.[94]

In both cases, however, the Court still confirmed the flexibility of its trademark use concept with regard to the use made by keyword advertisers themselves. In *Google France*, the Court recalled the general principle that relevant

im Lauterkeitsrecht', *Gewerblicher Rechtsschutz und Urheberrecht International*, 549; R.M. Hilty and F. Henning-Bodewig (eds) (2009), *Lauterkeitsrecht und Acquis Communautaire*, Berlin/Heidelberg: Springer; R.M. Hilty and F. Henning Bodewig (eds) (2007), *Law Against Unfair Competition – Towards a New Paradigm in Europe?*, Berlin/Heidelberg/New York: Springer.

91 Cf. CJEU, 23 February 1999, case C-63/97, *BMW/Deenik*, para. 42, which concerned information on a car repair service specializing in BMW cars.

92 Cf. Kur, *supra* note 31, 11; P. Dyrberg and M. Skylv (2003), 'Does Trade Mark Infringement Require the Infringing Use be Trade Mark Use and if so, what is "Trade Mark Use"?', *EIPR*, 229, 232.

93 This may change with a change of the status of Art. 5(5) TMD in a mandatory provision of harmonized EU trademark law. In this way, forms of other use could be regulated by the CJEU without having to apply a broad notion of trademark use. See Max Planck Institute, *supra* note 59, paras 2.221–2.222 and 2.229, with regard to this solution. However, it seems that the adoption of Art. 5(5) TMD as a mandatory provision brings along the further expansion of trademark protection into fields that, so far, may largely remain unaffected, such as the educational, scientific and cultural use.

94 These rules, however, are approached differently by the courts in EU Member States. As a guideline, the CJEU held that, in order to invoke the safe harbour for hosting, the service provider had to be 'neutral, in the sense that its conduct is merely technical, automatic and passive, pointing to a lack of knowledge or control of the data which it stores.' See CJEU, 23 March 2010, cases C-236/08-238/08, *Google/Louis Vuitton et al.* paras 114–119. In CJEU, 12 July 2011, case C-324/09, *L'Oréal/eBay*, para. 120, the Court also established the requirement to act as a 'diligent economic operator'. These guidelines, however, will hardly be sufficient to prevent different national standards. Cf. Ohly, *supra* note 59, 784, van der Laan, *supra* note 88, pp. 608–9.

trademark use existed in any event where the trader buying keyword advertising services used another's trademark in such a way that a link was established with the goods or services offered in the keyword advertisement.[95] In *L'Oréal/eBay*, the Court had the opportunity to further elaborate on that point with regard to the keyword advertising made by eBay. By selecting keywords corresponding to L'Oréal trademarks, eBay had sought to draw the attention of users of the Google search engine to L'Oréal products offered for sale on the website www.ebay.co.uk. The promoted goods, obviously, were offered by eBay's customers and not by eBay itself. Invoking the general rule that the establishment of a mere link with the eBay online marketplace was sufficient,[96] the Court, nonetheless, came to the conclusion that eBay made relevant trademark use. Although the goods concerned were offered by third parties, eBay's advertisements created 'an obvious association between the trade-marked goods which are mentioned in the advertisements and the possibility of buying those goods through eBay.'[97] Triggering a mere association with the trademark, in other words, was deemed sufficient to establish trademark use.

Further incentive schemes in EU trademark law for a generous approach to infringement criteria can be identified in the field of anti-dilution protection under Art. 5(2) TMD. The low threshold established by the CJEU with regard to the central eligibility criterion of 'having a reputation', for instance, has been criticized above as a missed opportunity to confine problematic protection against dilution to those trademarks that are likely to be blurred, tarnished, or unfairly exploited. The low standard of niche reputation developed by the CJEU, however, may be deemed compatible with relevant international norms and soft law recommendations.[98] If Art. 16(3) TRIPS is read to formally recognize the trademark dilution doctrine, the indications given in Art. 16(2) TRIPS and Art. 2(2) of the WIPO Joint Recommendation Concerning Provisions on the Protection of Well-Known Marks suggest a rather low standard, according to which niche knowledge among only one specific target group of the products marketed under the trademark – consumers, distributors, or other business circles – is sufficient.[99]

---

95 See CJEU, 23 March 2010, cases C-236/08-238/08, *Google/Louis Vuitton et al.*, para. 72.

96 See CJEU, 12 July 2011, case C-324/09, *L'Oréal/eBay*, para. 92.

97 See CJEU, *ibid*, para. 93.

98 See Senftleben, *supra* note 4, 50–3.

99 See WIPO Joint Recommendation Concerning Provisions on the Protection of Well-Known Marks, WIPO publication No. 833, Geneva 2000, online available at <http://www.wipo.int/about-ip/en/development_iplaw/>. Cf. A. Kur (1999), 'Die WIPO-Vorschläge zum Schutz bekannter und berühmter Marken', *Gewerblicher*

Additional incentives for a niche reputation approach can be identified in the EU. In a regional common market with national sub-markets that differ considerably in size, a niche approach offers equal access to anti-dilution protection because it constitutes the smallest common denominator. A standard of nationwide reputation, arguably, would require less effort in small EU Member States. Community-wide reputation, by contrast, may be beyond reach for brands stemming from small countries.[100] Practical considerations of this nature may induce the CJEU to set a low threshold for the required territorial expansion of a mark's reputation even in the case of Community trademarks that enjoy protection across the entire EU territory. The *Pago* decision of the Court points in this direction.[101]

Considering these various incentives, it would be naive to assume that the Court is prepared to limit trademark rights to basic protection against confusion with minor extensions concerning dilution. By contrast, the Court is likely to stick to the expansion of trademark protection at least in respect of the flexible concept of trademark use and the low standard of 'having a reputation'. The doors to brand protection will thus remain wide open. In the field of infringement criteria, the Court already refused adopting a stricter approach to unfair advantage under Art. 5(2) TMD in *Interflora/Marks & Spencer*.[102] Moreover, the Court confirmed in this decision its intention to protect communication, investment, and advertising functions in the context of Art. 5(1)(a)

Rechtsschutz und Urheberrecht, 866. With regard to the question whether Article 16(3) TRIPS sets forth an obligation to adopt anti-dilution legislation at the national level, see particularly M. Handler, 'Trademark Dilution in Australia?', *European Intellectual Property Review* 2007, p. 307. For further commentary on the TRIPS provisions, see N. Pires de Carvalho (2011), *The TRIPS Regime of Trademarks and Designs*, Austin/Boston/Chicago/New York: Wolters Kluwer, pp. 343–82; D. Gervais (2008), *The TRIPS Agreement: Drafting History and Analysis*, 3rd ed., London: Sweet & Maxwell, 274–9; A. Kur (1996), 'TRIPS and Trademark Law', in F.-K.Beier and G. Schricker (eds), *From GATT to TRIPs – The Agreement on Trade-Related Aspects of Intellectual Property Rights*, Studies in Industrial Property and Copyright Law, Vol. 18, Weinheim, p. 93 at pp. 107–8).

[100] A requirement of Community-wide reputation could not be established under the Trademark Directive anyway. Art. 5(2) TMD refers to trademarks having 'a reputation in the *Member State*' (emphasis added).

[101] See CJEU, 6 October 2009, case C-301/07, *Pago/Tirolmilch*, para. 29: 'As the present case concerns a Community trade mark with a reputation throughout the territory of a Member State, namely Austria, the view may be taken, regard being had to the circumstances of the main proceedings, that the territorial requirement imposed by Article 9(1)(c) of the regulation is satisfied.' As to the territorial scope of prohibitions against infringement, see CJEU, 12 April 2011, case C-235/09, *DHL/Chronopost*, paras 46–50.

[102] See CJEU, 22 September 2011, case C-323/09, *Interflora/Marks & Spencer*, para. 89.

TMD.[103] Hence, a fundamental departure from *L'Oréal/Bellure*, in the sense of a return to the high dilution threshold established in *Intel/CPM* and the abandoning of the newly created function theory, cannot be expected. Trademark rights in the EU, in other words, are not unlikely to remain relatively close to exploitation rights granted in other fields of intellectual property.

6. NEED FOR A NEW LIMITATION INFRASTRUCTURE

Given this low probability for a fundamental departure from the problematic status quo, the time is ripe to devise appropriate limitations on trademark rights instead of waiting for the CJEU to change its expansionist course.[104] On the basis of the foregoing analysis, the need for a new limitation infrastructure in trademark law is evident for at least three reasons.

Firstly, the architecture of the Trademark Directive was not designed to counterbalance the current scope of protection. As explained above, the Directive focuses on protection against confusion. Against this background, it is not surprising that the Directive specifically provides breathing space for the use of (trade) names and addresses, descriptive indications, and indications of the purpose of products in Art. 6 TMD, whereas it remains silent on other fundamental concerns, such as safeguards for freedom of expression and information. As the extension of the notion of trademark use to referential and decorative use was not necessarily foreseeable, precautions in this regard seemed dispensable. Only the anti-dilution regime in Art. 5(2) TMD was equipped with the flexible defence of 'due cause' that can be invoked to satisfy freedom of speech interests. This flexible defence, however, cannot generally be applied to all exclusive rights. It is confined to the regulation of brand protection in Art. 5(2) TMD. The moment the Court incorporates brand protection into other

103 See CJEU, *ibid*, para. 40.

104 For similar conclusions with regard to the situation in the US, see G.B. Dinwoodie (2009), Lewis & Clark Law School Ninth Distinguished IP Lecture: 'Developing Defenses in Trademark Law', *Lewis and Clark Law Review*, **13** (1), 99, 152:

> However, as the scope of trademark protection expands and the metes and bounds of protection become more uncertain, we cannot rely exclusively on creative interpretation of the prima facie cause of action to establish limits. Trademark law must more consciously develop defenses that reflect the competing values at stake in trademark disputes.

exclusive rights,[105] the system, therefore, inevitably becomes imbalanced. The newly introduced protection of typical brand functions under Art. 5(1)(a) TMD testifies to this weak point in the architecture of the Trademark Directive.

Secondly, it was not foreseeable that the Court would use the Trademark Directive to absorb more and more unfair competition law. With the extension of the notion of trademark use to referential and decorative use, the Court brought forms of use 'other than for the purposes of distinguishing goods or services' under the umbrella of harmonized EU trademark protection standards. Considering Art. 5(5) TMD, it becomes clear that these forms of use were not intended to fall under the harmonized rights of trademark owners. By contrast, Art. 5(5) seeks to leave national provisions dealing with 'other use' unaffected by the harmonized provisions in Art. 5(1) to (4) TMD.[106] If Member States decide to include forms of other use in their trademark statutes, Art. 5(5) TMD, moreover, ensures appropriate counterbalances by also providing for the flexible defence of 'due cause'. The CJEU, however, included referential and decorative use in the general notion of trademark use. In consequence, these forms of use become subject to the much less flexible Art. 5(1) TMD that grants exclusive rights without providing for an open defence that can be used to safeguard freedom of speech. As discussed above, particularly Art. 5(1)(a) TMD can easily become too heavy a burden for comparative advertising and parody. In the absence of a due cause defence, the breathing space for (commercial) freedom of expression is insufficient in this area of protection.

Thirdly, the existing limitations in the EU Trademark Directive are not necessarily applied in an efficient way by the CJEU. In *Portakabin/ Primakabin*, for instance, the Court had to decide on the selection of the trademark PORTAKABIN (and variations with minor spelling mistakes) for Primakabin's advertising of the sale of new and second-hand mobile building units, including those manufactured by Portakabin. To defend this keyword advertising, Primakabin invoked the exemption of the use of descriptive indications and indications of the purpose of products in Art. 6(1)(b) and (c) TMD, as well as the exhaustion of trademark rights under Art. 7 TMD. These limitations require compliance with a loyalty obligation in the sense of use of the trademark in accordance with honest practices in industrial or commercial

---

[105] For a description and assessment of this development, see Quaedvlieg, *supra* note 12.

[106] However, see F. Henning-Bodewig (2008), 'Nicht markenmäßiger Gebrauch und Art. 5 Abs. 5 Markenrichtlinie', *Gewerblicher Rechtsschutz und Urheberrecht International*, 301, with regard to the influence of Art. 5(5) TMD itself on national unfair competition law in EU Member States.

matters. Instead of applying these rules flexibly to create an efficient counterbalance to continuously expanding trademark rights, the CJEU aligned the loyalty obligation with the applicable infringement criteria. Recalling the above-described market transparency obligation imposed on keyword advertisers in *Google France* and *Bergspechte*, the Court concluded that keyword advertisers could not rely on the limitations in Arts. 6(1) and 7 TMD, if the advertisement was vague to such an extent that Internet users were unable to determine whether the advertiser was a third party vis-à-vis the trademark proprietor or, on the contrary, an economically linked undertaking.[107]

While the conclusion as such may be reasonable, it is remarkable that the Court uses exactly the same considerations which support a finding of infringement, to reject the application of the limitations in Arts. 6(1) and 7 TMD. Defences must have an independent meaning different from relevant infringement criteria. Otherwise, a finding of infringement inevitably precludes the invocation of limitations and renders them meaningless. In *Portakabin/Primakabin*, the CJEU only partly complies with this basic prerequisite for balanced trademark protection. The Court admitted that in exceptional cases, Art. 6(1) TMD may still be available even though there is some likelihood of confusion.[108] In the case of Art. 7 TMD, the indication 'used' or 'second-hand' would be unproblematic. Moreover, Primakabin could not necessarily be prevented from including, in the marketing message appearing as a result of a search for 'Portakabin', second-hand goods bearing other trademarks.[109] With these additional considerations, the Court created loopholes for resellers. A real counterbalance to broad trademark protection, however, would require more flexibility.

The corrosive effect of these shortcomings in the architecture and application of the Trademark Directive must not be underestimated. Once the door to scrutiny in the light of trademark rights is opened wide on the basis of a broad concept of trademark use, the continuous relaxation of infringement requirements in recent years enhances the risk of a rash finding of infringement. Without appropriate defences, the reaction of EU trademark law to forms of referential and decorative use, for instance for the purposes of comparative

---

107 See CJEU, 8 July 2010, case C-558/08, *Portakabin/Primakabin*, paras 68–72 and 81.

108 See CJEU, *ibid*, para. 71, referring to CJEU, 7 January 2004, case C-100/02, *Gerolsteiner/Putsch*, paras 25–26, in which the Court explained that '[t]he mere fact that there exists a likelihood of aural confusion between a word mark registered in one Member State and an indication of geographical origin from another Member State is therefore insufficient to conclude that the use of that indication in the course of trade is not in accordance with honest practices.'

109 See CJEU, *supra* note 107, paras 84 and 91.

advertising and parody, will most probably be too harsh. Therefore, an enhanced limitation infrastructure is needed to re-establish a proper balance between rights and freedoms.

In fact, the process of devising new limitations has already started. In *O2/Hutchison*, the CJEU itself took first steps to create additional breathing space for comparative advertising:

> Consequently, in order to reconcile the protection of registered marks and the use of comparative advertising, Article 5(1) and (2) of Directive 89/104 and Article 3a(1) of Directive 84/450 must be interpreted to the effect that the proprietor of a registered trade mark is not entitled to prevent the use, by a third party, of a sign identical with, or similar to, his mark, in a comparative advertisement which satisfies all the conditions, laid down in Article 3a(1) of Directive 84/450, under which comparative advertising is permitted.[110]

As pointed out above, the Court confirmed this new limitation in *L'Oréal/Bellure*.[111] In this context, the rules of the EC Comparative Advertisement Directive are openly applied as an external balancing tool that is not reflected in harmonized EU trademark law itself.[112] The explicit recognition of this new limitation in EU trademark law would give evidence of the particular importance attached to commercial freedom of speech in the context of trademark protection.[113]

With regard to parody, criticism and comment,[114] comparable external

---

110 See CJEU, 12 June 2008, case C-533/06, *O2/Hutchison*, para. 45.

111 See CJEU, 18 June 2009, case C-487/07, *L'Oréal/Bellure*, para. 54.

112 In *O2/Hutchison*, the CJEU could establish a link between the prohibition of confusion in Art. 3a(1)(d) of the Comparative Advertisement Directive and the likelihood of confusion test in Art. 5(1)(b) TMD. See CJEU, 12 June 2008, case C-533/06, *O2/Hutchison*, para. 69 and operative part. The balancing via external norms was less obvious under these circumstances.

113 Cf. Max Planck Institute, *supra* note 59, paras 2.260–2.262, proposing the inclusion of an explicit limitation regarding honest referential use that, besides comparative advertising, would cover use for purposes of indicating replacement or service, use for purposes of commentary and criticism, and parody.

114 For case law reflecting the need for appropriate balancing tools, see the aforementioned cases of the German Federal Court of Justice, 3 February 2005, case I ZR 159/02, *Lila Postkarte*, *Gewerblicher Rechtsschutz und Urheberrecht* 2005, 583, and 11 March 2008, case VI ZR 7/07, *Gen-Milch*, *Neue Juristische Wochenschrift* 2008, 2110, both online available at www.bundesgerichtshof.de. See also District Court of Amsterdam, 22 December 2006, case KG ZA 06-2120, *Denk vooruit*, *Intellectuele eigendom en reclamerecht* 2007, 139; Paris Court of Appeals, 14th chamber, Sec. A, 26 February 2003, *Greenpeace France/Esso and SPCEA/Greenpeace et al.*, *IIC* 35 (2004), 342; Constitutional Court of South Africa, 27 May 2005, *Laugh it Off Promotions CC v South African Breweries Int. (Finance) B.V. t/a Sabmark Int.*, case CCT 42/04, *IIC* 36 (2005), 868. Cf. Z.M. Navsa (2009), 'Trademark Dilution – No Laughing Matter',

balancing tools are not readily available. The EC Copyright Directive[115] provides for limitations for the purposes of criticism and review, and caricature, parody and pastiche.[116] However, in spite of the growing overlap between the two fields of intellectual property,[117] copyright and trademark law are not intertwined to such an extent that copyright limitations could generally be applied analogously in trademark law.[118] Instead, the CJEU would have to directly invoke the fundamental guarantee of freedom of expression in Art. 11 of the EU Charter of Fundamental Rights and Art. 10 of the European Convention on Human Rights.[119] Therefore, the need to enshrine appropriate

---

EIPR, 455; C. Geiger (2006), '"Constitutionalising" Intellectual Property Law? The Influence of Fundamental Rights on Intellectual Property in the European Union', *IIC* **37** , 371, 395–7.

115 Directive 2001/29/EC of the European Parliament and of the Council of 22 May 2001, on the harmonisation of certain aspects of copyright and related rights in the information society (OJ 2001 L 167, 10).

116 See Art. 5(3)(d) and (k) of the Copyright Directive.

117 With regard to cumulative copyright and trademark protection, see S. Carre, 'Marques et droit d'auteur: Métaphore d'une belle rencontre', in Geiger and Schmidt-Szalewski, *supra* note 18, p. 25; M.R.F. Senftleben (2010), 'Der kulturelle Imperativ des Urheberrechts', in M. Weller, N.B. Kemle and Th. Dreier (eds), *Kunst im Markt – Kunst im Recht*, Baden-Baden: Nomos; V. Vanovermeire (2009), 'Inschrijving als merk van een in het openbaar domein gevallen werk', in A. Cruquenaire and S. Dusollier (eds), *Le cumul des droits intellectuels*, Brussels: Larcier, p. 177; A. Ohly (2007), 'Areas of Overlap Between Trade Mark Rights, Copyright and Design Rights in German Law', *Gewerblicher Rechtsschutz und Urheberrecht International*, 704; D.W.F. Verkade (1998), 'The Cumulative Effect of Copyright Law and Trademark Law: Which Takes Precedence?', in J.J.C. Kabel and G.J.H.M. Mom (eds), *Intellectual Property and Information Law – Essays in Honour of Herman Cohen Jehoram*, Den Haag, London and Boston: Kluwer, p. 69; J.H. Spoor (1990), *De gestage groei van merk, werk en uitvinding*, Zwolle: Tjeenk Willink.

118 This may be advisable, however, in cases where both rights apply cumulatively. Cf. M.R.F. Senftleben (2007), 'De samenloop van auteurs- en merkenrecht – een internationaal perspectief', *Tijdschrift voor auteurs-, media- en informatierecht*, 67; P.B. Hugenholtz (2000), 'Over cumulatie gesproken', *Bijblad bij de industriële eigendom*, 240.

119 With regard to the impact of the fundamental guarantee of freedom of expression on trademark protection, see the in-depth analysis conducted by Sakulin, *supra* note 21, and C. Geiger, 'Marques et droits fondamentaux', in Geiger and Schmidt-Szalewski, *supra* note 18, p. 163; L. Timbers and J. Huston (2003), 'The "Artistic Relevance Test" Just Became Relevant: the Increasing Strength of the First Amendment as a Defense to Trademark Infringement and Dilution', *Trade Mark Reporter*, **93**, 1278; R. Cooper Dreyfuss (2008), 'Reconciling Trademark Rights and Expressive Values: How to Stop Worrying and Learn to Love Ambiguity', in G.B. Dinwoodie and M.D. Janis (eds), *Trademark Law and Theory: a Handbook of Contemporary Research*, Cheltenham, UK and Northampton, MA: Edward Elgar Publishing, p. 261.

defences for parody, criticism and comment in EU trademark law can be deemed even more pressing than in the case of comparative advertising where the specific rules laid down in the Comparative Advertisement Directive are readily available.

Inspiration for this internalization of safeguards for freedom of expression can be found, for instance, in the US trademark system. After the US Supreme Court required 'a showing of actual dilution, rather than a likelihood of dilution' in *Moseley v V Secret Catalogue*,[120] the 2006 Trademark Dilution Revision Act amended the anti-dilution provisions in the US Lanham Act. The threshold for giving proof of dilution was lowered in this context.[121] Accordingly, the question of appropriate counterbalances arose and led to the introduction of a statutory, open-ended fair use provision that explicitly offers breathing space for parody, criticism and comment. To safeguard the freedom of the press, the provision also limits trademark rights with regard to news reporting and news commentary.[122]

When comparable limitations are included in EU trademark law, these new limitations should be brought in line with existing limitations in the EC Copyright Directive that serve the same purposes.[123] In this way, a consistent system of corresponding limitations can be created that prevents the erosion of the freedom offered in copyright law in cases of overlap with trademark protection.[124]

---

120 See Supreme Court of the United States of America, March 4, 2003, *Moseley v V Secret Catalogue, Inc.*, 537 U.S. 418 (2003). Cf. Moskin (2004), 'Victoria's Big Secret: Wither Dilution Under the Federal Dilution Act', *Trademark Reporter,* **93**, 842–59.

121 See Trademark Dilution Revision Act of 2006 (H.R. 683) amending the US Trademark Act of 1946 (15 U.S.C. 1125). With regard to the required proof of dilution, this new legislation clarifies that protection against dilution is to be granted 'regardless of the presence or absence of actual or likely confusion, of competition, or of actual economic injury'. Cf. Beebe, *supra* note 26, 1143; C. Chicoine and J. Visintine (2006), 'The Role of State Trademark Dilution Statutes in Light of the Trademark Dilution Revision Act 2006', *The Trademark Reporter,* **96**, 1155.

122 See Section 43(c)(3) of the US Lanham Act, as amended by the 2006 Trademark Dilution Revision Act. For a description of the situation under the former US Federal Trademark Dilution Act, see M.K. Cantwell (2004), 'Confusion, Dilution and Speech: First Amendment Limitations on the Trademark Estate: An Update', *The Trademark Reporter,* **94**, 549. With regard to common law fair use defences in the US, see J. Moskin (2005), 'Frankenlaw: The Supreme Court's Fair and Balanced Look at Fair Use', *Trademark Reporter,* **95**, 848.

123 See the aforementioned Art. 5(3)(d) and (k) of the Copyright Directive 2001/29/EC. With regard to use privileges for the press, see Art. 5(3)(c) of the Copyright Directive covering the reporting of current events.

124 Cf. M.R.F. Senftleben (2011), 'Overprotection and Protection Overlaps in Intellectual Property Law: The Need for Horizontal Fair Use Defences', in A. Kur and

Finally, it is remarkable that, besides the aforementioned specific limitations, the US provision generally exempts '[a]ny fair use, including nominative or descriptive fair use, or facilitation of such use.'[125] This safety net of an open-ended limitation recalls the general defence of 'due cause' in Art. 5(2) TMD. The US example shows that, irrespective of the introduction of several specific limitations, it is advisable to also provide for a general safeguard clause that can be invoked in the case of new, unforeseen developments that require additional balancing tools.[126] With a general limitation of this type, courts are rendered capable of reacting adequately to new technologies. The problems raised by keyword advertising can serve as an example in this regard. As trademark rights become broader, they also become more likely to absorb forms of use that serve important competing interests and should remain free for this reason. In this situation, the safety net of a flexible defence enables the courts to maintain a proper balance between rights and freedoms.[127] As pointed out above, the CJEU relied on the flexible 'due cause' defence in *Interflora/Marks & Spencer* to create breathing space for keyword advertising informing consumers about alternative offers in the market.[128]

A comparable need for additional flexibility may arise, for instance, with regard to research and teaching, and the use of trademarks for cultural purposes. Admittedly, activities in these fields do not necessarily occur 'in the context of commercial activity with a view to economic advantage and not as a private matter.'[129] Accordingly, they may be unlikely to constitute 'use in the course of trade' in the sense of EU trademark law and would remain outside

V. Mizaras (eds), *The Structure of Intellectual Property Law: Can One Size Fit All?*, Cheltenham, UK and Northampton, MA: Edward Elgar Publishing, p. 136, available online at http://ssrn.com/abstract=1597123. With regard to proposals concerning the convergence of infringement criteria, see F.W. Grosheide (1998), 'Zwakke werken – Een pleidooi voor een merkenrechtelijke benadering van de inbreukvraag in het auteursrecht', in D.W.F. Verkade and D.J.G. Visser (eds), *Intellectuele eigenaardigheden: Opstellen aangeboden aan mr Theo R. Bremer*, Deventer: Kluwer, p. 121.

125 See Section 43(c)(3) of the US Lanham Act, as amended by the 2006 Trademark Dilution Revision Act.

126 See Max Planck Institute, *supra* note 59, para. 2.266, also proposing a general fair use clause to allow for flexibility in situations not previously envisaged by the legislator, particularly with regard to new business models emerging in the digital environment.

127 For a more detailed discussion of this point, see Senftleben, *supra* note 124, pp. 170–9.

128 See CJEU, 22 September 2011, case C-323/09, *Interflora/Marks & Spencer*, para. 91.

129 For this definition of 'use in the course of trade', see CJEU, 23 March 2010, cases C-236/08-238/08, *Google/Louis Vuitton et al.*, para. 50; CJEU, 12 November 2002, case C-206/01, *Arsenal/Reed*, para. 40.

the reach of trademark rights from the outset.[130] With increasing partnerships between private companies and educational, scientific, and cultural institutions, however, the absence of use in trade may become less evident, while the socially valuable objectives of sponsored activities still justify an exemption from the control exerted by trademark owners. In the case of cultural activities, it can be added that freedom of art may be understood to cover accompanying promotion and marketing activities.[131] From this perspective, it would also make sense not to rely exclusively on an exemption based on the condition of use in the course of trade.

A final lesson can be learned from the limited scope of the due cause defence in the current Trademark Directive. As indicated above, this open defence only applies to brand protection under Art. 5(2) TMD and the extension of trademark protection to use 'other than for the purposes of distinguishing goods or services' under Art. 5(5) TMD. As the CJEU decided to offer brand protection and protection against other use also under Art. 5(1)(a) TMD, this limited scope of the defence led to imbalanced protection. Against this background, it is advisable to generalize this safety net and render the due cause defence applicable across all exclusive rights granted in EU trademark law. The proposed specific limitations for the purposes of comparative advertising, criticism and review, caricature,[132] parody and pastiche, and the report-

---

130 However, see the analysis conducted by the Max Planck Institute, *supra* note 59, para. 2.66, according to which 'it appears that "in the course of trade" must be distinguished primarily from private use.' Cf. also paras 2.160–2.162 of the analysis. Educational, scientific and cultural use does not constitute private use in a strict sense. Hence, it may qualify as use in the course of trade in certain cases and become subject to the exclusive rights of trademark owners.

131 For an approach to the fundamental freedom of art covering both creation ('Werkbereich') and dissemination ('Wirkbereich'), see German Federal Constitutional Court, 3 November 1987, case 1 BvR 1257/84, *Herrnburger Bericht*, published in the official collection *BVerfGE* 77 (1987), 240, where the Court held that the freedom of art covered advertising for a work of art. If the trademark of a third party is used for the purpose of advertising an art work, this freedom of art, necessarily, must be reconciled with the fundamental guarantee of property, including intellectual property. Cf. H.D. Jarass and B. Pieroth (2010), *Grundgesetz für die Bundesrepublik Deutschland – Kommentar*, 11th ed., Munich: C.H. Beck, pp. 207–12. A new trademark limitation regulating this field could provide guidance for an appropriate balancing of interests in this context. As to the status of intellectual property within the EU system of human rights, see the critical comments by C. Geiger (2009), 'Intellectual Property Shall be Protected!? – Article 17(2) of the Charter of Fundamental Rights of the European Union: A Mysterious Provision with an Unclear Scope', *EIPR*, 113.

132 The reference to caricature stems from Art. 5(3)(k) of the EC Copyright Directive and is proposed here, as pointed out above, also in the context of trademark law to harmonize the limitation infrastructure in the two – often overlapping – fields of intellectual property law. While the category of caricature may perhaps be deemed less

ing of current events should also be implemented as defences that can be applied to all exclusive rights. In other words, these specific limitations and the open due cause defence should be added to the catalogue of limitations in Art. 6 TMD.

7. CONCLUSION

In recent years, the CJEU has broadened the scope and reach of EU trademark protection constantly, in particular in the area of brand protection. Developing a flexible concept of trademark use that encompasses referential and decorative use, the Court opened the doors to trademark protection wide. With the adoption of a remarkably low threshold for a showing of reputation, these doors are kept wide open also with regard to enhanced protection against dilution. In addition, the Court found mere attempts to ride on the coat-tails of a mark with a reputation to amount to trademark infringement under Art. 5(2) TMD. Use having an adverse effect on typical functions of marks with a reputation – communication, investment, and advertising functions – became actionable under Art. 5(1)(a) TMD.

This systematic relaxation of eligibility and infringement criteria can hardly be justified. The rationales underlying the protection of brand investment and brand communication are rather weak. In particular, the incentive and reward rationales that serve as a basis for exploitation rights in other fields of intellectual property are inapplicable in this context. Unlike inventors and authors, the brand owner cannot validly claim to have created intellectual property that furthers science or art. The trademark does not fall into the public domain after a limited period of time to enrich mankind's universal treasury of intellectual creations. Against this background, it remains unclear why the CJEU paved the way for more generous and readily available brand protection. With these steps, the Court approximated trademark rights to exploitation rights without a sound policy justification.

With the challenges arising in the digital environment, the imbalances caused by this jurisprudence clearly come to the fore. As the limitations recognized within the EU trademark system are incapable of coping with the excessive protection following from the extensions in recent years, the CJEU had to invoke the rules of the Comparative Advertisement Directive as an external balancing tool to create breathing space for comparative advertising. To offer

relevant in a trademark context, it may still become important with regard to portrait trademarks. For a discussion of developments in this area, see C. Gielen (2009), 'Portretmerk: een non-merk?', in D.J.G. Visser (ed.), *Commercieel portretrecht*, Amstelveen: deLex, p. 113.

even more space, the Court supplemented the application of the Comparative Advertisement Directive with an open-ended 'due cause' defence that also serves the purpose of informing customers about alternatives in the market. It remains to be seen whether the Court will develop comparable balancing mechanisms with regard to parody, criticism, and comment. Otherwise, an encroachment upon freedom of expression and information seems inevitable.

While the questions raised by keyword advertising may lead to the development of a more nuanced coat-tail formula in the context of Art. 5(2) TMD, and a cautious approach to the function theory governing Art. 5(1)(a) TMD, a fundamental departure from *L'Oréal/Bellure*, in the sense of a return to a high threshold for anti-dilution protection, cannot be expected. By contrast, trademark rights in the EU are not unlikely to remain relatively close to exploitation rights granted in other fields of intellectual property. Furthermore, the CJEU is unlikely to change its expansionist course in the area of eligibility criteria. A broad concept of trademark use allows the Court to bring more and more non-harmonized unfair competition law under the umbrella of harmonized EU trademark law. The lax reputation test in the field of anti-dilution protection may be deemed inevitable to offer equal access to anti-dilution protection in a regional common market with national sub-markets that differ considerably in size. The doors to generous brand protection will thus remain wide open.

For this reason, the time is ripe to devise an appropriate limitation infrastructure that is capable of counterbalancing the broad grant of protection. The limitation for comparative advertising that the Court deduced from the Comparative Advertisement Directive should be reflected in EU trademark law. Additional limitations are indispensable with regard to criticism and review, and caricature, parody and pastiche. To secure the freedom of the press, they should be accompanied by safeguards for the reporting of current events. Measures could also be taken with regard to the use of trademarks for research, teaching, and cultural purposes. In any case, the updated limitation infrastructure should provide for a general due cause defence that can be used in unforeseen circumstances requiring the further limitation of trademark rights. As the CJEU tends to trespass across the boundary lines between protection against confusion in Art. 5(1) TMD and protection against dilution in Art. 5(2) TMD, the new limitations and the general due cause defence should be applicable across all exclusive rights of trademark owners. They should be added to the list in Art. 6 TMD.

8. The simplification and codification of European legislation for the protection of geographical indications

Gail Elizabeth Evans

From the outset, the legislative rationale for the Community-wide protection of geographical indications (GI) was based upon the need to simplify the diversity of national laws protecting the various kinds of designations for agricultural products. In 1992 Regulation 2081 On the Protection of Geographical Indications and Designations of Origin for Agricultural Products and Foodstuffs (GI Regulation)[1] was enacted on the basis that codification would promote fair competition between producers and enhance consumer perceptions of product authenticity.[2] The Regulation created a *sui generis* system of registration characterized by two of indications of source, Protected Designations of Origin (PDO) and Protected Geographical Indications (PGI), the PDO being distinguished from the PGI by the need for a stronger link between the product and the place of production. In coverage, the range of agricultural products permitted was reasonably broad, but applications in respect of foods were restricted to basic items such as meat, fish and dairy products.

That same year saw a second legislative instrument enacted, Regulation (EEC) No 2082 on certificates of specific character for foodstuffs such as pasta, ice cream and chocolate.[3] It created a Community-wide scheme for the registration of Traditional Specialities Guaranteed (TSG), a term that refers to the name of a food that is produced using traditional raw materials, composition, or method of production. TSGs were also conceived as a Community-wide instrument entitling rightholders, where registration is 'with reservation

[1] Regulation No 2081/92 of 14 July 1992 on the protection of geographical indications and designations of origin for agricultural products and foodstuffs. Throughout the chapter 'geographical indication' ('GI') will be used in its broader sense to include both PDOs and PGIs.

[2] Regulation No 2081/92, Recital 7.

[3] Regulation No 2082/92 of 14 July 1992 on certificates of specific character for agricultural products and foodstuffs. For a complete list of the foods covered see Annex I of the Regulation.

of the name',[4] subject to compliance with the specification and to participation in an inspection regime, to produce and market the traditional product using the protected name.

The first major amendment of the GI Regulation occurred in 2006 pursuant to the complaint by Australia and the US to the WTO that the EU law was discriminatory of foreign applicants seeking to register GI in the EU. In order to remedy the Panel's finding of discrimination, amended Regulation 510/2006 sought to remove differences in the registration procedure for GI belonging to producers in third countries.[5] Although TSGs were not the subject of the WTO dispute Panel, a new regulation was enacted, which includes similar reforms respecting the procedures to be followed by applicants from non-EU countries.[6]

The impetus for the latest proposal to further simplify the regulation of GI derives from the need to strengthen the EU's competitive position in world agricultural markets. It provides a comprehensive codification of the system for protecting designations of product quality.[7] In view of increasing interna-

---

[4] In the case of TSGs, there are two different levels of protection: 'registration with and without reservation of the name' (Article 6(2)(a)). 'With reservation of the name': in such cases the name, even where unaccompanied by the indication 'traditional speciality guaranteed'; the abbreviation 'TSG'; or the associated EU logo; may no longer be used on the labelling of similar foodstuffs not satisfying the registered specification (e.g. 'Jamón Serrano'): DG Agriculture and Rural Development, 'Traditional Specialties Guaranteed', Background Paper To The Green Paper On Agricultural Product Quality", Working Document (October 2008) at pp. 2–3.

[5] Concerning discrimination in regard to the registration of foreign GI, the panel recommended that the EU, (a) bring the Regulation into conformity with the TRIPS Agreement and the GATT of 1994; (b) amend the Regulation to remove conditions requiring reciprocity of inspection procedures as they applied to applications for registration of GI located in third countries. Accordingly, Regulation 2081/92 was repealed and replaced by Regulation 510/2006 on the protection of geographical indications and designations of origin for agricultural products and foodstuffs of March 20, 2006 (in force on 31 March 2006).

[6] Regulation No 509/2006 of March 20, 2006 on Agricultural Products and Foodstuffs as Traditional Specialities Guaranteed replaced Regulation No 2082/92; Regulation 1216/2007 laying down detailed rules for the implementation of Regulation 509/2006 on Agricultural Products and Foodstuffs as Traditional Specialities Guaranteed, see art. 7 on the applications for registration, especially regarding third-country producers at art. 7(7); see also Recitals 8, 11, 12 and 14.

[7] Proposal for a Regulation of the European Parliament and of the Council on Agricultural Product Quality Schemes, COM(2010) 733 Final, Brussels, 10 December 2010; see Recital 1 referring to the quality and diversity of European Union agricultural production as a competitive advantage for European Union producers. The Quality Schemes Regulation is part of the 'Quality Package' that also includes a proposal to modify Regulation (EC) No 1234/2007 (Regulation (EC) No 1234/2007 of 22 October 2007 establishing a common organisation of agricultural markets and on

tional competition for agricultural markets, the Green Paper of 2008 argues that, given its trade advantage in 'finished' products, the best response is to strengthen Europe's reputation for quality.[8]

In light of consumer concern over provenance and safety, the term 'food quality' has acquired a new relational significance, where, quality is related not only to the product's physical characteristics, but also its farming attributes, to the extent that production methods are considered to reflect nutritional, food safety and environmental values. In turn, the significance of the GI has redoubled as, by linking the product to the place of production, coupled with modern advertising techniques, they become the media via which assurances of quality are communicated to consumers.

The Green Paper evinced strong support for the use of GI as a means of informing consumers about the qualities of products. To this end, both Commission Communications and stakeholder consultations, advised that the regulation of GI needed to be simplified in order to promote increased access and more widespread adoption of the registration system.[9] Thus the rationale for simplification of the GI legislation is said to rest both on the heightened need for producers to differentiate their products, and the increasing demand by consumers for assurances of product quality.

The broader rationale for continuing codification of Agricultural Product Quality Schemes relates to the Commission's programme for the simplification

---

specific provisions for certain agricultural products (the single Common Market Organisation); guidelines setting out best practice for the development and operation of certification schemes relating to agricultural products and foodstuffs; and guidelines on the labelling of foodstuffs using Protected Designation of Origin (PDIO) and Protected Geographical Indications (PGI) as ingredients: Quality Schemes Regulation, Explanatory Memorandum, at 2.

8 European Commission (2008), 'Green Paper on Agricultural Product Quality: Product Standards, Farming Requirements and Quality Schemes', at p. 4. Although the EU remains an important producer of basic commodities, two thirds of its annual agri-food exports worth around €70 billion a year are 'finished products', such as meat, dairy products, wine and vegetable oils: Communication from the Commission to the European Parliament on Agricultural Product Quality Policy (SEC(2009) 670) (SEC(2009) 671).

9 Simplification is recognized as a major objective in developing a coherent approach to quality policy: see Commission of the European Communities, Communication from the Commission to the European Parliament, the Council, the European Economic and Social Committee and the Committee of the Regions on Agricultural Product Quality Policy, COM(2009), Brussels, 28.5.2009 at pp. 10-11; see also on the simplification of rules and procedures: European Commission, Directorate-General for Agriculture and Rural Development, 'Conclusions from the Consultation on Agricultural Product Quality', Brussels (2009) <http://ec.europa.eu/agriculture/quality/policy/green-paper/index_en.htm.> at pp. 9–11.

of EU legislation.[10] Pursuant to the Lisbon Strategy,[11] the simplification programme is designed to provide a stimulus to innovation by recasting EU legislation with a view to improving its transparency, effectiveness and efficiency, thereby reducing the administrative burden stemming from regulatory requirements.[12] Realizing this goal involves a variety of methods, including the repeal of legal acts which are irrelevant or obsolete, and so-called 'recasting' that is, the simultaneous amendment and codification of legal acts.[13]

The Proposal for a Regulation on Agricultural Product Quality Schemes (2010)[14] (Quality Schemes Regulation), would repeal and amend the existing, individual regulations to provide a unified framework for the protection of

---

10 In October 2005, the Commission launched a further phase for the simplification of existing EU law by setting out a rolling programme, covering the years 2005–2008 (based on its 2002 Action Plan for simplifying and improving the regulatory environment). This programme drew extensively on stakeholder input and focused on sectoral simplification needs. See Commission Working Document, 'Third progress report on the strategy for simplifying the regulatory environment' COM(2009) 17 Final, Brussels, 28 January 2009. For updates of the Commission's simplification programme see 'Third strategic review of Better Regulation in the European Union', Commission Communication, COM(2009) 15 final (2009); and 'Smart Regulation in the European Union', Commission Communication, COM(2010) 543 Final (8 October 2010).

11 The Lisbon Strategy (adopted 2000) intended to deal with the low productivity of economic growth in the EU. The main fields were economic, social, and environmental renewal and sustainability. The Lisbon Strategy was based on the concepts of: Innovation as the engine for economic change (following the writings of Joseph Schumpeter); and social and environmental renewal, <http://europa.eu/legislation_summaries/research_innovation/research_in_support_of_other_policies/n26021_en.htm>.

12 'Smart Regulation in the European Union', Commission Communication, COM(2010)543 final (8 October 2010) at pp. 3–4.

13 'Smart Regulation in the European Union', Commission Communication, COM(2010)543 final (8 October 2010) at pp. 7–8.

14 Proposal for a Regulation of the European Parliament and of the Council on agricultural product quality schemes, COM (2010) 733 final, Brussels, 10.12.2010 2010/0353 (COD) ('Quality Schemes Regulation'). Proposal for a Regulation of the European Parliament and of the Council on agricultural product quality schemes, COM (2010) 733 Final, Brussels, 10.12.2010 2010/0353 (COD) ('Quality Schemes Regulation'). See also Committee on Agriculture and Rural Development, Proposal for a Regulation on Agricultural Product Quality Schemes, Presidency compromise text (February 23, 2011) (COM(2010)0733–C7-0423/2010–2010/0353(COD)): http://www.europarl.europa.eu/oeil/popups/ficheprocedure.do?lang=en&reference=2010/0353(COD). Adopted by the EU Parliament 12.09.2012: http:www.europarl.europa.eu. For an analysis of the amendments contained in the compromise text see G.E. Evans, 'The Simplification of European Legislation for the Protection of Geographical Indications. The Proposed Regulation on Agricultural Product Quality Schemes', EIPR, Volume 34, Issue 11, October, 2012, pp. 33–49.

PDOs, PGIs and TSGs.[15] In light of the significance of the simplification programme, wine is significant by its absence from the Quality Schemes Regulation.[16] Historically, Community regulations for wine have been the subject of a separate instrument, and recent reform of the legislation has seen the convergence of quality schemes for other agricultural products. Regulation No 479 of April 2008 on the Common Organization of the Market in Wine[17] provides both PDOs and PGIs in respect of certain wine sector products. Nonetheless, in response to an industry consultation, for the present, the Commission has proposed maintaining a regime for wines differentiated from that for other food products.[18]

If successful, the programme for legislative simplification and the policy on agricultural product quality should increase the effectiveness and efficiency of the law by strengthening the reputation of quality products among consumers; creating new markets; streamlining the registration and protection of GI. However, apart from the difficulty in measuring these projected outcomes, we are faced initially with the question of how to define efficiency and effectiveness in reference to the regulation of GI? Economic analysis informed by efficiency and effectiveness is about the relationships between inputs, outputs and outcomes. In institutional terms, it refers to the minimization of the extent of expenditure of resources, financial, temporal and informational, in a process to obtain an output defined as 'efficiency'. 'Effectiveness' is how well the process achieves its desired output, the latter being constituted by those features that meet the expectations of consumers.

Thus the speed with which applicants may be able to register GI constitutes a measure of 'efficiency'; but when the procedure leads to greater transparency of the register for potential competitors and consumers, that is an effective outcome. 'Effectiveness' is about achieving objectives consistent with wealth maximization; 'efficiency' is reaching such objective with the use of optimal resources.[19] In terms of effectiveness, stakeholders highlighted the need to:

---

15 A full list of the Regulations that the Quality Schemes Regulation would replace is given in Recital 7 of the Proposal for a Regulation on agricultural product quality schemes.

16 This Regulation shall not apply to grapevine products with the exception of wine vinegars, or to spirit drinks or to aromatized wines, Quality Schemes Regulation, Article 2(2).

17 Council Regulation (EC) No 479/2008 of 29 April 2008 on the common organisation of the market in wine, entered into force in 2009.

18 Proposal for a Regulation of the European Parliament and of the Council on agricultural product quality schemes, COM(2010) 733 final, Brussels, 10.12.2010 2010/0353 (COD) ('Quality Schemes Regulation'): Explanatory Memorandum, at 5.

19 C. Veljanovski, 'The Economics of Law'. Institute of Economics Affairs Hobart Paper No 157, at 58. Available at SSRN: <http://ssrn.com/abstract=935952>.

increase the reputation of products by promoting consumer recognition of geographical indications and; ensure the use of sustainable farming methods; and improve the enforcement of geographical indications.[20]

Moreover, the concepts of efficiency and justice are related not only from an economic perspective but also from a philosophical one. Thus from a utilitarian perspective governments should consider not only the cost of maintaining the institutions associated with the protection of GI, but also the justice involved in maximizing the overall utility to society.[21] Therefore an analysis of the simplification of the regulation of GI might just as well be based on the economic costs of protecting geographical names long considered to have been generic for a type of agricultural product on the one hand,[22] as the benefits of sustainable agriculture, environment conservation and rural development in seeking to promote monopolies in GI on the other. Prior to considering the most efficient use of resources, legislators need to question the extent to which the Quality Schemes Regulation is capable of realizing the most desirable outcomes.

As a means of evaluating the proposed Quality Schemes Regulation, this chapter considers the concept of efficiency in light of the criteria identified by stakeholders as indicative of a more effective system for the protection of geographical indications. It argues that the simplifying assumptions which the Quality Schemes Regulation makes in respect of GI may not necessarily be the most efficient or effective in maximizing the social utility of the system. In the exposition of this argument, the chapter examines the proposed amendments to the registration system for GI, as well as opportunities missed in the Quality Schemes Regulation to address particular issues, which case law has highlighted as needing the attention of the legislature, notably the use of names

---

20 Commission of the European Communities, Communication from the Commission to the European Parliament, the Council, the European Economic and Social Committee and the Committee of the Regions on Agricultural Product Quality Policy, COM(2009), Brussels, 28.5.2009 at pp. 10; see also on the simplification of rules and procedures: European Commission, Directorate-General for Agriculture and Rural Development, 'Conclusions from the Consultation on Agricultural Product Quality', Brussels (2009) <http://ec.europa.eu/agriculture/quality/policy/green-paper/index_en.htm.> at pp. 11-14.

21 According to current thought intellectual property law seeks to maximize the net social benefit of the practices it regulates. Thus the utilitarian notion of the greatest good for the greatest number is expressed in terms of financial reward: Robert P. Merges, *Justifying Intellectual Property*, (2011) Cambridge, MA:Harvard University Press at p. 2.

22 Regulation, Article 3(1) defines a 'name that has become generic' as the name of an agricultural product or a foodstuff which, although it relates to the place or the region where this product or foodstuff was originally produced or marketed, has become the common name of an agricultural product or a foodstuff. For instance, the names 'Mozzarella' and 'Camembert' for cheese, when used without qualification are not currently protected as geographical indications in the EU.

widely considered to have become generic. The chapter concludes with a finding that the Quality Schemes Regulation has yet to effectively address the needs of small-scale producers in disadvantaged areas, whether as potential users of the system or competitors.

1. UNITY OF STRUCTURE AND CONCEPTUAL COHERENCE

The logic of the Quality Schemes Regulation's unified regulatory structure is not entirely coherent from a legal perspective. The first and most significant change wrought by the codification is one of legislative structure. The legislation is set within a single, unified structure for various kinds of 'quality schemes' that are currently the subject of separate regulations. Thus PDOs and PGIs are incorporated as Title II within the Quality Schemes Regulation on agricultural product quality schemes. Traditional Specialties Guarantees are found in Title III. In addition, a new category of *indicia* has been created, 'optional quality terms' such as 'first pressed' with reference to olive oils, which are found in Title IV. [23]

Arguably, the conceptual basis of the Quality Schemes Regulation is flawed in so far as it contains an unprecedented combination of intellectual property and so-called 'optional quality terms' that are also to be accorded statutory protection. Admittedly, industrial property is broadly defined in the Paris Convention for the Protection of Industrial Property as applying to 'agricultural industries and to all manufactured or natural products'.[24] Industrial property rights in commercial designations are also characterized by certain limitations, definition and scope. The PGI is limited by the linkage with the territory, the specification, the defined geographic area of usage and generic usage. In contrast, the list of 'optional quality terms' appears to belong more properly within a regulatory framework for marketing standards or product labelling than one for intellectual property. Proposed 'quality terms' common to customary usage in the sector such as 'free range' or 'reduced fat', do not conform to any accepted definition of industrial property. 'Optional quality terms' are so vaguely defined as to be subject only to a list of general criteria: to the effect that the term relates to a characteristic of a product, or a farming or processing attribute.[25]

---

23 Quality Schemes Regulation, *supra* note 14 above.

24 Quality Schemes Regulation, Article 1(3).

25 See Quality Schemes Regulation, Article 29 regarding additional optional quality terms; and Article 28 regarding Commission power to reserve, amend or cancel such terms.

Ostensibly, TSGs are included in the Quality Schemes Regulation with comparatively greater justification. Traditional food names reserved under the TSG Regulation may constitute industrial property in so far as they are subject matter protectable under unfair competition law.[26] However, if the aim is to simplify the legislation, why was the TSG not abolished and traditional foods incorporated as PGIs? The rationale for the retention of the TSG within the Quality Schemes Regulation appears to rest on the assumption that in order to increase the number of applications, it is necessary to: incorporate the TSG within a consolidated legislative instrument for indications of geographical origin; and increase the period of traditional practice from 25 years to 50 years. This rationale is questionable in view of the fact that over some 20 years there have been only 30 names registered. Can this evident lack of success in producer adoption of the TSG really be cured by such legislative action? It is arguable whether the reserved names would not be better incorporated within the GI Regulation as PGIs. As L. Bérard and P. Marchenay observe, most of the products registered as TSGs correspond more closely to PGIs, being largely inseparable from local culture and fairly typical of their roots.[27] Alternatively, TSGs, particularly those with names that are not reserved, might be included with 'quality terms' in marketing standards or labelling regulations.

2. AMENDMENT OF DEFINITIONS OF DESIGNATION OF ORIGIN AND GEOGRAPHICAL INDICATION

As with the trade mark, so the definition of a PDO and PGI is directly related to the scope of protection accorded the rightholder. In the case of the trade mark, the law limits registrable signs to those that are capable of distinguishing the goods of one undertaking from those of other undertakings. In the case of the GI only names that possess the requisite link between the specific place of production and the reputation or quality of the product, are protectable. The definition of a PGI and PDO is therefore critical to establishing a minimum standard for protection. Each form bears a distinct relationship to the place of production; each differs in the character of that relationship. Currently, the

---

26 Paris Convention for the Protection of Industrial Property, Article 10(*bis*).

27 The existing Regulations for GIs and TSG both cover beer, chocolate and derived products, bread, pastry, cakes, confectionery, biscuits and other baker's wares, beverages made from plant extracts, and pasta. The only products not included in the current list for PGIs are 'pre-cooked meals, prepared condiment sauces, and soups or broths'. See L. Bérard and P. Marchenay, 'A Market Culture: "Produits de Terroir" or the Selling of Heritage' in Sarah Blowen, Marion Demossier and Jeanine Picard, *Recollections of France, Memories, Identities and Heritage in Contemporary France, Contemporary France Series,* Vol. 4 (Oxford: Berghahn Books, 2001), pp. 154–160.

PGI[28] is defined broadly enough for most locally based products to take advantage of its protection.

Nonetheless, the Quality Schemes Regulation would amend the current definition of a PGI to conform more closely with that of the TRIPS Agreement.[29] Proposed Article 5(1)(b) defines a 'geographical indication' as a name which identifies a product:

(i) originating in a specific place, region or country,
(ii) where a given quality, reputation or other characteristic of the product is
(iii) essentially attributable to its geographical origin, and at least one of the production steps of which take place in the defined geographical area.

Arguably, the amended definition of a PGI has the potential to increase the scope of protection, less with respect to the form of the indication of geographical origin,[30] than with the character of the link between product and place. On the one hand, the retention of the term 'name' in reference to a 'geographical indication' in contrast with TRIPS' use of the term 'indications' suggests a desire to restrict the kinds of designations eligible for protection to direct and indirect geographical indications, the latter not constituting a geographical name as such, but a description capable of informing consumers of the place of origin of the product. On the other hand under the proposed definition, the current requirement for linkage between the product and the territory may well be attenuated to the point where reputation alone would be sufficient to achieve protection. As the definition stands, the PGI requires the product to be produced, processed or prepared within the defined geographical area, and the quality, reputation or other characteristics to be generally 'attributable' rather than 'essentially due' to that area. In fact, adopting the terms of the TRIPS Agreement would likely bring uncertainty to the definition of a 'protected geographical indication' and obscure its existing relationship with the

---

28 In Article 2(1)(b) of the Quality Schemes Regulation, a protected geographical indication is defined as 'the name of a region, a specific place or, in exceptional cases, a country, used to describe an agricultural product or a foodstuff originating in that region, specific place or country, and which possesses a specific quality, reputation or other characteristics attributable to that geographical origin and the production and/or processing and/or preparation which take place in the defined geographical area'.

29 Article 22 of the TRIPS Agreement.

30 E.g. 'Bud' makes it clear to Czech citizens that beer with that name comes from the town of Ceské Budejovice: see Budějovický Budvar National Corporation v Rudolf Ammersin GmbH (C-478/07) [2009] E.C.R. I-7721; [2009] E.T.M.R. 65, Opinion of A.G. Ruiz-Jarabo Colomer at [35], [68] and [69]. Regulation 510/2006 allows for indirect GI by referring, in art. 1(2), to 'traditional names', even though they may not be place names.

'protected designation of origin'. The definition of 'geographical indication' in Article 22 of TRIPS is an amalgamation of the variety and breadth of terminology that distinguishes the 'appellation of origin' from the 'geographical indication' and the 'indication of source.'[31] On the one hand, to include the phrase 'essentially due' within the definition of PGI is to invoke the more narrowly delimited PDO where factors of physical and human geography lend distinctive features to product quality.[32] On the other hand, to define a PGI to accord exactly with the text of TRIPS, in terms of 'a given quality, reputation or other characteristic of the good' risks changing the existing character of the link between product and place within Community law. At its most attenuated point the definition of a PGI simply requires a description of how the quality or reputation is attributable to the defined geographical area.[33] Thus, the PGI for Cornish Sardines describes a 'specific link between the geographical area and the fishing practices including the catching, landing and processing of Cornish Sardines' that comprise 'well documented traditional fishing methods'.[34] Specificity of the geographical area] If the amended definition of a 'geographical indication' is adopted, the current requirement for linkage between the product and the territory may be attenuated to the point where reputation alone would be sufficient to achieve protection.

---

[31] The term 'appellation of origin' is defined in Article 2 of the Lisbon Agreement for the Protection of Appellations of Origin and their International Registration of 1958: it 'means the geographical denomination of a country, region, or locality, which serves to designate a product originating therein, the quality or characteristics of which are due exclusively or essentially to the geographical environment, including natural and human factors'. Article 1(1) of the Madrid Agreement on Indications of Source defines the term 'indication of source' as an indication referring to a country or to a place situated therein as being the country or place of origin of a product; note that an indication of source does not require that the product should have certain qualities or characteristics, which are derived from its geographical origin.

[32] Proposal for a Regulation of the European Parliament and of the Council on agricultural product quality schemes, COM(2010) 733 final, Brussels, 10.12.2010 2010/0353 (COD)): Article 5(1)(b)(ii).

[33] The Green Paper and the Impact Assessment question whether such scope risks diminishing the intensity of the link between product and place. Specifically, it inquires whether the criteria for PGIs as distinct from PDOs should be made stricter to strengthen the link between the product and the geographical area: see European Commission (2008), 'Green Paper on agricultural product quality: product standards, farming requirements and quality schemes', Brussels , pp. 13–14; and European Commission of Agricultural Product Quality Policy: Impact Assessment Agricultural Product Quality Policy: Impact Assessment, Part B, Geographical Indications, p. 122.

[34] Cornish Sardines (registered 03.03.2010): see Commission Regulation (EC) No 1182/2009 of 30 November 2009 entering a name in the register of protected designations of origin and protected geographical indications (Cornish Sardines (PGI)), <http://ec.europa.eu/agriculture/quality/door/list.html>. For details of the specification see Official Journal of the European Union, 12 May 2009 at para. 5.1.

In comparison, the proposed definition of PDO is ostensibly unchanged in substance if not in expression. While the existing definition is specific in referring to 'the production, processing and preparation of which take place in the defined geographical area', the Quality Schemes Regulation refers simply to 'the production steps'.[35] It is an open question whether this attempt to simplify the wording may have unintended consequences with respect to the drafting of the product specification, and the scope of protection accorded the PDO.

In all, the proposed simplification might well alter the internal coherence between the PDO and PGI. The single, consolidated definition of 'geographical indications' in Article 22 of the TRIPS Agreement functions within a two-tiered scheme of protection which, lacking any specific provision of exclusive rights for agricultural products, other than wines and spirits, relies on the various unfair competition laws of WTO Member States. In contrast, Regulation 510/06 is a *sui generis* system of registration which contains a two-fold definitional structure for PGIs and PDOs. Recall that the differences between the PGI and the PDO are marked by the character and extent of the linkage of production to the defined geographical area. Any expansion of the definition of the PGI would alter the interrelationship and balance between the two kinds of indication, giving rise potentially to additional pressure on the scope of the PDO as, given its more restrictive character, it is perceived by applicants as the more valuable intellectual property to possess. On the one hand, the specificity of criteria in the definition of PDO is more closely associated with the French notion of terroir with its the focus on the constitutive qualities of the product and production process.[36] On the other hand, the PGI accommodates with greater ease the English and German approach to the relationship between product and place, with its focus on unfair competition, trustworthy consumer information and the associated criteria of deception and misrepresentation. Two key objectives of the Quality Schemes Regulation are to improve communication between producers and consumers about agricultural product qualities and; increase the coherence of the relevant legislative instruments.[37] Considering

---

35 Quality Schemes Regulation, Article 5(1)(a) stipulates: (a) 'designation of origin' is a name which identifies a product: (i) originating in a specific place, region or, in exceptional cases, a country; (ii) where the quality or characteristics of the product are essentially or exclusively due to a particular geographical environment with its inherent natural and human factors; and (iii) the production steps of which all take place in the same defined geographical area.

36 L. Bérard and P. Marchenay, 'A Market Culture: Produits de Terroir or the Selling of Heritage' in Sarah Blowen, Marion Demossier and Jeanine Picard, *Recollections of France: Memories, Identities and Heritage in Contemporary France*, Berghahn Books, v.4, Contemporary France series, Oxford, UK, 2001 at pp. 154, 155, 160.

37 Proposal for a Regulation of the European Parliament and of the Council on agricultural product quality schemes, COM(2010) 733 final, Brussels, 10.12.2010

the greater emphasis the amendments to the definition of a PGI would lend the communication function, it is possible to see the intention of legislators, to ensure that consumers are accurately informed about the characteristics and farming attributes of agricultural products.[38] Moreover, in view of ongoing international efforts to increase harmonization of GI, in so far as the proposed definition of a 'geographical indication' seeks to synthesize differing national approaches to protection, it might be seen as a positive initiative. However, the probable effectiveness of the amendments in achieving these objectives is open to question. The amendments may well call into question the internal coherence of the legislation by altering the conceptual understanding of the relationship between product and place.[39] In the event such a reconceptualization were to set at risk the link between product and place, two decades of judicial decision-making might be rendered uncertain. Currently, the PGI is defined broadly enough for most locally based products to take advantage of its protection.[40] Given the normative differences underlying the markedly different regulatory approaches within civil and common law jurisdictions, it seems preferable continue to allow harmonization to evolve gradually within the case law of Community courts.[41]

3. MISSED OPPORTUNITY TO EXTEND PRODUCT COVERAGE

PDOs, PGIs and Community Trade Marks (CTMs) are each subject to the principle of 'specialty', in so far as they are protected in relation to certain

---

2010/0353 (COD) ('Quality Schemes Regulation'): Explanatory Memorandum, at 3.

[38] Proposal for a Regulation of the European Parliament and of the Council on agricultural product quality schemes, COM(2010) 733 final, Brussels, 10.12.2010 2010/0353 (COD) ('Quality Schemes Regulation'): Explanatory Memorandum, at 2.

[39] Further on the relationship between product and place see Dev Gangjee *Relocating the Law of Geographical Indications* (Cambridge University Press, 2012) at 141–146.

[40] 'Article 2(1)(b) of Regulation No 510/2006 defines a protected geographical indication as: the name of region, a specific place or, in exceptional cases, a country, used to describe an agricultural product or a foodstuff: originating in that region, specific place or country; and which possesses a specific quality, reputation or other characteristics attributable to that geographical origin; and the production and/or processing and/or preparation of which take place in the defined geographical area.'

[41] G.E. Evans, 'A Comparative Analysis of the Protection of Geographical Indications in the European Union and the United States under *Sui Generis* and Trademark Systems' in T. Takenaka ed. *Intellectual Property Systems in Common Law and Civil Law Countries,* Edward Elgar (2013, forthcoming).

kinds of products. Within the Quality Schemes Regulation, the relatively limited scope of product coverage has been generally maintained. Under existing legislation, both TSGs and PGIs cover those agricultural products intended for human consumption listed in Annex I to the Treaty, such as edible oils, cheese, and fish.[42] However, applications in respect of foods are comparatively more restricted.[43]

The TSG Regulation No 509/2006 alone covers a variety of foods to include, pre-cooked meals, prepared condiment sauces and soups.[44] Should the EU adopt a more inclusive coverage of food products under the Quality Schemes Regulation it would serve not only the possible incorporation of TSGs within the PGI scheme, but also meet the developmental objective to assist producers, in promoting the use of the registration system for GI, with their efforts in producing quality products, that might benefit the rural economy.[45]

A similar and stronger argument may be made in respect of the traditional products known as handicrafts such as woollen knitwear, carpets and mosaic work. An extension of product coverage under the Quality Schemes Regulation to include handicrafts would meet the broader goal of the Quality Schemes legislation in promoting agricultural and processing activities, particularly in less favoured rural areas.[46] In 2009 the Commission conducted a feasibility study into the protection of geographical indications for handicrafts.[47] When producer representatives were asked about the possible inclusion of handicrafts within the registration system for GI, there was majority support for such a proposal. Producers considered the registration system to

---

42 With the exception of the addition of dark chocolate, Quality Schemes Regulation at para. 3.1.1.

43 Registration may be sought for those agricultural products for human consumption referred to in: the Treaty Establishing the European Community (EC Treaty), Chapter 20, Annex I; Lisbon Treaty, Consolidated versions of the Treaty on European Union and the Treaty on the Functioning of the European Union, Official Journal, Vol. 51, May 2008, Annex I, list referred to in Article 38 of the Treaty On The Functioning of the European Union; GI Regulation, Annex I – Foodstuffs covered in Article1, paragraph 1: Regulation (EC) No 417/2008 (OJ L 125 of 9 May 2008); Regulation (EC) No 510/2008 (OJ L 149 of 7 June 2008), Annex II – Agricultural products covered in Article1, paragraph: Regulation (EC) No 417/2008 (OJ L 125 of 9 May 2008); Regulation (EC) No 510/2008 (OJ L 149 of 7 June 2008): <http://europa.eu/legislation_summaries/agriculture/food/l66044_en.htm>.

44 The TSG regulation alone covers a variety of foods listed in Annex I to Regulation (EC) No 509/2006.

45 Quality Schemes Regulation, Recital 4 and Article 1.

46 Quality Schemes Regulation, Article 1.

47 Insight Consulting (2009), 'Study on the protection of geographical indications for products other than wines, spirits, agricultural products or foodstuffs', commissioned by the Directorate General for Trade of the European Commission, <http://trade.ec.europa.eu/doclib/docs/2011/may/tradoc_147926.pdf>.

constitute an effective means of promoting agricultural products.[48] If the registration system for GI were to include handicrafts, such extended coverage might have the further advantage of reviving traditional crafts in remote areas of the EU.[49] For example, communities in remote areas such as the Shetland Islands might well benefit from the ability to file for a PGI for hand-made woollen garments. Moreover, given the share of exports that such handicrafts enjoy, their limited legal protection at the EU level should be a source of concern.[50]

In recognition of the fact that agricultural enterprise from both European and third countries may be prevented from obtaining the most effective form of registration, the Green Paper on Agricultural Product Quality Policy of 2008 identified the scope of products covered by the GI Regulation as an issue meriting comment through public consultation.[51] Should the EU adopt a more inclusive coverage of products under the GI Regulation, as recommended by the Economic and Social Committee, it would not only assist producers to develop export markets but also to promote the authenticity of handicrafts, and reduce misleading claims as to product origin.[52]

---

48 Insight Consulting (2009), 'Study on the protection of geographical indications for products other than wines, spirits, agricultural products or foodstuffs', commissioned by the Directorate General for Trade of the European Commission at pp. 7-10.

49 Doha, WIPO Agenda. At the fifth session of the WIPO Intergovernmental Committee on Intellectual Property and Genetic Resources, Traditional Knowledge and Folklore, it was pointed out that some traditional cultural expressions (TCEs), such as handicrafts made using natural resources, may qualify as 'goods' which could be protected by geographical indications.

50 M. Blakeney (2009), 'Protection of Traditional Knowledge by Geographical Indications', in C. Antons (ed.), *Traditional Knowledge Traditional Knowledge, Traditional Cultural Expressions and Intellectual Property Law in the Asia-Pacific Region* (Max Planck Series on Asian Intellectual Property Law) Kluwer Law International, p. 108.

51 Further to the 'Green Paper on Agricultural Product Quality Policy', the European Commission consulted the public on agricultural products and foods covered by the Regulation with particular consideration to salt, mixed herbs, wicker products and condiments: <http://ec.europa.eu/agriculture/quality/policy/index_en.htm>. The European Economic and Social Committee on Geographical indications and designations also launched a policy consultation process (Opinion 2008/C 204/14) at para. 1.2.3.

52 The EESC recommends that the product listings accompanying Regulation No 510/2006 should include non-agricultural products, with a view to promoting the rural culture of an area: Opinion of the EESC on GIs, OJ, 2008, C 204/57 at para. 1.2.3. Further, Insight Consulting conducted a study with the aim of ascertaining the feasibility of protecting handicrafts: 'Study on the Protection of Geographical Indications for Products Other than Wines, Spirits, Agricultural Products or Foodstuffs', 2009, <http://ec.europa.eu/trade/creating-opportunities/trade-topics/intellectual-property/geographical-indications/>.

4. AMENDMENT OF THE APPLICATION PROCEDURE

The Quality Schemes Regulation sets out to streamline the application and registration process for PDO and PGI, including opposition and cancellation procedures; scrutiny by the Commission; and decisions on registration. As stated in the Explanatory Memorandum, one of the aims in revising the registration process is to render the system more effective by shortening time delays and stipulating specific periods of time for the completion of procedures.[53] To this end, under Article 47 concerning scrutiny and publication for opposition, the Commission is to scrutinize applications to check that they meet the necessary conditions within a period not exceeding six months.

The most significant, and potentially controversial change, is that respecting permitted time periods in relation to opposition procedures in Article 48, where the period during which an interested party may object to the registration of the name has been shortened from six to two months.[54] The intention is to reduce delays by having the European Commission (EC) complete its analysis and reach a final decision more quickly, partly by early rejection of clearly insufficient submissions. Subsequently, where a statement of opposition is admissible, the Commission is to invite the opponent and the authority that lodged the application to engage in appropriate consultations for a reasonable period that shall not exceed three months. On the one hand, the clarification of procedures for opposition and shorter time periods should increase the effectiveness of the system, given that they are designed to maintain a register that is more efficient to register names, one that is transparent and reflects the competitive realities of market conditions. On the other hand, some flexibility may need to be allowed in the case of applicants from outside the EU, if producer groups in less developed countries are not to be disadvantaged by their comparative lack of legal resources.

---

53 Proposal for a Regulation of the European Parliament and of the Council on agricultural product quality schemes, COM (2010) 733 final, Brussels, 10.12.2010 2010/0353 (COD) ('Quality Schemes Regulation'): Explanatory Memorandum, at p. 8.

54 See Regulation No 510/2006, Article 7; and Quality Schemes Regulation, Article 48. It is notable that in the compromise text agreed by the Council and the European Parliament representatives (adopted by the EU Parliament on September 12, 2012), not only has the opposition period been extended to three months, but a clause has been inserted stating that 'the Commission may ... extend the deadline of the consultations by a maximum of three months if the Commission deems that extending the deadline contributes to reaching an agreement or if one of the participants is a of a third country': draft art. 48 at p 41: *Committee on Agriculture and Rural Development, Proposal for a Regulation on Agricultural Product Quality Schemes, Presidency compromise text (February 23, 2011) (COM(2010)0733C7-0423/2010-2010/0353(COD)): http:www.europarl.europa.eu/oeil/popups/ficheprocedure.do?lang=en&reference=2010/0353(COD).*

Two further potentially constructive steps are the clarification in Article 51 of the criteria for cancellation to specify that in addition to non-compliance with the specification, names may also be cancelled on the ground that no product has been 'placed on the market under [...] the protected designation of origin or the protected geographical indication for at least five years'.[55] Secondly, in the interests of greater transparency and enhanced competition, Article 11 affirms that the register of GI, including those belonging to producer groups in third countries, shall be 'publicly accessible'.[56]

5. AMENDMENT OF PRODUCTION STANDARDS AND PRODUCT SPECIFICATION

The product specification governs production standards. It details the sourcing of raw materials; and the standards applicable to production and processing.[57] As a result, it is possible for producer groups to exert a considerable degree of control over the processing and distribution, and ultimately over the scope of protection accorded the product. Given the opportunity producers have in setting down the terms of production and at the end of the day, the scope of protection accorded to the product, concern has arisen over the sourcing of raw materials and the lack of controls carried out in order to ensure compliance with the specification.

In particular, since the PGI requires only that production or processing should take place in the defined geographical area, all the raw materials may be sourced from outside.[58] Thus, in the case of the PGI, the product need not originate entirely from within the designated region and need only have one particular quality that is attributable, rather than exclusively due to, the geographical area. Research conducted prior to the proposed legislative changes indicated that in some Member States consumer groups expressed concern that consumers are being misled with regard to the origin of raw mate-

---

55 Cf. Regulation No 510/2006, Article 12 regarding cancellation.

56 Cf. Regulation No 510/2006, Article 7(6): 'The Commission shall maintain updated a register of protected designations of origin and protected geographical indications'.

57 See Article 4(2) of the GI Regulation setting out the requirements of the product specification.

58 In the case of *Spreewälder Gurken* the CJEU ruled that a foodstuff may be treated as originating from the geographical area concerned if it is processed or produced in that area, even if the raw materials are sourced from outside the defined area: Case C-269/99, *Carl Kühne GmbH & Co. KG and Others v. Jütro Konservenfabrik GmbH & Co. KG*, CJEU (2001), para. 61.

rials. For example, where a PGI product is concerned, the origin of the raw materials such as beef, may even be sourced internationally.[59]

The legislative response is to be found in Articles 5 and 7 of the Quality Schemes Regulation, which contain new provisions concerning additional controls on production. Article 5(3) would allow the legislature to provide 'restrictions and derogations regarding the steps of production, which shall take place in the defined geographical area or regarding the sourcing of raw materials'. Similarly, Article 7(3) is drafted to allow the EC to 'lay down further rules as to the content of a product specification'. In future, if the Quality Schemes Regulation is accepted, the EC intends to supervise more closely both the production steps, including the sourcing of raw materials; and the controls provided over those production steps.

On the one hand, the possibility of sourcing all raw materials from outside the defined geographical area makes the registration of PGIs a very effective form of protection for the broadest possible constituency of producers. Given the breadth of the amended definition, there would be few producers groups, having the capacity collectively to mobilize production that would be unable to apply for protection.

On the other hand, in view of the fact that all raw materials may come from outside the area, the current absence of control over the external sourcing of raw materials in processed foods risks impugning credibility of the geographical indications in the eyes of consumer, doing little to reassure consumers that in paying a premium, the product has been certified as complying with verifiable standards of food safety.[60] When seen from the viewpoint of the credibility of GI in the eyes of consumers, there is a decided advantage in the additional scope the Quality Schemes Regulation gives the Commission to require producers in certain sectors to inform the public about the place of farming of raw materials where this is different from the place indicated by the geographical indication; and to identify the origin of raw materials, in cases where they come from somewhere outside the defined geographical area.[61]

---

59 In Italy, in the case of PGI Bresaola della Valtellina (a processed meat product) the product is being produced by some firms using meat from Bovine-Zebu in Brazil: European Commission of Agricultural Product Quality Policy: Impact Assessment Agricultural Product Quality Policy: Impact Assessment, Part B, Geographical Indications, p. 39.

60 See European Commission (2008), 'Green Paper on Agricultural Product Quality: Product Standards, Farming Requirements and Quality Schemes', Brussels , p. 13, discussing the criteria for registration of geographical indications.

61 Communication from the Commission to the European Parliament, the Council, the European Economic and Social Committee and the Committee of the Regions on Agricultural Product Quality policy (SEC(2009) 670). Further, the Commission is contemplating the possible extension of certification requirements to different operators in the supply chain including importers and distributors.

6. MISSED OPPORTUNITY TO DEFINE THE GEOGRAPHICAL AREA OF PRODUCTION?

If the application for GI protection to proceed without undue legal expense; we might enquire why legislators did not address the issues that have arisen concerning the demarcation of the geographic area of production. Article 7(1) of the Quality Schemes Regulation stipulates that to be eligible for 'designation of origin' or 'geographical indication' the specification must include a definition of the geographical area. Only those producers who are established in the defined geographical area are entitled to exercise the rights attached to the PDO or PGI. Difficulties may therefore arise over the exclusion of producers from the defined geographical area. The definition of geographical area has the potential to upset established market shares and can readily give rise to objections by competitors who are excluded from the defined area and, at worst, to litigation.[62] Any conflict over the definition of the geographical area needs to be resolved expeditiously. Those producers outside the defined area, who are unable to use the PGI or PDO labels, must either re-brand their product or move their production within the protected territory, as a successful application means that producers outside the defined area will normally be given five years to phase out their use of the geographical name in relation to production.[63]

Significantly, no specific criteria exist for delimiting the geographic area. For example, when the initial specification for the PGI 'Melton Mowbray' excluded Northern Foods Plc, a large producer, from the defined geographic area, the company sought to oppose the application. While the proposed area encompassed a large 1800 square mile region of the English East Midlands, including Leicestershire, where the market leader, Samworth Brothers, produced 62 per cent of the product; it excluded those towns in Shropshire and Wiltshire, where Northern Foods held 28 per cent of the market. In *Northern Foods Plc v The Department for Environment, Food and Rural Affairs*, the opponent challenged, albeit without success, the decision of DEFRA to forward the application to the Commission.[64]

Query whether the legislators missed the opportunity to clarify the defined geographical area of production? The issue of whether the definition of the geographical area satisfies the required elements of Article 2 of the GI

---

[62] See *Northern Foods Plc v The Department for Environment, Food and Rural Affairs* [2005] EWHC 2971.

[63] Quality Schemes Regulation, Article 5(1)(b).

[64] In 2005, the High Court dismissed Northern Foods' complaint concerning the description of the geographic area, thereby allowing the application to proceed to the Commission for further examination: *Northern Foods Plc v The Department For Environment, Food And Rural Affairs* [2005] EWHC 2971.

Regulation might have been referred to the various criteria linking the product with a specific place. The key question is whether the geographical area, as defined, constitutes an environment which possesses the specific natural and human factors capable of giving the product its particular characteristics.[65]

7. AMENDMENT OF CONTROL AND INSPECTION STRUCTURES

A PGI or PDO is only valid in so far as the product is certified to be in conformity with the specification.[66] While the GI Regulation requires the specification to include details of inspection structures, the effectiveness and impartiality of those procedures has been questioned.[67] The inspection process may not necessarily cover the mode of production, such as the rearing of livestock or choice of meat, when raw materials are drawn from outside the defined geographical area.

Currently, the responsibility for establishing and maintaining systems for inspection and compliance rests with the national authorities. They are obliged to have in place inspection systems, which are able to provide the monitoring and compliance structures necessary to ensure that the product conforms to the specification.[68] However, due to the lack of a supervisory authority at the EU level, problems have arisen with the standard and objectivity of inspection procedures.[69] The added value of the products bearing a PDO or PGI, based as it is on consumer trust, is only credible when accompanied by effective verification and controls.[70]

The Quality Schemes Regulation proposes to address this lack of rigour in quality control by providing for supervision of Member State control activities

---

[65] Joined Cases C-465/02 and C-466/02 *The Federal Republic of Germany and the Kingdom of Denmark v Commission*, Judgment of the Court, Grand Chamber, 2005, *Feta*, paras 48–51.

[66] Regulation No 510/2006, Article 4.1 of stating unequivocally that to be eligible to use a PGI or PDO a product must comply with the specification.

[67] See Articles 4(2)(g), 5(3) and (4) concerning inspection structures.

[68] Article 10(1) requires Member States to ensure that inspection structures are in place. To this effect see also *Parmesan*, para. 74. Note that the inspection bodies can be private bodies approved for that purpose by the Member State: Case C-132/05, *Commission of the European Communities v Germany,* CJEU, Grand Chamber, 2008 (*Parmesan*), para.75.

[69] The task of establishing controls is, in line with Regulation (EC) No 882/2004 on official feed and food controls, to be undertaken in the first place under the responsibility of national competent authorities.

[70] Quality Schemes Regulation, Recital 46.

to be undertaken at Union level.[71] The Quality Schemes Regulation proposes minimum common rules on official controls to ensure a product follows the specification and correct labelling in the marketplace. The proposal is to render protected products at each stage of production, processing and distribution, subject to inspection procedures that are consistent with general EU controls for the monitoring of animal health, animal feed and food law.[72] To better comply with EU controls, references to the most relevant articles are incorporated in the Quality Schemes Regulation;[73] in addition, so as to ensure greater objectivity and effectiveness, the legislators intend that the competent authorities should meet certain operational criteria;[74] that international standards are used for the operation and accreditation of the control bodies;[75] and that there is an annual review procedure, whereby information on control activities for GI is included in reports prepared by the Member States.[76]

On the one hand the proposal to have GI inspection procedures comply with EU standards for verification and control of agricultural and food production constitutes a constructive development; and one that is needed to improve consumer confidence in the certification process. On the other hand, we might question the efficiency of this proposal when the additional costs of compliance will be incurred by producer groups. In fact, the proposal recommends Member States be authorized to charge a fee to cover the costs incurred.[77] Therefore the immediate cost of verifying compliance with the specification will likely be borne by the producer groups subject to those controls.[78] In terms of effectiveness, producers will only be in a position to reap the benefits of registration provided their undertaking is able to sustain the costs of regular inspection.[79]

---

71 Provisions common to each scheme have been consolidated: Title V contains the common provisions; and Chapter I is devoted to 'official controls for protected designations of origin, protected geographical indications and traditional specialities guaranteed'.

72 See Regulation (EC) No 882/2004 of the European Parliament and of the Council of 29 April 2004 on official controls performed to ensure the verification of compliance with feed and food law, animal health and animal welfare rules, including a system of checks at all stages of production, processing and distribution.

73 See Quality Schemes Regulation, Recital 46.

74 See Quality Schemes Regulation, Recital 48.

75 See Quality Schemes Regulation, Recital 49.

76 See Quality Schemes Regulation, Recital 50.

77 See Quality Schemes Regulation, Recital 51.

78 Under Article 11(1) (Regulation No 510/2006) the costs of inspection and verification of compliance with the specification 'shall be borne by the operators subject to those controls'.

79 Langinier and Babcock argue that certification costs are the key determinant of distributional effects and social welfare associated with GI: C. Langinier and B.A. Babcock (2008), 'Agricultural Production Clubs: Viability and Welfare Implications', *Journal of Agricultural and Food Industrial Organization*, **6** (1), 1–29.

The Quality Schemes Regulation recognizes that small-scale producers in particular often find the EU GI system burdensome in terms of inspection procedures and the associated costs involved in compliance with the product specification.[80] The impact assessment for geographical indications highlighted the widespread failure of the system to attract applications from small-scale producers, notwithstanding that those producing artisanal products might benefit from a system that would assist in promoting traditional methods of manufacture. Consequently, for all the competitive benefits that producer groups may derive from the registration of GI, there may be practical and resource-based considerations that make it a less effective, more costly and possibly uncertain form of protection.[81] In recognition of the obstacles that the requirements of certification can pose for the very smallholders the registration system for GI was designed to assist, the Quality Schemes Regulation intends to monitor the related burdens faced by small-scale producers.[82]

8. MISSED OPPORTUNITY TO ADDRESS THE USE OF GENERIC NAMES

Recital 52 of the Quality Schemes Regulation identifies the need to clarify existing rules concerning the continued use of names that are generic. To this end, generic terms that are similar to, or form part of a denomination that is protected, are to retain their generic status.[83] Subsequently, in respect of 'certain prior uses' proposed Article 38 of the Quality Schemes Regulation saves 'terms that are generic in the Union, even if the generic term is part of a

---

[80] Therefore, further research is to be carried out in order to assess the problems faced by small-scale producers in participating in Union quality schemes. On the basis of the results of this analysis, the Commission may propose appropriate follow-up. See European Commission (2008), 'Green Paper on Agricultural Product Quality: Product Standards, Farming Requirements And Quality Schemes', Brussels, pp. 20–1.

[81] Concerning the comparative advantage of the trade mark system, see G.E. Evans (2010), 'The Comparative Advantages of Geographical Indications and Community Trade Marks for the Marketing of Agricultural Products in the European Union', *International Review of Intellectual Property and Competition Law*, **41**, IIC, 645-674.

[82] The 'Green Paper on Agricultural Product Quality' invited public submissions on how the administrative costs and burdens associated with membership of quality certification schemes could be reduced and the European Commission (2008), 'Green Paper on Agricultural Product Quality: Product Standards, Farming Requirements and Quality Schemes', Brussels, p. 21.

[83] 'Existing rules concerning the continued use of names that are generic should be clarified to the effect that generic terms that are similar to or form part of a name or term that is protected or reserved should retain such generic status' (Quality Schemes Regulation, Recital 52).

name that is protected [as a PDO or PGI]'. The definition of 'generic' in proposed Article 3(6)[84] ostensibly differs little from the existing definition in so far as it refers to 'terms which include those names of [the] product which, although relating to the place, region or country where the product was originally produced or marketed, have become the common name of a product'.[85] Nonetheless, the addition of the phrase 'in the Union' at the close of the definition, is likely to prompt debate over the extent of generic use throughout the EU necessary to invoke a successful defence to an action for infringement, as set out in proposed Article 13(1):

> Where a protected designation of origin or a protected geographical indication contains within it the name of a product which is considered generic, the use of that generic name shall not be considered [contrary to the exclusive rights of the GI holder].

Article 13 of the Quality Schemes Regulation continues to provide that PDOs and PGIs shall be protected both against 'any direct or indirect commercial use of a registered name' in respect of identical or comparable products, and any evocation of the name, even if the true origin of the product is indicated, or if the protected name is translated or accompanied by expressions such as 'style', 'type', 'method' or 'imitation'.[86]

The limitation on the rights of producer groups in respect of generic terms remains a controversial issue for applicants of GI and competitors alike. For example, in the case of *Parmesan*,[87] in response to an action for infringement, Germany claimed that although the term 'parmesan' had historical roots in the region of Parma, it had become a generic name for hard cheeses of diverse origins, grated or intended to be grated, as distinct from the PDO 'Parmigiano Reggiano'.[88]

---

84 Provisions common to each scheme are consolidated in separate Titles. Notably, key definitions common to each product quality scheme, such as 'generic terms', are consolidated in Title I; Quality Schemes Regulation, Article 3.

85 Likewise see Regulation No 510/2006, Article 13(1) to the effect that where a registered name contains within it the name of an agricultural product or foodstuff which is considered generic, the use of that generic name shall not be considered as an infringement.

86 Quality Schemes Regulation, Article 13(1)(a) and (b).

87 Case C-132/05 *Commission of the European Communities v Germany,* CJEU, Grand Chamber, 2008.

88 Under Article 13(1)(d) of Regulation 510/2006 (and former Regulation No 2081/92), where a registered name contains within it the name of an agricultural product or foodstuff which is considered generic, the use of that generic name on the appropriate agricultural product or foodstuff shall not be considered to be contrary to points (a) or (b) in the first subparagraph.

In establishing whether or not a name has become generic, Article 38 of the Quality Schemes Regulation directs the Court to take account of all factors, in particular:

(a) the existing situation in the Member States and in areas of consumption;
(b) the relevant national or Union legal acts.

In this regard, the criteria for assessing genericness do not differ substantively from Article 3(1) of the existing Regulation.[89] In its case law, the CJEU elaborated these factors at length, finding that, when determining the status of a name, it is necessary to consider the following criteria:

- Supply, that is, the places of production of the product concerned both inside and outside the Member State;
- Persistence of geographic connotation;
- Demand, that is, the consumption of that product inside and outside that Member State;
- How it is perceived by consumers inside and outside the Member State concerned; and
- The existence of national legislation specifically relating to that product, and the way in which the name has been used in Community law.[90]

Recent case law highlights the way in which the Court has succeeded in giving a restrictive interpretation to genericness, to the effect that, if the name retains the ability to evoke the place of production, it will likely be allowed to proceed to registration. In *Feta*, the Court found a persistence of geographical connotation based on the fact that, the majority of cheeses bearing the name 'feta' produced in Member States other than Greece, make explicit or implicit reference to Greek territory, culture or tradition. By inference therefore, the Court determined that consumers in those Member States perceived 'feta' as a cheese associated with Greece, even if in reality it had been produced in another Member State.[91] The decision confirming PDO status for Feta was followed in *Parmesan* where the Court reasoned that were 'parmesan' a neutral term without geographical connotation, there would be no plausible explanation for the persistent efforts of manufacturers elsewhere to establish through words or images a link between their products and Italy.[92] The Grand Chamber of the

89 Article 3(1) of the Regulation directs the court to take account of all factors, in particular: (a) the existing situation in the Member States and in areas of consumption; and (b) the relevant national or Community laws.

90 *Parmesan*, paras 53 and 101; see also Joined Cases C-465/02 and C-466/02 *Germany and Denmark v Commission* [2005] ECR I-9115 ('*Feta*'), paras 76–99.

91 *Feta*, para. 87.

92 *Parmesan*, para. 37.

CJEU took a broad view of the protection accorded such compound designations, rejecting the contention that they are infringed only when used in the exact form in which they are registered.[93]

Likewise, in the case of the PGI 'Bayerisches Bier',[94] the defendant, a Dutch beer producer, failed to convince the Court that the term 'Bayerisches' or translations of it had become generic for beer produced in accordance with 'the Bavarian method' of production which originated during the nineteenth century in Bavaria, from where it spread throughout Europe. The PGI 'Bayerisches Bier' was considered not to have become generic even when the European market for beer contained trade marks that included the word 'Bayerisches' or translations as synonyms for the Bavarian bottom-fermentation brewing method.[95] The Court concluded that registration of the PGI was justified by the need to prevent the disappearance of reputation as a result of 'popularisation through general use outside its geographical origin'.[96] There appears to be a serious case for codifying additional criteria to be applied to the test for genericness, to render the test more rigorous.

While those producers in the defined areas benefit from the increased marketing exclusivity which results from such an attenuated connection with the place where the product was originally produced, the economic impact on the interests of competitors, who must go to the expense of re-branding and re-labelling, is relatively discounted. The economic efficiency of the practice is surely open to question where restitution of the value in GI, has been achieved at the cost of litigation and expense for competitors. While it might have been anticipated that the Quality Schemes Regulation would seek to redress the balance of interests in favour of a derogation for long-held generic usage, proposed Article 38 merely reserves a right of the legislature 'to lay down additional rules for determining the generic status of names or terms' that conflict with a registered PDO or PGI.[97] Given the status of the decisions in

---

93 *Parmesan*, para. 31.

94 Case C-343/07 *Bavaria N.V. and Bavaria Italia Srl v Bayerischer Brauerbund*, CJEU, 2009 (*'Bavaria'*).

95 *Bavaria*, para. 105.

96 *Bavaria* [2009] E.C.R. I-5491; [2009] E.T.M.R. 61 at [106]. Also note that the geographical name that is the subject of an application for registration as a PGI or PDO cannot be regarded as generic pending the possible forwarding of the application for registration to the Commission of the European Communities by the national authorities: *Grandi Salumifici Italiani SpA v Regione Emilia-Romagna* (C-446/07) [2009] E.C.R. I-8041; [2009] E.C.R. I-8041; [2009] E.T.M.R. 64, Opinion of A.G. Sharpston at [36]; followed by the CJEU at [49].

97 The 'Green Paper on Agricultural Product Quality' calls for public consultation concerning the criteria that should be used to determine whether a name is generic European Commission (2008), 'Green Paper on Agricultural Product Quality: Product Standards, Farming Requirements and Quality Schemes', Brussels, p. 13.

Feta and *Parmesan*, legislators might have sought to codify the criteria elaborated by the Grand Chamber. Query whether their choice not to do so indicates that the Commission is keeping a watching brief on the balance of interests at play in conflicts over generic terms. Thus, for the present, the position is maintained, whereby the Court's restrictive interpretation of generic terms means that producer groups established within the EU, stand a good chance of recovering exclusive rights to a name.[98]

9. MISSED OPPORTUNITY TO CLARIFY THE INTERRELATIONSHIP OF GIS AND TRADEMARKS?

The interrelationship of the two distinct systems for the registration of GI and trade marks is another highly controversial issue. On the one hand, where an applicant attempts to register a Community trade mark (CTM) containing an earlier registered PGI or PDO, the classic rule of priority will apply to prevent registration.[99] [100] Article 14(1) of the GI Regulation and likewise the proposed Quality Schemes Regulation, require the refusal or invalidation of a trade mark, in circumstances where it would constitute the infringement of a PDO or PGI.[101]

On the other hand, in the case of conflicts between GI and earlier trademarks the rules do not strictly follow the principle of priority. In a reversal of the priority rule, an application to register a later GI that conflicts with an earlier trade mark is allowable, provided the application has been made in

---

98 See further G.E. Evans (2010), 'The Comparative Advantages of Geographical Indications and Community Trademarks for the Marketing of Agricultural Products in the European Union', **41** *IIC*, 663–4.

99 This is in accordance with the classic rule of priority that the first in time has the better entitlement. See also Article 7(1)(k) of Regulation No 207/2009 of 26 February 2009 on the Community trade (CTMR), stating that trade marks which contain a designation of origin or a geographical indication registered under the Regulation 510/2006 when they correspond to one of the situations covered by Article 13 of that Regulation and regarding the same type of product will be refused.

100 Similarly, the GI registration system allows interested parties to lodge an objection to the application for a PDO or PGI. It is possible to object in the case of an EU internal application at the national stage. Objections are also received in the six-month period after publication of the PGI application: Regulation 510/2006, Article 7.

101 Article 13 of Regulation 510/2006 sets out the scope of protection accorded PDOs and PGIs, and includes any direct or indirect commercial use of the registered name for comparable products and any misuse, imitation, or evocation. To the same effect see CTMR, Article 7(1)(k). Regarding Biraghi's defence that the term 'grana' is generic, see Case T-291/03, *Consorzio per la Tutela del Formaggio Grana Padano v OHIM, Biraghi SpA*, Court of First Instance, 2007, where the General Court held that the OHIM Board of Appeal had erred in finding that the existence of the PDO 'Grana Padano' did not prevent registration of the mark 'Grana Biraghi' at para. 89.

accordance with honest practice.[102] In the case of an earlier registered trade-mark, the GI Regulations mandate the coexistence of the two systems.[103] Article 14(2) of the GI Regulation applies in respect of conflicts between earlier trade marks and a registered GI:[104]

> With due regard to Community law, a trade mark the use of which corresponds to one of the situations referred to in Article 13 which has been applied for, registered, or established by use, in good faith within the territory of the Community, before either the date of protection of the designation of origin or geographical indication in the country of origin or before 1 January 1996, may continue to be used notwithstanding the registration of a designation of origin or geographical indication.[105]

Thus, the use of an identical and later registered GI will be allowed as an exception to the trade mark owner's rights, provided the use of the GI is in accordance with honest commercial practice.[106]

During the consultation phase for the Quality Schemes Regulation, several significant stakeholders, including the International Trademark Association

---

[102] Some likelihood of confusion between the trade mark and the later GI may even be tolerated: see Case C-100/02 *Gerolsteiner Brunnen*, CJEU, 2004, para. 24.

[103] CTMR, Article 164, states that the Trade Mark Regulation 'shall not affect Council Regulation (EC) No 510/2006, and in particular Article 14 thereof'. The term 'coexistence' refers to a legal regime under which a GI and a trade mark can be used concurrently to some extent, even though the use of one or both of them would otherwise infringe the rights conferred by the other.

[104] The scope of Article 14(2) is confined in time to those trade marks applied for, registered or established by use either before the GI is protected in its country of origin or before the date of submission to the Commission of an application for GI registration. See further G.E. Evans (2006), 'The Protection of Geographical Indications after Doha: Quo Vadis?', *Journal of International Economic Law*, **9** (3), 575–614 (with Michael Blakeney).

[105] That is provided that no grounds for its invalidity or revocation exist as specified under the Trade Mark Directive (EEC) No 89/104 of 21 December 1988; or the CTMR (EC) No 40/94 of 20 December 1993 on the Community trade mark (as codified in Regulation (EC) No 207/2009 of 26 February 2009), Article 12(b). The reference in Article 14(2) to 'Community law' alludes to certain exceptions to the rights of the trade mark owner. Specifically, the CTMR provides an exception where an unauthorized third party is using the name in question to indicate the kind, quality, geographic origin or other characteristics of the goods or services.

[106] The EC successfully argued before the WTO that GI and trade marks constitute independent but equal forms of intellectual property in accordance with the structure of the TRIPS Agreement and in particular Article 24.5 of that Agreement concerning their interrelationship. Their coexistence turns on the general exception as to trade mark rights in TRIPS, Article 17, as constituting a valid defence against the exclusive rights of trade mark holders: See WTO, 'EC – Protection Of Trademarks And Geographical Indications For Agricultural Products And Foodstuffs', Report of the Panel, 2005, WT/DS174/R, paras 7.512–7.531.

(INTA), expressed concern that the coexistence provisions of Article 14(2) of Regulation 510/2006 were not without ambiguity. INTA submitted that these provisions could be read in a manner as to suggest that the use of a trade mark filed long before the geographical indication application, but later than 1 January 1996, might be prohibited if the geographical indication had been protected in the country of origin at an earlier date.[107]

INTA considered this would be a violation of Article 16 of the TRIPS Agreement, and the basic principles of priority and territoriality. In this regard it recommended that the language of the coexistence provisions of Article 14(2) of GI Regulation[108] be amended so as to clearly reflect the priority principle.[109] In addition, it was suggested that the text of Regulation 510/2006 clarify that the beneficiaries of GI protection are not entitled to object to the use of a trade mark that is filed in good faith before the date on which the application for protection of the GI was submitted to the European Commission.

In response, proposed Article 14(2) has been redrafted to reflect the concern over the ambiguity with reference to pre-existing trade mark rights, and to affirm the principle of coexistence of the trade mark and GI systems.

> ...a trade mark the use of which contravenes Article 13 which has been applied for, registered, or established by use, if that possibility is provided for by the legislation concerned, in good faith within the territory of the EU, before the date on which the application for protection of the designation of origin or geographical indication is submitted to the Commission, may continue to be used and renewed for that product notwithstanding the registration of a designation of origin or geographical indication, provided that no grounds for its invalidity or revocation exist under Council Regulation (EC) No 207/2009 of 26 February 2009 on the Community trade mark or under Directive 2008/95/EC. In such cases, the use of the protected designation of origin or protected geographical indication shall be permitted as well as use of the relevant trade marks.

Thus the Article no longer refers to '1 January 1996' in connection with the date of registration (or application) of the allegedly conflicting trade mark.

---

107 See INTA letter to the Office of the United States Trade Representative (USTR) concerning Regulation 2081/92 governing geographical indications and its amendment, submitting that amended Regulation 510/2006 continues to violate the TRIPS Agreement, in that it does not fully ensure the exclusivity of prior trade marks, no matter their level of fame and degree of use: www.inta.org/Advocacy/Documents/March262004.pdf

108 Regulation (EC) No 110/2008 of the European Parliament and of the Council of 15 January 2008 on the definition, description, presentation, labelling and the protection of spirit drinks, Article 23(2).

109 And to bring it in line with and the previous provision of Article 14(2) under the original Regulation (EC) No 2081/92.

The final sentence is an additional provision which, consistently with Recital 54, affirms the principle of coexistence to the effect that 'the provisions for refusal or coexistence of a designation of origin or a geographical indication on the ground of conflict with a prior trade mark should be continued'. It affirms that the life of the trade mark continues with the addition of the words 'renewed for that product' at the same time making it clear that there is to be no expansion of trade mark rights in respect of the conflicting name. Further, the concern expressed by stakeholders that a prior trade mark was nevertheless open to challenge by beneficiaries of GI, and the expense such litigation poses for trade mark owners has been assuaged to some extent in the express statement of the principle of coexistence of the two systems and the effect of its operation in proposed Article 14(2).

In view of the legislation, cases such *Bavaria NV and Bavaria Italia Srl v Bayerischer Brauerbund*[110] should not arise in future. In that case, the geographical name at issue was Bavaria for beer. The parties concerned in the dispute were the earlier trade mark owner, the Dutch company Bavaria NV, and Bayerischer Brauerbund, a longstanding association of Bavarian brewers, holders of a PGI for Bavarian beer.[111] Brauerei Bavaria NV, one of the Netherlands' biggest producers of beer, began to use the designation 'Bavaria' in 1925, and it became part of its company name in 1930. Bavaria NV was the proprietor and the user of several international trade marks, in force in Italy and elsewhere, which contained, together with other expressions or figurative elements, the name 'Bavaria', with registration dates as early as 1947.[112] Many decades later, in 2001, the PGI 'Bayerisches Bier' was registered to the Bayerische Brauerbund eV (the Bavarian Brewers Association) of Munich.[113]

Subsequently, the Bavarian Brewers' Association began proceedings against Bavaria NV in Italy, seeking to prevent the Dutch company from using the name Bavaria in Italy and to have the company's trade mark rights to the name cancelled. When the matter came before the Turin Court of Appeal, it referred to the CJEU the question whether the fact that the PGI had been

[110] Case C-343/07 *Bavaria NV and Bavaria Italia Srl v Bayerischer Brauerbund*, CJEU, 2 July 2009.

[111] The statutes of the Bavarian brewers association (*Bayerischer Brauerbund*) dated back to 1917; and it had been the proprietor of the registered collective trade marks 'Bayrisch Bier' and 'Bayerisches Bier' since 1968.

[112] The registration dates, the Court noted, included 1947, 1971, 1982, 1991, 1992 and 1995 *Bavaria*, para. 17.

[113] Article 1 of Regulation (EC) No 1347/2001 registered the name 'Bayerisches Bier' as a PGI and Recital 3 in the preamble to that Regulation stated that that the PGI and the trade mark 'Bavaria' would not mislead the public as to the identity of the product, which is the standard embodied in Article 14(3) of the original Regulation (EC) No 2081/92.

granted protection after registration of the trade marks meant that the Dutch company might nevertheless continue using the marks.[114] In July 2009, the CJEU affirmed the principle of coexistence, holding that trade marks of third parties, registered prior to the date on which the application for registration of the PGI 'Bayerisches Bier' was filed and in which the word 'Bavaria' appears, might continue to exist.[115]

The strict application of the principle of coexistence means that the trade mark applicant is open to challenge from a later registered PGI or PDO, unless the mark is so well known and its usage of such duration, that consumers would be misled by use of the name as a protected GI.[116] The principle of coexistence means that a later applicant may successfully register a GI, and the trade mark owner will have to accept their coexistence with one exception. In accordance with Article 3(4), it is mandatory to refuse or cancel the registration of the proposed geographical denomination, where 'in the light of a trade mark's reputation and renown and the length of time it has been used, registration is liable to mislead the consumer as to the true identity of the product.'

While corresponding Article 6(4) of the Quality Schemes Regulation appears to be no different in substance, the ostensibly small change in the text from the actual and present tense of 'is liable to mislead' to the possibility posed by the future conditional 'would be liable to mislead', tends to confirm the view that this is a limited derogation, based on the reasoning of the Court in the case of Bavaria Holland. Although well-known and of long usage in Italy, the Bavaria Holland mark was not considered by the Court to be so well-known and its usage of such duration, that consumers would be misled by use of the name as a PGI.[117] In the case of Bavaria, the CJEU emphasized the coexistence of the two systems for the registration of GI and CTMs; finding that the mere existence of marks in the market which incorporate the name, is not an indicator that the geographical denomination is unregistrable under the GI Regulation.[118]

---

114 The Bavarian Brewers' Association also brought suit in Germany. A second question was referred to the CJEU, and considered concurrently, in Case C-120/08 *Bavaria NV v Bayerischer Brauerbund eV:* the referring court asked whether Article 14(1) of Regulation (EC) No 510/2006 applies in the case where the protected indication has been validly registered in accordance with the simplified procedure under Article 17 of Regulation (EEC) No 2081/92 of 14 July 1992.

115 As the registration of the PGI was interpreted as having no adverse impact upon the validity of the 'Bavaria' trade marks, coexistence as provided for in Article 14(2) of former Regulation (EEC) No 2081/92 of 14 July 1992, could continue: *Bavaria*, para. 125. Similarly, see the Opinion of *AG Mazek*, at para. 161.

116 Article 3(4) of the GI Regulation. Quality Schemes Regulation, Article 6(4) no change (or to the structure of provisions).

117 Note 116.

118 *Bavaria* [2009] E.C.R. I-5491; [2009] E.T.M.R. 61 at [123]–[125].

In the case of conflicts between a CTM and later registered GI, the latter enjoys a privileged position in relation to the CTM, in so far as the principle of priority is qualified by that of the coexistence of GI and CTMs. The breadth of rights the law accords GI combined with their characterization as an exception to trade mark rights, give the GI a decided advantage in the event that the registration of a geographical denomination is disputed. In response to stakeholders' concern that the GI Regulation should expressly stipulate that GI holders cannot object to the use in good faith of a prior mark, the Quality Schemes Regulation clarifies the operative dates for assessment in cases of conflicts between trade marks and GI. Recital 53 states that the:

> dates for establishing the seniority of a trade mark and of a designation of origin or a geographical indication should be that of the date of application of the trade mark for registration in the Union or in the Member States and the date of application for protection of a designation of origin or a geographical indication to the Commission.[119]

However, in view of the action in 'Bavaria Holland' the question arises as to whether the legislators should have gone further to clarify the rights of prior trade marks with a reputation that are alleged to conflict with a later IGO. Moreover, the fact that Recital 55 states that the criteria by which subsequent conflicting trade marks should be refused or invalidated, should correspond to the scope of protection provided in Article 13, is problematic in view of the breadth and absolute nature of the protection accorded GI.

10. AMENDMENT OF ENFORCEMENT PROVISIONS

There are two tiers to the enforcement of GI: enforcement of the product specification as provided in Article 4 of Regulation 510/2006; and enforcement under Article 13 in regard to the infringing misuse of GI. In respect of the former controls on the production process, according to Article 10(3) of the GI Regulation, the Commission shall make public names and addresses of the competent authorities and control bodies. These controls can result in the exclusion of producers and operators, within the defined area, who do not fulfil the requirements of the specifications. Enforcement of the specification is a mix of administrative protection and private legal action. In the first place, checks that producers are complying with the product specification are undertaken by public authorities or by private certification bodies. Member States

[119] Proposal for a Regulation of the European Parliament and of the Council on Agricultural Product Quality Schemes, COM(2010) 733 Final, Brussels, 10 December 2010.

may also conduct administrative controls on the use of registered names on products in distribution and retail, under specific legislation as part of the official control of EU food law.

Secondly, enforcement may involve the producer association commencing private legal action in the courts of Member States. Article 13 of the GI Regulation provides that registered names shall be protected against any direct or indirect commercial use of a name registered in respect of identical or comparable products; and any evocation of the name, even if the true origin of the product is indicated, or if the protected name is translated or accompanied by expressions such as 'style', 'type', 'method' or 'imitation'. In this last respect, the protection goes well beyond that accorded trade marks, which is limited, except in the case of well-known marks, to the goods for which the mark is registered or those sufficiently similar to cause consumer confusion.

Nevertheless, during the consultation phase, a majority of stakeholders were of the view that there is a need for better enforcement within and between Member States.[120] Stakeholders also referred to differences in outcomes among Member States in judicial decisions and remedies involving registered GI. The current GI Regulation does not specify the responsibility of Member States in relation to enforcement, whether administrative enforcement or action against misuse of the GI. Further, although the system of registration and protection involves exclusive EU competence for all GI registered under the Regulation and registered GI are enforceable in the courts of Member States, problems have arisen over the character and extent of enforcement outside the Member State of origin of the PDO or PGI. The nature of the problem is illustrated by the action brought by the Parma Ham Association to enforce the product specification in England. In *Consorzio del Prosciutto di Parma v Asda Stores Ltd*[121] the Consorzio di Parma, the association responsible for the administration of the PDO 'Prosciutto di Parma', brought proceedings against the defendant companies, seeking an injunction against Hygrade and Asda, to prohibit their activity on the ground that the slicing and packaging of the product outside the area of Parma was contrary to the product specification.

The dispute concerned the sale of 'Prosciutto di Parma' by defendant Asda Stores Ltd, the operator of a chain of supermarkets in the UK. The product,

---

[120] Respondents included farming organizations, regional authorities, individuals from the farming sector, processing organizations, consumer organizations, academic organizations and one retail organization: European Commission of Agricultural Product Quality Policy: Impact Assessment Agricultural Product Quality Policy: Impact Assessment, Part B, Geographical Indications pp. 37–8.

[121] Case C-108/01, *Consorzio del Prosciutto di Parma & Salumificio S. Rita SpA v Asda Stores Ltd & Hygrade Foods Ltd*, CJEU, 2003 ('*Parma Ham v Asda*'). Similarly see the potential scope of protection conferred by a broadly drawn specification in Case C-469/00 *Ravil SARL v Bellon Import SARL and Biraghi SpA* (*Grana Padano* cheese).

bearing the description *Parma Ham*, had been purchased pre-sliced from the second defendant Hygrade Foods Ltd, in packets that bore the words 'Genuine Italian Parma Ham'. For its part, Hygrade purchased the ham from an Italian producer who was a member of the *Consorzio*, then undertook the packaging, labelling and slicing for Asda supermarkets. It was only after the Consorzio appealed to the House of Lords that the activities of Hygrade and Asda were found to be in violation of the product specification, which clearly set out the terms of slicing and packaging within the area of production.[122]

The Explanatory Memorandum to the Quality Schemes Regulation states that 'the respective roles of Member States and groups applying for registration have been clarified with regard to the enforcement of protection of the registered names throughout the European Union'. To this end, the Quality Schemes Regulation contains additional provisions respecting inspection structures; specifies in some detail the roles and responsibilities of producer groups and Member States. With the explicit aim of improving enforcement of product specifications, Article 13(3) of the Quality Schemes Regulation states:

> Member States shall take the appropriate administrative and judicial steps to prevent or stop the unlawful use of protected designations of origin and protected geographical indications as referred to in paragraph 1, in particular at the request of a producer group as provided for in point (a) of Article 42.

Further specific provisions ensure the identification and coordination of control bodies throughout the EU, overseen by a single Agricultural Product Quality Policy Committee. In this regard, proposed Articles 33 to 35 mandate that Member States designate the details of competent authorities responsible for official controls to verify compliance with product specifications, as a matter of public record. In the event the competent authorities delegate specific tasks, Article 36 provides that such delegated bodies must be duly accredited according to EU standards.[123] Finally, Article 42 is concerned with

---

[122] In accordance with Article 4(e) of the GI Regulation, packaging may take place in the defined geographical area provided reasons are given for doing so that relate to the quality control of the product. E.g. in the case of Parma ham, slicing and packaging must take place in approved 'laboratories' within the traditional area, supervised by inspectors of the Association, who keep records of hams received: *Parma Ham v Asda* (House of Lords), para. 6.

[123] 'Such control bodies shall be accredited in accordance with European Standard EN 45011 or ISO/IEC Guide 65 (General requirements for bodies operating product certification systems)': Article 36(2), Proposal for a Regulation of the European Parliament and of the Council on agricultural product quality schemes, COM (2010) 733 final, Brussels, 10.12.2010 2010/0353 (COD). See also para. 3 to the effect that accreditation referred to in para. 2 may only be performed by: (a) a national accreditation body in the Union in accordance with the provisions of Regulation (EC) No

the role of producer groups in ensuring and monitoring the use of the name in trade and, if necessary, informing competent authorities with a view to preventing the unlawful use of protected PDOs and PGIs.

It is a constructive development that legislators have sought to address within the Quality Schemes Regulation the problems identified by stakeholders in respect of enforcement. Nevertheless, the question arises as to whether there is a need to expressly affirm that protected names create a valid EU right, directly enforceable in courts of Member States; and to specifically provide for the issue of both interlocutory and permanent injunctions as well as damages or an account of profits in cases where defendants either fail to observe the specification or misuse the name.

The general reference to 'appropriate ...judicial steps' in draft Article 13(3) may be subject to ambiguity. Are provisions needed to specify sanctions, provisional and protective measures in cases of infringement of GI? Have the legislators missed an opportunity to expressly affirm that a registered PDO or PGI creates a valid EU right; and to clarify questions of jurisdiction and procedure in legal actions relating to GI? In the case of *Parma Ham v Asda*, the English High Court at first instance, held that the claimant had no rights under Community law and this decision was affirmed by the Court of Appeal. The House of Lords stayed proceedings in order to refer the question of the enforcement of the specification in the UK to the CJEU. On reference, that Court of Justice affirmed that as the proprietor of the PDO, the *Consorzio*, had the right under the GI Regulation, to restrain the retail sale of Parma Ham which had not been sliced, packaged and labelled in the region of production, provided that it was consistent with the conditions of the specification.[124]

During the consultation process, stakeholders also commented on the need to address the 'counterfeiting' of names.[125] Had legislators taken the opportunity to elaborate provisional measures, civil and administrative procedures, remedies and border measures, it might have affirmed the scope of protection

765/2008, or (b) an accreditation body outside the Union that is a signatory of a multilateral recognition arrangement under the auspices of the International Accreditation Forum.

124 Compare the outcome in 12 January 2010 (Decision No 65/2010) where the Commercial Court of Oviedo (*Juzgado de lo mercantil no 1 de Oviedo*) issued an injunction against the Spanish company ILAS (Industrias Lacteas Asturianas) SA, holding that use of the term 'PARMESO' in relation to grated cheese was in violation of Protected Designation of Origin Parmigiano Reggiano under Article 13(1)(b) PDO/PGI Regulation (EC) No 510/2006, in addition to being an act of Unfair Competition ex Article 15(2) of the Spanish Unfair Competition Law.

125 See e.g. comments by a Greek producer group relating to misuse and lack of enforcement (Survey to producers, 2007): European Commission of Agricultural Product Quality Policy: Impact Assessment Agricultural Product Quality Policy: Impact Assessment, Part B, Geographical Indications pp. 37–8.

to be accorded a validly registered name as the nature of the EU enforceable right; and established a model for enforcement in third countries where EU names are not adequately protected.

11. MISSED OPPORTUNITY TO ADDRESS RESTRAINT OF TRADE?

Questions concerning the misuse of GI remain. The TRIPS Agreement recognizes that the enforcement of intellectual property rights should be to the mutual advantage of producers and consumers; and in a manner conducive to social and economic welfare.[126] It also recognizes that appropriate measures may be needed to prevent the abuse of intellectual property rights or the resort to practices which unreasonably restrain trade.[127]

On the one hand, legislators appear to take the view that GI pose little threat to competition, no doubt on the assumption that they are normally not linked to the size of the market for the product; and are applied to products of different kinds, with widely varying production structures.[128] The Quality Schemes Regulation affirms the need for producers to differentiate their products in order to respond to competitive pressures associated with the globalization of agricultural markets; and the concentration of power in the retail sector.[129] Notwithstanding, it does not neglect to refer to the potential abuse of GI in Article 43, concerning the right to use the system, wherein paragraph 1 provides: 'Member States shall ensure that operators willing to adhere to the rules of [the GI system] … are able to do so and do not face obstacles to participation that are discriminatory or otherwise not objectively founded.' Where the scale of production is too small for individual firms to establish reputations on a stand-alone basis, recent research on the economics of collective brands has found that GI serve to improve communication between sellers and consumers.[130] This has important implications for the debate concerning the

---

126 TRIPS, Article 7: 'Objectives'.

127 TRIPS, Article 8: 'Principles'.

128 The only reference to the potential abuse of GIs is found in draft Article 43 concerning the right to use the system, whereby paragraph 1 provides that: 'Member States shall ensure that operators willing to adhere to the rules of [the GI system] … are able to do so and do not face obstacles to participation that are discriminatory or otherwise not objectively founded.'

129 '…quality schemes contribute to and complement rural development policy as well as market and income support policies of the common agricultural policy (CAP)': Explanatory Memorandum at para. 1.1; and Recital 4, at 14.

130 A. Fishman, I. Finkelshtain, N. Yacouel and A. Simhon (2008), 'The

anti-competitive potential of protected GI. The same research also suggests that these institutions, by facilitating collective branding, can have positive welfare effects in promoting more efficient investment in product quality.[131]

Nevertheless, the breadth of intellectual property rights accorded EU producer groups, continues to stimulate academic debate as to whether the protection of GI reduces welfare and market efficiency by endowing producer groups with unnecessary market power.[132] It is submitted that any revision of GI Regulation, particularly in light of the potential increase in the scope of protection presaged by the amendment to the definition of a PGI, should take into account that unjustified restrictions, even in the case of products that have a quantitatively limited production, might possibly pose obstacles to the free movement of goods in the single market.[133]

12. CONCLUSION

The foregoing analysis set out to examine the Quality Schemes Regulation on Agricultural Product Quality Schemes in view of the criteria identified by stakeholders as necessary to a more effective system for the protection of GI. It argued that the simplifying assumptions which the Quality Schemes Regulation makes in respect of GI are not necessarily the most efficient or effective in maximizing the social utility of the system. It considered amendments to the definitions of PDO and PGI; the application procedure; production standards and product specification; control and inspection structures; as well as the enforcement of GI. It also examined the potential cost to competitors of protecting geographical names widely considered by the public to have become generic.

In a number of cases it might be concluded that legislators have yet to fully question the extent to which the Quality Schemes Regulation is capable of realizing its key objectives in promoting the effectiveness and use of the system; and enhancing the coherence of the legislation. Given the paucity of empirical evidence, the extent to which the amendments might create new markets by strengthening the reputation of quality products among consumers remains uncertain. Claims made in favour of the capacity of the system for the

---

Economics of Collective Brands' (17 December 2008). Available at SSRN: <http://ssrn.com/abstract=1317262>.

131 Note 130 at 5..

132 TRIPS, Article 8: Principles.

133 Article 101 of the TFEU (ex Article 81 EC) prohibits measures which may affect trade between Member States and which tend to restrict competition within the internal market in such a way as to provide a particular advantage for the domestic market of the State in question.

registration of GI, to provide the most effective means of marketing agricultural products, often overlook the fact that reputation based on place largely follows a pre-existing link with geographical origin. While the GI may be a particularly effective form of protection for producer groups able to take advantage of a well-known geographical name; a PDO or PGI is not the optimal form of intellectual property with which to build a reputation for the product outside the local area.[134] Where reputation is lacking, the launch of an advertising campaign is a costly undertaking, particularly in case of very small-scale producers from economically disadvantaged areas. Equally, while standardizing procedures for certification will increase the effectiveness of the system in the eyes of consumers, disadvantaged small-holders will likely struggle to find the resources to adequately enforce the product specification.

If effectiveness is about achieving objectives consistent with wealth maximization,[135] then in the interests of justice, action should be taken in order to alleviate the additional administrative burden on small-scale producers. Indeed, the Green Paper on Agricultural Product Quality, in drawing attention to the need for further research into the problems faced by small-scale producers, recognizes that a number of the simplifying assumptions which the Quality Schemes Regulation makes in respect of GI, are not necessarily the most efficient or effective in maximizing the social utility of the system.[136] The number of opportunities missed in the Quality Schemes Regulation to address substantive issues, notably to extend product coverage; to define the geographical area of production; and to clarify the use of generic names; might have gone some considerable way in stimulating greater economic efficiency for small-scale producers.

134 G.E. Evans (2010), 'The Comparative Advantages of Geographical Indications and Community Trademarks for the Marketing of Agricultural Products in the European Union', **41**, *IIC*, 645.

135 C. Veljanovski, 'The Economics of Law'. Institute of Economics Affairs Hobart Paper No 157. Available at SSRN: <http://ssrn.com/abstract=935952> at 61.

136 European Commission (2008), 'Green Paper on Agricultural Product Quality: Product Standards, Farming Requirements and Quality Schemes' at pp. 20–21.

Section 4

Patents and Plant Variety Protection

9. Constructing an efficient and balanced European patent system: 'muddling through'

Jens Schovsbo

1. SETTING THE SCENE

The title I have been given calls for a number of clarifications:

A *patent system* consists of both of rules and institutions. At the core are the specific patent rules and the patent offices (PTOs) which are dedicated to the issuing of patents. Often complications will arise at the interface between the patent system and the general legal system consisting of e.g. contract law, competition law and procedural law, the general court system, and the international framework found in the IPR conventions and treaties. In the following my focus will be limited to the specific patent rules and institution of the EU.

An *efficient* patent system is one that achieves the overall goals set out for it and a *balanced* system is one that does so in a way which maximizes the overall societal interests. The notion of 'balance' implies that patents incur costs on society. The aim of the legislator, therefore, should be to balance the costs with the gains. Behind these points, is the general idea that issuing patents is not in itself the goal of the patent system. Instead, patents are the means for achieving certain overall societal goals.

A *European* (in the following 'EU') patent system (as opposed to a global or national one) seeks to protect specific EU policy interests and to provide EU companies (and ultimately the EU citizens) with the advantage of efficient protection on their home market. The development on the EU level needs to be synchronized with the developments on the global scene. For the following my focus will be on the regional/national interface. Any EU legislative harmonization initiative thus also needs to take into account the specific European historical and cultural background. Because of the expansion of the patentable subject matter and since patent harmonization now also covers matters of procedural law and issues such as litigation the task of finding common EU grounds has become more difficult.

2. TRADITIONAL STARTING POINTS

The central goal of patent law always has been to further economic growth through innovation ('dynamic efficiency'). Technical knowledge is normally costly to produce but cheap to copy and without effective legislation in the form of patents, companies would therefore copy rather than innovate. The patent system incentivizes innovators by providing them with exclusive rights, which make it possible for patent holders to internalize their costs of R&D in the price of the patented products (or processes). This ability does not in itself 'reward' the patent holder. The patent system presupposes a *market place* where the patent holder can reap the economic reward of the patent by working the invention to sell the patented product or process. It is also part of the standard assumption that the patent merely provides the patent holder with an advantage on the market. The patent is not supposed to place the patent holder in a monopoly position and normally consumers will have access to substitutes. This reflects the more general point that the compensation offered by society (and paid by the consumers of the patented products etc.) should correspond to the contribution the patent holder made to society when he decided to patent (and thus to publish) his invention.

It is a special characteristic of the EU patent system that it not only aims at fostering innovation but at promoting innovative and competitive advantages for EU-innovators and to further market integration.[1] The European Commission has described a modern, integrated EU IPR system as a key element of its broader policies aimed at growth, development, and competitiveness[2] and as an essential condition in making the 'fifth freedom', i.e. the free movement of knowledge, a reality.[3] The Lisbon Treaty has identified even

1 Consolidated Version of the Treaty on the Functioning of the European Union (TFEU), Article 26 and see also the Preamble to the proposed Council Regulation on the Community Patent, Working document of 30 October 2009 (15149/09) of the Council of the European Union and Conclusions on an Enhanced Patent System in Europe adopted by the Council of the European Union on 4 December 2009.

2 The latest expression came in the document with the following (simple yet elegant and unpretentious) title A Single Market for Intellectual Property Rights Boosting creativity and innovation to provide economic growth, high quality jobs and first class products and services in Europe, Communication from the Commission to the European Parliament, the Council, the European Economic and Social Committee and the Committee of the Regions, Brussels, 24 May 2011 COM (2011) 287 final. See also Enhancing the patent system in Europe, Communication from the Commissions to the European Parliament and the Council, Brussels 3 April 2007 COM (2007) 165 final and Europe 2020 – a strategy for smart, sustainable and inclusive growth, Communication from the Commission, Brussels, 3 March 2010 COM (2010) 2020.

3 An Industrial Property Rights Strategy for Europe, Communication from the Commissions to the European Parliament, the Council and the European Economic and Social Committee – Brussels, 16 July 2008, COM (2008) 465 final, 3.

broader goals which need to be taken into account including the 'respect for fundamental rights and the different legal systems and traditions of the Member States', 'access to justice'[4] and '...the flowering of the cultures of the Member States'.[5] The Charter on Fundamental Rights of the European Union protects intellectual property rights as (other) property rights (Article 17(2)) and includes as part of the 'Right to the integrity of the person' in Article 3 a prohibition *inter alia* on making the human body and its parts as such a source of financial gain.

Traditionally, the patent system has been regarded as being 'value-neutral'. The argument has been that the patent system only entails a right to exclude and not a (positive) right to work an invention. Value oriented concerns such as ethical concerns and morality therefore are to be dealt with outside of the patent system e.g. in rules on marketing approval or on research. The rules on *ordre public* found in the European Patent Convention (EPC) may be said to constitute an important limitation to this view. Traditionally, however, these rules only serve as a safety valve for 'rare and extreme cases'[6] where the patent will be '*exploited*' commercially (as opposed to being granted) in a way which is contrary to *ordre public* or morality.[7]

As far as the patent institutions – in the following in particular the PTOs – are concerned it is the traditional starting point that they serve as neutral administrators and 'gate keepers' of the system. It is their main task to administer the patent rules by refusing applications of inventions which do not live up to the (rigid) standards set out in the patent statutes after a careful examination. As far as the administrative procedure is concerned, the patent offices are expected to function within the traditional (national) principles for good governance and thus to provide for an effective, accessible, fair and transparent process for the grant, maintenance, and enforcement of patents. The examination focuses on the technical aspects of the inventions and the staff consists of engineers. The role of the offices has traditionally been limited to the granting of the patents. Issues after grant (*post grant*) have not involved the offices.

---

4 TFEU, Article 67.

5 TFEU, Article 167.

6 EPO Examination Guidelines, April 2010 Part C Ch. IV-8.

7 See EPC, Article 53. The Agreement on Trade-Related Aspects of Intellectual Property Rights, Annex 1C of the Marrakesh Agreement Establishing the World Trade Organization, signed in Marrakesh, Morocco on 15 April 1994 (TRIPS) also recognizes the protection of *ordre public* or morality as grounds for exclusions from patentability, see Article 27(2) which contains a rather broad definition which includes the protection of human, animal or plant life or health or the avoidance of serious prejudice to the environment.

3. CHALLENGES

Following the traditional positions identified above I will describe and present on a very basic level some of the challenges to the patent system, as seen from three different perspectives: innovation challenges, non-economic challenges (morality) and governance challenges. These perspectives are arguably closely interconnected but for the present purposes it makes sense to try to simplify. In the subsequent part 4 of the chapter I will move on to propose ways to deal with the challenges.

3.1 Innovation Challenges

At the core of the innovation challenges lies a claim that the patent system to a problematic degree harms rather than promotes innovation. This claim has been made throughout the history of the patent system. At this place, I will focus only on what could be called the 'modern' critique, i.e. that the patent system has become 'outdated' because of changes in the nature of innovations and in the behaviour of inventors and/or patent owners.

It is a recurrent argument that patents hamper innovation because access to patented technology is blocked by a 'tangled, twisted mass of IPRs, which criss-cross the established walkways of commerce'.[8] [9] Such 'thickets' or 'anti-commons' increase transaction costs and in this way may slow down innovation which requires access to previous, protected technology. These risks have been reported in a variety of technical fields relating to biotechnology,[10] diagnostic testing,[11] computer programmes,[12] nano,[13] and microprocessors.[14] The risks are thus particularly pertinent to component technologies where innova-

---

8 R.P. Mergers (1996), 'Contracting into Liability Rules: Intellectual Property Rights and Collective Rights Organisations', *Calif. L.R.*, **84**, 1293–393, at 1295.

9 The literature is vast. An excellent overview and several in-depth studies are provided in G. Van Overwalle (ed.) (2009), *Gene Patents and Collaborative Licensing Models*, Cambridge: Cambridge University Press. See in particular the concluding chapter by G. Van Overwalle, 'Of thickets, Blocks and Gaps', *ibid*, pp. 383–463.

10 M.A. Heller and R.S. Eisenberg (1998), 'Can Patents Deter Innovation? The Anticommons in Biomedical Research', *Science,* 1 May **280** (5365), 698–701, and M.M. Hopkins et al. (2007), 'DNA Patenting: the End of an Era?', *Nature Biotechnology,* **25**, 185–7.

11 Van Overwalle, *supra* note 9 and e.g. B. Verbeure et al. (2006), 'Patent Pools and Diagnostic Testing, *TRENDS in Biotechnology* **24** (3), March, 115–20.

12 J. Bessen and M.J. Meurer (2008), *Patent Failure: How Judges, Bureaucrats, and Lawyers Put Innovators at Risk*, Princeton: Princeton University Press, pp. 190–93.

13 M.A. Lemley (2005), 'Patenting Nanotechnology', *Stan. L. Rev.* **58**, 601.

14 D.L. Rubinfeld and R. Maness (2005), 'The Strategic Use of Patents:

tion is characterized by small incremental steps and where the individual inventions cannot form the basis of economic exploitation. What is needed in such situations to stimulate innovation is not exclusive rights but mechanisms which facilitate access to use previous inventions in order to 'stand on the shoulders of Giants'.[15] [16]

Some commentators would point out that the heart of this challenge lies in the nature of the *patent exclusivity model*. This can be described as 'absolute permission rules'[17] which can be enforced by the use of injunctions. This entitlement model is problematic in a thicket situation because it makes it possible for holders of the patents which are needed to block for the use of their technology. The effect of this is particular damaging if there are no easy substitutes (e.g. the use of a gene as part of a diagnostic kit) or if inventing around patented technology is costly. The ability of patent holders to rely on injunction is normally not dependent on the nature of the use and e.g. uses which were not anticipated at the time of the patenting, uses which improve the patented invention or even uses which do not compete with the patent holder's use can normally be prevented.

Another way to explain the challenge would be to focus on the *administration of the system* and to point to the 'patent explosion' which has taken place in recent years. Arguably, a high number of patents could in itself increase transaction costs. This argument finds ample empirical support in the statistics which report an extraordinary growth in the number of patents within some of the sectors mentioned above, i.e. biotech, computer programmes, and nano.[18] Another and related argument would focus on the character of some patents. In the same way as many small and/or overlapping rights can limit access so can a few broad and 'strong' rights restrict access to downstream

---

Implication for Antitrust', in F. Lévêque and H. Shelanski, *Antitrust, Patents and Copyright – EU and U.S. Perspectives*, Cheltenham, UK and Northampton, MA: Edward Elgar Publishing, pp. 85–102 at p. 88.

15 S. Scotchmer (1991), 'Standing on the Shoulders of Giants: Cumulative Research and the Patent Law', *Journal of Economic Perspectives,* **5** (1), Winter, 29–41.

16 In its sector inquiry the European Commission identified alleged thickets in the pharmaceutical sector as part of a strategy to delay or block the market entry for generic medicines in connection with the expiration of patents on chemical substances ('evergreening'), Pharmaceutical Sector Inquiry – Preliminary Report, DG Competition Staff Working Paper, 28 November 2008.

17 Mergers, *supra*, note 8, 1293–393.

18 E.g. the 'STOA Report' Policy options for the improvement of the European patent system, Report from the European Parliament Scientific Technology Options Assessment – STOA – September 2007, IP/A/STOA/FWC/2005-28/SC16 (available at <http://www.europarl.europa.eu/stoa/publications/studies/stoa16_en.pdf>), 31. In its *Scenarios for the Future*, 2007, 17 and 37, the EPO described thickets as a consequence of an increase in the number of patents.

uses. 'Strong patents' have been reported to be particularly pertinent to patenting of 'emerging technologies', where patent offices may tend to issue patents which in hindsight and as the technology emerges turn out to be overly 'strong' (i.e. broad).[19]

A final method of explanation points towards *the behaviour of the users* of the patent system including innovators and third parties. This argument includes a claim that patents are to an increasing extent taken out for strategic reasons as 'bargaining chips'[20] or to simply block competitors rather than to serve as safe havens for real working of the invention. Such practices may even involve abusive behaviour if they are part of a scheme to force competitors out of the market (by raising costs) or if patents are used to 'ambush' competitors.

3.2 Non-economic Challenges: Morality

The traditional description that the patent system is 'value neutral' is flawed. The patent ideology is that of the liberal Western societies which see the market as the central mechanism for the creation and distribution of wealth. If one is opposed to those views, one would be critical towards the very idea of the patent system. Such a critique would be based on 'values'. Here I will, however, focus not on the idea of patenting as such but on the claim that the patenting of some specific and novel technologies is morally problematic as such.

The discussion of these issues has been particularly prominent regarding biotechnological inventions and the patenting of 'life'. The debate had a deep impact on the Biotech-Directive[21] where it is flatly recognized in the Preamble that the patenting of genes is controversial[22] and is pointed out that 'patent law must be applied so as to respect the fundamental principles safeguarding the dignity and integrity of the person'.[23] The morality concerns have been inter-

---

19 STOA Report, *supra* note 18, 15, 22, 30 and 39–40.

20 W.M. Cohen, R.R. Nelson, and J.P. Walsh (2000), 'Protecting their Intellectual Assets: Appropriability Conditions and why U.S. Manufacturing Firms Patent (or not)', *NBER Working Paper*, 7552.

21 Directive 98/44/EC of the European Parliament and of the Council of 6 July 1998 on the legal protection of biotechnological inventions, OJ L 213 30 July 1998, 13–21.The Directive has been transposed to the EPC by an amendment to the Implementation Regulation *to the Convention on the Grant of European Patents* (as last amended by decision of the Administrative Council of the European Patent Organisation of 26 October 2010), Rules 26–29.

22 Point 22.

23 Point 16.

nalized in the substantive rules of the Directive[24] and are also reflected in the institutional set up.[25] Despite these steps the area remains controversial and some legislators (Germany and France) have even limited the scope of protection of patents on certain human biological material to cover only the specific uses indicated in the patent claims.

The morality issues raised by the patenting of biotechnological inventions and in particular those relating to human substances are inherently complicated. In the EU legal set up the complications are given an extra twist because of the nature of harmonization. The complications were clearly spelled out by EPO's Board of Appeal in its 2001 decision on the Onco-mouse where it was made clear that the notion of '*ordre public*' must be established '... primarily by looking at laws and regulations which are common to most European countries'.[26] Whereas most EU countries would find it uncontroversial to subscribe to the economic rationale behind the patent system it is obviously much more difficult to find common ground on issues of morality. Not only is the very concept of 'morality' vague and complex but arguably values are varying between the 27 different countries and the 'laws and regulations' of 'most European countries' will only provide a very imprecise proxy for the underlying concerns relating to morality. The latest example of the problems can be found in the remarks of the Advocate General in Case C-34/10 on the definition of a 'human embryo' regarding a stem cell patent where the Advocate General succinctly put the problem in the way that the '[EU] is not only a market to be regulated, but also has values to be expressed'.[27] The Advocate

---

24 E.g. Article 5(1) (excluding 'the human body, at the various stages of its formation and development, and the simple discovery of one of its elements, including the sequence or partial sequence of a gene' from patentability). Article 6 reiterates the prohibition against patents on inventions if their commercial exploitation would be contrary to *ordre public* or morality and excludes in particular certain particularly controversial areas from patentability e.g. processes for cloning human beings (a) or uses of human embryos for industrial or commercial purposes (c).

25 See Article 7 (requiring the Commission's European Group on Ethics in Science and New Technologies to evaluate all ethical aspects of biotechnology) and Article 16 (requiring the Commission to report on any problems encountered with regard to the relationship between this Directive and international agreements on the protection of human rights).

26 Opposition Division of 7 November 2001 – *The British Union for the Abolition of Vivisection et al. v the President and Fellows of Harvard College ('Onco-Mouse')*, 2003, Official Journal EPO 473.

27 Opinion of Advocate General Bot delivered on 10 March 2011 in Case C-34/10, *Oliver Brüstle v Greenpeace eV*. The Opinion sets out the complications in a clear and precise way see e.g. point 45:

> The question which the Court is asked is certainly a difficult one. However, it is

General furthermore recommends that the concept 'human embryo' found in the Biotech-Directive should be defined autonomously and specifically for the purpose of the Directive.[28] Such an interpretation certainly makes sense as seen from a legal technical perspective and it is also completely logical as seen from the perspective of harmonization. As a consequence, however, the Directive leaves it completely to the EU legal system to define when human life begins for the purpose of patent law. As already pointed out this is an inherently difficult task and even though the Advocate General rightly points out that it is a legal task which has been left to the courts by the legislator it is at the same time obvious that deciding on such matters requires the decision making body to be able to balance a broad array of very different issues.

3.3 Governance Challenges

The European Patent Convention (EPC) came into force in 1977 and provides a legal framework for the granting of 'European patents'[29] by an intergovernmental organization (in practice by the European Patent Office (EPO))[30] on the basis of a single application. The EPC has established a European system for the granting of patents. *After grant*, a European patent is split up into a bundle of national patents, which in each of the (38) EPC contracting states become subject to the same rules and territorial limits that apply to other national patent rights in that state.[31]

---

exclusively legal in nature. The intrinsic difficulty in the question asked is accompanied by a reference, which is ever present in law but is particularly pregnant here, to the notions of ordre public, morality and ethics, as a result of the clarifications made by the legislature itself, for example in recital 16 in the preamble to Directive 98/44 or Article 6 of that directive, irrespective of the principles laid down in the Charter of Fundamental Rights which feed into all Union law.

28 *Ibid*, point 53.

29 The European patents granted by the EPO are in reality only 'European' until they leave the EPO (enter the 'national phase'). They then, as a point of departure, live their lives according to national patent legislation, see inter alia EPC, Articles 2 and 64. After grant, a European patent may, however, at the request of the proprietor, be revoked or limited by an amendment of the claims by the EPO, see EPC, Articles 105a–105c.

30 The European Patent Organization was set up on 7 October 1977 on the basis of the EPC. It has two bodies: a) the European Patent Office (EPO), which is the executive arm of the organization; and b) the Administrative Council, which supervises the EPO.

31 A European patent thus confers on its proprietor the same rights as would be conferred by a national patent granted in the state in question, see EPC, Articles 2 and 64.

In this way no 'EU patent system' – i.e. a system based on a unitary right and central enforcement – currently exists. This is obviously problematic both as seen from the point of view of the users of the system and from a policy point of view. From the users' perspective the problem is that the current system based on national validations and litigation is expensive and uncertain. From a policy perspective the problem is that the EPC system is outside of (direct) EU political and legal control even though an effective system for the protection of patents is seen as instrumental for the broader innovation policies of the EU.

In its 2011 Communication the Commission identifies inter alia the need for unified EU systems for patenting and for litigation as pivotal elements in the development of an efficient EU patent system.[32] These points are obvious and need to be urgently addressed. At long last it would also seem that real progress is being made and that the pending proposal for a 'unitary patent protection' stands a good chance of being agreed upon perhaps already in 2012.[33]

With a further harmonization and centralization of the EU patent institutions more interest should be devoted to the role and function of these institutions. The first thing to recognize is that PTOs are not neutral agents and passive gate keepers who simply administer the law. *Drahos* puts it in the following way:

> Patent offices are hybrid creatures, business bureaucracies which make their living from granting more rather than less patent registrations, from ensuring the repeat custom of their transnational clientele and from going on proselytising missions in those developing states or markets which are in the middle of acquiring patent systems.[34]

PTOs should thus be perceived as important agents in the making and development of patent law. In the same vein *Schneider* points to the role of PTOs in having fuelled a pro-patent bias which in turn has expanded the limits of patent

---

32 *Supra*, note 2.

33 Proposal for a Regulation of the European Parliament and of the Council implementing enhanced cooperation in the area of the creation of a unitary patent protection, Brussels COM (2011) 215/3. See also the Proposal for a Council Regulation implementing enhanced cooperation in the area of the creation of unitary patent protection with regard to the applicable translation arrangements, Brussels COM (2011) 216/3.

34 P. Drahos (1999), 'Biotechnology Patents, Markets and Morality', *EIPR*, **21** (9), 441–9, 442. See also and in the same direction, I. Schneider (2009), Governing the Patent System in Europe: the EPO's Supranational Autonomy and its Need for a Regulatory Perspective, *Science and Public Policy*, **36** (8), October, 619–29.

eligibility.[35] A centralization of EU's patent law with a unitary right and a central court system will further solidify the position of the EPO and thus increase its power in developing the EU's patent law.[36] As seen from a public policy perspective it therefore becomes a central challenge to make sure that the EPO will continue to administer the patent system in a way which is in conformity with the general public interest, i.e. in a way which is 'effective' (i.e. aims at achieving the overall goals of the system) and 'balanced' (does so in a way which maximizes the overall interests without favouring certain stake holders at the expense of others).

The development is already underway. In recent years the EPO has been focusing on 'raising the bar' and since 2008 and 2009 the office has reported grant rates below 50 per cent (2009: 42 per cent, 2008: 49 per cent, and 2010: 43 per cent).[37] The initiative to 'raise the bar' would certainly seem to be well founded in meeting the innovation challenges discussed *supra* ('thickets'). It is also, however, important to point out that it should not be an aim in itself for any patent system to reduce (or for that matter, increase) the number of patents. The goal should be to make sure that the patent system is working i.e. that it continues to contribute to the realizations of the goals of the system. To do so the PTOs should neither protect 'more' nor 'less' inventions. Instead they should protect the 'right' inventions, i.e. the inventions which are identified in the legislation. A broad perspective on 'quality' is therefore needed and this should include both the risk of over-protection and of under-protection and arguably, raising the bar involves a risk that the innovation losses from denying protection to certain 'small' inventions which have till now been protected diminishes the innovation gains from limiting the thickets generated by other small patents. My intention here is not to evaluate the effects of the initiative to raise the bar but merely to point out that the case illustrates the pivotal role of the PTOs in the functioning of the patent system and thus the importance of integrating the offices in the broader superstructure of the national and EU innovation policies.

---

35 Schneider, *supra* note 34, 622.

36 See on the role of the proposed central patents court from this perspective C.S Petersen and J. Schovsbo (2010), 'On Law and Policy in a European and European Union Patent Court (EEUPC) – What will It do to Patent Law and What will Patent Law do to It?', in H. Koch, K. Hagel-Sørensen, U. Haltern and J.H.H. Weiler (eds) *Europe – the New Legal Realisms*, DJØF Publishing: Copenhagen, pp. 609–38. The EUCJ in Opinion 1/09 of the Court from 8 March 2011 found that the proposal for a European and European Union Patent Court would contravene EU law. The proposal is therefore currently off the table but new initiatives can probably be expected shortly.

37 Source: <www.epo.org>.

3.4 Summing Up

The traditional patent law positions are being challenged. It can no longer be taken for granted that exclusivity automatically translates into innovation, and the perception of patent law as being 'neutral' and of the PTOs as passive administrators cannot be upheld. The driving forces behind these challenges have been changes in terms of the way innovation is done and in behaviour and an expansion of patent law to controversial areas such as human stem cells. Also the increased interest on 'soft' values in the Lisbon Treaty has put further pressure on traditional positions and so the increasing political interest in the area has dragged patent law into the arena of innovation policies. As seen from an EU position the challenges are particularly difficult to face because of the lack of a solid a EU system for the granting and enforcement of rights.

4. POSSIBLE WAYS FORWARD: 'MUDDLING THROUGH'

In one of the most cited surveys on the effects of the patent system the economist Fritz Machlup famously concluded that 'If one does not know whether a system "as a whole" [. . .] is good or bad, the safest "policy conclusion" is to "muddle through" . . .'.[38] The advice to 'muddle through' is admittedly neither precise nor bold. For those reasons it is also very practical. For the following thoughts on ways to 'Construct an Efficient and Balanced European Patent System' I take it to mostly include a warning: The patent system as it stands today is the bearer of immense values and one should only make (or suggest) dramatic changes if one is very certain about the nature of the problems and the effects of the solutions. Rather than promoting fundamental changes, I will therefore propose to look for ways to better understand and work with the

---

[38] F. Machlup, An economic review of the patent system, Senate Judiciary Comm., Subcomm. on Patents etc., Study no. 15, 85th Cong., 2nd Sess. (1958). The whole paragraph reads:

> If one does not know whether a system 'as a whole' (in contrast to certain features of it) is good or bad, the safest 'policy conclusion' is to 'muddle through' – either with it, if one has long lived with it, or without it, if one has lived without. If we did not have a patent system, it would be irresponsible, on the basis of our present knowledge of its economic consequences, to recommend instituting one. But since we have had a patent system for a long time, it would be irresponsible, on the basis of our present knowledge, to recommend abolishing it.

existing system. To provide concrete suggestions to meet the present challenges I will use the suggestions contained in the Science and Technology Options Assessment (STOA) Report on 'Policy options for the improvement of the European patent system' as my starting point, i.e.:

- Insertion of the economic mission of the patent system in the European Patent Convention;
- Enhancing governance within the European patent system;
- Improving quality aspects in regard to patentability standards and patent grant procedures;
- Dealing with emerging technologies;
- Increasing access to patented inventions; and
- Facilitating defensive publications.[39]

4.1 A Mission Statement

The purpose of a mission statement[40] in the EPC is to define more clearly the legal framework for the development of the law. This proposal in this way recognizes that patent law to a large extent develops through the practices of PTOs and national courts and not through changes in the written 'law' (statues or conventions). This raises special difficulties in steering the development. A mission statement would ideally help to solve some of these problems and to provide clarity while at the same time allowing for a high degree of flexibility in the development of the law. The main effect would probably be seen in the 'hard cases' and notably those which involve new subject matters or on setting the 'bar' for deciding on inventive steps. Special care should be made to make it clear that the guiding principle should be the general interest in the patent system and not the interests of special interest groups. For the reasons set out by *Drahos* this is probably a difficult task to overcome as there would seem to be a cultural bias in the system in favour of the patent holder and of 'expand-

---

[39] *Supra*, note 18. I was a member of the working group which prepared the Report.

[40] The STOA report suggested a Preamble to the EPC with the following wording:

> The granting of patents serves the purpose of enhancing social and economic welfare by means of encouraging inventions and their diffusion. The protection provided by patents should be sufficient to ensure proper incentives to inventors. This should imply that patents should be granted in a proportionate and transparent manner, so as to ensure legal certainty.

Supra, note 18, p. 34. Footnote with references omitted.

ing' the system. In this way the preamble should be phrased to make it easier for PTOs to refuse applications than to accept them.

The idea to strengthen the framework for the development of IPR towards a more fair and balanced situation has recently been developed in a more daring way as part of the so called 'IPT-project' and its proposal to amend the TRIPS.[41] The proposal includes an amendment of TRIPS Article 7 on 'Objectives' to include a reference to 'the promotion of competition and fairness in trade in the interests of [...] inventors and other producers, traders and consumers'[42] and an obligation to ensure that 'the scope of protection conferred by an intellectual property right corresponds to the contribution made to [...] innovation'.[43] This proposal would seem to offer some important insights also for the EU developments. More particularly the proposal points to the importance of rules and mechanisms also found outside of the patent law system notably in competition law. The importance of competition law and competition law thinking to the developments of patent law has now also been broadly accepted by the Commission, which has stressed that as a matter of policy 'strong protection of industrial property rights should be accompanied by rigorous application of competition rules'.[44]

4.2 The Innovation Challenge

The STOA Report contains several recommendations aimed at dealing with the problem of thickets including 'raising the bar' and taking special initiatives

---

41 The proposed amended text with commentaries and supporting articles are collected in A. Kur (2011) (ed.), *Intellectual Property Rights in a Fair World Trade System*, Cheltenham, UK; Northampton, MA: Edward Elgar. I participated in the working group which prepared the proposal.

42 Proposal for Article 7(a)(iii), *ibid,* p. 464.

43 Proposal for Article 7(b), *ibid.* It also includes a new Article 8a on 'Balancing of Interests' which is intended to operate as guidelines for the legislatures and courts concerning the introduction and interpretation of limitations to IPR. This clause includes a reference to Article 7 and thus internalizes the links to competition law and the basic notion of correspondence between the reward offered to the right holders and the benefits gained by society, *ibid*, pp. 465–7 for the text of the proposed amendment and pp. 538–51 for comments. Finally, it is being proposed to address the interface to competition law directly by a special provision (Article 8b) which requires Members to provide for measures (in particular, in the form of limitations of the rights or in the form of compulsory licences) 'if the use of the product protected by an intellectual property right is indispensable for competition in the relevant market, unless the application of such measures would have a significantly negative effect on the incentives to invest in research and development'.

44 Rights Strategy for Europe, Communication from the Commissions to the European Parliament, the Council and the European Economic and Social Committee, Brussels 16 July 2008, COM (2008) 465 final, 9.

to avoid overly broad patents in emerging technologies.[45] Another set of recommendations addresses the problem post grant and seeks to encourage ways of dealing with patent rights that promote access. The Report more concretely suggests to 'explore and support more flexible, non-exclusive exercises of patent rights, such as license of right, patent pools and clearing houses'.[46]

'Patent pools' and 'clearing houses' are contract based models which patent holders can employ to translate their individual exclusive rights into useable 'bundles' of technology.[47] In this way (some of) the transaction costs in navigating through the thickets may disappear and this may open to more innovative activities. The initiatives are based on the traditional patent system of exclusivity and do not as such require any changes in patent law in order to be implemented. At the same time, however, it would also seem to be clear that if one wants to encourage the use of such collaborative models some supportive mechanisms should be implemented such as setting up standards or providing for external funding.[48]

A broader endorsement of initiatives such as pooling would probably also require a clarification of some issues relating to competition law. TFEU Article 101 prohibits agreements between undertakings which restrict competition and since pooling and clearing houses would often involve agreements between competing undertakings a competition law intervention could be raised. The position in EU competition law was originally quite hostile towards pooling but gradually a more positive position has evolved. It is now generally recognized that pooling involving blocking and complementary ('essential') patents benefits competition by allowing for a one stop licensing of technology.[49] This benefits competition because it reduces transaction costs and opens up markets which would otherwise be closed and because it may also reduce the price of access to the package compared to a price based on the individual rights.

---

45 *Supra* note 18, 38–40.

46 *Supra* note 18, 40. I have elsewhere elaborated on this suggestion see J. Schovsbo (2009), Increasing Access to Patented Inventions by Post-grant Measures, *Science and Public Policy*, **36** (8), October, 609–18 (discussion compulsory licensing, licenses of right and behavioural rules).

47 M.A. Heller (1998), 'The Tragedy of the Anticommons: Property in the Transition from Marx to Markets', 111 *Harv. L. Rev.* **111**, 621–88.

48 See for detailed and careful analyses and studies Van Overwalle, *supra* note 9 (pointing out that a broader endorsement of collaborative models and the development of concrete initiatives require a careful examination of the issues).

49 E.g. J. Schovsbo (2011), 'Fire and Water Make Steam – Redefining the Role of Competition Law in TRIPS' in A. Kur (ed.), *supra* note 41, pp. 308–58 at pp. 336–8.

By joining a pooling arrangement the individual patent holders normally give up their ability to enforce their rights by injunctions vis-à-vis other members of the pool. In this way the effect of pooling agreements is to basically transform the exclusivity model offered in patent law with a liability model. Pooling shows how patent holders will sometimes have an interest in making such a transformation. One could, however, also consider whether the law should more proactively support the development towards liability models. One way of doing so would be to include a *Licences of right* option in the patent system. Such a model is included in the pending Proposal for a Council Regulation on the Community Patent.[50] If enacted it would make it possible for a patent holder to declare his intention to enter into an agreement with anyone who is prepared to accept the conditions including the payment of an 'appropriate return'.[51] A broader use of competition law to prevent the abuse of patent holders would also point in the direction of a liability system and so would more specific rules such as those found in the Swiss Patent Act which provide that anyone who wants to use a patent for a biological invention as a tool or means for research has a right to a non-exclusive licence to do so.[52]

The examples show how sometimes, the shift from a regime based on property rights (exclusivity) towards one based on liability rules takes place because of an active choice made by the patent holder. Sometimes, the shift is the consequence of a choice made in the legislation or it is the result of a sanction imposed by competition law. Even though it would on the face of it seem to be controversial to consider allowing for more 'lapses' from the exclusivity model which constitute the base line of patent protection one should not shy away from using alternative ways to open access to patented technology.[53]

4.3 Governance

The STOA Report suggests to 'enhance governance within the European patent system'. The need to enhance governance is due partly to the position of the EPO outside of the EU institutional and legal set up and partly to the general developments in patent law including the expansion of protection to new and controversial areas. In this way the call for enhanced governance is at the same time a call for more political accountability of the EPO system and

---

50 COM (2011) 251/3, *supra,* note 32, Article 11.

51 Schovsbo, *supra,* note 46, 614–15.

52 *Ibid*, 613–14.

53 A. Kur and J. Schovsbo (2011), 'Expropriation or Fair Game for All? The Gradual Dismantling of the IP Exclusivity Paradigm' in A. Kur (ed.) *supra* note 41, pp. 408–51 at pp. 444–5.

a broader call for 'democratizing'[54] of EU patent law to legitimize the decision making which takes place in the EPO.

5. CONCLUSIONS

The 'EU patent system' consists of rules and institutions and any initiative to improve the system should be aimed both at the rules and at the institutions to establish a patent system for the EU which is both 'effective' and 'balanced'. No ready-to-use toolkit is available to 'fix' the EU (nor indeed the global) patent system to make it better suited for the governance and stimulation of technology and innovation but any attempt to 'muddle through' would have to take into account both the substantive rules of the patent system and the way these rules are being administered. The challenges addressed above are general in the sense that any patent system in the world has to find ways to deal with them. The solutions, however, need to take account of the specific European circumstances. The challenge is to create a system which not only benefits innovation but can also deal with the sensitive issues involving morality and does so in a way which is at the same time effective and centralized and respects the cultural and legal diversities of the EU-countries.

---

54 Schneider, *supra,* note 34, 628 (pointing out that democratization would include attention to three dimensions: 'Accountability' (meaning that the EPO takes responsibility for the public good rather than its 'clients'), 'transparency' (access not just to files and records but also to decisions-making), and 'democratic control' (the EPO and the EU must be regarded as elements within a broader European governance framework)).

10. Smart innovation and inclusive patents for sustainable food and health care: Redefining the Europe 2020 objectives[1]

Geertrui Van Overwalle

INTRODUCTION

'May you live in interesting times'. This phrase is reputed to be the English translation of an ancient Chinese curse.[2] Gazing around in the intricate world of patents and biotechnology, it seems that patents hold great promise, but may appear as a curse as well. Patents may well fuel the development of the most fascinating and 'smart' innovations in the field of life sciences: re-engineered micro-organisms producing medicines, re-constructed plants killing insects, re-modeled animals delivering human hormones, harvested human stem cells repairing human body parts, just to name a few. But patents may also have some unintended, over-exclusive ('under-inclusive') consequences and hinder access and further research and development in the area of biotechnology:

---

[1] The author is paraphrasing the three mutually reinforcing priorities and objectives of Europe 2020: 'smart, sustainable and inclusive economy'. These should help the EU and the Member States deliver high levels of employment, productivity and social cohesion, see http://ec.europa.eu/europe2020/index_en.htm. The current chapter is partly based on G. Van Overwalle (2008), 'Biotechnology and Patents: Global Standards, European Approaches and National Accents', in *Genetic Engineering and the World Trade System,* D. Wüger and T. Cottier (eds.), Cambridge University Press, 77-108 and on G. Van Overwalle, (2009) 'Of Thickets, Blocks and Gaps: Designing Tools to Resolve Obstacles in the Gene Patents Landscape', in *Gene Patents and Collaborative Licensing Models. Patent Pools, Clearing Houses, Open Source Models and Liability Regimes*, Van Overwalle, G. (ed.), Cambridge: Cambridge University Press, 381-463.

[2] Differences of opinion exist as to the origin of the phrase. Some claim that it is an authentic Chinese saying, whereas others state (e.g. *Yale Book of Quotations* with reference to the American Society of International Law Proceedings, vol. 33, 1939) that no authentic Chinese saying to this effect has ever been found, and that it may have originated among the English or the Americans themselves.

25% of the human genome is said to be patented at present,[3] truly complicating access and freedom to operate in health care and possibly compromising 'sustainable' welfare for all.

The aim of the present analysis is twofold. First, the chapter aims to portray the current state of play and the impact of patent law and practice in two disputed domains which show some remarkable linkages, namely plant biotechnology and human genetics.[4] Second, the chapter tries to sketch how to maintain the fuelling capacity of patent law whilst mitigating some (unintended) negative effects in these innovative sectors.

The chapter is structured as follows. The chapter starts with an overview of the current multilevel framework protecting technological achievenements in the area of plant and human biotechnology (section 1). The chapter then provides an analysis of recent case law, responding to challenges testing the limits of current patent legislation (section 2). Next, the chapter zooms in on some perceived problems (section 3), and suggests avenues for improvement (section 4). The chapter concludes that next to (further) narrowing down the scope of patentable subject matter and restricting the coming into *existence* of patent rights, mechanisms should be put in place which restrict the room to manoeuvre for patent holders, in particular the way in which they *exercise* their rights. In this regard, patents should no longer simply be viewed as exclusive rights, but as tools to protect and share, giving rise to 'inclusive patents', in sectors which are vital for our well-being, such as food and health care.

1. SETTING THE SCENE: CURRENT PATENT LEGISLATION

The intellectual property rights (IPR) regime in general, and the patent system in particular, is shaped as a multi-level legal framework. At the **international** level, the key international standards with regard to patents are consolidated in the Agreement on Trade Related Aspects of International Property Rights (TRIPS Agreement).[5] The TRIPS Agreement introduces a worldwide frame-

---

3 K. Jensen and F. Murray (2005), 'Intellectual Property Landscape of the Human Genome', *Science*, **310**, 239.

4 The present analysis will not focus on the debate surrounding patents, *ordre public* and morality. Hence, the area of human stem cell technology has not been selected for further examination in the present paper.

5 Agreement on Trade-Related Aspects of Intellectual Property Rights (TRIPS Agreement), included as an Annex to the WTO Agreement (see www.wto.org/english/tratop_e/trips_e/t_agm0_e.htm). Membership of the WTO implies adherence to the TRIPS Agreement.

work of minimum standards with regard to the grant, scope and use of patents (Articles 27–34). The general principle with regard to patentable subject matter defines that patents shall be available for any invention, whether products or processes, in all fields of technology, provided that they are new, involve an inventive step and are capable of industrial application (Article 27(1)). Patents shall be available, and patent rights enjoyable, without discrimination as to the place of invention, the field of technology, and whether products are imported or locally produced (Article 27(1)). Since patents shall be available irrespective of the field of technology, patent protection is in principle possible for achievements in the life sciences.

At the **European** level, patent law is dominated by the European Patent Convention (EPC).[5] As a matter of principle, it is possible to obtain a European wide patent for any invention which is new, involves an inventive step and is susceptible of industrial application (EPC Article 52(1)), by applying for a patent at the European Patent Office (EPO). On the basis of a single application and examination procedure it is possible to protect an invention in up to 38 European countries, all Contracting States which have ratified the EPC.

In a direct bid to resolve some lacunas and confusing issues with regard to bio-patenting in Europe, and to harmonize Member States' legislations on this point, a Directive on the legal protection of biotechnological inventions was adopted by the European Parliament on 6 July 1998.[7] At the same time, the Directive also represented a subtle attempt, the EU having no authority over the EPO, to steer the granting policy of the EPO indirectly. The Directive was indeed incorporated into the EPC in 1999,[8] thus providing for the EPO more detailed guidelines with regard to the patenting of human material.

The EU Biotechnology Directive officially proclaims for the first time in Europe that patent protection is no longer restricted to inanimate objects, but is also principally accessible with regard to living matter. In that regard, the Directive stipulates that inventions 'which are new, which involve an inventive step and which are susceptible of industrial application, shall be patentable even if they concern a product consisting of or containing biological material or a process by means of which biological material is produced, processed or used' (Article 3(1)). 'Biological material' means any material

6 European Patent Convention of 5 October 1973 (see www.epo.org/).

7 Directive 98/44/EC of 6 July 1998 of the European Parliament and of the Council on the legal protection of biotechnological inventions (OJ L 213, 30/07/1998, p. 0013) (see http://europa.eu.int).

8 Notably as Rule 29 of the Implementing Regulations to the EPC, which was inserted by decision of the Administrative Council of 16 June 1999, and which came into force on 1 September 1999.

containing genetic information and capable of reproducing itself or being reproduced in a biological system (Article 2(1)(a)).

The EU Biotechnology Directive also takes into account the ethical concerns in the field of bio-patenting. Echoing EPC Article 53(a), the Directive stipulates that inventions the commercial exploitation of which is considered to run counter to *ordre public* or morality shall be excluded from patentability (Article 6(1)). EPC case law clarified that the concept of *ordre public* covers the protection of public security and the physical integrity of individuals.[9] The concept also encompasses the protection of the environment.[10] Furthermore, EPC case law pointed out that the concept of morality is related to the belief that whereas some behaviour is right and acceptable, other behaviour is wrong; this belief is founded on the totality of the accepted norms which are deeply rooted in a particular culture.[11] In legal doctrine, especially in civil law countries, it is generally confirmed that the twin concept of *ordre public* and morality is used to define the outer limits of what society tolerates at present and to delimit the absolutely unacceptable. The notion of *ordre public* refers to the legal principles which touch upon the essential interests of the state, whereas the concept of morality encloses extra-legal norms based on the prevailing values held by the public. According to legal writers, the *ordre public*/morality concept offers only a 'narrow gate of entry' to exclude inventions, especially inventions in the area of the life sciences, from patent law.[12]

For the time being, it is also possible to obtain patent protection in Europe for biotechnological inventions by separate application to each of the **national** patent offices within Europe. The national systems are relevant to a degree, since certain events of primary interest have recently taken place at the national level, on the occasion of the implementation of the EU Biotechnology Directive.

Let us now investigate how these general rules play out in two currently highly contested domains of innovation in the life sciences.[13] First, plant

---

9 Technical Board of Appeal, 21 February 1995 (T 356/93) (Appeal on the decision of the Opposition Division, 15 December 1992).

10 See Point 5 of the aforementioned decision, Official Journal EPO, 1995, (545), 557. Cf. point 14, Official Journal EPO, 1995, (545), 560.

11 See Point 6 of the aforementioned decision, Official Journal EPO, 1995, (545), 557.

12 R. Moufang, R. (1998), 'The Concept of "Ordre Public" and Morality in Patent Law', in G. Van Overwalle (ed.), *Octrooirecht, ethiek en biotechnologie [Patent Law, Ethics and Biotechnology], Droit des brevets, éthique et biotechnologie*, (CIR-Reeks, 13) , Brussels: Bruylant, pp. 65–77 and the references cited there.

13 As said earlier the present analysis will not focus on the debate surrounding patents, *ordre public* and morality. Hence, the area of human stem cell technology has not been selected for further examination in the present paper.

biotechnology, with controversial patent claims on plant traits and on essentially biological processes for the production of plants. Second, human genetics, with debated patent claims on human genes and on diagnostic methods.

1.1 Plant Biotechnology

At the international level the TRIPS Agreement sets forth that Members may exclude **plants** from patentability (Article 27(3)(b), first sentence). The optional nature of that statement has led to a variety of approaches to the patent protection of plants, but the most dominant view so far was that patents on biological resources are useful and that the exclusionary TRIPS provision is not to be implemented. In addition, TRIPS stipulates that Members shall provide for the protection of plant varieties either by patents or by an effective *sui generis*[14] system or by any combination thereof (Article 27(3)(b), second sentence). In the context of TRIPS, it was usually understood that the reference to a *sui generis* system pertained to the system of plant breeders' rights, based on the International Convention for the Protection of New Varieties of Plants of 1961 (the so-called UPOV Convention).[15] [16]

Turning to Europe, the central provision states that European patents shall not be granted in respect of plant varieties (EPC Article 53(b)). One reason for the exclusion of plant varieties from patent protection is the fact that several European countries have introduced special legal protection for the results of plant breeding, based upon the International Convention for the Protection of New Varieties of Plants of 1961 (UPOV Convention) and forming the basis for the national laws on breeders' rights.[17]

---

[14] A *sui generis* system means a regime 'of its own kind': the term is used to identify a legal system that exists independently of other, major categorizations.

[15] This Convention was signed by several European countries and thus created a Union for the Protection of New Varieties of Plants, commonly known under its French abbreviation UPOV (Union pour la Protection des Obtentions Végétales).

[16] This interpretation met with criticism in some Member States (See D. Gervais (2003), *The TRIPS Agreement. Drafting History and Analysis*, London: Sweet & Maxwell, pp. 227–34, especially last paragraph on p. 229). During the Doha WTO Ministerial Conference of 2001, and the subsequent Ministerial Declaration of 14 November 2001, it was suggested that the notion should be given wider scope, and that TRIPS Article 27(3)(b) could serve as a legal basis for the introduction of a *sui generis* protection regime for traditional knowledge related to plant genetic resources (See para. 19 Ministerial declaration, adopted on 14 November 2001 (WT/MIN(01)/DEC/1). Also see D. Gervais, *ibid*, pp. 227–34.

[17] For more, see G. Van Overwalle (1997), *The Legal Protection of Biotechnological Inventions in Europe and in the United States,* Leuven: University Press, p. 78.

EPO practice,[18] prior to the promulgation of the EU Biotechnology Directive, generally accepted that subcellular fragments instrumental to plant modification (like DNA sequences, genes, plasmids and vectors), genetically modified plant cells and transgenic plants *per se* (where specific plant varieties are not individually claimed),[19] could be the subject of patent protection. An analysis of a series of European patents for plants *per se* shows that as far as the kind of technology was concerned, patent protection has been granted for new realizations in the field of in-vitro culture, as well as for recombinant DNA technology or protoplast fusion. As far as the type of claims was concerned, the analysis showed that in the case of in-vitro culture and protoplast fusion it was almost exclusively process claims that were set forth, whereas in the case of recombinant DNA technology, product claims which relate to the end-product (modified plant cells, plants and seeds) or to intermediate products (e.g. vectors and plasmids), were applied for as well.[20]

The EU Biotechnology Directive aligned itself with the prevailing EPO granting policy.[21] The Directive excludes plant varieties from patentability (Article 4(1)(a)). The exclusion applies to plants or their propagating material in the genetically fixed form of the plant variety, and does not apply to plants that do not meet the profile of a variety and which belong to a classification unit taxonomically higher than that of a variety, in other words for the plant *per se*.[22] Inventions which concern plants *per se* shall be patentable if the

18 In other words, before the enactment of the EU Biotechnology Directive. For more details, see Van Overwalle, *supra* note 17, p. 78.

19 Technical Board of Appeal, 13 October 1997 (T 1054/96 – Novartis), Official Journal EPO, 1998, 511 (see http://legal.european-patent-office.org/dg3/biblio/t961054ep1.htm); Enlarged Board of Appeal, 20 December 1999 (G 1/98 – Novartis), Official Journal EPO, 2000, 111–141; Technical Board of Appeal, 6 December 2000 (T 1054/96 – Novartis) (see http://legal.european-patent-office.org/dg3/biblio/t961054eu1.htm).

20 For a detailed analysis of the aforementioned plant patents, see G. Van Overwalle (1996), *Octrooieerbaarheid van plantenbiotechnologische uitvindingen. Een rechtsvergelijkend onderzoek naar een rechtvaardiging van een uitbreiding van het octrooirecht tot planten. [Patentability of Plant Biotechnological Inventions. A Comparative Study towards a Justification of Extending Patent Law to Plants (Substantive Summary)],* Brussels: Bruylant , pp. 139–45. Also see, G. Van Overwalle, 'Patent Protection for Plants: a Comparison of American and European Approaches', 39 *IDEA-Journal of Law and Technology* (USA), 1999, 143–194.

21 For details, see Van Overwalle, *supra* note 17, p. 78.

22 A little explanation might clarify this situation. The differentiation between plants *per se* and plant *varieties* as deployed in the Directive is based on the modern biological division of the animal and plant world into groups, or taxa, i.e: division, subdivision, class, order, family, genus and species, whereby each 'higher' taxon subsumes all 'lower' taxa. The application of these groups to the plant kingdom results in its being classified in a hierarchy with five divisions which, in turn, are divided into

technical feasibility of the invention is not confined to a particular plant or animal variety (Article 4(2)). So, in providing patent protection for plants *per se*, the Directive does not make use of the flexibility offered in TRIPS (Article 27(3)(b), first sentence) to exclude plants from patent protection.

As to the patentability of **plant genes** or gene sequences, TRIPS does not contain any specific provision relating to their patentability. Therefore, plant genes can probably be regarded as patentable subject matter under TRIPS. No specific provisions are foreseen in the EU Biotechnology Directive either. Therefore, plant gene sequences which have been isolated and characterized can be assumed to be patentable subject matter as long as they fulfil the criteria of novelty, inventive step, industrial applicability and enabling disclosure.

At the international level the TRIPS Agreement further sets forth that Members may exclude plants and **essentially biological processes for the production of plants** from patentability. At the European level, the EPC gives way to the suggested exclusion and stipulates that essentially biological processes for the production of plants are excluded from patentability (EPC Article 53(b)). The EU Biotechnology Directive equally stipulates that essentially biological processes for the production of plants shall not be patentable (Article 4(1)(b)). It is further clarified that a process for the production of plants or animals is essentially biological if it consists 'entirely' of natural phenomena such as crossing or selection (Article 2(2)). However, the exclusion of essentially biological processes for the production of plants shall be without prejudice to the patentability of inventions which concern a microbiological or other technical process or a product obtained by means of such a process (Article 4(3)).

1.2 Human Biotechnology

The TRIPS Agreement does not explicitly refer to the **human body.** However, states may take a decision to deny patents on their territory for inventions claiming **human genes** based on ethical grounds in case the commercial exploitation of such patents runs counter to *ordre public* or morality (TRIPS Article 27(3)(b)). Till now, few countries have used the option to carve out human genes from their patent laws.[23]

Even though the EPC, in the pre-Directive-era, did not contain specific provisions concerning the admissibility of patents on human beings and

---

subdivisions, classes and orders. Orders are, on the basis of flower structure, further subdivided into families. Families are, in turn, divided into genera and species. For an actual example – the potato – clarifying the current taxonomy of the plant kingdom, see G. Van Overwalle (2008), *supra* note 1, p. 77–108.

[23] See *ibid*.

human body material, European patents have been granted for human genes and the majority of recombinant DNA achievements. Thus, European patents were issued for the production of alpha-type interferon,[24] gamma-type interferon,[25] coagulation factor VIII,[26] tissue-type plasminogen activator or t-PA,[27] erythropoietin[28] and others. A good example in this connection is the patent granted for alpha-type interferon. An examination of the description and patent claims of the interferon patent reveals that protection was granted for a well-defined DNA sequence, a recombinant DNA molecule, a host transformed with the said recombinant DNA molecule, an alpha-type interferon produced by the said transformed host for a process for producing the recombinant DNA molecules, a process for the transformation of the host, and a process for the production of an alpha-type interferon.[29]

The EU Biotechnology Directive offered some refinement as to the patentability of the human body in general and human gene sequences in particular. The Directive posited that neither the human body at the various stages of its formation and development, nor the simple discovery of one of its elements including the sequence or partial sequence of a gene, can constitute a patentable invention (Article 5(1)), whereas an element isolated from the human body or otherwise produced by means of a technical process, including the sequence or partial sequence of a gene, may constitute a patentable invention, even if the structure of that element is identical to that of a natural element (Article 5(2)).

After the EU Biotechnology Directive was passed by the European Parliament, the EPO amended their Regulations and added a rule confirming the patentability of isolated human genes (EPC rule 29(2)). The question then arose to what extent this new rule was in conformity with the exclusion of inventions the publication or exploitation of which would be contrary to *ordre*

---

24 European patent with publication number 32.134, entitled 'DNA sequences, recombinant DNA molecules and processes for producing human interferon-like polypeptides'.

25 European patent with publication number 77.670, entitled 'Human immune interferon'.

26 European patent with publication number 83.483, entitled 'Ultrapurification of factor VIII: C preparation'.

27 European patent with publication number 93.619, entitled 'Human tissue plasminogen activator, pharmaceutical compositions containing it, processes for making it, and DNA and transformed cell intermediates therefore'.

28 European patent with publication number 148.605, entitled 'Production of erythropoietin'.

29 European patent with publication number 32.134, entitled 'DNA sequences, recombinant DNA molecules and processes for producing human interferon-like polypeptides'.

public or morality (EPC Article 53(a)). Based on earlier case law,[30] the EPO adopted the view that the new rule 'only gave a more detailed interpretation of the meaning of Article 53 EPC as intended from its inception'. It thus followed from the text of the rule itself that genes were not to be considered as an exception from patentability on grounds of *ordre public* or morality.[31]

On the international level it is also generally agreed that national patent legislatures can exclude **diagnostic, therapeutic and surgical methods**[32] for the treatment of humans from patentability (TRIPS Article 27(3)(a)). The option to exclude such methods is based on public health considerations: medical and veterinary practitioners should be free to take the action they consider adequate to diagnose and treat illnesses. In other words, those who carry out diagnostic, therapeutic or surgical methods as part of a medical treatment of humans should not be inhibited by patents. It was agreed that this exclusion shall not apply to products, in particular substances or compositions, for use in any of these methods.

Long before the TRIPS Agreement came into being, the EPO decided to exclude diagnostic methods from patent protection when 'practiced *on* the human or animal body'. The exclusionary provision in the EPC is constructed more narrowly than its TRIPS counterpart, implying that the *only* methods excluded from patent protection are diagnostic methods practised *on* the human body. Unfortunately, the EPO legislator did not define the term 'diagnostic method', so it was left to the courts to delineate the exact scope of the exclusion. In short, current EPO case law suggests that diagnostic methods carried out *in vivo* are considered unpatentable, whereas diagnostic methods not carried out on the human or animal body, but practised *in vitro* are considered patentable.[33]

---

30 EPO EBoA G1/98, 1999 (Novartis AG.).

31 EPO TBoA T272/95, 2002 (Howard Florey Institute).

32 Generally speaking, genetic testing relates to identifying changes in chromosomes, genes, or proteins to find changes that are associated with inherited disorders (http://www.ghr.nlm.nih.gov/handbook/testing/genetictesting). More narrowly, *medical* genetic testing aims at probing genetic material for disease associated geno- or karyotypes (medical applications of cytogenetics, DNA and biochemical tests):J. Sequeiros and Guimarães G. 'Definitions of Genetic Testing in European and other Legal Documents', Study for Unit 3 EuroGentest (WP3.4), in collaboration with Unit 6 (WPs 6.6 and 6.4), 10th (final) draft version of 16 June 2009, available at: http://www.eurogentest.org/web/files/public/unit6/core_competences/BackgroundDoc DefinitionsLegislationV10-FinalDraft.pdf (last accessed 30 April 2012). The present contribution focuses, even more specifically, on medical genetic *DNA/RNA* testing. See, J. Sequeiros (2010), 'Definitions of Genetic Testing', in U. Kristoffersson, J. Schmidtke and J.-J. Cassiman, (eds), *Quality Issues in Clinical Genetic Services*, Berlin-Heidelberg: Springer.

33 For more details, see e.g. G. Van Overwalle (2010) 'IPR Issues and High

2. TESTING THE LIMITS: RECENT CASE LAW

The limits of current patent legislation are put to test. Various recent judicial decisions offer some guidance and provide valuable insights on where the exact limits of patent law should be drawn in the area of the life sciences.

Overlooking the current European legal framework, it is crystal clear that in the realm of plant biotechnology, current patent legislation allows the patentability of transgenic plants *per se,* isolated plant genes as well as genetic modification techniques (see Table 10.1) and excludes plant varieties and essential biological processes for the production of plants. However, new techniques have come to the fore, putting the current framework to test. This is particularly true in the plant field, where queries have emerged about the interpretation of the concept of biological processes and its potential ability to qualify as patentable subject matter, and where questions arose about the exact scope of protection for plant genes.

Overlooking the patent framework in the field of human genetics, it is undisputed that the European legislator embraces the patentability of human genes, as well as genetic diagnostic methods carried out *in vitro*. However, in the domain of human genes, the principle debate on the patentability of human genes is (re)opened, and the alleged distinction between (non-patentable) discoveries (EU Biotechnology Directive, Article 5(1)) and (patentable) inventions in the area of human genetics.

2.1 The Soy Meal Case

The question at the heart of the debate in the Soy Meal *Monsanto* case related to the scope of biotechnology patents, more in particular, the scope of patents awarded for genetically modified plants and plant genes. The question was decided by the Court of Justice for the European Union (CJEU) in July 2010,[34] following a request for a preliminary ruling from the Court of The Hague (the Netherlands), which had to decide on the alleged infringement of a patent from Monsanto related to glyphosate resistant plants (European patent with publication number 546.090).

Glyphosate resistant plants express the CP4 EPSPS gene, rendering the plant – in case: soya – resistant to the herbicide *Roundup Ready*. The *Roundup*

Quality Genetic Testing', in *Quality Issues in Clinical* Genetic Services, Kristoffersson et al, *supra* note 32, pp. 251–65 (full paper available at http://ssrn.com/abstract=1720008); D. Thomas (2007), 'The EPC and the Granting Policy and Case Law of the EPO', in G. Van Overwalle (ed.), *Gene Patents and Public Health,* Brussels: Bruylant , pp. 61–71; D. Thomas (2003), 'Patentability Problems in Medical Biotechnology', *IIC* , 847–994.

34 *Monsanto Technology LLC v Cefetra BV et al.*, ECJ, C-428/09, 6 July 2010.

Table 10.1 Overview types of patents in the realm of plant biotechnology

Invention	Subject matter		Claims
Product	Plants *per se*	e.g. genetically modified plants (transgenic plants)	– end product: modified plant cells, plants, seeds – intermediate products: vectors, plasmids, etc
	Plant traits	– native traits: e.g. drought resistance, reduced water content, increased anti-oxidant content – newly inserted traits: e.g. herbicide resistance, insect resistance	
Method	Genetic transformation techniques	Recombinant DNA technology	*Agrobacterium* mediated gene transfer
	(Mix) conventional breeding (and molecular breeding) techniques		

Ready soya was cultivated on a large scale in Argentina and the resulting soy meal was then imported into the Netherlands. Monsanto did not hold a patent in Argentina, but did so in the Netherlands, including product claims on the CP4 EPSPS gene and on plant cells and plants transformed with this gene. Tests showed the presence of said DNA sequence in the imported soy meal. The question then arose whether the import of the soy meal infringes Monsanto's product claims on the gene, when the product of the plant in which the gene has been inserted, i.e. meal, is imported.

The general principle regarding the scope of biotechnology patents implies that patent protection shall extend to any biological material possessing the same characteristics as the initial biological material (EU Biotechnology Directive, Article 8). The principle as applied to genes includes that 'The protection conferred by a patent on a product containing or consisting of genetic information shall extend to all material … in which the product is incorporated and in which the genetic information is contained and performs its function' (Article 9).

The CJEU ruled that Article 9 is to be interpreted as not conferring patent right protection:

> in cases where the patented product [read: the DNA sequence, in case the CP4 EPSPS gene] is contained in the soy meal, where it does not perform the function [in case protecting biological material in which the DNA sequence is incorporated against the effect of herbicides] for which the product is patented, but did perform that function previously in the soy plant, of which the meal is a processed product, or would possibly again be able to perform that function after it had been extracted from the soy meal and inserted into the cell of a living organism.

The CJEU verdict responds to a long felt need for guidance in the debate on the scope of protection for biotechnological inventions and for genes in particular. The merit of the CJEU verdict lies in its pointing to actual performance of the function of the DNA sequence in the material in which it is incorporated as an essential *condition* for deserving patent protection. Contrary to what many commentaries suggested, the CJEU does not offer a clear answer as to the exact *scope* of the protection for DNA sequences.[35] The answer developed by the CJEU does not provide a fine-meshed and thorough argumentation on scope of protection in the area of genetics. It may well be, however, that the CJEU meant to say that the scope of protection for DNA sequences is to be restricted to the function(s) mentioned in the patent application, and thus opted for a purpose bound protection regime.[36] *If* the CJEU indeed intended to postulate a restricted, purpose bound regime in the plant domain, then the CJEU ruling may be regarded as a landmark case with epic proportions, being one of the very first manifestations of the European judiciary calling a halt to the ongoing expansion of patent law in the area of biotechnology, and calling for a halt in further stretching the limits of patent law in this area.

---

[35] See my critical analysis in G. Van Overwalle (2011), 'The CJEU Monsanto Soybean Decision and Patent Scope: As Clear As Mud', *IIC* , 1–3. Also see C. Heath (2009), 'The Scope of DNA Patents in the Light of the Recent *Monsanto* Decisions', *IIC*, 940; M.A. Kock (2010) , 'Patent Protection for DNA sequences – to be or not to be?', *JIPLP*, 5, 754–6; C. Seitz (2010), 'The European Life Science Law and the Protection of Biotechnological Inventions – New Developments for Patent Protection under the European Biotechnology Directive (Monsanto Technology LLC / Cefetra BV and others, ECJ (Grand Chamber), Judgment of 6 July 2010, C-428/08)', *European Law Reporter*, 276–80.

[36] For a challenging discussion on the choice between absolute and purpose bound protection, see I. Schneider (2003), 'Funktionsgebundener Stoffschutz auf DNA-Sequenzen? Policy-analytische und wissenschaftstheoritische Anmerkungen zu einer zentralen Kontroverse in der Biopatentierung', in C. Baumgartner and D. Mieth (eds), *Patente am Leben? Ethische, rechtliche und politische Aspekte der Biopatentierung*, Paderborn: Mentis, pp. 179–211.

2.2 The Tomato and Broccoli Cases

The key issue at stake in the Tomato and Broccoli cases decided by the Enlarged Board of Appeal of the EPO[37] related to the patentability of essentially biological processes for the production of plants. The decision followed the decisions of the Technical Boards of Appeal.[38] The methods at stake do not relate to the development of genetically modified plants, but cover conventional breeding methods and conventional seeds.

The broccoli in suit has elevated levels of glucosinolates, a class of compounds with anti-cancer potential. The method of obtaining the broccoli involves locating the relevant genes for higher levels of glucosinolates on the broccoli genome, identifying them with genetic markers, crossing wild broccoli plants with cultivated lines, and subsequently selecting the lines containing the desired substance by means of markers. A European patent was awarded with claims on this breeding method.[39] The tomato in case has reduced fruit water content, which is useful in the tomato industry for manufacture of products such as ketchup or sauces. The method of obtaining the tomatoes with reduced fruit water content includes the steps of crossing tomato plants from one subspecies (*Lycopersicon esculentum*) with other (wild) species, allowing plants to remain on the vine past the point of normal ripening, and subsequent screening of the plants for reduced fruit water content by extended preservation of the ripe fruit and wrinkling of the fruit skin, which is related to dehydration. A European patent was granted with claims on this breeding method.[40]

In the opinion of the Enlarged Board of Appeal, the legislator's intention was to exclude conventional methods (including sexual crossing of (whole

---

[37] Decision of the Enlarged Board of Appeal of the European Patent Office, 9 December 2010, G 2/07 (Broccoli case) and G 1/08 (Tomato case). By decision of 21 April 2008 the Enlarged Board decided to consider the points of law referred to it by Technical Board of Appeal in case T 83/05 (G 2/07) and in case T 1242/06 (G 1/08) in consolidated proceedings.

[38] Interlocutory decision of the Technical Board of Appeal, 22 May 2007 in case T 83/05 (Broccoli), and interlocutory decision of the Technical Board of Appeal, 4 April 2008 in case T 1242/06 (Tomato).

[39] EP 1 069 819 entitled 'Method for selective increase of the anticarcinogenic glucosinolates in brassica species', granted to Plant Bioscience on 24 July 2002. The central claim encompasses a method for the production of *Brassica* with elevated levels, which comprises crossing wild broccoli species with cultivated lines, and selecting hybrids with elevated levels (Claim 1). Further, claims include a method which additionally comprises screening for the specific traits with RFLP markers (Claim 4).

[40] EP 1 211 926 entitled 'Method for breeding tomatoes having reduced water content and product of the method', awarded to the State of Israel on 26 November 2003.

genomes of) plants, and the subsequent selection of the plants having the desired trait) for the breeding of plant varieties from patentability. The application of technical means or other forms of human intervention in such processes which helped to perform crossing and selecting was already common, even though the natural phenomenon of meiosis ultimately determined the genetic make-up of the plants produced. The Enlarged Board of Appeal takes the view that the use of the word 'essentially' reflects the legislative intention that the mere fact of using a technical device in a breeding process (e.g. a special greenhouse) should not be sufficient to give the process as such a technical character and should not have the effect that such process can avoid the exclusion.[41] The Enlarged Board is unable to see why the legislator's decision to provide appropriate patent protection for 'secondary' features such as technical devices or means (today e.g. markers) by allowing them to be patented in themselves but not to extend protection to the biological process in which they are used, would no longer be justified today, merely because today many more such technical possibilities exist. The Enlarged Board of Appeal finally concludes that a non-microbiological process for the production of plants which contains the steps of crossing and selecting plants does not escape the exclusion of essentially biological processes merely because it contains, as a further step or as part of any of the steps of crossing and selection, an additional feature of a technical nature.[42] [43]

The answer provided by the EPO is well reasoned and restores the legislator's intent to give a sensible interpretation to the exclusion of essentially biological processes for the production of plants. The decision excludes conventional plant breeding methods in which human intervention assists, including the provision of a technical means serving to enable the performance of the process. The products of such methods of breeding, cannot be covered

---

41 Cf. Decision of the Enlarged Board of Appeal of the European Patent Office, 9 December 2010, G 0001/08, p. 67, explanatory notes.

42 However, if a process of sexual crossing and selection includes within it an additional step of a technical nature, which step by itself introduces a trait into the genome or modifies a trait in the genome of the plant produced, so that the introduction or modification of that trait is not the result of the mixing of the genes of the plants chosen for sexual crossing, then that process leaves the realm of the plant breeding, which the legislator wanted to exclude from patentability. Therefore, such a process is not excluded from patentability under EPC Article 53(b) but qualifies as a potentially patentable technical teaching.

43 It has to be noted that the decision of the Enlarged Board has the objective of clarifying the legal meaning of the concept of 'essentially biological processes' under the EPC, and that a first concrete application will be provided by the Technical Boards of Appeal, which had referred the questions to the Enlarged Board of Appeal and are now called to decide upon the individual cases in the light of the guidance provided by the Enlarged Board of Appeal.

with a patent either, but may in principle be protected as a plant variety. On the other hand, the decision leaves patent protection available for methods of genetic engineering, inserting certain features into a plant, as well as the resulting genetically modified plants.[44]

2.3 The Breast Cancer (BRCA) Case

The core question in the decision in March 2010 of Judge Robert W. Sweet of the District Court for the Southern District of New York revolved around the patentability of isolated human genes and associated diagnostic methods.[45] The decision to deny patent protection to some breast cancer genes swept through the US biotech community as a shock wave and ruffled feathers in Europe as well.

The case related to genetic tests for familial breast and ovarian cancer developed by the company *Myriad Genetics*. The product claims were directed to isolated DNA containing human BRCA1 and BRCA2 gene sequences. The method claims covered the process of identifying certain mutations in the BRCA genes. The US District Court held that the claimed isolated DNA 'is not markedly different from native DNA as it exists in nature' and constitutes unpatentable subject matter.[46] The court also ruled that the claimed method is 'directed only to the abstract mental process of comparing or analyzing gene sequences', fails the so-called 'machine or transformation test',[47] and is unpatentable as well.[48] The *Myriad* decision has been appealed and the Court of Appeal for the Federal Circuit (CAFC) came to a different conclusion.[49] In December 2011, ACLU petitioned the Supreme Court to hear the Myriad Genetics case.[50]

---

[44] For some other critical comments, see S. Bostyn (2006–2007), 'Do you Want Biological or Essentially Biological Vegetables', *BioScienceLawReview*, 146–55; A. Hübel (2011), 'Essentials on Essentially Biological Processes for the Production of Plants: Decisions G2/07 (Broccoli Case) and G1/08 (Tomato Case) of the Enlarged Board of Appeal of the EPO', *EIPR*, 328–30.

[45] *Association for Molecular Pathology v US Patent and Trademark Office*, Southern District of New York (29 March 2010).

[46] Ibid.

[47] As cited in *Bilski v Kappos*, US Supreme Court (28 June 2010), referring to *In re Bilski*: '[a] claimed process is surely patent-eligible under §101 if: (1) it is tied to a particular machine or apparatus, or (2) it transforms a particular article into a different state or thing'.

[48] See *supra* note 45.

[49] *Association of Molecular Pathology v US Patent and Trademark Office*. USDC SDNY 09 Civ. 4515 (2010).

[50] For more details, see I. Huys, G. Matthijs and G. Van Overwalle, 'The Fate and Future of Patents on Human Genes and Genetic Diagnostic Methods', 13 *Nature Reviews Genetics*, 2012, 441–448.

The case has received much attention and has been commented upon broadly and vigorously in Europe. In Europe, more or less similar claims to the BRCA genes and genetic diagnostic methods were granted. Even though the European patents survived during the EPO opposition and appeal proceedings (albeit with narrower scope), the current US suit may well (re)open a principled discussion on the patentability of human genes and genetic diagnostic methods in Europe.[51]

3. OVERSTEPPING THE BOUNDARIES? HINDERING EFFECTS OF PATENTS

An overview of current trends in patent legislation and case law in the field of plant and human biotechnology reveals two opposing tendencies. On the one hand, there is an increasing trend to award patent protection for biotech inventions such as transgenic plants, plant genes, related biological processes, and human genes and genetic diagnostic methods. Witness the growing numbers of patents on plants *per se* and (native) plant genes, and the boosting numbers of patents on human DNA and related diagnostic tests. The patent system applies to an ever broadening range of new techniques that make plant breeding and human genetic testing more efficient and effective. A steady growth of patents for biotech inventions of this type is hardly surprising in view of the EU *legislator* having put in place the EU Biotechnology Directive, which unequivocally proclaims patent protection for biological material, including plants and human genes.

On the other hand, there is a clear call for attenuating the grip of patents and toning down the alacrity with which patent protection is being awarded for biological material. Witness the positions taken in recent European *case law,* in particular the *Monsanto* verdict from the CJEU, and the decision of the EPO Enlarged Board of Appeal in the Broccoli and Tomato cases, complemented with the stance taken in the recent US *Myriad* ruling.

It remains to be seen, whether the judicial treatment of patent principles in these cases is different from the application of patent doctrines in other industry sectors or technologies.[52] For example, the question arises to what extent

[51] For a better understanding of the differences between the US and the European legal framework and underlying policy options, see I. Huys, G. Van Overwalle and G. Matthijs (2011), 'Gene and Genetic Diagnostic Method Patent Claims. A Comparison under current European and US Patent Law', 19 (10) *European Journal of Human Genetics (EJHG)*, 2011, 1104-1107.

[52] G. Van Overwalle (2011), 'Policy Levers Tailoring Patent Law to Biotechnology. Comparing European and US Approaches', *University of California Irvine Law Review,* 2011, 435-517 (full paper available at http://ssrn.com/abstract=1720875).

the *Monsanto* verdict differs from the principles envisaged for the scope of protection of human genes in diagnostic tests, and to what extent the ruling of the Enlarged Board of Appeal in the Broccoli and Tomato cases is in line with the principles developed for computer-implemented research.[53] This differentiation issue deserves further attention and definitely calls for closer examination.

In any case, even though recent case law may apply the same principle differently in biotechnology compared to other (sub)sectors, and well tends to narrow down the patentability and scope of some categories of biotechnological inventions, compared to many public policy issues relating to the impact of plant and gene patenting may well persist in the (near) future,[54] as similar problems pop up in both the plant and the human biotechnology area.

3.1 Restrictive Licensing

The increasing amount of patents in plant biotechnology sparked a wide debate on the (potential) negative effects of patents. Discussions with stakeholders[55] pointed to problems with licence conditions, more in particular the (sometimes excessive) costs breeders have to pay for the use of a patented construct.[56] Costly and obstructive licensing strategies for patents on breeding techniques and properties can have a negative effect on further innovation in the sector when patent rights stretch to a plant that can be used as a parent in breeding. This is even more so for patents on native plant 'traits', but less for breeding methods such as new marker systems.[57]

---

[53] See Hübel (2011), *supra* note 44.

[54] On the complex but inescapable relation between patents and the public, see K. Murray and E. van Zimmeren (2011), 'Dynamic Patent Governance in Europe and the United States: the *Myriad* Example', *Cardozo Journal of International and Comparative Law*, **19**, 287–342.

[55] See N. Louwaars, H. Dons, G. Van Overwalle, H. Raven, A. Arundel, D. Eaton and A. Nelis (2009), *Breeding Business. The Future of Plant Breeding in the Light of Developments in Patent Rights and Plant Breeder's Rights* (Study on request of the Netherlands Ministry of Agriculture, Nature and Food Quality (LNV) via the Policy Support Cluster Economically Promising Agro-chains (BO-3)), Wageningen: Centre for Genetic Resources (CGN) – Wageningen University and Research Centre, p. 61 (CGN Rapport 2009-14 EN) (study available at http://ssrn.com/abstract=1720088).

[56] One case has been described by the World Bank (World Bank (2006), *Intellectual Property Rights. Designing regimes to support plant breeding in developing countries*, Washington DC: World Bank Agriculture and Rural Development. Report # 35517, p. 77; see: http://siteresources.worldbank.org/INTARD/Resources/IPR_ESW.pdf) where the licence costs for a Bt construct (insect resistance) for use in cotton in India were twice as high as hybrid cotton seed, resulting in a threefold increase of the final seed price for the farmer. Also see Louwaars, *supra* note 59, p. 45.

[57] See *ibid*, p. 50.

The growing number of patents on human genes and genetic tests also led to significant public concern. Newspapers commenting on patent cases, quite often, portrayed gene patents as a negative story.[58] The commotion surrounding the current patent framework for genetic inventions points to a typical phenomenon in the area of genetics and intellectual property. Claims on genes are generally difficult, if not impossible, to circumvent, or 'invent around'[59] and problems arise when gene patents are licensed too restrictively. Restrictive licensing practices could further hamper research and development[60] – and in the case of human genes – clinical access, and availability of high-quality tests for patients. The *Myriad* case exemplifies such a restrictive licence policy, resulting in public disapproval. Studies have documented similar restrictive licensing practices for other tests as well.[61]

3.2 Patent Thickets

Another frequently heard complaint in the plant biotech field, is that patent rights generate patent thickets, webs of overlapping patents through which a company must 'hack' in order to commercialize a technology.[62] A high number of patents and the uncertainty about their precise scope makes it very

---

58 See T. Caulfield, T. Bubela and C.J. Murdoch (2007), 'Myriad and the Mass Media: the Covering of a Gene Patent Controversy', *Genetics in Medicine*, **9**, 850–5; T. Caulfield, R.M. Cook-Deegan, F. Scott Kieff and J.P. Walsh (2006), 'Evidence and Anecdotes: an Analysis of Human Gene Patenting Controversies', *Nature Biotechnology*, **24**, 1091–4; E.R. Gold, J. Carbone (2010), 'Myriad Genetics: In the Eye of the Policy Storm', *Genet. Med.* **12** (4 suppl.), S39–70.

59 I. Huys, N. Berthels, G. Matthijs, G. and Van Overwalle (2009), 'Legal Uncertainty in the Area of Genetic Diagnostic Testing', *Nature Biotechnology*, October, **27**, 903–9.

60 In some empirical studies, a negative impact of patents could not be found. However, these studies focused on biomedical research, not downstream product development.

61 M.K. Cho, S. Illangasekare, M.A. Weaver, D.G. Leonard, J.F. Merz (2003), 'Effects of Patents and Licenses on the Provision of Clinical Genetic Testing Services', *J. Mol. Diagn.* **5** (1), 3; J.P. Evans (ed.) (2010), 'Patently Complicated: Case Studies on the Impact of Patenting and Licensing on Clinical Access to Genetic Testing in the United States', *Genet. Med.* **12** (4 suppl.), S1–S211 (http://www.nature.com/gim/journal/v12/n4/full/gim201034a.html).

62 C. Shapiro (2001), 'Navigating the Patent Thicket: Cross Licenses, Patent Pools, and Standard Setting', in A. B. Jaffe et al. (eds), *Innovation Policy and the Economy*, vol. 1, Cambridge, MA: MIT Press), pp. 119–50. Concerns about the detrimental effect of patent thickets have recently loudly been voiced (again), see *Digital Opportunity. A review of Intellectual Property and Growth,* An independent report commissioned by Prime Minister David Cameron and carried out by Ian Hargreaves, 2011 (available at http://www.ipo.gov.uk/ipreview.htm).

difficult to establish whether certain techniques can be used without infringing or not. Even though evidence is (still) rather anecdotal,[63] complaints regarding the dense patent landscape have fuelled a debate on the (alleged) hindering impact of patents on access to plants *per se,* and of plant traits in particular, and, subsequently, on access to genetic diversity.

Also in the human genetics area, problems of patent thickets have been signalled. Accumulation, or 'stacking', of royalties that have to be paid when confronted with a patent thicket may lead to a 'tragedy of the anticommons',[64] affecting research and development and harming clinical and patient access in the long run. Empirical data do not yet confirm existence of a patent thicket in genetics at large.[65] However, thicket problems in genetic diagnostics could grow with shifts from monogenetic to multifactorial testing (multiplex diagnostics) and toward diagnostics based on genome-wide association studies driven by the high-throughput of single nucleotide polymorphism platforms and next-generation sequencing possibilities.[66]

3.3 Monopolistic Behaviour

Growing patent positions[67] in the plant biotech area, in combination with technological developments, have furthermore led to concerns about the large consolidation move among breeding companies. Such concentration may entail strategic use and monopolistic behaviour. It may also result in a few companies controlling a large part of the world market for some crops, making a growing part of the global food supply dependent on a few actors.[68]

---

[63] An often cited story is the alleged patent thicket in the case of Golden Rice, where some 70 patents were uncovered which were necessary to develop the rice. See G. Graff and D. Zilberman(2001), 'Towards an Intellectual Property Clearinghouse for Agribiotechnology', *IP Technol. Today*, **3**, 1–12.

[64] M.A. Heller and R.S. Eisenberg (1998), 'Can Patents Deter Innovation? The Anticommons in Biomedical Research', *Science* 280, 698–701.

[65] M.M. Hopkins et al. (2007), 'DNA patenting: the end of an era?', *Nat. Biotechnol.* 25, 185; K. Jensen, F. Murray (2005), 'Intellectual Property Landscape of the Human Genome', *Science* 310, 239.

[66] SACGHS (2010), *Revised Draft Report on Gene Patents and Licensing Practices and Their Impact on Patient Access to Genetic Tests* (Bethesda, MD: SACGHS, NIH). Also see J.H. Barton (2009), 'Emerging Patent Issues in Genomic Diagnostics', *Nat. Biotechnol.* 24, 939.

[67] See Table 3.7 'Top 10 applying companies for process-GM-plant patents between 2003 – 2007', in Louwaars et al., *supra* note 59, Table 3.7 shows that the share of the top 10 companies in the United States is no less than 75.1%, whereas the concentration level in Europe remains lower, with 42.5% of all patent applications.

[68] See Louwaars et al., *supra* note 59.

3.4 Erosion of Genetic Diversity

Last but not least, concern has been expressed that patent rights – especially patents on native plant traits – interfere with access to genetic variation, a very important source of innovation.[69]

4. CONSTRUCTING THE FUTURE: RECONCEPTUALIZING PATENTS

Both in the plant biotech and in the human biotech area, the behaviour of unwilling or powerful patent owners may result in hold ups and refusals to license. Wide patenting may lead to patent thickets, royalty stacking and, ultimately, a tragedy of the anti-commons. When reflecting on how to redress these unintended consequences of the patent system, it is important to recall the rationale of patent law. The major objective of patent law is to offer protection to the inventor against free riding and to encourage the development and disclosure of knowledge and innovation with a view to fostering scientific, technical and social progress in the interest of society at large, in other words, providing 'sustainable' welfare. In order to pursue this objective, inventors are given the opportunity to recoup their investments by way of an exclusionary right. It is widely accepted that patent systems are premised on an implicit 'social contract'[70] aimed at balancing private and public interests. Changes to the system should acknowledge this social contract and explore options that preserve the positive incentive for the production ofcrops, drugs and therapies and remedy some perceived hindrances in the field of agriculture and human genetics.

4.1 Tackling Restrictive Licensing

Patent and antitrust law leave considerable freedom to patentees to set up licensing agreements and do not prohibit exclusive licensing. The perceived problems in the plant biotech and human genetics area resulting from restrictive licensing practices may be tackled with *legislative* measures, such as compulsory licences. A compulsory licence has been introduced in the plant arena already to enhance the accessibility of genetic material (EU Biotechnology Directive Article 12(1)). However, the conditions set forth (EU

---

69 See Louwaars et al., *supra* note 59 and the references cited there.

70 L.H Hoffmann, in *Kirin-Amgen* v *Hoechst Marion Roussel*, House of Lords (21 October 2004).

Biotechnology Directive Article 12(3)(b)) make effective use of this instrument very difficult. For example, proving that the invention (e.g. trait) constitutes 'significant technical progress of considerable economic interest' when it can be used in the variety of a certain company cannot be demonstrated a priori.[71] Legislatures also imposed compulsory licences in the health area, forcing patent holders to grant use in the name of public health in Belgium, France, and Switzerland.[72] Although these compulsory license mechanisms have not yet been put to work in Europe, they may have an indirect, preventive effect on unduly restrictive licensing behaviour by patent owners.[73]

Another potential legislative measure to restrict patent holders' rights is the establishment of an exemption. An exemption may be conceived as a 'safety valve' in a property rule dominated regime, such as the patent system.[74] Suggestions in this regard have been made to introduce a breeder's exemption in patent law, providing immunity to breeders making use of native plant traits during research and development.[75] Various scenarios have been set forth, ranging from the introduction of a full breeder's exemption[76], to the introduction of a restricted breeder's exemption.[77] A restricted type of exemption has been introduced in France and in Germany.[78]

---

71 See Louwaars et al., *supra* note 59, 50.

72 See E. van Zimmeren and G. Van Overwalle (2011), 'A Paper Tiger? Compulsory License Regimes for Public Health in Europe', *IIC*, 4–40 and the references cited there.

73 *Ibid.*

74 Cf. E. van Zimmeren and G. Van Overwalle (2011), 'A False Sense of Security Offered by Zero-Price Liability Rules? Research Exceptions in the US, Europe and Japan in an Open Innovation Context', in R. Okediju and M. Bagley (eds.), *Global Perspectives on Patent Law*, Oxford: Oxford University Press (in press).

75 See Louwaars et al., *supra* note 59; P.H. Feindt,. and the Advisory Board on Biodiversity and Genetic Resources at the Federal Ministry of Food, Agriculture and Consumer Protection (BMLEV), *Biopatents – A Threat to the Use and Conservation of Agrobiodiversity? Position Paper of the Advisory Board on Biodiversity and Genetic Resources at the Federal Ministry of Food, Agriculture and Consumer Protection (translation of German original paper)*, 26 May 2010.

76 I.e. an exemption of the use in plant breeding of genetic material falling under the scope of the patent, and also of the commercialization of the new varieties (plant propagation material) originating from such breeding)

77 I.e. an exemption of the use of genetic material for plant breeding, but not of the commercialization of the varieties originating from this activity when these varieties carry this patented trait). See Louwaars et al., *supra* notes 57 and 59.

78 See s. 11(2)(a) of the German Patentgesetz, Article L 613-5-3 of the French Code de la Propriété Intellectuelle and art. 9(e) of the Swiss Bundesgesetz über die Erfindungspatente and for a critical analysis, see Van der Kooij (2010), 'Towards a Breeder's Exemption in Patent Law?', *EIPR*, **32**(11), 545–52.

Introduction of a diagnostic-use exemption in Europe, shielding diagnostic testing from infringement, as suggested by SACGHS,[79] may also be worthwhile considering. SACGHS recommends that this exemption would equally apply to (commercial and non-commercial) service providers using laboratory-developed tests and to test-kit makers. However, in view of the uncertain (and possibly stifling) impact of the exemption on kit development – requiring approval by the Food and Drug Administration, which would raise costs for entering the market – its scope should be restricted to clinicians using their own 'homemade' gene-based tests.[80]

4.2 Redressing Patent Thickets

Legislative tools may be helpful in the attempt to deal with patent thickets. In the area of plant (bio)technology altering patent law to exclude plant traits could be contemplated.[81] Patent protection of technological processes in support of plant breeding would remain possible but should not stretch to plant genetic traits. At present, Switzerland is contemplating the exclusion of plant genes.[82] Natural gene sequences as such would not be patentable, including isolated gene sequences, and this would apply indiscriminately to human, animal and plant genes.[83] It has also been suggested to exclude plants *per se* from patent law, but before introducing such a U-turn, more detailed empirical evidence is necessary on the alleged negative effect of patents on plants *per se* on (follow on) innovation.

In the human genetics area, patent law may also be modified to ban human genes from its field of application. Deeming gene patents ineligible for protection may be valuable in view of fostering (upstream) research and the provi-

---

[79] SACGHS (2010), *supra* note 70.

[80] G. Van Overwalle (2010), 'Turning Patent Swords into Shares', *Science*, 17 December (issue 6011), **330**, 1630–1.

[81] Cf. Louwaars et al., *supra* note 59, 57.

[82] See Article 1(b) of the bill, reviewing the current Swiss Patent Act (Project Loi fédérale sur les brevets d'invention): 1. Une séquence génique ou une séquence génique partielle existant à l'état naturel n'est en soi pas brevetable; 2.Une séquence dérivée d'une séquence génique ou d'une séquence génique partielle existant à l'état naturel constitue toutefois une invention brevetable lorsqu'elle est préparée techniquement, que sa fonction est décrite concrètement et que les autres conditions de l'art. 1 sont remplies; l'art. 2 est réservé [1. A genetic sequence or a partial genetic sequence existing in a natural state is not patentable in itself; 2. However, a sequence derived from a genetic sequence or a partial genetic sequence existing in a natural state constitutes a patentable invention when it is technically prepared, its function is described concretely and the other conditions of art. 1 are fulfilled; art. 2 is reserved].

[83] See the Explanatory Memorandum accompanying the bill for some further background.

sion of genetic testing, but may be detrimental to incentivizing (downstream) development of drugs and therapies. A more moderate alternative may be to focus on the scope of patent rights and to introduce a purpose-bound protection regime for gene patents.[84] Under such a rule, a patent for a DNA sequence no longer encompasses all possible future applications but is restricted to the specific use described in the patent application. However restrictive it may seem, purpose bound protection may still prevent free use of a gene patented for diagnostic applications.[85]

Providing swift, flexible responses to changing conditions through formal, legal avenues may be hard because of legal complexity and political reality in Europe. In the meantime, as a substitute or as a complement, *rules of contract* may offer a partial solution. Navigating the patent landscape in plant and human biotechnology, may even be achieved more adequately and rapidly through private, collaborative efforts. These could take the form of specially tailored genetic patent pools and clearinghouses.[86] Some genetic pools and clearinghouses have been established in the agricultural and in the health care field for humanitarian purposes.[87] For-profit initiatives, however, remain scarce. One exception is the proposal to establish an 'Industry licensing platform providing access to patented non-regulated native traits', launched by Syngenta.[88] Another example is the establishment of a diagnostic genetics patent clearinghouse or named *Librassay*^{TM} – *Molecular Diagnostics Patent Supermarket* by MPEG LA.[89] Given the complexity

---

84 Van Overwalle, *supra* note 84.

85 *Ibid.*

86 There is a growing literature on how to tackle the issue of patent thickets. The interested reader might wish to consult *Digital Opportunity. A review of Intellectual Property and Growth,* An independent report commissioned by Prime Minister David Cameron and carried out by Ian Hargreaves, 2011 (available at http://www.ipo.gov.uk/ipreview.htm) where one of the recommendations to alleviate the problems with thickets is the development of patent pools.

87 E.g. the well-known Golden Rice pool (see http://www.goldenrice.org/) or the Medicines Patent Pool (http://www.medicinespatentpool.org/). For an overview and an in-depth analysis of these and other pools and clearinghouses, see G. Van Overwalle (ed.) (2009), *Gene Patents and Collaborative Licensing Models. Patent Pools, Clearinghouses, Open Source Models and Liability Regimes*, Cambridge: Cambridge University Press, p. 477. Also see E. van Zimmeren, S. Vanneste, G. Matthijs, W. Vanhaverbeke and G. Van Overwalle (2011), 'Patent Pools and Clearinghouses in the Life Sciences', 29 (11) *Trends in Biotechnology,* 2011, 569-576.

88 See M. Kock, presentation at the PPP Innovation Platform Workshop, Zürich Oerlikon, 31 May 2011. Also see http://www.syngentafoundation.org/index.cfm?pageID=708. The proposal is currently circulating in the European Seed Association for discussion.

89 See http://patentdocs.typepad.com/files/neuman.pdf./

surrounding the establishment and operation of collaborative initiatives, such as patent pools and clearinghouses, efforts should probably concentrate indeed on pools and clearinghouses set up around single genes or gene panels.[90]

CLOSING REMARKS

Various remedies have been suggested to deal with potential hindering effects of patents in the area of plant and human biotechnology – two areas which show remarkable linkages and share similar problems. What many of these suggestions have in common, is their call for a more responsible behaviour of patent owners in the exercise of their patent rights. In light of the controversies surrounding patents on plant traits and on human genes, and the growing discontent with some undesirable effects of the current patent system, there is a need to reconceptualize patent rights, all the more so in the life sciences area. A patent can no longer be viewed as a title giving (almost) complete freedom to exclude others from use, but rather as a temporary permit to exploit monopoly rights under fair and reasonable conditions, investing technology owners with the authority to invent and share. In other words: patents may be looked at as tools to reshape exclusions into inclusions, giving rise to 'inclusive patents'. A patent should be seen as a duty-bearing privilege,[91] especially in areas which are vital for our basic well-being, namely food and health care.

Compulsory licences (e.g. for crop breeding and public health) and exceptions (e.g. a restricted breeder's exception for the use of native plant traits and a narrow diagnostic-use exemption) can function as a safety valves and discourage exclusive or overly restrictive licensing. Narrow(er) claim drafting (e.g. purpose-bound protection for gene patents) and collaborative licensing (e.g. genetic patent pools and clearinghouses single genes or gene panels) may help overcome patent thickets. All such measures will establish 'inclusive patents', fuelling 'smart' innovations assisting in achieving 'inclusive' welfare in Europe in the food and health care sector by 2020[92] and far beyond.

---

90 G. Van Overwalle (2009), *supra* note 1, 381–463.

91 P. Drahos (1996), *A Philosophy of Intellectual Property,* Sudbury, MA: Dartmouth Publishing.

92 Cf. the objectives of 'Europe 2020'. 'In a changing world, we want the EU to become a smart, sustainable and inclusive economy. These three mutually reinforcing priorities should help the EU and the Member States deliver high levels of employment, productivity and social cohesion.' See http://ec.europa.eu/europe2020/index_en.htm

11. Construction of an efficient and balanced patent system: patentability and patent scope of isolated DNA sequences under US Patent Act and EU Biotech Directive

Jan Krauss and Toshiko Takenaka

1. INTRODUCTION

European countries started their efforts to develop an efficient and balanced patent system in the 1970s. Regarding harmonization of procedural and substantive aspects of patent granting, the signing of the European Patent Convention ('EPC') [1] in Munich in 1973 marked the beginning of these efforts, and the Convention entered into force in 1977. This process continued under the leadership of the European Patent Office ('EPO'), in refinement of examination guidelines and its own case law. In parallel with these efforts, the European Union ('EU') expanded its interests in patent systems, and published green papers and proposals for furthering the harmonization of patentability and patent scope of inventions in particular technology fields through EU directives. Inventions in these technology fields include computer programs and biotechnology because patentability of these inventions is most controversial for important public policies competing with the patent public policy for promoting these inventions. The EU made an attempt to enact a directive for computer software inventions by publishing a proposal.[2] This attempt failed because the EU was unable to find a compromise between different industry sectors representing competing interests after an extensive debate on

---

1 Convention on the Grant of European Patents art. 100, 5 October 1973, 1065 UNTS 255.

2 Proposal for a Directive of the European Parliament and of the Council on the Patentability of Computer-Implemented Inventions (Commission Proposal COM (2002) 92).

whether patent protection promotes or hinders innovations.[3] For biotechnological inventions, the EU was successful in enacting the Biotechnology Directive ('Biotech Directive').[4] However, texts of the Biotech Directive represent compromises and thus include a lot of ambiguity in key terms defining the scope of protection.[5] This led to different interpretations adopted by national courts in EU member states. Further, patent owners need to file multiple suits with national courts to enforce national patents resulting from the same European patent because the enforcement of European patents has not been uniform, which may lead to different results of patent validity and infringement for the same European patent against the same defendant. To remove the non-uniformity in interpretation and inefficient parallel litigations, the EU is working to develop a uniform patent enforcement system.[6]

However, the US is no better than EU countries for harmonizing patentability of inventions in these controversial technology fields. Although the US is one jurisdiction and has a uniform patent enforcement system, it is not easy for US judges to agree on a uniform interpretation of texts in the US Patent Act. In *Bilski v. Kappos,*[7] US Supreme Court justices were highly divided with respect to the same question that European legislators debated, i.e., whether patent protection promotes or hinders innovations. They were unable to agree whether the text under Patent Act §101 categorically excludes business methods from patent eligibility. Although the majority rejected the categorical exclusion approach with a five to four vote, it was unable to give lower courts and the United States Patent and Trademark Office ('USPTO') a clear instruction regarding how to decide patent eligibility when claims are directed to business methods. Instead, it instructed them to examine patent eligibility on a case-by-case basis by comparing subject matter under examination with those examined by the Supreme Court in its precedents.

---

3 S. Schohe, C. Appelt and H. Goddar (2008), 'Patenting Software Related Inventions in Europe', Toshiko Takenaka (ed.), *Patent Law & Theory*, 325. Particularly, open source software license groups are strongly opposed to patent protection of software.

4 Directive 98/44/EC of the European Parliament and the Commission of 6 July 1998 on the legal protection of biotechnological inventions, OJ L 213, pp.13–21 (30 July 1998).

5 J. Straus (2008), *The Scope of Protection Conferred by European Patents on Transgenic Plants and Methods for Their Production*, in A. Bakardjieva Engelbrekt, U. Bernitz, B. Domeij and A. Kur (eds), *Festschrift for Marianne Levin*, Stockholm: Norstedts Juridik, pp. 643, 647. Prof. Straus gives a further clarification of 'biological material' and 'function' in Biotech Directive.

6 EU Council's draft agreement to a unified patent court (14 June 2011). The main features of the proposal are available at: http://www.epo.org/law-practice/legislative-initiatives/eu-patent.html (last visited 23 July 2012).

7 *Bilski v. Kappos,* 130 S. Ct. 3218, 3221 (US 2010).

Non-uniformity in interpreting the text under Patent Act §101 is even worse with respect to biotechnological inventions. Not only judges but also different sectors of the federal government are divided as to whether the text excludes DNA sequences in isolated form. In *Ass'n for Molecular Pathology v. United States,* ('Myriad'),[8] the US Department of Justice filed a brief with the US Court of Appeals for the Federal Circuit ('CAFC'), advancing the interpretation that the text of Patent Act §101 excludes patent eligibility of DNA in isolated form as being a product of nature. This interpretation is contrary to the well-established examination practice at the USPTO.[9] Reflecting the divided positions of the federal government, three CAFC judges were divided as to whether isolated DNA sequences are identical to naturally occurring DNA sequences. Two judges with science backgrounds joined to create the majority and upheld patent eligibility for isolated DNA as described in the *Myriad* claims. However, the Supreme Court vacated the *Myriad* judgment and remitted the case to CAFC for further consideration in light of its recent *Prometheus* decision.[10] In *Prometheus,*[11] the Court rejected patent eligibility for claims directing a customized method for drug administration because it found the claims directing to a law of nature.

On remand, the same CAFC panel upheld patent eligibility of isolated DNA claims, using the same analysis as the vacated first judgment. Both vacated and remanded judgments highlight a similar approach that US and European judges adopt when analyzing a claim directing to isolated DNA. In the vacated judgment, CAFC judges' analysis focused on the function of claimed isolated DNA sequences to distinguish them from patent ineligible natural products. In *Monsanto v Cefetra* ('*Monsanto*'),[12] the Court of Justice for European Union ('CJEU') also emphasized the function of isolated DNA sequences for supporting patent eligibility of the sequence under the Biotech Directive and adopted a special rule for limiting the scope of patent protection for the sequence.

On remand, CAFC judges made clear that *Prometheus* does not control patent eligibility of claims directing to DNA in isolated form because such claims are directed to compositions of matter, which is explicitly listed in §101, in contrast to medical methods examined in *Prometheus.*[13] The majority and

---

8 *Ass'n for Molecular Pathology v. U.S. Patent & Trademark Office*, 653 F.3d. 1329 (Fed. Cir. 2011).

9 *Ibid.* at 1358 (Moore J., concurring).

10 *Ass'n for Molecular Pathology v. Myriad Genetics, Inc.*, 132 S. Ct. 1794 (U.S. 2012).

11 *Mayo Collaborative Servs. v. Prometheus Labs., Inc.,* 132 S. Ct. 1289 (2012)

12 Decision of 7 July 2010; Case C-428/08.

13 *Ass'n for Moleculor Pathology v. United States PTO*, 689 F.3d 1303, 1325. (Fed. Cir. 2012).

dissent continued the same discussion engaged in the vacated first judgment in focusing on the functional difference between a native DNA in the human body and the same DNA in isolated form. Accordingly, this chapter will compare CAFC's *Myriad* and ECJ's *Monsanto* focusing on the role of function in determining patent eligibility and protection scope for isolated DNA sequences. It will also examine a unique feature of isolated DNA sequences and explain why the function plays a more important role in patentability and infringement analysis for isolated DNA sequences than analyses of other types of technologies. Further, it will discuss the challenge to reward inventors of isolated DNA sequences for the contribution they have made through the inventions.

2. US: *MYRIAD*

In *Diamond v. Chakrabarty*, the US Supreme Court confirmed patent eligibility of a man-made living microorganism by commenting that 'Congress intended statutory subject matter to include anything under the sun that is made by man.'[14] The Supreme Court reinforced this wide scope of protection given by the patent law in a recent decision, *Bilski v. Kappos*, by citing *Chakrabarty*.[15] However, this broad patent eligibility subject matter principle is subject to three exceptions: (1) laws of nature, (2) physical or natural phenomena and (3) abstract ideas.[16] In *Bilski,* the dispute focused on the third exception regarding the question whether a business method that claims are drawn to is an abstract idea and thus patent ineligible. In *Myriad,* the dispute focused on the second exception regarding the question whether isolated DNA sequences that claims are drawn to are natural phenomena or natural products.

The subject matter at issue in *Myriad* relates to BRCA1 and BRCA2 DNA sequences which are closely correlated to a risk of breast and ovarian cancer. Research teams including researchers at the University of Utah and Harvard University identified the precise BRCA genes in the human body, funded at least partially by the federal government.[17] These researchers eventually joined to found a molecular diagnostic company called Myriad in Salt Lake City, Utah. They obtained patents for their inventions based on the discovery of BRCA1 and BRCA2 genes. As a result, Myriad holds, either through ownership or exclusive licence, a number of patents on medical technologies relating to these genes.

---

14 *Diamond v. Chakrabarty*, 447 U.S. 303, 309 (1980).
15 *Bilski v. Kappos,* 130 S. Ct. 3218, 3221 (U.S. 2010).
16 *Ibid.*
17 *Ass'n for Molecular Pathology v. US Patent and Trademark Office*, 669 F. Supp. 2d 365 (SDNY, 2009).

Myriad is a unique case in which a group of cancer patients and medical doctors who treat these patients sued USPTO, Myriad and the Myriad inventors-researchers for challenging the validity of patents held by Myriad. In the United States, a party can file a declaratory judgment ('DJ') action to seek a court's decision for declaring a patent being issued by USPTO invalid as long as there is a case or controversy between the DJ plaintiff and a defendant.[18] The District Court for the Southern District of New York found such a controversy and exercised the DJ jurisdiction. This decision was affirmed by CAFC when Myriad filed an appeal to CAFC.[19]

Claims that the plaintiff group challenged are classified into (1) a group of composition claims directing to isolated DNA molecules or sequences; and (2) a group of method claims directing to methods of using the DNA molecules to identify a risk of breast and ovarian cancer.[20] CAFC found patent eligibility of the composition claims but rejected patent eligibility of some of the method claims as being directed only to abstract mental processes. Among CAFC's discussions on patent eligibility, an analysis of the composition claims is most relevant to the comparison with the *Monsanto* ECJ decision because both decisions' patent eligibility analysis focuses on the function of invention.

Authored by Judge Lourie, a judge with a PhD in chemistry, the majority CAFC opinion carefully reviewed the Supreme Court's analysis in *Chakrabarty*[21] and *Funk Brothers*[22] and compared subject matter in these precedents and the isolated DNA sequences that the claims are drawn to because these cases are most relevant to *Myriad* in dealing with living subject matter. To distinguish a patent eligible human-made product from a patent ineligible product of nature, the majority held that the former must have a marked difference from the latter. Relying on the distinctions made by the Supreme Court with respect to the patent eligible man-made bacteria in *Chakrabarty* and the patent ineligible mixture of culture capable of inoculating the seeds of leguminous plants in *Funk*, the majority concluded that the comparison to identify the necessary difference to give rise to patent eligibility should focus on the structure rather than the function.[23]

---

18 28 USC §2101(a).

19 *Ass'n for Molecular Pathology* 653 F.3d at 1353-54.

20 Representative composition claims are as follows:

1. An isolated DNA coding for a BRCA1 polypeptide, said polypeptide having the amino acid sequence set forth in SEQ ID NO:2.
2. The isolated DNA of claim 1, wherein said DNA has the nucleotide sequence set forth in SEQ ID NO:1.
5. An isolated DNA having at least 15 nucleotides of the DNA of claim 1.

21 *Diamond v. Chakrabarty*, 447 U.S. 303 (1980).

22 *Funk Bros. Seed Co. v. Kalo Inoculant Co.*, 333 U.S. 127, 130 (1948).

23 *Ass'n for Molecular Pathology*.

In analyzing the claimed DNA sequences, the majority found that the sequences contain the necessary structural difference and thus are patent eligible because molecules of these claimed sequences are substantially different from molecules that exist in nature with respect to its chemical identity and nature.[24] The majority first defined 'a native DNA' in the human body as a one of 46 large, contiguous DNA molecules in which each DNA molecule is itself an integral part of a larger structural complex, a chromosome. In contrast, 'an isolated DNA' such as one that *Myriad* patent claims are drawn to is a free-standing portion of a native DNA molecule, frequently a single gene, which has been cleaved or synthesized to consist of just a portion of native DNA being removed from its chromosomal structure. The subject matter of *Myriad* composition claims is markedly different from native BRCA1 and BRCA2 genes, because isolated BRCA1 and BRCA2 in the isolated form consist of approximately 80,000 nucleotides in contrast to BRCA1 in the native form which is part of a chromosome and consists of 80 million nucleotides and BRCA2 in the native form which is part of another chromosome and consists of 114 million nucleotides. The majority distinguished a purified DNA from isolated DNA because only the latter DNA is removed from the chromosomal structure by a chemical process to produce a molecule which is markedly different from a native DNA in the human body.[25]

The majority rejected the plaintiffs' argument that an isolated DNA is not markedly different from a native DNA in including the same information content carried in both nucleotides sequences.[26] It found the plaintiff's analysis improper because the analysis focuses on the use or benefit of DNAs instead of the nature or structure of DNA molecules as isolated compositions of matter. Because the isolated BRCA1 and BRCA2 DNA sequences as claimed in the *Myriad* claims are markedly different in structure from BRCA1 and BRCA2 DNA sequences in the human body and created by man through a chemical process (cleaving) and covalently bonding the DNA to other genetic materials, the majority concluded that all composition claims are patent eligible.

The dissenting judge, Judge Bryson, intensively disputed the majority's distinction between native and isolated DNA sequences. In his view, to constitute the change necessary for giving rise to patent eligibility, claimed subject matter must be markedly different from a natural product not only structurally but also functionally.[27] BRCA1 and BRCA2 DNA sequences in natural and isolated forms are the same because they have the same sequence code for the same proteins and present the same units of heredity. Therefore, the isolated

24 *Ibid.* at 1415.
25 *Ibid.* at 1415.
26 *Ibid.* at 1416.
27 *Ibid.* at 1435 (Bryson J., dissenting).

DNA sequences have no significant difference in function for coding BRCA genes.

Judge Moore, who holds electrical science bachelor and master degrees, concurred with the majority for supporting its conclusion of patent eligibility but agreed with Judge Bryson for requiring a marked difference structurally and functionally between claimed subject matter and naturally occurring products.[28] She upheld patent eligibility of the compound claims because she found sufficient difference in structure and function with respect to the isolated BRCA1 and BRCA2 DNA sequences. In her analysis, the isolated BRCA1 and BRCA2 DNA sequences, particularly those which are significantly shorter than the sequence of entire gene, are functionally different from naturally occurring BRCA1 and BRCA2 DNA sequences in the human body because only the former can provide a function of diagnostic genetic testing. Only isolated DNA sequences can be used as primers in a diagnostic method for detecting gene mutations and as the basis for probes and therefore have a function markedly different from the function of naturally occurring DNAs such as BRCA1 and BRCA2 DNA sequences in the human body. These naturally occurring DNAs cannot provide a diagnostic function.

As a result, two judges of the three-judge panel adopted a test to focus on the function of claimed subject matter to distinguish isolated DNAs from patent ineligible naturally occurring DNAs.

3. EU: *MONSANTO*

In *Monsanto*, the ECJ emphasized the function of an isolated DNA for supporting patent eligibility and used the function for determining the scope of patent protection for the DNA. In Europe, the Biotech Directive makes it clear that an isolated DNA is patent eligible in EU member states even if the isolated DNA is structurally identical to a naturally occurring DNA.[29] This makes it impossible for defendants to challenge the validity of Monsanto patents for lack of patent eligibility. However, the Biotech Directive limits the scope of patent protection through function by requiring an accused material to perform its function. Thus, defendants tried to avoid a claim of infringement, asserting that their products do not perform a function which is described in the patent application to support the industrial applicability.

---

28 *Ibid.*, at 1425 (Moore J., concurring).

29 *See supra* note 4. Biotechnology Directive, Biotechnology Directive, Art. 5 para. 2 provides: 'An element isolated from the human body or otherwise produced by means of a technical process, including the sequence or partial sequence of a gene, may constitute a patentable invention, even if the structure of that element is identical to that of a natural element.'

The main claim of European Patent EP 0 546 090 ('`090 Patent') in suit in *Monsanto* is directed to an isolated DNA sequence, which renders a soybean plant resistant against a herbicide, glyphosate, when it is introduced into the plant.[30] The specification of the `090 Patent discloses how the isolated DNA sequence functions to give the resistance to soybean plants. Such herbicide resistant soybean plants are called Roundup Ready® or RR ('RR') and commonly used in agriculture. Although Monsanto secured patent protection in EPC countries including the Netherlands through the `090 patent, it does not have any patent in Argentina. Cafetra and Toepfer imports soybean meal including meal made of the genetically modified RR soybeans. RR soybeans were harvested and processed into meal in Argentina. Such meal was then imported into Europe. Although the imported RR soybean meal contained the patented DNA sequence, it could no longer function as a resistance marker. In other words, it was merely contained as a 'residue' in the soybean meal. Nevertheless, Monsanto initiated an action to block the import of the meal into the European Union. It filed for injunctive relief, asserting infringement of the `090 Patent at the Court of the Hague (Rechtbank's-Gravenhage) when RR soybean meal arrived in a port of the Netherlands.

The Court of the Hague found that the imported RR soybean meal no longer performs the herbicide resistant function and held that the meal does not infringe the `090 Patent. The Hague Court rejected Monsanto's argument that mere presence of the patented DNA sequence in the meal is sufficient to uphold a claim of infringement as long as the sequence once performed the herbicide resistance function and will perform the function again after it is

---

[30] Claims 1 to 6 of the EP patent read (Please note that only the scope of Claim 6 was referred to CJEU for interpretation of Directive Art. 9):

1. An isolated DNA sequence encoding an EPSPS enzyme having a Km for phosphoenolpyruvate (PEP) between 1-150 pM and a K(glyphosate)/Km(PEP) ratio between 3-500, which DNA sequence is capable of hybridizing to a DNA probe from a sequence selected from the group consisting of SEQ ID NO:2, SEQ ID NO:4, and SEQ ID NO:6.
2. A DNA molecule of claim 1 wherein said Km for phosphoenolpyruvate is between 2-25 1M.
3. A DNA molecule of claim 1 wherein said Ki/Km ratio is between 6-250.
4. An isolated DNA sequence encoding a protein which exhibits EPSPS activity wherein said protein is capable of reacting with antibodies raised against a Class II EPSPS enzyme.
5. The DNA sequence of Claim 4 wherein said protein is capable of reacting with antibodies raised against a Class II EPSPS enzyme selected from the group consisting of SEQ ID NO:3, SEQ ID NO:5, and SEQ ID NO:7.
6. The DNA sequence of Claim 5 wherein said antibodies are raised against a Class II EPSPS enzyme of SEQ ID NO:3.

isolated from the soybean meal and transferred into a living material. The Hague Court interpreted the extent of patent protection for biotechnological inventions under Article 9 of Biotech Directive and Dutch Patent Law, Article 53a(3)[31] which corresponds to Article 9. [32] It concluded that an accused DNA sequence must perform the expected function although it does not need to continuously perform the function if it is necessary to activate the function of the sequence under certain conditions such as heat, dry conditions or disease.

However, the Court of Hague was not sure if the language of Biotech Directive Article 9 is sufficiently clear to support its function-limited protection. To avoid a conflict with the Biotech Directive, the Court stayed the infringement proceedings and referred four questions to the ECJ.[33] Among these questions, the appropriateness of the function-limited protection is most relevant to *Myriad* because it examined the scope of patent protection for isolated DNA sequences in the context of patent eligibility and industrial applicability. Advocate-General Mengozzi issued an opinion agreeing with the Court of Hague's interpretation of Article 9 in limiting the patent protection of isolated DNA sequences by function.[34]

---

[31] Art. 53(a) of Dutch Patent Law reads:

1. In respect of a patent on a biological material possessing specific characteristics as a result of the invention, the exclusive right shall extend to any biological material derived from that biological material through propagation or multiplication in an identical or divergent form and possessing those same characteristics.
2. In respect of a patent on a process that enables a biological material to be produced possessing specific characteristics as a result of the invention, the exclusive right shall extend to biological material directly obtained through that process and to any other biological material derived from the directly obtained biological material through propagation or multiplication in an identical or divergent form and possessing those same characteristics.
3. In respect of a patent on a product containing or consisting of genetic information, the exclusive right shall extend to all material in which the product is incorporated and in which the genetic information is contained and performs its function … .

[32] Art. 9 of the Directive reads: 'The protection conferred by a patent on a product containing or consisting of genetic information shall extend to all material save as provided in Article 5(1) in which the product is incorporated and in which the genetic information is contained and performs its function.'

[33] C-428/08, Reference for A Preliminary Ruling from the Rechtsbank's-Gravenhage (Netherlands) logend on 29 September 2008, OJ C 313 of 06 12 2008, p.16 (2008).

[34] C-428/08, Opinion of Advocate General, available at http://curia.europa.eu/jurisp/cgi-bin/form.pl?lang=EN&Submit=Submit&numaff=C-428/08 (last visited 23 July 2012).

The ECJ agreed with the Advocate-General relying on the present verb tense in Article 9 to require the isolated DNA in the accused material to perform its function.[35] The Court clarified that the required function is the function described in the specification for supporting the requirement of industrial applicability: with respect to the '090 Patent, the function is protecting soybeans from the effect of herbicide.[36] Because the RR soybean meal no longer performs the function of the invention, herbicide resistance effect, protection of the '090 Patent does not extend to the soybean meal. In other words, it is insufficient for the patent owner of a patent on an isolated DNA to assert infringement by an accused material including the DNA under Biotech Directive Article 9 if the DNA in the material once performed the function of invention in the past (i.e., in the living soybean plant.) It is also insufficient that the DNA in the accused material would resume the function of the invention if it is isolated from the material in respect of which the patent protection is asserted and introduced into a new material, such as a living organism. In the latter case, the patent owner can obtain protection under Article 9 only with respect to the new material.[37]

To support its function-limited patent protection for isolated DNA sequences, the ECJ relied on Recital 23 in the preamble of the Biotech Directive that makes clear that DNA sequences contain technical information and thus are patent eligible only if the sequences have a function. The Court also relied on Recital 24 which requires a description of a function in the specification to support industrial applicability if a claim is directed to a sequence or partial sequence of a gene and the sequence is part of a protein or used for producing a protein. Because the patentability of a DNA sequence under the Biotech Directive depends on the description of the function that the sequence performs, the patent protection of the sequence should be available only if the sequence performs the function.[38] If patent protection for an isolated DNA sequence extends to a material as long as the patented sequence is contained in the material regardless of the performance of its function as Monsanto argued, the text of Article 9 requiring the performance of the function would become meaningless.[39] As a result, the ECJ adopted a special rule, a function-limited patent protection, for isolated DNA sequence patents.

Although the ECJ decided the scope of patent protection under Biotech Directive Article 9, which provides for an additional protection for a patent on

---

35 C-428/08 Judgment of the Court (Grand Chamber) , 6 July 2010, OJ C 234, 28 08 2010, I (2010) (*Monsanto* CJEU Judgment).

36 *Ibid.*, para 36.

37 *Ibid.*, para 39.

38 *Monsanto* CJEU Judgment at note 11, para 45.

39 *Monsanto* CJEU Judgment at note 11, paras 46 and 47.

a claim directing to an isolated DNA, the Court did not distinguish the additional protection from the regular protection under EPC Article 69.[40] It follows that *Monsanto* can be read to require patent owners to show that an accused isolated DNA performs its function which is described in the specification for supporting industrial applicability when they want to enforce their patents on isolated DNA sequences. This situation is different from *Monsanto* where the patented isolated DNA was contained in a material, soybean, and infringement is asserted against *the material* under the Dutch Patent Law Article 53(a), Paragraph 1 which is implementing the additional protection under Biotech Directive Article 9 instead of against *the isolated DNA sequence*, which is governed by a different Article of the Dutch Patent Law which is implementing the regular protection under EPC Article 69. DNA sequences in isolated form which are removed from chromosome structure cannot provide the function of invention to support industrial applicability unless the industrial applicability is a diagnostic use or a use as a primer *in vitro* reaction such as the isolated DNA sequences in *Myriad*.[41] For example, the Monsanto's DNA sequence does not perform its herbicide resistant function unless it is incorporated into its chromosome structure. As a result, the ECJ's restrictive interpretation prevents enforcement of all isolated DNA patents except for DNAs which are used for diagnostic methods.[42]

4. PATENT PROTECTION OF DNA SEQUENCES: DOUBLE NATURE

Why did these courts care about the function of isolated DNA sequences for giving patent protection? It is likely that judges of both courts acknowledged a unique feature of DNA sequences and tried to balance the reward for inventors and contribution through disclosure of isolated DNA sequences by the inventors. DNA sequences have a double nature: (1) nature as a chemical compound and (2) nature as a carrier of genetic information. If judges focus on the compound nature and limit the protection by the structure, the scope of patent protection for an isolated DNA sequence is very limited even if a patent

40 J. Krauss and T. Takenaka (2011), 'A Special Rule for Compound Protection for DNA Sequences – Impact of the ECJ "Monsanto" decision on Patent Practice', *J. Pat. & Trademark Off. Soc'y*, **93**, 189.

41 *Ibid* at 199. Judge Moore also discussed this point in Myriad. Ass'n for Molecular Pathology v. United States PTO, 653 F. 3d 1329, at 1365 (Moore J., Concurring in part).

42 M.A. Kock (2010), 'Purpose-Bound Protection for DNA Sequences: in Through the Back Door?', *JIPLP*, **5**, 495.

is granted for the sequence because any isolated DNA sequences which are incorporated in any chromosome structure are excluded from the patent protection.

Moreover, DNA sequences in isolated form do not have any biological function although they may function to give a diagnostic use or a use as a primer *in vitro* reactions. Thus, inventors of these isolated DNAs for non-diagnostic uses receive only very small rewards for identifying the function of a gene and isolating the precise sequence of the gene. This protection would not be sufficient for a big contribution made by the inventors for making it possible for researchers to develop new materials with the identified function by incorporating the gene.

In contrast, if courts focus on the nature of genetic information carrier, patent protection should extend to any material regardless of the structure of the compound. DNA sequences can be read as means-plus-function claims under US Patent Act §112 to cover the structure disclosed in the specification and their equivalents as long as DNA sequences perform their function through the genetic information they carry.[43] In this sense, DNA sequences function like software inventions which are frequently drafted in means-plus-function claims. The expansive protection fully rewards inventors who identify the function of a gene and isolate the precise sequence of the gene with respect to the contribution they have made. However, such protection may extend beyond what inventors actually invented and contributed to the state of the art if the protection goes far beyond the disclosure made by the inventors.

Obviously, as a chemist, Judge Lourie in *Myriad* viewed isolated DNA sequences as chemical compounds and did not pay much attention to the information carrier nature of the sequences. Therefore, he focused on the nature of the compound and found patent eligibility. However, it is likely that he refuses to extend the protection of an isolated DNA sequence beyond the compound that the claims are drawn to. Such narrow claim scope facilitates courts in finding patent eligibility but makes it difficult for them to find infringement. Unless defendants use exactly the same compound as the claimed compound, courts would not find infringement. Thus, it is necessary to include separate claims directing to materials including isolated DNAs if patent owners want to assert infringement against other forms than the exact structure of DNA in isolated form that claims are drawn to.

In contrast, the Biotech Directive was drafted to acknowledge the double nature of DNA sequences and focuses on the nature of information carrier in extending its protection to any material including patent DNA sequences as long as the sequences perform the function of industrial applicability under

---

43 35 USC § 112, para. 6.

Article 9. Focusing on the function, there is no difference in DNA sequences in isolated form and natural form. Thus, it was necessary for the Biotech Directive to expressly endorse patent eligibility of an element isolated from the human body such as the isolated DNA sequences in *Myriad* 'even if the structure of that element is identical to that of a natural element.'[44] Accordingly, the Biotech Directive does not find identity between two DNA sequences which do not have the same function, such as the herbicide resistant DNA sequence in living material and the same sequence in dead soybean meals regardless of the structural identity between the sequences. In other words, a DNA sequence does not infringe a claim directed to the isolated DNA unless the sequence performs the function of the isolated DNA. It is likely that this thought led the ECJ to an adoption of its function-limited protection.

Judge Bryson also adopted this approach and thus did not distinguish the two forms. Judge Moore also adopted this approach but distinguished BRCA DNA sequences because these DNA sequences are used for a diagnostic use and can perform the function to support utility even if the sequences are in isolated form. She may reject patent eligibility if the isolated DNA sequence at issue has a use other than a diagnostic use such as use for giving plants the herbicide resistance in *Monsanto* because the sequence in isolated form cannot perform any use. However, this issue should be examined under the utility or industrial applicability requirement rather than patent eligibility although the two issues are intertwined to determine patentability.

Between the two approaches, the US has been subscribing to the first approach in focusing on the structure instead of function or property to evaluate the difference of subject matter for patentability and infringement. In the determination of non-obviousness, the prima facie obviousness focuses on structural differences.[45] An unexpected result is merely a factor of secondary consideration to rebut the prima facie obvious.[46] In determining literal infringement, the all elements rule focuses only on structures except for means-plus-function claims.[47] Function plays an important role only in deter-

---

[44] *Supra* note 4, Biotech Directive Art. 5, para. 2.

[45] *KSR Int'l Co. v. Teleflex Inc.*, 550 US 398, 127 S. Ct. 1727, 167 L. Ed. 2d 705 (2007). For a general discussion of obviousness determination, D. S. Chisum, *Chisum on Patents*, Chapter 5 (1973, Supp. 2011), New York, USA: Matthew Bender & Company.

[46] *In re Dillon*, 919 F.2d 688, 16 USPQ 2d 1897 (Fed. Cir. 1990) (en banc), cert. denied, *Dillon v. Manbeck*, 500 U.S. 904, 111 S. Ct. 1682, 114 L. Ed. 2d 77 (1991).

[47] *Warner-Jenkinson Co. v. Hilton Davis Chem. Co.*, 520 U.S. 17, 117 S. Ct. 1040, 137 L. Ed. 2d 146 (1997); *Pennwalt Corp. v. Durand-Wayland, Inc.*, 833 F.2d 931, 4 USPQ 2d 1737 (Fed. Cir. 1987). For a general discussion of claim construction, see Chisum, *supra* note 45, Ch. 18.

mining infringement of means-plus-function claims[48] and infringement under the doctrine of equivalents.[49] However, US courts historically disfavoured a claim defining an invention by its function.[50] Thus, means-plus-function claims are subjected to a restrictive claim interpretation.[51] Moreover, US courts are very reluctant to find infringement under the doctrine of equivalents after the Supreme Court indicated a serious concern over an uncertainty introduced by the doctrine because the doctrine is decided by jury.[52]

Therefore, additional protection available under Article 9 is not available under the US Patent Act. A claim for an isolated DNA sequence covers only the isolated sequence and does not extend to a sequence in a chromosome. If courts find infringement of a claim directed to an isolated DNA sequence with respect to the same sequence in a chromosome, they erroneously interpret the claim in violating the all elements rule by ignoring the limitation requiring the sequence in isolated form.[53] Courts cannot erase such limitation under the doctrine of equivalents.[54] A separate claim directed to a biological material such as a cell or plant in which the sequence is incorporated is necessary if the patentee wants to assert infringement by the material. Even if an applicant obtains a patent including a claim directed to an isolated DNA sequence and separate claims directed to different materials including the sequence, the material claims are invalid unless the material is enabled and supported by the written description of specification. In *Monsanto v Syngenta Seeds, Inc.*,[55] Monsanto asserted infringement of US patents covering the same recombinant DNA technology in ECJ *Monsanto* for producing herbicide resistant plants. To obtain patent protection as broad as additional protection under Biotech Directive Article 9, Monsanto included claims directed to a chimeric plant gene being limited by its function, giving herbicide resistance to plants.[56] Such

48 In re *Donaldson Co.*, 16 F.3d 1189, 29 USPQ 2d 1845 (Fed. Cir. 1994); *Al-Site Corp. v. VSI Int'l, Inc.*, 174 F.3d 1308, 50 USPQ 2d 1161 (Fed. Cir. 1999).

49 *Warner-Jenkinson Co, supra* note 47.

50 *Gen. Elec. Co. v. Wabash Appliance Co.*, 304 U.S. 364, 37 USPQ 466 (1938).

51 35 USC §112, para. 6.

52 *Warner-Jenkinson Co., supra* note 47 at 39 n. 8.

53 *Unique Concepts, Inc. v. Brown,* 939 F.2d 1558, 19 USPQ 2d 1500 (Fed. Cir. 1991).

54 *Warner-Jenkinson Co. supra* note 47 at 29.

55 *Monsanto Co. v. Syngenta Seeds, Inc.*, 503 F.3d 1352, 84 USPQ 2d 1705 (Fed. Cir. 2007)

56 Claim 1 of the '835 recites:

> A chimeric plant gene which comprises:
> (a) a promoter sequence which functions *in plant cells*;
> (b) a coding sequence which causes the production of RNA, encoding a chloroplast

claims may extend patent protection to any plant as long as the DNA sequence in the plant performs the herbicide resistant function. CAFC invalidated the claims for lack of enablement, finding the functional terms in the claims analogous to the functional language *In re Vaeck*.[57] Whether the DNA sequence can give the herbicide resistant function to all flowering plants was not known to one skilled in the art on the filing date of the patents. In denying the protection for plants which are not enabled and described, the US patent system guarantees a freedom to use materials which are not covered by valid claims and leaves competitors opportunities to obtain separate patents for materials in which the performance of the sequence's function is unexpected.

As a result, as far as patent protection for isolated DNA sequence is concerned, the balance of interests between competing interests in the EU under the Biotech Directive leans toward interests for inventors in contrast to the balance leaning toward the public under the US Patent Act. ECJ judges are not well experienced in patent and may not have acknowledged the double nature of isolated DNA. It is possible that the ECJ felt a need to shift the balance to protect public interests and introduced the special rule for limiting the patent protection for DNA sequence patents. However, such a special rule is inconsistent with the general rule under EPC Article 69 and introduced a lot of uncertainty in claim drafting practice and validity of patents which were already issued before *Monsanto*.[58]

ECJ judges are not familiar with the rule under the EPC and claim drafting practice and thus may not have expected these results. *Monsanto* highlights an inefficiency of a patent enforcement system with a highest court which has no patent experienced judges. The EU tried to remove this inefficiency by proposing a system avoiding a review by the ECJ. However, this proposal was rejected by the ECJ[59] as inconsistent with the EU treaty.[60]

---

transit peptide/5-enolpyruvylshikimate-3-phosphate synthase fusion polypeptide, which chloroplast transit peptide permits the fusion polypeptide to be imported into a chloroplast *of a plant cell*; and
(c) a 3'non-translated region which encoded a polyadenylation signal which functions *in plant cells* to cause the addition of polyadenylate nucleotides to the 3'end of the RNA; the promoter being heterologous with respect to the coding sequence and adapted to cause sufficient expression of the fusion polypeptide to enhance the glyphosate resistance *of a plant cell* transformed with the gene.

57 *In re Vaeck*, 947 F.2d 488, 20 USPQ 2d 1438 (1991).

58 Krauss and Takenaka, *supra* note 40, at 203.

59 Opinion of European Court of Justice, 8 March 2011, available: http://curia.europa.eu/juris/celex.jsf?celex=62009CV0001&lang1=en&type=NOT&ancre= (last visited 23 July 2012).

60 Treaty on the Function of the European Union (TFEU).

The US system shares the same inefficiency because none of the Supreme Court justices has patent experience. Although the Court's precedent emphasizes a fundamental rule that every element in a patent claim is deemed material to determining the scope of a patented invention[61] and the invention as a whole must be considered for patent eligibility without disregarding old elements,[62] the *Prometheus* Court discounted some elements in the *Prometheus* claims as being well-understood, routine, and conventional and concluded the claims direct to nothing more than a law of nature.[63] The Court focused on the inventive concept instead of the claim language and required a claim to describe subject matter significantly different from a law of nature. Although the *Myriad* isolated DNA claims are product claims and thus distinguishable from the process claims in *Prometheus*, the Supreme Court may read the isolated DNA claims parallel to a process claim by focusing on the function of DNA instead of the claim language distinguishing the native DNA in the human body. Further, as highlighted by Judge Bryson's analysis, a function-focused analysis may lead to a conclusion that a native DNA and its isolated form are not distinguishable. Unlike the EU Biotech Directive, the US Patent Act does not have any provision expressly endorsing patentability of isolated DNA. In short, the chance that the Supreme Court would find patent ineligibility with respect to the *Myriad* patent claims is very high even if CAFC affirms patent eligibility on remit. Such a decision will have significant impact on the validity of patents held by US biotech firms and universities.

5. CONCLUSION

Constructing an efficient and balanced patent system is a continuous exercise with no end. Courts in US and EU countries strive to develop such a system by interpreting texts in the Patent Act and EU directives while balancing competing interests. Because these texts often reflect compromise in legislative process and cannot be clear and unambiguous on their face, judges are often divided in interpreting these texts. Because of the double nature of DNA sequences, courts in the EU and the US face even bigger challenges for balancing competing interests, which may lead to an unexpected impact on prosecuting and enforcing patents for DNA sequences. It seems impossible to have a complete harmonization between the EU and US. Instead, each country should learn from each other through respective case law and adopt the best balance reflecting public policies unique to DNA related inventions.

---

61 *Warner-Jenkinson Co. v. Hilton Davis Chem. Co.,* 520 U.S. 17 (1997).

62 *Bilski v. Kappos,* 130 S. Ct. at, 101 S. Ct. 1048, 1058 (1981).

63 *Prometheus Labs., Inc.*, 132 S. Ct. at 1294.

Section 5

Copyright Protection in the EU

12. The dynamics of harmonization of copyright at the European level*

P. Bernt Hugenholtz

1. INTRODUCTION

Over the past twenty years, the European Union (formerly the European Community) has carried out an ambitious agenda of copyright harmonization, with the aim of promoting the Internal Market by removing disparities between the laws of the Member States. This has resulted in seven directives on copyright that were adopted between 1991 and 2001. While these directives have created a measure of uniformity between the laws of the Member States, harmonization has come at considerable cost to the Member States. Also, the directives have largely ignored the single most important obstacle to the creation of an Internal Market in content-based services: the territorial nature of copyright. Despite extensive harmonization, copyright law in the European Union is still largely linked to the geographic boundaries of sovereign Member States. Consequently, copyright markets in the European Union remain vulnerable to compartmentalization along national borderlines.

This chapter critically assesses the results of copyright harmonization in the EU, and argues that territoriality in national copyright law should be confronted in the light of the emerging European market for copyright-based services. It commences with an assessment of the benefits and costs of copyright harmonization in the European Union; thereafter explains the still-prevailing rule of territoriality in national copyright law in the Member States; goes on to discuss various legal doctrines that mitigate its detrimental effect on the Internal Market; then examines in which way territoriality affects authors, other right holders, service providers and consumers; and finally looks at the prospect of unitary copyright protection by way of a true *European Copyright Law*.

* Parts of this chapter were previously published in: P. Bernt Hugenholtz et. al. (Institute for Information Law) (2006), 'The Recasting of Copyright & Related Rights for the Knowledge Economy', Report to the European Commission.

2. THE PROS AND CONS OF HARMONIZATION

At first impression, twenty years of harmonization of copyright and related rights have been remarkably productive. Despite initial scepticism about the European Union's legislative competence in the realm of copyright, the EU legislature has carried out an ambitious and broad ranging agenda of harmonization that has touched upon many of the most important issues in the field of copyright and related rights. From the early directives dealing primarily with specific subject matter or rights to the later 'horizontal' Information Society Directive, the harmonization process has produced a sizeable body of European law on the subject matter, scope, limitations, term and enforcement of copyright and related rights.

Although many inconsistencies remain, the harmonization machinery has undeniably produced a certain *acquis communautaire*. While far from complete it has normative effect not only in the Member States that are obliged to transpose the directives, but also at the international level. Where the directives have provided precise instructions, leaving the Member States little discretion for deviation, such as in the case of the Computer Programs Directive, the harmonization process has led to fairly uniform legal rules throughout the EU, and thereby enhanced legal certainty, transparency and predictability of norms in these distinct sectors.

But these results have come at considerable expense, in terms of time, public finance and other social costs, to the organs of the European Union and its Member States. Due to the complexity of the European law-making procedure, even a relatively non-controversial directive takes several years to complete, from its first proposal to its final adoption, including translation into the many official languages of the Union. Upon adoption of a directive, another round of lawmaking will commence at the level of the Member States. Twenty-seven governments will consult local stakeholders, draft implementation bills, and discuss these with twenty-seven parliaments often ignorant of the fact that the directives leave limited discretion to national legislatures. The step-by-step approach towards harmonization that the European legislature has followed has placed an enormous burden on the legislative apparatus of the Member States. For national legislatures, the harmonization agenda of the EU has resulted in an almost non-stop process of amending the national laws on copyright and related rights.

In all, the time span between the first proposal of a directive and its final implementation can easily exceed ten years. Despite the 'Better Regulation' agenda that includes proposals to speed up, simplify and make more transparent the European Union's legislative process and its various end products, it is not to be expected that the duration and costs of this entire process will be significantly reduced. Even if 'Better Regulation' will lead to a speeding-up of lawmaking at the Community level, this will not affect the transposition process at the national level which may take over five years from adoption of a directive. On the contrary, given the rapid expansion of the EU with new Member States that have only limited experience with the transposition process, it can be expected that a new harmonization initiative will require even more time to complete.

Clearly, directives, the instruments of a harmonization, are ill suited to quickly respond to the challenges of a constantly evolving, dynamic information market. But even a relatively un-ambitious consolidation exercise, such as a 'recasting' of the acquis,[1] would take several years to complete and then transpose, assuming that Member States and stakeholders could exercise enough self-restraint to refrain from adding new policy options to the agenda.

Another structural deficiency of the harmonization process is the asymmetric normative effect of harmonization by directive. The harmonized norms of copyright and related rights in the seven directives in many cases well exceed the minimum standards of the Berne and Rome Conventions to which the Member States have adhered. More often than not the norms also exceed average levels of protection that existed in the Member States prior to implementation, as exemplified by the Term Directive that has harmonized the duration of copyright at a level well above the normal European term of 50 years *post mortem auctoris*. Surely, this trend of 'upwards' harmonization is driven, in part, by the desire of the European legislature to seek 'a high level of protection of intellectual property', which would lead to 'growth and competitiveness of European industry'[2] – a proposition that has yet to be proven.[3] But some up-scaling of protection is probably inevitable, considering the political and legal problems that a scaling back of intellectual property rights would cause those Member States offering protection in excess of the European average.

A related problem is the 'ratcheting-up' effect that a harmonization directive inevitably has on national levels of protection, even in the rare case that a

---

1 Communication 'Updating And Simplifying The Community Acquis', COM(2003) 71 final, Brussels, 11 February 2003. See also European Commission, 'A Single Market for Intellectual Property Rights Boosting creativity and innovation to provide economic growth, high quality jobs and first class products and services in Europe', COM (2011) 287 final, Brussels, 24 May 2011 (proposing a 'European Copyright Code' that might consolidate the existing directives).

2 Recital 4 of the Information Society Directive.

3 See European Commission, First evaluation of Directive 96/9/EC on the legal protection of databases, 12 December 2005, available at http://ec.europa.eu/internal_market/copyright/docs/databases/evaluation_report_en.pdf. (arguing that positive effect of the introduction of the sui generis right on the EU information economy cannot be proven).

directive would later be repealed. Repealing a directive does not automatically lead to the undoing of implementation legislation at the national level, unless a national legislature has provided for a sunset clause. This makes harmonization by directive essentially a one-way street, from which there is no turning back.

The phenomenon of 'upwards' approximation is inherent to the process of harmonization by directive, and a reason for serious concern. The effectiveness, in economic and social terms, and credibility, in terms of democratic support, of any system of intellectual property depends largely on finding that legendary 'delicate balance' between the interests of right holders in maximizing protection and the public at large, in having access to products of creativity and knowledge. Moreover, a constant expansion of rights of intellectual property due to 'upwards' harmonization is likely to create new obstacles to the establishment of an Internal Market, rather than remove them, as long as exclusive rights remain largely territorial and can be exercised along national borders.

Another weakness of the harmonization process lies in its short-term negative effect on legal certainty in the Member States, especially where a directive introduces new rights or novel terminology. Harmonization by directive creates additional layers of legal rules that require interpretation first at the national level of the local courts, and eventually by the European Court of Justice. This extra legislative layer is the cause of great legal uncertainty, as long as the European Court of Justice (ECJ) had not pronounced its final 'verdict' on the most contentious issues.

Yet another structural draw-back of the instrument of harmonization is its limited potential to provide true unification. Harmonization directives usually leave a broad measure of discretion to the Member States, and are often vague as a result of political compromise. It is common for directives to provide minimum standards of protection, or optional provisions. In some cases, the norms in a directive leave national legislatures so much leeway that their actual harmonizing effect must seriously be called into doubt. An example here is article 5(2) and (3) of the Information Society Directive, that allows Member States to 'pick and mix' limitations from a 'shopping list' of some twenty-one broadly worded categories of exemptions. This kind of *faux harmonization* merely creates havoc among Member States and interested parties, and does not bring the Internal Market much closer.

Yet another criticism concerns the lack of transparency of the legislative process. Law-making by directive involves a highly complex interplay between all three legislative powers of the Community. Almost inevitably this complexity reduces the transparency of the legislative process, and invites lobbying, rent-seeking and overregulation. More often than not, harmonization initiatives are driven by hidden political agendas. Indeed, the stated aim of a directive ('removing national disparities') rarely tells the full story, and in some cases appears to be wholly far-fetched.

A final critique concerns the quality of the legislative product. The complex legislative procedure leading to a harmonization directive, involving input from three EU institutions and twenty-seven Member States, simply can not produce norms of the quality that the EU – the largest market in the world – requires. To make matters worse, pressure from powerful lobby groups and from the EU's main trading partners, does not allow enough time for the reflection needed to produce good-quality regulation. At the national level, to avoid the risk of rushing into immature or unnecessary legislative initiatives, legislatures often seek advice from (committees of) academic advisors. Similarly, academic experts could play an important role as quality controllers at the European level.

On balance, the process of harmonization in the field of copyright and related rights has produced mixed results at great expense, and its beneficial effects on the Internal Market are limited at best, and remain largely unproven. Twenty years of harmonization of copyright law have not produced a solid, balanced and transparent legal framework in which the knowledge economy in the European Union can truly prosper. Even worse, the harmonization agenda has largely failed to live up to its promise of creating uniform norms of copyright across the European Union. This sobering conclusion calls for caution and restraint when considering future initiatives of harmonization by directive.

3. TERRITORIALITY IN EUROPEAN COPYRIGHT

But the real Achilles heel of harmonization is territoriality. Despite twenty years of harmonization, copyright law remains essentially national law, with each of the European Union's Member States having its own national law on copyright and neighbouring (related) rights. The exclusivity that a copyright confers upon its owner is, in principle, limited to the territorial boundaries of the Member State where the right has been granted. In its *Lagardère* ruling[4] the ECJ has confirmed the territorial nature of copyright and related rights. The territorial nature of copyright has various legal consequences.

---

4 *Lagardère Active Broadcast*, ECJ 14 July 2005, case C-192/04, para. 46: 'At the outset, it must be emphasised that it is clear from its wording and scheme that Directive 92/100 provides for minimal harmonisation regarding rights related to copyright. Thus, it does not purport to detract, in particular, from the principle of the territoriality of those rights, which is recognised in international law and also in the EC Treaty. Those rights are therefore of a territorial nature and, moreover, domestic law can only penalise conduct engaged in within national territory.'

In the first place, since copyright is granted autonomously by each Member State for its own territory, rules on copyright may vary from one Member State to the other. Although the seven harmonization directives in the field of copyright and related rights have removed these disparities in distinct fields (e.g. computer programs, rental and lending, satellite broadcasting and cable retransmission, term of protection, databases, artists' resale right, rights of reproduction and communication), important areas have remained largely or completely unharmonized. This is the case, for example, for the notion of a work of authorship. Whereas the Dutch Supreme Court has qualified the fragrance of a perfume as a 'work of literature, science or art', the French Cour de Cassation has excluded fragrances from the domain of copyright altogether, holding that 'a perfume fragrance, which is the result of the simple application of know-how, does not constitute the creation of a form of expression [...] capable of benefiting from the protection afforded to intellectual works by copyright'.[5] As a consequence of such differences, 'smell-a-like' perfumes that are perfectly legal in some EU countries are illegal in others. Other unharmonized areas include moral rights, rules on authors' contracts and rules on the collective administration of rights.

A second and related aspect of territoriality is that according to the rule of private international law, the law of the country where protection is sought (the so-called *Schutzland*) governs instances of copyright infringement.[6] This rule implies that making a work available online (i.e. over the Internet) affects as many copyright laws as there are countries where the posted work can be accessed. In other words, copyright licences for such acts need to be cleared in all countries of reception – normally, all twenty-seven Member States of the EU.

Due to the rule of national treatment found inter alia in article 5(2) of the Berne Convention, works or other subject matter protected by the laws of the Member States are protected by a 'bundle' of twenty-seven parallel (sets of) exclusive rights. A third consequence of territoriality is, therefore, that copyright in a single work of authorship can be 'split up' into multiple territorially defined national rights, which may be owned or exercised for each national territory by a different entity. This is the case, for instance, with copyrights in musical works. In practice, composers, song writers and music publishers grant their copyrights to collective rights management organizations that operate on the basis of strictly nationally defined legal mandates.

---

5 *Kecofa v Lancôme*, Dutch Supreme Court (Hoge Raad) 16 June 2006, case C04/327HR, [2006] ECDR 26; *Bsiri-Barbir v Haarmann & Reimer*, Cour de Cassation 13 June 2006, 210 R.I.D.A. 348 (2006).

6 Article 8 of the Rome II Regulation.

Over time, the ECJ and the EU legislature have responded to the problems of territoriality, by mitigating its consequences in various ways. These responses, however, have been uneven and remain incomplete, particularly with regard to making works available online.

3.1 Community Exhaustion

The ECJ has recognized early on that the territorial exercise of rights of intellectual property negatively affects the free circulation of goods, which is a core characteristic of the Internal Market. In a series of decisions preceding the harmonization of copyright and related rights, the ECJ held that the right to control the distribution of copyright protected goods is exhausted following the initial putting on the market of these goods inside the Community with the consent of the right holder(s).[7] This so-called rule of 'Community exhaustion' was codified, much later, in article 4(2) of the Information Society Directive. As a consequence, markets for copyright protected goods can no longer be partitioned according to national borders; parallel importing of goods that incorporate copyrighted works, such as books or CDs, that originate from other EU Member States, is legitimate. No exhaustion, however, occurs if these goods have their origin outside the European Union, e.g. from the United States; in such cases, right holders in the EU may legitimately oppose parallel imports.

No similar rule of exhaustion, however, has been developed in respect of the provision of content-related services. These services therefore remain vulnerable to the concurrent exercise of rights of public performance, communication to the public, cable retransmission or making available in all the Member States where the services are offered to the public. In its *Coditel I* decision, the European Court of Justice expressly refused to recognize a rule of Community exhaustion in respect of acts of secondary cable transmission.[8] The right holder in a neighbouring Member State (in this case Belgium) could legitimately oppose the unauthorized retransmission of a film broadcast in another State (Germany) via cable networks, without unduly restricting trade between Member States. The EU legislature has, much later, codified the *Coditel I* rule in respect of the rights of communication and making available to the public in article 3(3) of the Information Society Directive.

[7] See for instance *Deutsche Grammophon v Metro SB*, ECJ 8 June 1971, case 78/70, ECR [1971] 487.

[8] *Coditel v Ciné Vog Films*, ECJ 19 March 1980, case 62/79, ECR [1980] 881.

3.2 The Satellite Broadcasting Solution

Apart from the codification of the rule of Community exhaustion, which permits the further circulation of copyrighted goods within the European Union upon their introduction on the market in the EU with the local right holder's consent, the only structural legislative solution to the problem of market fragmentation by territorial rights can be found in the Satellite and Cable Directive of 1993. According to article 1(2)(b) of the Directive, a satellite broadcast will amount to communication to the public only in the country of origin of the signal, i.e. where the 'injection' ('start of the uninterrupted chain') of the program-carrying signal can be localized. Thus the Directive departed from the so-called 'Bogsch theory', which held that a satellite broadcast requires licences from all right holders in all countries of reception (i.e. within the footprint of the satellite). Since the transposition of the Directive, only a licence in the country of origin (home country) of the satellite broadcast is needed. As a result, at least in theory, a pan-European audiovisual space for satellite broadcasting has been created, and market fragmentation along national borders is avoided, by steering away from the cumulative application of several national laws to a single act of satellite broadcasting. Paradoxically, in those markets where the problem of territoriality has now become acute[9] no similar legislative solution has been achieved. But unlike in the realm of satellite broadcasting, content providers offering trans-border online services across the European Union will have to clear the rights from all right holders concerned for all the Member States of reception.

3.3 The Online Music Recommendation

Providers of online services comprising musical works may find some comfort in the Online Music Recommendation, which was adopted by the European Commission in 2005.[10] This non-binding recommendation seeks to facilitate the grant of Community-wide licences for online uses of musical works by requiring collective rights management societies to allow right holders to

---

9 See Communication from the Commission to the European Parliament, the Council, the European Economic and Social Committee and the Committee of the Regions, on Creative Content Online in the Single Market, Brussels, 3 January 2008, COM(2007) 836 final.

10 Commission Recommendation 2005/737/EC of 18 May 2005 on collective cross-border management of copyright and related rights for legitimate online music services, OJ L 276/54, 21 October 2005. See also European Parliament Resolution of 13 March 2007 on the Commission Recommendation of 18 October 2005 on Collective Cross-Border Management of Copyright and Related Rights for Legitimate Online Music Services, T6-0064/2007.

withdraw their online rights and grant them to a single collective rights manager operating at Community level. Nevertheless, the Recommendation does not address the more fundamental problem of territorially divided rights. Moreover, its scope is limited to musical works, phonograms and performances – subject matter that is traditionally exploited through collecting societies. The Recommendation does not concern existing contractual arrangements between, for instance, film producers and distributors or broadcasters, or writers and publishers.

In view of its non-binding status it is difficult to assess whether the Recommendation has had any real effect on the behaviour of right holders and rights managers. Nevertheless, there is a noticeable tendency amongst holders of large catalogues of music copyrights, particularly music publishers, to withdraw their 'online rights' from smaller national collecting societies, and entrust these to larger societies that operate on a European scale.

3.4 EU Competition Law

Even less structural, but sometimes effective nonetheless, are the remedies found in EU competition law, notably articles 101 and 102 of the Treaty on the Functioning of the European Union (TFEU), formerly articles 81 and 82 of the EC Treaty, against the exercise of intellectual property rights along national borders that result in the unjustified partitioning of the Internal Market. The European Court of Justice has produced extensive case law on the issue, applying both former articles 81 (anti-trust) and 82 (abuse of dominant position). With regard to the former articles, the Court has held in *Coditel II* that a contract providing for an exclusive right to exhibit a film for a specified time in the territory of any Member State may well be in violation of that provision if it has as its object or effect the restriction of film distribution or the distortion of competition on the cinematographic market.[11] In *Tiercé Ladbroke* the Court of First Instance ruled that an agreement by which two or more undertakings commit themselves to refusing third parties a licence to exploit televised pictures and sound commentaries of horse races within one Member State:

> may have the effect of restricting potential competition on the relevant market, since it deprives each of the contracting parties of its freedom to contract directly with a third party and granting it a licence to exploit its intellectual property rights and thus to enter into competition with the other contracting parties on the relevant market.[12]

[11] *Coditel II*, ECJ 6 October 1982, Case 262/81, ECR [1982] 3381, paras 17 et seq.

[12] *Tiercé Ladbroke SA v Commission*, CFI 12 June 1997, case T-504/93 ECR [1997] II-923, paras 157 et seq.

The *GVL* case demonstrates that article 102 TFEU may also serve as a remedy against the territorial exercise of copyright. According to the European Court of Justice:

> a refusal by a collecting society having a *de facto* monopoly to provide its services for all those who may be in need of them but who do not come within a certain category of persons defined by the undertaking on the basis of nationality or residence must be regarded as an abuse of a dominant position within the meaning of Article [82] of the Treaty.[13]

Issues of territorial exclusivity are also at the heart of several more recent competition cases concerning licensing practices of collecting societies.[14] In the *Santiago Agreement* case, the European Commission prohibited a large number of European collecting societies, members of CISAC, from restricting competition as regards the conditions for the management and licensing of authors' public performance rights for musical works. The collecting societies were found to have restricted the services they offer to authors and commercial users outside their domestic territory.[15]

The groundbreaking *Premier League Decoder* cases that were decided by the Court in October 2011 confirm that EU competition law militates against licensing contracts that confer absolute territorial exclusivity.[16] These cases turned on the trade in satellite decoder cards that provide access to encrypted foreign satellite transmissions of live Premier League football matches from Greece at lower prices than domestic pay television services in the United Kingdom. According to the Court the exclusive licensing contracts that the Premier League had entered into with the Greek satellite pay television vendor, which included an obligation not to sell decoder cards to consumers abroad, led to absolute territorial exclusivity, which the Court held not to be justified and therefore in conflict with both the freedom to provide services and competition law. Interestingly, the Court expressly rejected the argument of price discrimination – i.e., the possibility of differentiating consumer prices – as a valid justification for segmenting markets inside the EU.[17]

---

13 *GVL v Commission*, ECJ 2 March 1983, case 7/82, ECR [1983] 483, para. 5.

14 Commission Decision 2003/300/EC of 8 October 2002 relating to a proceeding under Article 81 of the EC Treaty and Article 53 of the EEA Agreement (case No COMP/C2/38.014 [IFPI Simulcasting].

15 Commission Decision of 16 July 2008, case COMP/38698 (CISAC).

16 *Football Association Premier League Ltd a.o. v QC Leisure a.o.; Karen Murphy v Media Protection Services Ltd*, CJEU 4 October 2011, joined cases C-403/08 and C-429/08.

17 CJEU 4 October 2011, case C-403/08, para. 115.

4. ECONOMIC AND CULTURAL IMPACT OF TERRITORIALITY

The territorial nature of copyright, and the fragmentation of the Internal Market that it fosters, affect the emerging 'knowledge economy' in the EU in various ways – both negative and positive. In addition, territoriality in copyright has certain cultural ramifications. It would however require extensive empirical study to precisely assess the impact of copyright territoriality on the European cultural economy. Such analysis being well outside the scope of the present study, this chapter will content itself with briefly indicating some possible positive and negative effects on the stakeholders most directly concerned.

4.1 Authors

For authors, territoriality implies that they need to ascertain, and enforce, their copyrights in all Member States of the EU concurrently. For some authors this may entail increased transaction and enforcement costs, although in practice copyright enforcement will often be left to publishers, broadcasters and other intermediaries that have contractually secured the rights to sue.

In book publishing, authors will hardly be affected by territoriality. Licences are normally not granted on a per-country basis; instead, licensing practices differentiate between language editions. For example, a German writer is likely to grant publishing rights in the German (original) language to a German publisher, while licensing English language translation rights to a British publisher. The Community exhaustion rule will guarantee that these various book editions can be freely distributed across the entire EU territory.

For composers and song writers, territoriality does have more immediate consequences. Although EU competition law has forced collecting societies to accept membership from foreign (non-national) authors, membership in practice is still largely determined by local circumstance. In practice, composers and song writers have little alternative but to join a national, often monopolistic collecting society.

4.2 Other Right Holders

The impact of territoriality on publishers, film producers, music publishers and other derivative right holders is much greater. On the positive side, territoriality allows these intermediaries to engage in certain practices that might be beneficial to their commercial interests. In the first place, territorial compartmentalization facilitates price discrimination. If average price levels for a product or service vary from one Member State to the next, a provider might maximize profits by offering the same content in different states at different prices. Market segmentation, including territorial segmentation, can also be a way to influence competition. By restricting the provision of goods or services to the territory of one country, providers can avoid competition with services or goods outside the country.[18] In the third place, marketing cultural goods in foreign countries will sometimes call for territorial licensing, for instance, when the good needs to be customized to cater for local audiences. This may be the case, in particular, for the cinema release and broadcasting of foreign films.

On the negative side, territoriality entails increased costs of licensing and enforcement. If right holders own rights for multiple territories, they will need to ascertain and enforce their copyrights in all Member States of the EU concurrently. The existing disparities in national law, particularly as to subject matter and scope of protection, create additional costs, as right holders are forced to seek legal counsel per country as to the exact state of the law.

Right holders are also affected by the territorial practices of collecting societies, not only in the field of music performance rights, but also regarding reprography (photocopying), cable retransmission rights and private copying remuneration rights (levies). In all but a few exceptional cases, collective administration of rights and remunerations is still undertaken at the national levels.

4.3 Collecting Societies

Most collective rights management societies currently derive their existence from rights granted or entrusted to them on a national, territorial basis – sometimes protected by a government licence or monopoly. Proceeds from the collective exploitation of these rights flow not only to entitled right holders, whereby local authors are sometimes favoured over foreign right holders, but are also channelled to a variety of cultural and social funds, mostly to the benefit of local authors and performers and local cultural development. By protecting and promoting local authors and performers, collecting societies thus play an important role in fostering 'cultural diversity' in the EU. Removing the territorial aspect of performance and communication rights would not only affect these de facto cultural subsidies, but might also undermine the societies' very existence, except for a handful of societies that are

---

18 See N. Helberger (IViR), 'Refusal to Serve Consumers because of their Nationality or Residence – Distortions in the Internal Market for E-commerce Transactions?', Briefing Note for European Parliament Committee on Internal Market and Consumer Protection, January 2007.

large enough, or sufficiently efficient, to compete at the European level. Indeed, under the influence of the Commission's Online Music Recommendation a struggle for survival among collecting societies is already evident.

4.4 Broadcasters

Broadcasters play a dual role both as owners of copyrights and neighbouring rights, and as users of copyright works. Over time broadcasters have been increasingly confronted with territoriality-related problems, as terrestrial transmissions are increasingly complemented or substituted by broadcasting media that more easily transcend national borders. Whereas the Satellite and Cable Directive has brought some relief to broadcasters using satellite platforms, no similar legal solution presently exists in respect of web-based broadcasting services. As a consequence, providers of such services are compelled to clear rights for all the countries where such broadcasts are received,[19] or, if this is infeasible, restrict access to their services to local audiences.

Disparities in national copyright protection, particularly as regards limitations of copyright, may cause additional impediments for transnational broadcasters. Statutory limitations permitting, for instance, incidental uses of audiovisual content for news reporting or quotation purposes may vary significantly from country to country.

4.5 Libraries and Archives

Libraries and audiovisual archives engaging in mass digitization also suffer from problems associated with copyright territoriality. Whereas the problems of securing licences from thousands or even millions of – often hard to identify – right holders are already enormous at the national level, these problems are multiplied for digitization projects with transnational ambitions, such as *Europeana*. In cases where these problems become insurmountable, remote access to digitized collections will necessarily have to be restricted to national audiences.[20]

Limitations and exceptions relevant to libraries and archives differ spectacularly between Member States. While digital archiving or document delivery

---

[19] See EBU Response to the EC Commission Communication on the Management of Copyright and Related Rights in the Internal Market, 24 June 2004, available at http://ec.europa.eu/internal_market/copyright/docs/management/consultation-rights-management/ebu_uer_en.pdf.

[20] See, for example, the BBC Archive, http://www.bbc.co.uk/archive/index.shtml.

on demand may be perfectly legitimate in some Member States, the same activities may require licenses in others, thereby raising impediments to the establishment of trans-national library services.

The Google Book Settlement that would allow Google to digitize and make available online for American users millions of books, illustrates – perhaps better than any other recent development – the shortcoming of a European market still divided by national copyrights and divergent copyright limitations, and the urgency to pursue supranational solutions.[21]

4.6 Providers of Online Content Services

Arguably, providers of content-related services are the most hard-hit by copyright's rule of territoriality. The fragmentation of online rights along the national borders of Member States requires such providers to clear *a priori* all relevant rights for all Member States (and other non-EU countries) for which these services are made available. Offering content online across the European Union therefore entails huge transaction and licensing costs. This puts European content service providers at a large competitive disadvantage, particularly when compared to competitors in the United States, where copyright is regulated at the federal level and no state-by-state licensing is required.

4.7 Consumers

Consumers of content-related online services are increasingly confronted with access denials on grounds associated with territoriality. For example, online music stores based in Member States routinely deny sales to consumers from other Member States,[22] presumably because licences granted by phonogram producers or collecting societies do not allow extraterritorial sales. For similar reasons, as explained above, consumers will often be denied access to audiovisual services abroad, either transmitted by satellite or offered online. Territorial fragmentation appears to be particularly rampant in respect of online television sports coverage. Whereas, for example, many national broadcasters transmitted the 2010 Winter Olympic Games online on multiple broadband channels, access to these channels from abroad was usually restricted,

---

21 See 'It is time for Europe to turn over a new e-leaf on digital books and copyright', joint Statement of EU Commissioners Reding and McCreevy on the occasion of the Google Books meetings in Brussels, 7 September 2009, available at http://europa.eu/rapid/pressReleasesAction.do?reference=MEMO/09/376&format=HTML&aged=0&language=EN&guiLanguage=en.

22 See Helberger, *supra* note 18.

apparently for copyright-related reasons. Clearly, for consumers of such services, the Internal Market has yet to materialize.[23]

5. CONCLUSIONS

As this chapter demonstrates, the territorial nature of copyright, while undeniably offering specific benefits to certain stakeholders concerned, profoundly affects the Internal Market. Despite decades of harmonization, territoriality, as an essential characteristic of copyright and related rights, remains a common instrument for partitioning markets within the EU – a practice 'repugnant to the essential purpose of the treaty, which is to unite national markets into a single market', according to the ECJ.[24] As a consequence, as long as national copyrights and related rights persist, no single market will be attained, not even if total harmonization of national laws is achieved.

The harmonization directives in the field of copyright and related rights adopted by the European legislature since 1991 have largely ignored the territorial nature of the economic rights. As a consequence, even in 2012 content providers aiming at European consumers need to clear rights covering some twenty-seven Member States. This clearly puts them at a competitive disadvantage vis-à-vis their main competitors outside the EU, such as the United States, where copyright is regulated at the federal level.

Whereas European (case) law has tackled the problem of territoriality head-on for the distribution of physical goods, by establishing a rule of Community exhaustion incorporating intellectual property, the territorial nature of rights of communication online has been left intact. While the Commission's Online Music Recommendation does address some of the problems caused by territoriality in the field of collective rights management of musical works, the Recommendation does not question the territorial nature of copyright and related rights as such.

The question, therefore, must be addressed whether similar solutions can be found in respect of copyright-related online services. In search of such solutions, three different approaches might be considered.

---

23 See European Parliament, Resolution of 21 June 2007 on consumer confidence in the digital environment, Strasbourg, 21 June 2007, A6-0191/2007, sec. 30: 'it is unacceptable that certain entrepreneurs who supply goods or provide services and content via the internet in several Member States deny consumers access to their website in certain Member States and force consumer to use their websites in the State in which the consumer is resident or whose nationality he or she holds'.

24 *Deutsche Grammophon v Metro SB*, ECJ 8 June 1971, case 78/70, ECR [1971] 487.

5.1 Extending the Satellite Broadcasting Model to the Internet

One possible solution would be to extend, or apply by analogy, to the Internet the 'injection right' model of the Satellite and Cable Directive, which was explained above. This is by no means a novel idea. Already in the 1995 Green Paper that preceded the Information Society Directive,[25] the European Commission toyed with the idea of applying to the Internet the country of origin approach that typifies the Satellite and Cable Directive. But this suggestion was immediately and unequivocally discarded by all right holders consulted. Right holders feared they would lose control over copyrighted content once it was offered online, under a licence, somewhere within the European Union. It was also pointed out that transmission of works over the Internet is not merely an act of communication to the public, as is satellite broadcasting, but also concerns the right of reproduction. Works made available online are stored on servers and copied repeatedly on their way from the content provider to the end user.

In a Staff Working Document that accompanies the Communication of the Commission on 'Creative Content Online', the possibility of extending the Satellite and Cable Directive's country-of-origin approach to the Internet is once again extensively discussed:

> Some stakeholders, including representatives from the broadcasters suggest that the country-of-origin principle should be considered for online services along the lines of the Satellite and Cable Directive. They consider that in particular, Internet streaming/simulcasting is comparable to the case of satellite broadcasting. While internet streaming and indeed simulcasting may indeed be structurally similar to broadcasting, this is less true for a host of 'on-demand' services and 'online retail' of music or film. In the case of online purchases, legal doctrine has established that the relevant act under copyright laws takes place in the country where the consumer has access to the relevant services. In depth analysis will be needed before considering the extension of a technology specific solution. [...] Furthermore, the extension of the country of origin principle raises a number of concerns, such as the difficulties of locating the relevant act of transmission in the digital environment, the risk of devaluation of copyright if a single tariff and licence were to be applied to the whole Internal Market, or of a 'race to the bottom' both regarding the emergence of the protection and the scope of the protection. Hence, the question of whether or not the Satellite and Cable Directive (93/83/EEC) should be made technologically neutral by extending the country-of-origin principle to online services should be addressed through a review of this Directive.[26]

---

[25] European Commission, 'Copyright and Related Rights in the Information Society', Green Paper, COM(95) 382 final, Brussels, 19 July 1995, pp. 41 ff.

[26] Commission staff working document – Document accompanying the Communication from the Commission to the European Parliament, the Council, the European Economic and Social Committee and the Committee of the Regions on

5.2 Promoting Multi-territorial Licensing

A much less ambitious approach would be to keep the territorial nature of copyright as a matter of principle intact, but to promote multi-territorial licensing. This is the approach apparently advocated by the Commission in its 2011 IPR Strategy paper. The Commission no longer discusses the country-of-origin approach of the Satellite and Cable Directive as a viable solution. Instead, the Commission announces its intention 'to create a legal framework for the collective management of copyright to enable multi-territorial and pan-European licensing'. This 'framework', presumably a directive, would partly reiterate the approach of the Online Music Recommendation, while taking into account the interests of smaller collecting societies. The Commission proposes:

> To foster the development of new online services covering a greater share of the world repertoire and serving a greater share of European consumers, the framework should allow for the creation of European 'rights brokers' able to license and manage the world's musical repertoire on a multi-territorial level while also ensuring the development of Europe's cultural diversity. To that end, an enforceable European rights management regime that facilitates cross-border licensing should be put in place.[27]

5.3 Unification of EU Copyright Law

Nevertheless, if the European Union is really serious about achieving the Single Market for content-related goods and services, the problem of territoriality in copyright must be confronted in a more fundamental way. As the Institute for Information Law has suggested in a major study on the future of European copyright law that was carried out for the European Commission,[28] a truly structural and consistent solution, which would immediately remove all copyright-related territorial obstacles to the creation of the Single Market, would be the introduction of a unified European Copyright Law. Long

---

creative content online in the Single Market, COM(2007) 836 final, Brussels, 3 January 2008, pp. 25–6.

27 European Commission, 'A Single Market for Intellectual Property Rights – Boosting creativity and innovation to provide economic growth, high quality jobs and first class products and services in Europe', COM(2011) 287 final, Brussels, 24 May 2011, p. 11.

28 P. Bernt Hugenholtz et al., 'The Recasting of Copyright & Related Rights for the Knowledge Economy', Report to the European Commission, DG Internal Market, November 2006, p. 210. See also M. van Eechoud, P. Bernt Hugenholtz et al. (2009), *Harmonizing European Copyright Law. The Challenges of Better Lawmaking*, Alphen aan den Rijn: Kluwer Law International, pp. 317 ff.

considered taboo in copyright circles, the idea of the European Copyright is gradually receiving attention it deserves, both in scholarly debate[29] and political circles. For example, in one of her last public speeches on copyright, former Commissioner Vivian Redding expressly endorsed the idea of the European Copyright Law:

> Last, but not least, one could think of a more profound harmonisation of copyright laws in order to create a more coherent licensing framework at European level. A 'European Copyright Law' – established for instance by an EU regulation – has often been mooted as a way of establishing a truly unified legal framework that would deliver direct benefits. This would be an ambitious plan for the EU, but not an impossible one.[20]

Importantly, the Lisbon Reform Treaty has introduced a specific competence for Union-wide intellectual property rights. Article 118 TFEU provides:

> In the context of the establishment and functioning of the Internal Market, the European Parliament and the Council, acting in accordance with the ordinary legislative procedure, shall establish measures for the creation of European intellectual property rights to provide uniform protection of intellectual property rights throughout the Union and for the setting up of centralised Union-wide authorization, coordination and supervision arrangements.[31]

Arguably, article 118 TFEU would allow not only for the introduction of Union-wide copyright titles, but also for the simultaneous abolishment of national titles, which would be necessary for such an initiative to take its full effect and remove territorial restrictions.

The potential advantages of such a Union-wide copyright title are undeniable. A European Copyright Law would immediately establish a truly unified legal framework, replacing the multitude of – sometimes conflicting – national rules of the present. It would have instant Union-wide effect, thereby creating

---

29 See, for example, the 'European Copyright Code' that was published by a group of European copyright scholars (the 'Wittem Group') in 2010, available at www.copyrightcode.eu.

30 Viviane Reding, Speech delivered at Visby/Gotland on 9 November 2009, available at http://europa.eu/rapid/pressReleasesAction.do?reference=SPEECH/09/519&format=HTML&aged=0&language=EN&guiLanguage=nl. Similar ideas our expressed in a 'Reflection paper' on 'Creative Content in a European Digital Single Market: Challenges for the Future', which was jointly issued by the DG's INFSO and MARKT, available at http://ec.europa.eu/internal_market/consultations/docs/2009/content_online/reflection_paper%20web_en.pdf.

31 The 'ordinary procedure' that article 118 refers to is the co-decision procedure. The European Parliament has to agree to a proposal, and the Council must adopt the proposed law with a qualified majority vote.

a single market for copyrights and related rights, both online and offline. It would enhance legal security and transparency, for right owners and users alike, and greatly reduce transaction costs. Unification could also restore the asymmetry that is inherent in the current *acquis*, which *mandates* basic economic rights, but merely *permits* limitations.

Devising this European Copyright Law would be an ambitious undertaking – at best a project of the long term. With copyright law today in a state of immediate crisis, due in particular to the problems of mass infringement associated with the Internet, the question arises whether time would allow the EU legislature to embark on such an undertaking. The answer, in the opinion of this author, is yes. Work on the European Copyright Law could be undertaken in parallel with improvement, at the national level or in the form of further harmonization, of copyright in the EU. Indeed, such work could be less dependent on the mood of the day, and might allow sufficient reflection, thereby enhancing the quality of the final legislative product. In this respect, the slow but certain development of a body of European contract law in an institutionalized cooperation between the Commission and a group of qualified academic experts might serve as an example.[32] Ideally, such an 'unhurried' drafting process could produce the technologically neutral norms that make up a transparent, consistent, supranational legal framework, free from territorial restrictions, for many years to come.

The European Commission's 2011 IPR Strategy paper entertains the possibility of consolidating the entire body of harmonized copyright law into a single 'European Copyright Code'.[33] According to the Commission, '[t]his could encompass a comprehensive codification of the present body of EU copyright directives in order to harmonise and consolidate the entitlements provided by copyright and related rights at EU level.' The paper also states the Commission's intention to examine the feasibility of creating an optional 'unitary' copyright title based on article 118 TFEU, which would exist in parallel to national copyrights. While these statements demonstrate that the prospect of a unification of European copyright is no longer beyond the political horizon, the European Commission apparently is not yet ready to consider the creation of a truly unified European Copyright Law that would replace national copyright laws in the Member States.

---

32 See Communication from the Commission to the European Parliament and the Council, European Contract Law and the Revision of the Acquis: The Way Forward, COM(2004) 651 final, Brussels, 11 October 2004.

33 European Commision, *supra* note 28, p.11.

13. The Wittem Project of a European Copyright Code

Thomas Dreier

1. COPYRIGHT IN THE EU

1.1 Unification of Civil Law

In the European Union with its focus on the single market, the question of unification of national legal systems is on the agenda. As is commonly known, the progress of unification has reached different stages. Partly, common law has been established; partly the efforts rather followed the path of harmonization of national laws, at least for the time being. As regards general civil law, which more than any other legal field has developed out of national traditions of EU Member States, the European Commission currently encourages the elaboration of transnational principles by legal scholars which shall lead to the creation of a European Contract Law.[1]

The law of intellectual property offers a mixed picture with regard to unification. Partly, unification was already advanced at a comparatively early stage owing to the permeability of national borders, particularly for new technologies, and due to the open markets. Community rights which are valid throughout the EU exist in the form of the Community trademark, the Community

[1] Commission Decision of 26 April 2010 setting up the Expert Group on a Common Frame of Reference in the area of European contract law (2010/233/EU) [2010] OJ L 105/109. The activities rely on the Draft Common Frame of Reference (DCFR); see the six-volume 'Principles, Definitions and Model Rules of European Private Law – Draft Common Frame of Reference (DCFR)', Munich and Oxford 2009, drawn up by the Study Group on a European Civil Code (www.sgecc.net) and the Research Group on EC Private Law (Acquis Group, www.acquis-group.org) and published by v.Bar/Clive/Schulte-Nölke and Beale/Herre/Huet/Storme/Swann/Varul/Veneziano Zoll, and the single-volume 'Interim Outline Edition (IOE)', Munich 2008; the latter is available under http://ec.europa.eu/justice/policies/civil/docs/dcfr_outline_edition_en.pdf. – See, in general the website of DG Justice http://ec.europa.eu/justice/policies/civil/policies_civil_contract_en.htm#cfr.

design and the Community plant variety right.[2] In parallel, national legislation of the Member States has been harmonized in these areas. Attempts to also create a Community patent have still not yet been completed, mainly due to the success of the European Patent Convention, which came into force in 1977.[3] In contrast, European copyright legislation has so far not gone beyond a wide, yet only partial harmonization of national laws. At the edges, as regards rules applying to cross-border situations, law scholars currently try to develop common principles which supplement the Rome I and II Regulations according to a method used in general civil law.[4]

1.2 Copyright in the Tension Between Territoriality and the Internal Market

The fact that a Community copyright regime has not yet been set up might be due to the specifics in cultural policy and the legal traditions that have evolved in the Member States. As a consequence of the principle of territoriality, absent a Community copyright, the internal market is governed by as many national laws as there are Member States. This may enter into conflict with the EU's fundamental principle of freedom of movement for goods and services. Consequently, the single market should be made subject to common rules. Moreover, the different national copyright regimes and the resulting issues of applicable law to cross-border uses and law enforcement may cause significant transaction costs.

This tension between the freedom of movement for goods and services and the principle of territoriality applying in copyright law was addressed by the European Court of Justice at a comparatively early stage in the history of the Union, albeit not immediately after conclusion of the Treaties of Rome. In a first phase, the principle of exhaustion of the distribution right was established as far as physical copies of copyrighted works are concerned.[5] In a second

---

[2] Council Regulation (EC) 207/2009 (replacing Regulation (EC) 40/94) of 26 February 2009 on the Community Trade Mark [2009] OJ L 78/1; Council Regulation (EC) 6/2002 of 12 December 2001 on Community Designs [2002] OJ L 3/1, amended by Regulation (EC) 1891/2006 of 18 December 2006 [2006] OJ L 386/14, and Council Regulation (EC) 2100/94 of 27 June 1994 on Community plant variety rights [1994] OJ L 227/1.

[3] For the current state of the eventful development see http://ec.europa.eu/internal_market/indprop/patent/index_en.htm.

[4] Cf. the draft of 'Principles for Conflict of Laws in Intellectual Property' (CLIP), available under www.ip.mpg.de/ww/de/pub/mikroseiten/cl_ip_eu/.

[5] Case C-78/70 *Deutsche Grammophon v Metro* [1971] ECR I-487; Case C-55/80 and 57/80 *Musik-Vertrieb Membran v GEMA* [1981] ECR I-147; and Case C-62/79 *Coditel I* [1980] ECR I-881.

phase, however, the European Court of Justice (ECJ) then gave precedence to differing national copyright provisions (duration; rental rights) over the fundamental freedoms under Community law, thereby upholding the freedom of Member States to pursue their own copyright and, in a broader sense, cultural policies.[6] In doing so, the ECJ likewise invited the Community legislature to remove existing differences in national copyright legislation which might have a negative impact on the functioning of the single market.

For the following 20 years, the Commission, the Council and the Parliament undertook efforts towards harmonization. Up until now, this has resulted in seven Copyright Directives so far plus the Enforcement Directive which affects all intellectual property rights including copyright; two additional proposals for directives are currently debated.[7] Thus, significant differences between the legal systems of the Member States were removed, which had been considered barriers to the free movement of goods and services. Nevertheless, the harmonization remained rather piecemeal. In particular, no real harmonization was achieved regarding the limitations to copyright. This is all the more deplorable since the exceptions to the exclusive rights form an integral part of copyright law.[8] In practice, the limitations often are the norm

6 Case C-158/86 *Warner Brothers v Christiansen* [1988] ECR I-2605 and Case C-341/87 *EMI Electrola v Patricia* [1989] ECR I-79. See for example T. Dreier (2007), 'The Role of the ECJ for the Development of Copyright in the European Communities', *J. Cop. Soc.* **54**, 183.

7 Directive 2009/24/EC (replacing 91/250/EEC) of 23 April 2009 on the legal protection of computer programs [2006] OJ L 111/16; Directive 2006/115/EC (replacing 92/100/EEC) of 12 December 2006 on the rental right and lending right and on certain rights related to copyright in the field of intellectual property [2006] OJ L 376/28; Directive 93/83/EEC on the coordination of certain rules concerning copyrights and rights related to copyright applicable to satellite broadcasting and cable retransmission [1993] OJ L 248/15; Directive 2006/116/EC (replacing 98/83/EEC) of 12 December 2006 on the term of protection of copyright and certain related rights [2006] OJ L 376/12; Directive 96/9/EC of 11 March 1996 on the legal protection of databases [1996] OJ L 77/20 ff.; Directive 2001/29/EC of 22 May 2001 on the harmonization of certain aspects of copyright and related rights in the information society [2001] OJ L 167/10; Directive 2001/84/EC of 28 September on the resale right for the benefit of the author of an original work of art [2001] OJ L 272/32, and Directive 2004/48/EC of the European Parliament and of the Council of 29 April 2004 on the enforcement of intellectual property rights [2004] OJ L 157/45, Corrigendum to Directive 2004/48/EC [2004] OJ L 195/16. In addition, two Directives are currently underway, the proposed Directive amending Directive 2006/116/EC of the European Parliament and of the Council on the term of protection of copyright and certain related rights, Doc. COM(2008) 464/3 prolonging the term of protection for performing artists and performers of phonograms, and the proposed Directive on certain permitted uses of orphan works, Doc. COM(2011) 289 final of 24 May 2011.

8 Critically, in particular, P. Bernt Hugenholtz (2000), 'Opinion, "Why the Copyright Directive is Unimportant and Possibly Invalid"', *EIPR* 499, 501; H. Schack

which is decisive for the outcome of a particular case. True, the Information Society Directive contains an exhaustive catalogue of 21 limitations, but all except one of them are optional. Not surprisingly, Member States' national copyright laws greatly differ in this respect.[9] Here, further harmonization by means of directives is faced with considerable difficulties within the 27 Member States.

Subsequent attempts of the Commission to promote market-driven self-regulation in line with competition and internal market requirements by way of a 'better regulation approach' in the form of non-binding recommendations[10] hardly proved to be successful,[11] not least because they bypassed the Member States. Moreover, the proposed EU-wide solution for so-called 'orphan works', preparing the way for 'Europeana' as the equivalent to the 'Google book search-project',[12] shall be restricted to a kind of framework legislation, rather than providing for full European harmonization (the core of the proposal is that a work which is considered an orphan work according to the European definition contained in the Directive in one Member State shall be considered an orphan work in all Member States). Obviously, the political will is currently not existing or not strong enough to reach further harmonization. This is the case even though art. 118(1) TFEU now provides an explicit basis to create a Community copyright, which is often regarded as inevitable in literature and which was at one point mentioned – albeit hesitantly – as a future option by the (old) Commission.[13]

(2009), 'Europäische Urheberrechts-Verordnung: erwünscht oder unvermeidlich?', *ZGE* 275, 278.

[9] An overview is given by L. Guibault (2010), 'Why Cherry-Picking Never Leads to Harmonisation. The Case of the Limitations on Copyright under Directive 2001/29/EC', *JIPITEC* **1**, 55, available at http://www.jipitec.eu/issues/jipitec-1-2-2010/2603/JIPITEC%202%20-%20Guibault-Cherrypicking.pdf.pdf.

[10] Commission Recommendation of 18 May 2005 on collective cross-border management of copyright and related rights for legitimate online music services [2005] OJ L 276/54, for comment see T. Lüder, 'Making Markets Work – the Case for EU-wide Online Licensing', http://www.fordhamipinstitute.com/media/IP2007Papers.zip.

[11] Critical statements from GRUR (2006), 'Stellungnahme zur Empfehlung und zur Studie der Europäischen Kommission über die Lizensierung von Musik für das Internet vom 18.10.2005', *GRUR* 303 and MPI (2006), 'Stellungnahme des Max-Planck-Instituts für Geistiges Eigentum, Wettbewerbs- und Steuerrecht zuhänden des Bundesministeriums der Justiz betreffend die Empfehlung der Europäischen Kommission über die Lizensierung von Musik für das Internet vom 18. Oktober 2005 (2005/737/EC)', *GRUR Int.* 222. For legal problems of CELAS see LG Mannheim ZUM 2009, 253 and LG München I ZUM 2009, 788.

[12] See http://ec.europa.eu/information_society/activities/digital_libraries/index_en.htm, and for 'Europeana' http://europeana.eu/portal.

[13] See – but without mentioning art. 118 (1) TFEU – Schack, *supra* note 8, 275 and the same earlier: (2000), 'Europäisches Urheberrecht im Werden', *ZEuP*, 799;

Especially in the age of the Internet, a fully functioning internal market is needed for cross-border exploitation of copyrighted works. Furthermore, transparent and consistent copyright rules will be necessary to ensure an increase in both supply and use of digital content as well as in services for information and entertainment purposes. These rules will have to bridge civil and common law traditions. Finally, a unified European copyright regime should not merely focus on the rights of authors and rights holders, but also consider other values embedded in the European legal culture such as freedom of expression and the idea of competition.

2. THE WITTEM PROJECT

2.1 Starting Point

As a result of these considerations, the 'European Copyright Code' was made accessible to the public at www.copyrightcode.eu on the occasion of the 10th World Day of Intellectual Property on 26 April 2010. The Code was developed within the framework of the Wittem Project, which was established in 2002 as a collaboration between copyright scholars across the European Union concerned with the future development of an optimal balanced European copyright regime while duly reflecting the affected interests and relevant issues.[14] It comprises the draft of a unified European Copyright, which reflects the core principles and provides a basis to continue the discussions about the future development of the European copyright law on the European or a national scale.[15] The aim of the Wittem Project and this Code was to keep the discussion process widely free from special interests and integrate both the civil and common law traditions. At the same time, the voice of academia

taking a critical position S. von Lewinski (2010), 'Introduction', in M. Walter and S. von Lewinski (eds), *European Copyright Law* Oxford: Oxford University Press. For the Commission statement see 'Creative Content in a European Digital Single Market – Challenges for the Future, A Reflection Document' by DG InfoSoc and DG Market of 22 October 2009, p. 18, n. 49 (http://ec.europa.eu/avpolicy/docs/ other_actions/col_2009/reflection_paper.pdf).

[14] The project is named after the Belgian conference place where the idea of a 'European Copyright Code' has been formulated for the first time. The project has its roots in an International Network Program run by three Dutch universities (Radboud University of Nijmegen, University of Amsterdam and Leiden University), and sponsored by the government-funded Dutch ITeR Program. It aims to promote transparency and consistency in the field of intellectual property.

[15] Cf. the penultimate recital of the preamble ('*Believing* that the design of a European Copyright Code might serve as an important reference tool for future legislatures at the European and national levels').

should be better heard which is not always adequately taken into account in the Brussels legislative process affected by huge lobbying interests and with a lack of transparency. This seemed particularly indicated, since the comprehensive study for harmonizing European copyright law, which was undertaken by the University of Amsterdam, Institute for Information Law (IVIR) on behalf of the European Commission, largely remained without results.[16]

2.2 Methodology

In general, the 'European Copyright Code' imitates the efforts towards harmonization in general civil law both as regards the objective and the methodology. However, even more than these larger sized ventures, the members of the Wittem Project Drafting Committee[17] were not solely interested in working out common *principles* underlying the national copyright legislation of the Member States.[18] Rather, exceeding the level of detail normally associated with common principles of law, the 'European Copyright Code' is drafted in a way which comes close to a *legislative instrument.*[19] Hence it might be possible to adopt the Code as law, though it has to be said that the 28 articles are drafted in rather lean language, which might not necessarily comply with the tradition of drafting statutory provisions in all Member States.

Moreover, it has to be noted that the 'European Copyright Code' is not comprehensive. Rather, it concentrates on the main elements of any copyright codification. It covers the subject matter of copyright (Chapter 1), authorship

---

[16] Published by M. van Eechoud, P. Bernt Hugenholtz, S. van Gompel, L. Guibault and N. Helberger (2009), *Harmonizing European Copyright Law – The Challenges of Better Lawmaking,* Alphen aan den Rijn: Kluwer Law International.

[17] Wittem Group Drafting Committee: Prof. *Lionel Bently* (Centre of Intellectual Property and Information Law, University of Cambridge, Emmanuel College, Cambridge); Prof. *Thomas Dreier* (Institute for Information and Economic Law, Centre for Applied Legal Science, Karlsruhe Institute for Technology, KIT); Prof. *Reto Hilty* (Max Planck Institute for Intellectual Property and Competition Law, Munich); Prof. *P. Bernt Hugenholtz* (Instituut voor Informatierecht, Universiteit van Amsterdam); Prof. *Antoon Quaedvlieg* (Radboud Universiteit Nijmegen); Prof. *Alain Strowel*, (Facultés universitaires Saint-Louis, Bruxelles) sowie Prof. *Dirk Visser* (Universiteit Leiden); responsible for the overall coordination was Prof. *Quaedvlieg*.

[18] See in particular for the Commission on European Contract Law (CECL; so called Lando-Group) O. Lando and H. Beale (eds) (1999), *Principles of European Contract Law, Parts I and II*, Leiden, The Netherlands: Nijhoff; and O. Lando, E. Clive, A. Prum and R. Zimmermann (eds) (2003), *Principles of European Contract Law, Part 3*, Alphen aan den Rijn, The Netherlands: Kluwer Law International. See also the project 'Common Principles of European Contract Law' (CoPECL; www.copecl.org) currently run by the Joint Network on European Private Law.

[19] Meanwhile, the DFCR also contains 'model rules'.

and ownership (Chapter 2), moral rights (Chapter 3), economic rights (Chapter 4, including provisions on the term of protection), and limitations (Chapter 5). However, the Code does not deal with remuneration rights such as public lending right and droit de suite, which are not established in each national copyright system. Also, apart from some exceptions, the Code does not deal with copyright contract law. Moreover, the Code does not touch upon neighbouring (related) rights, database rights, nor does it deal with rules on copyright liability or enforcement and the legal protection of technical measures. Rules related to the rights of foreigners, the applicable law and transitional provisions are also excluded. The same applies to the law of the copyright collecting societies.

Of course, preliminary documents exist in the form of explanatory memorandi drafted by the rapporteurs as well as of minutes of the meetings held by the Drafting Committee with the members of the Wittem Advisory Board and other ad hoc invited experts.[20] Nevertheless, the authors have refrained from making these preliminary documents accessible to the public. This should prevent that too much attention is paid to the past genesis of the 'European Copyright Code'. Rather, energy should be concentrated on its discussion and further development. However, for the avoidance of doubt, the authors used a total of 58 footnotes with further explanations, wherever appropriate. The footnotes serve several purposes. First, they help clarify the content and the meaning of the English legal terms used. Secondly, they contain additional information which has not been incorporated in the legislative text. Finally, the footnotes may indicate on which occasion the members of the Drafting Committee did not fully agree and to what extent differing views could be generally accepted.

2.3 Existing Legal Framework

On the one hand, it is important to note that both in form and in content the 'European Copyright Code' is not a mere restatement or consolidation of the

---

[20] The method of working chosen by the Wittem Group is similar to former projects (such as the Commission on European Contract Law, CECL) in other fields of law and operates with the support from an Advisory Board as well as from further experts that were invited ad hoc. Members of the Advisory Board: Prof. *Jon Bing* (Institutt for rettsinformatikk, Universitetet i Oslo); Prof. *Robert Clark* (University College Dublin); Prof. *Frank Gotzen* (Centrum voor Intellectuele rechten, Katholieke Universiteit Leuven); Prof. *Ejan Mackaay* (Université de Montréal); Prof. *Marco Ricolfi* (Università degli Studi di Torino); Prof. *Elzbieta Traple* (Uniwersytet Jagiellonski w Krakowie); Prof. *Michel Vivant* (Institut d'Études Politiques de Paris), and Prof. *Raquel Xalabarder* (Universitat Oberta de Catalunya). *Sophie van Loon* und *Liza Gerritsen* (Radboud University of Nijmegen) provided the secretariat for the Wittem Group.

existing '*acquis communautaire*', which has been undertaken at several instances.[21] Of course, the 'European Copyright Code' was not created in a vacuum. Rather, the international framework for copyright legislation is set by the Berne Convention (BC), the Trade-Related Aspects of Intellectual Property Rights (TRIPS Agreement) and the WIPO Copyright Treaty (WCT). It would also be difficult to ignore the *acquis communautaire* in the area of copyright, which is, after all, based on the common will of the EU Member States. In so far, it does not seem reasonable to give up the level of unification already achieved in the EU.

On the other hand, this framework should not be taken as entirely irreversible and necessary modifications not discarded a priori. Since the European legislator is at liberty to modify the *acquis*, the members of the Drafting Committee saw the possibility to deviate from the *acquis*, wherever it is not in conformity with fundamental beliefs of the Wittem Group. The Drafting Committee has especially been guided by three fundamental beliefs. Firstly, the Drafting Committee acted under the assumption that copyright law protects the moral and economic interests of the authors, while serving the public interest in the creation and dissemination of works in the fields of literature, art and science.[22] Secondly, in view of this a reasonable balance has to be found between the two conflicting interests of protection on the one hand, and access on the other. Finally, a minimum of flexibility is required, in order to respond appropriately to changes due to the rapid development of technology, which makes future modes of exploitation and the use of copyrighted works unpredictable.

In sum, the members of the Drafting Committee believe that the design of the present 'European Copyright Code' may serve as an important reference tool for future legislatures both at the European and the national level.[23] In

[21] See para. 6 of the introduction to the Code. Earlier considerations, that were also built for the Commission, about an update and consolidation of the Common law can be found in the lecture by *Walter* on the occasion of the conference in Santiago de Compostella in 2002 (http://ec.europa.eu/internal_market/copyright/docs/conference/2002-06-santiago-speech-walter_en.pdf); see furthermore the studies carried out by van Eechoud, Bernt Hugenholtz, van Gompel, Guibault and Helberger, *supra* note 16; K. Riesenhuber (ed.) (2007), *Systembildung im Europäischen Urheberrecht,* Berlin: De Gruyter; R. Hilty and C. Geiger (eds) (2007), *Impulse für eine europäische Harmonisierung des Urheberrechts,* Berlin: Springer; M. Leistner (ed.) (2010), *Europäische Perspektiven des Geistigen Eigentums,* Tübingen: Mohr Siebeck; and Schack, *supra* note 8, 277.

[22] See also M. Senftleben (2010), 'Der kulturelle Imperativ des Urheberrechts', in M. Weller, N. Kemle, T. Dreier and Peter Michael Lynen (eds), *Kunst im Markt – Kunst im Recht,* Baden-Baden: Nomos-Verlag, 75.

[23] See the call for elaborating a Copyright Regulation by Schack, *supra* note 8,

literature, the Code was criticized by some commentators as being too cautious since it followed new paths only as regards the limitations. Also it was said that the Code remained too faithfully within the international regulatory framework. Other commentators, however, have described it as ranging 'from cautious synthesis to radical prescription'.[24] But the project mainly focused on combining legal traditions rather than putting copyright onto new feet.[25] Altogether, it is hoped that the Code is not too utopian from the perspective of legal policy making, although it probably will not be taken over into future European or national copyright legislation of EU Member States on a verbatim basis.

3. THE SPECIFIC PROVISIONS OF THE 'EUROPEAN COPYRIGHT CODE'

3.1 Chapter 1: Works (Arts 1.1–1.2)

To begin with, the term 'work' is defined and illustrated by a non-exhaustive enumeration of examples following the definition of subject matter both of the

271, 291. Robert A. Gehring, Golem.de of 28 April 2010, www.golem.de/1004/74804.html takes a fundamentally positive position vis-à-vis Wittem Draft ('Even if it cannot be regarded as revolutionary, the proposed model at least goes beyond the status quo in many cases').

[24] So emphatically, R. Kuhlen (2011), 'Richtungweisend oder eine verpasste Chance? – Der Copyright-Code des Wittem-Projekts' ('A little more courage to enter unknown territory might have been expected'), *JIPITEC*, **2**, 18, available at www.jipitec.eu/issues/jipitec-2-1-2011/2960/jipitec_kuhlen.pdf; see also the detailed – and mostly critical – comment by Jane Ginsburg, 'European Copyright Code – Back to first principles (with some additional detail)', Public Law & Legal Theory Working Paper Group, Paper Number 11–261, available at http://ssrn.com/abstract=1747148, but at the same time honoring the attempt to bridge civilian and common law approaches ('the drafters therefore deserve applause'), 3. Critically regarding some of the rules regarding limitations P. E. Geller (2010), 'A German Approach to Fair Use – Test Cases for TRIPS Criteria for Copyright Limitations?', *J.Cop.Soc.* **57**, 901, 914 et seq., and J. Griffiths (2010), 'Unsticking the Centre-piece – the Liberation of European Copyright Law?', *JIPITEC* 87, available at www.jipitec.eu/issues/jipitec-1-2-2010/2617/JIPITEC%202%20-%20Griffiths-Unsticking.pdf. For discussion see also below under 3.5.2.

[25] For more comprehensive approaches see, e.g., T. Kreutzer (2008), *Das Modell des deutschen Urheberrechts und Regelungsalternativen: Konzeptionelle Überlegungen zu Werkbegriff, Zuordnung, Umfang und Dauer des Urheberrechts als Reaktion auf den urheberrechtlichen Funktionswande*, Baden-Baden: Nomos; G. Hansen (2009), *Warum Urheberrecht? – Die Rechtfertigung des Urheberrechts unter besonderer Berücksichtigung des Nutzerschutzes*, Baden-Baden: Nomos.

Berne Convention and of the many national copyright laws of the EU Member States (art. 1.1). Then, some works are excluded from copyright protection, even though they principally would have to be considered as copyrightable subject matter (art. 1.2). This reveals, in fact, a comparative approach rather than being directed at new forms of collaborative, open-ended work creation.[26]

According to the general term used in art. 1.1(1), any expression within the field of literature, art or science is copyrightable subject matter. A footnote clarifies that copyrightability is independent of the mode, form of expression or merit of a given work, and no fixation is required.[27] It is also explained in a footnote that an adaptation of a work may likewise qualify as a work itself.[28] This demonstrates the endeavour of the authors to be as concise as possible. Although adaptations of a work are treated separately by most national copyright regimes, the copyrightability of adaptations already results from the general definition of what constitutes a protected work.

As a general requirement for protection, the Code uses the term 'the authors' own intellectual creation', initially contained in the Computer Programs Directive of 1991[29] and subsequently used by the Copyright Term Directive[30] and the Database Directive.[31] Essentially, the Code covers what the ECJ seems to indicate in its *Infopac* decision (art. 1.1(1)).[32] A footnote explains that this notion can be interpreted as the 'average' European threshold, presuming it is set somewhat higher than skill and labour. This is possible if emphasis is put on the element of creation. For factual and functional works, the focus will be more on a certain level of skill (judgement) and labour, whereas for productions in the artistic field the focus will be more on personal expression.[33] However, the Code did not adopt the notion of originality.

The categories of works listed in art. 1.1(2) as non-exhaustive illustrative examples correspond to the categories usually to be found in national laws, including computer programs, collections, compilations and databases.

---

26 That has been criticised by Kuhlen, *supra* note 24, p. 20, para. 14.

27 Footnote 2 to the Code.

28 Footnote 2 to the Code.

29 Art. 1(3) of the Directive 2009/24/EC (91/250/EEC) of 23 April 2009 on the legal protection of computer programs [2009] OJ L 111/16.

30 Art. 6 of the Directive 2006/116/EC (replacing 93/98/EEC) of 12 December 2006 on the term of protection of copyright and certain related rights [2006] OJ L 372/12.

31 Art. 3(1) of the European Parliament and Council Directive 96/9/EC of 11 March 1996 on legal protection of databases [1996] OJ L 77/20.

32 Case C-5/08 *Infopaq* [2009] ECR-I 6569.

33 Footnote 7 to the Code.

According to art. 1.1(3), copyright protection shall, however, not extend to facts, discoveries, news and data ('in themselves'; the term 'as such' has built up a lot of jurisprudence under art. 52 of the European Patent Convention and was therefore avoided).[34] The same is true regarding ideas and theories, procedures, methods of operation and mathematical concepts.[35]

Art. 1.2 further excludes from copyright protection official texts of a legislative, administrative and judicial nature, including international treaties, as well as official translations of such texts, although they principally fall within the domain of copyright. As indicated in a footnote, 'official' works by private authors will be protected until they become 'official'. In addition, despite the exclusion, questions of moral rights could still arise.[36]

3.2 Chapter 2: Authorship and Ownership (Arts 2.1–2.6)

Chapter 2 deals with authorship (art. 2.1) and first ownership of moral rights (art. 2.2) as well as of economic rights (art. 2.3). The following provision enshrines the purpose-of-grant-rule (art. 2.4), and ownership of rights in the case of works made in the course of employment (art. 2.5) or on commission (art. 2.6) is defined. Surprisingly, despite the different approaches of civil and common law, the Drafting Committee rather quickly managed to agree on these points.

As a matter of principle, the author of a work is the natural person or group of natural persons who created it (art. 2.1). As regards films a footnote refers to the persons mentioned in art. 2(2) of the Copyright Term Directive.[37]

At the same time, the author enjoys the moral rights, which cannot be assigned (art. 2.2). The author is also the initial owner of the economic rights in a work (art. 2.3(1)), but these rights may be assigned and licensed[38] as well as passed by way of inheritance, in whole or in part, as stated in art. 2.3(2). An assignment is not valid unless it is made in writing (art. 2.3(4)). If the author has assigned economic rights, he shall nonetheless have a right to an adequate part of the remuneration (art. 2.3(3)).

---

34 Footnote 8 to the Code.

35 Inspired by art. 9(2) TRIPS.

36 Footnote 14 to the Code.

37 See footnote 15 to the Code (in which 'shall include' is to be understood in such a way that in individual cases co-authors could be other persons than those mentioned).

38 The term 'assignment' indicates a cession of economic rights; ownership of the rights is transferred to another person (see footnote 16 to the Code). The term 'license' indicates an act of authorization (permission) to use the work (see footnote 17 to the Code).

Art. 2.4 is a provision of contractual nature, borrowed from German law. According to this rule, the extent of a grant shall be determined in accordance with the purpose envisaged in making the grant, if the contract containing the assignment or an exclusive licence does not adequately specify the amount of the authors' remuneration, the geographical scope, mode of exploitation and the duration of the grant.

In accordance with art. 2(3) of the Computer Program Directive, the economic rights in works made in the course of employment are deemed to be assigned to the employer, unless otherwise agreed (art. 2.5). This is a significant difference to certain continental European copyright laws (such as the German Copyright Act). However, it is owed to the efforts towards harmonization throughout Europe. Moreover, different arrangements will probably be made in collective agreements. Anyway, the transfer of rights under art. 2.5 is called an 'assignment', which means that even employed authors retain their claims for remuneration pursuant to art. 2.3.

In contrast, in the case of commissioned works, the use of a work by the commissioner of that work is only authorized to the extent necessary to achieve the purposes for which the commission was evidently made (art. 2.6).

3.3 Chapter 3: Moral Rights (Arts 3.1–3.6)

The moral rights in a work, named in Chapter 3 following a general provision (art. 3.1), are the rights of divulgation (art. 3.2), attribution (art. 3.3) and integrity (art. 3.4). For each of these rights, the term of protection is regulated separately. Chapter 3 is completed by provisions concerning consent (art. 3.5) of the author as well as the interests of third parties (art. 2.6).

The right of divulgation is the right to decide whether and how the work is disclosed for the first time (art. 3.2). The right of attribution comprises the right to be identified as author, including the right to choose the manner of identification, taking into account the constraints resulting from the type of work evolved and the customary practices regarding attribution in his field.[39] In addition, the right of attribution comprises the right, if the author so decides, to remain unidentified (art. 3.3(1)(a)). In addition, the name or title given to the work are to be indicated, if requested by the author (art. 3.3(1)(b)). Contrary to current UK law, the existence of the right of attribution does not depend on any condition, such as claim or assertion by the author.[40] The right of integrity was copied from art. $6^{bis}(1)$ BC.

---

[39] See footnote 24 to the Code.

[40] This has been recognized by Jane Ginsburg, *supra* note 24, p. 4 ('an advance from the point of view of authors' rights, particularly for States, such as the UK, whose adoption of moral rights is both recent and reluctant'), who, however, deplores the lack

It was generally felt by the members of the Wittem Group that not all moral rights merit the same term of protection. The right of divulgation shall last for the life of the author (art. 3.2(2)). It should be noted, however, that general rights of privacy might still prevent unauthorized publication post mortem.[41] In contrast, the rights of attribution and integrity shall last for the life of the author and after his death, though the term is not exactly determined (art. 3.3(2) and 3.4(2)). After the death of the author the legal successor – as defined by the laws on inheritance – shall be entitled to exercise the moral rights. These are either the heirs or persons especially appointed by the author.[42]

The author can consent not to exercise his moral rights (art. 3.5), provided that such consent is limited in scope, unequivocal and informed. General waivers are not possible, but an author may consent to particular uses.[43]

Art. 3.6 is quite a special provision. Following the 'abus de droit' principle, the moral rights will not be enforced in situations where to do so would harm the legitimate interests of third parties (see also, with regard to limitations, art. 5.5) to an extent which is manifestly disproportionate to the interests of the author (art. 3.6(1)). The notion of 'interests of third parties' covers any legitimate interests both of private parties, such as those of publishers, and of the public in accessing the work.[44] After the author's death, the moral rights of attribution and integrity shall only be exercised in a manner that takes into account the interests in protecting the person of the deceased author, as well as the legitimate interests of third parties (art. 3.6(2)).

3.4 Chapter 4: Economic Rights (Arts 4.1–4.6)

After a general provision which also deals with the duration of the economic rights (art. 4.1), Chapter 4 contains the exclusive reproduction (art. 4.2), distribution (art. 4.3), rental (art. 4.4) and communication to the public (art. 4.5) rights as well as the adaptation right (art. 4.6). The list of economic rights as such is exhaustive ('closed'), with the right of 'communication to the public' being an open concept.[45] All the rights relate to protected works in whole or in part, provided the part qualifies, in and by itself, for copyright protection.

---

of a firm stance on the authors' rights position ('[o]n the other hand, the drafters appear, consciously or not, to have rejected the *jus naturalis* conception of copyright that animates many Continental European national laws and that underlies moral rights').

41 See footnotes 22 and 25 to the Code.

42 See footnote 26 to the Code.

43 For further explanations see footnotes 28–33 to the Code.

44 See footnote 34 to the Code. Critically, however, Jane Ginsburg, *supra* note 24, p. 15 ('a curious provision').

45 See footnote 37 to the Code.

The phrase 'in whole or in part' implies at the same time what constitutes an infringement.[46]

The economic rights expire at a time after the author's death. However, the Code does not state an exact duration (art. 4.1(2)). However, a footnote expresses the Drafting Committee's general feeling that the current term of protection of the economic rights expiring 70 years after the author's death is too long.[47]

The right of reproduction is defined in a way such as to absorb, from the outset, the limitation contained in art. 5(1) InfoSoc Directive. Hence, of the temporary reproductions only those are considered 'reproductions' within the meaning of the Code which have independent economic significance independent from a permitted use (i.e. permitted either by law or authorized by the rightholder, art. 4.2).[48] The right of distribution including the rule of exhaustion (arts 4.3(1) and (2)) is only described in its basic structure and it contains – in contrast to art. 4(1) InfoSoc Directive – neither a definition, nor further details as formulated by the case law of the ECJ. A footnote clarifies that the rule of exhaustion has to be interpreted coherently with the same concept in the law of industrial property.[49] The right of rental follows the Rental Directive and, just as the Directive, does not extend to the rental of buildings and works of applied art (art. 4.4). The right of communication to the public is divided into three main categories, including but not limited to public performance, broadcasting (including rebroadcasting and retransmitting, by wireless and wired (cable) means),[50] and making available to the public (art. 4.5(1)). A communication of a work shall be deemed to be to the public if it is intended for a plurality of persons, unless such persons are connected by personal relationship (art. 4.5(2)). The right of adaptation is formulated as an economic right of its own, circumscribed as the right to adapt, translate, arrange or otherwise alter the work (art. 4.6).

3.5 Chapter 5: Limitations (Arts 5.1–5.8)

3.5.1 Technical and policy approach

Chapter 5 of the 'European Copyright Code' concerning limitations is the most expansive Chapter and the one which differs most from the '*acquis communautaire*'. The Wittem Group placed great emphasis first on combing through and consolidating the historically grown limitations which had been rather

46 See footnote 39 to the Code.
47 See footnote 40 to the Code.
48 For critique see Jane Ginsburg, *supra* note 24, pp. 17 *et seq.*
49 See footnote 44 to the Code.
50 See footnote 47 to the Code.

randomly arranged in the InfoSoc Directive, and on completing them and arranging them in a reasonable order. Second, since the exclusive rights are broadly defined so that the main focus of balancing the protection interest with access and use interests[51] rests with the limitations, an appropriate balance had to be reflected in the drafting of the limitations.[52]

Thus, all limitations – not only a selection of the limitations – listed in art. 5 of the InfoSoc Directive have been reassembled in the 'European Copyright Code', including the limitations provided for in the Software Directive. To the extent necessary, the respective legislative texts have been reformulated and adapted to current media practices. Unlike the Directive, the Code does not aim at particular types of use (with the exception of reproduction for private use), but covers 'uses' in general. Consequently, the Code does not distinguish between analogue and digital uses. However, a footnote clarifies that the different intensity of use inherent in analogue and digital use may have relevance for the amount of remuneration to which the authors are entitled.[53] The reason why the Code incorporates all of the limitations listed in the InfoSoc Directive is justified by the fact that the European legislature has already accepted them. Moreover, in the opinion of the Drafting Committee, it was not quite clear whether a particular use should be covered by an exclusive right or fall under a limitation, in case of doubt, such a use should not require authorization but rather give rise to a claim for remuneration only. The reason is that in these constellations third parties and the public often have significant interests regarding access, whereas the authors' interests to participate in the proceeds generated by the use of the copyrighted works generally supersedes the authors' control interest.[54] The Code therefore distinguishes between uses

---

[51] For this tripolar approach (author, rightholder, user) see, for example, R. Hilty (2005), 'Vergütungssystem und Schrankenregelungen. Neue Herausforderungen an den Gesetzgeber', *GRUR*, 819, 820; C. Geiger (2004), 'Droit d'auteur et droit du public à l'information: approche de droit comparé', Droit des affaires, propriété intellectuelle, Vol. 25, No. 19–97, Paris: Litec; and for a quadrupolar diversification of the interests in play (author, rightholder, competitor, user) T. Dreier (2007), 'Regulating Competition by way of Copyright Limitations and Exceptions', in P. Torremans (ed.), *Copyright Law – A Handbook of Contemporary Research,* Cheltenham, UK and Northampton, MA: Edwar Elgar Publishing, 232. Critically, however, Jane Ginsburg, *supra* note 24, p. 4. ('"balance" often seems to resemble a coded version of "cutting back on exclusive rights" or "more baldly" "users' rights"').

[52] Critically as regards the balance struck in view of the three-step test, however, Jane Ginsburg *supra* note 24, p. 22 ('Examination of the scope of these exceptions suggests that assumption may not always be correct').

[53] See footnote 49 to the Code.

[54] For the interpretation of the three-step test under art. 13 TRIPS see the Declaration on the Three-Step Test, which can be found under http://www.ip.mpg.de/ww/en/pub/news/declaration_on_the_three_step_.cfm.

permitted without authorization and remuneration and such uses, which are permitted without authorization, but which are subject to remuneration.

Structurally, the Code then distinguished limitations with regard to their (primary) purpose defining limitations with regard to uses with minimal economic significance (art. 5.1), uses for the purpose of freedom of expression and information (art. 5.2), uses permitted to promote social, political and cultural objectives (art. 5.3) and uses for the purpose of enhancing competition (art. 5.4). Arts 5.1–5.4(1) to a large extent correspond with the limitations listed in art. 5 InfoSoc Directive, including some special provisions which originate from other directives, and also takes into account the jurisdiction of the ECJ. In contrast, the limitation for the purpose of enhancing competition contained in art. 5.4(2) is an innovative proposal. As another specialty, the Code exempts additional uses comparable to the uses enumerated in arts 5.1–5.4(1), provided a certain analogy can be established and that the conditions of the three-step test are met. It should be noted in this respect that in balancing the interests at the third step, the legitimate interests of both the author or rightholder and of third parties and the public shall be taken into consideration (art. 5.5). To the extent that uses are only permitted against remuneration, the claim for remuneration has to be exercised by a collecting society (art. 5.7(2)). In some cases, the compulsory licensing fee can also be negotiated individually. Furthermore, the relationship between uses permitted under Chapter 5 and moral rights (art. 5.6), as well as technical protection measures (5.8), was clarified.

3.5.2 Limitations in detail

According to art. 5.1, *uses with* no or at most *minimal economic significance* are: the making of back-up copies; the incidental inclusion of a work in other materials; and the use in connection with the demonstration or repair of equipment.

According to art. 5.2, *uses for the purpose of freedom of expression and information* cover: the use of a work for the purpose of the reporting of contemporary events; the use of published articles on current economic, political or religious topics or of similar works broadcast by the media;[55] the use of works of architecture or sculpture, made to be located permanently in public places; the use by way of quotation of lawfully disclosed works; as well as the use for the purpose of caricature, parody or pastiche (art. 5.2(1)). As clarified in a footnote, it may in certain cases be permitted to quote the entire work, although quotations normally will only imply partial use of a work.[56] While

[55] The limitations of the enumeration go back to art. 5.3(c) InfoSoc Directive and to art. 10 BC.

[56] See footnote 50 to the Code.

these uses are not subject to remuneration, the use of single articles for purposes of internal reporting within an organization (art. 5.2(a)) and the use for purposes of scientific research (art. 5.2(b)) are only permitted against payment of remuneration. This is a compromise, because, on the one hand, one could have excluded certain uses for scientific purposes in a more extensive way from the duty to pay remuneration.[57] On the other hand, the suggested solution already limits the space for business models on a contractual basis and it already goes beyond the existing privileges of uses in the field of science and research. It should be noted in this respect that the scope of each use permitted is limited by its particular purpose. At the same time, it has to be remembered that the claim for remuneration can only be exercised by a collecting society (as stated in art. 5.7 (2)), so that the provision anyway should not interfere with normal market development. If there should be a market failure in the form of lack of competition, art. 5.4(2) provides the appropriate remedy.

Feeling obliged to *promote social, political and cultural objectives*, the Code exempts use acts such as: the use for the benefit of persons with a disability, which is directly related to the disability and of a non-commercial nature; the use to ensure the proper performance of administrative, parliamentary or judicial proceedings or public security; and the use for the purpose of non-commercial archiving by publicly accessible libraries, educational establishments or museums and archives (art. 5.3(1)). It is understood that the exception only covers reproductions made in order to preserve documents, but not any subsequent commercial exploitation of the works that have been archived.[58]

While the aforementioned uses are permitted without remuneration, an appropriate remuneration is due for the uses covered by art. 5.3(2), i.e. for the reproduction by a natural person for private use – provided that the source from which the reproduction is made is not an obviously infringing copy – on the one hand, and the use for educational purposes on the other. It has been criticized by some commentators that art. 5.3 does not also privilege 'transformative use'.[59] The Code does indeed not, but it should be kept in mind that in defining the right of adaptation in art. 4.6, the Code refrains from being specific with regard to the exact boundary between adaptations subject to authorization and modifications of copyrighted works which may qualify as free use.

57 As demanded by Kuhlen, *supra*, note 24, p. 22, para. 26.
58 See footnote 52 to the Code.
59 Kuhlen, *supra* note 24, p. 20, para 13.

For the purpose of enhancing competition art. 5.4(1) contains two limitations, one of which is already codified in an EU directive and one which has been developed by the ECJ. The limitation allowing use for the purpose of reverse engineering in order to obtain access to information, by a person entitled to use the work is borrowed from the Computer Program Directive, and the limitation regarding use for the purpose of advertising public exhibitions or sales of artistic works or goods which have been lawfully put on the market has been taken from the *Evora* case.[60] Both uses are also permitted without remuneration.

Art. 5.4(2) is a novelty and aims to ensure competition in the field of information products and services for news articles, scientific works, industrial designs, computer programs and databases, provided that the owner of the copyright in the work has refused to license the use on reasonable terms, leading to the elimination of competition in the relevant market and the use does not unreasonably prejudice the legitimate interests of the owner of the copyright in the work. As such, art. 5.4(2) includes control criteria which have been drawn from antitrust law into copyright law. Not surprisingly, this proposal has already met with criticism in traditional copyright literature, which understands copyright not as a regulatory framework which balances the interests of all parties involved, but rather as a law whose purpose is to endow authors with the competitive advantage that exclusive rights confer. From this perspective, the incorporation of 'competition' limitations into copyright must indeed be seen as fundamentally incoherent.[61] However, the reason why the drafters of the Code have adopted art. 5.4(2) is that it seems appropriate to exercise not only an ex post control when competition has already been affected or even eliminated at the expense of competitors and consumers. Of course, notwithstanding its advantages, any ex ante control can only be based on a prognosis of future market development which always bears the risk of being uncertain. Since it is the purpose of art. 5.4(2) to safeguard competition, uses made under this provision give rise to payment of a remuneration, which – contrary to most other limitations of the Code – has to be negotiated by the parties concerned in each individual case and cannot be claimed by collecting societies.

Finally, according to art. 5.5 other use that is comparable to the uses enumerated in arts. 5.1 to 5.4(1) is also permitted,[62] provided that the use

---

60 Case C-337/95 *Dior v Evora* [1997] ECJ I-6013. Footnote 53 to the Code clarifies that the means of advertising should be normal and proportionate for the business.

61 Jane Ginsburg, *supra* note 24, p. 25.

62 In this regard, only an analogy to the limitation for purposes of enhancing competition which is already precisely defined in art. 5.4(2) is excluded.

remains within the framework of the three-step test, considering the legitimate interests of the author or rightholder and taking account of the legitimate interests of third parties. This means that the interests mentioned in arts 17, 30, but not in art. 13 TRIPS have to be considered as well. The limitations explicitly named serve as points of reference in view of the comparability and are of a normative nature.[63] A footnote clarifies that art. 5.5 does not allow new limitations by blending the criteria of arts 5.1 to 5.3.[64] This combination of the continental European approach and the British model ensures a flexibility missing in the InfoSoc Directive, which is often called for in literature and which, in the opinion of the Drafting Committee, is needed in view of the unpredictable technical and economic development. At the same time, recourse to the rather non-specific criteria of the US-American fair use doctrine has been avoided. Of course, some legal uncertainty remains which, however, was accepted in view of the increase in flexibility that has been gained. This provision gave rise to two critical remarks in legal literature. Firstly, it has been questioned whether analogue exceptions could be subjected to the three-step test, if they are based on fundamental rights.[65] However, in this regard the positive function of the criteria of the three-step test in art. 5.5 might be pointed out. Contrary to the classical three-step test which has the function to *limit* the scope of permissible exceptions, in the context of art. 5.5 the same criteria define the *outer* limits of what is permissible as an exception to the exclusive rights. Of course, this turn into a positive reading of the criteria seems to describe the same line of delimitation, but the change in perspective probably results in a change of the burden of proof.[66] Secondly, it has been criticized that although the flexibility is to be welcomed in principle, the provision will nonetheless be of limited use, since it is obviously directed at the legislature.[67] However, this is only true if the Code is regarded as the basis for further harmonization measures. But if the Code is regarded as a blueprint

---

63 See footnote 48 to the Code with further details.

64 See footnote 55 to the Code.

65 P.E. Geller (2010), 'A German Approach to Fair Use – Test Cases for TRIPS Criteria for Copyright Limitations?', *J.Cop.Soc.* **57**, 901, 914 et seq.

66 See also R. Hilty (2010), 'Declaration on the "Three-Step Test". Where do we go from here?', 2 *JIPITEC* **2**, 84, para. 13, available at www.jipitec.eu/issues/jipitec-1-2-2010/2614/JIPITEC%202%20-%20Hilty-Declaration-Three-Step-Test.pdf ('The charming thing about this opening clause is that it does to some extent turn the Three-Step Test into a positive reading'). J. Griffiths (2010), 'Unsticking the Centrepiece – the Liberation of European Copyright Law?', *JIPITEC* **2**, 87, 90, para. 18, available at www.jipitec.eu/issues/jipitec-1-2-2010/2617/JIPITEC%202%20-%20Griffiths-Unsticking.pdf, however, is sceptical whether the turn into a positive reading is in accordance with international law and, consequently, prefers a model following the US fair use doctrine.

67 Jonathan Griffiths, *supra* note 66, p. 89, para. 14.

for national legislature or European regulation – as the Drafting Committee had hoped – then art. 5.5 is directed at the courts[68] and gives them the opportunity to respond flexibly to rapidly changing circumstances and needs.

Arts. 5.1, 5.2(1), 5.3(1), 5.4(1) define uses which are permitted without remuneration. In contrast, uses according to arts. 5.2(2), 5.3(2), 5.4(2) are only permitted against payment of remuneration. In other words, apart from the uses with minimal economic significance, constantly permitted without authorization and without remuneration, it was decided for each other purpose whether an obligation to pay remuneration seems appropriate or not. This decision depends on the intensity of the intervention as weighed against the author's participation interest and the user's interest in access. Any remuneration provided for shall be fair and adequate, art. 5.7 (1). While no distinction of analogue and digital use acts shall be made with regard to the question of the permission of the use act as such, it seems appropriate that the amount of remuneration depends on the economic significance of the use act. If the use is made by a third party on behalf of beneficiaries of the limitations, the remuneration to be paid might be higher than if it is made by the privileged individual itself, since competition is affected by such uses.[69]

As stated in art. 5.7(2), a claim for remuneration according to arts. 5.2(2) and 5.3(2) can only be exercised by a collecting society, whereas the compulsory licensing fee arising from art. 5.4(2) shall be negotiated by the parties involved in each individual case.[70]

Furthermore, as stated in art. 5.6 uses pursuant to the limitations under Chapter 5 do not affect the author's moral rights. This fully applies to the right of divulgation. It applies to the right of attribution, unless such attribution is not reasonably possible, and, as regards the right of integrity, unless the applicable limitation allows for such an alteration or the alteration is reasonably due to the technique of reproduction or communication applied by the use.

According to art. 5.8, rightholders, who control the use of copyright protected works by technical measures, are under an obligation to make available to the beneficiaries of the limitation means of benefiting from the uses, on the condition that: (a) the beneficiary of the limitation has lawful access to the protected work; (b) the use of the work is not possible to the extent necessary to benefit from the limitation concerned; and (c) the rightholder is not prevented from adopting adequate measures regarding the number of reproductions that can be made. The uses mentioned in art. 5.3(2)(a) for the benefit of persons with a disability remain unaffected.

---

68 See also Kuhlen, *supra* note 24, p. 21, para. 22.

69 Footnotes 49 and 57 to the Code.

70 Footnote 54 to the Code.

6. OUTLOOK

Finally, it should be noted that although the outcome of the Wittem project has been formulated as a 'Code', the authors do not take a position on whether and to what extent a homogenous legal framework seems to be desirable at the European level. In the opinion of the authors, the Code could serve as a model for a future Community copyright, but the drafters did not take a position on the desirability of introducing a unified European framework.[71] This indecisiveness has been subject of criticism in literature.[72]

However, at the present time, two arguments can be pointed out in favour of the approach taken. Firstly, formulating substantive law rules is without prejudice to the question whether the further harmonization process should be just influenced or whether a truly unified European copyright regime should be designed. In any case, the thoughts and ideas contained in the Wittem Code should not only be considered if a Community copyright will be created. Already, it would be quite a success, if the results of the Wittem project entered the harmonization process. Secondly, the question whether homogenous rules in the Member States must effectively result in a unified law at European level requires further consideration beyond what was discussed in the process of drawing up the 'European Copyright Code' and to which the Code therefore takes no position. In this respect, the first issue to be decided is whether or not, and if so to what extent, a Community copyright should replace national copyright legislation.[73] Furthermore, it is not to be forgotten that due to language borders current exploitation of copyright protected works, especially by publishers and broadcasters, is more often than not confined to the territories of individual Member States if it does not take place at the regional level altogether. This raises the additional question whether the European legal framework should reflect existing market conditions or rather define the aim to be achieved in terms of completing the internal market. At any rate, as demonstrated by the discussion of the Services Directive,[74] a simple reference to the concept of the internal market as laid down in the EU Treaties,[75] is not by itself a complete answer to the question.

---

[71] See section 2 of the Code's introduction.

[72] A critical position is taken by Kuhlen, *supra* note 24, p. 19, para. 7 ('difficult to understand').

[73] The latter was, in particular, suggested by Reto Hilty, 'Declaration on the "Three-Step Test" Where do we go from here?' *supra* note 66.

[74] European Parliament and Council Directive 2006/123/EC of 12 December 2006 on services in the internal market [2006] OJ L 376/36.

[75] See, however, Schack, *supra* note 8, pp. 275, 280 ('logic of the internal market'; 'in a unified economic area monopoly rights with regard to intellectual goods have to be defined uniformly, in order to enable smooth transborder use').

As the result of several years of work of the Wittem Group, the 'European Copyright Code' will hopefully contribute at both the national and the European – and perhaps even the international – level to the discussion on and the creation of a transparent and consistent copyright legislation, which protects the interests of the authors in the same fair and balanced way as it takes into consideration those of the general public.

14. Consume and share: making copyright fit for the digital agenda*

Marco Ricolfi

1. WHAT ARE WE TALKING ABOUT?

As it often happens, the title of my chapter has an ambiguous ring to it. Are we trying to figure out which set of specific changes in copyright legislation would help in achieving the targets set by the specific policy document released by the EU Commission last year;[1] or are we supposed to deal with a broad new vision of the role of copyright intended to foster the generation and dissemination of creativity in the new digital environment? Are we talking about EU Directives or the Berne Convention; about short term or medium term?

Well, perhaps the two dimensions, different as they are, may go hand in hand. It stands to reason that a few ideas about the future – what could and indeed should happen in the next five or ten years or so – may also help us in transacting the business of today and of tomorrow. So let me start from the broader picture and come back to questions of more immediate concern in the final remarks.[2]

1 European Commission, Communication from the Commission to the European Parliament, the Council, the European Economic and Social Committee and the Committee of the Regions, A Digital Agenda for Europe, Brussels, 19 May 2010 COM (2010) 245.

2 In sketching out the broader picture, I draw on the final section of my paper *Copyright Policies for Digital Libraries in the Context of the i2010 Strategy*, presented at the 1st COMMUNIA Conference, Louvain-la-Neuve, Belgium (1 July 2008), available at http://www.communia-project.eu/node/110.

2. CREATORS AND THEIR PUBLIC: FROM THE LONG ROUTE TO THE SHORT ROUTE

The case is often made that copyright, as we have known it for three centuries, which after all is a brief parenthesis in the *longue durée* of the millennial history of information technology, may no longer be an appropriate tool for the needs of creators and society in a digital environment.

What is the basis for this – arguably bold, but also quite widespread[3] – argument? The reply is quite straightforward: in the last two decades or so, the social and technological basis of creation has been radically transformed.

The time has come for us to finally become aware that in our post-post-industrial age, the long route which used to lead the work from its creator to the public by passing through different categories of businesses is gradually being replaced by a short route, which puts in direct contact creators and the public. This development may be sketched as follows.[4]

1. In the analogue word, direct access to the market by creators was confined to a very limited number of very special cases.[5] Otherwise, it could be taken for granted that the intermediation of business was necessary to

---

[3] *See* L. Lessig (2008), *Remix. Making Art and Commerce Thrive in the Hybrid Economy*, New York: The Penguin Press; V. Grassmuck (2009), 'The World is Going Flat(-Rate): A Study Showing Copyright Exception for Legalizing File-Sharing Feasible as a Cease-Fire in the "War on Copyright" Emerges', *Intellectual Property Watch*, 11 May, http://www.ip -watch.org/weblog/2009/05/11/the-world-is-going-flat-rate accessed 12 May 2009; P. Aigrain (2008), *Internet & Création: Comment Reconnaître les Échanges sur Internet en Finançant la Création*, Cergy-Pontoise: Éditions In LibroVeritas; Y. Benkler (2004), 'Sharing Nicely: On Shareable Goods and the Emergence of Sharing as a Modality of Economic Production', *Yale L.J.*, **114**, 272. A very open minded approach is also advocated by the speech made by WIPO's Director General F. Gurry, *The Future of Copyright*, Sydney, 25 February 2011, available at http://www.wipo.int/about-wipo/en/dgo/speeches/dg_blueskyconf_11.html, accessed 2 March 2011. A theoretical framework to the re-orientation of the assessment of the rules concerning information products is arguably provided by the literature devoted to common pool resources and more specifically to its extension to knowledge and information commons: *see* in this connection C. Hess and E. Ostrom (2007), 'Introduction: An Overview of the Knowledge Commons', in C. Hess and E. Ostrom (eds), *Understanding Knowledge as a Commons. From Theory to Practice*, Cambridge and London: MIT Press, 3 ff.

[4] For additional references *see* M. Ricolfi (2008), 'Individual and Collective Management of Copyright in a Digital Environment', in P. Torremans (ed.), *Copyright Law. A Handbook of Contemporary Research*, Cheltenham, UK and Northampton, MA: Edward Elgar, 282, 285 ff. and 308 ff.

[5] Such as the bohemian painter personally seeking out patrons to sell his paintings or the wandering gipsy carrying around his violin.

bring works from creators to markets. In particular, books and records needed to be printed. For this purpose some kind of 'factory' was required, to manufacture what in effect were fixed, stable, material or – as the expression now goes – 'hard' copies of the work. In turn, these hard copies needed to be stored, transported, and distributed, before reaching the shelves where the public would finally find them.

It was difficult for creators to engage in all these steps; and this is why, as a rule, they preferred to resort to businesses to set up the characteristic trilateral relationship between creator, business and the public, which is typical of primary exploitation of copyrighted works.[6] The kind of business which appeared indispensable for this purpose had features which the last two centuries made familiar. To begin with, it had to make substantial outlays to figure out whether there was a market for the work; then again it had to invest and take large risks for the mass production of material copies of works and for their distribution; and this on a scale which increased in step with the extension of the markets. Publishers, Hollywood and the record labels are appropriate cases in point. Radio and TV came in to take care of so called 'secondary' utilization of work.

In all these regards, it certainly can be said that this was a quite long route to institute a contact between the creator and the public; and that business was a very valuable, indeed indispensable intermediary to achieve such a goal.

2. In the digital environment all this dramatically changes. On the production side, perfect digital copies make 'factories' of physical, material copies of works redundant, at least in principle.[7] What is especially remarkable is that this same development is now reaching the movie industry. Until recently this sector of the entertainment business appeared to be the last bulwark in which capital intensive business could be considered really indispensable. But this is becoming less and less true as each day passes. Jean Cocteau predicted that the tools required for the creation

---

6 *See* in this connection W.R. Cornish (1996), *Intellectual Property: Patents, Copyright, Trade Marks and Allied Rights,* London, Sweet & Maxwell, 401.

7 It may be argued that this is true only for additional copies, the ones which can be costlessly multiplied after what we could call the initial embodiment, the prototype or the 'master' has been first created; and to this it may be added that for the latter the required investment still is huge. This objection has indeed been raised a number of times (e.g. by P. Auteri (2006), 'Diritti d'autore, nuove tecnologie e Digital Rights Management', in M.L. Montagnani, M. Borghi (eds), *Proprietà digitale: diritti d'autore, nuove tecnologie e Digital Rights Management,* Milano: Egea, 23 ff); but the case becomes less and less defensible as the time passes. The role of software and of digital technology in the creation and initial fixation of music is increasing all the time, and their cost is decreasing in parallel.

of a movie would at some point in time become as cheap as paper and pencil; and digital technology may still prove his vision right.[8]

On the distribution side a similar – possibly less visible, but certainly even more striking – process is taking place. This is so because digital goods, which are distributed through the net, are light rather than heavy, and use up a limited amount of storage space. But even more so because the technological endowment held by the public at the receiving end has in the meantime deeply changed. Even in the past the end user had to make an investment in different kinds of technology, by purchasing a radio or a TV set, a record player or a tape recorder. The novel feature is that since the beginning of the digital age the scale of a minimum unit of the technological endowment at the receiving end – e.g. the memory of a PC – has started to be largely in excess of the average needs of the consumer;[9] and as a rule each unit is interoperable with all the others. A similar analysis can be reiterated in connection with file-sharing. Whatever legal assessment we may pass of this practice, its ultimate technological ramifications cannot be revoked in doubt.[10] Here we have enormous excess capacity residing with the public at large at the receiving end; and this excess capacity can be mobilized to create distributive networks of extraordinary scale, scope and effectiveness.

3. In this novel context, it would seem that the setting up of a relationship between creator and business no longer has the same compelling rationale as it used to have in the past. Digital copies are (nearly) perfect; and can be duplicated at no cost at the receiving end. Therefore, in a number of situations both the 'factory' and the physical distribution chain are no longer indispensable.[11] It appears therefore that creators can more and more often access markets without engaging in the trilateral relationship, which used to be characteristic of dealings in copyright. Indeed, these technological determinants enable creators to make works directly available to the public. It is even more remarkable that an increasingly large

---

8 For starters *see* on Open Source Cinema http://en.wikipedia.org/wiki/Open_Source_Cinema, accessed 23 February 2011.

9 As noted by Benkler, *supra* note 3, 277.

10 As indeed aptly described by the decision of the US Supreme Court of 27 June 2005, *Metro-Goldwin-Mayer Studios Inc. et al. v Grockster, Ltd. et al.*, 125 S. Ct. 2764 (2005). On the potential for distribution offered by open spectrum access *see* L. Lessig (2001), *The Future of Ideas. The Fate of Commons in a Connected World,* New York: Vintage Books, Random House, 78 ff, 218 ff, 240.

11 Both developments had been anticipated a number of years ago: *see* E. Volokh (1995), 'Cheap Speech and What it Will Do', *Yale L.J.*, **104**, 1805. and I. De Sola Pool (1983), *Technologies of Freedom,* Cambridge, MA and London, UK: The Belknap Press of Harvard University Press, 249–51.

number of members of the public itself are in turn grabbing the opportunity, offered by the technology available at the receiving end, and transform themselves into producers and distributors of works.

To cut a long story short: both the production and distribution functions migrate from business to the public and there they can rely on excess of resources available at each consumption unit. These, if individually of small scale, may be multiplied by very large numbers to provide almost infinite manufacturing and distribution capacity in a way that dwarfs past industry's investments and makes them to a large extent redundant.[12]

The stage scenario is indeed changing. Social sharing enters; business recedes. As a result, the long route from creators to the public may at some point become much shorter; and this is happening more and more all the time. Today creators set up their own sites and make books and music directly accessible to the public therefrom.[13] Currently, user generated content and social networks are growing exponentially:[14] creators and public are finally merging into each other.

3. THE THREE REQUIREMENTS FOR A LEGISLATIVE AGENDA FOR THE DIGITAL ENVIRONMENT

What are the implications of this upheaval for the legislative agenda? Of course, we do not know much about the future. So much is changing all the time and so quickly, that it is impossible to make predictions. Nevertheless, we can anticipate with some confidence that, in the future, production and distribution of works will continue to originate from two different segments: the

[12] It may be questioned whether cloud computing (on which *see* J. Zittrain, *Lost in the Cloud*, in *NY Times*, 20 July 2009; at the EU level Expert Group Report, *The Future of Cloud Computing*, in http://cordis.europa.eu/fp7/ict/ssai/docs/cloud-report-final.pdf) reinforces or calls in question the direction of this process: software-as-a-service, infrastructure-as-a-service and platform-as-a-service slim down the amount of technology which both businesses and the public require in order to generate and access content; and possibly announce the emergence of a new generation of powerful intermediaries.

[13] On the early beginnings of the phenomenon, when Stephen King set up a site to allow readers to download his latest short story, 'Riding the Bullet', at $ 2.50 per download, *see* J. Epstein (2000), 'The Rattle of Pebbles', *The New York Review of Books*, 27 April, 55, 57–8.

[14] For an early appraisal *see* Pew Internet & American Life Project, Home Broadband Adoption 2006, 28 May 2006, available at: http://www.pewinternet.org/~/media//Files/Reports/2006/PIP_Broadband_trends2006.pdf.pdf (accessed 14 May 2012).

one based on business and markets and the other – on the production and distribution mode which is based on decentralized non-market decisions, often referred to as 'social sharing'. The latter segment, currently encompassing creations which go from the open content made available by Wikipedia and Wikis, from free music and pictures to blogs plus the massive volumes of user-generated content not ascribable to these genres but still proceeding along the 'short route' I just sketched out, will exponentially grow, dwarfing the market segment based on the 'long route'; and the two components of creativity will not be mutually exclusive but will interact.

This is why any agenda for lawmaking for the digital environment should meet at least three requirements.

First, the agenda should incorporate rules which are appropriate not only for the long route but also for the short route.[15]

Second, it should allow for the 'peaceful coexistence' of the two sets of rules, making them interoperable, in such a way that the continued existence and specific contribution of the two sectors is maximized.

Third, obstacles inherited by the past, which unduly inhibit the emergence of the short route, should be gradually phased out in ways which should minimize the disruption of the workings of the old route.

4. COPYRIGHT 2.0: INTERESTS AND RULES

Against this background, let us think for a moment about the set of rules which would appear to be appropriate to meet the demands of creators operating along the short route.

4.1 The Interests

In the market based model it was essential for creators and even more so for businesses to control and restrict access to works, as the monopoly granted by expansive exclusive rights enabled them to charge whatever price the market would bear. However, this would not appear to be the goal of creators currently operating along the short route. The great majority of them, be it 9

[15] A similar idea would appear to be shared by proponents of 'dual', 'hybrid' or 'bipolar' systems of protection which have been cropping up in the recent past. *See* C. Geiger (2011), 'Promoting Creativity through Copyright Limitations: Reflections on the Concept of Exclusivity in Copyright Law', *Vanderbilt J. of Ent. and Tech. Law*, **12**, 515 and A. Peukert (2005), 'A Bipolar Copyright System for the Digital Networks Environment', *Hastings Comm. & Ent. L.J.*, **28**, 1. For a theoretical frame of reference *see* Hess and Ostrom, *supra* note 3.

out of 10 or 95 out of 100, do not make a living out of 'sales' of 'copies' of their works; they earn their livelihood in another activity or business and devote a portion – often a very large portion – of their spare time to creating, in a way which may give them a bit of extra income, professional credit and recognition which may have positive spill-over effects in their main line; or just fun (or a combination of the three). Even when the creators operating along the short route are professionally engaged in the creation of works, which is usually not the case, their business model usually is based on income flows different from the sale of copies as such. It would appear that there is a shift whereby even singers and songwriters increasingly rely on performances, tours, endorsements, merchandising and their likes[16] rather than sales of albums and tracks.

This is the business model which the Grateful Dead pioneered, possibly taking a clue from open source software and IBM, and is currently expanding to an increasing number of businesses. So that the eminent economist Paul Krugmann, a few years ago, made the case that the demise of reliance on income based on 'hard' copies was being generalized and, making his case, quipped that in the long run we will all be the Grateful Dead.[17] What is important for creators engaged along the short route is, it would appear, that their work can be disseminated as widely as possible, on two conditions: first, that the work is correctly attributed to them, and second, that the creators may, if they so choose, reserve the right to prevent third parties from making a commercial profit out of their work unless this is agreed to by the creator herself.

4.2 The Rules

If this is so, then what may currently be needed is a new kind of copyright, which we may, if you wish, label Copyright 2.0. I submit that the new system would have four basic features. Old copyright, or Copyright 1.0, would still be available, but it would have to be claimed for by the creator at the onset, e.g. by inserting the old copyright notice, ©, as the US did in the past, before its

16 Including revenue from product placement embedded in virally disseminated video clips (as magisterially shown by Lady Gaga).

17 P. Krugman, 'Bits, Band and Books', *New York Times*, 6 June 2008. This trend seems confirmed by the current behaviour of 'traditional' businesses, which are indeed seeking to obtain a share of these novel income streams: *see* J. Gapper, 'The music labels can take a punch', *Financial Times*, 3 July 2008, noting that labels have started 'to get a slice of the action from the artists' other earnings, including live performances and merchandising'. Accordingly, 'Universal is taking a share of touring and merchandise revenue in 90 per cent of contracts it signs with new artists'.

adhesion to the Berne Convention.[18] If no notice was given, Copyright 2.0 would apply, and this would give creators just one right, the right to attribution. The notice could also be added after creation, but then it would only have the effect of giving exclusivity against specified non-authorized uses (in particular: subsequent commercial uses). The Copyright 1.0 protection given by the original notice could be withdrawn, and may be it should be deemed withdrawn after a specified period of time (e.g. the 14 years of the original copyright protection), unless an extension period (of another 14 years) is specifically requested.

What is the purpose of the exercise I just sketched out? Well, I confess that, even a couple of years after airing this proposal, I am not so totally sure after all that the four features I just described are really what is appropriate for the needs of our societies and their creators.

The point I am making, however, is that thinking along these lines at least allows us to conceptualize how the different sets of rules correspond to the specific needs of the creators who create works along the long and short route. We assumed that Copyright 1.0 should survive; and we may anticipate that this is likely to be resorted to by creators (and businesses) choosing to operate along the long route. Indeed, the ultimate goal is not to displace old copyright, which seems to be alive and well in many situations, but to add to the menu a second possibility, Copyright 2.0, which should be better tailored to the characters of production and distribution of works prevailing in the current digital environment.

This line of reasoning might also help us in asking the next question. Which set of rules would then operate in each given situation? Well, in some way I already replied to this question: creators should opt in for Copyright 1.0 at the time of the original release of their work; otherwise the new and more flexible Copyright 2.0 would operate as a default set of provisions. This is why in the

---

[18] The question of 're-formalizing' copyright has come back to discussion in recent times: *see* S. van Gompel (2010), 'Formalities in the Digital Era: an Obstacle or Opportunity?', in L. Bently, U. Suthersanen and P. Torremans (eds), *Global Copyright. Three Hundred Years since the Statute of Anne, from 1709 to Cyberspace*, Cheltenham, UK and Northampton, MA: Edward Elgar, 395 ff. and C. Sprigman (2004), 'Reform(aliz)ing Copyright', *Stan. L. Rev.*, **57**, 485. The idea of a copyright notice is being upgraded into the notion of global copyright registries: today registration may become a precondition for protection, as state-of-the art technology enables the creation of global digital repositories, giving security on the integrity of the digital files embodying works and on the identity of the person or entity claiming copyright and makes the corresponding filings user-friendly and inexpensive. If one were to consider that making registration into a global registry, rather than notice, a precondition for protection is too harsh a requirement, then registration might at least be required as a precondition of *extension* of protection.

past I characterized this approach as 'Lessig by default' or, in a less personalized way, 'Creative Commons by default'. The idea behind the approach is that the very successful uptake of Creative Commons licences and other copyleft licences by creators operating along the short route[19] shows that out there, in the digital prairies and wilderness, is a very large number indeed of creators who prefer to reserve only some rights rather than all rights; and that the time has come for legal systems to recognize this fact of life by creating a regime in which downstream freedom is the rule and a system under which creators may have the option to reserve some rights or, if they like, all the old Copyright 1.0 rights, only if they wish and say so, giving appropriate notice.

5. THE NEW INTERNATIONAL FRAMEWORK AND THE ROLE OF THE EU

Of course, to go this way, one would have to change hundreds of laws and a few international conventions (including the Berne and TRIPs).[20] I do not know that this is impossible. I am among those who, at the beginning of the digital age, insisted that it was too early to legislate. In my opinion, however, the time has now come. It is for you to decide whether this is an impossibility, a dream or, may be, a vision. What I know is that the present time – and the present place – is the best to discuss this.

Let me also remark that the EU should take the lead in this regard, for a variety of reasons. First, because it has the legitimacy and the prestige to do it. The same States which currently are EU Member States to a large extent coincide with the ones which originally conceived and put in place the Berne Convention;[21] today they still have the cultural and international prestige required to take the initiative to adapt the Berne to the digital environment.

Second, I submit that taking up Copyright 2.0 is in the long term interest not only of our society and of our culture but also of our economy. To argue the case in a detailed and comprehensive way, one would need multiple interdisciplinary volumes rather than the end tail of a 15 minutes presentation. Let me therefore confine myself to two short – and admittedly a bit too assertive – remarks.

---

[19] In November 2009 the Creative Commons Monitor project calculated that more than 207 million web pages had been licensed under some Creative Commons Public Licence.

[20] For a discussion *see* Sprigman, *supra* note 18.

[21] *See* S. Ricketson (1999), 'The Birth of the Berne Union', in F.M. Abbott, T. Cottier, F. Gurry (eds), *The International Intellectual Property System: Commentary and Materials,* The Hague, London and Boston: Kluwer Law International, 861 ff.

In the last three decades much of IP policy in the developed world has turned around the idea that ratcheting up protection of IPRs is a good idea, as it protects by strong property rights assets which typically belong to US and EU rights holders, and that the other brilliant idea is to expand enforcement standards abroad, with a view to boosting revenue generated by exports of IP-protected goods or by inflows of royalties dutifully paid by foreign users. This approach has been put at the basis of the Uruguay Round negotiations which finally led to the adoption of the WTO and of its IP component, TRIPs.[22] It was also quickly taken up by the EU and particularly so in connection with copyright based products, as if our legacy of artistic creation could be a long lasting source of income flowing into Europe from the rest of the world until the (very long indeed) term of protection expires.

There are several grounds to believe that this strategy is both illusory and doomed. Here, leaving aside that it is easier for the Biblical camel to pass through the needle's eye than persuading our developing neighbours that strong enforcement of our rights is in their interest, I will only mention the fact that finally the domestic economies of our business partners have reached such a size that their demands that we give them access to our technology and IP as a precondition to our obtaining access to their markets are more and more successful.[23]

While IP-based exclusivity protection would (unsurprisingly) appear not to assist our economies as much as our trade negotiators had hoped, I suggest that we had better place our bets on the third paradigm of innovation which seems to be emerging: distributed innovation through digital network driven cooperation. In the beginning innovation was the preserve of individuals; at a later stage the engine was to be found in organizations, be they the firms or research entities. Both modes required appropriation of the results of innovation by means of property rights over IP, to provide the incentives to creation. This has changed radically in the last few decades: while classical property rights based IP protection has increasingly proved unequal to the new challenges of innovation,[24]

---

22 On the origins of the American idea, swiftly taken up by European trade diplomacy, that the lack of global IP protection and enforcement amounts to a 'trade barrier' *see* P. David (1993), 'Intellectual Property Institutions and the Panda's Thumb: Patents, Copyrights, and Trade Secrets in Economic Theory and History', in M.B. Wallerstein, M.E. Mogee and R.A. Schoen (eds), *Global Dimensions of Intellectual Property Rights in Science and Technology*, Washington, DC: National Academy Press, 19 ff. and J. Braithwaite and P. Drahos (2000), *Global Business Regulation*, Cambridge: Cambridge University Press, 61 ff.

23 Anecdotal evidence may be obtained by looking at procurement for nuclear plants and high speed trains.

24 As anticipated by J.H. Reichman (1994), 'Legal Hybrids Between the Patent and Copyright Paradigms', *Columbia L. Rev.*, **94**, 2432. For a confirmation of the short-

network driven innovation is seen to thrive in contexts where exclusivity has been relinquished and is to a large extent replaced by cooperative behaviour among the players, based on a combination of contractual arrangements and liability rules.[25]

I submit that our societies may obtain a genuine competitive advantage in fostering innovation based on this third paradigm rather than in insisting on global acceptance of strong IP rights, which have in part outlived their function; and that we should consider how to make the best of the new chances offered to us

Reforming old international IP conventions which are to a large extent based on the assumption of exclusivity, including the Berne and TRIPs,[26] should be part of this larger job.

6. THE 2010–2020 DIGITAL AGENDA FOR EUROPE

Of course, reforming international conventions takes time. In the past the EU has shown that it is able to take up the challenge of an economic crisis to explore new opportunities for innovation and growth. What are then the intermediate priorities? Which opportunities may we seize *now* in this regard, while the process leading to Copyright 2.0 and Berne 2.0 is – hopefully – kick-started?

It would seem that the 'Digital Agenda for Europe'[27] indicates a number of current priorities which perfectly fit the broader approach I just advocated. Let me mention just three of them.

comings of the classical approach in the new technological environment *see* M.A. Heller (1998), 'The Tragedy of the Anticommons: Property in the Transition from Marx to Markets', *Harvard L. Rev.*, 111. and M.A. Heller and R.S. Eisenberg (1998), 'Can Patents Deter Innovation? The Anticommons in Biomedical Research', *Science,* **280**, 698. A review of the relevant literature is to be found in M. Ricolfi (2006), 'Is There an Antitrust Antidote Against IP Overprotection within TRIPs?', *Marquette Intellectual Property Law Review*, **10**, 305.

[25] For examples of the working of this third paradigm *see* A.K. Rai, J.H. Reichman, P.F. Uhlir and C. Crossman (2008), 'Pathways Across the Valley of Death: Novel Intellectual Property Strategies for Accelerated Drug Discovery', VIII *Yale Journal of Health Policy, Law, and Ethics,* 1. (in connection with drug discovery) and J. H. Reichman and P. Uhlir (2003), 'A Contractually Reconstructed Research Commons for Scientific Data in a Highly Protectionist Intellectual Property Environment', *Law & Contemp. Probs.*, **66**, 315.

[26] But *see* the refreshing remarks showing that exclusivity is not even today mandated either by Berne or TRIPs *see* Geiger, *supra* note 15, 544 ff.

[27] European Commission, A Digital Agenda for Europe, *supra* note 1.

First, orphan works should be brought into the fold of the EU digital libraries initiative, just as advocated by the Digital Agenda,[28] by means of extended collective licences.[29] Under the mechanism, any rights holder may at any time reveal herself and opt out of the regime. If one stops for a moment to think about it, opting out of an extended collective licence scheme amounts to opting in to full copyright protection. In this perspective, the orphan works regime would be a nice, first experiment in the direction of requiring opting in to Copyright 1.0.

Second, collective rights management organizations (CRMOs) are aptly characterized as a fine example of contracting into liability.[30] Individual property rights are pooled into a collecting society, which converts the full property right over the individual work into a pro-rata share of the claim to global compensation agreed in advance with users. What is required in the digital age is that users should not have to go around, hat in hand, to all the 27 EU CRMOs to get from each of them clearance for the service; and that cross-border pan-European licensing takes off. The Digital Agenda is rightly looking into this as well.[31]

Third: Public sector information is an essential input for the emergence of the third paradigm of innovation I just sketched out in § 5. Maps, geo-data, environmental data-sets, laws, regulations and case law and the like may be brought together across jurisdictions through digital networks and contribute to the emergence of new aggregated information products and services at pan-European level. The current text of Directive 98/2003 still needs several upgrades to contribute to the goal, so that its revision is one more of the focal points of the Digital Agenda.[32]

---

28 European Commission, A Digital Agenda for Europe, supra note 1, 6–7; 29–30.

29 The literature on ECL is significantly growing: see, in addition to T. Koskinen-Olsson (2006), 'Collective Management in the Nordic Countries', in D. Gervais (ed.), *Collective Management of Copyright and Related Rights*, Wolters Kluwer, pp. 257 ff., the literature quoted in V. Grassmuck, *The World is Going Flat(-Rate)*, *supra* note 3.

30 R.P. Merges (1996), 'Contracting Into Liability Rules: Intellectual Property Rights and Collective Rights Organisations', *Cal. L. Rev.* **84**, 1293.

31 European Commission, A Digital Agenda for Europe, *supra* note 1, 7–8.

32 European Commission, A Digital Agenda for Europe, *supra* note 1, 9–10. The specific copyright issue in the PSI Directive is whether the rules concerning government IP right may help or hinder the process, as illustrated in detail by E. Derclaye (2008), 'Does the Directive on the Re-use of Public Sector Information affect the State's database sui-generis right?', in J. Gaster, E. Schweighofer and P. Sint P. (eds), *Knowledge Rights – Legal, Societal and Related Technological Aspects, Austrian Computer Society*, 137 ff.

If we combine the three ‘action plans’, we can see that, while certainly they do not amount – and do not intend to amount – to a roadmap to Berne 2.0, they bring together three components which are vital to reconciling IP and the new digital environment. CRMOs are called to overcome their national limitations to operate cross-border along the routes opened up by digital technology. Orphan works are seen as a possible area for a more flexible statutory licence regime, unless their holders show up and opt out of it. The enormous wealth of data-sets generated by public sector bodies engaged in their primary function is increasingly made available to the pioneers of the third innovation paradigm.

Whether these test beds of legislative innovation – the three action plans I briefly referred to – are to take off in actual legislative innovation and coalesce into a normative environment which brings us closer to a reconciliation of copyright law and the digital environment, we do not know yet. I surely hope so.

Section 6

Databases, Design Protection, Unfair Competition and/or New IP Rights in the EU

15. Unfair competition: complementary or alternative to intellectual property in the EU?

Anselm Kamperman Sanders

1. INTRODUCTION

The law of unfair competition can be characterized in that, unlike intellectual property rights, the scope of the legislation encompasses the functioning of the free market as a whole. The purpose of the law of unfair competition is to ensure that free and fair competition is maintained. Fair competition in a free market economy can be characterized by the fact that demand and supply determine the price of a product. This basic economic rationale that underlies a market economy requires that as a matter of principle there is freedom for competitors to copy and build upon the achievements of other market participants. Intellectual property rights can be justified as exclusive rights in relation to intellectual and industrial creativity only on the basis of the fact that they address specific instances of market failure in a market for original expressive works. In order to ensure a transparent and diversified market for products or services, the protection of trademarks or other badges of trade against confusing uses can equally be justified. Even the patent monopoly can be justified in the free market economy as it does not take away from the public something that existed before, but rather creates a competitive market in disclosed and novel inventive ideas themselves. In all instances public welfare is increased as more creative works will be produced, market transparency facilitates consumer choice, and technology can be incorporated in products, while disclosure opens claimed inventions up to scrutiny for improvement or alternatives.

In all these instances intellectual property rights govern competitive relationships in commerce, although copyright can also extend to the private sphere. The law of unfair competition is capable of supplementing intellectual property rights by reinforcing them in their prime function in rationale, but also in providing supplementary or alternative protection. And here it is important to realize that the law of unfair competition does so based on its distinct rationale of protection of the market as a whole.

This chapter considers to what extent the law of unfair competition serves as an alternative to or augmentation of protection by means of intellectual property rights. It also considers the way in which unfair competition law principles have pervaded European law. Although the Database Directive bears the unmistakable hallmarks of protection against misappropriation,[1] the spill-over effects seem to be far less noticeable in this domain as compared to the protection of trade marks against dilution[2] or free riding on the achievements of others.

Where cases are fought in multiple jurisdictions, actions in unfair competition often proved to be the proverbial joker in the deck, depending on the generosity of the national courts in cases involving passing off and slavish imitation.[3] This then also raises the question to what extent it remains possible to defend that the law of unfair competition as a whole need not be harmonized.

2. HARMONIZATION OF THE LAW OF UNFAIR COMPETITION?

That there is no mandate for harmonization of the law of unfair competition in the Member States of the European Union is a position that has been frequently advanced following the *Beele* case,[4] in which the ECJ, in consider-

---

1 On the concept of misappropriation, see M. Leistner (2011), 'The Legacy of *International News Service v. Associated Press (USA)*', in Heath and A. Kamperman Sanders, *Landmark Intellectual Property Cases and Their Legacy,* The Hague and Alphen a/d Rijn: Kluwer Law International, p. 33. Although pronounced close to death by Posner in his article (2003), 'Misappropriation: A Dirge', *Houston Law Review*, 40, 621, the doctrine appeared alive and well in the USA, see *Barclays Capital Inc. v TheFlyOnTheWall.com*, 06 Civ. 4908 (S.D.N.Y. 18 March 2010) until the decision was reversed by the Court of Appeal for the Second Circuit, see *Barclays Capital Inc. v TheFlyOnTheWall.com,* No. 10-cv-1372, 2011 WL 2437554 (2d Cir. 20 June 2011).

2 On the concept of dilution, see A. Kamperman Sanders, '*Odol*: The Introduction of a Watery Concept with Steeled Resilience, in Heath and A. Kamperman Sanders, *supra* note 1, p. 51.

3 See A. Nicotra, 'Hitting the Bricks – Protecting the LEGO® Brick around the World', in Heath/Kamperman Sanders, *supra* note 1, p. 135.

4 ECJ, 2 March 1982, *BV Industrie Diensten Groep v J.A. Beele Handelsgemeenschap* [1982] ECR 707, at para 7:

> Such an injunction constitutes an obstacle to the free movement of goods between the member states and in principle is caught by article 30 which prohibits all measures having an effect equivalent to quantitative restrictions on imports. However, the court has repeatedly held (for example, in the judgment of 20

ing an injunction granted for passing off, stated that the law of unfair competition falls within the 'mandatory requirements' exemption to Article 34 of the Treaty on the Function of the European Union (TFEU).[5] It held that:

> National case-law prohibiting the precise imitation of someone else's product which is likely to cause confusion may indeed protect consumers and promote fair trading; these are general interests which, according to the decisions of the court cited above, may justify the existence of obstacles to movement within the community resulting from disparities between national laws relating to the marketing of products. That such a rule does meet mandatory requirements is moreover borne out by the fact that it accords with the principle underlying article 10 bis of the Paris Convention for the protection of industrial property, as last revised on 14 July 1967 at Stockholm, which prohibits inter alia all acts of such a nature as to create confusion with the goods of a competitor, and by the fact that this rule is recognized in principle in the case-law of most member states.[6]

As long as the national rules on unfair competition are applied equally to domestic and imported product alike, any impact on the free movement of goods that may occur, but equally the possible disparity between national legislations and their different application, is covered by the exception.[7] One

---

February 1979 in case 120/1978, the Cassis de Dijon case, (1979) ECR 649 and in the judgment of 17 June 1981 in case 113/80 Commission v Ireland (1981) ECR 1625) that in the absence of common rules relating to the production and marketing of products, obstacles to movement within the community resulting from disparities between national legislation must be accepted in so far as such legislation, applying without discrimination to both domestic and imported products, may be justified as being necessary in order to *satisfy mandatory requirements relating in particular to the protection of consumers and fairness in commercial transactions* (emphasis added). Therefore the protection against imitation provided in the way described in the judgment making the reference for a preliminary ruling must be examined to determine whether it meets those conditions.

5 Treaty on the Functioning of the European Union (Consolidated Version), [2010] OJ C 83/47.

6 ECJ, 2 March 1982, *IDG v Beele* [1982] ECR 707, at para. 9.

7 ECJ, 2 March 1982, *IDG v Beele* [1982] ECR 707, at para. 15:

> The rules of the EEC Treaty on the free movement of goods do not prevent a rule of national law which applies to domestic and imported products alike, from allowing a trader, who for some considerable time in the member state concerned has marketed a product which differs from similar products, to obtain an injunction against another trader restraining him from continuing to market in that member state a product coming from another member state in which it is lawfully marketed but which for no compelling reason is almost identical to the first-mentioned product and thereby needlessly causes confusion between the two products.

could even argue that with any attempt at harmonization of the law of unfair competition by the ECJ it would be overreaching its mandate.[8]

While most European jurisdictions know a law against unfair competition comprising universally recognized concepts,[9] such as protection against passing off, misleading of consumers, discrediting competitors, or even dilution,[10] unfair competition law never became a common European concept.[11] In fact, English courts have continuously resisted any attempt at harmonization of the tort of passing off with more Continental notions of unfair competition,[12] and despite having broadened the law of passing off:[13] *Never has the tort shown even a slight tendency to stray beyond cases of deception.*[14]

---

8 D. Meale and J. Smith (2010), 'Enforcing a Trade Mark When Nobody's Confused: Where the Law Stands after L'Oreal and Intel', *JIPLP,* **2**, 96; M. Björkenfeldt (2010), 'The Genie Is Out of the Bottle: The ECJ's Decision in L'Oréal v. Bellure', *JIPLP,* **2**, 105.

9 See Article 10*bis* of the Paris Convention for the Protection of Industrial Property of 20 March 1883, as Revised at Stockholm in 1967 and as amended on 28 September 1979. See also G.H.C. Bodenhausen (1968), *Guide to the Application of the Paris Convention for the Protection of Industrial Property As Revised at Stockholm in 1967,* Geneva World Intellectual Property.

10 J. Passa (1997), *Contrefaçon et Concurrence Déloyale,* Paris: Litec; M. Berger (1997), *Die funktionale Konkretisierung von Art. 2 UWG,* Zürich: Schulthess; A. Kamperman Sanders (1997), *Unfair Competition Law,* Oxford: Oxford University Press.

11 F. Henning-Bodewig and S. Schricker (2002), 'New Initiatives for the Harmonisation of Unfair Competition Law in Europe', *EIPR,* 27; S. Schricker (1991), 'European Harmonisation of Unfair Competition Law – A Futile Venture?', *IIC,* 788; R.W. De Vrey (2005), *Towards a European Unfair Competition Law,* Leiden: Koninklijke Brill.

12 *Fry LJ in Mogul Steamship Co. v McGregor Gow & Co.* (1889) 23 QBD 598, 615: '[T]o draw a line between fair and unfair competition, between what is reasonable and unreasonable, passes the power of the courts.'

13 One only needs to read the following cases to see a development that comes close to recognizing dilution, but the requirement for misleading remains: *Erven Warnink v. Townend* [1980] RPC 31; *Reckitt & Colman v Borden* [1990] 1 WLR 491; *Cadbury Schweppes v Pub Squash* [1981] 1 WLR 193; *Taittinger v Allbev* [1993] FSR 641; see also C. Wadlow (2005), *The Law Of Passing-Off*, 3rd ed. London: Sweet & Maxwell.

14 Jacob J. in *Hodgkinson & Corby v Wards Mobility Services* [1995] FSR 169: 'There is no tort of copying. There is no tort of taking a man's market or customers. Neither the market nor the customers are the plaintiff's to own. There is no tort of making use of another's goodwill as such. There is no tort of competition.'

3. UNFAIR COMPETITION – COMPLEMENTARY TO OR PART OF EUROPEAN LAW?

Yet the ECJ has, in a number of trademark cases, made statements that indicate it considers the law of unfair competition to augment the Trade Mark Directive and Regulation, especially if the consumer is not confused.[15] It, however also seems to see the law of unfair competition as an integral part of Community law where the law protects beyond the traditional confines of protection against confusion and addresses issues such as 'taking unfair advantage of' the reputation, or 'causing detriment to' the distinctive character of a registered trademark.[16]

These concepts find their origins not so much in the law of unfair competition of the Member States but in the Uniform Benelux Trademarks Act 1971,[17] the appendix to the 1962 Benelux Convention on Trademarks[18] that entered into force on 1 January 1971, replacing in Belgium, the Netherlands and Luxemburg the national variants of the old French law of 1811. These three nations decided to enhance their common market, a precursor to the European Union, with a common trademark act that would reflect the most 'modern' thinking on trademark law at the time. Rather than confining this harmonization effort to ensure equal protection of unitary trademark rights against confusion, it was also to take into account changes in business practices, advertising and marketing in the Benelux countries. A Uniform Benelux Design Act of 1975[19] completed the picture. Of the two Conventions, the unitary trademark regime especially incorporated notions of passing off and protection against other forms of unfair competition, such as dilution and free riding from both internal national, as well as international examples.[20]

Without reference to the term 'dilution' or 'free riding' itself[21] the concepts

---

[15] ECJ, 9 January 2003, *Davidoff v Gofkid* [2003] 1 CMLR 35.

[16] ECJ 18 June 2009, *L'Oreal v Bellure* [2009] ETMR 13.

[17] Amended in 1986 to implement the First Directive 89/104/EEC of the Council, of 21 December 1988, to Approximate the Laws of the Member States Relating to Trade Marks (OJ EC No L 40 of 11 February. 1989, 1), and in 1996 due to TRIPS.

[18] Since replaced by the Benelux Convention on Intellectual Property (trademarks and drawings or designs) of 2005.

[19] Entry into force 1 January 1975.

[20] Of importance here is the reception of the the seminal article by F.I. Schechter (1926–1927), 'The Rational Basis of Trademark Protection', *Harvard L. Rev.*: **40**, 813.

[21] See J.T. McCarthy (2004), 'Dilution of a Trademark: European and United States Law Compared', *TMR* **94**, 1163, noting at 1165–1166 that the term 'Dilution' is not used in the European context, and if it is, it is by reference to US practice and Schechter's 1927 article. The irony being that dilution is a European invention that can

found their way into the First Trademark Directive[22] as well as the corresponding provisions of the Community Trademark Regulation,[23] by protecting marks *with a reputation* against use on dissimilar goods or services as 'taking unfair advantage of or causing detriment to the distinctive character or the repute of the trademark'.[24] The influence of the Benelux countries in this respect is clear, prompting AG Jacobs to state: '[I]n the course of negotiations in the Council, a provision protecting marks "with a reputation" was included at the request of the Benelux countries, and became Article 5(2) of the Directive'.[25] The issue of whether employment of the same or a similar mark on the same or similar goods, in other words, or whether the concept of dilution was encapsulated in the more nebulous criterion of 'likelihood of association', eventually culminated in a heated exchange. This exchange[26] was prompted by an obiter statement in the English decision on *Wagamama v City Centre Restaurants*,[27] in which Laddie J. dismissed the association criterion as a tautology, citing it as 'repetitive' or 'unnecessary'. Although the European Court of Justice (ECJ) at first appeared to follow the English vision in the landmark case *Puma v Sabel*, rejecting the view that 'likelihood of association' means that the accused mark merely 'calls to mind' the senior mark and that 'the concept of likelihood of association is not an alternative to that of

be traced to the case of *Odol*, Landgericht Elberfeld, 11 September 1924, *Juristische Wochenschrift* 1925, 502. See A. Kamperman Sanders, 'Odol: The Introduction of a Watery Concept with Steeled Resilience', in Heath and Kamperman Sanders, *supra* note 1, p. 51.

22 First Directive 89/104/EEC of the Council, of 21 December 1988, to Approximate the Laws of the Member States Relating to Trade Marks (OJ EC No L 40 of 11 February 1989, 1).

23 Council Regulation (EC) No 40/941 of 20 December 1993 on the Community trademark, since amended.

24 Article 5(2) of the Directive rather provides:

> Any Member State may also provide that the proprietor [of a registered trademark] shall be entitled to prevent all third parties not having his consent from using in the course of trade any sign which is identical with, or similar to, the trade mark in relation to goods or services which are not similar to those for which the trade mark is registered, where the latter has a reputation in the Member State and where use of that sign without due cause takes unfair advantage of, or is detrimental to, the distinctive character or the repute of the trade mark.

25 ECJ, 30 October 1999, *General Motors v Yplon* [1999] 3 CMLR 427, para. 28.

26 A. Kamperman Sanders 1996), 'The Wagamama Decision: Back to the Dark Ages of Trade Mark Law', *EIPR*, **1**, 3; P. Prescott (1996), 'Think Before You Waga Finger', *EIPR*, **6**, 317; A. Kamperman Sanders (1996), 'The Return to Wagamama', *EIPR*, **10**, 521; P. Prescott (1997), 'Has the Benelux Trade Mark Law Been Written into the Directive?', *EIPR*, **3**, 99.

27 English High Court, *Wagamama v City Centre Restaurants* [1995] FSR 713.

likelihood of confusion, but serves to define its scope',[28] it later[29] found there to be a lacuna in protection against dilution in the absence of confusion, which the Member States could fill by allowing action against a competitor for causing 'detriment to, or taking unfair advantage of the distinctive character or repute of a trademark', rather than someone who uses the sign on dissimilar goods or services.[30]

In the case of *Intel v Intelmark*, the renowned semiconductor manufacturer sought the revocation of a UK company's registration of 'Intelmark' for marketing and telemarketing services. There was no evidence of consumer confusion between the marks of both companies. The ECJ, however, reaffirmed[31] that causing detriment to the distinctive character of the mark is actionable when:

> such detriment is caused when that mark's ability to identify the goods or services for which it is registered and used as coming from the proprietor of that mark is weakened, since use of the later mark leads to dispersion of the identity and hold upon the public mind of the earlier mark. That is notably the case when the earlier mark, which used to arouse immediate association with the goods and services for which it is registered, is no longer capable of doing so.

The sting is in the tail, and the ECJ seemingly reversed on its route to expansion of protection against dilution. It also held that, in order to prove detriment to the distinctive character of the mark with a reputation, the proprietor must present evidence of a change in economic behaviour of the average consumer of the earlier goods or services as a consequence of the use of the later mark, or a likelihood that such a change will occur in the future. Although there is no need to show that the later user has obtained commercial benefit from the use of the earlier mark, the decision has been heralded as a firm restriction of the possibility to rely on dilution as a cause of action.[32]

Although the possibilities for action against dilution appear to be curbed after *Intel v Intelmark*, the ECJ did revisit the broader concept of parasitism or 'free riding' in *L'Oréal v Bellure*,[33] pointing to the existence of a European

---

28 ECJ, 11 November 1997, *Sabel v Puma* [1998] 1 CMLR 445, para. 18; See also ECJ, 29 September 1998, *Canon v Metro-Goldwyn-Mayer* [1999] 1 CMLR 77.

29 ECJ, 9 January 2003, *Davidoff v Gofkid* [2003] 1 CMLR 35.

30 *Ibid*, para. 25, indicating that Art. 5(2) 'cannot be given an interpretation which would lead to marks with a reputation having less protection where a sign is used for identical or similar goods or services than where a sign is used for non similar goods or services'; later affirmed in ECJ *Adidas-Salomon v Fitnessworld* [2003] 1 CMLR 14.

31 ECJ, 27 November 2008, *Intel v CPM* [2009] RPC 15.

32 J. Palm (2009), 'The ECJ's Puzzling Concept of a "Change in Economic Behaviour"', *Brands in the Boardroom,* 20, <www.iam-magazine.com>.

33 ECJ 18 June 2009, *L'Oreal v Bellure* [2009] ETMR 13, para. 79.

concept of unfair competition. The case dealt with the use of comparison lists for traders to market smell-alike perfumes by referring to the L'Oréal originals. In linking trademark law and the law on comparative advertising, the ECJ held that:

> Since, under Directive 84/450, comparative advertising which presents the advertiser's products as an imitation of a product bearing a trade mark is inconsistent with fair competition and thus unlawful, any advantage gained by the advertiser through such advertising will have been achieved as the result of unfair competition and must, accordingly, be regarded as taking unfair advantage of the reputation of that mark.

The case highlighted the dividing lines in European thinking on the role of unfair competition in trademark law in that, whereas Dutch commentators welcomed the decision in jubilant terms,[34] or even as a *Liberation! … As if a window has been opened, suddenly blowing a breath of fresh air in a stale room*,[35] English commentators[36] continued to question how the decision could be reconciled with the tort of passing off. A Swedish commentator even termed it a 'most controversial trademark case',[37] alluding to the fact that although the outcome may well be positive for big industry holding famous marks, the development is of no socially-beneficial worth to competition as a whole. Consumers are in fact worse off, being deprived of comparative information to base a purchasing choice on.

4. UNFAIR COMPETITION – ALTERNATIVE TO INTELLECTUAL PROPERTY LAW?

When considering the question whether the law of unfair competition can or should, in addition to being incorporated into intellectual property law, still serve as an alternative to intellectual property law, one could say that one needs to distinguish protection based on the obligations to prevent misleading, discrediting, or confusing acts, expressly mentioned in Article 10*bis*(3) of the Paris Convention from the more diverging national expressions of protection against slavish imitation or free riding. This is, however, a path that leads to insoluble discussions on what is fair in competition, opening up the chasm that

34 Gieler (2009), Case comment on *L'Oréal v Bellure* in *Intellectuele Eigendom en Reclamerecht*, 43.

35 Visser Case Comment on *L'Oréal v Bellure, Boek9.nl* – Monday 22 June 2009 –B9 7987.

36 Meale and Smith, *supra* note 8, 96.

37 Björkenfeldt, *supra* note 8, 105.

separates the English from the more Continental approach. The simple statement from the English High Court from 1889 in *Mogul Steamship Co. v McGregor Gow & Co* says it all: '[T]o draw a line between fair and unfair competition, between what is reasonable and unreasonable, passes the power of the courts.'[38]

It is therefore much more interesting to ask oneself what sets the law of unfair competition apart from intellectual property. If one reads Posner's 'Misappropriation: A Dirge',[39] who also asks himself this very same question, one could come to the conclusion that the sole supplementary role of the law of unfair competition lies in preventing free riding in direct market failure situations between two competitors, or as Posner calls it 'the danger of killing the goose that lays the golden eggs'.[40] True to the US tradition on the matter, he limits the application of the misappropriation doctrine to that of protection of time-sensitive information. In a recent case involving the repeated copying of information from online servers containing financial news and stock recommendations, the United States District Court for the Southern District of New York issued a permanent injunction, ordering the defendant to delay the publication of the information aggregated and analysed by the plaintiffs from the moment of the opening bell of the stock exchange with a time delay of at least two hours.[41] The District Court applied the test set out in the case *NBA v Motorola*,[42] which requires the plaintiff to show that (1) the plaintiff was generating or gathering information at a cost; (2) the information was time-sensitive; (3) the defendant's use of the information was free-riding on the plaintiff's efforts; (4) the defendant was in direct competition with a product or service offered by the plaintiff; and (5) the ability of the defendant to continue free-riding would 'so reduce the incentive to produce the product or service that its existence or quality would be substantially threatened'.

The injunction was, however, lifted by the Court of Appeals for the Second Circuit.[43] It held that, although the principles developed in *INS v AP*[44] and *NBA v Motorola* are still good law, the plaintiff's 'hot news' claim was preempted by federal copyright law. Under this principle the tort of misappropriation (or any state legislation on the matter) must be interpreted narrowly and should not encroach upon the balance struck by the federal legislator in

---

38 English High Court, *Mogul Steamship Co. v McGregor Gow & Co.* (1889) 23 QBD 598, per Fry LJ at 615.

39 (2003), *Houston L. Rev.*, 40, 621.

40 *Ibid* at 628.

41 *Supra* note 1.

42 105 F.3d 841, 852 (2d Cir. 1997)

43 *Supra* note 1.

44 248 U.S. 215 (1918).

terms of protectable subject matter and the scope of protection offered to copyright works (or other IP rights).[45] In the case at hand, the court held that the plaintiffs were 'making the news', which means that the reports produced fall within the subject matter and scope of the Copyright Act, but do not attract protection thereunder. Since the plaintiffs did not present any 'extra element' that makes it 'qualitatively different' from a copyright infringement claim, the cause of action against a competitor is preempted.[46]

The Continental European laws against unfair competition are, however, not limited to direct competition, but consider the functioning of the free market economy as a whole.[47] It is this rationale that gave rise to the dilution doctrine, as first established in the case of *Odol*,[48] decided in 1924 by the Landgericht at Elberfeld in Germany.[49] The case involved the use of the mark Odol on an area completely unrelated to the one for which the trademark holder had registered it. The existence of a competitive nexus between the two parties was deemed not necessary under unfair competition law. The frustration of the trademark owners' ability to compete on its own market for mouthwash, for which it was registered, is held as the central tenet for the decision. The use by the defendant, a steel producer of the mark 'Odol' for its unrelated products was held to be an unlawful interference, an act 'gegen den guten Sitten', in the market for mouthwash.

Although the concept of dilution is now firmly engrained in the law of trademarks, it would be unwise to forget the genesis and rationale of this doctrine, in order to give it a proper and purpose-limited reading. It is also the unfair competition rationale that should guide the ECJ to what extent protection ought to be granted in dilution or free riding cases. For the interpretation of the 'taking unfair advantage of the reputation of a trade mark with a reputation' section in the Trade Mark Directive, a lot of the restrictive reasoning in the case of *Intel v CPM*[50] can be directly traced to the unfair competition rationale in terms of defining markets and customer behaviour.

Although the law of unfair competition may give rise to alternative forms of protection in future, such as a broad Community reading on slavish imita-

---

45 *Erie Railroad Co. v Tompkins*, 304 U.S. 64 (1938).

46 *Computer Associates International v Altai*, 982 F.2d 693, 716 (2d Cir.1992).

47 R. Callmann (1926/27), 'Unlauterer Wettbewerb zum Wohl der Allgemeinheit?' *Markenschutz und Wettbewerb*, 378 and the seminal (1929), *Der Unlautere Wettbewerb*, Mannheim: Bensheimer.

48 Landgericht Elberfeld, 11 September 1924, *Juristische Wochenschrift*, 1925, 502.

49 For a history of the case and its impact on the law today, see Kamperman Sanders, '*Odol*: The Introduction of a Watery Concept with Steeled Resilience', in Heath and Kamperman Sanders, *supra* note 1, 51.

50 ECJ, 27 November 2008, *Intel v CPM* [2009] RPC 15.

tion,[51] caution should be exercised as we may find that protectionism or market segmentation is the direct result of national protection against unfair competition in whatever guise,[52] especially since there is thus far no harmonized notion of European Community preemption, as the perfume cases in the Netherlands and France have shown.[53] There are after all good reasons for the demarcation lines by which formal requirements for the acquisition of intellectual property rights leave certain forms of intellectual or industrial creativity in the public domain.

5. CONCLUSION

It is my submission is that unfair competition is an integral part of the law that governs our free market economy, and it therefore follows that a 'Community Law Against Unfair Competition' already exists. It can, however, not remain a nebulous concept that is merely defined by the treaty obligations in the Paris Convention. The notions contained therein elude categorization, appropriate limitation and principles of Community preemption.[54] Any Community Law Against Unfair Competition therefore should ideally be subject to a harmonization Directive or even a Regulation.

---

[51] See A. Kamperman Sanders (2009), 'Do Whiffs of Misappropriation and Standards for Slavish Imitation Weaken the Foundations of IP Law?', in E. Derclaye (ed.), *Research Handbook on the Future of EU Copyright*, Cheltenham, UK and Northampton, MA: Edward Elgar, p. 567, for a description of Lego's attempt to stretch the boundaries of unfair competition law, despite pre-emptive limitations present in the intellectual property system. For an overview of Lego's global litigation strategy and its success, see Nicotra, *supra* note 3.

[52] See on the different outlook on the protection of the scent of perfumes as copyright works, the Dutch Supreme Court in *Lancôme v Kecofa*, 16 June 2006, NJ 2006, 585, as opposed to the French Cour de Cassation, *Bsiri-Barbir v Haarmann & Reimer Civ.* (1re ch.), 13 June 2006; [2006] ECDR 28.

[53] T. Cohen Jehoram [2006], 'The Dutch Supreme Court Recognises Copyright in the Scent of a Perfume The Flying Dutchman: All Sails, No Anchor', *EIPR*, 629–31.

[54] Kamperman Sanders, *supra* note 51, at p. 574:

> What remains to be undertaken is a fundamental discussion of the appropriate ambit and place of the law of unfair competition in the context of European harmonisation, but most important of all on the role of unfair competition law as a supplementary, alternative, or subsequent method of protection for intellectual and industrial property rights.

16. Database rights: success or failure? The chequered yet exciting journey of database protection in Europe

Estelle Derclaye*

INTRODUCTION

It is a somewhat scary thought but there it is: it is over 20 years since the European database debate started. And the debate is still raging. Indeed, the Commission issued its initial proposal in 1992,[1] eventually giving birth to the Database Directive in March 1996.[2] But it had started considering harmonization of database protection as early as 1986.[3] As is known, the Directive harmonized copyright law for databases, providing protection only for their structure and only if the selection or arrangement is the author's own intellectual creation, and created a brand new *sui generis* right protecting the investment in collecting, verifying and/or presenting the contents of databases. Both before and after its adoption, the *sui generis* right has been, and still is very much criticized for its overreaching protective strength, which is not counterbalanced by sufficient limits.[4] Most Member States implemented the Directive

* © E. Derclaye 2011. The author welcomes comments and can be reached at ederclaye@hotmail.com or estelle.derclaye@nottingham.ac.uk

1 Proposal for a Council Directive on the Legal Protection of Databases, COM (92) 24 final – SYN 393 Brussels, 13 May 1992, OJ C156, 23 June 1992.

2 Directive 96/9/EC of the European Parliament and of the Council of 11 March 1996 on the legal protection of databases, OJ L77/20, 27 March 1996, further referred to as 'the Directive'.

3 Commission of the European Communities, Questionnaire Relating to Provisions of National Copyright Laws of Specific Importance for the Operations of Computerised Information Systems, submitted to the DGXIII Legal Advisory Board (1986). See thereafter, the Commission Green Paper on Copyright and the Challenge of Technology: Copyright Issues Requiring Immediate Action, COM (1988) 172 final (7 June 1988) and the Follow-up to the Green Paper, Working Programme of the Commission in the Field of Copyright and Neighbouring Rights, COM (1990) 584 final.

4 To cite but a few of those who criticized the *sui generis* right: M. Davison (2003), *The Legal Protection of Databases*, Cambridge: University Press; J. Reichman

in time in 1998 or thereabouts. Much litigation for infringement of the *sui generis* right ensued in many Member States, culminating in 2004 with the four rulings of the Court of Justice in the *BHB* and *Fixtures Marketing* cases.[5] Those decisions in many ways clarified and limited part of the scope of the *sui generis* right, quietening somewhat the initial criticisms.[6] The first evaluation report of the Directive came quite a bit later than expected, in 2005, with the Commission generally drawing the conclusion that the *sui generis* right has not really worked and thus proposing four options: the *status quo*, repeal the whole Directive, repeal or amend, the *sui generis* right.[7] Since then, nothing much has happened on the database topic except two decisions of the Court of Justice in 2008 and 2009.[8] In the main, these confirmed the interpretation given to the *sui generis* right in the previous 2004 rulings. The second evaluation report is now also long overdue and still awaited but was not on the agenda of the Commission's work program for 2011. In fact, no aspect concerning the Database Directive was.[9] However, 2010 saw the surprising *Football Dataco* ruling in the United Kingdom[10] which was referred in December 2010 to the Court of Justice[11] and whose decision on 1 March 2012 proved decisive in the area.[12]

---

and P. Samuelson [1997], 'Intellectual Property Rights in Data?', *Vanderbilt L. Rev.*, **50**, 51; N. Mallet-Poujol [1996], 'La directive concernant la protection juridique des bases de données: la gageure de la protection privative' *DIT*, 1, 6; P.B. Hugenholtz [1996], 'De databankrichtlijn eindelijk aanvaard: een zeer kritisch commentaar', *Computerrecht*, 131.

5 Case C-203/02 *The British Horseracing Board Ltd v William Hill Organisation Ltd* [2005] 1 CMLR 15; Case C-444/02 *Fixtures Marketing Ltd v Organismos Prognostikon Agonon Podosfairou* (OPAP) [2005] 1 CMLR 16; Case C-46/02 *Fixtures Marketing Ltd v Oy Veikkaus AB* [2005] ECDR 2; Case C-338/02 *Fixtures Marketing Ltd v Svenska Spel AB* [2005] ECDR 4.

6 T. Aplin [2005], 'The ECJ Elucidates the Database Right' *IPQ*, 204; M. Davison and P.B. Hugenholtz [2005], 'Football Fixtures, Horseraces and Spin Offs: the ECJ Domesticates the Database Right', *EIPR*, 113; E. Derclaye [2005], 'The ECJ Interprets the Database *Sui Generis* Right for the First Time', *ELR* **30**, 420–30.

7 DG Internal Market and Services Working Paper, First Evaluation of Directive 96/9/EC on the Legal Protection of Databases, 12 December 2005, available on http://europa.eu.int/comm/internal_market/copyright/prot-databases/prot-databases_en.htm.

8 Case C-304/07 *Directmedia Publishing GmbH v Albert-Ludwigs-Universitat Freiburg* [2008] ECR I-7565; Case C-545/07 *Apis-Hristovich EOOD v Lakorda AD* [2009] ECR I-1627.

9 Thanks to Jens Gaster for this information.

10 *Football Dataco v Brittens Pools* [2010] EWHC 841; [2010] 3 CMLR 25 (ChD).

11 *Football Dataco et al. v Yahoo UK! et al.* [2010] EWCA Civ 1380.

12 Case C-604/10 *Football Dataco & Others v Yahoo UK! & Others* 1 March 2012, nyr, available on www.curia.europa.eu

This chapter will first address the failings and successes of the Database Directive's *sui generis* right (1) and copyright (2). It will then conclude by suggesting what changes should be made and what the future holds (3).

1. THE *SUI GENERIS* RIGHT: A PARTLY MADE UP GAFFE

It is a euphemism to say that the *sui generis* right is in the main a failure. Some have gone as far as saying that adopting the Database Directive was a mistake.[13] Indeed, the database *sui generis* right suffers from a high number of birth defects which have been abundantly decried and will therefore be only summarized here.[14] Indeed, the paradox of the *sui generis* right is that an effort less creative than that involved in creating a copyright work is rewarded with more protection.

In a nutshell, the right has three important flaws.[15] First, not only are the exceptions (for private use, teaching and research, and public security and administrative or judicial procedures[16]) both too narrow and too scarce, they are in addition all optional. This makes the strong right (it has broad economic rights of extraction and reutilization) very unbalanced. Therefore, more exceptions should be introduced, and at the very least for criticism or review and news reporting. Ideally, they should be aligned with copyright law's exceptions applicable to databases.[17] Compulsory licences should also be imposed under

---

[13] M. Davison [2007], 'Database Protection: Lessons from Europe, Congress, and WIPO', Case Western Reserve L. Rev., **57**, 829.

[14] For detailed coverage, see e.g. V. Bensinger (1999), *Sui Generis Schutz für Datenbanken: Die E.G.-Datenbankrichtlinie vor dem Hintergrund des Nordischen Rechts,* Munich: C.H. Beck; M. Leistner (2000), *Der Rechtsschutz von Datenbanken im Deutschen und Europäischen Recht, Eine Untersuchung zur Rechtlinie 96/9/EG und zu ihrer Umsetzung in das Deutsche Urheberechtsgesetz*, Munich: C.H. Beck; Davison *supra* note 4; E. Derclaye (2008), *The Legal Protection of Databases, A Comparative Analysis,* Cheltenham, UK and Northampton, MA: Edward Elgar, Ch. 10.

[15] For more detail on these three flaws, see Derclaye, *ibid.*

[16] See article 9 of the Directive.

[17] R. Hilty et al. [2009], 'European Commission: Green Paper: Copyright in the Knowledge Economy – Comments by the Max Planck Institute for Intellectual Property, Competition and Tax Law', *IIC,* 309, at 317:

> Only coherence between the different bodies of law guarantees a free and unobstructed flow of scientific information. Therefore, limitations should also apply to the *sui generis* right in unoriginal databases, which has been stipulated by Directive 96/9/EC on the legal protection of databases. This would avoid disparities between the two most relevant protection regimes that are closely linked in the information society.

See also *ibid*, 319.

certain conditions on single source database makers. Second, the term of protection is indefinitely renewable, provided a new substantial investment can be proved.[18] However, especially in dynamic databases, users cannot identify whether the part they propose to extract or reutilize is one where a renewed substantial investment has taken place, thereby *de facto* protecting the entire database and therefore, elements which should no longer benefit from the right. Finally, the relationship between the *sui generis* right and other possible protections, namely contracts, unfair competition and anti-circumvention provisions, is not addressed appropriately, giving far too much protection to databases makers.[19] In addition to these three main flaws, a number of tweaks would need to be made to the definition of a database and the criteria of substantial investment and substantial part, in addition to the interpretation given by the Court of Justice in the *BHB*, *Fixtures Marketing*, *Directmedia* and *Apis* cases.[20]

More importantly, if the 2005 Commission evaluation report is to be believed,[21] the right may well have been a wasted effort or even more worryingly, have made things worse than they were before its adoption.[22] However, as has been noted, the empirical data is extremely thin[23] and the correlation between the *status quo* or decrease in the number of databases in the European Union – if, again, it is correct that there has been a *status quo* or decrease depending on the Member State in question as the data is very partial – and the introduction of the *sui generis* right is not entirely clear.[24] Therefore, at best, it is still unclear what effect the *sui generis* right has had.

---

18 See article 10 of the Directive.

19 Only one 'exception' (article 8(1) the lawful user's right to extract or re-use insubstantial parts) is made imperative.

20 For these suggestions, see Derclaye, *supra* note 14.

21 *Supra* note 7. And it may not be as it relies solely on only one source, the Gale Directory of Databases and a handful of replies from the industry.

22 M. Block, 'The Empirical Basis for Statutory Database Protection after the European Database Directive', pp. 6, 14–15, available at www.law.duke.edu/cspd/papers/empirical.doc.

23 Block, *ibid*, p. 5; J. Reichman [2002], 'Mondialisation et Propriété Intellectuelle' *Revue Internationale De Droit Économique*, **16**, 455, 463–64, translation available at http://www.cairn.info/load_pdf.php?ID_REVUE=RIDE&ID_NUMPUBLIE=RIDE_162&ID_ARTICLE=RIDE_162_0455; S. Scotchmer (2004), 'Innovation and Incentives' 82 ('there is little or no evidence that lack of protection has impeded the creation of new databases'), cited by D. Gervais [2007], 'The Protection of Databases', *Chicago-Kent L. Rev.*, **82**, 1109, at 1166.

24 Block, *supra* note 22, pp. 7, 11–12 noting at 12 that:

> That said, it would be premature to conclude from the evidence that database protection simply does not work to spur new production. Other explanations cannot be ruled out, including the simplest that complex database protection schemes will take a long time to have any appreciable effect. Thus, if there is a problem then database protection might be a way to solve it.

Despite all its birth defects, the *sui generis* right has been domesticated rather neatly by the Court of Justice in 2004, notwithstanding the fact it was constrained by the limits of the referred questions. In this respect, one can say that some measure of success has been achieved in the sense that many of the monopolistic or overprotective features of the right have been abolished, annihilated or severely curtailed. The most important part of the *BHB* and *Fixtures Marketing* rulings is the interpretation of the term 'obtaining'.[25] Obtaining data only means collecting it. Therefore, no investment in creating data can ever trigger a *sui generis* right. Spin-off databases are therefore excluded from protection if no separate investment in the collection, verification or presentation of the data is proved. This leaves out many important databases such as sports fixtures, television listings and timetables.[26] Secondly, the Court also established a necessary link between the substantial investment and substantial part, including a clarification of what 'qualitative' and 'quantitative' mean and that the concepts of substantial part and insubstantial part are mutually exclusive. Finally, the Court clarified a number of other points namely the definition of a database and the scope of the rights of extraction and reutilization, which are broad and include indirect acts although not mere consultation of the database.[27]

In 2008, the Court of Justice further clarified that extraction is not limited to physical copying of the database (i.e. copy/paste) but that the term 'transfer' is broad.[28] Therefore, it is irrelevant that the transfer is based on a technical process of copying the contents, such as electronic, electromagnetic, electro-optical or any other similar processes or on a simple manual process and that the transfer may lead to an arrangement of the elements concerned which is different from that in the original database. The following year, the Court again restated the broad concept of extraction and the link. Mainly, it further clarified that the type of system for database management, e.g. a computer program, is not a relevant factor when determining whether extraction has taken place. Also, it made clear that if a database is a Russian doll (comprised of several smaller sub-databases), the level at which infringement

---

25 *BHB*, supra note 5, paras 30–32.

26 Nevertheless, the ruling may have had the unintended consequence to force database makers to make 'unnecessary investments in presentation or artificial efforts to select and arrange the texts to generate copyright protection'. Gervais, *supra* note 23, at 1164–5 also noting that this criticism 'reminds one of older debates about the value of typographical copyright.'

27 For more detail, see E. Derclaye [2005], 'The Court of Justice Interprets the Database *Sui generis* Right for the First Time', *ELR*, **30** (3), 420–30.

28 *Directmedia*, *supra* note 8. For comments on these cases, see A. Christopher and K. Freeman [2009], 'Case Comment on Directmedia', *EIPR*, 151 and A. Koo [2010], 'Database Right Decoded', *EIPR*, 313.

must be examined, is the level of the smallest database. So courts must first determine if a module is a database itself and is protected. If yes, then 'the volume of materials allegedly extracted and/or reutilised from the module concerned must be compared with the total contents solely of that module'.[29] Thus all in all, these two decisions 'simply'[30] confirmed that exclusive rights must be broadly interpreted and that there is a necessary link between substantial investment and substantial part.

Hopefully, the Court of Justice will carry on its work in future rulings and soon, and most importantly, in *Football Dataco v Sportradar*[31] and *Innoweb v Wegener ICT Media*.[32]

2. COPYRIGHT: NOTHING TO REPORT, ALMOST

Copyright harmonization of databases was much less controversial and was really intended to clarify a few aspects of the Member States' copyright laws. First, databases comprising not only works but also data were to be protected.[33] Second, the level of originality was to be the author's own intellectual creation.[34] Provisions on authorship and ownership, rights and exceptions simply 'codified' the *status quo*.[35] Of course, for Europe's common law

---

29 *Apis*, *supra* note 8, paras 62–3.

30 The *Apis* ruling however added very valuable insights such as the level at which infringement must be determined in a database comprised of several smaller databases, something which did not go without saying on a reading of the Directive's provisions.

31 *Football Dataco et al. v Sportradar AG and Sportradar GmbH* [2011] EWCA Civ 330. In this case involving the same claimant but different defendants, the Court of Appeal of England and Wales asked the Court of Justice whether it is an act of extraction or reutilization for a party having a server in a Member State to send data (a substantial part from a protected database) to a user in another Member State in response to requests from that user (the data then being displayed on the user's computer) and if so, in which Member State the act occurs, in the first Member State, the second or both. Judgment of the CJEU, 18 October 2012, Case C-173/11, available on www.curia.europe.eu.

32 CFI The Hague, 15 February 2011, HA ZA 08–300, reported on http://www.ie-forum.nl/index.php?//Voornemens+vragen+te+stellen////27930/ – the Dutch court asks several questions on the interpretation of extraction and reutilisation along with a question on the meaning of article 8(2). Case C-202/12, available on www.curia.europa.eu.

33 Following the provisions of the TRIPs Agreement and the World Copyright Treaty.

34 Article 3(1) of the Directive.

35 Moral rights were not touched upon, as in none of the other directives in the field of copyright so far.

countries, such harmonization was much more of a change in terms of the level of originality required. Until 2010, no court in the United Kingdom had to discuss this new concept of originality. We now have one decision, *Football Dataco*, which touches on this very notion and on which the Court of Justice has pronounced itself,[36] in addition to what it said in its *Infopaq, Bezpečnostní softwarová asociace, Painer* and *FAPL* rulings.[37] And in view of the high number of pending references in the field of copyright,[38] there will be yet more developments which will probably also affect database copyright. So in respect of copyright, the Directive can be said to be a success but a moderate one since it really codified 'business as usual'. And probably, the only two defects are the scarce and narrow exceptions and the lack of appropriate provisions as to the relationship between copyright and other types of protection namely, unfair competition, contracts and anti-circumvention measures, as for the *sui generis* right.

While the Court of Justice case law on the copyright front is commonplace for the continental lawyer, it is not for the common lawyer. A discussion of the *Football Dataco* case is therefore in order. So what happened in *Football Dataco*?[39] The case concerned whether copyright and/or *sui generis* right subsisted in annual fixtures lists produced and published for the purposes of various football leagues. The claimants organize professional football matches and exploit the data in connection with those matches, including the fixture lists. The defendants exploited the said lists without a licence from the claimants. How are the lists drawn? A number of rules have to be followed, for instance none of the clubs can have three consecutive home or away matches. Other constraints are the start and end of the season, the number of matches that must be played and the dates of international matches and other competitions outside the league in question. Questionnaires are sent to clubs which can send in their requests i.e. specific date requests, non specific date requests or pairing requests. With all that information at hand, a computer engineer

36 Case C-604/10 *Football Dataco & Others v Yahoo UK! & Others* 1 March 2012, nyr, available on www.curia.europa.eu

37 Case C-5/08 *Infopaq International A/S v Danske Dagblades Forening*, [2009] ECDR 259; Case C-393/09 *Bezpečnostní softwarová asociace – Svaz softwarové ochrany v Ministerstvo kultury* [2011] ECDR 70; Joined Cases C-403/08 and C-429/08 *Football Association Premier League and others v QC Leisure and others and Karen Murphy v Media Protection Services* [2012] FSR 1; Case C-145/10 *Eva-Maria Painer v Standard VerlagsGmbH and others* [2011] ECR nyr, available on www.curia.europa.eu.

38 There are no less than 20 references at the time of writing. For a more or less complete list, see http://www.ipo.gov.uk/pro-policy/policy-information/ecj.htm.

39 *Football Dataco v Britten Pools* [2010] EWHC 841 (ChD); *Football Dataco et al. v Yahoo! UK et al.* [2010] EWCA Civ 1380 (CA).

prepares the lists. He follows the rules above and tries to accommodate each club's requests. Often he has to reject or accept a club's request because it would be unfair to another club. For some clubs, there can be many places where they can go on the grid the engineer prepares but for other clubs, there is only one place. When the table is completed, it is reviewed by employees of the leagues and the engineer tries to find a solution to problematic fixtures.

In the High Court, Floyd J held that the fixtures lists were protected by copyright but not the *sui generis* right and also that no other copyright subsisted. In other words, the only way the fixture lists can attract copyright is as databases. There is therefore no other copyright protection possible.[40] Not surprisingly,[41] the judge does not find any *sui generis* right, as he squarely follows the *BHB* ruling: '[t]he separate work which goes into obtaining, verifying or presenting the data in the Fixture Lists is trivial'.[42]

The interesting aspect of the judgment is the determination of originality. Floyd J seems to equate the old British test (skill, judgement and labour) to the author's own intellectual creation but distinguish it from the even lower criterion of 'sweat of the brow'. For Floyd J, the process of making the lists 'involves very significant labour and skill'.[43] Not everyone would come up with the same list because 'judgements have to be made as to the relative importance of certain rules in comparison to others'.[44] Thus making fixtures lists is not merely sweat of the brow. 'Unlike a "sweat of the brow" compilation, there are some solutions which will simply not work, and others which will be better'.[45] Then, the judge discusses the author's own intellectual creation criterion. For him, the author's own individual creativity is required but the Directive is not clear as to the amount/quality of such creativity. It will thus vary from case to case. What is clear though is that a sweat of the brow collection will not do; the author's creativity must be stamped on the collection. This means that 'the *author* must have exercised judgement, taste or discretion (good, bad or indifferent) in selecting or arranging the contents of the database'.[46] Thus, a list of all Acts of Parliament in the last 100 years would not qualify for example but a collection of the author's 1000 favourite poems would pass the test.[47] The test is both qualitative and quantitative. Indeed, as recital 19 of the database Directive provides, a CD compilation is

---

40 Para. 100 of the first instance decision.

41 Compare with TGI Paris, 20 June 2007, *PMU v Eturf*, available on http://legalis.net/ spip.php?page=jurisprudence-decision&id_article=1973, below note 66.

42 [2010] EWHC 841, para. 92.

43 *Ibid.*, para. 41.

44 Para. 42.

45 Para. 43.

46 Para. 86.

47 *Ibid.*

quantitatively not enough, even if it may be qualitatively so.[48] But the qualitative test is a low one. A modicum of creativity will suffice. Floyd J also makes clear that the selection or arrangement required for the collection to attract copyright is not confined to such selection or arrangement performed after the data is created but also before.[49] He then gives his test to determine database copyright:

(i) Identify the data which is collected and arranged in the database;
(ii) Analyse the work which goes into the creation of the database by collecting and arranging the data so identified, to isolate that work which is properly regarded as selection and arrangement;
(iii) Ask whether the work of selection and arrangement was the author's own intellectual creation and in particular whether it involved the author's judgement, taste or discretion;
(iv) Finally, one should ask whether the work is quantitatively sufficient to attract copyright protection.[50]

Applying these factors to the facts, the judge finds that there is copyright in the fixture lists as different persons can devise different lists. There is judgement and discretion in the selection and arrangement of match dates.[51] And this is also quantitatively sufficient. 'The quantum of relevant work involved in producing the Lists for any of the Leagues is considerably greater and made more complex by the fact that no two fixtures can be freely interchanged without affecting others'.[52]

According to Floyd J. it seems therefore, that the criterion of originality, now the author's own intellectual creation, for databases is very low indeed. Whereas both quality and quantity are required, only a modicum of creativity is necessary for databases. This seems to accord exactly with the US Supreme Court's *Feist* ruling.

On appeal the Court of Appeal, per Jacob J, decided to refer two questions to the Court of Justice. The first question (which has three subquestions) asks what is meant by the terms in article 3(1) of the Directive 'databases which, by reason of the selection or arrangement of their contents, constitutes the author's own intellectual creation' and 'in particular: (a) should the intellectual effort and skill of creating data be excluded? (b) does "selection or arrangement" include adding important significance to a pre-existing item of data (as

---

48 Para. 90.
49 Paras 81–82.
50 Para. 91.
51 Para. 97.
52 Para. 98.

in fixing the date of a football match)'.[53] Indeed, the defendants contend that the fixtures lists are not protected by copyright. Their argument is that copyright only subsists if there is selection or arrangement of *pre-existing data*. Therefore, for the defendants, Football Dataco does not have copyright because giving a date to a match (e.g. Arsenal v Chelsea on 26 April 2011) is creating data, not selecting or arranging it. They have a point because if copyright subsists in the lists, the 2004 *BHB* and *Fixtures Marketing* rulings on the *sui generis* right are completely bypassed. The Court of Appeal also wonders what exactly is meant by the author's own intellectual creation (subquestion c). Does it require more than significant labour and skill from the author, if so, what? Does it require some artistic aspect?

The second question is whether a database copyright independent of that harmonized in the Database Directive survives. This is what the claimants claim. But Jacob J does not agree that the relevant recitals mean that at all because if they did, 'harmonisation across the EU of laws as to the subsistence of rights in databases, would not have been achieved'.[54] But since the Court thinks that 'there is, perhaps, just enough of a lingering doubt on the point',[55] it decided to refer that question too.

At the time of this contribution's submission, in February 2011, I wrote: The ruling of the Court of Justice will therefore be fascinating. It will further expand on *Infopaq's* definition of the author's own intellectual creation and most importantly for databases, decide what selection means. The decision will be crucial because, if the Court of Justice decides that copyright can subsist in fixture lists and the like, the *sui generis* right for these at least, will become irrelevant and copyright will become the (super)protection *par excellence*, creating monopolies on information. Probably, the Court will not go there. It will also, hopefully, put the final nail in the coffin of 'any other remaining copyright' for databases in addition to that harmonized by the Directive.

On 1 March 2012, the Court of Justice did indeed decide both of these issues accordingly.[56] As to the first subquestion of the first question, the Court rightly held that the Database Directive's concepts of 'selection' and 'arrangement' refer to the 'selection and arrangement of the data through which the author of the database gives the database its structure'.[57] Selection and arrangement do not extend to the creation of the data contained in a database.

---

53 [2010] EWCA Civ 1380, para. 22.

54 Para. 14.

55 Para. 15.

56 Case C-604/10 *Football Dataco & Others v Yahoo UK! & Others*, nyr, available on www.curia.europa.eu

57 *Ibid.*, para. 32.

Therefore, the intellectual effort and skill expanded in creating data are not relevant in order to assess the eligibility of the database that contains them for copyright protection. The Court relies for this on the purpose of the Directive and its recitals 9, 10 and 12. In short, the Directive aims at stimulating the creation of databases. Its aim is not to protect the creation of data capable of being collected in a database. The Court then refers to its *Infopaq, Bezpečnostní softwarová asociace, Football Premier League* and *Painer*[58] rulings to reiterate once more its interpretation of the originality requirement, namely the author's own creation. Accordingly and applied to databases, the 'criterion of originality is satisfied when, through the selection or arrangement of the data which it contains, its author expresses his creative ability in an original manner by making free and creative choices [...] and thus stamps his "personal touch"'.[59] Therefore, the Court continues, the criterion is 'not satisfied when the setting up of the database is dictated by technical considerations, rules or constraints which leave no room for creative freedom'.[60]

This leads the Court to answer the second subquestion by saying that provided the selection and arrangement of the data in the case at hand is original, it is irrelevant whether or not this selection and arrangement includes 'adding important significance' to that data. Indeed, article 3(1) of the Database Directive provides that no other criterion than that of originality is to be applied to determine whether the database is original. Adding significance to the data has to do with the creation of the data. Therefore, adding significance to the data as such is not relevant anyway because it is something done to the data, not the structure of the database. Hence, the Court already implicitly provided an answer to this subquestion in its answer to the previous subquestion.

---

[58] For these cases, see *supra* note 37. In those cases, the Court held that the author's own intellectual creation means creativity. In respect of literary works, the *Infopaq* Court held that '[i]t is only through the choice, sequence and combination of those words that the author may express his creativity' (para. 45). For comments, see e.g. E. Derclaye [2010], 'Wonderful or Worrisome? The Impact of the ECJ Ruling in *Infopaq* on UK Copyright law', *EIPR*, **32** (5), 247–51 and E. Derclaye [2011], 'L'arrêt *Softwarová:* une révolution en droit d'auteur ou une "erreur de jugement"?', *Revue du Droit des Technologies de l'Information,* **43**, 57–62. In the *Painer* case the Court held that during the preparation phase, the photographer can choose the background, the pose, the lighting, the framing, the angle and atmosphere. When selecting the snapshot, the author can choose from several developing techniques including software. Therefore, these choices 'can stamp the work created with his "personal touch"'. The Court concluded that 'a portrait photograph can (...) be protected by copyright if (...) such photograph is an intellectual creation of the author reflecting his personality and expressing his free and creative choices in the production of that photograph'.

[59] Case C-604/10, para. 38.

[60] *Ibid*, para. 39.

The crux of the judgment comes at paragraph 42 when the Court clearly states that skill and labour in the selection or arrangement of the data, even if significant, is not sufficient as such to trigger copyright protection. The labour and skill must express the originality in the sense defined by the Court (i.e. creativity) for it to give copyright protection to the database. The Court of Justice then leaves it to the national court to decide if this is the case. However, it then seems to retract from this leeway given to the national court in the next paragraph, probably leaving in effect no room for manoeuvre to the Court of Appeal of England and Wales on remittal. Indeed, it states that the procedures for creating the fixtures lists, as described by the national court, are not original. Unless these procedures are supplemented by elements reflecting originality in selecting or arranging the data contained in the lists, the national court will then be forced to find that the database is not original and thus not protected by copyright law.[61]

As the Court of Appeal of England and Wales surmised in its own judgment and like the Advocate General, the Court of Justice replies fairly quickly to the second question. It holds that the Database Directive precludes national legislation which grants databases copyright under conditions which are different than those set out in its article 3(1), i.e. under conditions other than originality.[62] The Court reasoned that the aim of the Directive was to remove differences in national legislation particularly on the scope and conditions of copyright protection which adversely affected the functioning of the internal market, free movement of goods and services and the development of an information market in the EU. It also relies on recital 60 to say that article 3(1) carries out a 'harmonisation of the criterion for determining whether a database is to be protected by copyright'.[63] It reminds that of course, transitional provisions kept the status quo for databases created before 27 March 1996, which can remain protected under prior, different, if at all, eligibility criteria. However, for 'new databases', no other copyright protection can exist apart from that provided in the Directive.

The Court of Justice's decision in *Football Dataco*, albeit not a surprising one, is welcome for its further clarifications. Apart from firmly grounding the originality requirement and definitely 'killing' the skill and labour doctrine, the Court's decision also means that the Dutch *geschriftenberscherming* and Nordic catalogue rule cannot protect 'new databases'. Nevertheless, the answer to the second question is not totally clarifying. How about 'copyright-like' protection such as protection against parasitism or slavish copying, which many national laws provide in their tort or special unfair competition statutes?

61 Para. 44.
62 Para. 52.
63 Para. 49.

The Court of Appeal of England and Wales had asked the Court more specifically 'Does the Directive preclude national rights *in the nature of copyright* in databases other than those provided for by [Directive 96/9]?' (emphasis added). Maybe the Court of Justice assumed that since the United Kingdom does not have an unfair competition law (except passing off), it did not refer to that type of protection. Nevertheless, the Luxembourg Court could have interpreted the question in a more extensive way since it was posed in such broad terms, i.e. capable of encompassing unfair competition-type legislation. The Court's answer is not entirely clear on this point if at all, but on a logical construction of its paragraph 49, it is fair to assume that that sort of protection is also out of the window. Indeed, it would adversely affect the functioning of the internal market and free movement of goods and services if databases could obtain quasi-copyright protection through unfair competition law provisions.

3. A SMALL BUT GROWING SUCCESS STORY?

Despite the relatively little change in copyright law effected by the Directive and the *sui generis* right's flaws, the Directive's success is nevertheless undeniable as the Directive, and the subsequent case law from the Court of Justice, have harmonized both copyright and the *sui generis* right in the EU's single market.[64] However, this success is relative. So long as the national courts do not follow the Court of Justice's rulings, harmonization is a dead letter. To take just three Member States, it is clear that the penny has yet to drop in respect of some notions that the Court of Justice has already ruled on. For instance, in a Belgian case,[65] the Court held there was a qualitative extraction when important information is extracted from the database. However, the value of the information is irrelevant in determining infringement. What is relevant is the amount of investment in the part taken by the user. In another case, the Court of first instance of Paris held that *sui generis* right subsisted in the database of French horse races (made by *PMU*, the French equivalent of *BHB*, and similar to that made by *BHB* in the United Kingdom) and therefore a typical spin-off database.[66] The French Court did not check whether there was a substantial investment separate from the creation of the data. Also, some French courts still persist and cumulate the tort of parasitism when the *sui generis* right is

64 D. Gervais, *supra* note 23, at 1159.

65 CA Anvers, 19 December 2005, *Omni Whittington v East-West Debt* [2007] Auteurs & Media 85–96.

66 TGI Paris, 20 June 2007, *PMU v Eturf,* available on http://legalis.net/spip.php?page=jurisprudence-decision&id_article=1973.

infringed whereas the *sui generis* right has replaced this tort.[67] In the United Kingdom, with its ambiguous ruling in *Newspaper Licensing Agency v Meltwater*, the Court of Appeal recently totally muddled the High Court's case law applying the author's own intellectual creation following *Infopaq*: the Court of Appeal agreed with the High Court which had upheld *Infopaq* on the one hand, and then stated, on the other, that the old law was still applicable.[68] Hopefully, this confusion will be overcome when the *Football Dataco* case is decided on remand.

CONCLUSION: IN WHICH DIRECTION ARE WE GOING AND WHAT SHOULD BE DONE?

It is clear that the main problem with databases lies with the *sui generis* right. Empirical research to ascertain the usefulness of introducing such a right was missing before it was adopted and is still missing now. It is simply blindingly obvious that we need this empirical data before we do anything in respect of the *sui generis* right.[69] The Commission would be more than well advised to base

---

67 See T. Commerce Paris, 8 December 2006, *Motor Presse France v Jean Marc R.-M.*, available on http://legalis.net/spip.php?page=jurisprudence-decision&id_article=1889; CA Paris, 14th ch B, 23 January 2009, *Sté IIEESS, Ditel v Société*, affirming Trib. Com. Paris (réf), 18 June 2008, available at www.legalis.net (the Paris Commercial Court and Court of Appeal of Paris have again accepted jurisdiction when the claimant brought an unfair competition action for extraction of data from a database without looking into the question whether a *sui generis* right subsisted and whether it was infringed). More recently TGI Paris, 1 February 2011, *Adenclassifieds v Solus'immo*, available on http://legalis.net/spip.php?page=jurisprudence-decision&id_article=3092 (while finding for the defendant – holding that a search engine does not extract or reutilize data, – the Court nevertheless said that the tort of parasitism can still be added to the *sui generis* right – although parasitism was not established in this case). For an overview of the recent French case law interpreting the database *sui generis* right and unfair competition, see E. Derclaye [2012], 'Recent French Decisions on Database Protection: Towards a More Consistent and Compliant Approach with the Court of Justice's Case Law?', *European Journal of Law and Technology*, **3** (2), available at ejlt.org//article/view/124.

68 [2011] EWCA Civ 890, available at www.bailii.org/ew/cases/EWCA/Civ/2011/890.html

69 Gervais, *supra* note 23, at 1160 and 1165, advocating empirical studies and also non legal perspectives; P. Yu [2010], 'The Political Economy of Data Protection', *Chicago-Kent L. Rev.*, **84**, 777, at 793:

> before intellectual property protection is strengthened or new *sui generis* rights are created, policymakers need to conduct impact studies to ensure a holistic evaluation of the ramifications of the proposed new standards. Those studies have been widely

its second evaluation report on such empirical data. Some have suggested that since the *sui generis* right is a purely economic right, surely a cost benefit analysis should govern its fate.[70] In the meantime, economists, who so far do not seem to have been much interested in the issue,[71] should carry out empirical studies on the effect of the database right in Europe, now that several years have passed and we can probably therefore have a more global, accurate, view, well, provided they can find this data. The Commission should also start taking action upon what it suggested in its 2005 evaluation report. Whilst waiting for the empirical studies, it is clear that it can address one of the major flaws allowed by article 13 of the Directive namely the possibility to cumulate copyright, the *sui generis* right and other laws protecting these same efforts.

Finally, for the remaining issues, we will have to wait for future judgments of the Court of Justice and hope they make as much sense as in its previous databases decisions, as opposed to some other decisions such as *Bezpečnostní softwarová asociace*.[72] Indeed, despite their considerable competence, the Luxembourg judges are frequently only trained in one system (civil law or common law) and seldom trained in the, often, quite arcane copyright, and more generally, intellectual property fields. Academics should therefore provide 'advice' to the Court of Justice in pending references perhaps similarly to the system of *amici curiae* briefs existing in the United States[73] or else provide specific intellectual property training to the Court. Conferences, such as that organized in January 2012 by the Oxford Intellectual Property Research Centre,[74] which invited some of the Court of Justice's judges and Advocate Generals along with national judges as speakers, are also an excellent step in attempting to insure a dialogue between the judiciary and academics and a coherent case law.

---

endorsed in the areas of human rights, public health, and biological diversity and within the WIPO Development Agenda.

And 801: 'The decision to introduce data protection laws needs to be guided not by faith or speculation, but by empirical data'.

70 Gervais, *supra* note 23, at 1165–6.

71 As illustrated by the dearth of economic studies, both theoretical and empirical, on the topic. This has also been confirmed to me by Richard Watt and Ruth Towse.

72 The Court's decision on the issue of communication of the public of a graphical user interface atttracted a lot of criticism. See e.g. Derclaye, *supra* note 58.

73 As explained by Advocate General Niilo Jääskinen at the 'European Methods and Interactions in the Field of Intellectual Property Law' conference in Oxford in January 2012, such briefs may be counterproductive as they add to the Court's workload.

74 See 'European Methods and Interactions in the Field of Intellectual Property Law', http://www.law.ox.ac.uk/news.php?id=353

17. Function, art and fashion: do we need the EU design law?

Uma Suthersanen

1. INTRODUCTION: WHAT IS A 'DESIGN'?

> It would not accord with the normal use of language to apply the term 'sculpture' to a 20th century military helmet used in the making of a film, whether it was the real thing or a replica made in different material, however great its contribution to the artistic effect of the finished film. The argument for applying the term to an Imperial Stormtrooper helmet is stronger, because of the imagination that went into the concept of the sinister cloned soldiers dressed in uniform white armour. [1]

It is well known that the meaning of 'design'.is fiendishly difficult to contain. In English, the word 'design' functions as a noun, a verb and an adjective. It can refer to the ornamentation applied to an invention or the stylization of a sign, or to the three dimensional aspects of a product. A holistic approach would lead one to conclude that 'design' refers to the process or an evolutionary medium of creation rather than a finished product.[2] Thus, one Court held that:

> Design means [...] a conception or suggestion or idea of a shape or of a picture or of a device or of some arrangement which can be applied to an article by some manual, mechanical or chemical means. It is a conception, suggestion, or idea, and not an article, which is the thing capable of being registered [. . .] it is a suggestion of form or ornament to be applied to a physical body.[3]

This notion of design encompasses technical or biological inventions, geographical and fashion works, engineering or architectural design documents, and packaging or trade dress of products. The concept can stand true

1 Per Lords Walker and Collins, *Lucasfilm Ltd. v Ainsworth*, Supreme Court [2011] UKSC 39, [2011] 6 ECDR, at para. 44.

2 This phenomenon also applies to other words used to describe artistic works; thus, for instance, sculpture is both applicable to a process and a product; *Lucasfilm Ltd. v Ainsworth* (2011) UKSC 39, [2011] 6 ECDR, at para. 33.

3 *Dover v Nürnberger Celluloidwaren Fabrick Cebrüder Wolff* (1910) 27 RPC 498, 503.

irrespective of the mode of production, or the nature of the substrate manifesting the design, or the purpose of the creator, or the context of the use.

At one point of the design circle lie the value- and emotion-laden sentiments of beauty, aesthetics and pleasure; at another point in this circle, design leads and is led by market conditions, including consumer perception, product identity and competitive edge. In between art and market, lies a nebulous and grey area in which most design products live. Business entities, creators, and consumers understand and navigate this grey area on a daily basis. These players know that 'art' no longer originates solely from professional painters, sculptors and artists but can arise from a complex relationship between public taste, merchandising, consumption habits, branding, visual appeal, and most importantly, pricing. If successful, the work will be misappropriated, copied, counterfeited, and pirated. As Hillel Schwartz points out, the notion that art loses its authority and aura in an age of industrial reproduction is inaccurate. Instead, he asserts: 'Only in a culture of the copy, do we assign such motive force to the original [...] the more adept the West has become at the making of copies, the more we have exalted uniqueness.'[4]

Designs exist in both forms – the unique 'one', and the ubiquitous 'many'. They can manifest themselves simultaneously as utilitarian helmets worn in a battle scene of a film, as general fancy costumes worn by infants, as component parts of an artistic film set, and as a collectible art work sold in Christies.[5] The design of GWR 4900 Class 5972 Olton Hall locomotive is highly functional, built for a specific purpose in 1937. The artistic need to make an authentic visual representation of J.K. Rowling's Hogwarts Express in the visionary world of Harry Potter has, however, shifted this utilitarian product into a highly stylistic and lucrative merchandising world.[6]

The hybrid nature of a design, as icons of art, as museum exhibits, as collectors' items, as practical everyday objects, and as industrial functional products, has made legal categorization difficult. The dilemma has also, to a certain extent, shaped intellectual property law typology, so that designs are perceived as industrial property, functional models, industrial designs, drawings, and artistic works. As we shall see in the discussion that follows, the word 'design' itself has evolved into a generic term which has led to various

[4] H. Schwartz (1996), *The Culture of the Copy: Striking Likenesses, Unreasonable Facsimiles,* New York: Zone Books, at pp. 140 and 211.

[5] See the discussion below in section 5.2 in relation to the litigation concerning the Imperial Stormtrooper helmet in the film *Star Wars IV: A New Hope* (Lucasfilm, 1977).

[6] This steam locomotive is used to haul the 'Hogwarts Express'. One can obtain an exact miniature reproduction made by Hornby, the leading producers of model railways in the UK since 1901 (the 'Harry Potter Hogwarts Express' set) for around £45 from eBay (accessed 9 September 2011).

narratives which revolve on certain key themes: the evolution of *sui generis* rights, a universal legislative ambiguity in relation to the nature of 'design law', a struggle for courts to understand that the role of designs is always dictated, to a certain extent, by how and why they manifest in different times, markets and spaces.

2. PHANTOM IPRS

> Intellectual property may be extended to new subject matter either by accretion or by emulation. Accretion involves redefining an existing right so as to encompass the novel material; emulation requires the creation of a new and distinct right by analogy drawn more or less eclectically from the types already known.[7]

Patent, copyright and trade mark laws are the three major bulwarks within an intellectual property regime that guards creative and entrepreneurial endeavours.[8] Within this framework, there is a further set of rights, which protect, *inter alia*, designs, plant varieties, databases, petty patents/utility models, and geographical indications. These rights have been termed in a variety of ways ranging from second tier rights to sub-patentable rights to legal hybrids to *sui generis* rights.[9]

A common characteristic of *sui generis* intellectual property rights is that they tend to emanate from the inability of legislators and jurists to stretch the existing three bulwarks of the intellectual property regime to accommodate new things to protect. The subject matter, criteria and scope of protection of *sui generis* intellectual property regimes inevitably incorporate an *ad hoc* mixture of copyright, patent or trade mark principles. *Sui generis* rights also reflect, to a certain extent, the legislative journey taken whereby the 'young'

---

7 W.R. Cornish (1993), 'The International Relations of Intellectual Property', CLJ, **52** (1), 46, at 54–5.

8 For varied definitions of intellectual property, see D. Vaver (2011), *Intellectual Property Law: Copyright, Patents, Trade Marks,* 2nd ed., Toronto: Irwin Law, Ch. 1; G. Dutfield and U. Suthersanen (2008), *Global Intellectual Property Law*, Cheltenham, UK and Northampton, MA: Edward Elgar, Ch. 1; W.R. Cornish and D. Llewelyn (2003), *Intellectual Property: Patents, Copyright, Trade Marks and Allied Marks*, 5th ed., London: Sweet & Maxwell, at p. 3 (the authors add, though, that 'it also shields much that is trivial and ephemeral'); and L. Bently and B. Sherman (2008), *Intellectual Property Law,* 3rd ed., Oxford: Oxford University Press, at p. 1; M. Spence (2007), *Intellectual Property*, Oxford: Oxford University Press, at pp. 12–13.

9 For example, M. Janis (1990), 'Second Tier Patent Protection', *Harv. Int'l L.J.*, **40**, 151; J. Reichman (1994), 'Legal Hybrids Between the Patent and Copyright Paradigms', *Columbia. L. Rev.* 94, 2432; U. Suthersanen [2001], 'Incremental Inventions in Europe: A Legal and Economic Appraisal of 2nd Tier Patents', *JBL*, 319.

subaltern right is justified and distinguished from its more elderly parent right. It is relatively easy to discern various legal families within the intellectual property legal spectrum. For instance, the novelty criterion in plant variety, utility model or design laws, betrays the patent origin of these rights. The legislative history of *sui generis* database and sound recording rights[10] indicates extensive discussion on whether such rights were justified within copyright law, and if not, should the characteristics of copyright law be incorporated within such *sui generis* rights. A similar legal angst was sounded when computer programs were accorded, first copyright, and then patent protection, with many strongly arguing that software should be accorded separate rights.[11] Geographical indication laws, with their roots in trade protectionism and product identity, adopt a trade mark approach, protecting the origin of the product against consumer confusion.[12]

Conversely, some of these *sui generis* intellectual property rights are incongruously described as being young intellectual property laws, or poor cousins, or legislative after-thoughts, or historical accidents within the intellectual property regime. This is not strictly accurate, as many of these rights have had long legislative histories. For instance, design laws have been around since 1711 in France in relation to textile production;[13] the protection of geographical indications was internationally dealt with in the 1883 Paris Convention, though national laws and regulations have been protecting usage of geographical names since the early Etruscan and Chinese civilizations;[14] and early plant variety laws include the 1833 Papal States Edict, conferring property rights on new agricultural innovations.[15] Even the concern for protection of databases

[10] Rights of phonogram producers, like those of performers and broadcasters, come within euphemistic terms such as 'related rights' or 'neighbouring rights'. They are, to all practical purposes, outside the traditional authors' rights paradigm as set out in the Berne Convention, being located within the Rome Convention for the Protection of Performers, Producers of Phonograms and Broadcasting Organisations, 1960. They are, it is submitted, *sui generis* rights.

[11] See for instance the debate in, P. Samuelson et al. (1994), 'A Manifesto Concerning the Legal Protection of Computer Programs', *Colum. L. Rev.* **94**, 2308; *Cf* P. Goldstein (1994), 'Comments on a Manifesto Concerning the Legal Protection of Computer Programs', *Colum. L. Rev.* **94**, 2573.

[12] See, for example, Council Regulation (EC) No 510/2006 of 20 March 2006 on the protection of geographical indications and designations of origin for agricultural products and foodstuffs, OJ L 93, 31 March 2006, pp. 12–25.

[13] See Part 6 below.

[14] Art. 1(2), Paris Convention for the Protection of Industrial Property, 20 March 1883; K. Shao (2004), 'Look at my Sign: Trademarks in China from Antiquity to the Early Modern Times', *JPTOS* **87**, 654; Dutfield and Suthersanen, *supra* note 8, at pp. 227–8.

[15] M. Blakeney (2009), *Intellectual Property Rights and Food Security*, CABI, at p. 79.

and collections is not novel. Early examples of rights extending to compilations include the1837 Prussian Law[16] and the 1886 Berne Convention[17].

Sui generis rights were justifiable at certain periods of time, especially as the notion of 'intellectual property' itself was a relatively new nineteenth century species of law that has been evolving slowly in the last three centuries.[18] Contrary to their previous important roles within very specific agriculture, textile fashion, food and wine, sound recording, or mechanical product industries, *sui generis* rights today are often confusing and contradictory. A constant battle is sometimes fought as to the rationale and scope of such rights. Should utility model laws protect all innovations, which show a modest level of inventiveness and novelty, thereby undermining patent law? Or should utility model laws be confined to minor innovations in the field of engineering and construction, and excluded from more 'important' new technologies such as computer programs, biotechnology and pharmaceuticals?[19] Should geographical indication laws be viewed as a *sui generis* intellectual property right, which protects one aspect of product branding, or can we dispense with this right and rely solely on trade mark law?[20] Should beneficiaries of *sui generis* rights, such as performers, obtain moral rights, which are usually the preserve of *auteurs*?[21]

---

16 Art. 8, Law of 11 June 1837, which provides that educational and research institutions enjoyed a 30 year right over new editions of their works, including 'works which in one or several volumes constitute a single edition and thereby can be regarded as belonging together' or 'collections of articles and studies of different aspects of academic research' – the duration for these works were computed from the time of completion or publication with ownership vested in the corporate body as producer of the compilation.

17 Art. 2(5), Berne Convention for the Protection of Literary and Artistic Works, (Paris version, 1971) see also a similar criterion of originality in the EU database legislation in Art. 3, European Parliament and Council Directive on Legal Protection of Databases, 96/9/EC, 11 March 1996, OJ L 77/20, 27 March 1996.

18 Vaver, *supra* note 8, at pp. 6–7.

19 U. Suthersanen and G. Dutfield (2007), 'Utility Models and other Alternatives to Protection', in U. Suthersanen, G. Dutfield and K. Boey Chow (eds), *Innovation Without Patents: Harnessing the Creative Spirit in a Diverse World*, Cheltenham, UK and Northampton, MA: Edward Elgar.

20 Note, for example, the reluctance of the United States to embrace *sui generis* laws in relation to geographical indications. Part of the problem stems from the fact that a majority of places of origin and products are European in nature, and have also become genericized within American culture and language. See E. Creditt [2009], 'Terroir vs. Trademarks: The Debate over Geographical Indications and Expansions to the TRIPS Agreement', *Vanderbilt J. of Ent. And Tech. Law,* **11** (2) 425; *cf* D. Gangjee [2007], 'Quibbling Siblings: Conflicts Between Trademarks and Geographical Indications', *Chicago-Kent L. Rev.*, **82**, 1253, 1263.

21 Art. 5, WIPO Performances and Phonograms Treaty 1996.

This internecine conflict is most often seen in relation to the legal protection of designs that lie at the boundary of art and function.

At times, patent law principles are applied to protect designs due to the industrial manufacturing process involved in creating the artefact. Conversely, the aesthetic aspects and visual appeal of many designs suggest that copyright law is the most suitable type of protection. This ambivalence is evidenced in international intellectual property laws. The Berne Convention, Paris Convention and the TRIPS Agreement have all embraced the ambiguous nature of designs by suggesting that designs are appropriate subject matter for both copyright and industrial property protection.[22] It may be that the preferred mode of protection is very much dependent on the nature of the design, the type of product it is applied to, and the market in which the product manifests itself. Add to this the fact that many designs function as product identifiers, and thus can also be registered as three-dimensional trade marks.

National design laws reflect this ambivalence. The words which have appeared historically in national design legislations in order to contain its meaning include eye appeal, pattern, shape, configuration, form, model, ornamental, functional, original, individual character, novelty. The concerns which arise from these terms are myriad and include the following questions. Should the law protect functional designs? If not, what type of functional designs should be excluded? If design law is about incentivizing the efforts of a designer to bring a product into the marketplace, must courts then take into account the eye appeal of the product, or the consumer's perception of it? Should aestheticism, artistic character, artistic merit or eye appeal even matter?

The US design regime, for instance, incorporates design protection within the federal patent statute, conferring protection on designs that are novel, inventive and useful. Nevertheless, the intrinsic element of 'art' is acknowledged as the design patent law requires a further threshold to be fulfilled i.e. a design must be *ornamental*.[23] Often, the analysis under US design patent law is reduced to the art/function dichotomy i.e. a design which is functional cannot be 'ornamental'.[24] Moreover, the ornamental requirement is twisted

---

[22] Collectively read, the three main international instruments allow contracting States to protect designs under patent, copyright or *sui generis* design laws. Art. 1(2), Paris Convention for the Protection of Industrial Property of 20 March 1883, Stockholm version (2 October 1979); Art. 2(7), Berne Convention for the Protection of Literary and Artistic Works of 9 September 1886, Paris version (24 July 1971); Arts 9(1), 25, 26, TRIPS Agreement 1994.

[23] 35 USC § 171 (1976).

[24] *LA Gear Inc v Thom McAn Shoe Co* 988 F.2d 1117, 1123; 25 USPQ 2d 1913, 1917 (Fed. Cir., 1993); see also *Seiko Epson Corp v Nu-Kote International, Inc* 190 F.3d 1360, 1363 (Fed. Cir., 1999).

into a subjective test of eye appeal, aesthetic emotion and beauty.[25] Recent scholarship suggests that the US design law never had strong historical roots within the patent regime, and should not even have adopted a patent approach at all, especially in relation to the construction and scope of design patent claims.[26]

Unsurprisingly, all these terms and conjectures have led legislatures and courts into long and somewhat bewildering discussions into the justification, remit and criteria of design law.

3. A NEW HOPE: THE EU DESIGN REGIME

A contrasting approach is the EU *sui generis* design law, as set out in the Community Design Regulation (CDR).[27] The law clearly and deliberately eschews any qualitative requirement of artistry or aestheticism. A design need not be pretty or attractive or have eye appeal to be protectable. In addition to this, the CDR deliberately omits the requirement of 'industrial character' or 'industrial application', and a product can be the result of an industrial process or be the result of traditional craftsmanship. The traditional demarcation between fine art, applied art, and industrial design is to be discarded.

---

25 *Wabern Packaging Indus., Inc v Cut Rate Plastic Hangers, Inc* 210 USPQ 777 (2nd Cir., 1981) (an article must be 'ornamental, a product of aesthetic skill and artistic conception'); *Design, Inc v Emerson Co* 168 USPQ 519 (S.D. Tex., 1970):

> Although it is not an object which is displeasing to the eye, it is far from what could be considered a thing of beauty. There is nothing either artistic or aesthetic about it. One who sees it does not take delight in its creation. It is an item which is more likely to be stored in a kitchen closet rather than on display in one's living room. The design embodied in the Schroeder patent is, therefore, not ornamental.

See also *Seiko Epson Corp* 190 F.3d 1360 at 1362 (Fed. Cir., 1999) (holding that the designs at issue in this case were for printer ink cartridges, which are not widely regarded as things of beauty). See U. Suthersanen (2010), *Design Law in the EU and US*, London: Sweet & Maxwell, paras 10–019 *et seq.*

26 J. du Mont and M. Janis, The Origins of American Design Protection, 2011, *Indiana Law Journal*, Vol. 88..

27 Council Regulation (EC) No. 6/2002 of 12 December 2001 on Community designs (OJ EC No L 3 of 5 January 2002, p. 1), amended by Council Regulation No 1891/2006 of 18 December 2006 to give effect to the accession of the European Community to the Geneva Act of the Hague Agreement concerning the international registration of industrial designs (OJ EC No L 386 of 29.12.2006, p. 14).

A design must satisfy three main conditions before Community design protection can be conferred: it must be a protectable design without falling within the exclusions, it has to be new, and it has to have individual character.[28] Upon satisfaction of these criteria, the CDR then offers a choice between a 25-year exclusive registered design right,[29] or a three-year anti-copying unregistered design right.[30]

In relation to what constitutes a protectable design, the initial definition of design adopted a holistic concept, which concentrated on the marketing role of the design. Design was the symbiosis of three elements: (i) functional improvement or technical innovation in the product; (ii) creative contribution of an aesthetic nature by the designer; and (iii) investment by the manufacturer to develop the two preceding elements.[31] This initial utopian concept of design was soon abandoned as having the potential to encompass bare concepts, principles of construction or purely functional elements, which would trespass into the world of ideas and inventions. The current definition within the CDR is: '"design" means the appearance of the whole or a part of a product resulting from the features of, in particular, the lines, contours, colours, shape, texture and/or materials of the product itself and/or its ornamentation.'[32]

The law offers some guidance as to the type of elements one may have to assess in order to gauge the appearance of the product, including such intriguing elements as texture and materials. The consideration of such elements would align the designed product to any economic value that may be attached to the appearance of the product, which in turn protects the marketing aspect of the designed product. 'Thus, the appearance of the product will refer to *any* element, which can be perceived by the visual sense such as the weight or flexibility of a product or the tactile impressions given, for example, by textiles' (emphasis added).[33]

The term 'product' is defined within the CDR to mean any industrial or handicraft item, including complex products, packaging, get-up, graphic symbols and typographic typefaces. 'Packaging, get-up, graphic symbols and typographic typefaces' suggests that EU design law will protect communicative and visual aspects of the design which will seal the product's identity; 'get-up' will presumably also extend to restaurant and window interiors and displays. One can stretch the concept of product design to environmental design and landscape design, including props and costumes used for a film set.

---

28 Arts 5 and 6, CDR.
29 Arts 12 and 19(1), CDR.
30 Arts 11 and 19(2), CDR.
31 Suthersanen, *supra* note 25, para.6–001.
32 Art. 3(a), CDR.
33 Suthersanen, *supra* note 25, para. 6.1.3.

If a proprietor wished, he could claim protection for a whole set of articles within a general space as a complex product, or for individual products within a set, if separate registrations are made for individual products.[34]

The trouble with this definition lies in the word 'appearance'. The word does not reflect the multi-faceted nature of design, especially in relation to designs that reflect functional considerations. A recent decision from OHIM suggests a return to the 'eye-appeal' test, which appears to call for a more subjective discussion of what is 'aesthetic'.

The difficulty is compounded by the twin criteria of novelty and individual character, which both registered and unregistered designs must fulfil. In the case of novelty, the law clarifies that designs 'shall be deemed to be identical if their features differ only in immaterial details'. The reasoning appears arbitrary as to whether a feature will be considered material or not.[35] Moreover, it is not clear whether we account for the views of the designer alone, or whether the consumer's view is considered. But the hurdle caused by the novelty provision pales in comparison to that placed by the individual character criterion. Art. 6 reads: 'A design shall be considered to have individual character if the *overall impression* it produces on the *informed user* differs from the overall impression produced on such a user by any design which has been made available to the public'(emphasis added).

These are not easy legal concepts to grasp, in spite of recent guidance from the General Court in *Grupo Promer Mon Graphic v OHIM, PepsiCo*:

> In the specific assessment of the overall impression of the designs at issue on the informed user, who has some awareness of the state of the prior art, the designer's degree of freedom in developing the contested design must be taken into account. [...] In addition, the more the designer's freedom in developing the contested design is restricted, the more likely minor differences between the designs at issue will be sufficient to produce a different overall impression on the informed user [...] as regards the assessment of the overall impression produced by the designs at issue on the informed user, the latter will automatically disregard elements 'that are totally banal and common to all examples of the type of product in issue' and will concentrate on features 'that are arbitrary or different from the norm'.[36]

---

34 Art. 3(c), CDR defines complex product as 'a product which is composed of multiple components which can be replaced permitting disassembly and re-assembly of the product'. See *Mobile Home* Hamburg DC, 20 October 2006; as reported in H. Hartwig (2009), *Designschutz in Europa/Design Protection in Europe,* Carl Heymanns Verlag, Vol. 3 at p. 351 (design of a mobile home as a whole protectable; moreover the applicant could have claimed protection on parts of the mobile home separately).

35 Art. 5 (2), CDR. See *Holey Soles Holdings Ltd v Crocs Inc* [2008] ECDR 8 OHIM; *Imperial International Ltd v Handle Cookware Ltd* (R1456/2006–3) OHIM (Third Board of Appeal) 2 September 2008 (available online at http://oami.europa.eu/LegalDocs/BoA/2008/en/R0196_2008-3.pdf).

36 *Grupo Promer Mon Graphic SA v OHIM (Trade Marks and Designs),*

As for the 'informed user', this hypothetical person is more than a mere consumer but less than a design expert. He is not the seller or the manufacturer either, though he will be aware of the existing design corpus in the relevant product category.[37] Despite the difficulties, it is clear that consideration of appearance, novelty and individual character do call for, to a certain extent, an appreciation of the spectator's judgement of the designed thing. The spectator, legally termed the 'informed user', is called upon not only to determine criteria of protection, but also the scope of protection.[38] The importance of the spectator is ignored, nevertheless, by courts within design and copyright laws, in relation to functional designs. Instead, the courts incarcerate the designer and his thing into a monastic cell.

4. THE 'FUNCTIONALITY' WARS

> All things in nature have…a form, an outward semblance, that tells us what they are, that distinguishes them from ourselves and from each other. Unfailingly, in nature these shapes express the inner life, the native quality, of the animal, tree, bird, fish… it seems ever as though the life and the form were absolutely one and inseparable…Whether it be the sweeping eagle in his flight, or the open apple-blossom, the toiling work-horse, the blithe swan, the branching oak, the winding stream at its base, the drifting clouds, over all the coursing sun, form ever follows function, and this is the law.[39]

As suggested above, where *sui generis* rights are concerned, parent rights do affect the scope and nature of a subsidiary hybrid right. In the case of designs, for instance, case law in the areas of copyright and trade mark laws, in relation to artistic works and shape marks, affects how provisions within *sui generis* design law are interpreted, and *vice versa*. Thus, the debate as to how the law should discriminate against the functional aspects of a product without embarking on aesthetic discrimination is also to be found within trade

---

Pepsico. Inc Case T-9/07, [2010] ECDR 7, General Court (Fifth Chamber), paras 72 and 74.

[37] *Procter & Gamble Co* [2007] ECDR 4 (Court of Appeal, UK); *Grupo Promer Mon Graphic* (T-9/07), [2010] ECDR 7 (General Court (EU)); *Normann Copenhagen ApS* [2010] ECDR 3 OHIM (Trade Marks and Designs), (Third Board of Appeal).
71 See *Honda Giken Kogyo Kabushiki Kaisha v Wuxi Kipor Power Co Ltd* [2009] ECDR 4 OHIM (Third Board of Appeal).

[38] Art. 10, CDR.

[39] Louis Sullivan, the American architect who is often referred to as the father of skyscrapers and modernism, in L. Sullivan (1947), *Kindergarten Chats and Other Writings*, New York: Wittenborn, Schultz, Inc., at p.141, cited in S. Lambert (1993), *Form Follows Function? Design in the 20th Century*, Victoria & Albert Museum, at pp. 6–7.

mark and copyright laws.[40] This in turn affects the continued cohesion and viability of 'design law'.

4.1 'Functionality' Within the CDR

Recital 10, CDR suggests that certain types of functional designs are excluded. The reason is that: '[t]echnological innovation should not be hampered by granting design protection to features dictated solely by a technical function. It is understood that this does not entail that a design must have an aesthetic quality'.

The reasoning is that certain features of functional designs should be excluded, but other more ambivalent features which are both functional and have market appeal (whether because it is pleasant to look at or fashionably functional) should be protected. Art. 8(1), CDR explicitly states that protection is denied to 'features which are solely dictated by its technical function'.

The wording of Art. 8(1) suggests that design protection will only be denied to such features which have no alternative design features available which will achieve the product's technical function. What if there are only two or three available forms which can fulfil the technical function? Does the exclusion bite if the technical function is fully capable of being realized or is the mere possibility of a technical effect sufficient to exclude the design features from protection? Thus, a design may have been designed to be an ornament but it may, in time, acquire a technical purpose. Conversely, a design may have had a functional purpose when created, but with time, it is treated as an adornment or sculpture. Is 'function' to be determined from the perspective of the objective user, a panel of experts in the relevant product design field, the consuming public, or the 'informed user', who is the reference point in respect of individual character and scope of protection under the EU design law regime? Many products are perceived by the consuming public to be technically or functionally superior through astute marketing techniques,[41] though in actuality no real advantage is revealed. What, in any case, constitutes 'function'? And what if the 'functional design' gets elevated into a museum collection?[42]

---

40 Art. 26(1), TRIPS Agreement also provides that WTO Members have the option of excluding designs which are dictated essentially by technical or functional considerations.

41 See U. Suthersanen (2003), 'The European Court of Justice in *Philips v Remington – Trade Marks and Market Freedom*, [2003] 3 IPQ 256, at pp. 280 *et seq.* on the how the perception of a product is shaped by the producers' advertising message.

42 An example is Philippe Starck's 'Juicy Salif' (designed to be used for squeezing juice and is available in most shops in Europe). It is an iconic design and is much

4.2 The Traditional Functionality Doctrine

One manner of interpreting Art. 8(1), CDR is to adopt the 'multiplicity of forms' doctrine which had its genesis in the pre-harmonized French design law. The latter law excluded patentable designs by developing the '*multiplicite des formes'* doctrine. This doctrine preaches that technical features should be excluded from design protection only if the technical function cannot be achieved by any other configuration; if the designer has a choice between two or more configurations, the logical conclusion is that the appearance of the design is not solely dictated by its technical function.[43] This is the traditional OHIM approach, and was also adopted by the UK,[44] Spanish[45] and French[46] national courts.

In doing so, the courts were adopting the approach suggested by the Advocate-General, in *Koninklijke Philips Electronics NV v Remington Consumer Products Ltd,*[47] which concerned a trade mark decision on the three-dimensional shape of an electric shaver. Art. 3(1)(e) of the EU Trade Marks Directive excludes 'signs which consist exclusively of the shape of goods which is necessary to obtain a technical result'.[48]

The underlying purpose behind this provision is to prevent trade mark law, which has the potential to confer a permanent period of protection, from extending the life of other more short-lived rights, such as patents and design

---

used in the marketing literature of Alessi, the Italian designer firm which commissioned the design. Alessi claims to manufacture 'handicraft items made with the aid of machine'? Alessi further boasts on its website that it has more products than other design firms, which are part of 'permanent museum collections' including the MOMA, (New York), Met Museum of Art (New York), Centre Pompidou (Paris), and Victoria and Albert Museum (London). Why would such a consideration be important to them? See http://www.alessi.com/en/company/history.

43 U. Suthersanen (2000), *Design Law in Europe*, 1st ed., London: Sweet & Maxwell, paras. 13–24 *et seq*.

44 *Landor & Hawa International Ltd v Azure Designs Ltd* [2006] EWCA Civ 1285, [2006] ECDR 31; followed in *Bailey (trading as Elite Anglian Products) v Haynes (trading as RAGS)* [2006] EWPCC 5, [2007] FSR 10.

45 *Silverlit Toys Manufactory Ltd v Ditro Ocio 2000 SL*, Juzgado de lo Mercantil PTO Número Uno de Alicante, 20 November 2007, unreported, cited in *Lindner Recyclingtech GmbH v Franssons Verkstäder AB*; also see (1999) ITMA Review, April 2009, at p. 19. A summary is also provided at http://design-law.wikispaces.com/Silverlit+Toys+v+Ditro+OCIO+2000

46 *Procter & Gamble Co. v Reckitt Benckiser France SAS*, Tribunal de Commerce d'Evry, 5 April 2006; as reported in H. Hartwig (2009), *Designschutz in Europa/Design Protection in Europe*, Vol. 2, Carl Heymanns Verlag, at p. 167.

47 C-299/99; [2002] ECR I-5475.

48 First Council Directive (89/104/EEC) of 21 December 1988 to approximate the laws of the Member States relating to trade marks, OJ 1989 L 40, p. 1.

rights. The linkage between EU trade marks and design law was thought to be pertinent enough for the Advocate-General, to compare the markedly different statutory versions of the functionality test within the EU Trade Mark and Design Directives. From this difference, the Advocate General concluded that:

> the level of functionality must be greater in order to be able to assess the ground for refusal in the context of designs; the feature concerned must not only be *necessary* but *essential* in order to achieve a particular technical result: form follows function. This means that a functional design may, none the less, be eligible for protection if it can be shown that the same technical function could be achieved by another different form.[49]

This approach has been recently rejected by OHIM, in favour of an old British test – the eye appeal test.

4.3 The Return of the Amp Functionality Doctrine

Prior to the implementation of the EU design regime, British registered design law was confined to designs that exhibited features which 'appeal to and are judged by the eye'.[50] This was interpreted to mean that the design must offer some visual impact or at least, the features should seize the attention of a potential customer because their appearance is appealing. The landmark decision was *Amp v Utilux*[51] which concerned the design of an electrical terminal for use within a domestic washing machine. The (then) House of Lords held that the eye-appeal requirement meant that, not only must the features of a design be visible in the finished article, but it should also be noticeable and eye catching. However, this did not necessarily mean that a qualitative test of artistry or aestheticism was applied, but merely that there must be 'a special, peculiar, distinctive, significant or striking appearance – something which catches the eye and in this sense appeals to the eye …'[52]

As another judge in the case emphasized:

> The phrases 'appeal to' and 'judged solely by the eye' denote features which will or may influence choice or selection. The eye concerned will be the eye, not of the court, but of the person who may be deciding whether or not to acquire the finished article possessing the feature in question. This does not mean that the 'appeal' or the attraction must be to an aesthetic or artistic sense – though in some cases it may be.

---

[49] [2002] 2 CMLR 1329 (AGO), para. A.34. For the historical provenance and possible interpretation of this provision, see Suthersanen, *supra* note 43, paras. 6–018 to 6–024.

[50] s.1(1), Registered Designs Act 1949, 12, 13 and 14 Geo. 6 c. 88.

[51] (1972) RPC 103.

[52] *Per* Lord Pearson, at 121.

> The features may be such that they gain the favour of or appeal to some while meeting with the disfavour of others. Beyond being merely visible the feature must have some individual characteristic. It must be calculated to attract the attention of the beholder.[53]

However, if the sole appeal of the product was on the basis of its fitness for purpose, then, clearly the design did not satisfy the criterion. Here we have two conflicting notions. On the one hand, the judgment as a whole suggests that 'eye-appeal' demands a consideration of consumer taste and fashion. A product may be functional, but if it was visually arresting, it could be regarded as having eye appeal. On the other hand, the courts go further to state that in deciding whether a design was dictated by functional considerations, it was the designer's motivation which counted. The conundrum then is that a designer may have had functional motivations, which can be, with time, trumped by consumers' taste. And yet, the time of consideration is affixed to the moment of creation, and the motivation of the designer.

In *Lindner Recyclingtech GmbH v Franssons Verkstäder AB,*[54] the Third Board of Appeal, for the first time, declared a Community design invalid because it was found to be solely dictated by the technical function of the product in which it was incorporated. In doing so, the Board deliberately eschewed the Advocate-General's suggestion in *Philips* and the current 'multiplicity of forms' approach of national courts. Instead, the Board adopts the alternative *Amp* approach, and in doing so, aligns the technical result exclusion in design law to that adopted by the ECJ in trade mark law.

The Board argued that the phrase 'solely dictated by its technical function' does not, on its natural meaning, imply that the feature in question must be the only means by which the product's technical function can be achieved. Moreover, the Board emphasized the importance of the 'visual' aspect of design protection; if the visual appearance of a design is irrelevant, then protection must be denied as it is obvious that the functional aspect reigned supreme.

> Community design law is concerned with the visual appearance of products. That is clear from the definition of 'design' in art. 3(a) CDR and from the requirement of visibility in normal use for component parts in art.4(2)(b) CDR. [. . .] The significance of limiting protection to the visual appearance of products is that aesthetic considerations are in principle capable of being relevant only when the designer is developing a product's visual appearance. [...] As long as functionality is not the only relevant factor, the design is in principle eligible for protection.

---

53 *Per* Lord Morris of Borth-y-Gest, at pp. 112–13.

54 *Lindner Recyclingtech GmbH* (R 690/2007–3) [2010] ECDR 1 OHIM (Trade Marks and Designs) (Third Board of Appeal) 22 October 2009.

In short, the product design (irrespective of the nature of the product) has to look good enough for someone to care about its looks. Surely, this can only be gauged from the perspective of the consumer, and not, as suggested under the previous *Amp* decision, of the designer. Or should it be the guardian of EU design law, the 'informed user', who is employed in gauging individual character as well as the scope of protection? As previous case law from the EU General Court and OHIM has confirmed, the informed user can range from an adult consumer to an intermediate user (such as a retailer) or a five-year-old end user.[55] According to the *Lindner* tribunal, these matters are assessed objectively from the 'standpoint of a reasonable observer who looks at the design and asks himself whether anything other than purely functional considerations could have been relevant when a specific feature was chosen'.

In an effort to clarify that the EU design law does *not* ban designs that lack aesthetic quality or aesthetic merit, the Board states:

> It is only when aesthetic considerations are completely irrelevant that the features of the design are solely dictated by the need to achieve a technical solution. This is not, it must be stressed, tantamount to introducing a requirement of aesthetic merit into the legislation. It is simply recognition of the obvious fact that when aesthetics are totally irrelevant, in the sense that no one cares whether the product looks good, bad, ugly or pretty, and all that matters is that the product functions well, there is nothing to protect under the law of designs. [...].

One concern with the decision is that consumers do not ask the sort of question the tribunal calls for. Another concern is that subjective terminology such as 'aesthetic considerations' have been brought back into the discussion on functionality. Is there truly a difference between requiring 'aesthetic merit' being present in a design, and requiring that 'aesthetic considerations play a part in the development of the design'? The next section on copyright law emphasizes the point that there is no magical line dividing function, form, eye appeal and art. And the law should not struggle so valiantly to find such a line.

5. THE UK SUPREME COURT STRIKES BACK

5.1 The Duchamp Perspective on Artistic Work

Proprietors of 'design' products have various means of protecting their intellectual property under EU law. There is nothing within the CDR that prevents

---

55 *Grupo Promer Mon Graphic SA v OHIM (Trade Marks and Designs), Pepsico. Inc* Case T-9/07, [2010] ECDR 7, General Court (Fifth Chamber).

the co-existence of parallel protection under copyright, design, patent, utility model, trade mark or unfair competition laws (whether under national or EU regimes) save in certain specific instances (for example, where the novelty of the design is threatened if the design anticipates itself).[56]

If the design incorporates both artistic and functional features, the proprietor is faced with a conundrum. Should he choose the registration path and opt for a registered Community or national design right? Would this, however, prejudice any future claim under copyright, unfair competition or passing off? Courts have been reluctant to extend the protection accorded under registered design law, especially where the term of protection has expired.[57] Moreover, for SMEs and individual proprietors, design registration and enforcement can appear expensive and cumbersome.

The alternative is to rely on unregistered rights such as the unregistered Community design right (which still follows the complex criteria rules for the registered system) or national copyright law. Where copyright law is concerned however, this rather depends on the attitude of the national courts tó three-dimensional designs. One school of thought – let us call it the Marchel Duchamp approach – is that all art is protectable. There should be no judgement as to its aestheticism, its industrial nature, nor as to its purpose. This approach explains the ambivalence in the Berne Convention in relation to copyright protection of designs.[58]

The approach is reasonable if one accepts that art only becomes art when the reaction and input of the spectator (or consumer) has been assimilated into the work. It may look and feel artistic or functional, but the market may treat it otherwise.[59] Thus, designs can be transformed by the market into identifiers

---

[56] This multi-faceted protection regime is implicitly recognized in recitals 16, 31, 32, and Art. 96, CDR.

[57] Under German unfair competition law, for instance, the imitation of the product will be only considered unfair if special circumstances are met. Such particular circumstances arise from an avoidable deception as to origin or from the exploitation or impairment of the esteem in which the goods copied are held. German Act Against Unfair Competition, sec. 4, No. 9(a) and 9(b); *Construction Component (Baugruppe)* (I ZR 67/05), [2009] 40(8) IIC 985 BGH.

[58] Art. 2(7), Berne Convention. This provision resulted as a compromise solution between proponents of the l'unite de l'art approach, led by France, and the proponents of the 'industrial design' approach, comprising, at various stages of United Kingdom, Switzerland, Italy, Norway, Hungary and Japan. S. Ricketson and J. Ginsburg (2005), *International Copyright and Neighbouring Rights: The Berne Convention and Beyond*, 2nd ed., Oxford: Oxford University Press, Ch. 8.

[59] See, for instance, *Norris International v International T&T Corp.* 696 F.2d 918 (11th Cir., 1983) (US 11th Circuit court denied copyright protection to a wire wheel design, despite its primarily ornamental purpose. The Court looked at its potential utilitarian function: the wheel covers served as hubcaps to protect the wheel, brakes and

not only of the product but of the moral values of those who habitually use the product.

A case in point is *Plesner v Louis Vuitton*.[60] Plesner created a mural painting entitled 'Dafurnica', inspired by Picasso's 'Guernica', which showed a starving, poor African child holding a Chihuahua dressed in pink and a Louis Vuitton Audra handbag. These artefacts were a visual reference to Paris Hilton, a media personality. Louis Vuitton sued as the design of the bag was a protected registered Community design. Plesner argued successfully under her right to freedom of expression,[61] that it was necessary to incorporate the exact reproduction of the design in her painting as it conveyed the work's social message i.e. the difference in attention in the media between the situation in Darfur and other areas in crisis on the one hand, and the attention given by the media to the entertainment industry, on the other hand (as represented by the Hilton/Louis Vuitton imagery).[62]

Marcel Duchamp set out this alternative view of art. According to him, the audience (who can be another creator or parodist) has a vital role in validating something as an artwork: 'The artist may shout from all the rooftops that he is a genius: he will have to wait for the verdict of the spectator in order that his declarations take a social value and that, finally, posterity includes him in the primers of Artist History'.[63]

Duchamp's view of the artist is that he is but one consideration when determining whether a work is artistic or not. The artist is merely the medium of the work, without full consciousness of what is being produced. This goes against the grain of tribunals, especially in the UK, and more recently in the OHIM, that appear to place heavy reliance on the intention of the designer/artist.[64]

---

axles from damage and corrosion. The plaintiff's argument that the wheel covers did not actually accomplish these objectives was rejected, the Court holding that for the purposes of copyright, the efficiency of a utilitarian article is irrelevant.)

60 [2011] ECDR 4.

61 Art. 10(1), European Convention on Human Rights.

62 *Nadia Plesner Joensen v Louis Vuitton Malletier SA* [2011] ECDR 4. Louis Vuitton invoked not only its Community design rights in the handbag but also its right of property under Protocol 1, ECHR.

63 Marcel Duchamp, 'The Creative Act', paper given in Convention of the American Federation of Arts, Houston, 1957, available at http://eunchurn.com/mvio/Duchamp_Creative_Act.pdf.

64 The intention to mass manufacture a design was historically held, in the UK, to show an intention to create an 'industrial design' rather than an 'artistic work'; s.22(1), Copyright Act 1911; Registered Designs Act 1949, 12, 13 and 14 Geo. 6 c. 88, read with Rule 26 of the 1949 Designs Rules (now repealed). Also see *George Hensher Ltd v Restawile Upholstery (Lancs) Ltd* [1976] AC 64; *Metix (UK) Ltd v G H Maughan (Plastics) Ltd* [1997] FSR 718.

> All in all, the creative act is not performed by the artist alone; the spectator brings the work in contact with the external world by deciphering and interpreting its inner qualification and thus adds his contribution to the creative act. This becomes even more obvious when posterity gives a final verdict and sometimes rehabilitates forgotten artists.[65]

The Marchel Duchamp approach would treat industrial art and industrial literature in a similar manner, and protection would be accorded without much debate to computer programs,[66] advertising posters,[67] trade labels,[68] drawings, maps, plans,[69] and even perfumes.[70] It is the view of the spectator/consumer as to whether such works convey valuable, aesthetic, functional or moral information. Moreover, courts would need to look not only at the intention of the creator, the process of creation and manufacture, and the initial purpose of the artefact, but also at the acquired meaning the product gains with time and consumer appreciation. What was once utilitarian (e.g. the design of a train engine) can become popular, fashionable and even artistic (e.g. Hogwarts Express). On the other hand, what was once avant-garde 'art' (e.g. the Alvar Aalto Armchair) can become commonplace mass-manufactured furniture (e.g. Ikea's POÄNG chair).

5.2 The *Star Wars* Perspective

The UK Supreme Court has adopted another approach in its recent decision in *Lucasfilm Ltd. v Ainsworth*.[71] This decision was about the various intellectual property rights residing in artefacts and props used in the first Star Wars film – *Star Wars IV – A New Hope*. The film had received accolades, both in commerce and artwork, and won an Oscar for best costume design. One of the primary costumes was the Imperial Stormtrooper helmet.

---

65 Marcel Duchamp, 'The Creative Act', paper given in Convention of the American Federation of Arts, Houston, 1957, available at http://eunchurn.com/mvio/Duchamp_Creative_Act.pdf.

66 After much debate, computer programs were accepted as literary works, both under national and international copyright laws. See Art. 10(1), TRIPS Agreement 1994.

67 *Bleistein v Donaldson Lithographing Co* 188 US 239 (S. Ct., 1903).

68 *Elanco Products v Mandops* [1979] FSR 46 (CA).

69 See for example, s.4(1)(a), Copyright, Designs and Patents 1988 which protects graphic works, photographs, sculptures and collages, irrespective of artistic merit. *Cf Lucasfilm Inc. v Ainsworth* High Court [2008] EWHC 1878 (Ch), [2008] ECDR 17; Court of Appeal, [2009] EWCA Civ 1328; [2010] ECDR 6; Supreme Court, [2011] UKSC 39, [2011] 6 ECDR

70 *Kecofa BV v Lancome Parfums* [2006] ECDR (26) 363.

71 *Lucasfilm Ltd v Ainsworth*, High Court [2008] EWHC 1878 (Ch), [2008] ECDR 17; Court of Appeal, [2009] EWCA Civ 1328; [2010] ECDR 6; Supreme Court, [2011] UKSC 39, [2011] 6 ECDR

> The purpose of the helmet was that it was to be worn as an item of costume in a film, to identify a character, but in addition to portray something about that character – its allegiance, force, menace, purpose and, to some extent, probably its anonymity. It was a mixture of costume and prop.[72]

The main issue was whether copyright subsisted in the helmet as an artistic work.[73] The first instance judge dismissed all Lucasfilm's claims based on English copyright law because the helmet was not a work of sculpture. The Court of Appeal and the Supreme Court concurred with this aspect of the decision i.e. that the helmet was not an artistic work, as it failed to qualify as a sculpture.[74]

The major difficulty with the notion of 'artistic work' under UK law is that moveable three-dimensional works can only qualify as such if they fall within the statutory categories of sculpture or work of artistic craftsmanship. The statute expressly states that copyright protection is available to sculptures, 'irrespective of artistic quality'. The same is not true of works of artistic craftsmanship.[75] At the heart of this decision was the question: should all functional

---

[72] *Per* Mann J, [2008] EWHC 1878 (Ch), [2008] ECDR 17. The helmet served as the paradigm case, that would be decisive of the outcome.

[73] George Lucas conceived the story line and the characters, including the concept of the Imperial Stormtroopers as threatening characters in 'fascist white-armoured suits'. Other artists and prop makers were involved in drawing and painting the costume. The defendant Ainsworth, who is a designer, produced several prototype vacuum-moulded helmets, based on initial drawings, with a final version was approved by George Lucas. Mr. Ainsworth made 50 helmets for use in the film. From 2004 onwards, Ainsworth used his original tools to make versions of the Imperial Stormtrooper helmet and armour, and other artefacts for sale to the public.

[74] An intriguing aspect of this case was that Lucasfilm held a default judgment based on copyright law in a US district court, and a further issue based on the justiciability in England of the US copyright claims. In 2006, Lucasfilm obtained a default judgment in the United States District Court, Central District of California, for $20 million, $10 million of which represented triple damages under the Lanham Act. Lucasfilm sought an order for the enforcement of the US judgment, and a claim based on US and English copyright laws. Both the trial judge and the appellate Court held that the US judgment was unenforceable. The trial judge further held that Lucasfilm's United States copyright claims were justiciable in England; the Court of Appeal disagreed with the trial judge on this point. The only issues before the UK Supreme Court were whether the helmet was a sculpture, the defences under the UK copyright law, and the justiciability in England of the US copyright claims. The decision is also remarkable in that the UK Supreme Court held that the US copyright claims were justiciable in UK courts.

[75] s.4(1)(a), (c), CDPA 1988. There is a further possibility of convincing courts that some movable three-dimensional works qualify as 'works of architecture' which are defined widely enough to possibly include individual sculptural elements of building such a stained glass window or an intricately designed balcony.

and industrially manufactured three-dimensional artefacts be considered 'sculptures'? And if not, what is the qualifying criterion, which shifts it from non-protectable things to an 'artistic work'?

There was a commendable attempt in all three *Lucasfilm's* judgments to come to some agreement as to what constituted a sculpture. All three tribunals were in agreement, for instance, that it was important to keep to the normal English usage of the word 'sculpture', though this usage was not necessarily determinative. All judges were similarly in agreement that no judgement must be made about artistic worth. The Court's task, instead, is to discern artistic purpose ('the artist's hand'). This was related to a further definition of a sculpture – a three-dimensional work made by an artist's hand.[76]

The analysis in the New Zealand decision of *Wham-O Manufacturing Co. v Lincoln Industries Ltd*[77] was cited by counsel for the claimants as one whereby purely functional and industrial objects (such as wooden moulds for producing the flying plastic Frisbee toy) can be held to be sculptures, especially as modern copyright law eschews such notions as artistic merit, artistic taste, judgement or arrangement.[78] The trial Court in *Lucasfilm* held, however, that while utilitarian or functional objects could be regarded as a sculpture, not every three-dimensional object could be a sculpture unless some element of 'artistic expression' was present.[79]

The question of functionality inevitably arose, in the attempt to capture the meaning of 'sculpture'. Counsel for the claimants argued that the issue of functionality could not possibly arise as the articles in question had no functional purpose whatever. The Stormtroopers' helmets did not exist in order to keep their wearers warm or decent or to protect them from injury in an inter-planetary war. Their sole purpose was to make a visual impression on the filmgoer.

Moreover, if we look at the impact of the Stormtroopers' helmets in the marketplace, it is clear that these items function in the grey world of fashion wear, product identifiers and design icons. In fashion terms, there are countless websites retailing Stormtrooper helmets and costumes to suit every age and taste. For instance, the ever-popular infant sized Strormtrooper costume, with a look-alike helmet, retails at £14, whilst a full-sized Stormtrooper replica helmet for adults costs approximately £249.[80] These are made from

---

76 This refers to the oft-cited definition of Laddie J. in *Metix (UK) Ltd v G H Maughan (Plastics) Ltd* [1997] FSR 718, at pp. 721–2.

77 [1985] RPC 127.

78 *Per* Mann J, [2008] EWHC 1878 (Ch), [2008] ECDR 17, paras 97 *et seq*.

79 *Per* Mann J, [2008] EWHC 1878 (Ch), [2008] ECDR 17, para. 112.

80 See, for example, http://www.funwarehouse.co.uk/ and http://www.stormtroopershop.com/. A Google search for these item retrieves over 260 000 websites. The original Ainsworth site is available at http://www.sdsprops.com/. All sites were accessed on 8 September 2011.

unauthentic moulds; if a Stormtrooper helmet is cast from the 'original Ainsworth' mould, it would cost £500. If one wished to step across from the 'mass-produced industrial design' to 'art', the Ainsworth-made unfinished Stormtrooper helmet sold at a Christies auction in 2002 for £4465.[81] Under the Marcel Duchamp approach suggested above, these are art works. The spectator has made his views known, has lifted it to a profitable merchandising status, and more importantly in the contemporary world, has priced the work in Christies.[82]

> However, the Courts thought differently, and held that it was utilitarian. Here are some passages of the reasoning employed by the judges: Although invented, the helmet and armour are still recognisable as such and have a function within the confines of the film as the equipment of the stormtrooper.
>
> There must [...] be some element of artistic expression however unsuccessful...Sculpture, like painting (however good or bad it may be), does connote the work of the artist's hand and the visual purpose attributed to it by the judge in this case. Put simply, it has, broadly speaking, to be a work at least intended to be a work of art.[83]
>
> The issue in this case and the judge's approach to it does not turn on the purpose for which it is actually used but on the purposive nature of the object: what the judge described as its 'intrinsic quality of being intended to be enjoyed as a visual thing'. A medieval suit of armour, however highly decorated, is no different. Although now of largely historical interest, it was made for a practical purpose which, again, characterises it as an object of utility rather than an artistic work.[84]
>
> The relative significance of the functional and the artistic is central to this appeal.[85]
>
> But it was the Star Wars film that was the work of art that Mr. Lucas and his companies created. The helmet was utilitarian in the sense that it was an element in the process of production of the film.[86]

---

[81] Sale 9538 (Film & Entertainment), December 2002, London, available at http://www.christies.com/lotfinder/star-wars-1977/4036538/lot/lot_ details.aspx?from=searchresults&pos=3&intObjectID=4036538&sid=de84c410-0056-4209-a068-f87e281f5684&page=10.

[82] 'The easiest definition of contemporary art [...] is what is sold by major auction houses in contemporary art sales.', D. Thompson (2008), *The $12 Million Stuffed Shark: The Curious Economics of Contemporary Art and Auction Houses*, London: Aurum Press, at p.10.

[83] *Per* Lord Justice Jacob, [2009] EWCA Civ 1328; [2010] ECDR 6, at paras 66 and 70.

[84] *Per* Lord Justice Jacob, [2009] EWCA Civ 1328; [2010] ECDR 6, at paras 73–5.

[85] *Per Lords Walker and Collins,* [2011] UKSC 39, [2011] 6 ECDR, at para. 29.

[86] *Per Lords Walker and Collins,* [2011] UKSC 39, [2011] 6 ECDR, at para. 44.

It is submitted that much of the Courts' reasoning is historically biased. In terms of legislative history, the Supreme Court's hesitance to extend the copyright label of sculpture to the helmets derives from the evolution of design law. The Court emphasized this much when it pointed out that UK Parliamentary policy has been to develop three separate tiers of graduated protection: copyright, registered design right and unregistered design right. This was to be contrasted to the 'indiscriminate protection of literary copyright'. Thus, artistic works of art (sculpture and works of artistic craftsmanship) have the fullest protection; then come works with 'eye appeal' (as discussed in *AMP Inc v Utilux Pty Ltd* above), and then a modest level of protection to purely functional objects under the UK unregistered design right system.[87]

Despite the lengthy discussion on what constituted an artistic work, the Supreme Court's final stance on this was largely attributable to their view that there were 'good policy reasons for the differences in the periods of protection, and the Court should not, in our view, encourage the boundaries of full copyright protection to creep outwards'.

Put simply, terms such as functionality and artistic are part of the Court's arsenal of weapons to cut back on cumulative protection of designs under two intellectual property laws. With its policy-clad armour, the Court was not about to embark on questions such as market prices for original moulds or the purpose of the helmets by end-users or modern consumer tastes. This attitude may mean that UK courts would be reluctant to view designer fashion goods, for example, as artistic works. And this would be the result, irrespective of the spectators' view. Louis Vuitton handbags, for example, may have been exhibited in the past in the Guggenheim Museum in New York (as 'art'), and in the Victoria and Albert Museum in London (as 'design'), but to the UK Supreme Court, such works should seek *sui generis* copyright protection.[88]

---

[87] No mention was made of the EU design law. Moreover, it should be noted that UK intellectual property law offers two types of unregistered design right protection. One right is available under ss. 213 *et seq*, CDPA 1988; the other is available as a Community design right under the CDR. Subject matter, criteria, scope and terms of protection differ considerably. For an overview of the two, see Suthersanen, *supra* note 25, para. 5.3.2.

[88] Thompson, *supra* note 82, at p.11.

6. CONCLUSION: REVENGE OF THE FUNCTION/ART DICHOTOMY

> The reason that parallel rights can exist is simple: each form of right is created by statute. Unless there is a specific provision preventing rights from co-existing, they just do. *Jacob J, in Philips v Remington.*[89]

> It is improbable that a design rights framework optimised to support innovation and growth would feature a multiplicity of overlapping rights. *Hargreaves Report, 2011.*[90]

What the paper attempts to unravel is a *sui generis* regime in struggle with the inherent contradictions of a discipline-hopping subject matter. The official EU stance has been that we need a 'third way' in order to conclude years of debate as to whether designs should be protected under a patent approach or a copyright approach. Under the EU approach, proprietors can now opt for the registered design right, or the 'new', cheaper, and shorter unregistered right if this is suitable for the product. The exclusion of functional features was to demarcate design law from patent law. And yet, this approach has seemingly unearthed fundamental flaws.

The first flaw concerns the width of protection offered under the unregistered design right. As Jeremy Phillips recently mused:

> Small- and medium-sized enterprises (SMEs), as well as micro-enterprises, have been increasingly calling for more and better protection for designs. Yet it is unclear whether this is even worth achieving for them. In so many instances, the protection accorded by a design, whether registered or not, is so narrow that a competitor can lawfully and confidently make a few changes and sell a similar product without fear of legal action. Designs take time and effort to register and are usually of short-term protection unless renewed. Litigation is expensive and uncertain. So why bother at all?[91]

Most intellectual property lawyers would disagree with Phillips and assert the 25-year exclusive right created under the registered system offers advantages to large manufacturing industries and trade associations.[92] Nevertheless, they

---

89 *Per* Jacob J., in *Philips Electronics NV v Remington Consumer Products* [1998] RPC 283 (H.Ct).

90 I. Hargreaves, *Digital Opportunity: A Review of Intellectual Property and Growth*, a review for the UK government, May 2011, para. 7.4. available at http://www.ipo.gov.uk/ipreview-finalreport.pdf.

91 J. Phillips (2011), 'Editorial: The Great Design Conundrum', *JIPLP*, **6** (8), 507.

92 The advantages of a registration-based system are as follows: it functions as a source of information and certainty; it offers prima facie evidence of validity; it can

would agree with him that the scope of registered designs is indeterminate due to the difficulty in applying individual character and functionality. Moreover, many lawyers and jurists would remain sceptical as to the efficacy or use of the three-year unregistered anti-copying design right system. Many reasons were given as to why an anti-copying right (or *quasi* copyright) was necessary, including the following: automatic protection which is useful for short-lived products; lower threshold of originality (not applicable under the CDR); no application or registration costs; and the long duration (not applicable under the three-year unregistered Community design right).[93] These reasons may be valid but what was being argued by the fashion and consumer goods industries was for copyright or unfair competition protection, and especially for a scheme of protection that understood that products and consumer taste are cyclical in nature. Instead, industries with short-lived goods have been offered an extremely restrictive anti-copying right.

The second flaw concerns the embracing of a multi-tiered protection regime for a subject matter that defies strict definitional parameters. The contentious issue of simultaneous protection under design and other intellectual property rights was decided in favour of a cumulative regime ethos, which is enshrined in Art. 96(1). The CDR is without prejudice to EU or national laws on unregistered designs, trade marks or other distinctive signs, patents and utility models, typefaces, civil liability and unfair competition. Art. 96(1), CDR emphasizes the inextricable link with copyright law by stating:

> A design protected by a Community design shall also be eligible for protection under the law of copyright of Member States as from the date on which the design was created or fixed in any form. The extent to which, and the conditions under which, such a protection is conferred, including the level of originality required, shall be determined by each Member State.[94]

The 'cumulative protection' principle offers, however, no clear guidelines save that designs must be eligible for copyright protection, even when protected under design law. The final line of the provision exacerbates the problem as it gives 27 Member States within the EU the complete freedom to enact any extra conditions which must be satisfied before designs are protected, including the level of artistic expression required. This serves as an invitation to lawmakers to return to the art/function debate, which in turn has made both

enhance the proprietor's ability to gain financial benefits through licensing opportunities or using it as a security interest. See Suthersanen, *supra* note 25, paras 11–004, *et seq.*

[93] *Ibid*, at paras 11–009 *et seq.*

[94] This is repeated in Art. 17, Directive 98/71/EC of the European Parliament and of the Council on the legal protection of designs.

national and EU design law unnecessarily complex. Indeed, the UK Supreme Court makes specific reference to the abysmal British legislative history as being the reason there must be a demarcation between 'sculpture' and 'design', between function and art, and between 'mass manufacture' and 'by the artist's hand'.[95]

The third flaw lies in the functionality criterion that is employed by the legislature and the judiciary in attempting to draw the art/function dichotomy. It has become unwieldy as it is flows simultaneously, in different permutations, within copyright, design and trade mark laws. Theoretically, the criterion is important to ensure that protection is accorded to goods which should seek patent protection. And yet, in practical terms, should we revisit this criterion and ask ourselves whether it is necessary? Under EU law, the difference between the terms of protection is five years.[96] Are our industries and markets so fragile that competition will be stifled if the shape of a consumer product is protected under the wrong intellectual property right?

If the answer is yes, we then turn to the fourth fundamental flaw. We have no valid rationale to grant property rights to designs which do not satisfy the criteria of patent, trade mark or copyright laws. The first design-related regulations in 1711 in Lyon were enacted as local regulations based on a misappropriation approach, rather than the conferment of a property right. They were designed specifically for the textile industry.[97] Even the subsequent

---

[95] For a historical account, see J. Lahore (1971), 'Art and Function in the Law of Copyright and Designs: The Need for a Reappraisal', *Adelaide Law Review*, **9**, 182.

[96] Patent law offers a 20-year term of protection whereas registered design law grants a 25-year protection term. Under international law, the minimum term of protection to be accorded under a *sui generis* design system is 10 years.

[97] Ordinance of the Consuls of Lyons (1711), approved by the Council of State (1712) and registered in Parliament (1717). It reads:

> All master merchants, working masters, journeymen and others employed in the manufacture of fabrics of silk, regardless of sex and age, are expressly prohibited and enjoined from taking, stealing, selling, lending, transferring and using directly or indirectly any designs which have been entrusted to them for manufacturing purposes.

Translation from F. Prager (1944), 'History of Intellectual Property From 1545 to 1787', *Journal of the Patent Office Society*, November, **26** (11), 711–60. See generally L.E. Miller (1999), 'Innovation and Industrial Espionage in Eighteenth Century France: An Investigation of the Selling of Silks Through Samples', *Journal of Design History,* **12**, 271–92; and also L. Pérez (2008), 'Inventing in a World of Guilds: Silk Fabrics in Eighteenth-century Lyon', in S. R. Epstein & M. Roy Prak (eds), *Guilds, Innovation and the European economy, 1400–1800,* Cambridge: Cambridge University Press, at p. 238.

design laws in France and England were short-lived measures, which were more concerned with offering immediate relief within the textile design industry against misappropriation.[98] Could we perhaps revisit misappropriation laws in order to protect designs? This discussion has already been had in the past, with the first working party on design being proposed in 1959.[99] In fact, most of the dilemmas discussed in this paper, from copyright protection to the nature of registration, have been highlighted in many commentaries and reports.[100]

In an ideal, non-Berne/Paris/TRIPS world, we could start by repealing all design-related legislation, and removing the term 'artistic works' from copyright law. Instead, misappropriation of works of art, design, sculpture, fashion and anything not falling within the general notion of 'design' would be protected under national unfair competition laws. Such protection could be offered irrespective of the criterion of protection and functionality tests. Using historical precedents, we could argue that narrow laws are the best means to encourage and support innovation in certain sectors, especially in relation to new industries or arts.

However, it would be foolish to offer this suggestion seriously in light of international conventions, national legislations and the great European design scheme. Moreover, one should not be misled by the complexity of the laws into thinking no protection is required. However, the type of protection required is very dependent on the designed product, and the copied feature. The design proprietor needs protection to cover all aspects of the designed product – visual impression, brand identity, artistic value, fashion status, and functional innovation. The current paradox of a complicated, art/function led multi-tiered protection system does lead one naturally to question the very rationale of *sui generis* design law.

The conclusion is more pessimistic. There is probably nothing we can do about the current state of legal protection of designs. The result is a moribund

---

98 French Law of 18 March 1806; An Act for the encouragement of the arts of Designing and Printing of Linens, Cottons, Calicoes and Muslin, 1787, 27 Geo. 3, c.38 (UK). Prior to the 1787 design law, early design protection was under the English engraving Acts. The first engraving Act, secured in 1734 as a result of William Hogarth's campaign against illegal copies of his prints, was narrow in its scope of protection, 1734 (8 Geo. 2, c.13). This was expanded in 1766 to extend protection to other types of prints, including any historical print or prints, or any print or prints of any portrait, conversation, landscape, or architecture, map, chart or plan or any other prints, and any print taken from any picture, drawing, model or sculpture, either ancient or modern (Act of 1766 (7 Geo. 3, c. 38); replaced by the Prints Copyright Act 1777 (17 Geo. 3, c.57), which enlarged the remedies for piracy).

99 Rosconi Designs Working Party report, 2143/IV/62, 17 December 1962.

100 Max Planck Institute.

law, which eventually will be of little use to design proprietors, but will give rise to much academic discussion. The problem is not that the law needs to be changed, but rather the attitudes of the legislators and judiciary need to be revised. As mentioned in the introduction, design products lie in a grey area which is understood, recognized and appreciated by business entities which use designs to sell highly functional products, by creators who use it to constantly beauty and function, and by consumers who do appreciate well-designed and highly functional products, whether it is to be viewed and displayed in the living room, or viewed and displayed in the utilities room. The change in the law will come when, perhaps, our lawmakers can also embrace the modern notion of design, and let go of the nineteenth century notion of art divorced from function. That design *is* art, even if it is bad, functional, and ugly, and not necessarily appealing to the eye.

Section 7

IP Enforcement in the EU

18. IP enforcement in Europe: acquis and future plans

Jacques Raynard

The action taken by the European Community in the field of intellectual property has focused mainly on the harmonization of national substantive law and the creation of a unitary right at Community level. Certain national intellectual property rights, such as trademarks, designs, patents for biotechnological inventions and certain aspects of copyright and related rights, have been harmonized. The Community has also created some unitary rights at Community level such as the Community trademark and, more recently, Community designs. Discussions are also under way with regard to creating a European Union patent, but I must confess I feel somewhat bewildered on this last topic.[1]

These initial steps are aimed at producing a certain harmonization in the regulation of intellectual property rights. A second step was to strengthen existing provisions to punish infringement and counterfeiting.

1 The European Parliament approved on 17 February 2010 the use of enhanced cooperation procedure to create a unified patent system. Introduced by the Treaty of Amsterdam, the enhanced cooperation procedure allows those Member States that wish to, to establish closer cooperation among them. In December 2011, the European Parliament and the Member States agreed on a regulation on the unitary patent and a regulation on translation arrangements for the patent. 29 June 2012, the European Council concluded negotiations on the outstanding and final element of the unitary patent system in the EU, the Unified Patent Court. The Central Division of the Court of First Instance of the Unified Patent Court (UPC) will have its seat in Paris. Specialised thematic clusters will be created in two sections of the Central Division, one in London and the other in Munich. Conclusions of the European Council (28/29 June 2012), EUCO 76/12, available at: http://www.consilium.europa.eu/uedocs/cms_data/docs/pressdata/en/ec/131388.pdf (last accessed 19 July 2012). However, due to the suggested by the Council deletion of the three key Articles, 6, 7 and 8, the European Parliament at its recent plenary session, 2–5 July 2012, postponed its scrutiny of the EU draft patent legislation. Press Release, European Parliament, EU unitary patent: Council move would infringe EU law, says EP rapporteur, REF.: 20120709IPR48484, available at: http://www.europarl.europa.eu/news/en/press-room/content/20120709IPR48484/html/EU-unitary-patent-Council-move-would-infringe-EU-law-says-EP-rapporteur (last accessed 19 July 2012).

For this purpose, some legal measures have been taken. The Commission has implemented a legal framework. The Intellectual Property Rights Enforcement Directive of 29 April 2004 is one of the cornerstones of this. It has harmonized the laws of Member States with regard to civil measures for the enforcement of all intellectual property rights. As you know, Article 18 of the Directive requires Member States to submit to the Commission a report on the implementation of the Directive three years after that date. A Commission Report, complemented by a staff working document, was provided in December 2010.[2] The report includes an assessment of the effectiveness of the measures taken, as well as an evaluation of its impact on innovation and the development of the information society. The report sets out a series of concrete issues where clarification may be needed, in particular to adapt the Directive to the new challenges inherent in a modern digital society.

I will focus my chapter on certain new measures provided by this Directive, more specifically regarding the French transposition of this text. But this Directive is not the only tool set up by the EC.

The European Customs Regulation 1383/2003, of 22 July 2003, which allows for the detention of goods suspected of infringing IPR, is another pillar of this legal framework. A proposal on criminal sanctions is currently under discussion in the Council.

Meanwhile, the Commission proposed to supplement the legal framework with complementary non-legislative measures, in line with Competitiveness Council Resolution of 25 September 2008 on a comprehensive European anti-counterfeiting and anti-piracy plan.

This Resolution endorsed the need to step up the fight against fake goods and called for the creation of a European Observatory on Counterfeiting and Piracy. On 11 September 2009 the Commission adopted a Communication on enhancing the enforcement of intellectual property rights in the internal market and deciding the creation of the Observatory.

The Observatory has been launched to:

- improve the quality of information and statistics related to counterfeiting and piracy on the internal market of the EU
- identify and spread national best practice strategies and enforcement techniques from both the public as well as the private sector
- help raise public awareness.

---

[2] Report from the Commission to the Council, the European Parliament and the European Social Committee on the application of Directive 2004/48/EC of the European Parliament and the Council of 29 April 2004 on the enforcement of intellectual property rights, 22 December 2010, COM(2010) 779 final.

The Observatory provides studies on different topics such as:

- damages in intellectual property rights
- corrective measures
- evidence and right of information
- cross border measures in the EU
- border risk management and cooperation with the carriers and shippers in the fight against counterfeiting and piracy
- counterfeits and postal sector.[3]

The Commission communication was followed by two Council Resolutions[4] that supported the Commission's policy. The report adopted by the European Parliament also expressed support for an enhanced policy, including a strong legal framework to combat counterfeiting and piracy.[5]

Infringements of intellectual property rights taking place outside of the EU also constitute a major source of concern. The Commission is tackling this question through participation in international initiatives, such as the negotiation of the Anti–Counterfeiting Trade Agreement (ACTA).[6]

---

3 European Observatory on Counterfeiting and Piracy: http://ec.europa.eu/internal_market/iprenforcement/observatory/index_en.htm (last accessed 19 July 2012). The name of the European Observatory on Counterfeiting and Piracy was changed to the European Observatory on Infringements of Intellectual Property Rights by Recital 5 of Regulation (EU) No 386/2012 of the European Parliament and of the Council of 19 April 2012 on entrusting the Office for Harmonization in the Internal Market (Trade Marks and Designs) with tasks related to the enforcement of intellectual property rights, including the assembling of public and private-sector representatives as a European Observatory on Infringements of Intellectual Property Rights. Article 1 of this Regulation entrusted Office for Harmonization in the Internal Market (Trade Marks and Designs) with the Observatory.

4 Council Resolution of 25 September 2008 on a comprehensive European anti-counterfeiting and anti-piracy plan, OJ C 253, 4.10.2008, p.1; Council Resolution of 1 March 2010 on the enforcement of intellectual rights in the internal market, OJ C 56, 6.3.2010, p.1.

5 European Parliament, Resolution of 22 September 2010 on enforcement of intellectual property rights in the internal market (2009/2178(INI)), A7-0175/2010.

6 Although the European Parliament rejected the agreement by its vote on 4 July 2012, the European Commission will continue to consider other options to enhance protection of intellectual property at international level. Announcement, European Commission, Statement by EU Trade Commissioner Karel De Gucht on European Plenary Vote on ACTA (Anti-Counterfeiting Trade Agreement), 4 July 2012, available at: http://trade.ec.europa.eu/doclib/press/index.cfm?id=818 (last accessed 19 July 2012). For details on enforcement policies of the EU see Strategy for the enforcement of intellectual property rights in third countries 2005/C 129/03, available at: http://eur-lex.europa.eu/LexUriServ/LexUriServ.do?uri=OJ:C 2005:129:0003: 0016:EN:PDF (last accessed 19 July 2012).

As already mentioned, the Directive 2004/48 must be considered as the masterpiece of the European system intended to enhance enforcement of IP rights. Some provisions, like the presumption of authorship or ownership (Article 5), the possibility of 'sampling' in the context of information gathering (Article 6), provisional measures to preserve evidence (Article 7) and the possibility of injunctions against intermediaries (Articles 9 and 11) have helped render the enforcement of intellectual property rights in the EU more effective. Due to late transposition of the Directive in many Member States (the transposition process was achieved in France with the law of 29 October 2007) experience in applying the Directive is limited. And only few court cases have been reported by the Commission report, and I have been somewhat frustrated by the study of this material.

So, I will focus on certain particular questions. As a French academic lawyer, I would like to emphasize some questions and new rules provided by the Directive with the perspectives that they offer under French law.

- I will speak about:
- the scope of the directive,
- the right of information,
- damages questions.

1) First, I would like to speak about the *scope of application of the Directive*. As you know, the Directive covers all infringements of intellectual property rights without containing any definition of intellectual property rights. The scope is not limited to those rights harmonized at EU level, but also covers rights protected as intellectual property rights by national law. Of course, this method provides flexibility to the scope of the Directive, but some questions remain open. One of them is the status of unpatented know-how, often taken into account as trade secrets pursuant to American doctrine.[7] According to the Commission staff working document '*It seems to derive from the wording of the Directive that, in cases where they are protected as an intellectual property right at national level, they should be understood as being covered by the scope of the Directive*'.[8]

---

7 See F Dessemontet (1997), 'Les secrets d'affaires dans l'Accord sur les aspects des droits de propriété intellectuelle qui touchent au commerce', *Mélanges Junod*, Fac. Genève, n°1s.

8 Commission Staff Working Document, Analysis of the application of Directive 2004/48/EC of the European Parliament and the Council of 29 April 2004 on the enforcement of intellectual property rights in the Member States, 22 December 2010, SEC(2010) 1589 final, § 2.1, p. 5.

I think the uncertain status of know-how is very dangerous if we take into account the often valuable asset for the company. At the same time, unpatented know-how is often the purpose of international contracts which achieve a technology transfer. Differences of opinion about its protection could be the cause of tricky disputes.

Under French doctrine, unpatented know-how is only protected by contractual commitments and unfair competition.[9] This approach seems to be in compliance with internationals treaties, and more specifically with Article 39 of the TRIPS agreement.[10] It is a natural consequence of the rule that a property right begins only by filing a patent application: before this step there is no property right, no infringement action, no right to take measures for preserving evidence such as *saisie-contrefaçon* in France; damages for misappropriation of unpatented know-how will be set under general rules of civil liability upon *Article 1382 of Code civil*, without any consideration for the unfair profits made by the other party.

In light of this understanding of the notion, I believe that it would be irrelevant to include unpatented know how in the scope of the Directive. The introduction of criminal provisions for the protection of trade secrets seems a more appropriate way to fight against practices of industrial espionage, a French bill was filed on 13 January 2011, in this way.[11]

We could have a similar discussion about domain names.

2) Let us go now to the *right of information* which is set up by Article 8 of the Directive. As you know, according to this provision, the competent judicial authorities can order that information be provided by the infringer or another person on the origin and distribution networks of the goods which infringe intellectual property rights.

After the transposition of the Directive, national courts have seen a significant increase in requests for information: this provision has had a significant impact on the possibilities to establish the 'exact quantities of infringing products involved' and therefore on the accuracy of the calculation of damages.

---

[9] See J. Raynard (2010), *Retour sur le savoir-faire non breveté*, Mélanges G.Bonnet, Litec, p. 451.

[10] See Agreement on Trade-Related Aspects of Intellectual Property Rights, Art. 39§1:

> In the course of ensuring effective protection against unfair competition as provided in Article 10*bis* of the Paris Convention (1967), Members shall protect undisclosed information in accordance with paragraph 2 and data submitted to governments or governmental agencies in accordance with paragraph 3.

[11] Proposition de loi n° 3103, relative à la protection des informations économiques.

A first issue is to appreciate the group of persons who can be forced to provide information: the Directive goes beyond the infringers. It is widely extended to any other person who was found in possession of the infringing goods on a commercial scale, or who was involved in the infringing activities. This provision, due to its limitation to activities carried out on a commercial scale, does not apply to consumers. Such information may be requested also from other actors like intermediaries, for example Internet service providers, transporters or online market places. Intermediaries are also likely to be subject to injunctions and provisional measures, under Articles 9 and 11; pursuant to the last provision the notion of 'intermediary' is understood broadly by the Directive and includes all persons 'whose services are used *by a third party* to infringe an intellectual property right'. This implies that even intermediaries who do not have a direct contractual relationship or connection with the infringer may be considered as intermediaries in the scope of the Directive.

In the French case law, another issue is to know if an injunction ordering the provision of information can be issued before the decision on the merits, at the level of *juge de la mise en état*, in order to gather evidence of infringement. On this topic, there is currently a discrepancy within the *Tribunal de grande instance de Paris*, one section of the tribunal deems that the *juge de la mise en état* has no jurisdiction for ordering to provide information, while two others sections of the Tribunal consider that they are able to do it.[12] Actually, this dispute concerns the nature of the right to information: is it only a measure intended to allow the calculation of damages or is it also possible to use the right of information to get evidence of infringement?

But the main question that arises on this topic, is how to strike the balance between property rights, on the one hand, and right to privacy on the other. According to the Commission report on application of the Directive, it seems that in some Member States the disclosure of the relevant information is practically impossible in both criminal and civil proceedings; it seems to be the case in Spain and Austria.[13] Meanwhile, a European legal framework on the

[12] TGI Paris, 3e ch. 1Re sect, ord. Juge de la mise en état, 4 mai 2010, PIBD 2010, 924, III, 598, and case law quoted.

[13] In Spain, data may only be disclosed for the purposes of prosecution or investigation of serious criminal offences (infringement of intellectual property rights do not seem to fall within this category), and any extension would be illegal unless it would be embedded in the law. In Austria, the reform of the criminal procedure removed the possibility to bring a private criminal action ('Privatanklage') without knowing the identity of the infringer. The only possibility for rightholders now seems to be to launch a civil information claim under copyright law, which is not effective in the case of temporary IP addresses. Study on Online Copyright Enforcement and Data Protection in Selected Member States, Hunton and Williams, November 2009 available at: http://ec.europa.eu/internal_market/iprenforcement/docs/study-online-enforcement_en.pdf, (last accessed 19 July 2012).

protection of personal data has been set up in particular with Directive 95/46/EC on the protection of individuals with regard to the processing of personal data and on the free movement of such data, and Directive 2002/58/EC on the processing of personal data and the protection of privacy in the electronic communications sector.

Both protection of privacy and IP rights are recognized as fundamental rights by the Charter of Fundamental rights of the European Union.[14] So the European Court of Justice issued two decisions in which it emphasized the need to balance enforcement of IP rights and protection of personal data.[15] According to the Commission report, the European framework on protection of personal data, on the one hand, and enforcement of IP rights on the other, is neutral, in that there is no rule implying that the right to privacy should take precedence over the right to property or vice versa. So, the official advice given by the report is that national laws implementing the various directives must be construed in a way that allows a balance to be struck between these rights. But, obviously, one can think that implementation of the right of information will be restrained by protection of personal data.

3) But one of the most innovative provisions for the French jurist relates to the *repair mode of counterfeiting*.

Currently, under the French law, damages are calculated in accordance with general rules of civil liability set by Article 1382 of Code civil. The mere aim of awarding damages is to place the rightholders in the same situation as they would have been in the absence of the infringement. If we consider the patent rightholder, the system of damages will depend on whether or not the owner had operated the patent. If the owner carried out sales, he will get as damages the lost profits which he suffered; if the same did not operate the patent, he will get the amount of royalties which would have been paid if the infringer had requested authorization.[16] Under this system, damages awards do not currently appear to effectively dissuade potential infringers from engaging in illegal activities: it is a criticism frequently made of the application of general rules of liability. So, if we consider the French hit parade of the largest damages awarded by the *Tribunal de Grande Instance de Paris* for patent counterfeiting since 1990, the most important damages were awarded in 1994

---

[14] Arts 7, 8 and 17(2) of the Charter of Fundamental Rights of the European Union. Art. 17(2) states that intellectual property shall be protected.

[15] Judgment of 29 January 2008 in the case C-275/06, *Productores de Música de España (Promusicae) v Telefónica de España SAU*; judgment of 19 February 2009 in the case C-557/07, *LSG-Gesellschaft zur Wahrnehmung von Leistungschutzrechten GMBH v Tele2 Telecommunication GMBH*.

[16] See J. Azéma and J.-C. Galloux (2006), *Droit de la propriété industrielle*, 6e édition, Paris: Dalloz, n° 697 s., pp. 422ff.

in the case *Ciba Geigy Rhône poulenc v Interphyto*, for an amount of a little over 6 million euros; in 2009 the *Tribunal* granted an amount of around 4.3 million euros in the case *Agilent Technology Deutschland v Waters corp*. And, for the same period, there were no more than ten cases in which the compensation awarded exceeded one million euros. We are so far from the largest US awards for patent counterfeiting such as the famous case *Centocor v Abbott*, deemed in June 2009, in which an Eastern District of Texas jury held Abbott liable for $1.67 billion in damages for infringing Centocor's patents covering antibodies against tumour necrosis factor.

Damages under the Directive are intended to achieve two goals: compensation but also deterrence: damages must be effective and dissuasive (Art. 3–2). So, to set damages, the Directive states that the national judge must take into account all appropriate aspects such as negative economic consequences, lost profits, but also unfair profits made by the infringer and, in appropriate cases, moral prejudice caused to the rightholder. As an alternative, the judge may, in appropriate cases, set damages as a lump sum on the basis of elements such as, at least, the amount of royalties or fees which would have been paid by a licensee.

The European Observatory on Counterfeiting and Piracy carried out a report to provide analysis of damages awards in the Member States, especially after implementation of the Directive. This report includes also some recommendations and best-practice examples. Under this submission, it would appear that courts face difficulty in calculating and awarding compensation comprehensively; most often, they grant a lump sum damages, based on the relevant licence fee which can be the full price of a licence, but may also be a lower amount Outside of lost profits, rightholders may not, in practical terms, be compensated for other negative economic consequences resulting from an infringement, such as reputational damages, price declines, damage to the distinctiveness or value of a trademark. Damages for non-economic harm are often unavailable, and moral damages are rarely awarded.

Meanwhile, the costs of investigating, taking legal actions against an infringement are often not compensated in full. For example, courts may have awarded lawyers' fees below the amount actually spent, as seems to be the case in countries like Denmark, Greece, Luxembourg or Spain. Finally, in some cases, infringers may retain some of their profits, or otherwise have an economic incentive to engage in infringement: for example, according to European Observatory report, damages may be reduced when an infringer gets a licence post-infringement (e.g. in the UK).

In this context, the Commission report is making some proposals.

In such cases, it could be considered whether the courts should have the power to grant damages commensurate with the infringer's unjust enrichment, even if they exceed the actual damage incurred by the rightholder. Equally, there could be a case for making greater use of the possibility to award damages for other economic consequences and moral damages. In cases where the infringer is a legal person and the rightholder fails to obtain damages because the infringer has no assets – has been liquidated or is in any other way insolvent – an assessment could be made as to whether the rightholder is able to claim damages from the company's managing director(s) under national law, and if so under what conditions.[17]

I would like to make a last observation on this point. If we read, again, the recitals of the Directive, the first justification of this text lies in the achievement of the internal market which entails eliminating restrictions on freedom of movement and distortions of competition (Recitals 1–12). This is the genuine foundation of the legal framework set up by the EC, not only in the area of IP rights. So the Directive on the enforcement of IP rights must be understood as a tool to set up the internal market. As a result of this consideration, significant discrepancies in the assessment of damages between national judges could appear as a failure of competition, and so would be unacceptable. In this case, of course, the European Court of Justice would have to construe this provision. But in any event, the national judge will have to take into account sentences issued by their foreign counterparts. That should be a subject of dialogue and provides opportunities of new meetings of this kind in the future.

17 *Supra* note 2.

19. The impact of the Anti-Counterfeiting Trade Agreement on the legal framework for IP enforcement in the European Union

Roberto D'Erme, Christophe Geiger, Henning Grosse Ruse-Khan, Christian Heinze, Thomas Jaeger, Rita Matulionyte and Axel Metzger

In October 2007, the US, Japan, South Korea, Mexico, New Zealand, Switzerland and the EU announced their intention to negotiate a new Anti-Counterfeiting Trade Agreement (ACTA). The expressed idea is to 'establish new international norms, helping to create a new global gold standard on IPR enforcement'.[1] ACTA has caused controversy not only because the treaty obligations it creates seem to go significantly beyond the existing international standards in TRIPS, but also due to the almost complete absence of transparency in access to any draft negotiating texts.[2] After years of secrecy and forced by various leaks,[3] the ACTA negotiating parties – the EU, the US, Japan, Australia, New Zealand, Canada, South Korea, Singapore, Morocco, Mexico and Switzerland – finally released an 'official' draft text in April

---

[1] European Commission (2007), European Commission seeks mandate to negotiate major new international anti-counterfeiting pact, Press Release of 23 October 2007 (IP/07/1573).

[2] M. Geist (2010), *ACTA Guide, Part Three: Transparency and ACTA Secrecy*, available at: http://www.michaelgeist.ca/content/view/4737/125/ (last accessed 17 July 2012).

[3] *See, e.g.*, Anti-Counterfeiting Trade Agreement Informal Predecisional/Deliberative Draft: 18 January 2010, PIJIP IP Enforcement Database, available at: http://sites.google.com/site/iipenforcement/acta ('Full Leaked Text Dated January 18, 2010', available at: https://docs.google.com/a/student.american.edu/viewer?a=v&pid=sites&srcid=ZGVmYXVsdGRvbWFpbnxpaXBlbmZvcmNlbWVudHxneDozNWJiMzU4ODljYjIzNWQ1) (hereinafter: January 2010 ACTA draft) (last accessed 17 July 2012).

2010.[4] After its release, subsequent rounds of negotiations produced revised ACTA drafts which again leaked to the public. On 2 October 2010 finally, the negotiating parties released a new consolidated text reflecting the 'outcome of the 11th and final round of negotiations'. This October text is almost identical to the final ACTA version which the negotiating parties made available in early December 2010.[5] The final text allows insights into the 'new gold standards' the negotiating parties aim at.

ACTA has faced criticism ever since news about its negotiation became public. In particular NGOs, academics and officials from developing countries have voiced concerns regarding, inter alia, access to medicines, the protection of privacy, the free flow of information on the Internet and criminal enforcement measures.[6] To alleviate these concerns, the European Commission in a press release after the first official release, emphasized that 'the overall objective of ACTA is to address large-scale infringements of intellectual property rights which have a significant economic impact', and stressed that 'ACTA will by no means lead to a limitation of civil liberties or to "harassment" of

---

4 *See* Anti-Counterfeiting Trade Agreement Informal Predecisional/Deliberative Draft: April 21, 2010, PIJIP IP Enforcement Database, available at: http://sites.google.com/site/iipenforcement/acta ('Official Consolidated ACTA Text Prepared for Public Release, April 21, 2010', available at: http://www.wcl.american.edu/pijip/go/acta04212010) (hereinafter: April 2010 ACTA draft) (last accessed 17 July 2012).

5 The October text, *see* Anti-Counterfeiting Trade Agreement Informal Predecisional/Deliberative Draft: 2 October 2010, PIJIP IP Enforcement Database, http://sites.google.com/site/iipenforcement/acta ('Official Text – October 2 2010', available at: http://www.wcl.american.edu/pijip/download.cfm?downloadfile=7E80577D-97C5-C65E-26F54A14686C8F00&typename=dmFile&fieldname=filename) (hereinafter October 2010 ACTA draft). Final ACTA text, see Anti-Counterfeiting Trade Agreement, 3 December 2010, available at http://www.dfat.gov.au/trade/acta/Final-ACTA-text-following-legal-verification.pdf (hereinafter ACTA) (last accessed 17 July 2012).

The Agreement was signed on 1 October 2011 in Tokyo by the representatives of eight of the negotiating parties (Australia, Canada, Japan, Republic of Korea, Morocco, New Zealand, Singapore and the United States) and on 26 January 2012 by the European Union and 22 of its Member States (Austria, Belgium, Bulgaria, Czech Republic, Denmark, Finland, France, Greece, Hungary, Ireland, Italy, Latvia, Lithuania, Luxemburg, Malta, Poland, Portugal, Romania, Slovenia, Spain, Sweden and the United Kingdom). The United States of Mexico signed ACTA on 11 July 2012. See Press Release in English available at: http://www.impi.gob.mx/work/sites/IMPI/resources/LocalContent/3388/4/IMPI_010_2012_en.pdf (last accessed 18 July 2012

6 *Text of Urgent ACTA Communique: International Experts Find that Pending Anti-Counterfeiting Trade Agreement Threatens Public Interests*, Am. U. Wash. Coll. L. Program Info. *Just. & Intell. Prop.* (23 June 2010), available at: http://www.wcl.american.edu/pijip/go/acta-communique (last accessed 17 July 2012).

consumers'.[7] The Commission also points out that ACTA 'will not hamper access to generic medicines'.[8] In the following, this chapter describes the concerns (European) academics and scholars nevertheless have with regard to the consistency of ACTA with international and European law, especially on IP enforcement as well as on other areas such as fundamental freedoms and data protection. One venue where these concerns have been expressed is an opinion on ACTA issued by a group of prominent European academics in January 2011.[9] The opinion identifies the most critical aspects of ACTA and invites European and national institutions to carefully consider the opinion before ratifying the Agreement or withholding consent.[10] It received significant support in the academic community[11] and has subsequently been submitted to the European Parliament and other relevant European and national institutions. The text of this opinion is reproduced below.

As a response, the European Commission has published a comment on the opinion.[12] In its Comments, the Commission recognizes the 'expertise of

---

7 *See* Press Release, European Commission, Anti-Counterfeiting Trade Agreement: European Commission welcomes release of negotiation documents (21 April 2010), available at: http://trade.ec.europa.eu/doclib/press/index.cfm?id=552 (stressing that ACTA will not modify IP law, but will create rules for enforcing IP rights in 'courts, at borders, and over the internet') (last accessed 17 July 2012).

8 *Ibid.*

9 The text of the opinion and further information is available at http://www.iri.uni-hannover.de/acta-1668.html (last accessed 17 July 2012). The Opinion has also been published in: 2011 *Journal of Intellectual Property, Information Technology and E-Commerce Law (JIPITEC)* Vol. 2, 65.

10 In the meantime, another study drafted on the request of the European Parliament's Committee on International Trade by the Institute for Globalisation and International Regulation of the University of Maastricht expressed similar concerns and recommended that 'unconditional consent would be an inappropriate response from the European Parliament given the issues identified with ACTA as its stands' (European Parliament, Director-General for External Policies, Policy Department, 'The Anti-Counterfeiting Trade Agreement (ACTA): An Assessment', June 2011, EXPO/B/INTA/FWC/2009-01/Lot7/12, PE 433.859, Recommendations 8.1 (p. 65).

On 1 March 2012 the Committee on International Trade also hosted a public workshop on ACTA aimed at discussing the problems raised in regard with the Agreement. The opinions of the experts invited to analyse different aspects on ACTA were published in the study: European Parliament, Director-General for External Policies, Policy Department, 'Workshop The Anti-Counterfeiting Trade Agreement (ACTA)', March 2012, EXPO/B/INTA/FWC/2009-01/Lot7/25, PE 457.105, available at: http://www.europarl.europa.eu/committees/en/inta/studiesdownload.html?languageDocument=EN&file=73311 (last accessed 17 July 2012).

11 A list of signatories is available at: http://www.iri.uni-hannover.de/acta-1668.html (last accessed 17 July 2012).

12 The Comments on the 'Opinion of European Academics on Anti-Counterfeiting Trade Agreement' of the European Commission are available at:

those producing and putting their name to the Opinion' and welcomes 'a serious, text-based, legal analysis of ACTA' but disagrees with those findings in the opinion which point to inconsistencies and tensions between ACTA and international and European Law.[13] While this is not the appropriate place to analyse the Commission's response in any detail, the following must be emphasized: The Commission acknowledges that 'ACTA is written in more general terms than EU legislation, or that the exceptions, procedural guarantees and safeguards in ACTA are less precise, and less specific than those of the relevant EU legislation'.[14] This generality, and its resulting ambiguity, paired with the absence of specific (procedural) checks and balances is one of the key features of ACTA that has triggered a significant number of the concerns expressed in the opinion.[15] In this regard, the opinion aims to point to the potential problems, tensions and inconsistencies which may arise if these general provisions are *not* translated in specific safeguards and guarantees in the implementation stage. A good faith effort in implementing ACTA may alleviate the tensions and potential inconsistencies addressed in the opinion. In light of the specific responses by the Commission,[16] one would hope

---

http://trade.ec.europa.eu/doclib/docs/2011/april/tradoc_147853.pdf (last accessed 17 July 2012), reproduced in: Journal of Intellectual Property, Information Technology and E-Commerce Law (JIPITEC) 2011, Vol. 2, p. 171.

[13] See also the Communication from the Commission to the European Parliament, the Council, the European Economic and Social Committee and the Committee of the Regions, 'A Single Market for Intellectual Property Right, Boosting creativity and innovation to provide economic growth, high quality jobs and first class products and services in Europe', Brussels 24.5.2011, COM (2011) 287 final, p. 20, stating that ACTA is 'fully in line with the EU acquis'.

[14] See Comments of the Commission, at p.1.

[15] *See* also the concerns expressed by the European Data Protection Supervisor in its Opinion of 24 April 2012 on the proposal for a Council Decision on the Conclusion of the Anti-Counterfeiting Trade Agreement: 'The drafting of the Agreement which came out as a result of the negotiations lacks a sufficient level of precision and leaves much room for interpretation open to contracting parties. Such lack of precision is regrettable as the Agreement does not lay out with sufficient legal certainty the types of mechanisms that could be put in place as a result of entering into ACTA and the safeguards against the misuse of personal data or to protect the right of defence' (para 33), available at: http://www.edps.europa.eu/EDPSWEB/webdav/site/mySite/shared/Documents/Consultation/Opinions/2012/12-04-24_ACTA_EN.pdf (last accessed 17 July 2012).

[16] Further efforts were made by the European Commission to answer to the expressed concerns on ACTA. The Commission referred the Agreement to the European Court of Justice on 10 May 2012 with the following question: 'Is the envisaged Anti-Counterfeiting Trade Agreement (ACTA) compatible with the European Treaties and in particular with the Charter of Fundamental Rights of the European Union?' (European Commission officially referred ACTA to the European Court of Justice, Statement by John Clancy, EU Trade Spokesman, Notice, Brussels, 11 May

that implementing ACTA in the EU[17] and its Member States[18] is driven by such an implementation which upholds existing checks and balances and introduces new ones that correspond to the new measures to protect the enforcement interests of right holders.

Another aspect of the Commission's response needs highlighting. In disputing potential inconsistencies with existing international law, mainly the TRIPS Agreement, the response clarifies that the often more specific safeguards contained in TRIPS remain applicable and relevant for all WTO Members implementing ACTA.[19] This acknowledgement by the Commission is an important sign that ACTA is not self-standing body of law which re-writes and overrides existing treaty obligations, but subordinates itself to the checks and balances contained in TRIPS. Such an understanding of the ACTA–WTO/TRIPS relationship reasonably follows from Art.1 ACTA which confirms that 'Nothing in this Agreement shall derogate from any obligation of a Party with respect to any other Party under existing agreements, including the TRIPS Agreement'. However, given that ACTA often goes beyond some of TRIPS' concrete enforcement obligations without any mention of the often equally concrete safeguards contained in TRIPS, the operation of the – again very general – clause in Art.1 ACTA needed clarification. This clarification that the existing TRIPS checks and balances remain intact and applicable is a welcome development.

2012, available at: http://trade.ec.europa.eu/doclib/press/index.cfm?id=799 (last accessed 17 July 2012).

17 Nevertheless, it has to be mentioned that the European Parliament declined to consent to conclusion of the Agreement on 4 July 2012. Press Release of the European Parliament is available at: http://www.europarl.europa.eu/news/en/head-lines/content/20120220FCS38611/1/html/European-Parliament-rejects-ACTA, and the adopted text is available at: http://www.europarl.europa.eu/sides/getDoc.do?type=TA&reference=P7-TA-2012-0287&language=EN&ring=A7-2012-0204 (last accessed 17 July 2012).

18 Due to the concerns on the Agreement, Cyprus, Estonia, Germany, and Slovakia decided not to sign ACTA until the European Parliament expresses its vote. Other Member States of the European Union which signed the Agreement, such as Poland, Czech Republic, Latvia, Austria, Bulgaria and Romania, decided to freeze the ratification of ACTA. Moreover, the Dutch Parliament has announced that it will not ratify ACTA, and on 26 June 2012 the Dutch government stated that it will not sign the Agreement regardless of the decision of the European Parliament.

19 See for example the statements in the Commission response on the safeguards in art.56 and art.53.2 TRIPS at pp.16–17.

APPENDIX

OPINION OF EUROPEAN ACADEMICS ON ANTI-COUNTERFEITING TRADE AGREEMENT THE SIGNATORIES OF THE OPINION

following the adoption of the Anti-Counterfeiting Trade Agreement (ACTA) on 3rd December 2010

recognizing that

(a) *the extensive international trade in goods infringing intellectual property rights prejudices the legitimate interests of right holders and thus appropriate enforcement standards as well as international cooperation are needed;*
(b) *ACTA does not intend to extend the scope of protection of intellectual property rights granted under national laws and contains general provisions committed to balanced enforcement procedures;*
(c) *the most controversial enforcement measures proposed in the initial stages of the negotiations of ACTA have been narrowed down or abandoned in its final version;*
(d) *the appropriate balance needs to be effectively ensured between the enforcement of intellectual property rights and the fundamental rights of users such as the right to information and education, the freedom of expression, the right to accessible health care, the right to privacy and protection of personal data, the right to due process as well as other human rights and good governance in general;*
(e) *the protection and enforcement of intellectual property is one of the means to promote technological and creative innovation and its dissemination to the public; it thus must be seen together and not in conflict with other EU internal and external policies such as the promotion of the information society, the fostering of education, health care and development in third countries, and the promotion of biological and cultural diversity on an international scale;*
(f) *the Commission repeatedly reassured and the European Parliament welcomed in its Resolution of 24 November 2010 that ACTA is entirely compatible with existing EU law, but in fact this is not clear;*
(g) *certain controversial provisions were not fully removed from ACTA but are in some cases formulated as non-binding ('may') clauses, which signifies international political incitement to implement these clauses into contracting Party`s law;*
(h) *ACTA, being plurilateral in its nature, contains numerous provisions*

requiring higher enforcement standards than those set under existing international agreements; no state shall be put under pressure to adopt standards negotiated in a forum in which it did not participate;

draw the attention to the following points:

I. EU Law

Contrary to the European Commission's repeated statements and the European Parliament's resolution of 24 November 2010, certain ACTA provisions are not entirely compatible with EU law and will directly or indirectly require additional action on the EU level.

The following is a non-exhaustive list of illustrations that indicate the general tendency of ACTA:

Civil enforcement

1. Injunctions: art. 8.1 ACTA requires Contracting Parties to grant an order against a party to desist from an infringement, and *inter alia,* an order to that party or, where appropriate, to a third party to prevent infringing goods from entering into the channels of commerce. While the wording of art. 8 1 ACTA itself appears to be similar to the corresponding provision of art. 11 Directive 2004/48, it is worth mentioning that art. 12 of Directive 2004/48 gives the Member States an option to order pecuniary compensation to be paid to the injured party *instead* of applying the measures provided for in art. 11 Directive 2004/48, if the conditions specified in art. 12 are met. It seems that this option would be lost or at least called into question if art. 8.1 ACTA were enacted in its present form. It should not be forgotten that the US Supreme Court has recently upheld the traditional equitable four-factor test for injunctions in patent law and rejected an approach which favours automatic injunctive relief.[20]
2. Damages: art. 9.1 ACTA refers to a set of criteria which specifies the amount of compensatory damages. Some of the factors mentioned at the end of the provision are not provided for in art. 13.1 Directive 2004/48. These factors should not be adopted in European law since they are not appropriate to measure the damage. 'The value of the infringed good or service, measured by the market price, [or] the suggested retail price', as indicated in art. 9.1 ACTA, does not reflect the economic loss suffered

[20] eBay Inc. v MercExchange LLC, 547 US 388 (2006).

by the right holder. Furthermore, according to art. 9.4 ACTA pre-established damages or presumption based damages (especially reasonable royalties) may only be ordered as an alternative to the damages referred to in art. 9.1 (compensatory damages) and art. 9.2 (infringer's profits). In the absence of a clear rule on the alternative application of art. 9.1 or art. 9.2, it may be argued that compensatory damages and infringer's profits may be ordered cumulatively which is not explicitly stated in art. 13 Directive 2004/48. This would raise the amount of damages for the infringement of intellectual property.

3. Other Remedies: for corrective measures, art. 10 ACTA shifts the focus from 'disposal outside the channels of commerce' to outright destruction ('except in exceptional circumstances'), while art. 10 Directive 2004/48 provide several options, destruction only being one of them. Also, it may be asked why the caveat of proportionality which exists in art. 10.3 Directive 2004/48 is omitted. In particular, the interests of non-infringing third parties may need to be protected (e.g. property rights in the infringing goods which may have been acquired by a *bona fide* consumer; property of third parties in the materials/implements used to create the infringing goods). It is true that art. 6.3 ACTA provides for a general requirement of proportionality, but the same holds true for art. 3 Directive 2004/48, and still there is a specific reference to proportionality in the specific provision on corrective measures.
4. Provisional Measures: art. 12 ACTA does not make specific reference to the procedural guarantees for the defendant laid down in Directive 2004/48 (arts. 9.4, 9.5 Directive 2004/48). This is unfortunate, as the European Court of Justice has stressed the importance of these provisions 'to ensure that a balance is maintained between the competing rights and obligations of the right holder and of the defendant'.[21] Both the Luxembourg and the Strasbourg[22] courts have repeatedly held that the right to be heard occupies an eminent position in the organisation and conduct of a fair legal process. While the specific rules concerning the right to be heard may vary according to the urgency of the matter (and thus allow the adoption of provisional measures *inaudita altera parte* as provided for in art. 12.2 ACTA), 'any restriction on the exercise of that right must be duly justified and surrounded by procedural guarantees ensuring that persons concerned by such proceedings actually have the opportunity to challenge the measures adopted in urgency'.[23] It is not easy to understand why ACTA provides for provisional measures *inau-*

---

21 ECJ Case C-89/99, [2001] ECR I-5851 paras 38 et seq. – *Schieving-Nijstad*.
22 ECHR App.-No. 17056/06 paras 78 et seq. – Micallef v Malta.
23 ECJ Case C-341/04, [2006] ECR I-3813 para 66 – *Eurofood*.

dita altera parte, but does not at the same time take up the procedural guarantees which have been introduced in Directive 2004/48 and which are necessary to ensure that persons concerned by such proceedings have a later opportunity to challenge these measures.

Border measures

5. Definition: ACTA's provision on the scope of the border measures section contains an ambiguity giving rise to potential misuse. Whereas art. 2.1(a) Border Measures Regulation 1383/2003/EC (BMR) specifically narrows the scope of application of border measures for trademark infringements to 'counterfeit goods' only, art. 13 ACTA instead allows border measures in the case of 'intellectual property rights' in general and thus applies to all kinds of trademark infringements. IP rights are defined in art. 5(h) ACTA as all categories of IP covered by TRIPS. This suggests an interpretation of art. 13 ACTA that includes not only cases of counterfeiting, but also all other forms of trademark infringements based on mere similarity of signs, risk of confusion and even the protection for well-known trademarks against dilution. This is not only a clear extension of the EU *acquis*, but presents a particular problem for international trade in generic medicines which could be seized based on allegations of 'ordinary' trademark infringements. For all these reasons, art. 13 ACTA requires re-wording or, at least, a narrow interpretation and implementation. As art. 13 ACTA allows Contracting Parties to exclude certain forms of IP infringements as long as this does not amount to 'unjustifiable discrimination', public health grounds can justify the exclusion of ordinary trademark infringements from the scope of border measures. This would also ensure that ACTA parties live up to their general obligation in art. 6.1 ACTA not to create barriers to legitimate trade.

Criminal enforcement

6. No EU *acquis* on criminal measures: within the EU legal framework there are currently no provisions on criminal enforcement of intellectual property rights. ACTA, therefore, is by nature outside the EU law and would require additional legislation on the EU level.
7. Scope: art. 23.1 ACTA provides for a broad definition of 'commercial scale' covering all acts carried out on a commercial scale including at least those carried out as commercial activities for direct or indirect economic or commercial advantage. By contrast, in its Position of 25 April 2007, the European Parliament (EP) expressly excluded acts 'carried out by private users for personal and not-for-profit purposes'.[24]

The EP also declared that 'the fair use of a protected work, including such use by reproduction in copies or audio or by any other means, for purposes such as criticism, comment, news reporting, teaching (including multiple copies for classroom use), scholarship or research, does not constitute a criminal offence'. ACTA does not reaffirm these safeguards for private users and for limitations and exceptions.

8. Parallel imports: art. 23.2 ACTA prescribes criminal procedures and penalties on the wilful importation and domestic use on a commercial scale of goods infringing trademark rights. The vague language of the article could seem to cover importation and domestic use of products which, although lawfully marketed in the exporting country, have not been authorized in the importing country. Such interpretation would hinder parallel imports in the EU. The EP in art. 1 of its Position suggested that parallel imports should be specifically excluded from the scope of criminal offences. Such exclusion is not reflected in ACTA.
9. Cinematographic works: while according to art. 23.3 ACTA criminal measures for the unauthorized copying of cinematographic works are merely optional, ACTA prompts Contracting Parties to criminalize such an action without the commercial scale assessment and without any assessment of the intention of the defendant. Again, this disregards the exception in relation to fair use and copying for private and not-for-profit purposes repeatedly stressed by the EP.
10. Safeguards: while strengthening criminal enforcement measures, ACTA at the same time does not provide any of the safeguards needed to ensure the balance of interests between parties and guarantee a due process. In comparison, art. 7 of the EP Position of 25 April 2007 required the prohibition of the misuse of criminal procedures and sanctions, especially when they are employed for the enforcement of the requirements of civil law. Such guarantees, for instance, would be of particular importance in *ex officio* proceedings allowed under art. 26 ACTA. Also, art. 8 of the EP Position required that the rights of infringers are duly protected and guaranteed. Meanwhile, art. 25 ACTA authorizes judicial national authorities to issue seizure, forfeiture and destruction orders. However, it does not guarantee the infringer's right to be heard in these procedures.

---

[24] Position of the European Parliament adopted at first reading on 25 April 2007 with a view to the adoption of Directive 2007/.../EC of the European Parliament and of the Council on criminal measures aimed at ensuring the enforcement of intellectual property rights (EP-PE_TC1-COD(2005)0127).

II. INTERNATIONAL LAW

As recognized and welcomed by both the European Commission and the European Parliament, ACTA introduces enforcement standards higher than those existing under current international law. However, certain ACTA provisions do not ensure a balance between the interests of different parties, since they either eliminate safeguards existing under international law or after strengthening enforcement measures, fail to introduce corresponding safeguarding measures.

Most issues discussed above in relation to EU law are also of concern at the level of international law and go beyond TRIPS. The following points are pertinent only for the international law level. The list contains the most important provisions where the balance of interest is lacking and is meant to be illustrative and non-exhaustive:

Civil enforcement

11. Right of information: art. 11 ACTA strengthens the right of information as already found in art. 47 TRIPS. First, under ACTA it becomes compulsory (voluntary under art. 47 TRIPS). Second, the list of information that might be requested is expanded and the right may be directed both against infringers or alleged infringers (only against infringers under art. 47 TRIPS). Meanwhile, the proportionality requirement, as available under art. 47 TRIPS (and art. 8.1 EU Directive 2004/48), has been eliminated. Also, ACTA contains no effective provision against misuse of acquired information (e.g. comparable to art. 8.3(c) EU Directive 2004/48).

Border measures

12. Scope: while TRIPS requires border measures only against the importation of counterfeit trademark goods or pirated copyright goods, ACTA parties have to provide border enforcement against imports and exports of goods infringing *any* IP right covered in TRIPS – except patent rights and test data which are excluded by virtue of fn. 6 ACTA. However, these exemptions as such do not offer sufficient safeguards for the international trade in generic drugs. Extending border measures to goods suspected of 'ordinary' trademark infringement can create barriers to global trade – in particular if applied to generics in transit. ACTA parties hence must take their general obligation, under art. 6.1, '*to avoid the creation of barriers to legitimate trade*' seriously and establish systems which safeguard international trade and public health.
13. Safeguards: ACTA eliminates the following safeguards available under TRIPS. First, art. 56 TRIPS contains a mandatory requirement that customs must have '*authority to order the applicant to pay the*

importer, the consignee and the owner of the goods appropriate compensation for any injury caused to them through the wrongful detention of goods'. ACTA, however, has no directly equivalent provision for compensation in cases of wrongful detentions. Further, art. 18 ACTA widens the options for right holders to provide securities, while it does not include the (mandatory) option for the goods owner/importer to provide a security under art. 53.2 TRIPS. Instead, it contains a limited allowance for the latter to provide securities to obtain possession of the goods '*in exceptional circumstances*' (art. 18, 4th sentence ACTA). Finally, art. 55 TRIPS contains mandatory limits to the duration of the initial detention of goods suspected of infringement within which proceedings leading to a decision on the merits of the case have to be initiated or the goods released. Again, ACTA does not contain an equivalent rule – art. 19 ACTA merely demands the initiation of infringement proceedings '*within a reasonable period*'.

Criminal enforcement

14. Definition of 'commercial scale': art. 23 ACTA defines acts carried out on a 'commercial scale' as 'commercial activities for direct or indirect economic or commercial advantage'. It is doubtful if this is compatible with a more flexible market/product-based interpretation of commercial scale adopted by the WTO Panel, which refers to 'counterfeiting or piracy carried on at the magnitude or extent of typical or usual commercial activity with respect to a given product in a given market'.[25]

Digital chapter

15. Technological measures: arts. 27.5–6 ACTA require stronger protection of technological measures than set under art. 11 WIPO Copyright Treaty and art. 18 WIPO Performances and Phonograms Treaty (no similar provisions exist in TRIPS). In particular, ACTA provides a broad definition of technological measures (no definition under WIPO Treaties), it prohibits both acts of circumvention as well as preparatory acts, and covers technological measures having dual (both legal and illegal) functions. Although art. 27.8 ACTA allows preservation of exceptions and limitations, it does not provide any mechanisms to ensure their exercise and enforcement.
16. Disclosure of subscribers' data: art. 27.4 ACTA regulates disclosure of subscribers' data and is broader than the (non-mandatory) right of

[25] China – Measures Affecting the Protection and Enforcement of Intellectual Property Rights (China – IPRs), WT/DS362/R, 09/0240, 26/01/2009.

information under art. 47 TRIPS. Most importantly, whereas ACTA poses a duty to disclose subscribers' data both on infringing and non-infringing intermediaries, art. 47 TRIPS refers only to an infringer. Also, ACTA mentions that fundamental principles 'such as freedom of expression, fair process, and privacy' shall be preserved. However, it does not provide more specific provisions on how these rights should be effectively ensured (compare with detail provisions on privacy in EU Directives 95/46/EC, 2002/58/EC, and 2006/24/EC).

Taking above into account, **the Signatories of the Opinion invite the European institutions, in particular the European Parliament, and the national legislators and governments, to carefully consider the above mentioned points and, as long as significant deviations from the EU *acquis* or serious concerns on fundamental rights, data protection, and a fair balance of interests are not properly addressed, to withhold consent.**

Drafting committee:

Roberto D'Erme	Research Assistant, Centre for International Intellectual Property Studies (CEIPI), University of Strasbourg
Christophe Geiger	Associate Professor, Director General and Director of the Research Department, Centre for International Intellectual Property Studies (CEIPI), University of Strasbourg
Henning Grosse Ruse-Khan	Senior Research Fellow, Max Planck Institute for Intellectual Property, Competition and Tax Law, Munich
Christian Heinze	Senior Research Fellow, Max Planck Institute for Comparative and International Private Law, Hamburg
Thomas Jaeger	Senior Research Fellow, Max Planck Institute for Intellectual Property, Competition and Tax Law, Munich
Rita Matulionyte (coord.)	Senior Research Fellow, Institute for Legal Informatics, Leibniz University Hannover
Axel Metzger (coord.)	Professor of Civil Law and Intellectual Property, Institute for Legal Informatics, Leibniz University Hannover

First Signatories:

Lionel Bently	Herchel Smith Professor of Intellectual Property Law, Director of the Centre for Intellectual Property and Information Law, University of Cambridge
Michael Blakeney	Professor of Law, University of Western Australia and Visiting Professor, Queen Mary Intellectual Property Research Institute
Thomas Dreier	Professor of Intellectual Property Law, Director of the Institute for Information and Economic Law, Karlsruhe Institute of Technology (KIT), Karlsruhe
Josef Drexl	Director of Max Planck Institute for Intellectual Property and Competition Law, Munich
Mireille van Eechoud	Associate Professor at Institute for Information Law, Faculty of Law, University of Amsterdam
Nikolaus Forgo	Professor of Information Technology Law, Institute for Legal Informatics, Leibniz University Hannover
Jonathan Griffiths	Senior Lecturer, School of Law, Queen Mary University of London
Reto Hilty	Director of Max Planck Institute for Intellectual Property and Competition Law, Munich
Thomas Hoeren	Professor and Head of the Institute for Information, Telecommunications and Media Law (ITM), University of Münster
Bernt Hugenholtz	Professor of Intellectual Property Law, Director of the Institute for Information Law, Faculty of Law, University of Amsterdam
Matthias Leistner	Professor of Civil, Intellectual Property and Competition Law, University of Bonn
Ansgar Ohly	Professor of Civil Law and Intellectual Property Law, University of Bayreuth
Miquel Peguera	Associate Professor of Commercial Law, Department of Law and Political Science, Universitat Oberta de Catalunya, Barcelona
Nikolaus Peifer	Professor and Director of the Institute for Media and Communications Law, University of Cologne

Alexander Peukert	Professor of Civil, Commercial and Intellectual Property Law, Goethe University Frankfurt am Main
Haimo Schack	Professor of Civil, International Private and Copyright Law, Christian Albrecht University Kiel
Martin R.F. Senftleben	Professor of Intellectual Property, Faculty of Law, University of Amsterdam
Gerald Spindler	Professor of Civil, Business and Commercial Law, Comparative Law, Multimedia and Telecommunications Law, University of Göttingen
Malte Stieper	Professor of Civil Law, Intellectual Property and Competition Law, University of Halle
Uma Suthersanen	Professor in International Intellectual Property Law, Queen Mary University of London
Guido Westkamp	Reader in Intellectual Property Law, Queen Mary University of London
Andreas Wiebe	Professor of Civil, Competition and Intellectual Property Law, Media and Information Law, University of Göttingen
Dan Wielsch	Professor of Civil Law and Legal Theory, University of Cologne

For further information see http://www.iri.uni-hannover.de/acta-1668.html

20. Checks and balances in the intellectual property enforcement field: reconstructing EU trade agreements

Xavier Seuba*

1. THE THIRD GENERATION OF ISSUES IN THE GLOBAL INTELLECTUAL PROPERTY RIGHTS AREA

The recent emphasis on the enforcement of intellectual property rights (IPR) has given place to a third generation of issues and debates in the IPR international policy-making area since the entry into force of the Agreement on Trade-Related Aspects of Intellectual Property Rights (TRIPS). In effect, right after the TRIPS was adopted, most of the research and policy proposals focused on its impact on public goods and social interests. The implications of the TRIPS were so broad that, even today, analysis of the TRIPS in search of policy space to protect the public interest continues to be fruitful. Later on, in the first years of the twenty-first century, a related but distinct debate re-emerged, this one focusing on relationships between IPR, innovation and the public interest. While some sustain the validity of the present IPR system to deliver meaningful innovation, others claim that the costs of the system go beyond its current benefits, which only arise when there is a market-based interest. More recently, intellectual property enforcement[1] has been placed at

* The author wishes to thank Thomas Colon and Pedro Roffe for their comments.

[1] 'Enforcement' is an English term which is presently widely used by scholars all over the world. However, this term has no exact translation into other languages, as can be seen in the TRIPS agreement's different versions. In effect, the Spanish term 'observancia' would be better translated as 'fulfilment', which is wider in scope than enforcement. In the French version of the TRIPS the translation of 'enforcement' is not a term but a definition: 'moyens de fair respecter les droits de propriérté intellectuelle', and could probably be shortened to 'mise en ouvre'. In either case, the translation is not exact. This is similar to the case of other English words in related fields, such as

the forefront of the international activity in the IPR field, in sharp contrast with the traditional autonomy left to national jurisdictions in this regard. Promoters of new enforcement undertakings assume that the enforcement of IPR is a neutral endeavour limited to implementing what has already been agreed upon. Others, however, question the priority character put on the enforcement of IPR;[2] claim that enforcement is not addressed in a balanced manner;[3] and sustain that enforcement, as presently promoted, impacts the substantive breadth of IPR.[4]

A myriad of ongoing international initiatives foster the enforcement of IPR as the main objective among the range of IPR related activities.[5] The number, scope and reach of the new endeavours for IPR enforcement have expanded considerably. Some of them are private,[6] others are public in nature[7] and there are also public and private partnerships[8] which promote the enforcement of IPR. From the international point of view, the focus is placed on activities such as the adoption of new norms,[9] the improvement of the cooperation among national IPR-related authorities,[10] the strengthening of institutions dealing with IPR enforcement, and the identification and retaliation against countries which are considered to not do enough to

---

'accountability or 'empowerment', which, though successful, provoke difficulties when trying to delimit a field of research.

2 See. X. Li and C.M. Correa (2008), 'Conclusions and Strategic Recommendations', in X. Li and C.M. Correa, *Intellectual Property Enforcement. International Perspectives*, Cheltenham: Edward Elgar, p. 210.

3 H. Große Ruse-Khan, 'Re-delineation of the Role of Stakeholders: IP Enforcement beyond Exclusive Rights', in Li and Correa, *supra* note 2, p. 56.

4 X. Seuba, J. Rovira and S. Bloemen, 'Welfare Implications of Intellectual Property Rights Enforcement Measures', *PIJIP Research Paper no. 5*, American University Washington College of Law, Washington, D.C., http://digitalcommons.wcl.american.edu/cgi/viewcontent.cgi?article=1005&context=research (accessed 23 July 2012).

5 C.M. Correa (2009), 'The Push for Stronger Enforcement Rules: Implications for Developing Countries', *The Global Debate on the Enforcement of Intellectual Property Rights and Developing Countries*, Geneva: ICTSD, pp. 27–80.

6 Such as the Business Action to Stop Counterfeiting and Piracy (BASCP) or the International Trademark Association (INTA), International Chambers of Commerce (ICC) initiatives.

7 The most related with the object of this chapter is the EU Strategy for the enforcement of intellectual property rights in third countries.

8 The International Medical Products Anti-Counterfeiting Taskforce (IMPACT) is probably one of the most known and ambitious.

9 Through the adoption of multilateral, plurilateral, regional, multi-party and bilateral agreements containing IPR enforcement obligations.

10 North-to-South' programs of cooperation among IPR offices and agencies have become frequent.

protect rightholders' interests.[11] This chapter focuses on the normative aspects of the enforcement debate.

In the normative field, existing international substantive standards are increasingly supplemented with secondary norms of adjudication, which in principle deal with the fulfilment of the former,[12] and therefore with the end of the infringing activities. In a short period of time, countries, and in particular developing countries, have faced a cascade of new norms and policies pertaining to the fields of civil, criminal and administrative IPR enforcement. The origin of these norms is diverse: plurilateral and multilateral initiatives, free trade agreements (FTA) and World Trade Organization (WTO) accession compromises are, among others, the main sources.

Numerous academic studies have reported, classified and analysed enforcement treaties and initiatives. The existing academic *acquis* mapping enforcement initiatives permits entering into substantive areas of research. The work ahead is considerable and it is foreseeable that the analysis of new IPR enforcement norms will boost an intense academic activity. A relevant area of research should be the policy space available in the context of the new IPR enforcement obligations. That is, the performance in the enforcement area of a similar endeavour to that conducted in relation with primary norms contained in the TRIPS and in other international agreements containing IPR substantive norms.

For the past 15 years a tremendous effort has been made to identify the policy space existing in substantive provisions enshrined in international IP agreements, mainly the TRIPS agreement. Invoking various arguments and pursuing distinct hermeneutic paths, provisions contained in the TRIPS and in some FTAs have been clarified in benefit of development, human rights and other relevant social interests.[13] The public health field is a good example in that regard, and right now the so-called 'TRIPS flexibilities' are already part of any relevant document dealing with the TRIPS.[14] However, and although it

---

11 Either unilaterally through procedures such as the US Special 301, or in the context of multilateral forums such as the Dispute Settlement Understanding at the WTO.

12 In this group, H.L. Hart gathered norms enshrining the procedure to be used in determining and judging infringements, and to identifying who is to judge. That is, these norms regulate the establishment and identification of the corresponding sanctions if the violation of a primary norm occurs.

13 A comprehensive book and good example in that regard is the ICTSD-UNCTAD (2005), *Resource Book on TRIPS and Development*, New York: Cambridge University Press.

14 There are probably hundreds of books, articles, book chapters and reports dealing with the TRIPS flexibilities. Probably among the most representative – because of the forum, the process and the outcomes – is Commission on Intellectual Property

is frequently stated that countries should make use of flexibilities available to tailor enforcement of IPR in line with their needs and level of development, that same exercise has not yet been undertaken with regards to new IP enforcement provisions contained in recent treaties.[15] In fact, most of the articles enshrined in FTA enforcement chapters remain intact as academic focus of research. Some countries have partially imported enforcement legislation originating in other countries without probably fully knowing its real significance and reach.

2. THE DIRECTIVE 2004/48 ON THE ENFORCEMENT OF INTELLECTUAL PROPERTY RIGHTS AS POINT OF DEPARTURE

There exist several potential approaches to identify some flexibility in the enforcement field. This chapter follows a path based on a comparative analysis of the European Union (EU) text for civil enforcement harmonization and several EU trade agreements. In effect, a comparison is made between the *Directive 2004/48 on the enforcement of intellectual property rights (Enforcement Directive)*[16] and one association agreement (with Central America states), one multi-party trade agreement (with Peru and Colombia), one bilateral free trade agreement (South Korea) and one economic and partnership agreement (Cariforum). The objective is twofold. First, to identify checks and balances present in the EU legislation but absent in the treaties promoted by the EU. Second, to signal out the most suitable provisions to

---

Rights (2006), Innovation, and Public Health, *Public Health, Innovation and Intellectual Property Rights*, Geneva: WHO; UNCTAD, *Using Intellectual Property Rights to Stimulate Pharmaceutical Production in Developing Countries: A reference guide*, GE. 11–50568, 2011–500.

[15] The research conducted on enforcement initiatives has delivered proposals that impact enforcement management. Among the most refreshing proposals, mention can be made of the identification of ceilings in the TRIPS which would limit the adoption of new and enhanced IPR standards. In parallel, it has also been argued that enforcement does not only imply the entry into force of rightholders rights, but also the rights of consumers. *See*, for the first, H. Große Ruse-Khan and T. Jaeger (2009), 'Policing Patents Worldwide? EC Border Measures against Transiting Generic Drugs under the EC – and WTO Intellectual Property Regimes', *IIC*, **40** (5); and for the second, Große Ruse-Khan, *supra* note 3, pp. 43–4; H. Xue, 'Enforcement for Development: Why not an Enforcement Agenda for the Developing World', in Li and Correa, *supra* note 2, p. 148.

[16] Directive 2004/48/EC of the European Parliament and of the Council of 29 April 2004 on the enforcement of intellectual property rights, *Official Journal of the European Union* L157 of 30 April 2004.

achieve a balanced IPR enforcement, which may be present in some treaties but not in others. Both comparisons should, ideally, permit amending national laws taking the best from the EU legislation and from other EU FTA.

In 2004 the DG Trade adopted the *Strategy for the Enforcement of Intellectual Property Rights in Third Countries*,[17] which opened a new era and mapped EU future actions in the IPR enforcement field. The *Strategy* responded to the view that, at the present stage of the global IPR legal evolution, the focus must be placed on vigorous enforcement of IPR legislation. The *Strategy* anticipated numerous activities intended to guarantee the enforcement of IPR in third countries, among others the promotion of new legal undertakings on enforcement. In congruence with that goal, the EU has inserted powerful IPR enforcement chapters in 'ambitious'[18] economic treaties subscribed with both developed and developing countries, and has sponsored similar initiatives in multilateral fora.

In the civil enforcement area, the *Enforcement Directive* is the basis of new international legal undertakings promoted by the EU. The Directive set the framework to harmonize the means available for rightholders to fight against the infringement of IPR, and hence to enforce their rights. The European legal framework for civil enforcement went beyond the measures enshrined in the TRIPS, and promoted the adoption of the practices and legislation of the Member States that had proved to be the most effective[19] for the protection of rightholders. Therefore, national procedural sovereignty was partially sacrificed in favour of stronger and more harmonized enforcement legal frameworks.

The *Enforcement Directive* was not passed without criticism, something worth taking into account when accepting it as the basis for new IPR enforcement frameworks. The reasons for criticism were numerous, some of them were grounded in EU law[20] while others were of more conceptual nature.

---

[17] European Commission, *Strategy for the enforcement of intellectual property rights in third countries*, 10 November 2004, *Official Journal of the European Union*, 26/6/2005, C 129/3 – C 129/16.

[18] Report from the Commission to the European Parliament, the Council, the European Economic and Social Committee and the Committee of the Regions, *Application of the Directive 2004/48/EC of the European Parliament and the Council of 29 April 2004 on the enforcement of intellectual property rights*, Brussels, 22–12–2010, COM (2010) 779 final, p. 4.

[19] *Ibid*, p. 5. The so called 'best-practices approach'.

[20] Probably the most important is the affirmation that the constitutional basis for action was not met: to contain harmonizing provisions which have as their object the establishment and functioning of the internal market. *See*. W.R. Cornish, J. Drexl, R. Hilty and A. Kur (2003), 'Procedures and Remedies for Enforcing IPRs: the European Commission's Proposed Directive', *EIPR*, **25** (10), 447.

Among these last, mention must be made at least of two arguments which are of application everywhere the EU Directive is exported. First, the mixture in a sole document of measures devoted to very distinct IPR categories has been contested, because many of these categories have their own principles and particularities [21] Second, and particularly important, the harmonization of the procedural institutions contained in the Directive impacts on local visions of fairness and equity, as well as on national approaches to fundamental freedoms. Professors Cornish, Drexl, Hilty and Kur were clear about this 'In procedural law lie the real tests of how punitive, and therefore preventive, legal redress should be. The tests have evolved in different countries out of long experiences with their own system, each with its virtues and idiosyncrasies'.[22]

Given the similarities between the *Enforcement Directive* and the EU FTA, it becomes apparent that the Directive has not only been the point of departure to negotiate the treaties, but the destination itself. In effect, when a comparison is made between the recent EU treaties containing obligations on civil enforcement, it becomes clear that they include almost the same wording as the Directive. In fact, as far as the rights granted to the title holders, the five texts are almost identical. The differences are located in the provisions (or the absence therein) that deal with the limits of rightholders' entitlements and with the rights of their competitors and IPR protected goods users. The absence of balancing provisions in the EU treaties when compared with the Directive might seem surprising, since the Directive has traditionally been considered one-sided in favour of the rightholder. However, the fact is that the *Enforcement Directive* contains several provisions that oblige to take into account interests distinct to those pertaining to IPR holders.

3. GENERAL STRUCTURAL AND CONTENT COMPARISON

Chapter II of the *Enforcement Directive* is organized in seven sections. The first, on general provisions, contains three articles: one introduces the general obligations, the next indentifies the entitled applicants and the third includes a presumption of authorship or ownership. The second section of Chapter II deals with evidence and also lays down two articles, one on evidence, the other

21 In 2004 it was certainly noticeable the inclusion in a legal text intended to fight 'piracy and counterfeiting' of IPR infringements that have nothing to do with piracy and counterfeiting. Presently it is probably not as noticeable as it was.

22 W.R. Cornish, J. Drexl, R. Hilty and A. Kur, *supra* note 20, 448.

on measures to preserve evidence. Section 3, on the right of information, and Section 4, on provisional and precautionary measures contain in both cases a single but lengthy article. Next, the measures resulting from a decision on the merits of the case are regulated in Section 5, which includes three articles dealing with corrective measures, injunctions and alternative measures. Damages and legal costs are foreseen in Section 6, while Section 7 includes a short article dealing with publication of legal decisions.

When provisions for civil enforcement contained in the four agreements under analysis are compared with the *Enforcement Directive*, some structural differences can be identified. The *Enforcement Directive's* Chapter II was carefully divided into seven sections, each one dealing with distinct legal institutions pertaining to the civil enforcement area. By contrast, the EU agreements gather in a single section all civil enforcement provisions.[23] Furthermore, sometimes this section also includes administrative enforcement measures,[24] or even all IPR enforcement provisions of the treaty: civil, administrative and criminal – and specific references to the liability of Internet service providers.[25] However, leaving aside the number of sections, there is a great coincidence with regards to the order, the naming and the content related to the rights of the rightholders of the articles that deal with civil enforcement.

All agreements concluded by the EU contain an article on general obligations, on the entitled applicants, on evidence, on measures to preserve evidence, on the right of information, on provisional and precautionary measures, on corrective measures, on damages, on legal costs and on the publication of judicial decisions. Only in the case of the treaty with the Cariforum there is no article on the presumption of ownership or authorship, while the agreement with Central America does not foresee any article on injunctions nor on alternative measures. But the rest, both in content and title, greatly coincides.

Although coincidences are important, they are not absolute. At least three main areas of differentiation can be identified. In the first, the differentiation is drawn between the *Enforcement Directive* and the EU treaties. EU promoted treaties do not enshrine the guarantees for competitors and IPR-protected goods users contained in the *Enforcement Directive*. The second area has to do with a differentiation found among the EU treaties themselves. In effect, while some treaties contain let-out clauses, these are absent in other treaties. 'National conformity clauses', that is, a reference to the need that the obligation undertaken must be implemented in a manner consistent with national

---

23 Or sub-section, in the case of the Cariforum (pertaining to the intellectual property section).

24 This is the case of the treaty with Peru and Colombia.

25 This is the case of the Central America treaty and the Cariforum treaty.

legislation, are particularly present in the treaty with Colombia and Peru.[26] A third difference has to do with the IPR categories covered by civil enforcement measures in general, as well as with the categories affected by specific provisions in particular. For instance, if attention is paid to the wording of the treaty, civil (and all) enforcement measures of the Cariforum agreement also impact on utility models and protection of undisclosed confidential information. This is a possibility that the other agreements discard. On the other hand, there are some further restrictions, such as the ones found in the Central America treaty, which reserves corrective measures to the cases of counterfeit and pirated goods.

The following sections identify the main differences with the objective of selecting the crafting favouring a more balanced approach to the enforcement of IPR. Once differences are identified, countries should be able to incorporate them in their respective legislations or to claim the review of their respective agreements. Most of the time, however, the incorporation of these references should be unproblematic, since they are already foreseen in the EU legislation.

4. GENERAL PROVISIONS

A very important provision of the *Enforcement Directive* is its article 3. It lays down the general requirements and characteristics of enforcement remedies, procedures and measures. The conditions set up therein permeate the entire Directive and constitute the basic framework to enact balanced national laws for IPR enforcement in the EU Member States.

Some of the requirements enshrined in article 3 refer to the interests of the rightholder, this being the case of the requirement that establishes that procedures must be 'dissuasive'. Other conditions that enforcement provisions must fulfil are of interest for rightholders, competitors and IP-protected goods users. This is the case of the 'affordable' nature of said procedures. Most importantly, article 3 contains some balancing requirements that must guide the characteristics and the implementation of the provisions for IPR enforcement. The corresponding procedures, remedies and sanctions must be fair, equitable and proportionate. This call for fairness, equity and proportionality is a useful reference when specific consequences of enforcement procedures and remedies seem out of balance or, simply, not appropriate in a given situation.[27] And, importantly, article 3 also establishes that the creation of barriers to legitimate trade must be avoided and safeguards against their abuse shall be provided.

---

[26] It alludes to the need to respect national legislation in the case of the precautionary and provisional measures and legal costs.

[27] See below references to permanent injunctions, or recall the *eBay* case, rejecting automatism in the granting of injunctions.

The abovementioned requirements have also been introduced in all the agreements under analysis. The Colombia and Peru multi-party agreement contains an additional general provision. In this case, echoing the TRIPS, reference is made to the absence of obligation to put in place a system for the enforcement of IPR distinct from that for the enforcement of law in general.[28] Also echoing the TRIPS,[29] the Colombia and Peru agreement alludes to the freedom existing with respect to the distribution of resources.[30] The absence of these references in the rest of the treaties can be solved through distinct paths. One possibility is to invoke the general referral to the TRIPS contained in all agreements,[31] which reaffirms the commitments of the parties under TRIPS Part III. As the TRIPS also contains the stated obligations, the EU partners can invoke them regardless of not having been expressly included in their respective texts. A matter pertaining to a distinct order of things is the real impact of provisions of this sort. Enforcement sections are expensive to implement. New judges, administrative buildings and personnel, among other investments, may be necessary to honour them. To fulfil this obligation and at

---

[28] The TRIPS 41.5 states that the Part on IPR enforcement 'does not create any obligation to put in place a judicial system for the enforcement of intellectual property rights distinct from that for the enforcement of law in general' while the Peru and Colombia agreement affirms that the enforcement Chapter 'does not create for the Parties any obligation to put in place a judicial system for the enforcement of intellectual property rights distinct from that for the enforcement of law in general'.

[29] The reason is not clear to enshrine again, in a FTA, a right which is already foreseen in the TRIPS. There are some potential justifications, but none without speculative content. It is possible, for instance, to claim that the EU thinks that through the repetition of the same provision while not mentioning others the balance is struck in favour of the former. It is also possible that the intention was merely to underpin the priority character permeating specific provisions, without intent to disregard the unmentioned articles. Is it also speculative to state that a hope of oblivion when enshrining only the rights of rightholders and not the matching balancing provisions existed? On the other hand, the same kind of questions apply to the incorporation in FTA IPR chapters of provisions which had already been enacted in an FTA concluded by the trade partner with another state (for instance, to repeat in the agreement between the EU and Central America what has already been enshrined in the CAFTA).

[30] Art. 41.5 of TRIPS states 'Nothing in this Part creates any obligation with respect to the distribution of resources as between enforcement of intellectual property rights and the enforcement of law in general', while the Peru and Colombia agreement affirms that 'this Chapter does not create [...] any obligation with respect to the distribution of resources for enforcement of intellectual property rights and the enforcement of law in general'.

[31] More questions arise: can conflict of treaties be identified between the TRIPS provisions and FTA IP provisions? If this is the case, which would prevail? Although we seem to have a conflict of treaties clause (the TRIPS apply), *lex specialis* and *lex posterior* rules indicate that precedence must be given to the IPR provisions contained in the FTA.

the same time make use of the right to not modify the distribution of resources seems difficult to harmonize.

One article in the general provisions section refers to the entitled applicants. As the EU Directive, almost all EU agreements distinguish four distinct entitled applicants: the holders of IPR, other persons authorized to use those rights – in particular licensees, – IP collective rights-management bodies and professional defence bodies.[32] It is important to note that a reference is made to the fact that action on the part of those applicants will be carried out 'in so far as permitted by and in accordance with the provisions of the applicable law'. This can be either construed as a let-out clause, or as a provision granting an important margin to legislate.

5. EVIDENCE

Rules for obtaining evidence are essential in a world of intangible assets.[33] Fundamental issues for the rightholder such as the determination of the moment of the commencement of the infringement, or the quantity of infringing goods that have been marketed, depend on the existence of effective rules on evidence. On the other hand, the infringer will be frequently requested to provide information lying in his control. This information will probably involve sensitive data, regardless of its real contribution to assess the existence of an infringing activity. The provision of these data might be linked either to the right to privacy, or the right to not self-incriminate, which will have to be appropriately balanced against the interest existing in requiring the evidence.

5.1 Evidence

Article 6 of the *Enforcement Directive* obliges Member States to empower the judicial authorities to order the opposing party to present evidence lying in his control. It clarifies that this possibility must follow an *ex parte* petition, that it is subject to several guarantees to balance the interests of both parties (6.1) and that the information that may be ordered to be produced includes relevant banking, financial or commercial documents when the case has to do with an infringement committed on a commercial scale (6.2). This same possibility is

32 In the case of the Agreement with Central America, IP collective rights-management bodies are not included among the potential applicants.

33 C. Heath (2005), 'Comparative Overview and the TRIPS Enforcement Provisions', in C Heath and L. Petit, *Patent Enforcement Worldwide. A Survey of 15 Countries*, Oxford and Portland: Hart Publishing, p. 15.

established in all the agreements under study.[34] Differences between the *Enforcement Directive* and the EU agreements, however, can be identified with regards to the guarantees foreseen in benefit of the opposing party.

The *Enforcement Directive* requires the applicant to specify and identify the requested evidence that lies in the control of the opposing party. This prevents unspecific searches and protects the normal functioning of the economic activity of the opposing party, whose privacy and/or business will not be, at least in principle, unjustifiably intruded in search of unknown evidence. In this same line of reasoning, the Directive also requests the applicant to present 'reasonably available' evidence in order to substantiate his claims, and makes the communication of banking, commercial or financial information conditional upon the protection of confidential information.

When these limits and guarantees are contrasted with those included in the agreements concluded by the EU, only the treaty with Central America stands the comparison. In effect, neither the specification of the evidence, nor the presentation of evidence by the applicant ('reasonably available' or not), is required in the agreements concluded with Cariforum, South Korea and Colombia and Peru. Hence, unless a legal framework conditioning the production of evidence to some procedural and substantive guaranties is adopted – at least with the same wording as in the EU Directive – present articles on evidence will be easily abused by rightholders, who would be allowed to fish for evidence. Right now, the only common denominator in all EU treaties under analysis is the reference to the protection of confidential information.

In the agreements with the Cariforum and Central American states there is another potential avenue for exploring some flexibility when deciding whether or not evidence lying in the control of the opposing party must be produced. In effect, both agreements state that the provision of evidence will only be requested 'when appropriate' (Central America agreement) and 'where appropriate' (Cariforum agreement). 'Appropriate' remits to 'suitable' or 'proper'. These terms open an important window either for policy definition through additional legal specification, or for judicial autonomy to decide whether or not any obligation to show the requested documentation exists.

5.2 Measures for the Preservation of Evidence

Safeguarding of evidence on the alleged infringement – even when the proceedings have not been initiated – is an important measure to foster the

---

34 Art. 237 of the Colombia and Peru agreement, art. 262 of the treaty with Central America, art. 10.43 of the agreement with South Korea and art. 153 of the Cariforum agreement.

efficiency of IPR infringement procedures, particularly patent proceedings.[35] The *Enforcement Directive* regulation of the measures for obtaining evidence mixes features originating from the French *saise de contrafaçon* and the British *Anton Piller orders*. Although inquisitive in nature, and in the case of the *Anton Piller order* even described as an 'instrument of oppression',[36] the *saise de contrafaçon* and *Anton Piller order* have been progressively carved out so that the alleged infringer is not found defenceless. Some of the guarantees enshrined in France and in the United Kingdom have been transferred to the *Enforcement Directive*. However, the transposition of the resulting EU checks and balances has not occurred in the texts that the EU proposed and has concluded with its trading partners.

According to article 7 of the *Enforcement Directive* judicial authorities must be able to order provisional measures to preserve relevant evidence in respect of the alleged infringement. This is further defined with the identification of two potential actions: detailed description, with or without taking samples, and physical seizure of the infringing goods and, in appropriate cases, of the materials and implements used and related documents. These *ex parte* measures are subject to the presentation of reasonable available evidence to support that the right has been or is about to be infringed. The measures, which must be prompt and effective, may be taken even without the other party having been heard and even before the commencement of judicial proceedings.[37]

The general legal regime described greatly coincides with the regulation foreseen in the agreement with Peru and Colombia,[38] the treaty with South Korea,[39] the agreement with Cariforum[40] and the treaty with Central America.[41] The main general difference when the treaties are compared

35 D. Stauder affirms that safeguarding of evidence is one of the most special features that determine the efficiency of patent infringement procedures, the other one being the granting of speedy injunctive relief. D. Stauder, 'Introduction', in Heath and Petit, *supra note 33*, p. 1.

36 Mr Justice Brightman is quoted in *Anton Piller K.G., -and- Manufacturing Processes Limited, Bernard Preston Wallace and Alfred Henry Stephen Baker* saying: 'it seems to me that an Order on the lines sought might become an instrument of oppression, particularly in a case where a plaintiff of big standing and deep pocket is ranged against small man who is alleged on the evidence of one side only to have infringed the plaintiff's rights'. See *Anton Piller K.G. v Manufacturing Processes Limited, Bernard Preston Wallace and Alfred Henry Stephen Baker* [1975] EWCA Civ 12, 8 December 1975.

37 Art. 7.1 of the Enforcement Directive.

38 Art. 238 of the multi-party treaty with Peru and Colombia.

39 Art. 10.44 of the agreement with South Korea.

40 Art. 154 of the Cariforum agreement.

41 Art. 263 of the agreement with Central America.

among themselves and not with the *Enforcement Directive* is found in the agreement with Colombia and Peru. First, this treaty contains a national conformity clause regarding the physical seizure of the infringing goods.[42] Second, it states that measures must be not only prompt and effective, but also proportionate. This last is an important feature not foreseen in the rest of the texts. It implies a call for proportionality that gives to Colombian and Peruvian legislators and judges a broader margin to fine-tune measures for the preservation of evidence in a balanced manner.

Measures for the preservation of evidence as defined in the *Enforcement Directive* can become powerful tools to interfere with a competitor's activity unless safeguards are provided. The possibility to enter the competitor's premises and to inspect, and even to seize allegedly infringing goods, is prone to be abused if no clear limits are established. The EU Directive has introduced several guarantees to avoid such an undesired outcome.

As the measure for the preservation of evidence may be adopted *inaudita parte,* the *Enforcement Directive* states that notice must be immediately given after the execution of the measure.[43] The affected party has the right to ask for a review of the measure, a process that will oblige the judge to reconsider whether the measure must be revoked, maintained or modified.[44] Moreover, in case proceedings leading to a decision are not instituted in a reasonable period of time, the revocation will also be granted.[45] Very importantly, these measures may be subject to the lodging by the applicant of adequate security or an equivalent assurance,[46] and where measures are revoked or lapse, or no infringement is found, the defendant may be awarded appropriate compensation.[47] Therefore, notice, review revocation, security and compensation are the guarantees instituted to try to mitigate potential harmful effects of the measures.

Again, none of these checks and balances has been introduced in the agreements under study. This absence allows some deviations from the original intent of this provision. For instance, if title holders know that no compensation in favour of the defendant will be awarded when no infringement is found, they may be tempted to use measures for the preservation of evidence as an additional offensive commercial tool at their disposition. EU trading partners should, therefore, consider the introduction of at least the same level of EU protection by their own, having in mind that the EU legislation in this field not

---

42 'If the domestic legislation permits'.
43 *Enforcement Directive*, art. 7.1.
44 *Enforcement Directive*, art. 7.1.
45 *Enforcement Directive*, art. 7.3.
46 *Enforcement Directive*, art. 7.2.
47 *Enforcement Directive*, art. 7.4.

only originates from diverse traditions, but also that it has been transferred and implemented in very diverse ways. Openness to find alternative methods for implementation can be fruitful in this very sensitive area.

6. RIGHT OF INFORMATION

The *Enforcement Directive*'s article 8 regulates the right of information. This is an important provision for rightholders, particularly in their fight against counterfeiting and piracy, and it is also a potentially controversial right from the perspective of protection of personal data. The origin of article 8 can be traced back to the German Anti-Piracy Law of 1990, which enshrined the *Auskunftsanspruch* (right of information) and permitted requesting information on the identity of infringers, their suppliers, and their customers.

For many European States the level of detail of the *Enforcement Directive*'s article 8 implied the introduction of relevant changes in their legislations. This article permits obtaining information on the origin of the infringing goods or services, the distribution channels and the identity of any third parties involved in the infringement of any IPR. This is clearly an important departure from TRIPS, where the right of information is an optional remedy. Rightholders claim that this knowledge is important to prosecute the infringing activity from the root. However, it is also recognized that the right of information can be abused if no strict limits are laid down, something which should be particularly worrying given its close relationship to privacy and the protection of personal data.[48] Moreover, its legitimacy could

---

[48] In *Promusicae*, the European Court of Justice stated that:

> Article 8(1) of Directive 2004/48 admittedly requires Member States to ensure that, in the context of proceedings concerning an infringement of an intellectual property right and in response to a justified and proportionate request of the claimant, the competent judicial authorities may order that information on the origin and distribution networks of the goods or services which infringe an intellectual property right be provided. However, it does not follow from those provisions, which must be read in conjunction with those of paragraph 3(e) of that article, that they require the Member States to lay down, in order to ensure effective protection of copyright, an obligation to communicate personal data in the context of civil proceedings.

The ECJ concluded that 'Directives 2000/31, 2001/29, 2004/48 and 2002/58 do not require the Member States to lay down, in a situation such as that in the main proceedings, an obligation to communicate personal data in order to ensure effective protection of copyright in the context of civil proceedings'. *Productores de Música de España (Promusicae) v Telefónica de España SAU* Case C-275/06, 28 January 2008, paras 58 and 70.

also be challenged in many legal orders since it may imply obliging suspected infringers to self-incriminate.

According to the *Enforcement Directive* and the texts of the agreements under study, judges may order to make available information on the origin and distribution networks of the goods or services which infringe an intellectual property right. The *ex parte* request for information must be justified and proportionate, and it can be made not only to the infringer, but also to the person found in possession of the infringing goods, using the infringing services or providing services used in infringing activities.[49] Except in the case of the infringer itself, in the rest of situations the activity must be performed on a commercial scale.

Article 8 of the Directive establishes several guarantees aimed at fostering a balanced implementation of the right of information.[50] These guarantees have been transferred to the agreements with South Korea,[51] Cariforum[52] and Peru and Colombia,[53] but not to the treaty concluded with Central American countries. In this last case, there is no reference to the precedence of rules relating to civil and criminal proceedings on this kind of information, or to rules that govern the responsibility for the misuse of information. Moreover, the agreement with Central America does not mention some regulatory aspects closely related with fundamental rights. One is the right to not admit one's – and that of a close relative's – culpability by not providing the requested information. Another is the precedence of rules on protection of the confidentiality of information and the processing of personal data.

7. PROVISIONAL AND PRECAUTIONARY MEASURES

Provisional and precautionary measures are crucial in IPR proceedings. In categories such as patents, their effects on competition are so powerful that in some jurisdictions the expectations of the parties are placed even more in provisional measures than in the final decision on the merits of the case. The

49 *Enforcement Directive*, art. 8.1.

50 *Enforcement Directive*, art. 8.3(b) through (e): i) Prevalence of statutory provisions that govern the use in civil or criminal proceedings of the information communicated pursuant to the right of information; ii) prevalence of provisions that afford an opportunity for refusing to provide information which would force to admit oneself participation – or that of his/her close relatives – in an infringement of an intellectual property right; iii) prevalence of statutory provisions that govern the protection of confidentiality of information sources or the processing of personal data.

51 South Korea treaty, art.10.45.3(b) through (e).

52 Cariforum agreement, art. 155.3(b) through (e).

53 Peru and Colombia treaty, art. 239.3(b) through (e).

case of interim injunctions is clear. If, for instance, the alleged infringer is ordered to shut down its activity until the final decision is delivered, that competitor will be irremediably placed out of the market. Certainly, some measures for preserving evidence such as the seizure of infringing goods and the materials and tools used in their manufacture may result in the same outcome, but in principle the intended goal is distinct.

The *Enforcement Directive* sets up three main options regarding provisional and precautionary measures: the issuance of interlocutory injunctions,[54] the seizure or delivery up of allegedly infringing goods[55] and the seizure of both movable and immovable property of the alleged infringer.[56] Each option has its own regulation, with specific requirements and guarantees. These specific regulations are accompanied by some general conditions applicable to all three of them, as well as by references to the potential consequences if they are abused. When the EU trade agreements are compared with one another and with the *Enforcement Directive*, it becomes apparent that in the field of provisional and precautionary measures there is more diversity than in the rest of civil enforcement measures.

In the *Enforcement Directive* the first provisional and precautionary measure mentioned is the issuance of interlocutory injunctions. This possibility is meant to address three distinct situations: to prevent an imminent infringement of an IPR, to stop the continuation of the alleged infringement, and to subject the continuation of the infringement to the lodging of guarantees. In these cases, interlocutory injunctions may be issued both against the infringers and intermediaries, and with respect to all IPR categories.[57]

Although the EU agreements follow a similar pattern with respect to interlocutory injunctions, there are also some differences. Together with the 'national conformity clause' found in the agreement with Peru and Colombia,[58] the main differences can be found in the Central America agreement.[59] In this case there is no mention of the possibility to subject the continuation of the infringement to the lodging of guarantees, or to the possibility to grant interlocutory injunctions against intermediaries. Moreover, when reference is made to interlocutory injunctions to forbid the continuation of the alleged infringement, there is no mention of the possibility to request a recur-

[54] Art. 9.1(a).

[55] Art. 9.1(b).

[56] Art. 9.2.

[57] Having in mind that copyright interlocutory injunctions have their own *lex specialis*: injunctions against intermediaries in copyright cases are covered by Directive 2001/29/EC.

[58] 'In accordance with their domestic legislation, the Parties shall provide that the judicial authorities'.

[59] Agreement with Central America, art. 265.

ring penalty payment, as it is foreseen in the EU Directive, the Cariforum agreement, the treaty with South Korea, and the treaty with Peru and Colombia.

As aforesaid, the second option among precautionary measures is the judicial seizure of goods to prevent their entry into or movement within the channels of commerce. This legal institution, originating in the British freezing orders, is again absent in the agreement with Central America. By contrast, the rest of agreements have enacted this possibility in the same terms as the *Enforcement Directive*.[60]

The third option implies the seizure of the property of the alleged infringer, including the blocking of bank accounts and other assets, in case of infringement on a commercial scale. This is a possibility not included either in the agreement with Peru and Colombia, nor in the agreement with Central American states. As a guarantee for the opposing party, included both in the agreement with South Korea and in the treaty with Cariforum,[61] the injured party that asks for the seizure of movable and immovable property, must prove circumstances likely to endanger the recovery of damages.

As a general guarantee applicable to the three stated options, the Directive establishes that the applicant may be required to provide 'any reasonable available evidence' in order to satisfy with 'sufficient degree of certainty' that he is the rightholder, that the corresponding right is being infringed or that such infringement is imminent. In other words, it is required to show a good case, something that 'can be considered a basic issue of justice: No defendant shall be made subject to a measure that presumably would not stand up to a proper trial'.[62] The requirement to establish satisfaction with a 'sufficient degree of certainty' permits adopting a high threshold for the adoption of the provisional and precautionary measures, which will probably differ in each IPR category. Whatever the specific interpretation, this is an option of the utmost importance that, nevertheless, neither the agreement with Peru and Colombia, nor the South Korean agreement, foresee.

It is again noticeable that the *Enforcement Directive* references aimed at ensuring that provisional measures are not abused have not been included in the treaties concluded with the EU's trading partners. The first instance is the obligation to revoke the measures if the applicant does not institute, within a reasonable period of time, proceedings leading to a decision on the merits of the case. The second is the option to subject the measures to the lodging of an

---

60 Art. 240.2 of the treaty with Colombia and Peru; art. 10.46.2 of the treaty with South Korea; art. 156.2 of the Cariforum treaty.

61 It is however enacted in the South Korean agreement (art. 10.46.3) and in the Cariforum agreement (art. 156.3).

62 Heath, *supra* note 33, p. 28.

adequate security or an equivalent assurance. And the third is the reference found in the *Enforcement Directive* to the compensation that will follow if measures are revoked, they lapse due to any act or omission by the applicant or if it is found that there has been no infringement or threat of infringement.[63] That is, according to the EU Directive, compensation would follow even where the plaintiff did not act maliciously: 'after all, the plaintiff entertains a calculated risk when requesting a provisional measure'.[64] But it seems that this will not be the case for EU partners, unless they supplement the wording of the respective agreements in the implementation process.

8. MEASURES RESULTING FROM A DECISION ON THE MERITS OF THE CASE

In the *Enforcement Directive,* measures resulting from a decision on the merits of the case are regulated in three provisions dealing with corrective measures, injunctions, and alternative measures. The EU treaties contain some slight but important differences with regards to corrective measures and injunctions, while they are identical with regards to alternative measures. The exception can be found in the agreement with Central America, which does not include provisions on injunctions and alternative measures.

8.1 Corrective Measures

The *Enforcement Directive*[65] and the EU agreements[66] permit three distinct actions with regards to goods found to be infringing IPR, and in appropriate cases also with regards to materials used to produce those goods. The first is to recall infringing goods from the channels of commerce, the second is the definitive removal from the channels of commerce and the third is their destruction. These measures will be applied with respect to infringements of all IPR, except in the case of the Central America agreement, which limits corrective measures to pirated and counterfeited goods.[67]

As a balancing criterion when considering the request for corrective measures, the *Enforcement Directive*, the EU agreement with Central America, and the treaty with South Korea allude to the need for proportionality, as well

---

63 See, respectively, arts. 95, 9.6 and 9.7 of the Enforcement Directive.

64 Heath, *supra* note 33, p. 27.

65 Enforcement Directive, art. 10.

66 Art. 241 of the Peru and Colombia agreement; art. 266 of the treaty with Central America; art. 10.47 of the South Korean treaty; and art. 157 Cariforum.

67 Art. 266.1 of the Central America Agreement.

as to the need to take into account the interests of third parties. These are important and useful references to deliver balanced decisions on corrective measures. Colombia, Peru and Cariforum members could probably benefit from the incorporation of these principles in their domestic legislations, regardless of its absence in the treaties concluded with the EU.

8.2 Injunctions

Once a judicial decision is taken and an infringement is found, an injunction prohibiting the continuation of the infringing activity can be ordered. Hence, injunctions are intended to stop the infringing act and to forbid its reoccurrence in the future. They are probably one of the most valued remedies in the civil enforcement field, since they permit restoration of market exclusivity for the rightholder.

Leaving aside the Central America agreement, which is silent on this matter, the rest of the EU trade agreements[68] repeat the same pattern of the *Enforcement Directive* as far as the provision on injunctions is concerned:[69] in case of infringement, judicial authorities may issue an injunction against the infringer to prohibit the continuation of the infringement. In all cases this possibility is subject to national legislation, and will be implemented 'only if appropriate'.

Injunctions may also be issued against intermediaries whose services are used to infringe an IPR. The *Enforcement Directive* opens this possibility in cases of infringements of 'an intellectual property right', and recalls article 8.3 of the *Information Society Directive*.[70] This, in principle, means that all IPR categories would be covered, as happens in the case of the treaty with Cariforum and in the text with Peru and Colombia. The agreement with South Korea, however, limits actions against intermediaries to copyright and related rights, geographical indications, and trademark infringements.[71]

An important difference is found in the treaty with Colombia and Peru, which expressly mentions TRIPS article 44.2.[72] The reference to this article makes it possible to limit the remedies available to payment of adequate remuneration in the circumstances of each case, taking into account the

---

68 Art. 242 in the Peru and Colombia agreement; 10.48 in the South Korean treaty; and art. 158 of the Cariforum.

69 Enforcement Directive, art. 11.

70 The content is coincidental. According to Directive 2001/29/EC, aspects of copyright and related rights in the information society, 'Member States shall ensure that rightholders are in a position to apply for an injunction against intermediaries whose services are used by a third party to infringe a copyright or related right.'

71 See art. 10.48.2.

72 See art. 242 of the multi-party treaty between the EU, Peru and Colombia.

economic value of the authorization, or to issue a declaratory judgment and grant adequate compensation. The objective of this provision is to permit the continuation of infringing activities pursuant to the adequate remuneration and compensation of the injured party. There may be different circumstances in which it will be socially preferable or more equitable to allow the continuation of the infringing activity, something that this reference to TRIPS article 44.2 permits if certain conditions are fulfilled.

Although the reference to TRIPS article 44.2 is absent in the rest of agreements, a call for equity considerations in granting injunctions can be introduced due to the presence of conditional language ('judicial authorities *may* order', 'judicial authorities *may* issue'...). These enabling references may be understood as meaning that a permanent injunction does not necessarily or automatically follow a decision finding an infringement. The US Supreme Court backed this view in the *eBay, Inc. v MercExchange* decision, which reversed a Court of Appeals for the Federal Circuit decision while stating that 'the decision whether to grant or deny injunctive relief rests within the equitable discretion of the district courts, and that such discretion must be exercised consistent with traditional principles of equity'.[73]

9. DAMAGES AND LEGAL COSTS

9.1 Damages

The initial wording of the *Enforcement Directive* article 13 frames damages as a compensatory remedy: the infringer must pay damages 'appropriate to the actual prejudice suffered'. Although the EU Commission defends a new and opposite interpretation,[74] this means that the operation will be devoid of punitive nature and that many factors shall be taken into account to determine the

[73] *eBay, Inc. v MercExchange*, L.L.C., 547 US 388, 391 (2006).

[74] In its evaluation of the *Enforcement Directive,* the Commission frames damages as a dissuasive instrument – and not only as a compensatory one. It furthermore seems to re-open the door of a proposal that attracted a very intense opposition when the *Enforcement Directive* was drafted: punitive damages. It does not say it explicitly, but it affirms that 'it could be considered whether the courts should have the power to grant damages commensurate with the infringer's unjust enrichment, *even if they exceed the actual damage incurred by the rightholder*'. Report from the Commission to the European Parliament, the Council, the European Economic and Social Committee and the Committee of the Regions, *Application of the Directive 2004/48/EC of the European Parliament and the Council of 29 April 2004 on the enforcement of intellectual property rights*, Brussels, 22 December 2010, COM (2010) 779 final, p. 8.

awarded damages. As in the case of alternative measures and other already analysed provisions, EU treaties have copy-pasted the wording of the article on damages contained in the *Enforcement Directive*.[75]

The provision on damages draws a distinction between the infringer who knowingly infringed or had reasonable grounds to know, and the infringer that did not know or had no reasonable grounds to know. With regards to the 'conscious' infringer there are two alternatives. In the first case, when judicial authorities set damages they shall take into account lost profits, unfair profits realized by the infringer and elements other than economic factors. The second alternative permits setting damages as a lump sum on the basis of elements such as the amount of royalties and fees which would have been due if an authorization had been requested. By contrast, in the case of the infringer that did not know, judicial authorities may order the recovery of profits or the payment of damages.

All the EU agreements under study contain the aforementioned regime for assessing damages. A shorter version of the text, however, can be found in the agreement with Central America. In that text mention is made only of the obligation to allow judicial authorities to order the payment of damages to the rightholder to compensate for the injury. However, no references to specific consequences are made in the case of the infringer who knowingly infringed or had reasonable grounds to know. This leaves open, for instance, the question of whether unfair profits made by the infringer or elements such as the moral prejudice caused to the rightholder can be computed. By contrast, the agreement with Central American states alludes to the case of the infringer that did not know or had no reasonable grounds to know, and states that judicial authorities may order the recovery of profits or the payment of damages.

9.2 Legal Costs

All the texts under examination prescribe, as a general rule, that legal costs and expenses incurred by the successful party shall be borne by the unsuccessful party. Both the Directive and the treaties[76] – except the Cariforum text – establish that costs must be reasonable and proportionate, and all the texts – this time also including Cariforum – establish that equity considerations must be introduced when deciding whether or not to adjudicate the costs to the unsuccessful party.

[75] Art. 13 of the *Enforcement Directive*; art 244 of the treaty with Colombia and Peru; art. 267 of the treaty with Central America; art. 10.50 of the agreement with South Korea; and art. 160 of the Cariforum agreement.

[76] Art. 14 of the *Enforcement Directive*; art. 245 of the Colombia and Peru treaty; art. 268 the Central America text; art. 10.51 in the agreement with South Korea; and art. 161 the Cariforum text.

Interestingly, a 'national conformity clause' or let-out clause is foreseen in the treaty between the EU, Peru and Colombia, and in the treaty between the EU and Central America. In effect, the attribution of legal costs to the unsuccessful party will be performed 'in accordance with domestic legislation', in the case of Peru and Colombia, and 'in accordance with domestic law', in the case of Central American states. This reference, added to the reasonability, proportionality and equity mandated in the same provision, are decisive criteria when deciding who will bear the legal costs.

10. PUBLICATION OF DECISIONS

The articles dealing with the dissemination of information regarding judicial decision have almost the same wording in the texts under study.[77] Following an *ex parte* petition, judicial authorities may order the dissemination of information concerning the decision, including displaying and publishing. The costs of these measures will fall on the infringer. The unique difference in this regards can be found in the South Korean treaty, which establishes that judicial authorities will order the publication 'where appropriate'.

11. CONCLUSIONS

Chapter II of the *Enforcement Directive* contains 'measures, procedures and remedies' for IPR civil enforcement. The seven sections of Chapter II set up general provisions and lay down articles on evidence, the right of information, provisional measures, measures resulting from a decision on the merits of the case, damages, legal costs, and publicity measures. This scheme is systematically repeated in the IPR chapters of the EU recent trade agreements, which also include the content of the *Enforcement Directive* that benefits rightholders.

The texts concluded by the EU with developed and developing trade partners enshrine almost solely the *Enforcement Directive* institutions that are of interest for title holders. This means that the checks and balances present in the already controversial *Enforcement Directive* are neither proposed nor included in the treaties with the EU partners. This absence raises questions from the angle of the obligation to negotiate treaties in good faith. Whatever the case,

[77] Art. 15 of the *Enforcement Directive*; art. 246 of the Colombia and Peru treaty; art. 269 the Central America text; art. 10.52 in the agreement with South Korea; and art. 162 the Cariforum text.

the analysis presented in this chapter, showing the differences between the *Enforcement Directive* and the EU trade agreements, and among the EU association agreements themselves, could be helpful in integrating into the legislations of the respective EU partners the public-interest balancing provisions that the *Enforcement Directive* foresees.

Countries have an initial and straightforward option to redress the mentioned shortcomings: to implement the EU FTA adding the checks and balances absent in the *deconstructed* EU proposals and in the presently unbalanced texts of the treaties. This option, which seems reasonable given the current state of things and the consequences of implementing the treaties with the EU simply as they read right now, raises, however, some fundamental questions related to the convenience of globalizing the EU legislation on civil enforcement.

The proposed exportation of the *Enforcement Directive* balancing provisions should not be equated to the acceptance of the resulting overall outcome. The *Enforcement Directive* Recital 10 states that the Directive is aimed at establishing 'high, equivalent and homogenous level of protection', and recently the EU Commission has stated that the Directive 'created high European legal standards to enforce different types of rights'.[78] While this is a foreseeable goal in the EU and in other similar contexts, it is indeed not a policy priority of developing countries. In fact, it is difficult to justify the prioritization of the enforcement of economic and private legal interests in contexts where daunting basic human needs are not satisfied.

---

78 Report from the Commission to the European Parliament, the Council, the European Economic and Social Committee and the Committee of the Regions, *Application of the Directive 2004/48/EC of the European Parliament and the Council of 29 April 2004 on the enforcement of intellectual property rights,* Brussels, 22 December 2010, COM (2010) 779 final.

Section 8

Making the European IP System Work: Further Steps to Take

Raimund Lutz

1. THE EPO'S ROLE IN FOSTERING THE EUROPEAN PATENT SYSTEM

1.1 Introduction

The European Patent Organisation is an institution which over the past three decades, has emerged as a success story of European integration and cooperation, enabling Europe-wide patent protection to be garnered through a single, centralized and rationalized patent grant system whose proven high quality has made it a global benchmark.

Today, the European Patent Organisation has 38 Member States. Extension Agreements are in force with Bosnia Herzegovina and Montenegro. Moreover, very recently, a validation agreement – the first of its kind – has been concluded with Morocco. This means that with a single European patent application, protection can now be obtained in up to 40 countries, covering an overall market of 600 million people. This market is greater than the US, Japanese and South Korean markets combined.

There is strength in such numbers, but, as we know, there are also weaknesses: taken individually, huge competing markets such as the US, Japan and South Korea operate in a single language, under a single court jurisdiction and enjoy a unitary patent covering their territory. In contrast, a patent holder choosing to have Europe-wide protection ends up with a bundle of 40 European patents covering territories speaking more than 30 different languages and subject to 40 different court jurisdictions.

In today's world of intensifying economic competition, Europe cannot afford to lose ground in a sector as vital for innovation as patent policy. For this reason, it is my profound conviction that we must finish building the European patent system, creating the structures which were envisaged and embraced over half a century ago.

1.2 Creating a Unitary European Patent System

I fully embrace the ideal of a unified Europe. The European patent system can only be considered complete with a unitary patent and a centralized, specialized patents court, and this is clearly an economic imperative. Therefore, I am particularly happy to observe that the Member States of the EU, with the exception of Spain and Italy, have decided to establish enhanced cooperation between themselves in the area of the creation of unitary patent protection.

The European Commission, on 13 April 2011, tabled a package of two legislative proposals under enhanced cooperation containing the provisions that are necessary to implement unitary patent protection in the participating 25 Member States. The EPO strongly welcomes this decisive step forward towards improving the European patent system. It is hoped that the Council and the European Parliament will soon reach agreement on the two Regulations.

The proposals envisage a central role for the EPO: applicants will have to file an application for a European patent with the EPO the same way as they do today. Once the European patent is granted, and the mention of the grant is published in the European Patent Bulletin, the patentee would request the EPO to register the unitary effect in a new Register for unitary patent protection. Indeed, it is vital that the creation of the unitary patent should not call into question the principle that the processing of European patent applications is centralized at the EPO. That is crucial to ensure uniform treatment leading to high-quality patents. In other words: if the system is to operate smoothly, it is essential for European patent applications to be entirely governed by the EPC.

The EPO is envisaged to take over a number of additional administrative tasks with regard to the unitary patent. It will, in the post-grant phase, in particular be responsible for the requests for unitary patents, the translation system, for collecting and distributing the renewal fee payments and for the register for unitary patents. I am confident that the EPO is best placed and well prepared to smoothly carry out the additional tasks that it will be entrusted with. For the Office and the European Patent Organisation it is crucial that full cost coverage of the EPO expenses incurred in carrying out the additional tasks is guaranteed and that the overall system maintains the financial sustainability of the European Patent Organisation.

As regards reduction of the translation requirements, the unitary patent has a significant cost reduction potential which will enable applicants from countries which up to now do not play a major role in the European innovation landscape to take advantage of the benefits inherent to sound patent protection. In this context it is to be welcomed that the language arrangements for the EU patent are based on the EPO's three-language system for the grant procedure. This balanced solution of proven effectiveness and with broad user acceptance.

The European Commission proposal regarding the translation arrangements provides for transitional measures to be applied during a certain period before a system of high quality machine translations becomes available. The

EPO will make every effort to accelerate, in close cooperation with the Commission, the provision of high-quality machine translations with a view to shortening the transitional period under which additional translations will have to be filed by patentees. I sincerely believe that the EPO can contribute to a possible language regime for the unitary patent insofar as proposals for the EU patent's language regime are also based on production of machine translations of the application and granted unitary patent into all EU official languages, for information purposes. In this respect, the Office is making the development of 'fit-for-purpose' machine translation technology one of its top priorities. The aim is to provide users with machine translation services from and into English (and, later, French and German) for all the languages of the EPC contracting states. I believe that in due course, together with the national offices, we can achieve a reliable and high-performance system.

Finally, needless to say how fundamental a unified, centralized patent litigation system is, as the natural sequel to the centralized grant procedure. The current fragmentation of jurisdiction, after the centralized patent-granting structure, is a serious weakness in our system.

1.3 Enhancing Efficiency while Maintaining High Quality Standards: the Example of the European Patent Network (EPN)

High quality patents offering maximum legal security, and protecting the interests of both innovators and the public, are the cornerstone of a patent system which is fit for purpose. If the EPO's standing as one of the leading patent granting authorities in the world is to be upheld, we must focus our energies on maintaining the strength of our procedures, and if possible, improve upon the already high quality and efficiency of the EPO's search and examination procedures.

World-wide, patent offices are battling crushing workloads and increasing backlogs. To give an idea of the magnitude of the phenomenon: In 2010, 235 000 applications were filed at the EPO, an increase of 11% over 2009, and of 62% over the filing rate at the turn of the new Millennium in 2000, which stood at 145 000. Hence, the most recent figures clearly indicate that demand for patent protection is on the rise again, after the economic downturn of the previous two years and we expect a further increase for the current year.

The EPO's increasing workload is not only due to the sheer volume of applications: as innovation rates rise and human knowledge accumulates, technology is becoming more complicated. Applications have grown in size and complexity to reflect those developments. Also, the pool of prior art to be searched has exploded as a function of global integration and digitalization.

Facing these challenges necessitates a multi-pronged strategy: this includes among other things tightening up granting procedures, increasing operational efficiency through automation, and optimizing the benefits of work sharing. But in a globalized patent system quality cannot be improved in isolation or through individual effort alone. What is required is a concerted effort at international level to enhance the quality of patent examination and to guarantee the stability of patent rights. Since the world-wide trend in obtaining broader geographic protection leads to duplication of filings in many patent offices, work-sharing or utilization is a major element in attempting to deal with the workload, by reducing the duplication of unnecessary work performed by patent offices on corresponding applications.

In the context of this contribution, I would like to focus on one of the numerous EPO initiatives aiming at enhancing efficiency whilst maintaining a very high quality standard: the European Patent Network (EPN). The purpose of this cooperation is to create synergies aiming at further improving the functioning of the European patent system as a whole, whilst taking into account European diversity. The framework for this cooperation, the EPN, is a two-tier environment within which the EPO maintains its central role throughout the entire patent grant procedure, whereas the national patent offices (NPOs) of the Member States complement the role of the EPO, while developing dynamic innovation policies.

In terms of synergies, amended Rule 141 EPC which entered into force on 1 January 2011 and which implements the EPO's permanent utilization scheme, which grew out of the European Patent Network's Utilization Pilot Project,will play a significant role. Under amended Rule 141 EPC, any applicant claiming priority of a previous application will have to file a copy of the results of any novelty search carried out by or on behalf of the office of first filing, upon filing of the European application, or upon entry into the regional phase, in the case of a PCT application. A key principle of this scheme is that the extent of utilization of such search results will remain at the discretion of the patent examiner. In the interests of efficiency and in order to reduce the burden on applicants, our medium-term goal is to move from an applicant-driven submission of search results to an inter-office electronic exchange. Till date agreement on inter-office exchange of search results has been reached for first filings from the Intellectual Property Office of the UK (UKIPO), the United States Patent and Trademark Office (USPTO), the Japan Patent Office (JPO) and the Austrian Patent Office.

One should emphasize that Rule 141 EPC only marks the first step towards the establishment of the EPO's utilization scheme. The challenge now lies in extending the systematic utilization to other products such as written opinions and examination results. In the medium-term, under the so-called Utilization Implementation Project (UIP), measures will be adopted in particular to enhance access of EPO examiners to documents form national patent offices such as written opinions or examination reports. Possible data exchange models are currently being investigated and will be coordinated with the national patent offices.

Our view is that the systematic availability of first filing work results paired with the safeguard of examiner discretion is the best manner to harness efficiencies from the reduction of duplication of work, without putting the quality of European patents or the coherence of the European patent system at risk. This will, ultimately, also lead to a higher presumption of validity of patents granted by the EPO. The challenge now lies in extending this systematic utilization to other products such as examination results.

1.4 Conclusion

Bearing in mind the threats the present economic situation and world-wide backlogs pose to innovation, how can we make the European patent system work and which are the further steps to take? Well, the EPO's response to the challenge is to concentrate on long-term solutions which promote quality, efficiency and legal certainty, control costs, facilitate the diffusion of new technologies and provide a sustainable environment for innovation and economic growth for the benefit of both industry and society at large. This task can not be performed alone. This is why we will develop cooperation with the patent offices in our Members States and around the world.

Christian Archambeau

1. HOW TO MAKE THE EUROPEAN IP SYSTEM WORK

The past few decades have seen many advances in the European IP system. When OHIM was established as the intellectual property office for the EU in 1994, its founders had ambitious goals: naming it the Office for Harmonization in the Internal Market (Trade Marks and Designs). The Community trade mark (CTM) officially came into being on 1 January 1996, in an important first step towards the completion of the internal market for protection of industrial property rights. In 2004 we started registering Community designs which were also an immediate success.

From the start, demand for CTMs was two to three times higher than had been initially expected. This created a challenge to deliver the fast, high-quality service desired by customers. The early years were dominated by the need to keep up with the pace of applications, and the subsequent legal steps associated with administering registrations, such as oppositions, appeals and cancellations.

By the end of 2010, with CTM applications reaching 98 000, the time to register a CTM had dropped to 26 weeks for straightforward files – less than one-third of the time taken in 2004. For Community designs, with just under 82 000 received last year, for customers adopting some simple filing rules, 48-hour design registration is now a reality, and we have committed to informing customers about any problems in other files within 10 days. In effect, 2010 was the year when the Office finally caught up in a race against generally rising demand that started when it opened for business in 1996.

2. E-BUSINESS

The launch of the CTM in 1996 was paralleled by the expansion of popular use of the Internet in the mid-1990s and the rise in acceptance of instant communication media such as e-mail. By 1998 the first OHIM website was up and running. The following year online services for downloading CTM data, and allowing free Internet searches of a CTM database, were made available to the public. OHIM had taken the first steps towards becoming part of this new online business culture.

The rise of e-Business and the existing success of the Community trade mark and the Community design are closely linked. The Office's physical location is relatively remote from the main European business centres. The 350 000 companies from 170 countries who have registered Community trade marks range from large multinationals to small SMEs.

Around 70% of CTMs go to European companies but the customer-base is worldwide, diverse, and seeking service on a 24-hour basis, since they are based in many different time zones. At present almost 95% of CTM applications and 70% of registered Community design (RCD) applications are received electronically, meaning that for customers the Office's physical location has become truly irrelevant.

3. EMPLOYMENT AND INCOME

These improvements in performance were achieved with relatively modest employment growth, thanks to the Office's decision to embrace the e-Business model. OHIM currently has fewer than 650 European civil servants, supported by around 300 others employed through sub-contractors.

Our income, which was around €180m last year, is derived entirely from fees charged to users so we are not a burden on the EU's budget. Since the Community trade mark's introduction we have been able to more than halve the fees. The last reduction was in 2009 and a Community trade mark now costs just €900 to register online.

In terms of how we spend money, an important part, around 45%, goes on staff costs. Other significant costs include almost 15% on IT and data processing and slightly more on translations as we operate in 22 EU languages at the filing stage, and in five main languages for more complex matters.

These figures make us one of the most important EU agencies, if not the largest, in terms of employment and income.

OHIM's presence in Alicante has been an economic boon for the region, attracting well-qualified personnel from every part of the EU. In addition to having five working languages – English, French, German, Italian and Spanish – the office handles applications in 22 languages in all. Computerization and an online business model have allowed the office to adopt flexible working practices that are in line with modern family needs, and there are currently around 140 teleworkers.

4. NEED FOR REVIEW

By the end of 2010, when a new President, António Campinos, was appointed to the Office, it became evident that there was an urgent need to look at the consequences of some early decisions made in order to meet the hectic pace of initial growth in demand for the Office's services.

At the same time the European Commission's important legislative review covering the functioning of the trade mark system in Europe was also under way.

With regard to this legislative process, OHIM's position can be summarized as follows:

The Community trade mark is one of the most significant achievements of the internal market in the field of IP, and its unitary character must be preserved.

The system is working well for the benefit of users. As a result, the final outcome of the legislative process should lead to an improvement but not to structural changes.

OHIM's view is that we need 'evolution' not 'revolution'. But we do need to strengthen the system by improving, simplifying and adapting it, in particular to the new online era.

As the Community trade mark coexists with the national trade marks, together forming the European system, we need to assess this system in a comprehensive way. Hence OHIM has welcomed the Commission's decision to address the revision of both the CTM Regulation and the Trade Mark Directive at the same time.

The process has been launched, consultations are continuing, and we expect the Commission proposal during 2012. This will be sent to the Parliament and the Council for negotiation following the new 'ordinary procedure' for such legislation and, as usual, this process may take some time to complete.

With regard to what is at stake and the opportunity at hand, OHIM feels we owe it to all our stakeholders to be as ambitious as possible. Only once in a generation do we get the chance to revisit such important legislation. But while being ambitious, we must also keep our feet on the ground.

We must have the courage to touch upon all the issues but at the same time bear in mind the need for consensus if we are going to achieve anything worthwhile. We should also explore the idea of allowing those who are ready to move forward to do so now, allowing those who are not yet ready to join a consensus to do it when they are ready.

Having said that, a lot can be done within the existing legislation, and we have not explored all existing options so far.

5. COOPERATION

The Cooperation Fund, set up by OHIM in partnership with national IP offices and user organizations, is working to promote the convergence of tools including e-filing and file handling programs. There is scope for expanding this cooperation and a need for it to be continued in the future.

Meanwhile, we are also striving for convergence of practice in a spirit of mutual respect and understanding.

An example of convergence of practice is a proposal put to national offices by OHIM to try and reach agreement on how we treat Class headings in trade marks. There has been an excellent response to this initiative and we hope to follow the same pattern with regard to other divisive issues.

6. NEW RESPONSIBILITIES

In the early years of OHIM's operation, most attention had to be devoted to the task of becoming an efficient registration office for IP rights. However, it has become increasingly obvious that a healthy IP system in Europe also requires effective enforcement.

This is one area to which OHIM has been asked to contribute more, in partnership with stakeholders. Hence, on 19 April 2012, the European Parliament and the Council adopted Regulation (EU) No 386/2012 entrusting OHIM with tasks related to the enforcement of intellectual property rights, including the assembling of public and private-sector representatives as the European Observatory on Infringements of Intellectual Property Rights (formerly named the European Observatory on Counterfeiting and Piracy). The Regulation entered into force 5 June 2012.

We know that infringement of intellectual property rights is a threat to the wellbeing of the European and world economy, and we know that it goes on in a wide range of countries, whether at the production or the sales point.

The Observatory on Counterfeiting and Piracy, which was hosted and managed by DG Internal Market and Services, started operations in September 2009 as a 'platform coordinating IP enforcement-related strategies, bringing together experts from the public and private sectors'. Its creation followed a Council Resolution the previous year to develop a comprehensive European anti-counterfeiting and anti-piracy plan.

In 2011 OHIM and the European Commission reached an agreement to cooperate in the activities of the European Observatory on Counterfeiting and Piracy related to the protection of trade mark and design rights.

The agreement refers to statements by the Council and the European Parliament encouraging the creation of a legal basis for OHIM to become more widely involved in enforcement-related activities, particularly through fostering its cooperation with national IP offices and the Observatory.

It also acknowledges OHIM's previous involvement in enforcement through projects related to harmonization, protection, promotion and/or enforcement of trade mark and design rights.

Such activities include public awareness strategies, including the organization of events, training programmes, in particular for customs, police and the judiciary, and online databases relating to the infringement of trade mark and design rights, including relevant case-law and systems for exchanging information.

7. STRATEGIC PLAN

This need for increased emphasis on quality and cooperation, and the prospect of legislative change and wider competences such as enforcement being entrusted to the Office, were the background to the Office's Strategic Plan, launched in May 2010.

The Plan is, in effect, a road map until 2015, and is of critical importance to the Office's future.

The research leading up to the plan was designed to examine whether the previous strategy followed by the Office was sustainable, and more importantly, if it was the best way to fulfil the Office's full potential.

Certainly, there had been progress on the speed of publication and registration of Community trade marks, and also, in the opposition process. The registered Community design was another success story, delivering fast and cost-effective protection for industry designs.

However, not all areas of the Office's operations had moved forward at the same pace.

Three challenges for the years ahead were identified by the new President and his management team: the challenges of quality, cooperation and transparency.

Most of the early efforts made by the Office were calculated to deal with the unexpected popularity of the CTM and RCD and provide registrations of reasonable quality within a timescale acceptable to users.

Timeliness remains very important and OHIM continues to fine-tune and tighten standards, as well as introducing new timeliness standards in areas where none existed before. However, we know that we need to work harder on the other dimensions of quality.

The second major challenge identified in the Strategic Plan is that of cooperation, since OHIM does not exist in isolation. We are part of a wider EU system of intellectual property, and also part of a global system. In the global realm, there is, of course, WIPO, our Trilateral partners, and significant players such as the emerging giants in Brazil, Russia, India and China.

The Strategic Plan addresses both these challenges, taking as starting principles, participation and transparency.

Above all, the Plan is founded on two over-arching 'pillars' which are firstly, to develop our operational excellence, building on the successes of the last 15 years, and secondly, foster international cooperation and to develop a comprehensive European Network in which all have a key part to play.

The process of drawing up the Plan has been broad and inclusive, ensuring that all possible visions and aspirations are taken into account to build a strategy shared by all stakeholders and interested parties.

The resulting Plan has six major lines of action supporting three cumulative goals.

It includes specific goals and lines of action related to the challenges already mentioned.

The first goal is to build a strong, vibrant and creative organization. The second is to increase quality and optimize timeliness of operations. Goal three is to promote convergence of practice.

- The six Lines of Action supporting these three goals are:
- HR reform and cultural renewal
- Simplification and modernization of Information Systems
- Expansion and optimization of the working environment
- Establishment of the IP Academy and Knowledge Repository
- Improvement and broadening of quality
- Development of the European Network [/bl]

These Lines of Action are further broken down into a series of 33 Key Initiatives and each Initiative is associated with one or more detailed deliverables to track progress and achievement of results.

On HR Reform we will be introducing detailed job definitions, detailing the standard entry path to OHIM and new approaches for temporary agent contracting similar to the policies pursued in other EU agencies. We will also be taking steps to improve leadership training and our assessment systems.

The simplification and modernization of Information Systems involves taking back control of an increasingly complex web of 84 databases, 57 systems and 300 servers which have been set up over the years, and which is becoming impossible to maintain.

With regard to the working environment, we will, at last, be bringing the OHIM family together under one roof. In doing so we will provide an environment which is conducive to creating an integrated, modern organization committed to getting the best out of a highly-motivated staff.

The IP Academy will bring order and coherence to our existing investment in 'knowledge', broaden the scope of our communication policy, and provide the basis for a full range of Academy partnership programmes, based on the principle of inclusiveness. This will include a programme for learning on harmonization; the development and launch of learning programmes for the Observatory on Infringements of Intellectual Property Rights; the establishment of a database of IP experts and the launch of an e-learning platform.

The Quality line of action involves taking a holistic look at quality, revisiting the current quality criteria, creating new ones, and bringing ISO 9001 certification for the whole Office.

The final line of action is the development of a true European Trade Mark and Design Network dedicated to international cooperation. This involves many actions, which are detailed in the Plan, has links with the IP Academy and will lead to a reinvigorated approach to cooperation both within the EU and in the wider world.

8. WHY DO WE NEED A NETWORK?

At present, within the EU we have a system of legal co-existence with different options available to economic actors. But the systems are still far apart when it comes to many practices. They are not interoperable and lack harmonization. The levels of service provided by all offices need to converge so as to provide the user with a consistently high-quality experience regardless of whether they choose to protect their IP rights at national, regional or European level.

To ensure that the needs of all European stakeholders, especially users, are fully taken into account, closer cooperation and coordination between all the offices involved is necessary.

OHIM recognizes its special responsibility to support that process and at the same time, the Office is in a unique position to drive this convergence forward by harnessing its capabilities and its close working relationships with other multilateral bodies, both in Europe and beyond.

Just as the Cooperation Fund is promoting convergence of tools, we must also strive for convergence of practice in a spirit of mutual respect and understanding.

It is only by bringing closer together the national and Community systems with harmonized procedures, and harmonized twenty-first century tools, that we will at last be able to fully achieve the original vision of the legislators.

That vision was to create a European trade mark and design system where the choice of users to seek protection at national, regional or Community level was truly a free one.

It was to create a system where the choice of entrepreneurs was not driven by the differences in the quality of the services provided, or differences in cost-effectiveness, but only by strategic business decisions.

Michel Vivant

'Making the European IP System Work'. Here is a huge programme! And maybe an impossible programme!

Even with the subtitle: 'Further steps to take', many things can be said. Really many things...

As far as I was requested as an academic – in reality I claim myself as an academic who has also a practice – I shall choose to use the freedom of the academic world to stand back from the topic, strictly understood.

I) Most certainly, if we want to build a European System which works, we have to satisfy a certain number of concrete requirements. That is the first side of the question.

In broad outline, it is not very difficult to express an opinion about the need for unitary titles, for unitary policies, for a unitary judicial system...

About the first point, we already have a European trademark and European designs. It is certain that we need a European patent. Could we imagine today to have a patent for Burgundy, Wurttemberg or Wales? Such an affirmation would seem absolutely surrealistic. But, when we claim we have a sole economic territory – the territory of the European Union – it is no more preposterous to keep a patent for a small part of this territory, even if this part is Germany, France or the United Kingdom. On the other hand, in spite of that same economic reality, it would be, at least today, unrealistic, and inopportune to organize a European copyright – would it be European copyright or European *droit d'auteur*? The matter is too deeply linked to our different cultures. We can surely harmonize our approaches. It is false to say the contrary. But we are not ready to build a common right for all Europe. Our philosophies are too distant. All those observations are simply realism.

The question of the adoption of a unitary judicial system at least for the patent, is very specific and, for that reason, very different. For all the practitioners, it is a very practical question with very concrete issues. But we know that, for the Court of Justice, it is more a question of fundamental rights and of preservation of the European legal system. So in that view the further step on this topic would consist in imagining a perfect integration of this future patent court into the European system. Difficult programme! But not insuperable!

But, if all that is important, that is also very technical.

II) Opting for the standpoint I defined before, i.e. trying to stand back from the strict narrow approach, I shall favour a 'philosophical' approach: in this light we have to satisfy different imperatives if we really want to build something together.

I shall identify three or four main points.

First point: we must adopt a real regional approach, i.e. a common approach. Of course, we must adopt this common approach when it is possible (and it is for that reason I said before that it is too early to adopt a common system of copyright or *droit d'auteur* in Europe) or, at least, as far as it is possible (so we can have some convergent rules, even in this field). In that limit, we must not 'cobble together' short-sighted solutions, but we must try to define a real policy for our Continent within the international competition.

Second point: in a more immediately concrete way, I think, we must not hesitate to eliminate the unreasonable rules which create artificial obstacles between the States. That is first a question of national willingness but that is also a question of reason.

Dogmatic understanding and consequently dogmatic use of the 'moral right' of the author in the French system of 'author's right' is a good example of what I have in mind, when, for instance, 'right to respect' is understood as meaning absolute intangibility. But that interpretation is not necessary. A flexible understanding and a flexible practice is perfectly possible and compatible with the French system conceived with an open mind.

I shall give another example, this time from outside of Europe. When Article 102 35 USC states:

> [a] person shall be entitled to a patent unless (a) the invention was known or used by others in this country, or patented or described in a printed publication in this or a foreign country, before the invention thereof by the applicant for patent, or (b) the invention was patented or described in a printed publication in this or a foreign country or in public use or on sale in this country, more than one year prior to the date of the application for patent in the United States

it is the way open to biopiracy. A technique known and used in a country of the South but not described there in a printed publication can be patented in the United States! It is unreasonable and unfair. It is not possible to build a cross-border system on such basis.

Third point: if, in my view, such a solution is unreasonable, the third imperative that we might follow would be conversely to favour the reasonable rules. And, in my opinion, we must do that independently of the positive law.

I want to express the following idea. In many cases, a jurist is inclined to consider at first his own national system. In a certain way, it is natural. But on the other hand, beginning from the positive solutions given in a national system leads to think in accordance with this system and, in many cases, to consider with mistrust any change. Let us observe the mutual suspicion between 'copyright lawyers' and '*droit d'auteur* lawyers'! That is counter-productive. It is a way to tackle a problem with the eyes in the wing mirror! Contrary to that attitude, if we must surely respect our different traditions which are part of our culture, we must look together at the problems we have to face, because the problems are the same in London, in Paris or in Stockholm: which kinds of 'spaces of freedom' we want to recognize within the copyright system? Which kind of 'exception of experimentation' within the patent system can be beneficial for our societies? Etc.

Basically it is a matter of reasoning in terms of challenge and response.

Fourth point (or addition to the third): a further step, the ideal thing would be not only to find new common solutions for the future but, when it is necessary, to imagine new models, for instance to tackle challenges posed by the Internet.

But that is another story…

That being said, I would like, in order to conclude, to underline that the specific contribution of academics should be to take part in the debate . In this matter of IP, considerable interests are at work, ideology is omnipresent, geopolitical dimension is an element which cannot be neglected… So lobbies – and all kinds of lobbies – are very active, which, by the bye, is justified. But the role of the (true) academics would be to refuse connivance, to get the measure of things, to throw light on the real challenges we have to face, to 'flush out' the deceitful words... That can be a real help in making the European IP System Work..

Index

[Please note that IP stands for 'Intellectual Property' and 'IPRs', Intellectual Property Rights. References to Figures or Tables will be in *italic* print]